America's 100 Best Places to Retire

Edited by Elizabeth Armstrong

HOUSTON

America's 100 Best Places to Retire

Edited by: Elizabeth Armstrong

Art Direction and Cover Design: Fred W. Salzmann

Research Associates: Jennifer E. Davoren, Katie Solan, Michelle White

Back cover photo by Jynelle A. Gracia

Published by Vacation Publications, Inc.
5851 San Felipe Street, Suite 500
Houston, TX 77057

Library of Congress Control Number: 2007921224

ISBN 9780978607708

Printed in the United States of America

VACATION
PUBLICATIONS

The Contributors

Mary Lu Abbott

Ellen Barone

Ron Butler

Olin Chism

Jay Clarke

Steve Cohen

Julie Cooper

Jerry Camarillo Dunn Jr.

Katharine Dyson

Karen Feldman

Richard L. Fox

Lynn Grisard Fullman

Fred Gebhart

Mary Ann Hemphill

Linda Herbst

Bill Hibbard

Edie Hibbard

Carole Jacobs

Doris Kennedy

Jim Kerr

Bob Lane

Tracy Hobson Lehmann

Hilary M. Nangle

Adele R. Malott

Stanton H. Patty

Everett Potter

William Schemmel

Marcia Schnedler

Lan Sluder

Candyce H. Stapen

Molly Arost Staub

Nina Stewart

Catherine Watson

David Wilkening

Bob Woodward

Table of Contents

Low-Cost Edens 🛡   Undiscovered Havens ▪

By State

America's 100 Best Places to Retire

The Top 10

Best Art Towns
Ashland, OR
Beaufort, SC
Berkeley Springs, WV
Easton, MD
Hot Springs, AR
Jackson Hole, WY
Naples, FL
Santa Fe, NM
Sarasota, FL
Sedona, NM

Best Budget Towns
Danville, KY
Dothan, AL
Eufaula, AL
Hattiesburg, MS
Kerrville, TX
Mountain Home, AR
Natchez, MS
Rio Grande Valley, TX
Rockport, TX
San Antonio, TX

Best Undiscovered Towns
Cashiers, NC
Celebration, FL
Ferndale, CA
Grand Lake/Grove, OK
Mountain Home, AR
New Hope, PA
Poulsbo, WA
Seaside, FL
Shepherdstown, WV
Woodstock, VT

Best Lake Towns
Coeur d'Alene, ID
DeFuniak Springs, FL
Door County, WI
Eufaula, AL
Grand Lake/Grove, OK
Hot Springs, AR
Lake Geneva, WI
Mount Dora, FL
Mountain Home, AR
Saugatuck-Douglas, MI

Best Beach Towns
Carlsbad, CA
Delray Beach, FL
Hilton Head, SC
Myrtle Beach, SC
Naples, FL
Ocean County, NJ
Sanibel, FL
Siesta Key, FL
Southern Delaware
Whidbey Island, WA

Best Main Street Towns
Athens, GA
Dade City, FL
Danville, KY
Ferndale, CA
Hendersonville, NC
Port Townsend, WA
San Antonio, TX
Temecula, CA
Waynesville, NC
Winter Garden, FL

America's 100 Best Places to Retire

Best College Towns

Asheville, NC
Athens, GA
Brunswick, ME
Chapel Hill, NC
Charlottesville, VA
Fort Collins, CO
Gainesville, FL
Oxford, MS
Shepherdstown, WV
Williamsburg, VA

Best Small Towns

Cashiers, NC
Dade City, FL
DeFuniak Springs, FL
Edenton, NC
Ferndale, CA
Mount Dora, FL
Port Townsend, WA
Saugatuck-Douglas, MI
Waynesville, NC
Woodstock, VT

Best Four-Season Towns

Annapolis, MD
Bend, OR
Charlottesville, VA
Connecticut River Valley, CT
Door County, WI
Easton, MD
Grand Junction, CO
Prescott, AZ
Reno, NV
Santa Fe, NM

Best Mountain Towns

Asheville, NC
Bend, OR
Berkeley Springs, WV
Cashiers, NC
Fort Collins, CO
Jackson Hole, WY
Prescott, AZ
Ruidoso, NM
Santa Fe, NM
Waynesville, NC

San Juan
Islands
Port
Townsend ● Whidbey
Poulsbo ● Island

Coeur d' Alene

Bend

Grants Pass
Ashland

Jackson
Hole

Ferndale

Reno

Healdsburg

Fort Collins

Grand
Junction

St. George

Las Vegas

Rancho
Mirage
Temecula ● Palm
Desert

Sedona

Santa Fe

Prescott

Carlsbad

Scottsdale

Tucson

Ruidoso

Green Valley

Las Cruces

Sierra Vista

Wimberley
Kerrville ●
San Antonio

Rockport

Rio Grande
Valley

America's 100 Best Places to Retire

Door County

Lake Geneva

Galena

Saugatuck/
Douglas

Brunswick

Woodstock

Portsmouth

Connecticut
River Valley

New Hope

Berkeley
Springs

Ocean County

Annapolis

Shepherdstown

Southern
Delaware

Easton

Charlottesville

Williamsburg

Danville

Chapel Hill

Edenton

Grand Lake/Grove

Mountain
Home

Waynesville

Asheville

Pinehurst

Maryville

Hendersonville

Cashiers

Myrtle Beach

Oxford

Athens

Aiken

Hot Springs

Beaufort

Hilton Head

Eufaula

Natchez

DeFuniak
Springs

Dothan

Hattiesburg

Fairhope

Gainesville

Ormond Beach

Pensacola

Seaside

Ocala

Mount Dora

Tallahassee

Dade City

Winter Park

Bradenton

Winter Garden

Longboat Key

Celebration

Sarasota

Stuart

Vero Beach

Siesta Key

Jupiter

Venice

Delray Beach

Punta Gorda

Naples

Boca Raton

Sanibel

Fort Myers

Introduction

Welcome to the fourth edition of "America's 100 Best Places to Retire." The communities compiled here represent the best of the cities and towns that have been featured in *Where to Retire* magazine, each one updated to reflect the most current data available.

In this book, you'll find choices in 34 states. They include popular favorites such as Asheville, Myrtle Beach, Santa Fe and Sarasota, as well as destinations that are a bit off the beaten retirement relocation path — in Delaware, Kentucky, Maryland, New Hampshire and Oklahoma, for example.

In the mix, you'll find "Low-Cost Edens" (🌍) and "Undiscovered Havens" (▇). Check out our Top 10 lists on pages 6 and 7 to find the best small towns, college towns, beach towns, mountain towns, art towns and more.

Among our favorites is Ferndale, CA, a place so friendly that retiree Mike Bailey says, "You have to allow two hours to walk downtown because you're stopped by all your friends." And the top arts community of Berkeley Springs, WV, where resident Lynn Lavin creates ceramics that she sells at the local artists' co-op, and where musician Pat Spring started a piano lab for high school students. In Brunswick, ME, Jack Flynn takes classes at Bowdoin College, while wife Lorna praises the college's "hugely welcoming" attitude.

Regardless of where they choose to spend their retirement, most of the retirees we've met share some common desires for their new hometown: comfortable climates, nearby health-care facilities, homes within their budget, access to shopping and cultural venues, and perhaps opportunities for community involvement and continuing education. With these criteria in mind, we set out to find appealing retirement towns across the country and profiled them in *Where to Retire*.

The 100 towns featured in this book represent our top picks. Whatever your own dreams for retirement may be, we hope you'll find a place to indulge them within these pages. — *Elizabeth Armstrong*

Aiken, South Carolina

This small South Carolina town has warmly welcomed newcomers since the 19th century

By Jim Kerr

At the intersection of Whiskey Road and Grace Avenue in Aiken, SC, a rider halts his horse and leans toward a conveniently placed traffic signal button. Vehicles along busy Whiskey Road, with its walled mansions and majestic oaks, dutifully stop so that man and mount can proceed up unpaved Grace toward stables and equestrian training grounds.

Aiken is only 17 miles from the fabled links of Georgia's Augusta National, but decades before golf drew thousands each spring to this area from points north, Aiken was the winter home of well-to-do equestrians. Known as "winter colonists," they journeyed south by train, bringing their mounts with them, and while horse events still dominate the spring calendar in Aiken, horses and golf carts have become as compatible in this Southern town as the horse and carriage.

Today dozens of stables and 13 golf courses dot the landscape in and around Aiken, and a temperate year-round climate, combined with a strong sense of historic preservation, have made the small town a top choice for retirement.

"Golf and horses give Aiken additional dimensions," says active retiree Bill Reynolds, "but wonderfully warm and accommodating people, and a long tradition of welcoming newcomers, is what really got us hooked on the place."

Bill, 64, and his wife, Susan, 58, initially chose a retirement home in Boca Grande, a waterfront community on Florida's southwest coast. In 1994, they moved there from Cincinnati, where Bill had been an executive with Proctor and Gamble, and Susan had been a top sales executive for WLW Radio.

"It was very noncommercial and like being on vacation all the time," says Bill regarding Boca Grande's laid-back ambiance. "But ultimately it wasn't for us. Residents only stayed for six months, and we wanted more community involvement. I was on the board of the condo association, but it wasn't enough."

When they first started thinking about retirement in the 1980s, the couple searched both the east and west coasts of Florida, as well as the Carolinas, but they never considered Aiken until Susan's mother, who lived in Augusta, suggested they take a look. The town impressed them so much that they bought a large Charleston cottage-style house in the town's historic district on their first visit in March 2000. The house, built in the 1890s by polo enthusiast Fred Post, was a word-of-mouth find through a local real estate agent.

"If we had rented for six months, like many people tend to do, we might not have stayed," remembers Bill. "But the people we bought the house from immediately became our mentors and introduced us to most of the people who are today our friends. Because of this we became involved here fast. Within a week we had five dinner invitations."

Located in the far western midsection of South Carolina, and within three driving hours from Atlanta, Charleston and Columbia, Aiken rose from agricultural roots. A rail line was built in 1833 to transport the area's cotton, and the town was named for the Charleston-Hamburg Line's first president, William Aiken. Considered America's first real railroad, the original roadbed is today part of pleasant riding trails in a 2,000-acre urban forest called Hitchcock Woods.

From a bustling railroad center, the Civil War blasted Aiken back into relative obscurity, but only until 1870 or so, when its climate and a few prominent residents transformed the area into a health spa for wealthy Northerners and a training ground for their horses. They were the winter colonists, with elaborate mansions under towering magnolias and stables practically on their back doorsteps. Fox hunting, polo, steeplechasing and even golf were established by 1900.

The latter helped convince Jack and Jean Pilk that Aiken was a good retirement choice, even though a small Southern town with a population of 25,000 was not initially on their agenda. They had lived in Arlington, VA, where Jack, now 70, was an Army colonel working at the Pentagon, and Jean, a few years younger, was a highly successful portrait artist. Aiken seemed far away from her work, their five children and the energy of Washington, DC.

"It looked so small to me," remembers Jean, "but you're quickly indoctrinated into the easy lifestyle. It has a nice ambiance with lots going on, like music and art events. The USC campus is here, there are nice restaurants, a great staff in the hospital and easy shopping. Things are close, and finding a parking space downtown is rarely difficult."

They attend plays at the USC-Aiken Etheridge Center and at the Washington Center for the Performing Arts in downtown Aiken. There are plenty of art shows and guest speakers around town. But perhaps best of all, their community at Woodside Plantation has three challenging golf courses and an affordable country club membership.

"It's not a retirement community, either, and that attracted us," says Jean, who often works 10 hours a day on the portraits she paints under the natural northern light streaming into her studio. Her portrait commissions over many years have included Supreme Court justices, senators, governors and all the joint chiefs of staff.

While it was hard to pull up stakes and leave Arlington contacts behind, Jack's intuitions about Aiken have proved correct. It may be small, but a progressive and accommodating atmosphere has made them feel welcome, and the dramatic drop in the cost of living was only icing on the cake. The couple's 3,500-square-foot golf course home in Woodside Plantation was equal in price to a much smaller home in Arlington, and had many more amenities. The 1,400 houses in the development, which is minutes from downtown Aiken and shopping malls, cover a wide range of prices, with a full golf membership initiation fee of $15,000.

Posh hotels, many of them since restored, were built to host the friends and relatives of the early winter colonists. Homes along broad, leafy boulevards began to surround a downtown core of businesses, and industrial schools turned out skilled artisans who were attracted to the area by the building boom. But even though it was an American aristocracy that gave Aiken its initial push into the 20th century, it was, ironically, communism and the Soviet Union that altered the town's economy the most during the last half of the century.

As the Cold War heated up in the 1950s, thousands of engineers, academics, technicians and skilled laborers arrived in connection with the construc-

tion and opening of the Savannah River Site, a facility that designed and produced nuclear materials in competition with the USSR. While the plant, located on 310 square miles some 20 miles southwest of Aiken, is now largely in a decommissioning, decontamination and restoration mode, those employees and their families continue to have a profound effect on the economy. And Aiken's skilled labor pool draws not only Fortune 500 companies, but international businesses as well.

"There are 18 foreign firms or subsidiaries here now who see Aiken as an alternative to big cities, and Aiken has gone out of its way to establish industrial parks for them," says Robert Chelberg, a retired U.S. Army lieutenant general who is senior European adviser for Aiken's Economic Development Partnership.

His role with the EDP is only one of many consulting activities and community projects that keep him busy in Aiken, where he and his wife, Tricia, have lived in semiretirement since 1999. "We visited here several times from Fort Jackson, outside Columbia," Robert says. "It was much more than a nice Southern town. They work hard here to maintain the historical perspective of the place."

Aiken's progressive and friendly ambiance was a perfect fit for an active retiree like Robert, 63, but it was the town's horse-and-carriage mentality that appealed most to his 60-year-old wife. As a committed equestrian, Tricia has competed in dressage, polo, fox hunting and carriage-driving events for years, raising two children dedicated to the same sport.

The Chelbergs' ranch-style home, where bridles are draped on porch rail-

Aiken, SC

Population: 25,337 in the town of Aiken, 145,000 in the county.

Location: Aiken, the county seat, is about eight miles southwest of Interstate 20 in the far western midsection of the state. The town is less than 20 miles from Augusta, GA, 127 miles from Savannah, 126 miles from Charleston, 163 miles from Atlanta and 56 miles southwest of Columbia, the state capital.

Climate: High Low
January   58   36
July   90   75

Average relative humidity: 77%

Rain: 47 inches annually

Snow: 1 inch annually

Cost of living: Below average

Average housing cost: Single-family homes in Aiken's designated historic district range from $100,000 to $1 million

or more, depending on location, size, age and condition. In newer, upscale country club developments close to town, homes range from $300,000 to more than $1 million, and from $150,000 to more than $1 million in older golf subdivisions in town, depending on age, size and location. The average cost of a single-family home in Aiken is $162,000.

Sales tax: 5% state tax, plus a 1% Aiken County tax on all goods, including food.

Sales tax exemptions: Prescriptions, dental prosthetics and hearing aids. Persons 85 and older pay 1% less sales tax.

State income tax: Graduated in six tiers ranging from 2.5% on taxable income of $2,530 to 7% on taxable income of $12,650 (minus $367).

Income tax exemptions: Social Security benefits are exempt from state income taxes, and that portion of benefits taxed at the federal level is deductible from South Carolina taxable income. There is an exemption of up to $3,000 in any pensions if under age 65 and up to $10,000 in pensions if 65 or older. Each person age 65 and older receives an age deduction of $15,000 off any income, although that's reduced by the amount of retirement exemption taken.

Estate tax: None

Property tax: Owner-occupied homes are assessed at 4% of market value. In Aiken, there is a county rate of .2141 and a city rate of .071 for a total rate of $285.10 per $1,000. Taxes on a $162,000 home would be about $950 with homestead exemption, $1,520 without exemption. Both figures reflect a deduction of about $327 for the school tax exemption, set at a rate of .0818 on up to $100,000 of home value.

Homestead exemptions: The first $50,000 of the fair market value of a home is exempt from property taxes for citizens over 65.

Religion: More than 40 major denominations are represented in several dozen Aiken churches.

Education: The University of South Carolina at Aiken has approximately 3,200 undergraduate students, with degrees offered in 30 major areas of study as well as a master's program. Aiken Technical College is also located in Aiken.

Transportation: Aiken is about eight miles south of Interstate 20, which connects with Augusta, GA, 20 miles southwest, and Columbia, SC, 56 miles northeast. Columbia is a major interstate hub connecting I-20 with I-26 and I-77. Interstate 20 proceeds another 75 miles northeast to I-95 at Florence, SC. Colum-

ings and a stable is nestled out back, is within a mile of Winthrop Field, where Tricia competes in carriage driving as a member the Aiken Driving Club. Unpaved roads in the neighborhood, destined under town ordinance to remain that way for horses, border training tracks and stables. And at three different tracks in town, steeplechasers, thoroughbreds and polo ponies compete in Aiken's famous Triple Crown of Racing on three successive weekends every spring.

Other special equestrian events take place in the fall, but on any given day riders can be found in Hitchcock Woods, established by a foundation in 1939 and considered the largest urban forest in the United States. No vehicles are allowed on the forest's many miles of hiking and riding trails, which meander through 2,000 acres and are accessible through seven gates.

A county historical museum sits on the north end of the park, while Hopelands Gardens, a former plantation with a horse museum and outdoor concert pavilion, sits at the south end. And all of it is just a stone's throw from Aiken's historic downtown, where several excellent restaurants, upscale boutiques, outdoor cafes and gift shops have been established amidst the traditional hardware stores and banks.

"It's a perfect fit for us," says Susan Reynolds, who works two days a week at a new upscale dress shop downtown. "People are adamant about protecting the beauty of the city versus suburban sprawl." Adds Bill, "You need to strike a balance between preservation and economic opportunity and development."

Neither Bill nor Susan play golf or ride horses, but their recent fund-raising project called Horseplay touched on both Aiken's equestrian heritage and its tradition of community involvement. From October 2003 to March 2004, 30 to 35 life-sized fiberglass horses were sponsored and displayed around the town in conjunction with various community events. Local artists were commissioned to paint them, and all proceeds from the auction of the Horseplay statues went to a new arts program for seniors and children as part of Aiken's active Center for the Arts, which hosts classes, art camps and a variety of special events. The eight-member steering committee for the project was composed almost entirely of active retirees like Bill.

While it's possible to pass the time sitting in a sidewalk cafe or taking leisurely strolls through historic neighborhoods, many retirees find that the urge

bia and Augusta have regional and domestic air service. Charlotte, NC, and Atlanta, GA, both about two and a half hours away, are the closest international airports.

Health: Aiken Regional Medical Centers has 230 beds and a staff of about 1,000, including 120 doctors representing 39 specialties. The facility is equipped for a broad range of medical needs. Emergency care, open-heart surgery and coronary care are specialties, along with two other centers devoted to detection and treatment of cancer and diabetes. ARMC's Women's LifeCare Center concentrates on breast cancer detection, and a senior wellness program is dedicated to a variety of services to those over 50 at no charge.

Housing options: While the average home sold in Aiken is $162,000, there is a wide range of choices, from small starter homes to large elegant estates. In between are patio homes, condos, country houses and several golf communities where prices start at $150,000. One of the most established is **Houndslake**, (888) 346-8637, where patio homes start at about $300,000 and villas and bungalows begin at $150,000. Resales in Houndslake average about $90 per square foot. **Woodside Plantation**, (800) 648-3052, a gated country club community covering over 2,300 acres, contains three golf courses, including a Jack Nicklaus design. Patio and single-family home-and-lot packages begin at $225,000; cottage homes begin at $264,000. **Cedar Creek**, (800) 937-5362, a 14-year-old golf community several miles south of Aiken near the town of Ellentown, offers homesites from the mid $50,000s and custom homes with sites from $325,000. **Mount Vintage Plantation**, (803) 278-5000, is a golf course community about 16 miles west of Aiken. Many homesites border the 18-hole championship course. Lot prices start in the $40,000s, and larger estate tracts ranging from three to 10 acres can go up to $395,000. Single-family homes range from the $300,000s to the millions. While smaller houses in Aiken proper may approach the average cost, homes in the historic district often start at $500,000. Assisted-living communities include **Shadow Oaks**, (803) 643-0300, and **Eden Gardens**, (803) 642-8444. There are more than 30 apartment complexes in and around the town, including **Verandas on the Green**, (803) 649-3468, where two-bedroom, 1,000-square-foot apartments run $679 a month. A number of real estate agents operate in Aiken, including **Eulalie Salley & Co.**, (803) 648-7851. For equestrians, several agencies specialize in properties accommodating horses, including **Biddle Realty**, (803) 648-7871.

Visitor lodging: Hotel Aiken, (877) 817-6690, a completely remodeled, turn-of-the-century hotel in downtown Aiken, has rooms starting at about $65. The Guest House at Houndslake, (800) 735-4587, is a comfortable 34-room lodge on the golf course with rooms starting at $79. Special rates are available through the real estate office, (888) 346-8637. A number of bed-and-breakfast houses are located in Aiken, including Annie's Inn, (803) 649-6836; Carriage House Inn, (803) 644-5888; and Crossways Plantation, (803) 644-4746, with rooms starting around $90. A number of standard hotels and motels are available downtown, including Days Inn, from $42, (803) 649-5524; Quality Inn & Suites, $60-$80, (803) 641-1100; and Econo Lodge, from $45, (803) 649-3968. The fabulously restored Willcox Inn, (877) 648-2200, with only 22 rooms, runs $175 a night and up.

Information: Aiken Chamber of Commerce, 121 Richland Ave. East, P.O. Box 892, Aiken, SC 29802, (803) 641-1111 or www.aikenchamber.net.

to jump in with both feet is irresistible. When Chris and Thelma Lydle, both 58, moved here in 1999 from Montville, NJ, it was only three short months before Chris leaped back into the retail camera business, opening a shop in downtown Aiken. Life was just too easy, and the place needed a camera store.

Now, Chris says, "there is so much going on in Aiken, we're busier than ever." His centrally located store is on Laurens Street, which has a center divide. Chris describes the location as "delightful" because of its shops, restaurants and parking on four sides of the street instead of only two, even though spaces are often in short supply during peak business hours. "People are so polite, though," he reflects. "The other day I heard a horn honk — something so unusual it actually makes you turn around and look."

For recreation, Chris keeps a boat at J. Strom Thurmond Lake, a 70,000-acre reservoir located an hour from Aiken on the Georgia-South Carolina border just north of Augusta. "I've always been a boater," he says, "but I don't want to deal with coastal areas. People have always retreated from the coast to Aiken during hurricanes, and the lake is well protected."

Like the Pilks, Chris and his wife live in Woodside Plantation. There are several other residential golf communities, including Cedar Creek, located just outside Aiken and surrounded by horse farms. Among its amenities are an 18-hole golf course, lighted tennis courts, junior Olympic-sized swimming pool and bicycle paths. A scenic 3.5-mile walking trail wends through part of the 1,000-plus acres that have been set aside as a bird and wildlife sanctuary.

Another option is Houndslake, a rolling, wooded enclave in the heart of town where about 1,000 families live in a wide variety of homes ranging from cozy bungalows and cottages to elegant estates. Fifty thousand azaleas planted during the 1974 construction of the Joe Lee-designed golf course complement the dogwood, holly and kalmia. "We have so many people from just everywhere," says Peggy Penland, president of Houndslake Corp. "People sometimes just fall on Aiken by mistake, and then fall in love with it. One couple said, 'Build us a house,' and then handed me a checkbook."

About 16 miles west of Aiken, Mount Vintage Plantation opened in 2000 and is situated on 4,000 acres. The focal point of its championship golf course is an 1840s Piedmont plantation home that has been restored and now serves as the clubhouse. Homesites range from .25 to 17 acres, and many lots border the course.

A number of assisted-living facilities are scattered around town, as well as new condos. Kalmia Landing, an independent-living patio home and condominium neighborhood for seniors 55 and older, is located on the opposite side of Hitchcock Woods from Houndslake.

Louise Baker, who is Susan Reynolds' 78-year-old mother, moved to Aiken from Augusta only months ago and now lives in the new Sand River Condos near downtown. She easily walks to shopping and the town's stately brick library. But best of all, she can stroll five blocks under magnolias and oaks to her daughter and son-in-law's house. It's always a quiet walk — except on the mornings when thundering hooves from nearby polo matches or thoroughbred races rumble through the neighborhood. ●

Annapolis, Maryland

Maryland's capital revels in its Colonial history and sailing traditions

By Candyce H. Stapen

Douglas Klakulak, nattily attired in white breeches, red knee socks, a blue waistcoat and a brown tricorn hat, divulges that he stores both bullets and important papers in the haversack slung across his shoulder as he leads our small group on a walking tour of old Annapolis. He instructs the men in how a proper Colonial gentleman greets a lady: Stick out your belly to prove money enough to be well-fed, then place your left leg slightly in front of you. "That is putting your best foot forward," chuckles Doug, also known as Squire Doug.

The retired surgeon from Birmingham, MI, moved to Annapolis in 1999 and has been a volunteer guide since 2002. "I got to talk to people about the city's past, I get a lot of exercise, and the rest of the time I'm sailing on the Chesapeake," says Doug, 62. Like many retirees, Doug was drawn to Annapolis' combination of historic structures and bay location.

For centuries the Chesapeake Bay has attracted people. Long before Europeans arrived, American Indians fished the region's waters for terrapin, crabs and oysters. In 1649, Protestants from Virginia established Providence, a small hamlet on the Severn River. Arundelton, later known as Anne Arundel Town, developed along Spa Creek, the tributary that divides the City Dock area from the Eastport side of what is now Annapolis.

As the tobacco plantations flourished in the region's rich soil, the settlements grew. Anne Arundel Town became the Colonial capital in 1694, soon changing its name to Annapolis to honor Anne, the future queen of England. Now dubbed a "museum without walls," the old district of Annapolis encompasses 1,500 restored historic buildings and features the largest concentration of 18th-century architecture in the United States. This year the National Trust for Historic Preservation named the city to its annual list of a dozen distinctive destinations.

In old Annapolis, Federal-style brick homes, as well as boutiques and cafes, front streets initially laid out in the 17th century, giving the area a human scale. Stroll the cobbled walks and it's easy to imagine bewigged merchants hurrying to their shops and ladies in horse-drawn carriages being delivered to the parlors of the prominent for tea.

In the 18th century before the Revolution, Annapolis served as a busy customs port for the western shore of the Upper Bay. Ships unloaded spices and ceramics from China as well as rum, sugar and coffee from the West Indies, iron and wooden products from New England, and slaves from Africa and the West Indies. Alex Haley's ancestor Kunta Kinte, as chronicled in "Roots," was sold into slavery in Annapolis. He came to the New World in chains aboard the Lord Ligonier, which anchored in the harbor on Sept. 29, 1767. At City Dock, the Kunta Kinte-Alex Haley Memorial, a bronze sculpture of the Pulitzer Prize-winning author reading to three children sitting in rapt attention, commemorates Kunta Kinte's struggle.

Annapolis, with a population of 33,000, is manageable, especially when compared with much larger Washington, DC, 45 minutes away, and Baltimore, 30 minutes away. "Annapolis gives us the pluses of a small town as well as the big city," says Tricia Herban, 62, who moved to Annapolis with her husband, Mat, in 1996. "Today, I came back from the Eastern Shore. Saturday I was in DC, and Thursday I'm going to lunch with a friend in Baltimore."

Doug Klakulak and his wife, June Miller, 56, a retired naval nurse and part-time professor of nursing at Johns Hopkins in Baltimore, go to Baltimore and Washington two to three times a month to attend plays and the symphony as well as to visit museums.

Like the Klakulaks, many residents also pick Annapolis because of its sailing opportunities. The U.S. Naval Academy, established in 1845, anchors the city's east side. It's common to spot midshipmen in their dress whites moving briskly along Main Street. The forest of masts in the marinas in Back Creek and Eastport — fondly called "the Maritime Republic of Eastport" — attests to the city's popular pastime. Each October, Annapolis holds its annual sailboat show, the largest in-water sailboat show in the country.

"The neat thing about sailing the Chesapeake is that every five miles you find a place to pull in and spend the night. The water is beautiful, and there's lots of bird life," says Doug Klakulak.

Sailing also drew John and Kathy Deutsch to move to Annapolis from Allentown, PA, in October 2004. For about three years they visited the city on weekends and in summer to take sailing lessons. "That's when we fell in love with the bay area and Annapolis," says Kathy, 58, a former marketing director for an employee physicians group who works part time "just to get out of the house and into the community."

Notes John, 55, "With our children — 30 and 28 — both grown, we took a look at our lifestyle. We had a big house we didn't need. It was time to downsize and time for a life change." So they sold their house and purchased a 41-foot sailboat.

"Because I wasn't ready yet to throw out all my suits and shoes, we moved into a two-bedroom apartment," Kathy says. John, a training executive, still works for Fuji Medical Systems, but the couple sails whenever they can. "We hired a captain from the Annapolis Sailing School to go out with us on a few day sails so we could hone our skills and learn what our boat can do," John says.

When former investment banker and

sailing devotee Dick Franyo, 61, moved from Baltimore to Annapolis permanently in 2000, he decided to open a sailing bar, launching the Boatyard Bar & Grill in Eastport, just across Spa Creek from historic Annapolis, in October 2001. Rated by Sail magazine as one of the top 12 sailing bars in the world, the Boatyard is an airy eatery with lots of windows and good salads.

"Sailing is our soul," Dick says. "We devote a lot of our resources to sailing. We support all the major regattas with money. We film Annapolis' Wednesday night boat races and show the tapes here, and we give 1 percent of our sales to the Chesapeake Bay Foundation. We're a lifestyle place. We sell the Chesapeake Bay. "

Dick Franyo uses the Boatyard to support charities. "I wanted a platform for doing charity. You can do a lot more with a business than you can as a person. This April at our charity fishing tournament, we raised $25,000 for the Chesapeake Bay Foundation."

Dick covers the Boatyard's menus with photos of Annapolis' families on their boats. He also fully encourages Eastport's more eccentric traditions, such as sock burning, the official harbinger of warm weather. "On the first spring day, everyone rips their winter socks off their feet and throws them into a big bonfire at the Eastport Yacht Club," Dick says. "They don't wear socks again until winter. And, of course, they come back to the Boatyard for oysters and drinks."

Then there's the November Tug of War in which teams from Annapolis and the Maritime Republic of Eastport attempt to pull a 1,700-foot line strung across Spa Creek around various harbor markers. Celebrants return to the Boatyard to toast each other with Dark & Stormys, a drink made with dark rum and ginger beer that is a favorite with the sailing crowd.

The Deutschs ran in Eastport's .05K "marathon" across the very short Spa Creek Bridge. "When we reached the other side we received a passport that allows us to enter the Maritime Republic of Eastport," Kathy says. "The run benefited the local SPCA, and it was great fun. You've got to love an area that can laugh at itself."

"Annapolis is more than what we expected," says John Deutsch. "Along with sailing, the city has a close tie to tradition and history that you don't see in many places. You see the state flag flying a lot." Notes Kathy, "I've lived here eight months, and I can readily identify the flag of Maryland. I lived in Allentown for 34 years, and I have no idea what the state flag of Pennsylvania looks like. The idea of flying the flag is part of Annapolis' ties to history. It's a welcoming and comforting feeling."

The city's history also drew the Herbans. Tricia, a former fund-raiser, and Mat, a retired art professor, moved to the city from Columbus, OH. "I grew up near Rittenhouse Square, a historic area, and Mat and I lived in German Village, a historic district in Columbus," notes Tricia. "We always felt right in historic areas where the houses are old and the population is

Annapolis, MD

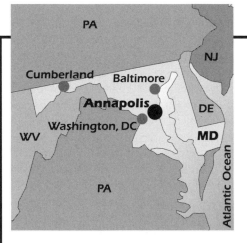

Population: 33,187 in Annapolis proper and 62,585 in greater Annapolis.

Location: Annapolis, Maryland's capital, is located on the Severn River. The city is 26 miles from Baltimore and 32 miles from Washington, DC. Annapolis is in Anne Arundel County.

Climate: High Low
January 41 24
July 87 67
The area has four definite seasons.

Average relative humidity: 65.5%

Rain: 39 inches annually

Snow: 14 inches annually

Cost of living: Higher than average

Average housing costs: The average rent for a two-bedroom apartment ranges from about $1,342 to $1,503 per month. The average price of existing homes in Anne Arundel County, based on sales in the fourth quarter of 2004, was $355,945. A two-bedroom, two-bathroom house in Annapolis' historic district typically ranges from $600,000 to $800,000.

Sales tax: 5%

Sales tax exemptions: Prescription drugs and most groceries

Income tax: Anne Arundel County has a local income tax rate of 2.56%. The state of Maryland has a graduated tax peaking at 4.75% on income over $3,000.

Income tax exemptions: The state does not tax Social Security or railroad retirement benefits. Maryland has a maximum pension exclusion of $22,600 for taxpayers who are 65 or older, totally disabled or whose spouse is totally disabled, and allows for an exemption of up to $5,000 on military retirement for those who are eligible. There is a personal exemption of

$2,400, and if the taxpayer is 65 or older, or blind, there is an additional $1,000 exemption. For a more complete list of exemptions, visit www. marylandtaxes.com.

Estate tax: The Maryland estate tax return is required if the decedent's federal gross estate plus adjusted taxable gifts equaled or exceeded $1 million and the decedent was either a resident of Maryland at the time of death or a nonresident who owned real or tangible personal property in Maryland.

Property tax: The county rate is 0.931 cents per $100 of assessed value. Within the city limits of Annapolis, the tax rate is $1.115 per $100 of assessed value. Assessments are made at 100% of market value. Maryland's rate is 0.132 cents per $100 of assessed value. Properties are assessed every three years. For more information, contact the Anne Arundel County Office of Finance, Customer Service Division, (410) 222-1144.

Homestead exemption: Maryland has a Homeowner's Tax Credit Program

denser than in the suburbs."

Like the Klakulaks, the Herbans wanted museums and concerts nearby. "We wanted to have access to the culture in East Coast cities and also easy access to Europe. BWI (Baltimore-Washington International Airport) gives us that in spades and at good prices."

However, the Herbans landed in Annapolis in 1996 by accident. "I thought Annapolis was out of our price range based on what I read in the papers when we were in Ohio," notes Mat. But when the Herbans stopped in Annapolis while researching places to live on the Eastern Shore, they went to a real estate agent and explained that they planned to retire in two years.

"She gave us a list and told us to check what we wanted to see. After lunch she showed us some houses, including the one we bought. We hadn't expected to buy it, but we did," says Mat, 67. "When we came to Annapolis and walked down Main Street, we felt that we had come home," Tricia says.

The Herbans purchased the historic 1860 house, renovated it and opened it in 1997 as a bed-and-breakfast inn with three guest rooms. "We didn't want to go into full retirement," Tricia says. "We wanted something that would engage us in the community, plus we collect art and we like to share the pieces we have with people."

The Herbans don't find their landlubber status a problem in this water-loving metropolis. "It's not a detriment to not be involved in sailing. There are plenty of ways to contribute to the community," Tricia says. Through the New Annapolitan, an organization for people who have relocated to the city within the past two years, the Herbans found ways to volunteer. Mat serves on the city's committee on art in public spaces. Tricia gives tours at the historic Paca House and is an information specialist at the convention and visitors bureau.

On our tour of the historic area with Squire Doug, we walked the manicured grounds of the U.S. Naval Academy, visited the chapel to view the elaborate stained-glass windows, including one designed by Tiffany, and saw the crypt of naval hero John Paul Jones. At the Maryland State House, built in 1772, Doug reminds us that the structure is the oldest state capitol in continuous operation in the United States. The U.S. Congress met in the old senate chamber from Nov. 26, 1783, until June 3, 1784. Here the delegates ratified the Treaty of Paris in January 1784 and accepted George Washington's resignation as leader on Dec. 23, 1783.

Pointing out Charles Willson Peale's painting of George Washington with his aide, Col. Tench Tilghman, and the Marquis de Lafayette that hangs on the wall, Squire Doug tells us to note that Washington's wrist is in his vest, a common pose in 18th-century portraits. "That's because in those days it cost more to paint hands and feet, and you wouldn't want to be 'charged an arm and a leg,'" says Doug, gleefully elucidating the 18th century once again. ●

based on income and the amount of property taxes due. In addition, the Homestead Property Tax Credit limits the increase in taxable assessments to 10% or less each year.

Religion: The county has 47 churches of various denominations that hold services each week.

Education: In Anne Arundel County, 30.6% of the population possesses a bachelor's degree and 86.4% are high school graduates. Annapolis has two four-year degree-granting institutions. St. John's College has an enrollment of 561 students, and the U.S. Naval Academy trains 4,335 undergraduates. Anne Arundel Community College, a two-year institution, has 14,290 students. About 65 accredited institutions of higher learning serve the nearby Baltimore-Washington area.

Transportation: Many major routes link to Annapolis. U.S. Highway 50/301 runs east and west, as do routes 32 and 100 and interstates 195 and 695. Interstate 97, the Baltimore-Washington Parkway (Route 295) and Route 2 run north and south. In addition, Annapolis offers easy access to I-95. Baltimore-Washington International Airport (BWI) is located 20 minutes from Annapolis. BWI offers approximately 715 U.S. and international flights daily. For more information, contact BWI, (410) 859-7111 or www.bwi airport.com.

Health: Anne Arundel Medical Center, located in Annapolis, is a full-service hospital with 260 beds and a 24-hour emergency room. Johns Hopkins University Medical Center, Baltimore, is about 26 miles away, and Washington, DC's hospitals, including Georgetown University Medical Center and the George Washington University Hospital, are 32 miles away.

Housing options: Properties in the historic district of Annapolis tend to be the most expensive, and properties farther out in the county tend to be less expensive. A two-bedroom, two-bath house in Crownsville, six miles from Annapolis' historic district, typically sells for $300,000 to $350,000. More than 5,000 units of over-55 housing are currently being developed nearby in three neighborhoods with resort-type amenities. Planned in Gambrills along the Patuxent River is a luxury development with a golf course, pools and fitness centers. It will have just under 2,000 units, both single-family homes and townhouses. Two other communities are being developed in Pasadena that combined will have more than 3,000 units, including condos, townhouses and single-family dwellings.

Visitor lodging: There are more than 2,000 rooms available in Annapolis and the greater Annapolis area, including rooms in 30 bed-and-breakfast inns. Rates for the Historic Inns of Annapolis in the heart of town start at $159, (800) 847-8882. Rooms at the Loews Annapolis Hotel start at about $149, (800) 526-2593. Visit www.visitannapolis.org for additional choices in various price ranges.

Information: Annapolis and Anne Arundel County Conference and Visitors Bureau, 26 West St., Annapolis, MD 21401, (410) 280-0445, (888) 302-2852 or www.visitannapolis.org.

Asheville, North Carolina

This small, vibrant city in the North Carolina mountains attracts active retirees from all over the country

By Mary Lu Abbott

While George W. Vanderbilt came to Asheville for its beautiful setting and built a 250-room chateau in the late 1800s, retirees today are finding they, too, can have the good life in the mountains of western North Carolina — and in smaller abodes.

On a high plateau surrounded by the gentle, often-misty Blue Ridge Mountains, Asheville has been a natural crossroads for centuries, creating a richly diverse community in the new millennium. Coming from such distant, and disparate, locales as New England and California, retirees today find a spirit that's simpatico with a variety of individual interests.

Settling here in 1994 from Connecticut, Jack and Sheila Ingersoll wanted a place they could truly call home after having moved many times.

"I wanted to put down roots, to know people in the town and to greet them as you walk around. I thought Asheville gave us that opportunity," says Sheila, 66. "It's somewhat a spiritual community. I thought the people had a caring spirit, and now I know they do."

Jack, 70, says, "I wanted to give back some of the good I had received over the years, and I thought there would be the opportunity here — and there has been."

An executive with IBM, Jack continued working as a consultant for several years after they moved to Asheville, then retired in 1998 and delved into a program called Leadership Asheville Seniors, which explores the history of the area, introduces participants to community leaders and matches work skills with volunteer needs.

From Marin County north of San Francisco, Louaine Elke focused on lifestyle rather than a region or particular towns for retirement. "I wanted a co-housing community, a concept started in Denmark," says Louaine, 67. While residents have their own private living unit, they also share some meals together in a community house and donate time keeping up the common grounds and tending to

community business, she says.

Louaine, a college instructor with degrees in fine arts and architecture, had investigated some co-housing communities in California after her husband died in 1994 but found them all too expensive. At the invitation of a former student, she came to Asheville in 1996 to see its architecture and crafts and discovered a co-housing unit was being developed in town. "I went to a meeting (of those planning the community) and I liked the people. I felt it would go. Sometimes people sit around and talk about doing this but it never goes. In a week, I made a deposit," she says.

Beyond the lifestyle concept, "I liked Asheville — the size, the old buildings, the university campus, the arts community," she says. She returned three times to watch progress of the community, located adjacent to a creek and wooded area, and moved here in 1998.

Rick and Linda Ricordati retired here from Rhode Island in 1997, after having lived most of their lives in the Chicago area. They discovered Asheville about 20 years ago when vacationing along the Blue Ridge Parkway and Skyline Drive, a scenic route that connects the Shenandoah Mountains in the north and the Great Smoky Mountains southwest of Asheville.

"Any time we traveled, we would look at a place and say, 'Could we live here?'" says Linda, 58. "The decision about Asheville was a process of elimination. I did not want a lot of heat and humidity. That ruled out Florida and Arizona — I don't care how dry it (Arizona) is, 110 degrees is 110."

Rick adds that they checked out San Diego but felt traffic was too congested, and it was too far from their children in the Midwest. "We looked at the coasts of North and South Carolina. The winters are mild, but the summers are brutal," he says.

"There are ocean people and mountain people, and we are mountain peo-

ple," says Linda.

On a master checklist of desirable qualities in a retirement destination, Asheville scores high — a small but sophisticated city with excellent health care, a reasonable cost of living and the added bonus of a university with a cutting-edge program for active seniors. Well-located, it's on Interstate 40 and the slow-paced Blue Ridge Parkway, approximately 200 miles from Atlanta, GA; 120 miles from Charlotte, NC; 110 miles from Knoxville, TN; and 60 miles from Greenville, SC.

Once they decided on the Asheville area, the Ricordatis visited several times and talked to many residents before buying property in a new development of free-standing homes. They like the diversity of Asheville. "It isn't filled with all the same types of people — all the same age or who all play golf," says Rick, 58, who retired from marketing. The cultural, educational and medical hub of a region that encompasses more than 200,000 residents, Asheville has a makeup that mixes retirees with college students, young families and professionals of all ages. Health care, manufacturing and tourism are major industries.

"We like the manageability of living here," says Linda. "It's easy to do things — to go to the grocery store or the cleaners. And if there's a little traffic, you don't mind it because the scenery is so beautiful."

"In general, the whole city is friendly and laid-back," Rick says. "It's unusual to bump into anyone who's not pleasant."

Since moving here in 1994, the Ingersolls have seen the city gain momentum. "It has gotten better. It's growing — but not too much — and downtown is really coming to life," Sheila says.

"We had dinner downtown the other night," says Jack, " and people were still walking around at 9 or 10. It's drawing a variety of ages."

Asheville entered its first boom in the early part of the 1900s, as Vanderbilt's elegant Biltmore Estate focused attention on the area. Its clean, cool mountain air soon made it a favorite resort among presidents and celebrities. Luxury accommodations opened, among them the still-grand 1913 Grove Park Inn, a massive hotel built in the style of a rustic lodge with walls of granite boulders. The downtown area blossomed with new buildings in art deco and modern designs, and farmland became housing developments with mountain views. When the Great Depression hit, Asheville and surrounding Buncombe County reeled under a massive debt and struggled for nearly five decades to pay off all its obligations rather than default on the loans. Only in the 1970s did the city really begin to recover, but there was an unexpected benefit to its long-term decline: Since the city had no extra funds for urban renewal projects popular in the '50s and '60s, its classic buildings didn't succumb to the wrecking ball.

Recognizing their architectural treas-

Asheville, NC

Population: About 70,000 residents in the city, 215,000 in Buncombe County. Asheville is the county seat and regional cultural, medical and educational hub.

Location: In the Blue Ridge Mountains of western North Carolina, about 200 miles northeast of Atlanta, GA, and 120 northwest of Charlotte, NC. It's on the Blue Ridge Parkway about 50 miles from Great Smoky Mountains National Park. Elevation varies, with the average being 2,200 feet.

Climate:

	High	Low
January	47	25
July	83	63

Average relative humidity: 58%
Rain: 48 inches
Snow: 15 inches
Cost of living: Slightly below average.
Average housing cost: $272,768 for a single-family home. The average monthly rent for a two-bedroom apartment is $799.
Sales tax: 7%
Sales tax exemptions: Prescriptions and services.
State income tax: For married couples filing jointly, the rate is graduated from 6% of taxable income up to $21,250 to 8.25% (plus $14,537.50) on amounts over $200,000. For single filers, it is graduated from 6% of income up to $12,750 to 8.25% (plus $8,722.50) on amounts over $120,000.
Income tax exemptions: Social Security and railroad retirement benefits are exempt. Up to $2,000 of distributions from private retirement benefits and IRAs (up to the amount reported in federal income taxes), or up to $4,000 of government pensions may be exempt. Total deductions may not exceed $4,000 per person.
Intangibles tax: None
Estate tax: Applicable to taxable estates

above $2 million.
Property tax: City residents pay a combined city-county tax rate of $1.13 per $100 of assessed value, with all homes assessed at 100% of market value. Annual taxes on a $272,768 home are about $3,082.
Homestead exemption: Those age 65 and older can exempt $20,000 or 50% off the assessed value of permanent residence if combined income is less than $19,700 annually.
Personal property tax: Same rate as home taxes noted above apply to vehicles, boats, motor homes, mobile homes and other specified belongings.
Religion: The city has about 300 places of worship, representing Protestant, Roman Catholic, Greek Orthodox and Jewish faiths.
Education: The city has several colleges and universities, augmented by campuses in surrounding communities. The University of North Carolina at Asheville has degree programs and is home to the North Carolina Center for Creative Retirement, which has numerous programs for retirees, including the College for Seniors with four terms of noncredit classes annually.
Transportation: Asheville Regional Airport provides commuter and jet service, and the Asheville Transit System runs buses in the city.
Health: A regional medical center, Asheville has five hospitals and more than 500 doctors, providing a range of health care including heart and cancer centers, trauma services and emergency air transport by helicopter.
Housing options: Some retirees choose to buy older homes in city neighborhoods, while others relocate to new developments in suburban areas or adjacent communities in Buncombe County. Some developments cater to active adults

but many are composed of all ages. Among choices: In the eastern part of the city, **ViewPointe** is a gated community of maintenance-free cluster homes for active adults, with a clubhouse for activities; homes are in the $240,000s to $270,000s. To the north in Weaverville, about 20 minutes to downtown Asheville, **Reems Creek Golf Club**, (828) 645-3110, attracts all ages, offering townhomes from the $200,000s and homes from $350,000. To the south at the community of Arden, about 10 minutes from Asheville, **High Vista Falls** is a gated community for all ages with golf course, clubhouse and patio homes from the $277,000s and townhomes from the low $300,000s.
Visitor lodging: A popular vacation hub, Asheville has a wide choice of lodging, from budget to luxury and including bed-and-breakfast inns. The grand dame is Grove Park Inn, (800) 267-8413, a legendary mountainside resort with a rustic elegance; rates start at $265. Contact the Asheville Bed & Breakfast Association, (877) 262-6867, for information on most of the B&Bs.
Information: Asheville Area Chamber of Commerce, P.O. Box 1010, Asheville, NC 28802, (828) 258-6101 or www.asheville chamber.org. North Carolina Center for Creative Retirement, (828) 251-6140 or www.unca.edu/ncccr.

ures from the early 20th century, residents and developers began restoring the art deco, Queen Anne, Revival and Romanesque structures and recycling them for new uses. Today more than $50 million is pledged for downtown redevelopment. Among the restorations downtown, Pack Place now houses three museums, a theater and cultural center. Galleries and shops showcase outstanding arts and crafts created in the region, augmenting the extensive collection of mountain crafts at the Folk Art Center outside town on the Blue Ridge Parkway.

Asheville's extensive cultural venues are a drawing card for many retirees who are eager to escape the hassles of living in metropolitan areas but still want some of the big-city amenities. "It's easy and inexpensive to go to performances here," says Louaine, noting that the area has community theater, university drama presentations and current productions by touring groups. It takes her as little as 10 minutes to get to performances, which usually cost less than $20 — "I figured it cost about $100 to go into San Francisco for an evening performance," she says.

Although the cost of living in Asheville runs slightly above average, it's less than metropolitan areas, and all those interviewed cited lower costs as a factor in choosing Asheville.

Each chose a different option for housing. The Ingersolls bought an older home, which they renovated. "It's 10 minutes from downtown but feels like it's in the country," says Sheila. The Ricordatis wanted a new development where they felt that making friends would be easier than in a neighborhood of longtime Asheville residents. "We pretty much built our house by phone and fax," Rick says, noting that they shuttled to and from Rhode Island during construction. They were pleased with the work, though. "The real surprise (of our move) was that we could build a house without being here, and it come out 98 percent the way we wanted," he says with a laugh.

Louaine's co-housing community has 24 units in close clusters of three or four attached homes that range from one to three stories and from one to five bedrooms. Each has a private back yard but the front yards are common. All parking is close to the street with walkways to the houses, an architectural design intended to encourage residents to meet and greet their neighbors as they go to and from their homes.

"We have a very interesting group (of residents), ranging from a 4-month-old baby to 70s," says Louaine. "This is part of the appeal to me — I didn't want all seniors." It's a friendly group that looks after each other, she says, and takes time to chat when crossing paths outside.

"In Denmark, co-housing residents eat dinner at the community house daily. Here we do it twice a week and sometimes the men do brunch on Sunday," she says. The community house has a restaurant-size kitchen, and residents sign up for work on the cooking team. A community garden provides vegetables and herbs for the shared meals, and residents also can have their own gardens. Louaine, who is an avid gardener, has an arbor where she grows Asian pears and kiwis, among other fruits.

A guiding force for many seniors who move to the Asheville area is the North Carolina Center for Creative Retirement, established in 1988 as part of the University of North Carolina at Asheville. With "creative" an operative part of its title, the center reached out to the growing number of seniors who want to stay active in retirement and designed programs that have become national models. Its mainstay is the College for Seniors, which offers four terms annually with classes in such far-ranging topics as Understanding the Balkans, King David vs. King James, Getting Started With Computers and U.S. Leadership in Today's Global Economy. UNCA faculty, community residents and retirees who are experts in varying fields teach the noncredit classes, which draw about 1,500 seniors annually.

The Ingersolls, Ricordatis and Elke are involved in classes at the College for Seniors, which they also found to be a good way to meet people, make new friends and learn more about the community. Jack serves on the boards of the College for Seniors and Leadership Asheville Seniors, another program of the center. Rick serves as the university's representative to United Way, and both he and his wife volunteer to assist with the center's Creative Retirement Exploration Weekend. Held over the Memorial Day weekend, the event annually draws about 150 seniors who attend workshops to discuss the economic, social and psychological factors of relocating to this region when they retire. Participants hear firsthand experiences from seniors who have come here from all parts of the country and have time to see Asheville and surrounding communities.

With mountains at their doorsteps, Asheville residents enjoy a variety of outdoor sports, including hiking, rafting, biking and fishing. The area has a mild four-season climate with a colorful spring and fall.

The retirees interviewed consider the health care here excellent, and Louaine notes that besides traditional medicine, the city has choices of alternative medicine. Although the crime rate is above average, many retirees agree that it didn't affect their decision to move to Asheville. "It's still a place where a lot of people don't lock their doors," says Rick.

All voice a common concern about increased air pollution, which usually occurs in summer. There has been a slight upward trend in air pollution recently, with the increased population driving more motor vehicles and pollutants drifting into the area from the west, according to representatives of the Western North Carolina Air Pollution Control Agency, which monitors air quality. They say that while in the summer of '99 Asheville had some days when the ozone level rose to moderate levels, the city had only two days when air quality was rated unhealthy for sensitive groups (those susceptible to asthma and other respiratory problems) and no days rated generally unhealthy.

Rick says most people who've relocated here like it so much they sound "like a voice for the chamber of commerce — we've become that way." As for seniors considering places to retire, Rick adds, "I think Asheville should be on your list. It was right for us but it may not be for everyone." He says a golfer would find plenty of courses to play but a "water person" or boating enthusiast might not be as happy here.

Jack says that after living so many different places, "This is home — where I want to be." Sheila adds, "No matter where I lived I enjoyed it, but I never made an attachment and I wondered if I would ever find a place I could. It's happened here." ●

Ashland, Oregon

Culture and climate blend for livability in Oregon's Rogue River Valley

By Bob Woodward

It is the theater that brings many visitors to Ashland, a small town of 20,085 nestled below the Siskiyou Mountains in southwest Oregon. Its Oregon Shakespeare Festival was cited in 2003 by Time magazine as one of the best of America's regional theaters — further evidence that theater-loving Ashland has achieved a national reputation with its festival. But the town also has found itself an equally enviable reputation as a special place to retire.

Bounded on the west and south by the mountains and U.S. Forest Service lands, Ashland has experienced controlled, well-managed growth.

This has allowed the town to retain the charm of handsome Victorian houses, bungalows and Craftsman homes on tree-shaded streets. The town also has a thriving downtown core area with verdant Lithia Park as its centerpiece. The 100-acre park is easily one of the loveliest city parks in the United States.

Add a moderate, year-round climate and a slower pace of life into the mix, and Ashland's overall livability is further enhanced. And for those who need a big-city fix from time to time, San Francisco and Portland are within easy reach by car or plane.

People who choose to forgo big-city pleasures for natural pursuits find Ashland an outdoor paradise. Residents can enjoy nearby hiking trails, fishing in lakes and rivers, paddling on the Rogue and Klamath rivers, and cycling or walking on city bikeways or along the Bear Creek trail linking Ashland to the nearby town of Talent. Come winter, there's cross-country skiing, alpine skiing and snowshoeing on Mount Ashland, 15 minutes from the snow-free heart of town.

But it was neither the outdoor recreation nor the theater that drew David and Deedie Runkel to Ashland from Washington, DC. "We'd heard about the town from friends in Seattle," says David, 62, "and then four summers ago, after visiting them and then our son in Portland, Ashland was on the way to our final destination to see our daughter in San Francisco. We decided to stop in and give the town a look-over."

They found Ashland completely booked up. But Deedie, 62, persevered and found a room for the night while David got lucky and acquired two tickets to that evening's Oregon Shakespeare Festival production. They spent that night and part of the next day in Ashland and left feeling drawn to the place.

But not enough to pick up their busy lives and immediately head west. Yet they knew they were ready for retirement. David had 20 years as a newspaper reporter on his resume, plus 20 years of public relations work for politicians in Pennsylvania and Washington, DC. Deedie had raised a family and then began a career working with various advocacy organizations, including a stint as project manager for the Peace Corps in Belize.

In looking at retirement, they wanted to stay active and do something together. They thought that running a bed-and-breakfast inn would be interesting and challenging, so they began to research B&B possibilities.

"We found a lovely old place on the Maryland shore," David recalls. "It had two 19th-century buildings, an 18th-century building and a huge formal garden. The place looked like way too much work."

"Then it came to us," Deedie says, "that we should be looking at a destination town, a place people really wanted to visit. Gettysburg, PA, kept coming up and looked promising until David started investigating Ashland online."

"We liked what we saw," says David, picking up the story, "and realized that there were plenty of B&B operations for sale in the town."

And so in July 2002, after helping organize the Peace Corps' 40th-anniversary celebration party in Washington, DC, they left the next day for Ashland. They wanted to get to Oregon as soon as possible to buy a B&B and begin operations before the theater season ended. They eventually chose a B&B named Anne Hathaway's Cottage.

They'd barely landed in town when Deedie joined the local Rotary Club and started volunteering at a soup kitchen in nearby Talent. Getting started in Ashland is easy because, as Deedie puts it, "everyone is relatively new here."

Now settled into the community, the Runkels came to enjoy the mild weather and the small-town atmosphere. "I like the fact that everything I need is within walking distance, and that I can take my dog everywhere," David says. Most of the merchants welcome dogs in their establishments and even have treats for them.

"I also like the fact that there are so many interesting people here who are leading or have led interesting lives," he says. And then there's the theater. "We try to see every production," Deedie says, "and we also try to do as many backstage things as we can." David adds, "The depth of the talent in the festival company is so good that even the minor roles are superbly acted."

Ever busy in retirement, the Runkels write for AARP's Modern Maturity magazine. David also does the occasional public relations consulting job. One of these engagements led him back to Washington, DC, to work for the World Bank this past winter. "That trip convinced me that we'd made the right choice in moving to Ashland," he says.

Deedie says she's convinced that the decision was right because of the proximity of their children still residing in San Francisco and Portland. "They can come and visit for the weekend, and that's important," she says.

Family is definitely the reason Barbara and Bill Rosen retired from Connecticut to Ashland. "Our daughter was a film and television actress in Hollywood," says Bill, 77, "and when she married a fellow actor and had children, they started looking for a better place to raise the kids. They made a long trip checking out places and found Ashland to their liking. We came out here four years ago to see them and look the town over."

"It was time to be nearer to the family," adds Barbara, 75, "and by the time we'd found a house we liked and decided to make the move, our second daughter had also moved to Ashland."

That settled it. The Rosens found a home in the Mountain Meadows retirement community that they liked and bought it. Then they rented it out for two years while they returned to Connecticut to settle affairs there. Eventually they made the move to Ashland.

"Mountain Meadows is not the sort of place where people sit around. It's a very active community of people," says Barbara. Adds Bill, "We love the fact that we have our own house but can go up to the clubhouse a couple of nights a week for a meal. It's wonderful to sit at the community table and have dinner with all the friends we've made here."

As many friends as the Rosens have made in Ashland, they continue to expand their friendships through teaching. Both are retired English professors from the University of Connecticut. Their expertise as tenured professors was, ironically, Shakespearean literature. Yet the fact that Ashland is the home of the Oregon Shakespeare Festival never played a part their retirement decision.

Now, however, their background in Shakespeare's literature plays an important part in their lives, as both instruct at Southern Oregon University's SOLIR (Southern Oregon Learning in Retirement) program for seniors. Among the courses the Rosens will teach this year are, "The Uses of Power in Shakespeare," "Tragedy of Youth and Age" and "Elizabethan Witchcraft."

When not teaching, they have become theater patrons like most other Ashland citizens. "We love the fact that we can be at the theater in 10 minutes," Bill says. "And besides the theater, there are so many good restaurants here to enjoy. Theater and good dining used to be an hour-and-a-half drive each way for us."

When they're downtown, Barbara appreciates that "in Ashland, pedestrians are sacred. This is a tourist town and cars go slowly, and drivers really pay attention to pedestrians." The Rosens say the community also pays attention to health care needs. After experiencing some medical problems, they learned firsthand that health care in the area was excellent, they say.

In their two years here, they both also found the religious community to be a

Ashland, OR

Population: 20,085

Location: Nestled in southwest Oregon's Rogue River Valley at an elevation of 2,000 feet above sea level, Ashland is just off Interstate 5. The California border is 15 miles to the south, San Francisco is 365 miles to the south and Portland is 290 miles north of Ashland on I-5.

Climate: High Low
January 45 30
July 90 54
The climate is mild with four distinct seasons.

Average relative humidity: 65%

Rain: 19 inches

Snow: 7 inches

Cost of living: Above average

Average housing cost: The median price for a single-family house in Ashland is $412,000; for a home in Jackson County, the median price is $268,100. Houses in Ashland rent for $850 to $1,500 per month. Two-bedroom apartments rent for $500 to $850 per month.

Sales tax: Ashland does not have a general sales tax but has a 5% tax on restaurant and take-out meals. Only food, not alcohol, is taxed.

State income tax: For single filers, it ranges from 5% of taxable income up to $2,650 to $413 plus 9% of the excess over $6,650. For married couples filing jointly, it ranges from 5% of taxable income up to $5,300 to $825 plus 9% of the excess over $13,300.

Income tax exemptions: Social Security benefits are exempt, as is all federal pension income based on service performed before Oct. 1, 1991. For federal pension income based on service before and after Oct. 1, 1991, the pension subtraction is prorated. Federal pensions for service after Oct. 1, 1991, and state and private pensions are not exempt.

Estate tax: Applicable to estates of $1 million or more. For estates exceeding $1 million, an Oregon inheritance return must be filed.

Intangibles tax: None

Property tax: The property tax rate in Ashland ranges from $9.07 to $14.51 per $1,000 of assessed value, depending on which fire and school district the property is located. Taxes are applied on approximately 67% of real market value on new construction, making taxes on a new $412,000 house about $2,504 to $4,005. The property tax rate in Jackson County is $9.97 to $17.27 per $1,000 of assessed value, depending on location.

Homestead exemption: The homestead deferral program exempts from property taxes those 62 and older or disabled who meet certain income requirements. There is a 6 percent interest on the deferred amount, payable at death or upon selling the home.

Religion: There are 36 churches in Ashland representing almost the same number of denominations.

Education: Ashland is home to Southern Oregon University, www.sou.edu. The 175-acre campus is minutes from downtown Ashland and serves 5,500 students with four-year degree programs in 100 areas of study. There are 35 majors in the arts and letters, social sciences and business departments. The student to professor ratio is 19 to 1. Southern Oregon offers three seniors-specific programs. Senior Ventures are for people

huge plus. Barbara is a Quaker, and Bill is a practicing Jew. "We like the fact that there's so much tolerance in this town, and how the various churches get together on civic projects," Bill says.

Barbara loves the sense of calm and space that she gets in Ashland. "For a small town, there's a lot going on, yet there's this great sense of calm. There's so much open, unspoiled country left around here," she says. "Everywhere you look there are mountains. It's that sense of space that we love."

Open space was something Mike and Kathe Nabielski had plenty of when they lived in Fairbanks, AK, a place they described as "romantic" when they first moved there. But the romance wore thin as the long, dark winters loomed each year. So, given the opportunity to retire early, they seized it. Kathe, 50, was employed for 27 years in Alaska's public school system, and Mike, 56,

worked in Alaska's State Department of Transportation.

After hours of laborious Internet research and reading every book on retirement communities that he could find, Mike determined that Ashland was the place that he and Kathe should retire. They visited on July 4, 1999, a celebratory occasion in Ashland with a parade and family-oriented activities. "We were so impressed with the celebration and the community spirit, the feel of the place and how safe we felt here," Kathe recalls.

So they bought a second home in a neo-traditional development just east of Ashland's downtown area. They paid a mortgage on it and their Alaska home until they could move to Ashland permanently in 2001.

"Right from the start we found, as expected, this to be a friendly community with so much to do," Mike notes.

"And we love the fact that we can walk or ride our bikes to the center of town in minutes," Kathe adds.

Another big plus is that Ashland is home to Southern Oregon University. "I think a university keeps a town on its toes — keeps people thinking," Mike says.

There's also plenty to do as far as part-time and volunteer work for active retirees like the Nabielskis. Last winter Kathe worked two days a week in the ski rental shop at the Mount Ashland ski area. She and Mike volunteer at the Habitat for Humanity thrift shop in nearby Medford and are active in the local chapter of the American Red Cross. Both are certified by the Red Cross to assist in national disasters. While they haven't been called out on a national emergency yet, they did spend weeks setting up camps for firefighters fighting the huge forest fires in the central Oregon moun-

over 50 and include field trips in Oregon, Texas, Canada and Washington. SOLIR (Southern Oregon Learning in Retirement) offers short-term educational experiences on the SOU campus. The university's Elderhostel program is one of the largest in the United States. Offering a wide variety of technical and traditional courses, Rogue Community College, www.roguecc.edu, has three campuses in Jackson County.

Transportation: Rogue Valley International Medford Airport, www.co.jackson.or.us, is the third-largest commercial airport in Oregon and is 15 miles north of Ashland. United Express and Horizon Air offer direct nonstop flights to locations including Portland, San Francisco, Seattle and Los Angeles. General (private) aviation facilities exist at the Ashland Municipal Airport. The Rogue Valley Transportation District (RVTD) offers bus service throughout Ashland on weekdays. Buses leave every 30 minutes, and the fare is 50 cents, (541) 779-2877.

Health care: Founded in 1906, the 49-bed Ashland Community Hospital, (541) 482-2441 or www.ashlandhospital.org, offers 24-hour emergency service, same-day surgery, an ICU unit, hospice room, CT scanning, ultrasound, gastroenterolo-

gy, mammography, bone density testing, MRI imaging, echocardiography, physical therapy and sports medicine, among other services. Five orthopedists and three retinologists are on staff. The hospital opened 10 new private rooms in 2004 and is in the process of expanding their surgery department. In nearby Medford, the 168-bed Providence Medical Center, (541) 732-5000, has a cancer care facility. The largest of Jackson County's hospitals is the 305-bed Rogue Valley Medical Center, www.asante.org, in Medford. The hospital offers home care, a hospice program and the Dubs Cancer Center, (800) 944-7073.

Housing options: Ashland offers a wide variety of housing options, from historic Victorian houses to modern single-family housing developments and many new condominium communities. Large parcels are available outside Ashland throughout Jackson County.

Mountain View Retirement Residence, (541) 482-3292, is located on Ashland's North Main Street two blocks from the hospital. It offers studio apartments, one- and two-bedroom apartments, and cottages on a month-to-month rental basis. Monthly rents for the studio apartments (325-493 square feet)

are $1,470 - $1,825. Rents for one-bedroom apartments (500-759 square feet) are $2,015-$2,475. Rents for two-bedroom apartments are $2,900-$2,965. Cottages, with family room, full kitchen and garage, rent for $3,025.

Visitor lodging: The 55-room Stratford Inn is less than five blocks from the Shakespeare Festival theaters. Rates for a room with two queen beds are $65-$130 per night, depending on season, (800) 547-4741. Newly remodeled Ashland Springs Hotel is in the center of downtown. Rates for a room with king-sized bed range from $129 to $169 per night in the spring and fall to $169 to $209 per night in the summer and $99 to $129 in the winter, (888) 795-4545. Ashland is home to numerous bed-and-breakfast establishments, most in charming old Victorian-era homes. Information on rates (expect to pay $90 to $200 per night, including breakfast) and locations can be obtained by contacting the 27-member Ashland B&B Network, (800) 944-0329 or www.abbnet.com.

Information: Ashland Chamber of Commerce, P.O. Box 1360, 110 E. Main St., Ashland, OR 97520, (541) 482-3486 or www.ashlandchamber.com.

tains in the summer of 2003.

Mike likes to run along the town's bike trails and in downtown Lithia Park. "Running in the park is special," he says. "It's so beautiful there any time of year." Kathe enjoys being around people. "I like the fact that Ashland is a tourist town because there are so many interesting people around during the theater season," she says.

And if retirees want to get away from Ashland and the theater crowds for a few days, that's easy. "We're a five-hour drive from California's wine country," Mike Nabielski says, noting that the Oregon coast is an easy drive, too. "Last year for fun we took the train from Klamath Falls (70 miles east) to Portland. Next year we plan to travel even more because we're so close to so many won-derful places living here," he says.

Ashland's location is ideal for the Nabielskis, and Mike is quick to point out the attractions: "The clean air, the low-key feel to the place, the sense of community, and the fact that all things and all points of view are open to dis-cussion." These qualities, he says, "are really what make Ashland a very special place." ●

Athens, Georgia

Low costs, a four-season climate and a college campus attract retirees
to this vibrant Georgia town

By Lynn Grisard Fullman

A snapshot on Mim and Nick Bourke's refrigerator door is a constant reminder, lest they forget, of why they forsook their Northern roots to retire to the South.

The photo captures an April day in Massachusetts when their home was blanketed in three feet of snow. Snow in April is something the two, married 38 years, likely will never experience again now that they have retired to Athens, GA. "It reminds us why we don't want to go back," says Mim, 59, who gave up a teaching job to raise the couple's two children.

Five years ago, when Nick, 60, was retiring as an executive with Johnson & Johnson, the two began considering where to retire. Their thoughts first fled to a town along the Georgia coast where they had often enjoyed vacations, but they soon realized that the seaside community, while outstanding as a vacation destination, was not suited to their full-time needs.

In due time, they remembered a stint in the early 1980s when they had lived in Athens, a college town in northeast Georgia. Nick, ever the businessman, jotted a few comparative figures on paper, but the decision was made more with their hearts than with their wallets.

"We did read some magazines that ranked cities and got a rough idea of the numbers," recalls Nick, an upstate New York native who met Mim on a blind date while both were in college. "From a numbers point of view, I don't know how Athens stacks up," he confesses, explaining that they wanted a place with all four seasons where he can "see some flowers and enjoy the shade of a live oak tree."

During his career, the couple lived in various parts of the country, including Savannah, GA, Massachusetts, Texas, North Carolina, Michigan and New Jersey. "We enjoy the quality of life here," Mim says, describing the ambiance as "nice and laid-back. We picked Athens

for a lot of reasons, including our familiarity and comfort with the area and the opportunities to get involved with social and volunteer activities."

The couple knew that the University of Georgia would "offer an awful lot of activities, including symphonies at the performing arts center, sporting events and renowned guest speakers. A lot of good events come into town, including road shows of Broadway productions," Nick says, noting that they have attended performances by the London Philharmonic and the Harlem Boys Choir, among others.

"The beauty of living here is that it is not congested — we can get around easily," Mim reports, explaining that traffic is heavier when the college's 30,000 plus students are on campus. Even so, her idea of gnarled traffic is having "to wait through two lights at the mall."

The sidewalk-laced town is filled with restaurants, clubs, galleries, newsstands, coffee shops — and Weaver D's, known for its collard greens and as the unofficial lunch spot of rock legends R.E.M. Long a musical mecca, Athens boasts a vibrant music scene that began gaining international recognition in the late 1970s. Bands such as R.E.M. and the B-52's rose to the top during the 1980s as other bands perfected their talents in area clubs.

While the Bourkes were certain Athens provided most of their retirement demands, they initially were disappointed to be so far from the coast, something they had enjoyed while living in New Jersey. "But then I realized that since we are retired and flexible, we can go to the beach anytime we want to," says Mim, adding that they are six hours from the Florida Panhandle and Seagrove and Santa Rosa's "absolutely lovely beaches."

The couple, however, feels that every day is a vacation in their golf-course community, Jennings Mill, where housing prices range from $250,000 to $1 million and a tee time is only a telephone call away. The nearby country club,

whose 13th hole has been ranked Georgia's best, has a beautiful new fitness center that Mim enjoys.

"Here you can get a very elegant home at a very reasonable price," Nick reports, describing their brick house as having some 3,000-plus square feet, crown moldings, tray ceilings and a terrace-level patio on a lot measuring almost an acre. The couple's home also is close to health-care facilities. The area's doctors and medical centers "are fantastic. I can get care here equal to the hospitals in Atlanta," Nick says.

The heartbeat of the city is the college, which sits smack-dab in the center of town, drawing students internationally and providing a kaleidoscope of faces, all of whom the Bourkes have found to be quite friendly.

"This town, surprisingly, has a lot of military retirees who have come to the Navy school in town (the Navy Supply Corps School) and decided to come back here to retire," Nick says. Another plus, Mim notes, is the availability of several independent- and assisted-living residences, making it easy to have older relatives nearby.

The Bourkes have had no problems settling in. Mim occasionally works in the boutique department of a local department store, and both volunteer with their church, the Catholic Center at the University of Georgia. Nick has been involved with Leadership Georgia and Leadership Athens and recently assisted with a Habitat for Humanity house. "Anybody can find a niche here," Mim says. "There are plenty of opportunities to get involved and to meet people."

"We are here to stay," concludes Nick. He says he'll reside in Athens as long as the photo of a snow-covered house remains on his refrigerator door.

But snow was not on the minds of Ruth Anne and John Hancock when they retired to Athens, a town whose name honors the classical Greek center of culture. "We literally chose Athens out of every place we'd ever been in our lives," Ruth Anne explains. While the strongest lure was a favorite niece who lived and worked there, the city itself intrigued the Hancocks, who have been married 22 years.

John's parents and several family members are buried in Athens, although neither he nor Ruth Anne ever expected to put down roots here. But put them down they did, especially after seeing all that the town has to offer. Having moved from Sarasota, FL, to Amelia Island and later to a gated community in Jacksonville, the Hancocks found themselves "free as a bird and looking for a nest," Ruth Anne says.

Long familiar with Athens, the couple took a closer look and "just decided that this is a nice place to be," remembers Ruth Anne, 66, a Humboldt, TN, native and former social worker. "We found it to be very attractive here," she says, noting that John is a native of Alma, GA, some 200 miles from Athens.

"We came and looked around one weekend and appreciated the architecture of the houses and the abundant trees, azaleas and camellias," she says, remembering being smitten by the town's "general atmosphere and (house) prices that are unbelievable."

On their sojourn through the streets and avenues of Athens, the couple happened upon "one house (that) reached its arms around us, saying, 'I've been waiting for you to come,'" she recalls. Built in the early 1990s, the one-story house has some 4,000 square feet, four bedrooms, three and a half baths and a floor-to-ceiling, stacked-stone fireplace that reminds Ruth Anne of the stacked-stone fences of Tennessee. A sunroom, bonus room and master bedroom with fireplace give the Hancocks, a blended family of six, room for visitors.

"It is nice to live in a university town where we get to enjoy so many activities," she notes, citing "excellent dining and fabulous restaurants, (including) the

Last Resort with eclectic food that is excellent" and lunches at the state botanical gardens in Athens.

Athens allows easy access for weekend getaways, whether to mountains or beaches, she says, adding that another plus is that "shopping is quite satisfactory. We have Macy's, Belks and Talbots and a host of small shops."

In addition, the area has a military base, Navy Supply Corps School, with a commissary and exchange. Retired from the U.S. Navy (with four years active duty and 24 years in the Reserves), John survived all the major battles in the Pacific during World War II, including battles of Coral Sea and Midway, where his ship, Yorktown CV-5, was sunk. He was among World War II veterans interviewed by news anchor Tom Brokaw, who visited the couple's Athens home in preparation for the national showing of "The Greatest Generation." Brokaw's interview with John framed Athens' lifestyle as one of the best.

Athens, GA

Population: 108,222 in Athens, with 8.1% age 65 and older. The total includes a limited number of University of Georgia students permanently residing in Clarke County.

Location: Athens is in north Georgia, 65 miles northeast of Atlanta.

Climate: High Low
January 52 32
July 90 69
The area has complete seasonal cycles with pleasant spring and fall seasons, typically mild winters and little snow.

Average relative humidity: 52%

Rain: 49.7 inches

Snow: Less than one inch annually

Cost of living: Lower than average

Average housing costs: In Athens, the median house value is $150,000. Typical cost of a new two-bedroom, three-bath home is about $160,000.

Sales tax: 7% (state 4%, city and county 3%)

Sales tax exemptions: Groceries are exempt.

State income tax: Georgia's personal income tax system consists of six brackets with a top rate of 6% kicking in at an income level of $7,000 for single filers and $10,000 for married couples filing jointly.

Income tax exemptions: For residents age 62 and older, retirement income up to $15,000 is not taxed. Up to $4,000 of earned income can be included in the $15,000. There is no tax on Social Security, interest on U.S. obligations or railroad retirement income.

Estate tax: Georgia does not levy estate tax on inheritances resulting from deaths after Jan. 1, 2005.

Property tax: Property is taxed on the assessed value, which is defined as 40 percent of the fair market value. Thus, the assessed value of a $150,000 house is $60,000, and the tax rate of $33.05 per

$1,000 of assessed value produces taxes of $1,983, without exemptions. You'll find more details on www.athensclarke county.com/tc.

Homestead exemptions: There is an exemption of $10,000 off assessed value. Therefore, on a $150,000 house, the net assessed value is $50,000. Its actual taxes are $1,653, but a credit for $264 provided by a grant to owners of homesteaded property reduces the owner's bill to $1,389.

Personal property tax: Household property is not normally taxable. Automobiles are taxed on the assessed value, which is defined as 40 percent of the fair market value. Thus, the assessed value of a $30,000 vehicle is $12,000, and the property tax rate of .03305 totals taxes of $397.

Religion: The Athens area has more than 86 houses of worship representing 17 denominations, including Protestant, Catholic, Jewish and Islamic.

Education: The community is home to the University of Georgia and satellite campuses of Gainesville College, Piedmont College, Old Dominion University and Athens Technical College. Affiliated

"The health care here has been fantastic," adds Ruth Anne, touting the town's "two excellent hospitals and many specialty physicians."

John, who golfed while living in Florida, has turned to gardening in Georgia, where he is involved with the local Purple Heart Association and a study group, the Torch Club. While John has discovered a passion for azaleas, Ruth Anne has found "wonderful, sweet water that does not have to be treated. It is delicious," she says.

John, who retired from the Bell Telephone System and later owned an automotive business, is taking ukulele lessons. The town's abundant musicians who offer music lessons are "an advantage of living here," says Ruth Anne.

"We fell into place as if we were mystically drawn to live here. There is a vibrant attitude, even among retirees. Athens is not a sit-on-the-front-porch place. It is electric. There is a lot of enthusiasm from people of all ages, and you feel it," she says. "There is no place like Athens — and we're so happy to call this town home."

Chet and Jeanne LaGrone are a bit more hesitant to extol the town's benefits. "I would like to keep it a secret," Jeanne admits, explaining that if too many people discover what Athens offers, the population might mushroom, traffic might become congested and shops could grow crowded.

"It's not so big that you can't get somewhere in a hurry, yet there are enough things to do," she reports, explaining that they have found all the things they expected and hoped for in a college town. "The city is just the right size," says Jeanne, who retired from public relations and newspaper work.

When Chet neared retirement, the couple drew up a list of factors — city size, taxes, climate, transportation, health care — that mattered most to them. Having narrowed their search to college towns in the Southeast, the LaGrones had no trouble selecting Athens, where their daughter had attended college. They knew that a college town would provide access to some of their favorite pastimes: sports, music and dance performances.

After working 35 years as an engineer with DuPont, Chet retired at 58. One month later, the couple moved to Athens, where they rented an apartment for one year and "looked at every corner of this county," Jeanne remembers.

Content that Athens was right for them, the LaGrones purchased a 1,800-square-foot, three-bedroom, two-bath, ranch-style house in Country Club Estates. Some five miles from the University of Georgia campus, the house has a current value of about $120,000. With no through traffic, their neighborhood is well suited for Chet's thrice-weekly, three-mile walks. He also swims several days a week at the YMCA, and Jeanne routinely does aerobics and weight training at an area health club.

---

with Elderhostel, Learning in Retirement (LIR) in Athens (www.geron.uga.edu/lir) from September through May offers daytime courses such as strength training, medieval and Renaissance papacy, French bistro cooking and computer skills. LIR year-round offers bridge, quilting and conversational French plus summer activities and a travel/study program with day trips.

Transportation: Athens-Ben Epps Airport is served by USAirways Express, which flies twice daily Monday through Friday and once daily on Saturdays and Sundays with service to Charlotte, NC. Most major airlines serve nearby Hartsfield-Jackson Atlanta International Airport, a major hub with connections to numerous destinations around the world. Bus service is provided by Greyhound. There is no passenger rail service. "The Bus" municipal transportation service is provided by the county.

Health: The area has 157 physicians, 42 dentists and two hospitals, St. Mary's Hospital with 196 beds and Athens Regional Medical Center with 319 beds. Athens has three immediate-care facilities, four outpatient surgery clinics, three mental-health centers, five rehabilitation centers and four nursing homes.

Housing options: Athens offers a variety of housing options ranging from downtown lofts to country estates. With no buy-in fees or leases, **Iris Place Retirement Residence**, (706) 425-0301, offers studios, one- and two-bedroom apartments and one- and two-bedroom cottages and garden suites. Monthly rent includes meals, weekly housekeeping, most utilities, transportation and activities. Apartment residents receive three meals daily; cottage and garden suite residents receive one. Because of the large number of students, there are multiple choices in rental opportunities with prices usually dependent upon location and the specific unit's amenities. The typical two-bedroom apartment rents for $700; a typical two-bedroom townhouse rents for $900 monthly. Several condominium communities house older citizens.

Visitor lodging: Athens boasts 1,637 guest rooms, including 73 at the recently constructed Comfort Suites. Hilton Garden Inn plans to open another 185 in January 2006. Overnight rates vary by seasons and community activities. Suburban Extended Stay of Athens has single nightly rates that begin at $49.99 and weekly rates from $209.99, (706) 208-8812. The Athens Holiday Inn, with more than 300 rooms and free parking, is $72-$130, (800) 862-8436. Holiday Inn Express, with deluxe continental breakfast, is $78-$83, (706) 546-8122 or (877) 500-6966. Dating to 1820 and once a stagecoach stop, the Grand Oaks Manor, on 34 acres five miles from downtown Athens, is $99-$169, (706) 353-2200. Magnolia Terrace Guest House, built in 1912 and with eight guest rooms, is $85-$150, (706) 548-3860. There are five campgrounds with RV parking.

Information: Athens-Clarke County Unified Government, P.O. Box 1868, Athens, GA 30603, (706) 613-3795 or www.athensclarkecounty.com. Athens Area Chamber of Commerce, 246 W. Hancock Ave., Athens, GA 30601, (706) 549-6800 or www.athenschamber.net. Athens Convention and Visitors Bureau, 300 N. Thomas St., Athens, GA 30601, (706) 357-4430, (800) 653-0603 or www.visitathensga.com.

"We walk all over the place," reports Chet, a Georgia Tech alumnus who spent his last 17 work years in Delaware. Before retiring to Athens, the couple had 10 different addresses, mostly along the East Coast. But when it came time to retire, they wanted a vibrant Southern college town with a favorable climate and cost of living.

"Crime is low here," adds Chet, who has spent countless hours volunteering as a tutor and with the Food Bank, Kiwanis Club and AARP's tax assistance to mid- and low-income retirees. Jeanne is involved with her church and helps with outreach programs and a soup kitchen. A Delta Gamma alumna, she is an adviser to the sorority's local chapter.

Climate was a consideration for the Louisiana natives, who wanted to avoid the heat and humidity of their youth. The moderate temperatures have been a joy, they report. Chet highly recommends Athens to those considering retiring to the town, and he remains pleased with the "nice climate, enough things to do (and) no waiting in lines of traffic."

After visiting Athens in 1867, naturalist John Muir later described the town as "a remarkably beautiful and aristocratic town." How good it is, after all these years, that some things never change. ●

Beaufort, South Carolina

Lovely waterscapes, live oaks and antebellum homes draw retirees
to this historic South Carolina town

By Jim Kerr

From their back yard atop a 25-foot-high bluff, Bob and Cindy Stoothoff look across a salt marsh waterway to one of the most picturesque and historic towns in the southeastern United States. Between the moss-draped branches of tall and twisting live oaks, the roofs and verandas of antebellum houses in Beaufort, SC, peek out over the banks of the Beaufort River.

Sailing schooners and Union warships once entered Port Royal Sound from the Atlantic near here, and while pleasure craft and shrimp boats with shallower drafts call these days, captains are still mindful of the six- to nine-foot tides as they maneuver vessels dockside. For Bob and Cindy, the flowing tides make for an interesting swim from their own dock, as tidal waters carry them along to neighboring landings. They have lived here on Lady's Island, across from Beaufort, since January 1998 after they bought and completely refurbished a 1940s Lowcountry cottage and guesthouse.

"We knew we wanted the southeastern U.S. for retirement," says Bob, now 63, "and while we weren't ready for retirement yet, we came down here to take a look." He grew up in suburban Chicago and worked there as director of sales for the food service division of Quaker Oats. Cindy, 55, was director of national account sales for Sara Lee, and while she wasn't ready to retire either, the couple began to look for a lifestyle that was substantially different from both Chicago and Vermont, where they owned a second home.

"In 1986, we saw an ad for Dataw Island, a few miles from Beaufort," Bob remembers. "We found Beaufort very appealing. But because we wanted a gated community that was both comfortable and secure, so we could both commute in our work, we bought a fully furnished model at Dataw with a beachy, bamboo look. It was wonderful, but two things propelled us to move to Lady's Island where we are today: the water

and proximity to downtown Beaufort."

Beaufort was established in 1711, and Lowcountry rice and indigo plantations made it one of the wealthiest hamlets on the continent by the 1750s. Water, as it always has, plays a key role in the lives of those who live, work, visit and retire here. There are 64 large and medium-sized islands and roughly 2,000 smaller ones spread over 587 square miles of Beaufort County, which includes the communities of Port Royal, Bluffton and Hilton Head Island.

The town of Beaufort (pronounced like the word "beautiful") is actually on Port Royal Island, located in the extreme southeast corner of South Carolina, midway between Savannah and Charleston. Rivers and sounds provide sparkling water vistas, and tall grasses in golden marshes wave lazily in the offshore breezes. Huge live oaks dripping with Spanish moss all but hide many of the 400-plus antebellum homes and historic sites designated in the National Historic Landmark District.

Shops, restaurants, offices and art galleries line Beaufort's East Bay Street, while elegantly restored homes, some dating to the American Revolution, stand regally along the west end of the street. A waterfront park and public marina occupy most of the shoreline along the Beaufort River.

Although the historic town is compacted into about 150 square blocks, its environs extend out miles in all directions into other towns, neighborhoods and gated communities, many of which were once part of prosperous plantations. A two-lane swing bridge connects Beaufort with several of these communities to the south, including Lady's Island, Cat Island, St. Helena Island, Dataw Island and Fripp Island.

When Bob and Cindy moved to Dataw Island in 1987, they were undaunted by the eight-mile commute up U.S. Highway 21 to Beaufort. It was a breeze compared to their daily trek to

work in downtown Chicago. They worked out of their Dataw house and played golf on an outstanding course that ran along a vast, fertile wetland.

But their growing interest in community projects and desire to live closer to the water spurred them to new quarters, and in 1998 they moved to 25-square-mile Lady's Island, which they consider part of downtown Beaufort. From here, Cindy makes the drive almost daily to Port Royal, where she spends up to 40 hours a week as the volunteer manager of the Habitat ReStore. The store accepts donated furniture and other goods that are sold to raise money for construction materials used in homes bought by qualified low income families.

Bob is also on the go most of the time, working as a volunteer in a variety of preservation and conservation projects, on government affairs committees and with various business and professional groups that address such issues as conservation and growth. The latter is a major issue. Beaufort County's population of 135,725 has grown 57 percent since 1990, although much of that has been on Hilton Head Island and nearby Bluffton.

The town of Beaufort has a population of around 15,000, and there are three military bases that contribute almost half a billion dollars annually to the local economy. When combined, the Marine Corps Air Station, Parris Island Marine Recruit Depot and the Naval Hospital account for an estimated 10,000 family members in the area. The retiree population has grown substantially and now includes Bob's 95-year-old father, who recently took up residence in the guest cottage. Still, the population is highly diverse, and the median age in the county is 35.

"There are wonderful examples of people who have retired here and plunged into the community, starting businesses and volunteering," says Billy Keyserling, a former state legislator, local real estate agent and current town council member. "There are more nonprofit organizations here per capita than most small towns. We use a lot of new people as volunteers. Our challenge is diversity, and the main question is, how do we absorb the people who want to come here?"

One answer appears to be the diversity of housing venues. While Beaufort is a town filled with families, many of whom have been here for generations, most newcomers gravitate to outlying developments. Dick and Arlene Porter moved a medically oriented publishing business here from New Jersey in 1993, renting a house in Beaufort while they

built at Callawassie Island, a 900-acre golf community with approximately 700 building lots 20 minutes south of downtown Beaufort.

"We did our homework," says Dick, 65. "We searched along the southeast coast from Charleston to Savannah on one-week to 10-day vacations every year for five years. It was actually fortunate we rented in town because we got to know a lot of people and made many close friends. Southern hospitality prevailed. I was introduced to the Beaufort County Arts Council and served on the board for three years."

Beaufort is ranked as one of the best fine arts towns in America, a legacy dat-

ing to pre-Civil War days. It was one of the wealthiest communities in the country when the war broke out, but when 60 warships and 12,000 troops from the Union army showed up one day in November 1861, the townspeople fled en masse in what became known as the Grand Skedaddle. Their homes became hospitals for the wounded and headquarters for the general staff, and while most residents never returned, the town, like Savannah, was spared in Union Gen. William T. Sherman's destructive drive north through the Carolinas.

Beaufort is a favorite with Hollywood, which has produced more than 20 major motion pictures here. Author Pat Con-

Beaufort, SC

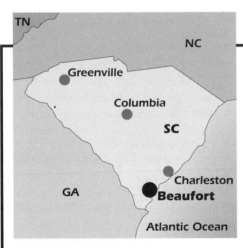

Population: About 15,000 in the town of Beaufort and 135,725 in Beaufort County.
Location: Beaufort, the county seat, is in the southeast corner of the state. A historic port city several miles inland from the Atlantic, it is situated on the Beaufort River 65 miles south of Charleston, SC, 30 miles north of Hilton Head Island and a 45-minute drive north of Savannah, GA.
Climate: High Low
January   58   38
July   90   74
Average relative humidity: 75%
Rain: 48 inches annually
Snow: None
Cost of living: Average to slightly above average
Average housing cost: Costs vary considerably among Beaufort's many housing venues, with premium prices for waterfront property. On Lady's Island, the median cost of a single-family home is about $400,000. Houses for sale in the historic district range from $700,000 to

$4.2 million. The median home price in Beaufort is $212,000. In outlying planned communities, homes with golf-course views average $275,000 to $550,000.
Sales tax: 5% state sales tax, with the occasional imposition of a county tax for special purposes.
Sales tax exemptions: Prescriptions, dental prosthetics and hearing aids. Persons 85 and older pay 1% less sales tax.
State income tax: Graduated in six tiers that range from 2.5% on taxable income up to $2,530 to 7% (less $367) on taxable income of more than $12,650.
Income tax exemptions: Social Security benefits are exempt from state income taxes, and that portion of benefits taxed at the federal level are deductible from South Carolina taxable income. Also, there is an exemption of up to $3,000 in any pension if under 65 and up to $10,000 in pensions if 65 or older. Taxpayers over 65 can take a $15,000 deduction off any income, although that's reduced by the amount of retirement exemption taken.
Estate tax: None
Property tax: Assessed value of homes is determined by multiplying market value by 4% for primary residents and by 6% for second homes and investment property. The tax rate is $19.86 per $100 of assessed value in the city and $19.70 outside the city. Annual taxes on a $212,000 primary home in the city would be about $1,684. Outside the city, the taxes would

be about $1,671. Personal property taxes are calculated at the same rates for motor homes, airplanes and boats, which are assessed at 10.5% of appraised value, and vehicles, which are assessed at 7.5% of appraised value.
Homestead exemptions: The first $50,000 of market value of a home is exempt from property taxes for citizens over 65.
Religion: There are 30 denominational churches, 12 nondenominational churches and one synagogue in greater Beaufort.
Education: The University of South Carolina at Beaufort offers associate degrees in arts and science as well as four-year degree programs. A south campus, adjacent to Sun City Hilton Head in Bluffton on U.S. Highway 278, openeds fall 2004. Residents over 55 can participate in a learning exchange program through the university in which retirees both teach and attend classes that last four to six weeks and cover a variety of subjects. The Technical College of the Lowcountry also has nearly 9,000 students annually in more than 70 programs.
Transportation: While somewhat off the beaten track, Beaufort is easily accessed from Interstate 95 via U.S. Highway 21 from the north and highways 278 and 170 from the south. The town has a small general aviation airport with commercial airline connections out of Charleston, 65 miles away, and Savannah, a 45-minute drive that meanders

roy, who grew up in Beaufort, further contributed to the town's popularity with novels such as "The Great Santini" and "Prince of Tides," the movie versions of which were filmed here. The Stoothoffs like to point across the river to a Colonial-style white house with a red roof poking through the trees along Beaufort's historical eastern shore. The 1850s house was used in "The Great Santini" and "The Big Chill," filmed in 1979 and 1983, respectively.

While houses can be found for sale in the historic district, few are priced under $700,000. Most newcomers opt for locations outside town, which range from raw land on undeveloped islands to planned communities where traditional living is replicated with classic coastal architecture.

Beale Cummings, a retiree from Maryland who works part time in real estate, bought six acres and built a house on St. Helena Island, a 47-square-mile, largely agricultural area where houses are still few and far between. "My wife wanted to be far enough south without being in Florida," Beale says. "We started in New Bern, NC, and moved our motor home 50 miles every other day for a month looking for property."

They found the combination of Beaufort's historic town and St. Helena's plantation and pastoral past to be exactly what they were looking for. "There was one porch light visible when we moved in three years ago," he laughs. "Now there are three, and I'm upset."

At Bull Point, an upscale real estate development some 15 miles northwest of Beaufort, there are no porch lights visible behind the plantation-style home of Wayne and Gladys Cousar. The 700-acre site is located on a wooded peninsula surrounded by creeks and salt marshes that once formed part of a large rice plantation. Of the 385 homes planned, about 20 have been built at press time and several more are under construction.

Wayne, 67, and Gladys, 64, lived for 32 years in Atlanta, where Wayne was a

around creeks and rivers. U.S. Airways Express has service between Hilton Head and Charlotte, NC, a U.S. Airways hub. Rental cars are available at the airports. Northbound and southbound Amtrak trains arrive daily in Yemassee, about 25 miles north of Beaufort. The train stops in both Charleston and Savannah and has sleeper cars.

Health. Beaufort Memorial Hospital has 150 board-certified specialists and a full range of medical care services with a 24-hour emergency department. BMH partners with Duke University Medical Center, giving physicians and patients access to Duke expertise in cancer and cardiac care. New cancer and heart centers opened recently with $10 million raised in a community campaign. The Naval Hospital provides health care for veterans, with a 20-bed hospital and emergency department.

Housing options: While there are homes for sale in Beaufort's charming historic district, few are priced below $700,000. Restored waterfront homes, many of which date from the mid-1700s to mid-1800s, generally cost well over $1 million when available. Anything on the water in or near Beaufort is premium property. In town, but not on the water, three-bedroom homes on small lots are priced from $145,000 to $305,000. A recent sampling of fast-growing Lady's Island, across the river, shows 156 homes from $49,000 for a mobile unit to $2.5 million for a large home on the water, a range that translates into an average price of $445,000. Nearby Port Royal is considered a good buy with strong investment potential, with modest homes selling from $185,000. Agents specializing in the area include Pat Harvey-Palmer, Hometown Realty, (800) 832-0066, and Beale Cummings, Coldwell Banker, (888) 838-3813. **Dataw Island**, (800) 848-3838, had several listings at press time, and they started at $250,000, plus substantial monthly homeowner fees. Homesites start at around $30,000. **Habersham**, (877) 542-2377, located in Beaufort, is a new master-planned community with traditional coastal architecture and homes priced from $250,000 to $1 million, flats from $248,000, and townhomes from $289,000. **Bull Point**, (800) 846-9003, 20 minutes northwest of Beaufort, has home sites from three-quarters of an acre to six acres ranging from $150,000 to more than $1 million. **Callawassie Island**, (800) 221-8431, midway between Beaufort and Hilton Head, has home sites from $25,000 and homes from $280,000 to $1.2 million. **Celadon**, (866) 525-9995, a new neighborhood on Lady's Island, features Colonial-style condominiums, two-story row houses and live-and-work homes with separate entrances for residence and business. Home sites start at $45,000 and homes from the $300,000s. **Islands of Beaufort**, (877) 334-7526, is a new and secluded, gated waterfront community 10 minutes from downtown with home sites starting at $86,000. Four assisted-living communities, plus a nursing home, provide specialized care for seniors, including **Morningside**, (843) 982-0270; **Helena House** in Port Royal, (843) 982-0233; and **River Oaks Residential Care**, (843) 521-2298.

Visitor lodging: Beaufort is a popular tourist town and stopover between Savannah and Charleston, with a variety of accommodations, including motels, hotels and bed-and-breakfast inns. Downtown hotels include the 43-room Best Western Sea Island Inn, with rates ranging seasonally from $109 to $139, (843) 522-2090; the 79-room Comfort Inn starting at $89, (843) 525-9366; and the 86-room Sleep Inn starting at $70, (843) 522-3361. Beaufort's B&Bs are the best bet for atmosphere and convenience. They include the luxury Beaufort Inn one block off the waterfront, built in 1897 and elegantly renovated with 21 rooms and suites starting at $145, (888) 522-0250, and the Rhett House Inn, with 18 rooms in the heart of the historic district, starts at $145, (888) 480-9530. Many hotels and B&Bs offer lower rates during the summer season.

Information: Greater Beaufort Chamber of Commerce, 1106 Carteret St., P.O. Box 910, Beaufort, SC 29901, (843) 986-5400, or www.beaufortsc.org. Ask for free relocation and tourism guides.

captain for Delta Airlines. "It's a home in a hometown community," he says of Bull Point, where the couple bought in 1997 and moved in 2000. "It's very low-density, and you get a chance to meet people slowly as they build and move in. It's not a resort thing."

He and Gladys were taken by the large forested lots, river views and array of wildlife, including deer, foxes, raccoons, bobcats and "tons of birds." They built a 4,200-square-foot Lowcountry plantation-style house that Wayne describes as "raised Greek revival." Wealthy plantation owners called them "cottages" back in the 1840s, but the description hardly fits today. The roomy, open-air, two-story house features a large screened veranda, a self-contained guest room linked by a breezeway, and a wooded back yard that slopes down to a dock. From here, it's a 45-minute boat ride into Beaufort aboard the Cousars' 27-foot Sea Ray, traveling along a creek that ultimately flows into the Beaufort River and Intracoastal Waterway.

When they are not involved in Beau-fort's Historic Foundation, the Rotary or church, the Cousars like to entertain their visiting children and grandchildren, who are delighted by the opportunities to swim, fish and drive around in Wayne's golf cart. "You can feel the wind and hear the birds," Gladys says. "You blend in with nature, and when you've had enough of peace and quiet, you go into Beaufort."

It's a perfect blend for many active retirees here. Arlene Porter at Callawassie found herself involved not only in wildlife projects such as the annual Audubon bird count, but also in community volunteer work, an ideal alternative to grueling production deadlines she once faced in the couple's publishing business. Dick Porter is an avid golfer, tennis player and kayaker who spent five years watching over loggerhead turtle eggs in a conservation program on Hunting Island, a state park and preserve east of Beaufort on the Atlantic seashore.

Beaches, wetlands, forests, waterways, wildlife, history, community life and recreation: It all seems to be here in some combination that suits retirees looking for the proper balance. When Frank and Linda Hager drove down from a vacation at Kiawah Island one rainy day in 1986, they were looking for a beach community. "We almost discarded the idea of Dataw Island because it had no beach," remembers Frank, now 65. "But when we crossed over the causeway onto the island, it was magical. The clouds parted and we saw white egrets in the trees with the sun shining through. There was already one 18-hole course and a marina, and we're both golfers and boaters."

They bought a patio home and used it as a getaway until moving permanently from Winston-Salem, NC, into a newer, larger house. Their large circle of friends includes the Stoothoffs, who sold them the Dataw Island home in 1999. And while the previous owners now have a view across the river to Beaufort's historic shoreline, Frank and Linda are equally content with the morning dew glistening off the 10th green of the Cotton Dike course, and the white egrets perched in the loblolly pines. ●

Bend, Oregon

On the sunny side of the Cascade Range, this central Oregon town is a natural paradise

By Bob Woodward

In the late 1800s, Farewell Bend was a small settlement on the banks of the Deschutes River. It was the last hospitable place pioneers visited before fording the river and starting the arduous trek west over the Cascade Mountains to the Oregon Territory's rich farmlands.

Today the village is a town called Bend (the Farewell was dropped by the U.S. Postal Service in 1905), and now it is even more hospitable — especially to retirees.

Located close to the geographical center of Oregon, Bend's attractions are many: a relatively mild high-desert climate, a variety of affordable housing options, a slower pace of life, clean air and water and a myriad of recreation opportunities minutes from town.

"My dream," says Joan Casey, "had always been to move to the country." Joan, 57, and her husband, John, 61, first came to central Oregon on a tour of the Northwest in 1990. "We were looking for a place to retire when we left California and Orange County," says Joan, "and our one-day planned stay in the Bend area turned into a five-day stay." They were booked at Sunriver Resort, 15 miles south of Bend, and ended up buying a condominium there.

In 1994, John sold his commercial pump business and officially retired. "When we finally decided to leave Orange County, we moved into our Sunriver condo for two years and started looking around the Bend area for something more permanent," John says.

"Something more permanent" had a ranch feeling for John, who envisioned himself as a rancher. But after looking at several ranches of 100 acres and larger on the outskirts of Bend, John had an epiphany. "I realized that I didn't need the responsibility that comes with a huge agricultural property," he laughs.

They settled for a smaller 15-acre tract closer to town — and even that proved, after a year and a half, to be too much work. So they bought a magnificent old house, built in 1907 on the banks of the Deschutes River, just minutes from Bend's downtown core. "Certainly being within walking distance of the downtown was a big plus," John says.

For Joan, her main reasons for moving to Bend were realized with their home on the river. "I came here to be in beautiful natural surroundings away from the sensory overload of Southern California," she says, "and to have other outdoor natural experiences close at hand. In short, I moved here to soothe my soul."

For John, the area's clean air, clean water and quiet were high on his list of reasons to move to Bend. Also important were the number of good golf courses and excellent fly-fishing opportunities in the area. Added incentive for the couple was the fact that their daughter and her husband had just completed a lengthy study of communities in the Pacific Northwest where they would like to live and start a business. They settled on Bend.

Getting started in the community after buying their new close-to-town home was easy for the Caseys. Joan, an avid art collector, went to work as a volunteer at a local art gallery.

Spurred on by what he'd seen happen to the open spaces in Orange County during his 30-plus years there, John became active as a volunteer with the Deschutes Basin Land Trust. "I saw a chance to help preserve open space and lands for future generations, and I jumped at it," he says. He has served as its president and is a current member of the executive board. Together the Caseys are involved in the Sacred Art of Living Center, which focuses on the healing arts. Joan says it has been "one of the true surprises and benefits of living in this community."

To the Caseys, Bend is all about community. "Most of the people we know who have come here to retire have really given back and continue to give back to the community," Joan says.

That's certainly true of Jim and Carol Bradfield, who retired to Bend from the San Francisco Bay Area. "After I retired from the food service industry in 1996, we sold our house in Mill Valley and started looking around for places to retire," says Jim, 62. "We looked around Santa Barbara, South Carolina and Mexico."

While mulling over these retirement possibilities, Jim and Carol decided to spend some time cruising on their sailboat.

"We'd been cruising for two years and were living on our sailboat in Mexico when our financial adviser recommended that we establish residence in Nevada for tax reasons," Jim says. "So we looked around the Minden-Gardnerville area south of Carson City and found a place to buy in the small town of Genoa. We liked the fact that Genoa didn't get much snow, yet was close enough to the Sierras and some excellent ski resorts."

Then fate intervened. The deal on the house fell through. Pondering what to do, Jim recalled a short stint he'd had as a sous chef at a resort near Bend years before and asked Carol if she'd be willing to give the town a look-over. "I'd really liked Bend when I was there, and the geography of place was similar to Genoa — mountains to the west and high desert country to the east of town," he says.

Carol, 58, immediately fell in love with Bend. "We were driving down the main (Wall) street, and I kept saying what a quaint, lovely town it was. And while I was going on enthusiastically, Jim was commenting on how much the town had changed since he'd been here," she says.

Once they stood in Drake Park in downtown Bend, looking out over the Cascade Mountains, they knew that this was to be their new home. They signed a one-year lease on a house and began looking for a permanent residence. Their search led them to purchase a five-acre parcel of land on the outskirts of Bend with a picture-perfect view of the Cascades' snowcapped volcanoes.

"But after a year of living in town" in the rental, Carol says, "we realized that what we wanted more than anything was to be within walking distance of the restaurants, the parks and the events."

So they sold their rural acreage and bought a house on Awbrey Butte just minutes from downtown Bend. Settled in, they dove into local activities. Jim found his niche at the parks and recreation district as a volunteer hiking, snowshoeing and cross-country skiing trip leader. He did such an outstanding job that he was named the Bend Metro Park and Recreation volunteer of the year in 2002.

In 1999, Carol put her background in clinical psychology and facilitating experience to use by volunteering at the local hospice as a grief and bereavement counselor. Jim joined Carol as a hospice volunteer in 2001.

Jim also became politically active as a founding father of the Truman Club, a social club designed to give busy professionals who vote Democratic a forum to discuss local, state and national issues. One of the benefits of this, Jim says, is "getting to know the governor of the state on a first-name basis."

Apart from their volunteer work, the Bradfields are active hikers, snowshoers and cross-country skiers, the latter two sports making Bend's wintry climate an attraction.

The amenities they felt they would surely miss when they moved to Bend were all cultural. "Frankly, we were expecting to travel regularly to Portland and even back to the San Francisco Bay Area to get cultural fixes," says Carol, who has been "pleasantly surprised" by the increase in performing arts and such endeavors since they moved to Bend. "We actually go to more concerts and shows here than we ever did in the Bay Area," adds Jim.

Last year Jim also discovered another good reason to live in Bend. "I was diagnosed by a local doctor as having multi-

Bend, OR

Population: About 65,000 in the city of Bend, the seat of Deschutes County. Nearly 20% of Bend's population is 55 or older. The county's population is 130,500.

Location: Bend is located close to the geographical center of Oregon at an elevation of 3,660 feet. To the west are the snowcapped Cascade Mountains; to the east stretches Oregon's vast sagebrush- and juniper-covered high desert country. Oregon's longest river, the 220-mile Deschutes, runs through the center of town. Bend is 500 miles in driving distance north of San Francisco, 327 miles south of Seattle and 175 miles southeast of Portland. Eugene, home of the University of Oregon, is 117 miles west, and Ashland, with its famous Oregon Shakespeare Festival, is 190 miles southwest.

Climate: High Low
January 40 21
July 82 44

Humidity: Bend has a dry mountain cli-

mate.

Rain: 12 inches

Snow: 33.8 inches

In the rain shadow of the Cascade Mountains, Bend has close to 300 days of sunshine per year. The number of sunny days fools people into thinking Bend is warm year-round. In fact, summers are short (usually mid-July until the end of September) and evening temperatures can drop below freezing 10 months a year. Bend has little or no spring season. The seasons almost always go directly from winter to summer, making for a short growing season.

Cost of living: Above average

Average housing cost: The median price of a single-family home is $258,000. The median price of a condo or townhome is $239,050.

Sales tax: None

State income tax: For single filers, it ranges from 5% of taxable income up to $2,650 to $413 plus 9% of the excess over $6,650. For married couples filing jointly, it ranges from 5% of taxable income up to $5,300 to $825 plus 9% of the excess over $13,300.

Income tax exemptions: Social Security benefits are exempt, as is all federal pension income based on service performed before Oct. 1, 1991. For federal pension income based on service before and after Oct. 1, 1991, the pension subtraction is prorated. Federal pensions for service on or after Oct. 1, 1991, and state

and private pensions are not exempt.

Intangibles tax: None

Estate tax: Applicable to estates of $1 million or more. For estates exceeding $1 million, an Oregon inheritance return must be filed.

Property tax: The property tax rate on a single-family dwelling in Bend is $15.1107 per $1,000 in assessed value, making taxes on a $250,000 home about $3,778 per year.

Homestead exemption: The homestead deferral program exempts from property taxes those 62 and older or disabled who meet certain income requirements. There is a 6 percent interest on the deferred amount, payable at death or upon selling the home.

Religion: Bend has more than 120 churches representing some 30 religions.

Education: Bend is the home of Central Oregon Community College (COCC), which offers two-year associate degrees. Oregon State University has a branch on the COCC campus. Through COCC, Oregon State offers 20 four-year degree programs in collaboration with partner institutions such as the University of Oregon and Eastern Oregon University (EOU). Central Oregon Community College serves 4,000 students and is located less than a mile from the center of town.

Transportation: Nearby (16 miles north), Redmond Airport serves the Bend and central Oregon area. Both United Express

ple system atrophy (MSA), a disease similar to Parkinson's. Specialists at Oregon Heath Sciences University in Portland corroborated that diagnosis. It made me feel very confident with the talent of the medical professionals and the medical facilities here in Bend."

Having first-class medical facilities close at hand wasn't even on Glen and Barbara Bates' list of needs when they started looking for a place to retire. Golf was a key ingredient in the search for the then Connecticut-based couple. "We started looking at communities about six years before we both retired," says Glen, 62. "We knew we wanted to be out West and started our search in Santa Fe, and in ensuing years covered Arizona, northern California, Idaho and Montana."

Both Barbara and Glen grew up in Washington state and met while attending Linfield College in Oregon's wet Willamette Valley. They had some idea of what the dry east side of Oregon was like. And with parents still residing in Washington, they thought they might give central Oregon a look.

Barbara, 60, picks up the story. "We planned a trip to see Glen's parents and did some research on golf possibilities in Oregon. Bend looked promising and so we stopped, stayed, golfed and left thinking this was the place for us."

They headed back to their home in Ridgefield, CT, where Glen eventually closed down his software consulting company. Soon afterwards Barbara retired from her position as a human resources manager at a computer company.

In February 2000, Glen and Barbara made a short visit to Bend where, in between looking for houses, they walked two golf courses. They returned home without having purchased a house — but they were new members of a golf club. Their friends in Connecticut thought they were nuts to make a permanent move out West without a place to live. "We'd tell them that we'd live in the car and shower at the clubhouse until we found a place to live," Barbara laughs.

---

and Horizon Air offer regularly scheduled daily flights to Portland, where connections can be made to all major domestic air carriers and to Lufthansa for flights to Europe. The flying time from Redmond to Portland is about 30 minutes. Horizon Air also offers morning and evening flights to and from Seattle's Sea-Tac International Airport. United Express offers daily flights to and from San Francisco International Airport. For more information: United Express at (800) 241-6522, Horizon at (800) 547-9308, or visit www.flyrdm.com. Portland International Airport and downtown Portland's Union Station are both accessible daily via the Central Oregon Breeze shuttle service. A senior round-trip ticket is $68, www.cobreeze.com. Bend's Dial-A-Ride van service offers shuttles around town seven days a week. Reservations are required. Fares range from 75 cents for disabled and low-income riders to $1.25 for the general public. U.S. Highway 97 (the Dalles-California Highway) runs through Bend. It's the main artery linking northern California with central Oregon, eastern Washington and eastern British Columbia.

Health: Bend is the primary medical center for all of central Oregon as well as parts of eastern Oregon and western Idaho. Cascade Healthcare Community operates the 220-bed St. Charles Medical Center in Bend and the 40-bed St. Charles Medical Center in nearby Redmond. Cascade Healthcare Community is the area's largest employer with 2,250 employees. The two hospitals offer a wide variety of services, including cardiology, critical care, emergency medicine, neurosurgery and oncology. Air Life helicopters provide emergency transportation.

Housing options: Bend is largely a town of single-family residences. However, an increasing number of condominiums and townhomes have been built in recent years. Those seeking more acreage can find it outside Bend city limits. Near St. Charles Hospital, the **Aspen Ridge Retirement Community**, (541) 385-8500 or www.frontiermgmt.com, rents studio apartments and cottage duplexes to seniors 55 and over. Rents range from $1,620 per month for a studio to $2,900 for a cottage. Located close to the banks of the Deschutes River just 2.5 miles from downtown Bend, **Touchmark**, (888) 231-1113 or www.touchmarkbend.com, offers a campus-style development for seniors over 55. Cliff Lodge, the newest phase of the community, is scheduled to open late 2006. Reservations are available for one- to three-bedroom lodge-style homes priced at $200,000 to $600,000. About 17 miles north of Bend, **The Falls at Eagle Crest**, (888) 703-2557 or www.fallsresortcommunities.com, is an active-adult community with 54 holes of golf, sports facilities, a day spa, trails for hiking and biking, two restaurants, fitness classes, and airport and ski shuttles. Homes start at $302,600.

Visitor lodging: Bend offers a wide variety of lodging from motels to hotels, resorts and bed-and-breakfast inns. In the heart of downtown, the 117-room Phoenix Inn has doubles and suites for $89-$179 per night, (541) 317-9292 or (000) 291-1761. Just a few miles out of town in a wooded setting, Mount Bachelor Village offers hotel rooms starting at $110 to luxury three-bedroom condos overlooking the Deschutes River for $235, (800) 452-9846. Close to downtown and Bend's verdant Drake Park, the Lara House B&B has six rooms with private baths, $90-$150 with breakfast included, (541) 388-4064 or (800) 766-4064. Located on Highway 97 minutes from downtown, the Riverhouse has 220 rooms with prices ranging from $82 to $172. The Deschutes River flows through the center of the property, (541) 389-3111 or (800) 547-3928.

Information: Bend Chamber of Commerce, 777 N.W. Wall St., Suite 200, Bend, OR 97701, (541) 382-3221 or www.bendchamber.com. A relocation package is available for $15. Bend Visitor and Convention Bureau, (877) 245-8484 or www.visitbend.com. Central Oregon Visitors Association, (800) 800-8334 or www.covisitors.com. Economic Development for Central Oregon, (800) 342-4135 or www.edforco.org.

In June, they found a place to live and settled in. Barbara found Bend perfect because of "the viable, lively downtown area, the good restaurants, the proximity to Portland for culture and the air links to get out of town as needed." Glen fell for Bend's "abundance of good golf courses, all the outdoor activities, particularly cycling and hiking, the small-town atmosphere and the Craftsman-style homes."

One chance moment made them realize that they'd made the right decision and had come to the right place. It happened at a local restaurant. "When we came to look around in February, we ate at an excellent restaurant and I had superb lamb shanks," Glen recalls, "and during our meal the chef stopped by our table and talked at length with us. We told him we were planning to move to Bend. Well, we finally moved here and went back to the restaurant for dinner. When I saw the chef, I said, 'See, we moved here as we promised.' And the chef replied, 'Oh, I remember you, lamb shanks back in February.'"

Although they felt at home immediately, it took Glen and Barbara time before they got involved in community life. Now Barbara is a volunteer with the Cascade Festival of Music and the Children's Museum and is a court-appointed special advocate on children's issues. She also helps with the newly formed, nonprofit Volunteers in Medicine, a group of doctors who provide medical services to low-income people who are employed but have no health insurance coverage. For his part, Glen is also involved with the Cascade Festival of Music and is a board member of their homeowners association.

Getting involved has been a pleasant surprise. "We've made more friends more quickly here than anyplace else we've lived," says Barbara. "It seems everyone loves being here." ●

Berkeley Springs, West Virginia

This pretty, historic spa town is perched in the mountains
of West Virginia's Eastern Panhandle

By Candyce H. Stapen

Larry and Pat Springer have been heading for the hills near Berkeley Springs, WV, since the 1970s for weekend getaways from Baltimore, MD. "Our kids used to be terrified of the quiet. They weren't used to it," Pat says. "Once when we had our cabin, it was midweek so there weren't many tourists, and it snowed. We took a walk, and we could hear the snow hit the ground. I told my kids, 'That's why we're here.'"

To savor the country calm, and to slide gradually into retirement, the Springers — musicians and teachers — commuted from Berkeley Springs to Baltimore two hours away several times a week from 1996 until they relocated permanently in 1999. "Every time we drove here, as soon as we crossed over the West Virginia line, the stress went away," notes Larry, a former educator, high school administrator and director of the Johns Hopkins University band. Pat taught music in Baltimore County and at Baltimore's Peabody Institute Elderhostel programs.

Berkeley Springs, the seat of Morgan County, sports a population of just 663. Add the outskirts and the figure jumps to a still manageable 2,500. The Star movie theater shows first-run features on Fridays, Saturdays and Sundays for $3.50 a ticket. Art galleries, craft shops, several restaurants and a hotel ring Berkeley Springs State Park, a 4.5-acre stretch of grass with bathhouses and a community pool in the heart of town. Ridges, rivers and mountains lace the surrounding landscape.

This combination of laid-back country charm and big city access also drew Dave and Eda Doyle, formerly of Potomac, MD. "Every time I go back to the Beltway and to the traffic, I remind myself of why I left," says Dave, who, along with his wife began Daveda Farms, a llama ranch on 46 acres on the outskirts of Berkeley Springs, when they retired from urban life in 1994.

"I'd been in office work. I'm not a golfer, and we wanted to do something outside, something with livestock that weren't going to market, and we wanted to stay within two hours of DC," says Dave, 77. "The Eastern Panhandle, Jefferson and Morgan counties, is growing, but in Berkeley Springs you get a bit more for your money," adds Dave, a former CIA reconnaissance officer.

"I like the location," says Eda, 65. "We go to Washington, DC, to the Kennedy Center and to museums every two months. We recently took friends visiting from New Jersey to see the new Air and Space Center near Dulles Airport. We're in the country, but we're not isolated."

Geography has always played a crucial role in Berkeley Springs, a mountain spot first made famous by its mineral waters. American Indians came to the springs long before the Colonists discovered them. On a map drawn in 1747 by Thomas Jefferson's father, the area was labeled Medicine Springs. In fact, the town is still officially known as Bath, named by the Virginia Legislature in 1776 when the region belonged to that colony.

The name Berkeley Springs came about in 1802 as a postal designation to distinguish this locale from other Baths in Virginia. The springs, rich in magnesium carbonate, emanate from a sandstone ridge 450 feet above the valley and release 1,000 to 2,000 gallons per minute at a constant water temperature of 74 degrees.

In the town park, you can still pump spring water into bottles for free and immerse yourself in a healing bath, followed by a 30-minute massage for the bargain price of $38. Centuries ago George Washington soaked here. Most likely the future president's first plunge in the soothing waters took place on March 18, 1748, when the 16-year-old Washington arrived as part of Lord Fairfax's surveying team.

In 1769, a more well-known and worldly Washington spent five weeks at the springs, bathing and enjoying afternoon tea and dinners with colleagues. To commemorate his dunks, the town placed "George Washington's Bathtub," a replica of a stone pool typical of those used by visitors in the late 1700s, in a section of Berkeley Springs State Park.

Washington was just one of the many socially prominent drawn to the region. In Berkeley Springs, as in many spas in the late 18th and the mid-19th centuries, the wealthy and the well-connected came "to take the waters." In between baths, mothers promenaded under the oak trees with their marriageable daughters while their fathers, rich plantation owners and merchants, gambled at billiards and bet on cockfights.

Now five full-service spa facilities, including Coolfont Resort, a few miles from town, wrap, knead, steam and soothe locals and visitors. "We have a lot more masseuses than lawyers in the county," notes Dave Doyle proudly.

"A lot of women do go regularly to Coolfont or to one of the places in town to soak in the mineral waters and have a massage," says Margaret Biggs, who with her husband, Charles, retired to Berkeley Springs from Warren County, NJ, in 1995. "We are just outside town on 40 to 50 acres against Sleepy Creek Preserve. We take our dog and walk two to four miles a day on our own property."

Awash in history, so to speak, Berkeley Springs sports another jewel: 6,000-acre Cacapon Resort State Park. Located 10 miles from town, this "poor man's country club" offers horseback riding, tennis, boating, lake swimming and fishing as well as golf at cut-rate prices.

Greens fees for the 18-hole course designed by Robert Trent Jones Sr. cost as little as $27 midweek, and cart rentals go for $14 for a single rider. The par-72 course, rated among the top 130 best-designed courses in the United States, tests your skill with 73 sand bunkers and three ponds.

In spring, rangers lead wildflower walks when the park blooms with dogwood, trillium and mountain laurel. Twenty miles of trails wind through meadows and woods and even along Cacapon Mountain, which at 2,300 feet has the highest peak in the Eastern Panhandle. In winter, you can cross-country ski near the river and through the snowy woods.

The hearty can pedal Morgan County's hills on mountain bikes, but for those who like the flat and narrow, it's just six miles to the C&O Canal towpath along the Potomac River. In the country, the stars glow with an intensity not visible in the city. The night sky pops into view with magnified clarity at the Morgan County Observatory, situated on a ridge 10 miles south of town. At the facility's public programs, you can trace the constellations, look for meteors and learn basic astronomy.

Besides nature, the nurture side of Berkeley Springs lures retirees. They especially like the lively arts scene and the volunteer opportunities.

"After my company was bought out four times in eight years, I decided to get out of the rat race," says Lynn Lavin, 63, a former manager in the medical technology field. When Lynn moved from Atlanta in 1998, she intended to co-own and operate a bed-and-breakfast inn in Berkeley Springs with a friend.

"I realized that wasn't for me, but I liked the town and the house next door to the one we looked at, so I bought it. It's a 1920s house with lots of nooks and crannies. Eventually I put the kiln in the double-car garage, and I've been doing my pottery ever since," says Lynn, who sells her ceramics at the Ice House Artists' Co-op, established by the Morgan Arts Council.

For the past four years AmericanStyle magazine has ranked Berkeley Springs as one of the top 20 small arts towns. About 120 working artists, including musicians, writers, potters, weavers, painters, glass artists and sculptors, reside in Berkeley Springs, a high percentage for a town not anchored by a college.

You can find Jerry Spaeth's work for sale at the Ice House as well. The retired auto body mechanic creates whimsical bicyclists, rock 'n' roll guitarists and other pieces from odd car parts. Jonathan Heath, a painter, and Jan Heath, a printmaker, show their work at the Heath Studio Gallery. Gallery sales aren't incidental to Berkeley Springs' economy. In 2004, the town sold more than $800,000 worth of art.

Then there's the active music community. On summer Saturday afternoons, courtesy of the Morgan Arts Council, you can listen to blues and jazz or toe-tap to

Berkeley Springs, WV

Population: The historic center and surrounding town, known officially by its Colonial designation of Bath, have a population of 663. Most people know Bath by its postal service designation of Berkeley Springs. About 2,500 people live in the historic area, plus the surrounding outskirts. Berkeley Springs is the county seat of Morgan County, population 15,514.

Location: Berkeley Springs is located six miles south of Interstate 70 and Interstate 68 in the Eastern Panhandle of West Virginia, approximately 90 minutes west of the Washington and Baltimore beltways.

Climate: High Low
January 45 20
July 90 70

Average relative humidity: 69%
Rain: 37 inches
Snow: 37 inches
Cost of living: Below average
Average housing cost: The average rent for a two-bedroom apartment is $609. In 2004, the average selling price for a home in Morgan County was $150,232. Homes sell from $100,000 to $650,000. A typical 1,800 square-foot, three-bedroom, two-bath house near town ranges from $200,000 to $250,000.
Sales tax: 6%
Sales tax exemptions: Prescription drugs and services.
State income tax: The minimum rate of 3% applies to income up to $10,000 and the maximum rate is 6.5% on income over $60,000.
Income tax exemptions: Under age 65, there is an exemption for federal and some state pensions of up to $2,000 per taxpayer and a full exemption for those in the state and local police, sheriff's and firefighter's pension system. For those age 65 and better, there is an exemption of up to $8,000 in all income. Social Security benefits subject to federal tax are taxable.

Estate tax: None, except for the state's "pickup" portion of the federal tax applicable to estates over $2 million.
Property tax: Within the city limits of the town of Bath, $1.3178 per $100 of assessed value; outside the city limits, $1.1366 per $100 of assessed value. Assessments are at 60% of market value. Tax on a $100,000 home after homestead exemption would be $527 a year within the city limits and $455 outside the city limits. The personal property tax is $2.2732 per $100 on automobiles, campers, motorcycles, above-ground swimming pools, golf carts and business equipment. There is no tax on intangibles.
Homestead exemption: The first $20,000 of assessed value of a homestead is exempt for persons at least 65 years old or certified as being totally and permanently disabled. One must also have lived in West Virginia for two consecutive years and apply between July 1 and Dec. 1 to qualify for the exemption.
Religion: There are 47 churches hold-

Irish folk melodies and country rhythms at a complimentary concert in Berkeley Springs State Park.

Musicians Larry and Pat Springer enjoy putting their talents to use in their adopted town. Larry serves on the Arts Council and performs in a community band while Pat plays in a viola, violin and piano trio and teaches piano to individuals.

Pat also started a piano lab for local high school students. Her dream is that this program will grow countywide. Notes Larry, "When you're younger, you tilt at windmills in the big city. When you get here you can narrow your sights down, and you can actually make a difference in things you care about." As the library director, Larry orchestrated a successful fund-raiser at Tari's, a local restaurant, and quadrupled the number of volumes in the children's section.

That ability to effect change, as much as the beautiful scenery and low-stress lifestyle, ranks high on a survey of retirees who chose Morgan County. "The retirees

wanted to be someplace they could make a difference," notes Jeanne Mozier, vice president of Travel Berkeley Springs, the official convention and visitors bureau for Morgan County. "People want their life to mean something. We're a small enough place to allow that to happen."

Although the Biggses came to Berkeley Springs because their daughter lives here, they found it easy to get involved. "There are a great many activities to volunteer for. The county government welcomes volunteers from locals as well as newcomers," says Charles, a former municipal engineer in New Jersey. "I saw a notice in the local paper for a meeting of the county's solid waste authority and asked them if they were looking for members." Now he's the treasurer.

Margaret, who taught kindergarten and first grade, volunteers in a program that offers reading and basic math assistance to local first-graders who need a bit of extra help. Margaret also put her love of plants to good use when she

served as president of the garden club. The club's current project is replanting the beds next to the old railroad station with chives, sage, rue, lavender, mint and other herbs. Even the Doyles' llamas do their part, visiting nursing homes or a Head Start program to charm seniors as well as the preschool set.

In this "almost heaven" slice of West Virginia, homes sell from $70,000 to $650,000 with a typical 2,000-square-foot, three-bedroom, two-bath house near town currently ranging from $150,000 to $200,000. At Cacapon South and Cacapon East, retirement and second-home developments bordering Cacapon State Park, lots range from $35,900 for one-half of an acre to $70,000 for three acres.

Between 1990 and 2000, the population of Morgan County increased 23.3 percent, the second-largest growth rate in West Virginia. And that's no wonder, considering all that Berkeley Springs has to offer retirees. ●

ing services each week in the county.
Education: In Morgan County, 11.2% of the population possesses a bachelor's degree and 76% are high school graduates. In Shepherdstown, WV, about 33 miles from Berkeley Springs, Shepherd University offers a four-year degree program and has an enrollment of 4,800 students. In Winchester, VA, about 35 miles from Berkeley Springs, Shenandoah University offers bachelor's degrees and has an enrollment of 2,900 students. In Keyser, WV, 60 miles from Berkeley Springs, Potomac State College, a regional campus of West Virginia University, offers two-year associate degrees and has an enrollment of 1,305 students.

Transportation: U.S. Route 522 runs north and south through Berkeley Springs, and West Virginia Route 9 cuts east and west. Interstate 70 leads to Baltimore, 100 miles away, and merges into Interstate 270 leading to Washington, DC, also 100 miles away. Pittsburgh, PA, is about 150 miles away. The Hagerstown Regional Airport in Hagerstown, MD, (240) 313-2777, is located a quarter of a mile from Inter-

state 81, 36 miles east of Berkeley Springs. Two major airports are within 90 miles of Berkeley Springs: Dulles International Airport, (703) 572-2700, and Baltimore/Washington International Airport, (800) 435-9294.

Health: Located in Berkeley Springs, the Morgan County War Memorial Hospital, operated by Winchester Regional Medical Center, has 25 beds, plus a 16-bed long-term care unit as well as a 24-hour emergency room. The Winchester Medical Center in Winchester, VA, is about 35 miles away. Johns Hopkins Hospital in Baltimore is about 100 miles away, as are the hospitals of Washington, DC, including Georgetown University Hospital and the George Washington University Hospital.

Housing options: Berkeley Springs recently underwent a housing boom, with 208 permits issued for new housing in 2004. Favorite retiree selections for new single-family home sites include **Cacapon South**, www.cacaponsouth.com, across Route 522 from Cacapon State Park, and **Cacapon East**, adjacent to a forest that is part of

Cacapon State Park. Together these developments currently have 160 lots. A new section of Cacapon South, with 35 more lots, opened in the summer of 2005. Lots are available from the developer, MDG Companies, www.mdgcompanies.com, ranging from one-half acre for $35,900 to three acres for $70,000. The company can recommend builders. In **Indian Run Village**, a section of Cacapon South, MDG is selling homes of approximately 1,200-1,680 square feet on one-acre lots, currently at prices of $190,000-$300,000, (888) 333-9336.

Visitor lodging: There are more than 100 lodging choices, including vacation homes. In the heart of town is the Inn and Spa at Berkeley Springs, $49-$150, (800) 822-6630. About two miles south of town, the Best Western offers rooms from $79, (866) 945-9400. Check www.berkeleysprings.com for other lodging choices.

Information: Berkeley Springs/Morgan County Chamber of Commerce, 127 Fairfax St., Berkeley Springs, WV 25411, (304) 258-3738 or www.berkeleyspringschamber.com.

Boca Raton, Florida

Arts, culture and cool sophistication characterize this beautifully maintained city
on Florida's lower Atlantic coast

By Jay Clarke

Boca Raton sparkles in many ways. In 2000, a magazine survey found that the average diamond ring in Boca Raton runs 2.2 carats, a size that puts a heftier sparkle on a lady's finger than in most other Florida towns. While this gem of a community no longer is a haven just for the wealthy, it definitely remains upscale.

"I don't miss anything from Elizabeth except my friends, and I get to see them on visits," says Jean McGrath, who moved from Elizabeth, NJ, to Boca Raton eight years ago. She and her late husband, Edward, a New Jersey judge for 28 years, moved here upon his retirement after visiting Florida many times.

Jean, who admits to being "in my 60s," is one of thousands of retirees who have settled in this southeast Florida city founded by Addison Mizner, the same 1920s architect who put Palm Beach on the social map. As with Palm Beach, Mizner envisioned Boca Raton as an upscale community with polo fields, grand plazas, lavish homes and a golden-domed city hall.

Some of his dream came true in the 1920s before the Florida boom collapsed, but most of Boca's growth has come in the past several decades. Today the village that Mizner founded is a city of about 87,000. Some of America's best-known companies have settled here, among them IBM, Siemens, Tyco and Applied Card Systems.

It is home to one of the state's four-year schools of higher learning, Florida Atlantic University, and to one of the country's most famous hotels, the Boca Raton Resort and Club. It also has a large and active senior center set on 17 acres of woodlands. In addition to many in-house programs and activities, the Mae Volen Senior Center has 25 vehicles to ferry seniors to shopping areas, movies and medical appointments.

And, of course, Boca Raton has the same beaches and weather that have attracted so many to Florida over the years. Like most retirees, Jean and her husband were lured to Florida by its salubrious climate, and like others she found it took awhile to get into the swing of things. "It was a bit lonely when we first moved down here," she recalls, "but I joined the garden club and that took care of that."

Jean served a term as president of the club, where she says she has made "a lot of nice friends." She also plays golf twice a week and enjoys the Broward Center for the Performing Arts and Boca's "lovely restaurants."

Another retiree who enjoys the year-round golf here is Bill Walsh, who moved from New York City with his wife, Barbara, in 1997. He had a successful business in Manhattan restoring European antiques, and he still misses it. "I didn't plan on retiring, but I had to cut short my career," he says. "I had to retire for health reasons."

But Bill, 65, has found other ways to keep busy. "I play golf and I volunteer at the Boca community hospital. That's very fulfilling," he says. Barbara, also 65, volunteers at the hospital and with a group that provides assistance dogs for handicapped seniors.

Bill believes Boca Raton has a lot going for it. "It has theater, arts, shops, beaches. There's so much going on. You don't have to spend a lot of money to see good theater here," he says.

Neither Bill nor Barbara has had any trouble getting to know their neighbors. "We're pretty friendly, and we also have a good corps of friends here from New York City. My next-door neighbor of 35 years (in New York) lives in Boca. Actually, he moved here before us," Bill says.

Though national surveys show that Boca Raton's living costs are significantly lower than New York's, Bill says he believes they are "perhaps a little less. Housing is not cheap in Boca; taxes are about even." He likes Boca's "cleanliness, the availability of good things to do, restaurants and the arts." Bill, who has a home on a golf course, also praises the area's golf opportunities.

On the other hand, winter, which is the prime season here, has lost some of its sheen for him. "It gets so jam-packed. You have to make reservations. It's tough just to go to movies. It's mobbed," he says. Still, though, Bill has no wish to move anywhere else. "I plan to spend the rest of my life here," he says.

It was also the climate that brought JoAnn Guise from the Chicago area to Boca Raton in the mid-1980s. But that wasn't the only factor.

"It was close to the Gulf Stream, less hurried and close to FAU (Florida Atlantic University) for culture. We also got into boating," says JoAnn, 62. She and her late husband also were well acquainted with the area. "We had vacationed in Florida before, and my parents were in Palm Beach."

They moved to Boca after her husband sold the golf course he owned. He spent seven years in Boca before he died in 1992. JoAnn has since remarried. Her husband, Ernie, 82, is a former Miami developer.

When she first moved to Boca, JoAnn says, "the lifestyle was more relaxed and the cost of living was less." Now, she says, costs are comparable to Chicago's and the living no longer is quite so easy. "Taxes are more here, but that's because we're on the water," she says.

"I missed the change of seasons at first. Then I began to realize there is a change of seasons here — you just have to look closer," says JoAnn, who enjoys gardening.

For Evelyn and Lewis Somerville, moving to Boca Raton was a move to stability. "This is the very first home we've owned," says Evelyn, 71. Lewis was in the Army and the Somervilles, like other military families, were nomads. "We moved here from everywhere — Italy, Idaho, Virginia, Oklahoma," Evelyn says. "We went to school together in a small Ohio town, Frazeysburg. It has just one traffic light. We don't miss it, but we have good memories."

Despite the constant changes in homes as they moved from base to base, Evelyn says their three children have done well. "They learned discipline, got a good education and were always ready to pick up and move on," she says.

The couple arrived in Boca after Lewis, now 73, left the Army in the late 1960s. "He needed a job and we saw an ad in a Tampa newspaper. I didn't even know where Boca was," Evelyn says. With their experience in moving every few years, Evelyn says they found it easy to make friends when they got to Boca.

What she likes best here, she says, is the ease in which she can get where she wants to go. "We don't miss winters, and we use air conditioning only from July to October," she says. That cuts electricity charges by a sizable amount, but Evelyn says she finds the cost of living here higher than in other locales where they have lived.

One way she keeps busy is working with a garden club that has 300 members. She and Lewis also do their own yardwork, but that's just the start of exercise for Lewis, who cycles 40 to 60 miles every day and 100 miles on his birthdays. "He's done them (the birthday rides) in the Blue Ridge Mountains, in the Grand Canyon — wherever we happen to be. This year it was at Camp Wekiva near Orlando," says Evelyn.

Moving from the North to Florida is a big step, and it can be an especially difficult transition when one leaves a large house to move into a less roomy apartment or condo. But Abe Forman, 83, took it in stride when he moved a year and half ago from Pottsville, PA, to Classic Residence by Hyatt, a retirement community in Boca Raton.

"What I like best is that basic needs are taken care of," he says. "In the latter part of life, you want someone to take

Boca Raton, FL

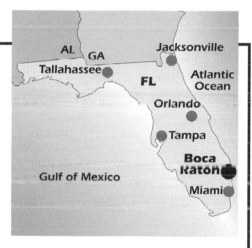

Population: 86,632

Location: On the Atlantic Ocean about 40 miles north of Miami and 27 miles south of West Palm Beach.

Climate:

	High	Low
January	74	58
July	90	75

Average relative humidity: 75%

Annual rainfall: 60 inches

Cost of living: Above average

Average housing costs: $384,700 for a single-family home, $220,400 for a condo.

Sales tax: 6.5%

Sales tax exemptions: Groceries and prescription drugs.

State income tax: None

Estate tax: None.

Inheritance tax: None

Intangibles tax: None. The tax was repealed as of Jan. 1, 2007.

Property tax: $19.2374 per $1,000 of assessed valuation. Homes are usually assessed at 80% of market value. Tax on a $384,700 home, with the $25,000 homestead exemption, would be approximately $5,440.

Homestead exemption: $25,000 off assessed value of primary, permanent residence. The county also offers an additional $25,000 exemption for seniors over 65 who meet certain income limitations, as well as exemptions for disabled veterans and widows.

Religion: There are more than 50 places of worship in the area.

Education: Three institutions of higher learning are located in Boca Raton. Florida Atlantic University, part of the state system, is a four-year university with a degree-seeking student population of 19,000. It has six campuses and eight colleges, plus a graduate school. Lynn University is a private, coeducational four-year university. It has about 3,000 students and awards associate, bachelor's, masters and doctoral degrees. Palm Beach Community College is a two-year, state-funded institution that awards an associate degree.

Transportation: The nearest major airports are Palm Beach International (25 miles north), Fort Lauderdale-Hollywood International (20 miles south) and Miami International (47 miles south). Boca Raton has a station on the Tri-Rail commuter train line, which runs between West Palm Beach and Miami.

Health: Boca Raton Community Hospital, with 394 beds and 24-hour emergency service, is the largest in south Palm Beach County. West Boca Medical Center is an acute-care facility with about 200 beds.

Housing options: Boca Raton real estate is expensive and escalating in price. The older coastal sectors tend to be most expensive while the new developments in unincorporated Boca Raton offer more value. The historic district in Old Floresta has homes designed by Addison Mizner. Other upscale neighborhoods include New Floresta and Woodfield Hunt Country Club. Near Boca Raton Resort and Club, plan to spend $1 million for a condo at The Addison. West Boca has country club communities like Arvida's Broken Sound. Mid-price communities include Boca Square, Lake Floresta, Boca Del Mar and Boca Pointe.

Visitor lodging: Rates are lowest in summer, highest in winter, and may vary also by availability and day of week. The Boca Raton Resort and Club, set on 356 acres, is one of America's most celebrated resorts, with 36 holes of golf, 30 tennis courts, a beach club, six pools, a marina and many shops. Rates begin at $149 in low season, (888) 491-2622. Boca Raton Marriott has convention facilities, a health club and an outdoor heated pool with wet bar, $209-$309, (561) 392-4600. Holiday Inn Express Boca Raton West, $88-$199, (561) 482-7070.

Information: Greater Boca Raton Chamber of Commerce, 1800 N. Dixie Highway, Boca Raton, FL 33432, (561) 395-4433 or www.bocaratonchamber. com. Relocation information is available.

care of everyday things. They do a marvelous job here."

Hyatt, known for its hotels, also operates several rental retirement homes like this one. For a monthly fee that ranges from $3,600 for a one-bedroom apartment to $4,500 and up for a two-bedroom apartment, renters at Classic Residence find that most of their needs are met. The rent includes two meals, weekly housekeeping service, fitness and computer centers, an arts and crafts studio, cable television and other facilities. Live entertainment is presented twice a week. Assisted living also is available at an extra cost for those who need it.

"They take care of you," says Abe, whose wife of 54 years died over five years ago. Back in Pottsville, Abe had a scrap iron brokerage firm. He still maintains an office there and keeps in touch by phone. But he feels firmly rooted in Boca Raton, which he says has given him more than he expected.

"I'm deeply impressed with the cultural life here," he says, "and Boca has excellent facilities — malls like Town Center and so many restaurants. You can do something every day, every hour."

Abe doesn't mind Florida's heat because he lives in an air-conditioned world. Nor does he miss Northern winters, but he does regret not experiencing the change of seasons. He also finds the cost of living a little cheaper here. "You don't need heavy clothing," he notes.

In Pottsville, Abe was president of his synagogue, and while he isn't as active here, he enjoys the many facets of Jewish life that his heavily Jewish residence offers. He also feels in tune with his Classic Residence neighbors in another way. "The majority of people who live here are people of means. Even if they're up in years, they are people who have been somebody, people who are reasonably affluent," he says.

One of those is Irving Perfit, who owned a paper mill and lived in Cliffside Park, NJ, until his retirement here seven years ago. Irving is 91, but he acts like a man in his 60s. Perhaps that's because this former Olympic athlete exercises daily. Irving was a speed walker in the 1932 Olympics, placing 28th.

Today, he's president of the community's residents council and takes an active role in life there. His lifestyle comes as a surprise to him because, he admits, "I never liked Florida." But he has a daughter and other relatives here, and his opinion of the state has changed. "I like Florida now," he says.

Apartment living is preferred by many who have retired to Florida, and a popular complex is Boca's Century Village. Al Sapadin and his wife, Blanche, have been residents almost from its beginning. They moved to Boca in 1982 from West Hempstead on Long Island, where he was with the Social Security Administration and a general insurance agency.

Al is 82 and Blanche is 80, but both look and act younger. Al writes for the community publication and does some tax work on the side, while Blanche has joined a study group and also does some writing. But both still find time to do volunteer work and enjoy the cultural offerings of nearby Florida Atlantic University.

The proximity of FAU, in fact, was one of the elements that persuaded the Sapadins to settle here. "Being close to the university was important," Blanche says. "This was a cultural wasteland" when she and Al first moved to Boca, she says. "Now we have music, plays from Broadway, the Boca Raton Museum of Art."

To make certain they would be content here, the Sapadins first rented when they came to Florida — something they advise others to do. After they decided they wanted to live here permanently they bought a two-bedroom apartment for $120,000 and settled in. They have a lake outside their back door, pay $300 a month in maintenance and enjoy a clubhouse, entertainment and other facilities. They live a happy life.

"Taxes are lower here; you don't have that $25,000 homestead exemption up North," Al says. "Food and restaurants are cheaper, too," adds Blanche. Not surprisingly, then, they don't miss Long Island — except perhaps for its change of seasons.

But that's the price anyone who moves to Boca Raton has to pay, and most retirees find it's a worthy trade. As Jean McGrath says, "I don't feel I've missed out on anything." ●

Bradenton, Florida

This city on Florida's Gulf Coast has a multitude of golf courses and access
to world-class cultural activities

By Karen Feldman

Spanish explorer Hernando de Soto landed in Bradenton in 1539 and trekked through the area in a fruitless quest for gold. Dave and Babbs Howland, on the other hand, struck pay dirt before they ever set foot in town.

The Howlands were living in Columbia, SC, when they decided to retire in 1998, after their children were out on their own. Dave, an entrepreneur who sold his computer graphics company, was 50. Babbs, a registered nurse, was 47.

They'd planned to move to Charleston, SC, and had been watching the real estate market there skyrocket for a while before they finally

decided to build a house. When they found out the home they'd selected had risen in price by $50,000 in a matter of months, they decided to look elsewhere for a retirement haven.

"We knew we liked Florida," Babbs says. "We liked the warm weather and the tropical plants, and we didn't want to live on the East Coast because it was so crowded."

"We got on the computer," Dave says. "We'd never been to this side of Florida, but we started looking at houses. The house we bought here was one of them."

That was in 1998, and the Howlands still enjoy their 5,500-square-foot, four-bedroom home on a canal. They swim in their pool daily, take their 10-year-old cocker spaniel for regular walks, go out to dinner a lot and throw frequent parties at their home. They are also active in the local Republican Party and have both served on the executive committee and as precinct captains.

"We love it here," Babbs says. "It's a wonderful place to live."

That's what a lot of active retirees are discovering about Bradenton, a midsized city situated between Sarasota and the Tampa-St. Peters- burg area.

In spring 2001, Ross and Kay Carter did some Web surfing in search of appealing communities as Ross prepared for retirement from the insurance industry, where he oversaw computer operations. They collected a box full of pamphlets from promising spots and kept sorting their favorites to the front. Time and again, the brochure for Lakewood Ranch, just south of Bradenton, made the cut.

Ross retired that fall. Thinking it would take a while to find a buyer, they put their Boston home on the market the day before the Sept. 11 terrorist attack. It sold three days later.

Although they'd planned to stay another year and not rush into a new life, it was suddenly time to move. "I said to Ross, 'If I don't get to be near one of my children, I'm simply going to die,'" says Kay, 61. With their daughters in San Francisco and Toronto, they decided that Florida, where their son lived, would be the best fit for them.

When they asked their son, Michael, what town he thought would best suit them, he didn't hesitate: Sarasota, he told them.

"He said it had the culture, the plays, the symphony, the things we love to do," Kay says.

They made a few stops on the East Coast, then headed west to Sarasota. They liked the area but didn't find a house they wanted there. They decided to check out Lakewood Ranch in person. "We loved it but didn't find anything right for us," Kay says. "We didn't know how to look."

They contacted a real estate agent and told her they liked to have a good time, wanted to be active, enjoyed music, sports and theater, and that Ross loved golf. She told them Lakewood Ranch would be a good fit and helped them find the lot in the Country Club community there where they built their 2,000-square-foot, three-bedroom villa.

"We found what we wanted, put the money down. We'd only been here three days and had never been to the area before. We were strangers in paradise," Kay says.

They didn't remain strangers very long. Shortly after moving into a rental, they headed to the Marie Selby Botanical Gardens in Sarasota in search of some Florida-style Christmas spirit. They met a man who also lived in Lakewood Ranch. Their new acquaintance called the next day to invite Ross to play golf. They've been friends ever since.

They met many other friends the same way, most from Lakewood Ranch, a 7,000-acre master-planned community that straddles the Sarasota-Manatee county line.

"There's some magic that seems to pull people together here," Kay says. "We find people who are willing to play, to help you out, to be a friend. They are so happy to be here that they greet you with a smile. We all practically hug ourselves each day thinking we are so lucky to be here."

From golf to country clubs, social and service groups within many planned communities, to 230-plus houses of worship, historic sites and other community organizations, the Bradenton area affords newcomers easy entree to a new life with new friends and a host of activities.

When Harold and Mary Benner moved south from the Columbus, OH, area in 1985, they looked along the west coast from Fort Myers north, finally buying a big house in St. Petersburg. Within a year, they knew they'd made a mistake.

"It was too much house and yard, and there was no way to make friends except our immediate neighbors — who were lovely people — but that was it," says Mary, 73.

"It was not what we retired for," says Harold, 75, a retired elementary school principal. "We wanted activity. We wanted the things Florida is known for."

So they retraced their steps and paid a second visit to a Bradenton condominium community called Country Village, which had been in the early stages of development when they first looked at it. This time it was different.

"It was an active community," Harold says. "There are lots of things going on. It suited our tastes." The 1,300-square-foot condo they bought has lots of wall space that accommodates their antique furniture, too. They've been in their two-bedroom, two-bath condo for 20 years.

In the early days, when there were fewer people there, everyone knew one another and they quickly made good friends. As time went on, some became closer than others, sharing the Benners' passion for bridge and Harold's taste for golf.

"There's something going on every night if you want to take part," Harold says. "We have great parties and dances, we have something for every one of the major holidays. There's the golf club, luncheon clubs," as well as spontaneous gatherings.

The Benners have headed up a number of Country Village parties, with Harold serving as the chairman of the condo activity committee for several years. He's also been active with Keep Manatee Beautiful, serves as head usher for the church they attend, works for Habitat for Humanity and finds time to enjoy a recently discovered talent for painting with watercolors.

Some Bradenton newcomers decide to start their own clubs. Babbs Howland found herself spending a lot of time among a congenial group of women that grew very close and wanted to make sure they stayed that way. They formed a group called Black and Pearls. "Once a month, we get into our black dresses and pearls and go out to dinner," Babbs says.

They'll eat, and sometimes have a speaker, but mostly it's about cama-raderie. In addition to the fun the group members have together, they enjoy the minor scene they cause in a restaurant as 30 or so well-dressed women gather.

The area provides lots of opportunities to give back to the community, too. Keep Manatee Beautiful helps coordinate groups of people who maintain designated roads and beaches. There are animal welfare organizations, state parks, hospitals and political groups all in need of motivated volunteers.

For those with an appetite for culture, Sarasota presents a gourmet smorgas-bord just south of Bradenton. It's the home of the Asolo Theatre Company, Sarasota Ballet, Sarasota Opera, the Flori-da West Coast Symphony, Van Wezel Performing Arts Hall, Florida State University Center for the Performing Arts, an annual film festival and a reading festi-val. The John and Mable Ringling Muse-um of Art includes the circus founder's bayfront home, art museum and sprawl-ing grounds and gardens.

Downtown's Palm Avenue is lined with art galleries. The nearby Towles Court has dozens of artists-in-residence. Marie Selby Botanical Gardens boasts a world-class orchid collection as well as other rare species, such as carnivorous plants, epiphytes and bamboo. Other attractions include Mote Marine Labora-tory and Aquarium and Sarasota Jungle Gardens.

Bradenton, FL

Population: There are about 53,330 residents in Bradenton, with more than 295,000 in Manatee County.
Location: Bradenton is the largest municipality in Manatee County. It is about 15 miles north of Sarasota, 51 miles south of Tampa and 119 miles west of Orlando.
Climate: High Low
January 72 51
July 92 75
Rain: About 55 inches annually
Average relative humidity: 74%
Cost of living: Slightly below average
Median housing cost: $316,000

Sales tax: 6.5%
Sales tax exemption: Food and medicine.
Intangibles tax: None. The tax was repealed as of Jan. 1, 2007.
Estate tax: The state eliminated the "pick-up" portion of the federal tax as of Jan. 1, 2005.
Inheritance tax: None
Property tax: $21.1462 per $1,000 of assessed value. On a $316,000 home with a $25,000 homestead exemption, annual taxes would amount to $6,154.
Homestead exemption: $25,000 off assessed value of primary, permanent residence.
Religion: There are 230 houses of wor-ship representing more than 65 denom-inations throughout Manatee County.
Education: Manatee Community Col-lege is a fully accredited two-year college offering Associate in Arts and Associate in Science degree programs and certifica-tion in a number of technical programs. The MCC Open Campus offers noncredit courses for personal enrichment and pro-fessional growth. University of South

Florida, Sarasota-Manatee, sits on the border between the two communities and shares a campus with New College, the state's public honors college. USF offers 34 degree programs and is one of three USF campuses, with the main one in Tampa. Other area colleges include the Ringling School of Art and Design, Eckerd College, the University of Sarasota and Keiser College.
Transportation: The Sarasota/Braden-ton International Airport is about 10 miles south of the city, with seven major carriers and four commuter airlines. Area residents have convenient access to interstates 75 and 275 as well as U.S. Highway 301, U.S. Highway 41 and state roads 64 and 70. Manatee Coun-ty Area Transit, (941) 749-7116, runs buses six days a week. Fares start at $1, and those 60 and older qualify for dis-counted fares. Greyhound Bus Line, (941) 747-2984, also provides daily service to a variety of destinations with-in the state and beyond.
Health: Manatee County has two full-service hospitals, one acute-care hospi-

Bradenton and surrounding Manatee County have their own attractions, as well. The city's downtown district has shopping, restaurants and a growing number of apartments and condominiums.

ArtCenter Manatee offers galleries and classes to professional and amateur artists of all skill levels. The 1920s bungalows in the Village of the Arts house the galleries and studios of 40 artists. The first two Friday nights and Saturday afternoons of the month, they are open to the public during ArtWalk. The Manatee Players perform shows at the Riverfront Theatre. The South Florida Museum affords visitors a look at the area's history, and the adjoining Bishop Planetarium allows them a glimpse into the heavens.

Carefully preserved buildings from the region's past — including a sugar cane mill and single-room schoolhouse — comprise Manatee Village Historical Park. In nearby Ellenton, visitors can explore the Gamble Plantation, furnished in the style of its 1844 heyday, when it was among the country's most successful sugar cane plantations.

Bradenton is proud of its Spanish roots and memorializes explorer Hernando de Soto's 1539 landing with the De Soto National Memorial along the Manatee River. And during the winter months, park rangers don period costumes and portray life as the early settlers lived it, including musket-firing demonstrations and basic cooking techniques.

And, of course, there are sports, especially Grapefruit League spring training when the Pittsburgh Pirates call Manatee County's McKechnie Field home. Nearby, the Cincinnati Reds train in Sarasota, the Yankees in Tampa and the Devil Rays in St. Petersburg. In Sarasota, fans can also see the Sarasota Red Sox, the Boston Red Sox farm league. Just north in Tampa, there are plenty of professional teams, including the Tampa Bay Devil Rays (baseball), the Buccaneers (football), the Storm (arena football), the Terror and the Mutiny (soccer), and the Lightning (hockey).

None of the three couples has plans to move, although the Howlands are a little gun-shy since the 2004 hurricane season. Their house has a 25-foot-high ceiling in the living room, and the pool cage soars to 35 feet. Between them are vast windows — the house has 68 in all, Dave says.

"Until last year the windows were kind of a plus," Babbs says. "The hurricanes last year made us a little more conscious about what glass could do if we have a lot of wind. This year we spent a good amount having film put on the windows to protect them."

Should they experience another hurricane season like last year's, they might consider a move, although they aren't sure where they would go. Meanwhile, there are plenty of people who would happily trade places. As a result, the real estate market in Bradenton is booming as people of all ages find themselves drawn to the location and lifestyle.

Real estate prices jumped 29.5 percent from August 2004 to August 2005, according to the county property appraiser's office. While that's good for current homeowners, it makes it harder

---

tal and a psychiatric facility. Blake Medical Center in Bradenton is ranked among America's top 100 hospitals by the Joint Commission on Accreditation of Healthcare Organizations. It is an acute-care, full-service hospital and offers a heart institute, rehabilitation center, 24-hour emergency center, outpatient services, a neuroscience center, orthopedics, oncology, a heartburn relief center, a women's center, and H2U, a wellness program for people 50 and older. Lakewood Ranch Medical Center is the county's newest health facility. It's a 120-bed, acute-care hospital with 24-hour emergency services, a women's center, critical care, outpatient and inpatient surgery and private rooms. Manatee Memorial Hospital is a 491-bed, full-service, acute-care facility with 24-hour emergency services, joint replacement, women's center, heart services and surgical weight loss. For those 50 and older, it offers the Senior Advantage Program, with periodic programs, talks and support groups. Manatee Glens provides psychiatric care for people in crisis, with mental illness and substance abuse treatment offered in both residential and outpatient settings.

Housing: Real estate prices have increased by almost 30% in the past year. An older two-bedroom, two-bath condo might start at about $245,000, while more modern units are rarely priced at less than $270,000. Beachfront homes start at about $1.8 million and sell quickly, while canal-front properties start at $500,000. Single-family homes in Bradenton golf communities sell for at least $350,000, but those directly on a course are higher in cost. Homes on the Manatee River can cost upward of $1 million, even a relatively modest home. **Lakewood Ranch**, (800) 307-2624, a 7,000-acre master-planned community just south of Bradenton, offers condos, detached villas, single-family homes and estate residences ranging from 1,100 square feet to 6,000 square feet and from $280,000 to $6 million. It has two Arnold Palmer-designed golf courses with a total of 54 holes and a full slate of amenities including 100 miles of sidewalks and trails and a dog park.

The area's supply of rental properties is plentiful, particularly homes in the $1,300- to $1,400-a-month range.

Visitor lodging: Days Inn Historic Bradenton is a 130-unit, pet-friendly motel with an outdoor pool, $59-$139, (941) 746-1141. Holiday Inn Bradenton-Riverfront is a 153-unit full-service hotel on the banks of the Manatee River, at the edge of the city's historic downtown district, $135-$209, (941) 747-3727. Fairfield Inn & Suites, Lakewood Ranch, has 87 units, some with whirlpool tubs, and is situated between Bradenton and Sarasota, $89-$199, (877) 552-3300. Tortuga Inn Beach Resort is a pet-friendly hotel on Bradenton Beach with standard units, efficiencies, two-bedroom units overlooking the Gulf, a pool and private beach, $115-$290, (877) 867-8842.

Information: Manatee Chamber of Commerce, 222 10th St. W., Bradenton, FL 34205, (941) 748-3411 or www.manateechamber.com. Bradenton Area Convention and Visitors Bureau, P.O. Box 1000, Bradenton, FL 34206, (941) 729-9177 or www.flagulfislands.com.

for some newcomers to afford a house, says Don Browning, a real estate agent with Coldwell Banker's North Lakewood Ranch office.

"The average cost of a home now is about $315,000," he says. "A year or so ago, the same house would have been $215,000 to $220,000."

A basic two-bedroom condo in an older development might still sell for about $245,000 and up, while those in newer communities start at $270,000 and rise from there. Beachfront homes start at about $1.8 million, while those on canals start at $500,000, Browning says.

Lakewood Ranch, with its range of communities and housing options, runs from about $335,000 to upward of $1 million. Single-family homes in Bradenton golf communities can be found starting at about $350,000, but prices are considerably higher for homes overlooking a course.

The prices don't seem to pose a problem for most retirees who are coming down with cash from the sales of their Northern homes, Browning says, but it's tough for younger people who make up the labor force. Despite the increases, it's still less expensive than neighboring Sarasota or Naples, which is about 90 minutes south.

"It's not quite as good a deal as it was before, but it's still a good deal when you consider there's no income tax and the proximity to culture and the beaches," Browning says. "It's so easy to get to and from anywhere. You can be at the beach in the morning and afternoon, then in the evening have an elegant dinner and see a show at Asolo (Theatre). That's a tremendous thing." ●

Brunswick, Maine

This pretty college town offers a lively arts and music scene on the Maine coast

By Hilary M. Nangle

Craggy fingers of land, tipped with granite fingernails and dotted with beaches, fishing villages, antiques shops and artisans' galleries, have long lured travelers to Midcoast Maine in summer. Many of these small towns and villages all but roll up their sidewalks after Columbus Day, sleeping quietly until Memorial Day announces the start of another tourist season.

Not so in Brunswick.

Conjure up images of a New England college town, and likely your dreams will depict something along Brunswick's lines. Bowdoin College, an oasis of ivy-covered brick buildings surrounding a grassy, tree-shaded quadrangle, anchors the south end of the downtown. Its alumni include Henry Wadsworth Longfellow, Nathaniel Hawthorne, U.S. President Franklin Pierce, Arctic explorers Robert Peary and Donald MacMillan and Civil War hero Joshua Chamberlain.

Brunswick's extra-wide Maine Street is lined with small shops and restaurants, many exhibiting a college-town funkiness. At its head is First Parish Church, where Harriet Beecher Stowe was inspired to write "Uncle Tom's Cabin." The adjacent Town Mall is a green where the twice-weekly Farmers Market and summer band concerts take place. Side streets display an eclectic mix of clapboard and brick Federal, Colonial, Victorian and Cape-style houses. The presence of Bath Iron Works and the Brunswick Naval Air Station provide a solid economic base and ethnic diversity.

Few places are all things to all people, but Brunswick, combined with its surrounding communities, comes close. Harpswell comprises two salty peninsulas and Orrs and Bailey's islands, connected to the mainland by bridges. Topsham, a mostly rural community with an excellent annual agricultural fair, is divided from Brunswick by the Androscoggin River. Freeport is a retail center that's home to L.L. Bean and more than 100 outlets, but also has Wolfe's Neck Woods, an oceanfront state park laced with walking trails. Bath, a small city with a proud shipbuilding heritage, has a nice shopping district and an excellent marine museum. And Popham Beach, which tips the Phippsburg Peninsula near Bath, is often voted the state's best beach.

"Moving to Brunswick was the best move we ever made," says Sherry Hanson, who moved here with her husband, Harry, from the rural farm country of Dixon, Il., in 1992. "We'd made other moves because of jobs, but we made this one because we wanted to. We never looked back; we never had even a moment of thinking, 'Oh my God, what have we done?'"

Sherry, 59, a freelance writer, and Harry, 69, who took early retirement from the YMCA, chose Brunswick because they wanted to return to the East Coast, knew the area from family camping trips, and both had distant family roots in Maine. Sherry did her homework and began subscribing to The Times Record, the local daily newspaper, about a year before they moved.

The Hansons knew that to manage the difference in housing costs between Dixon and Brunswick they needed to look at income properties. "We worked with Realtors from Sears-port through Brunswick," she says. Eventually they purchased an old house with a rental apartment in a neighborhood close to Brunswick's downtown. Although it was a big change from an area of Illinois where neighbors were few and far between, to the closeness of an in-town neighborhood in Maine, it was the right choice.

Convenience is a real plus. "We can walk or ride bikes to literally anything we want to do," Sherry says. When they want to relax over a cup of coffee, they bike to Wild Oats, a popular bakery cafe renowned for its breads and other fresh foods. Sherry bikes to the Maine Writers & Publishers Alliance (MWPA), a networking resource for freelance writers and Maine's small publishing houses.

Sherry found it easy to get involved in the community and meet folks. "I knew what I wanted to do and where to go," she says, thanks in part to having subscribed to the local paper. She immediately sought out MWPA and Maine Media Women, joining and becoming active in both. She also participates in poetry readings and Brunswick Area Arts and Cultural Alliance (BAACA) activities and teaches part time at the University of Maine in a continuing-education program in Portland, 26 miles south, and in an adult-education program at Gardiner High School, about 30 miles north. Last year she became active in the local chapter of Habitat for Humanity.

In winter, the Hansons occasionally go to a local golf course to cross country ski, but they prefer alpine skiing, and two major New England resorts, Sugarloaf and Sunday River, are each about two hours distant. Smaller areas such as Lost Valley, Mount Abram and Shawnee Peak are closer and deliver reliable conditions at affordable prices. Sherry and Harry visit Mount Abram often for its two-for-one days.

In the summer, Sherry often heads for Popham Beach. "That's my mental health place," she says. "I go there to walk, read, work on my poetry and catch a few rays." Recently, she and Harry have taken up sea kayaking, and Brunswick's location is convenient for short getaways for camping, hiking and sea kayaking in Acadia National Park on Mount Desert Isle, just over two hours northeast.

Being near the water was a key element in Lorna and Jack Flynn's search for a second home to which they could eventually retire. Jack, 60, who retired recently as vice president of human resources for International Paper, and Lorna, 58, who previously was the director of education for a rape crisis center, wanted a place on the water, one their children would want to visit with family. Cultural activities also were extremely important to the Flynns, who lived in New Canaan, CT, within easy reach of everything New York City offered.

One of the toughest parts of moving to Maine was giving up their New York Philharmonic tickets. "We like music and theater," Lorna says. "Living outside of New York, you get used to a certain level of culture, but we were ready for a different kind of life." A friend of Jack's recommended they look at Harpswell.

They did and were hooked. She immediately subscribed to the Bowdoin International Music Festival, a world-renowned summer chamber music school and concert series. "It was fabulous, with performers such as Eugenia Zuckerman. I can go to something every night," she says. Then she discovered the Maine State Music Theatre. "I grew up in a family that loves musicals, and having a world-class theater company is just great. These are things you're not expecting."

Although the local arts scene is somewhat diminished once summer fades, it doesn't go away. Bowdoin alone provides countless programs. "It has to provide opportunities for its students, who are really smart kids and demand good lectures and ancillary activities," Lorna notes. By joining the Association of Bowdoin Friends, Jack has been able to take courses, with the professor's permission, and his experiences while living in Russia are a plus in the classroom. "The kids love the geezers, as we're affectionately called," Lorna says.

The quality and quantity of other off-season cultural opportunities in the region were a pleasant surprise. In Brunswick, Eveningstar Cinema screens alternative movies, BAACA presents events, Theater Works stages plays and The Chocolate Church, a performing arts center in Bath, presents concerts and theater programs. Once a week Jack and Lorna go to Portland for a ballroom dancing class, and in winter, they go regularly for the museums and theater. And, of course, Bowdoin College offers a full

slate of opportunities as well as two museums. "Bowdoin provides us with a lot: classes, lectures, films, sports, use of the library, and Bowdoin's attitude toward the community is hugely welcoming," Lorna says.

Lorna has become involved in various aspects of the local community and, like Sherry, has found it surprisingly easy to do so. "We're way more social in retirement. We have a huge social life," Lorna says. She recently became president of the High Head neighborhood association. She also attends business breakfasts in Brunswick. But it's been her love of the arts where she's invested most of her volunteer time.

"When I first got here, I made friends with the crafts community; I became good friends with potters, painters, sculptors. Through them, I got involved with BAACA," she says. That led to her involvement with the Bowdoin International Music Festival and eventually to the Maine State Music Theatre.

When not volunteering in the arts, she's often puttering in her garden. "I've

Brunswick, ME

Population: 21,779
Location: Midcoast Maine, 26 miles north of Portland, Maine's largest city.
Climate: High Low
January   31   10
July   80   58
Average humidity: 69%
Rain: 45 inches annually
Snow: 75 inches annually
Cost of living: Above average
Average housing cost: About $285,000 in Brunswick, Harpswell and Topsham. Median selling price is about $230,000.
Sales tax: 5% on retail sales, 7% on pre-

pared food, lodging and alcoholic drinks, and 10% on short-term automobile rentals.
Sales tax exemptions: Grocery staples, prescription medicines.
State income tax: For single filers, ranges from 2% on taxable incomes of less than $4,450 to $907 plus 8.5% of taxable incomes over $17,700. For married couples filing jointly, ranges from 2% on taxable incomes of less than $8,900 to $1,817 plus 8.5% of taxable incomes over $35,450.
Income tax exemptions: For tax years beginning on Jan. 1, 2000, or later, residents may deduct up to $6,000 of federal, state and private pension income that is included in federal adjusted gross income. The $6,000 must be reduced by any Social Security or railroad retirement benefits received, whether taxable or not. For tax years 2001 and later, military pensions are fully deductible. For tax year 2005, the personal exemption amount is $2,850 and standard deduction amounts are as follows: $5,000 for single filers, $8,300 for married joint filers,

$7,300 for head-of-household filers, and $4,150 for married separate filers. There are additional exemptions for taxpayers age 65 and/or blind, as well as a low-income tax credit.
Intangibles tax: None
Estate tax: Applicable to taxable estates above $950,000 for deaths in 2005. Maine does not peg the estate tax filing threshold to the 2005 federal threshold of $1.5 million.
Inheritance tax: None
Property tax: In Brunswick, $21.90 per $1,000 valuation for fiscal year 2005-2006, with homes assessed at 70 percent of market value. The tax on a $285,000 home would be about $4,369, without exemptions.
Homestead exemption: Residents who have owned a home in Maine for at least 12 months can qualify for an exemption of $13,000 off the homes valuation. There are exemptions for veterans and legally blind homeowners.
Religion: There are numerous churches in Brunswick, including Apostolic, Assembly of God, Baptist (various sects), Church

never been able to have a garden, and now I have a huge garden; I trade vegetables with my neighbors." She's become treasurer of the Harpswell Garden Club and is active in the flower committee, which does the floral arrangements for a local church the club owns. "I've learned a tremendous amount. I've become an expert in boutonnieres and corsages," she says.

Cultural and recreational opportunities were also important for Rosemary and Gordan Brigham, who moved to the Highland Green retirement community in Topsham earlier this year. The Cambridge, MA, residents wanted to retire to a place within 2.5 hours from Boston. "We didn't want to give up all of what Cambridge offered, but we didn't want to live in the middle of it," Gordon says.

They looked at the Cape, Plymouth and various other places in Massachusetts, Rhode Island and even New Hampshire, but hadn't even considered Maine until they saw an advertisement for Highland Green. Its location just a few minutes from the Bowdoin College campus, its nine-hole golf course and nature preserve, and proximity to Portland and the ocean were all pluses in the Brighams' book. "This is a nice little place, off the tourist beat, relatively unaffected," Gordon says. "It's a quiet place to live and retire, but by no means inactive."

Already, the Brighams have joined the Brunswick-Topsham Land Trust, and they've been enjoying the Bowdoin International Music Festival and L.L. Bean concerts. Like the Flynns, they've joined the Association of Bowdoin Friends. "We get the Bowdoin calendar, and there is so much going on," Gordon says, comparing it to the Harvard calendar.

And Portland, just down the road, has the range of arts, culture, theater and restaurants that Boston offers. "It took us a half an hour to get into downtown Boston. In that same half hour, we're in Portland, and it's easier traffic-wise," Gordon says. "Everything is easier. That's part of the charm of being here. I know my stress level is zero," Rosemary adds.

Outdoor pleasures figured in their decision to locate here, too. "The closeness to the ocean is fantastic for us," Rosemary says. "We can drive up to Popham Beach late in the day and walk on the beach. It's like being in another world." Gordon took up golf over the summer, and Rosemary plans to start snowshoeing this winter to enjoy the preserve trails that ramble along the Cathance River.

Rosemary admits to having been very hesitant about moving to Maine because of the climate. "I was pleasantly surprised. I love the cool crisp days," she says. Gordon adds that they haven't found the winters all that different from Boston, perhaps just a little colder. But although they had laughed when they heard the term "mud season," they discovered that it does exist. "We wanted to live in a place that had real seasons. If you don't want to be bothered by weather, you shouldn't come to Maine, but if you enjoy seasonal pleasures, it's just great," he says.

of Christ, Christian Science, Episcopal, Independent Fundamental, Jehovah's Witness, Lutheran, Nazarene, nondenominational, Pentecostal, Roman Catholic, Seventh-day Adventist, Unitarian Universalist, United Church of Christ, Methodist and Word of God. The closest synagogue is in Bath.

Education: At Midcoast Senior College, part of the Osher Lifelong Learning Institute, members devise the curriculum and enroll in noncredit classes taught by peers. The program is an adjunct of USM's Center for Extended Academic Programs and is affiliated with the national Elderhostel Institute Network. At Bowdoin College, members of the Association of Bowdoin Friends can take courses (with the instructor's permission), participate in campus activities and use the athletic facilities. Courses are also offered through local adult-education programs at Southern New Hampshire University and University College at Bath/Brunswick.

Transportation: Vermont Transit/Greyhound Bus Lines and Concord Trailways connect Brunswick with Portland and Boston. Taxi companies and limousine services also provide local transportation. Air service is from Portland International Jetport.

Health: There are two hospitals in Brunswick: Mid Coast Hospital, with 71 inpatient beds, and Parkview Hospital, with 55 acute-care beds. Portland has two hospitals: Maine Medical Center, the state's largest, and Mercy Hospital. A veterans hospital is located in Togus, about one hour away.

Housing options: Homes and land are available in Brunswick as well as the neighboring communities of Topsham and Harpswell. Waterfront homes command the highest prices. According to Patty Sample at RE/MAX Riverside, (207) 725-8505, recent sales ranged from a low of about $85,000 to a high of $3 million. Area retirement communities include **The Highlands** in Topsham, (888) 760-1042; **Highland Green** in Topsham, (866) 854-1200; and **Thornton Oaks** in Brunswick, (800) 729-8033.

Visitor lodging: The region has plentiful lodging, including B&Bs, inns, motels and cottages. Reservations are essential. Among those open year-round: Brunswick Bed and Breakfast is in downtown Brunswick on the Town Mall, $120-$170, (800) 299-4914. Captain Daniel Stone Inn is a full-service inn within walking distance of downtown Brunswick shops and restaurants and convenient to Topsham, $89-$250, (877) 573-5151. Captain's Watch B&B in Harpswell has water views, $125-$175, (207) 725-0979. Black Lantern B&B is located in a Federal-style 1810 home in Topsham's historic district, $90, (888) 306-4165.

Information: Southern Midcoast Maine Chamber, 59 Pleasant St., Brunswick, ME 04011, (207) 725-8798 or www.midcoast maine.com. Also, visit www.maine.gov/portal/living/index.html for general information on living and retiring in Maine. The book "Where to Retire in Maine" covers 21 towns, including Brunswick. It is available for $15.95, plus $4.50 for shipping and handling, from Down East Books, (800) 685-7962 or www.down eastbooks.com.

While none of these couples has major misgivings about their moves to the Brunswick area, all wish there were more choice in restaurants. Rosemary praises the abundant fresh seafood available and especially enjoys the lobster rolls at Paul's Marina, but she bemoans the lack of a good Chinese restaurant.

The Flynns find Brunswick's restaurant choices limited, with one exception: "Henry and Marty's is as good as anywhere," Lorna gushes.

What Lorna misses most compared with New Canaan is quality shopping. "I want Lord & Taylor in Portland. I want that quality of store or Saks. But that's a small change," she admits, confessing, "I wake up every morning, look out the window and realize how lucky I am. We really hit it big here. It's a wonderful gift nature has given us, the ability to live on the water and be at peace with ourselves. I feel my pulse rate drop whenever I'm home." ●

Carlsbad, California

In Southern California, a picturesque city by the sea boasts
a springlike climate and lovely beaches

By Carole Jacobs

Last winter, Carlsbad resident Vicki Shepard, 54, was enduring high-level politics and bone-chilling temperatures as the deputy inspector general of the Department of Health and Human Services in Washington, DC. Weary of the workaday stress, snow and cold climate, but with a year to go before she could fully retire on a government pension, she decided to trade her high position in the government and the brutal winters for a lower role and the balmy winters of Carlsbad.

Today, Vicki says she's not only "fully entrenched in the Carlsbad lifestyle," but finally has the time — and the year-round mild weather — to pursue her favorite hobby, tennis. "It's great to be 3,000 miles away from all the politics," says Vicki, who now telecommutes from her single family home in an older section of Carlsbad about three miles inland from the ocean.

Vicki is no stranger to Southern California. "Before I lived in Washington, I worked for the Los Angeles regional office for 10 years and had offices in L.A., San Diego, Phoenix and Hawaii. I lived in Orange County (just a short drive north of Carlsbad), and I spent a lot of time driving up and down the I-5 freeway between Los Angeles and San Diego. Every time I went past Carlsbad, I thought to myself that it looked like the perfect place to live. The weather was perfect, it had a cute downtown, and just about everything else I wanted."

Vicki says a longtime friend and real estate agent helped her find the perfect house. When her agent called and said she had found an affordable single-family home just three miles from the beach, Vicki was sold. However, "affordable" is a relative term in a beach town where condos start at $400,000 and go into the millions.

But Vicki says the cost of housing in Washington, DC, is comparable to Carlsbad. "When I bought my house, which was built in 1978 and is located in an older cul-de-sac in Carlsbad, the first thing I did was rent a 40-cubic-yard dumpster, park it in the driveway, and rip out the popcorn ceiling," she says. Now that she's renovated the house, she says it's the perfect oasis.

"It's a small house on one level, which I prefer. After living in a lot of townhouses, it's nice not to have steps. And I have a very private back yard. I'm sitting out on my deck, and I can see the Four Seasons Resort as well as the fireworks from LEGOLAND," she says. She also appreciates that her home is just a half-hour north of the big-city attractions of San Diego, and a half-hour south from many friends she made during her 10-year stint in Orange County.

Vicki, who is single, was raised in Arkansas and lived in seven states during her government career. "I briefly considered retiring to Arkansas," she says. "I figured I could move back there and live like royalty on my government pension. But Arkansas has bugs and cold winters. Both are things I can live without. And even though the price of housing in Southern California is high, and, of course, there's also the traffic, I think moving here was worth the price."

Since moving to Carlsbad, Vicki says she has indulged herself by joining the tennis club at the world-renowned La Costa Resort and Spa, located less than a mile from her home. "I enjoy playing tennis outdoors all year around there, and I've met a lot of really nice people through the resort," she says. "People come in from all over the world, and the resort sets up matches for me with them on weekends."

Also retired from the Army Reserve, Vicki says she is "quite a patriot." While she misses attending national symphonies and functions on the White House Mall, and "rubbing elbows with all the dedicated people who can stay in DC and get what needs to be done," she says she's made friends with several neighbors who are stationed at a local Marine Corps base and share her patriotic spirit. "I live in a neighborhood where I still get to see people putting up American flags," Vicki says.

"I asked someone who has lived here forever if you ever begin to not notice the sunsets and the waves," Vicki says. "I've only lived here for a short time, but I still can't get over the beauty. Even when you get stuck in traffic on the freeway, it's not that bad. As you're creeping along, you get a great view of the sunset."

Russ Davis and his wife, Yvonne, both 61, bought a retirement home in Carlsbad two years ago. At the time, both were two years from retiring as assistant principals with a school district in Los Angeles County. "We had a mild familiarity with Carlsbad after visiting San Diego over the years," Russ says. "But the more we looked around, the more we liked its small-town atmosphere and easy access to San Diego. We already had friends who lived in Carlsbad, and our daughter goes to college at San Diego State, so it seemed like a natural choice for us," he says.

Russ says they "decided to buy a house before we retired so we could feel things out. Because we were both 12-month administrators, we didn't have summers off, but we were able to spend holidays and vacations in Carlsbad. By the time we were ready to retire and sell our house in Los Angeles, moving to Carlsbad full time was an easy transition."

Russ says he and his wife both love Carlsbad's scenic seaside location and year-round springlike weather. "We also enjoy living in a place that has a small-town feeling, but that's also very close to major cities with great theaters and restaurants," Russ says.

Unlike some Los Angeles residents, Russ and his wife never viewed Los

Angeles as a rat race that they wanted to escape. "We really enjoyed living in Los Angeles and its easy access to culture," says Russ, adding that they both miss Old Town Pasadena and enjoy going back to visit. "But as people who were entering a new part of life's journey, Carlsbad just seemed better for us," Russ says. "Carlsbad seems to be a little more slow-paced than Los Angeles. That could just be our new lifestyle, but the point is, there's just not much to not like about living in Carlsbad. Whether you want to relax at the beach or enjoy shopping in the city, it's all here."

One of the few beach towns in Southern California that didn't begin as a Spanish mission, Carlsbad was founded when the railroad came through in the 1880s. While stories differ on who discovered the natural springs that had nearly the same mineral properties as the spa waters in the popular resort town of Karlsbad, Bohemia (now in the Czech Republic), the springs lured hordes in search of the good life. A grand spa palace prospered until the 1930s. Despite the city's phenomenal growth and escalating housing prices that have nearly doubled in the past five years, today Carlsbad still calls itself a village by the sea where you can walk to nearly everything in town and then to the beach.

While Carlsbad has long been a retirement haven, there's a new breed of retiree moving to town, says Gary Nessim, 53, an agent with HomeLife Village Realtors in Carlsbad and himself a transplant from New York state.

"Five years ago, Carlsbad was still considered an affordable place to retire, and many people from the Midwest and Idaho moved in and bought down, or purchased smaller homes that cost less than the houses they had at home," Nessim says. "Back then, you could buy a small home in Carlsbad for $250,000, but those days are long gone. People from the Midwest who used to be able to afford to retire to Carlsbad have been totally priced out," he says.

"Lately, we're seeing more people coming in from high-cost communities like San Francisco, Washington, DC, and Los Angeles — major cities where costs are already very high," he says. "They are retiring to Carlsbad and buying brand-new homes in new planned communities that are as large as the homes they left behind." According to Nessim, the new breed of retiree "wants a custom home in a mixed community with lots of recreational facilities like golf courses and swimming pools, and where everything is immaculately maintained."

"If they owned a custom 3,000-square-foot house in Maryland or Connecticut, that's what they buy when they retire here," he says, adding that most new housing in Carlsbad is single-family, with just a few older developments building new luxury condos. With price tags starting in the $400,000s for small, single-family attached homes or condos, and from $600,000 into the millions for detached single-family homes, "Carlsbad has lost its reputation as an affordable place to retire," Nessim says. "Anything right on the coast is

Carlsbad, CA

Population: 96,000
Location: Carlsbad is located on the Pacific Coast in North San Diego County about 31 miles north of San Diego and 45 minutes south of Orange County. Interstate 5 intersects the city and parallels the coast.

Climate: High Low
January 65 44
July 73 62

Average relative humidity: 50-60%
Rain: 10 inches
Snow: None
Cost of living: Well above average
Median housing cost: $650,000 for single-family homes, $458,250 for new condos or townhomes.

Sales tax: 7.75%
Sales tax exemptions: Groceries, prescription drugs, services.
State income tax: For married couples filing jointly, the rates range from 1% on the first $12,638 to 9.3% (plus $3,652) on amounts above $82,952. For single filers, rates run from 1% on the first $6,319 to 9.3% (plus $1,826) on amounts above $41,476.
Income tax exemptions: Social Security benefits and railroad pensions are exempt.
Estate tax: The state's "pick-up" portion of the federal tax was eliminated Jan. 1, 2005.
Property tax: 1.1% to 1.4% of assessed value. Homes are assessed at 100% of purchase price plus 2% per year, whichever is lower.
Homestead exemption: There is a homeowner's exemption of $7,000 off the value of owner-occupied homes. The state's homeowner assistance program reimburses up to $473 to those who are 62 and older, blind or disabled, with incomes under $39,699.

Religion: Carlsbad and its adjacent beach communities have more than 50 churches representing all major denominations.
Education: Seniors can take continuing-education courses at a number of local colleges in town, including MiraCosta College in Oceanside and Cardiff-by-the-Sea, and Palomar College in San Marcos. National University and the University of Phoenix also provide services through their satellite campuses. In nearby San Diego, there's the University of San Diego, San Diego State University, Cal State San Marcos and the University of California at San Diego.
Transportation: Carlsbad is located on Interstate 5, which runs from San Diego north to the Canadian border. State Highway 78, North County's major east-west highway, connects Carlsbad with Escondido. Carlsbad's regional airport, McClellan-Palomar Airport, has six scheduled flights daily to Los Angeles (United Express) and four flights daily to Phoenix

going to cost in the millions."

Nessim says that most new development in Carlsbad is built for families rather than designated for retirees. "Most of the retirees we get in Carlsbad want to live in a mixed community rather than a retirement community," he says.

"There are far more new homes than existing houses on the market, and the new houses sell almost as fast as they can build them," he says. While the housing market has slowed a little from last year, and long waiting lines and bidding wars are somewhat a thing of the past, developers are still selling every new home they build, Nessim says. The resale market has also cooled, he adds. "We're seeing more people taking their homes off the market if they don't get the asking price."

Carlsbad's new master-planned family communities are built around golf courses and lakes and incorporate a lot of open green space. Most feature a variety of custom single-family homes, and many are gated and pedestrian-friendly, with shopping centers and schools that are within easy walking distance. Several offer membership in an upscale golf course for a fee, Nessim says.

Bressi Ranch is typical of Carlsbad's new master-planned developments. Designed as a pedestrian-friendly community, with a third of the land set aside as open space, the development has walking trails, a village green and, when completed, more than 500 single-family detached homes in an array of architectural styles and prices. In the Wisteria Place and Primrose Point subdivisions, two-story single-family homes with three to four bedrooms start in the low $700,000s. In the Gardenside and Heather Court subdivisions, homes with two to four bedrooms start in the $800,000s. In the more exclusive Canterbury subdivision, homes with four to five bedrooms start in the $900,000s.

Older planned communities like Calavera Hills and La Costa Greens are now expanding with new subdivisions that include condos as well as single-family homes on one or more levels. Calavera Hills, a large planned community set on a breezy hilltop with a large park, lake, hiking trails and summer concerts, has some of the lowest prices for new homes in Carlsbad. The Mystic Point subdivision features small, attached two- to three-bedroom condos of 1,363 to 1,535 square feet and priced from the $400,000s.

For retirees looking for luxury housing and golf club membership, La Costa Greens has expanded with new subdivisions like Isle Vista, featuring homes with up to six bedrooms in two-story architectural designs like Spanish Colonial, Monterey Ranch, European Cottage, Santa Barbara Mediterranean and Tuscan. Prices start in the $800,000s and include resort-style amenities like The Presidio, a private recreational club, neighborhood parks and tennis courts, an extensive trail system, and a 32-acre public community park with aquatic center.

Carlsbad's historic core also has become an attractive residential and shopping area, featuring a mix of restaurants, antique shops, boutiques, a farm-

(America West). John Wayne International Airport is about an hour north in Irvine. Amtrak offers service north to Los Angeles and south to San Diego from a station in nearby Oceanside. The Coaster commuter rail provides service from two stations in Carlsbad to downtown San Diego and points in between. The North County Transit District, a nonprofit, tax-supported modern and convenient bus system, offers service throughout Carlsbad and connects to other cities in San Diego County.

Health: Carlsbad has easy access to many state-of-the-art health facilities. The nationally recognized Tri-City Medical Center in neighboring Oceanside is a 450-bed facility with specialty care in cardiovascular, maternal, child health, behavioral health, occupational health, rehabilitation and imaging services. Scripps Memorial Hospital in nearby Encinitas offers 24-hour emergency service, intensive care, imaging services, cardio services, orthopedics, cancer care, urology, neurology and endoscopy, among other specialties. There are many top hospitals in nearby San Diego and Orange County. Carlsbad has outstanding senior living facilities offering various levels of continuing care. They include Carlsbad by the Sea, (800) 255-1556; La Costa Glen, (800) 333-7550; Las Villas de Carlsbad; (760) 434-7116; and Sunrise Senior Living, (888) 436-4648.

Housing: Carlsbad has a wide variety of new single-family homes and condos in upscale planned golf and lake communities, with prices ranging from $400,000-$600,000. New detached single-family homes in older planned communities like **Calavera Hills**, (760) 434-3477, range from $600,000 to $800,000 and into the millions for large, 2,000-square-foot condos and two- to six-bedroom single-family homes in planned communities like **Bressi Ranch**, (760) 431-8329. Rentals range from $750 to $2,000 per month, depending on size and location. Carlsbad has a limited amount of existing housing in older neighborhoods. Small condos, bungalows and single-family fixer-uppers in older neighborhoods start in the $400,000-$500,000 range. Carlsbad also has many apartment complexes where several or all units are designated for residents on limited or fixed incomes.

Visitor lodging: The Carlsbad area offers nearly 4,000 hotel and motel rooms in a wide variety of lodging options ranging from luxury beach, golf and spa resorts to moderately priced hotels and budget motels. Holiday Inn, Carlsbad by the Sea, is located near beaches, LEGOLAND, the Del Mar Racetrack and shopping, from $118, double occupancy, (800) 266-7880. Hilton Garden Inn is just steps from the beach and has a fitness center, from $135, (760) 476-0800. Grand Pacific Palisades Resort and Hotel is near downtown Carlsbad and has a water park and spectacular views of the ocean and flower fields, from $119, (800) 725-4723 or (760) 827-3200. Vacation rentals range from $1,000 to $4,500 a week.

Information: Carlsbad Convention and Visitors Bureau, 400 Carlsbad Village Drive, Carlsbad, CA 92008, (800) 227-5722, (760) 434-6093 or www.visitcarlsbad.com.

ers market, the Carlsbad Seawall, and new single-family homes and condos. "It has a very old-fashioned feel that appeals to a lot of retirees," Nessim says. Because The Village is just a block from the sea and beaches, real estate prices are high, he says, with new homes starting in the millions and new condos starting in the $700,000s.

For seniors looking for more affordable housing options, there's Rancho Carlsbad, an upscale manufactured home park for residents 55 and over, with a golf course, clubhouse and recreational activities. In addition, Carlsbad has apartment complexes where many or all of the units or condos are designated for people on limited or fixed incomes.

Nessim says most retirees move to Carlsbad for the same reason he did. "We have a great, springlike climate where you can play golf and tennis all year around, there's just enough humidity to keep your skin from getting dry, but not enough that we ever have a mold problem, and our beaches are beautiful and never crowded."

Carlsbad also boasts a wealth of outdoor recreation (surfing, swimming, fishing, strolling and sunbathing), including seven miles of breathtaking strands backed by 30- to 100-foot sandstone bluffs. Among them are the Carlsbad Boulevard Seaward Walk, a paved recreational path lighted for night strolling, and Carlsbad State Beach, a block from downtown with two four-mile beaches and jogging trails, one high on the bluffs and another down at the beach. South Carlsbad State Beach offers campsites on a cliff overlooking the beach and sea.

The city's many parks offer a variety of leisure activities, including free jazz concerts on Friday nights. The family-friendly beaches offer everything from surfing lessons to hiking on the Carlsbad trail system. Retirees eager to perfect their golf swing will find plenty of places to tee off in Carlsbad, which has two world-class golf resorts and more than 30 courses. The city also has many tennis courts and private clubs, and birders will find plenty to point their binoculars at in Carlsbad's beautiful lagoons.

Carlsbad is also world-famous for its flower fields, with acres of rainbow blooms planted in wide stripes of contrasting colors. Around the Christmas holidays, the fields are a sea of red poinsettias.

The town's latest claim to fame, LEGOLAND, is a popular place for kids of all ages, featuring historic cities, monuments and mountain ranges, all made of little plastic bricks. There's even an area where you can create a miniversion of your dream retirement home.

Carlsbad's active senior center is a modern, upscale facility. A walkable downtown is lined with Victorian, Dutch and Bohemian buildings that house a variety of boutiques, restaurants and shops. The chamber of commerce occupies the 1877 Santa Fe railroad depot, just one of several national historic landmarks in town. In recent years, downtown Carlsbad has become an antique mecca; the three-block district is lined with shops crammed with everything from estate jewelry and Depression glass to country quilts.

Berg Bak, a semiretired cosmetic manufacturer, jeweler and developer, lived all over the world (from Seattle and Idaho to Italy and Istanbul) before deciding to retire to Carlsbad last year. He and his fiancee settled into a beautiful luxury condo complex near the La Costa Resort that Berg says "looks like it could be in Paris."

Berg, a "very active 71" who has been married and divorced twice, says he and his fiancee chose Carlsbad as the home base for their jet-set lifestyle for several reasons. "First of all, I like living near San Diego because my son is a physician-bachelor in La Jolla, and I want to be close enough to keep my eye on him without living right on top of him," laughs Berg. "Aside from that, I'm a real beach boy. I do a lot of swimming, and you can also go jogging, walking, surfing, fishing — you name it. Retiring can be boring, but in Carlsbad, there's always something to do."

Berg says he's made many new friends since retiring to Carlsbad. "Most of the people in our condo complex are retired, and a lot of them have second homes in Palm Beach or Texas. Nearly everyone except us is a big golfer."

Berg says they considered other communities in the San Diego area, but ultimately chose Carlsbad because of its beautiful beaches and easy access to several international airports (in San Diego, Orange County and Los Angeles). "We do a lot of international traveling as well as cruising, and we like that the airports and the port are so convenient," he says. "You look around at all that Carlsbad has to offer, and you say to yourself, 'What's not to like?'" ●

Cashiers, North Carolina

Newcomers call this North Carolina mountain town a "great little spot"

By Jim Kerr

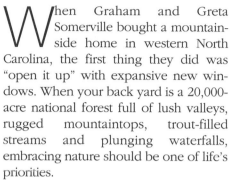

When Graham and Greta Somerville bought a mountainside home in western North Carolina, the first thing they did was "open it up" with expansive new windows. When your back yard is a 20,000-acre national forest full of lush valleys, rugged mountaintops, trout-filled streams and plunging waterfalls, embracing nature should be one of life's priorities.

Even though they only arrived here a few years ago, the Somervilles, who retired and moved from Pascagoula, MS, are in many ways like settlers who have been coming to this Blue Ridge Mountain area for the past 175 years — independent-minded, resourceful and ready to become part of a mountain community.

The place is called Cashiers, and while it embraces a dozen hamlets, more than 40 mountain neighborhoods and a dozen golf-course communities and resorts in its communal arms, there is no boundary-defined "town" per se. Its central business core is a crossroads with one stoplight at the intersection of U.S. Route 64 and North Carolina Highway 107.

Low-rise contemporary wooden structures house real estate offices, restaurants, shops and small businesses spread out in four directions for half a mile or so from the stoplight. A gas station or two occupy strategic positions as well, but there are no malls, neon signs, fast-food restaurants or man-made tourist attractions. Visitors, as well as those who live here either seasonally or full time, come for the fishing, hiking, golf, waterfalls and the simple pleasure of breathing cool, clean air at 3,500 feet.

The migration to Cashiers began in the 1820s, when settlers from South Carolina began grazing their horses and cattle in the lush valleys during the summer. They followed Cherokee Indian trails up the mountains, building cabins and planting crops. Legend has it that the name "Cashiers" derives from a resident horse named Cash, either because of his

cost or propensity for winning races. His domain became known as "Cash's Valley," later shortened to "Cashiers," or so the story goes.

The Civil War split the area and created severe conditions. Deserters trudged home to families while renegade bands and zealous home guards terrorized the population, events depicted in the best-selling novel and popular movie "Cold Mountain," a real place not far from here.

After the war, word spread rapidly about the natural beauty of the area and its cool summer climate. Summer homes were built, as were plush resorts and year-round communities. Today, summer residents number around 10,000 from mid-June through November, while the year-round population has leveled off at 1,700.

"We had lived in places like California and Hawaii, places with no real seasonal changes," says Graham Somerville, a retired manager with Chevron. "And for five years we lived in New Brunswick, Canada. We never ceased to be amazed at the changes there, and we felt the North Carolina mountains offered some of the same without the severe northern climate. Our house here was the last house we looked at on a weeklong trip to Cashiers in January 1999. It was snowing, and we knew if we loved it then, we would love it all year long."

The Somervilles live in Big Sheepcliff, a neighborhood of 52 elegant mountain homes along a gated road that winds up a mountain off Highway 107 just north of "downtown" Cashiers. Graham, 69, and Greta, 66, reflect the kind of involvement typical of retirees here. In addition to being the current homeowners association president at Big Sheepcliff, Graham tutors sixth-graders in arithmetic and reading, volunteers in the Highlands-Cashiers Hospital and helps out with fund-raisers for the library. Greta is president of the board of directors of the Cashiers-Highlands Humane Society, a

job that takes up to 30 hours a week.

"The sense of community here is amazing," says Greta, "especially when you consider that every fund-raiser has to be crammed into a May-to-November season."

Weather and logistics, including lengthy drives up and down sometimes slippery mountain roads, do not deter Cashiers-area volunteers, who have been instrumental in establishing a Village Green playground and school, a library, community center, museum and a tuition-free charter school for grades kindergarten through eight. The nearest movie theater may be 40 miles away, but Cashiers boasts several annual events, including a chamber music festival, symphony performances, arts and craft shows, house and garden tours, food festivals and holiday celebrations. In between, the great outdoors calls with some of the best trout fishing in the country, 12 area waterfalls to explore and hundreds of miles of hiking in the Nantahala National Forest.

All these things, plus outstanding golf, convinced Ethan Staats, a retired physician, to buy a home in Cashiers in 1985. At first his wife, Marilyn, was reluctant. The couple had lived for many years in Atlanta, where Marilyn, a published novelist, editor and travel writer, enjoyed ballet, theater and concerts.

"While I miss them," she says, "I've learned to love it here and to get into things I've never done before."

Her transformation from city to country life began with simple pleasures such as gardening and wildflower workshops. Later, through the Cashiers Historical Society, she became involved in the restoration of an early home, the only Greek revival house in western North Carolina, into a local museum. She became chair of the book sale committee for the Albert Carlton-Cashiers Community Library and wrote a history of the High Hampton Colony Club, a 1,000-acre resort and residential property founded by a Confederate general and former South Carolina governor, Wade Hampton, in the mid-1800s.

The Staatses live year round in Heaton Forest, one of four neighborhoods in the colony. Their contemporary mountain-view home is one of 25 along Heaton Road, but there are 220 homeowners in the colony, as well as the High Hampton Inn resort and its nationally recognized golf course.

Ethan, 72, is an eight handicapper and three-time club champion at High Hampton. He walks three to four miles a day, categorizing every wildflower he finds, and he says he has "probably fished for trout in every stream and river in the county." Yet he's on the go for many hours every week as the president of the library, founder of the fund-raising Cashiers Valley Book Club, and member of the Cashiers Valley Rotary Club and the Corridor Committee, a planning group dedicated to preserving Cashiers' country character by concentrating appropriate commercial and public entities into one business district.

Some say that won't be easy, considering the growth and transformation in the past 20 years. "Handmade crafts, old grocery stores and hardware stores that were typical of the area have disappeared," laments Fritz Alders, who splits his time between Cashiers and a home in Vero Beach, FL. "Now we have upscale dress and gift shops and a supermarket."

He and his wife, Pat, who have been part-time residents here since 1982, live in the mountain tennis community of Cedar Creek and belong to the nearby Wade Hampton Country Club, a Tom Fazio-designed course ranked among the top 20 private clubs in the country. Since they moved here, the number of members of the Cashiers Chamber of Commerce has risen from 61 to more than 400, many of them real estate offices. But while he protests the ever-increasing popularity and growth of Cashiers, Fritz says it "is one of the best-kept secrets in the country."

The state department of transportation is planning another stoplight to help traffic flow in the Cashiers business district. But while most residents express some concern with the growth, they are also confident that the area's main attraction will always be its natural wonders.

These are the oldest mountains in the nation, with valleys carved from the last ice age. A unique ecological zone exists here, split by the Eastern Continental Divide, located just north up Highway 107. East of it, streams and rivers flow to the Atlantic, while rainfall west of it runs down into the Gulf of Mexico. Less-traveled roads lead to tranquil valleys, majestic mountains rising to 5,000 feet and the

Cashiers, NC

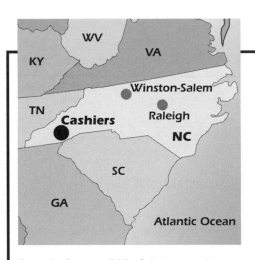

Population: 1,700 full-time residents, approximately 10,000 seasonal residents from June to November, 34,975 in Jackson County.

Location: In southwestern North Carolina on the southern crest of the Blue Ridge Mountains straddling the Eastern Continental Divide at 3,500 feet. The Cashiers business district is located at the intersection of U.S. Route 64 and NC Highway 107. The area extends south to the South Carolina border, north to Glenville, east to Lake Toxaway and west to Highlands.

Climate: High Low
January   54   27
July   86   65

Average relative humidity: About 45%

Rain: Average is 75 inches annually.

Snow: Average is 10 inches annually.

Cost of living: Somewhat above the national average.

Average housing costs: The median sale price of a home in the Cashiers area is $485,000, and the average price is about $800,000.

Sales tax: 7%

Sales tax exemptions: Prescription drugs, eyeglasses, some medical supplies and most services.

State income tax: For married couples filing jointly, it ranges from 6% on taxable income up to $21,250 to 8.25% (plus $14,537.50) on income over $200,000. For single filers, the rate is 6% on taxable income up to $12,750 to 8.25% (plus $8,722.50) of taxable income over $120,000.

Income tax exemptions: Social Security and Railroad Retirement Act benefits are exempt. Up to $2,000 of private retirement benefits, distributions from IRAs (up to the amount reported in federal income taxes) or up to $4,000 of government pensions may be exempt. Total deductions may not exceed $4,000 per person.

Estate tax: Applicable to taxable estates above $2 million.

Property tax: The Jackson County property tax rate is $0.36 per $100 of assessed value. There is no city tax in Cashiers, an unincorporated township. Tax on a $485,000 home would be $1,746 a year.

Homestead exemptions: North Carolina residents 65 and older, with combined incomes of $19,700 or less, are exempt from the first $20,000 or 50% of assessed value, whichever is greater. The home must be a permanent place of residence.

Religion: There are a dozen churches in Cashiers, including Baptist, Church of God, Episcopal, Jehovah's Witness, United Methodist, Roman Catholic, Presbyterian, Wesleyan Methodist and nondenominational.

Education: Southwestern Community College in Cashiers offers classes in language, business, trades and technical occupations. Western Carolina University, a four-year institution and a part of the North Carolina University system, is located 20 miles north in Cullowhee with 7,000 students and 312 faculty members. The University of North Carolina at Asheville and Clemson University in South Carolina are both about an hour and a half away. Brevard College, a private liberal arts school, is located 30 miles east in

thunder of waterfalls like Whitewater, the tallest in the eastern United States.

While there has been a building boom in the past decade, and a substantial influx of part-time homeowners, many locals see no reason to change the political complexion of Cashiers. In a 2003 referendum, they voted down an opportunity to incorporate the township by a ratio of 3-to-1. Cashiers had flirted with incorporation back in the 1930s, but unpopular restrictions and laws made the experiment short-lived.

That leaves Jackson County as the sole property-taxing authority. The county seat of Sylva, population 2,435, is an agricultural and college town 30 miles north up Highway 107. The county funds schools and other public projects, but Cashiers' residential property taxes are being reduced by more than 10 percent in light of substantial increases in assessed values. The median home price in the area is $485,000.

"In the big picture, the right kind of people are coming here, whether to retire or work," says Jessica Connor, editor of the local newspaper, appropriately named the Crossroads Chronicle. "There are a lot of new businesses, many geared toward homeowners, like interior decorating or design, painting, building and maintenance."

She and her husband moved here from Miami not long after the events of Sept. 11, 2001. Her mother-in-law moved here as well, opening a furniture store. "People seem to be grateful they're here in this great little spot, not battling it out somewhere. You want to embrace what's most important in life, and here you can get a taste of it," she says.

An army of workers — contractors, electricians, plumbers, landscapers, craftsmen and all manner of repairmen — service thousands of homeowners in the area, driving over the same twisty, two-lane blacktops used by tourists and residents. The workers generally live in more affordable communities, some of which are many miles away in Georgia, South Carolina and north Jackson County. They commute six days a week to Cashiers and nearby Highlands, 10 miles west, and traffic congestion is often exacerbated by summer road projects. Even so, Jessica Conner says, "Traffic problems are minuscule compared with Miami."

And despite a few drawbacks, the area has a way of enamoring almost everyone who comes here. Just as Marilyn Staats became a convert to mountain life, so did the couple's two children who live in Atlanta and Rome, GA. "They were very negative about us coming up here to live," remembers Ethan. "But their attitude changed drastically after they came to visit. Now they want to come all the time." ●

Brevard. The Cashiers area has a Union School with kindergarten through 12th grades, a private, nonprofit preschool and a tuition-free public charter school with grades kindergarten through eight.

Transportation: Cashiers is accessible from the east and west via U.S. Route 64 and from the south and north via NC Highway 107. The closest interstates are I-26 to the east and I-40 to the north, which intersect at Asheville, 65 miles from Cashiers. NC Highway 107 connects Cashiers with I-85 and Atlanta 150 miles southwest. The closest commercial regional airport is in Asheville, and the closest international airport is in Atlanta.

Health: The Highlands/Cashiers Hospital seven miles west of Cashiers is a well-endowed private hospital. There is a trained rescue squad funded by the county. WestCare Hospital is located in Sylva, the county seat, 25 miles north.

Housing options: Homes range from simple mountain cabins to elegant wooded retreats in gated golf communities, with prices ranging from $115,000 for a two-bedroom condo to $1 million-plus estates. "This is an area of affluent taste," says Marty Jones, owner of **Marty Jones Realty**, (828) 743-6445. "But $375,000 gets you a very nice home." He adds, however, that the median sale price of a home is $485,000. There are more than 40 developments in the area, including both public and private golf and tennis clubs. They range from exclusive **Trillium**, (888) 464-3800, where prices start at $350,000, to **Fairfield Sapphire Valley**, (828) 743-7110, and **Holly Forest**, (828) 743-7101, where homes start in the mid-$200,000s. As many as 10 real estate offices in Cashiers vie for the second-home and retirement markets. Some combine development with sales, such as **Keller Williams Realty**, (888) 743-2484. A recent sampling of the real estate market showed 140 homes for sale in Cashiers, ranging from $149,000 for a 25-year-old cabin to $5.4 million for an 80-acre mountaintop estate that includes a small guesthouse. Independent living for retirees is available at **Chestnut Hill**, (828) 526-5251 or www.chestnuthillofhighlands.com, on property adjoining the Highlands-Cashiers Hospital, with cottages starting at $210,000 and apartments at $3,381 a month. A 26-unit assisted-living facility opened October 2005 in the same location, with suites starting at $3,925 a month.

Lodging: Cashiers offers a versatile cross section of accommodations from cabins to luxury resorts and inns. At the upper end of the scale, the Greystone Inn on Lake Toxaway has 33 rooms, a golf course, spa and lake activities from $335 per night, double occupancy, including breakfast and dinner, (800) 824-5766. The High Hampton Inn has a golf course, 35-acre lake and scenic hiking trails with rooms for $96-$107 per person on weekdays, including three meals, (800) 334-2551. The Laurelwood Mountain Inn, located in the center of Cashiers, has motel rooms for $69-$98 per night, depending on season, and log cabin suites for $154 year-round, (800) 346-6846. The Millstone Inn, a B&B and mountain lodge with a restaurant two miles west of Cashiers, has 11 rooms and suites starting at $285, (888) 645-5786. Vacation homes and cabins are available on a weekly basis through individual Web sites and agencies, including Pebble Creek Village, (828) 743-0623; Mountain Lake Properties, (800) 352-2364; and Cashiers Resort Rentals, (877) 747-9234.

Information: Cashiers Chamber of Commerce, P.O. Box 238, Cashiers, NC 28717, (828) 743-5941 or www.cashiers-nc.com.

Celebration, Florida

Retirement dreams come true in this Florida town created by Disney

By David Wilkening

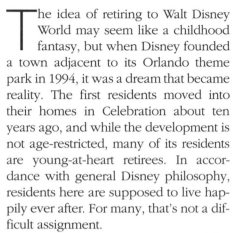

The idea of retiring to Walt Disney World may seem like a childhood fantasy, but when Disney founded a town adjacent to its Orlando theme park in 1994, it was a dream that became reality. The first residents moved into their homes in Celebration about ten years ago, and while the development is not age-restricted, many of its residents are young-at-heart retirees. In accordance with general Disney philosophy, residents here are supposed to live happily ever after. For many, that's not a difficult assignment.

New residents Rod Owens and his wife, Peg, found that it really is a small world after all, as the Disney ditty goes. They had planned a retirement relocation, and their search for a new community took them about 17,000 miles in a small motor home. But eventually they found their new home only 30 miles from the old one.

"After my husband retired, we started traveling. But we were always looking for someplace else to live," recalls Peg Owens. The couple had what seemed an almost perfect retirement location on a lake in Central Florida near the garden-rich tourist attraction of Cypress Gardens. But while living on a lake sounds like a fine lifestyle, "it was quiet but boring," says Peg.

The couple wanted to live in the South in a community with good sidewalks. "My husband jogs every day, and we knew we wanted somewhere with the mobility of being able to walk on sidewalks," she says. They were considering various places they visited, but their search came to an end on the day they read about a new community planned by Walt Disney World in Florida.

Celebration, less than an hour from their home, was so popular before it even opened that a drawing was held to determine the buyers of the first 500 homesites available. There were 5,000 entries, and Rod, a retired dentist, and Peg were among the lucky ones.

Their good fortune allowed them to become two of Celebration's first residents when they moved into their home in the summer of 1996. What they found when they arrived was a small-town atmosphere and a downtown that featured retail shops, restaurants, a town hall, a post office, grocery store, offices and cinema. Not only did they have sidewalks on which to jog, they also had access to a lake ringed with a wide promenade that is a focal point of the town.

One of Disney's theme parks, EPCOT (Experimental Prototype Community of Tomorrow) originally was to have been a place where people lived and worked. Walt Disney died long before that ever took place, but he probably would have approved of the magic of Celebration, a community with Southeastern ambiance and pre-1940s-style architecture. When complete, it will have 12,000 to 15,000 residents in homes overlooking plenty of green space. The 4,900-acre site just south of busy U.S. Highway 192 near Interstate 4 is surrounded by a 4,700-acre protected greenbelt.

Disney wanted its community to be perfect, just like its theme park, and it is said that the creators of Celebration spent a decade studying successful towns of the past and present to create a close-knit community — but one that also is technologically advanced to meet the needs of the 21st century. Famous architects of Disney's new town included Robert Stern, Aldo Rossi, Michael Graves and Philip Johnson.

The technology is evident in various ways, such as Florida Hospital Celebration Health, a 60 bed health-care facility offering comprehensive care and a 60,000-square-foot fitness and wellness center. Another example is the community's own Intranet, which links homes, schools, health-care facilities, office and retail areas, providing such online services as e-mail, chat rooms and bulletin board announcements.

But there are homey small-town touches such as homes with front porches designed to promote social interaction. Even the par-72 Celebration Golf Club has been designed to have the feel of a city park. Popular with retirees such as the Owenses are the many miles of nature trails and bicycle paths.

Also popular among retirees is an over-50 group of volunteers. But what the Owenses and others find particularly enticing about Celebration is its wide mix of age groups that all seem to share a sense of community.

"You get a great feeling of community here that I don't think you find at mobile home parks or retirement areas," says Peg Owens. Virtually everyone she knows at Celebration is involved in some type of charity or civic organization. Her husband, Rod, 57, helps out with Give Kids the World. Peg, 51, started a garden club when Celebration first opened and has watched it grow from 15 to almost 60 members.

If there is a negative side to Celebration, the Owenses feel it is nearby busy U.S. Highway 192. "We do hate the traffic there," Peg says. As best they can, the Owenses and other residents avoid getting out at rush hour and other peak traffic times.

The Owenses praise the wide choice of housing available, ranging from apartments to garden, village, cottage and estate homes. Prices start in the high $200,000s for a condominium and reach $1 million at the estate level. The Owenses chose a 2,400-square-foot home that has a small lot but provides them with plenty of privacy because of the layout.

Houses are designed in six styles: Classical, Victorian, Colonial Revival, Coastal, Mediterranean and French. There are six home types: estate, village, cottage, garden, townhouse and bungalow. These types allow for a variety of lifestyles that range from a traditional large home on a golf course that might be 90 feet wide by

130 feet deep to compact cottage homes like those found in the downtown areas of some of Florida's cities and towns. Bungalow homes, the smallest at 39 feet wide by 79 feet long, are reminiscent of Coral Gables, FL, or Pasadena, CA, in the early 1900s. Thirty-seven of 47 bungalow sites were snapped up the first day they became available in September 1999.

The community is not gated, but the Owenses say that's no detriment. Perhaps partly because there always are people out participating in various activities in the community, there is little concern about crime.

"All ages are here. We love seeing and hearing the children. There are wide sidewalks everywhere. Children are skating by. Families are walking by. You feel perfectly safe," says another resident, Melie Sue Ablang. She and her husband, Ernie, a physician, also were among the lucky lottery winners who first moved here. Like the Owenses, the Ablangs read about Celebration in a magazine.

At the time, they were living in Chesapeake City, MD. "Ernie had always loved Disney, so we flew down and took a look," Melie Sue says. They made up their minds almost immediately. Sight unseen, evaluating it from a picture, they bought a village home with a garage apartment.

"Back home in Chesapeake City, we told our kids we were packing up and retiring to Disney World. Their mouths were open. Their eyes were wide. They said, 'You're doing what?' But they quickly got over the shock," recalls Melie Sue.

The Ablangs helped start the Celebrators, an over-50 retirement club that now has about 60 members and meets monthly to hear guest speakers. Melie Sue is active in the garden club and does work with the Celebration Foundation, an independent, nonprofit organization established to promote and conduct activities in the town's community buildings. She and Ernie also are active in the local Presbyterian church.

Like the Owenses, Melie Sue and Ernie don't want to live in a community peopled entirely by retirees. They relish the variety of age groups they encounter daily. And, "there's always something going on," says Melie Sue.

Community-sponsored events range from St. Patrick's Day treasure hunts, periodic car shows, pumpkin-carving events at Halloween, founders day weekends, basketball tournaments and even artificial snow at Christmas.

Along with the Ablangs and the Owenses, Pat and Joe Storey also were among the first settlers here. And the Storeys have equal praise for Celebration, though they are moving — very reluctantly and by necessity, says Joe, a retired Navy pilot. He had already retired and they were living in another part of

Celebration, FL

Population: About 9,000, eventually reaching 12,000 to 15,000 when the development is complete.

Location: In the northwest corner of Osceola County, 10 miles southwest of downtown Orlando and just south of Walt Disney World, about 20 minutes from Orlando International Airport.

Climate: High Low
January 72 49
July 92 73

Average relative humidity: 55%

Rain: 48 inches annually

Cost of living: Slightly below average in Orlando. Housing costs in Celebration are above average.

Average housing cost: The average single-family home in Celebration costs about $800,000, according to Century 21 Premium Properties.

Sales tax: 7%

Sales tax exemptions: Groceries and prescription drugs.

State income tax: None

Intangibles tax: None. The tax was repealed as of Jan. 1, 2007.

Estate tax: None

Property tax: $16.4627 per $1,000 of assessed value. Real property is assessed at 100% of value. The annual tax on an $800,000 home, with exemption noted below is about $12,759.

Homestead exemption: $25,000 off the assessed value of a permanent, primary residence.

Religion: All major religions are represented in Osceola County. Community Presbyterian Church is located in Celebration.

Education: Four-year colleges in the area include the University of Central Florida and Rollins College. There also are several junior colleges, including Seminole Community College, Valencia Community College and others. Noncredit classes for adults are available at various outlets, including The Knowledge Shop.

Transportation: Orlando International Airport is a major airport providing direct service both nationally and internationally. But the area's major bus transportation system, Lynx, does not serve Celebration.

Health: Florida Hospital Celebration Health, a 60-bed facility that offers acute care, is located in Celebration. There are several other major hospitals in the Orlando area.

Housing options: New residents can choose from condominiums to estates. Prices start in the high $200,000s for condos, the $300,000s for bungalows and townhomes, $400,000s for cottages, $600,000s for village homes and $1 million and up for estates. There are no apartments in Celebration, as the last remaining units have been converted to condos.

Visitor lodging: The 115-room Celebration Hotel is built in 1920s-style wood-frame design, with rooms from $179 to $449, (888) 499-3800 or (407) 566-6000. Near the theme parks are other options in all price ranges.

Information: Celebration Realty, 910 Beak St., Celebration, FL 34747, (877) 696-8696, www.celebrationfl.com or Celebration Town Hall, (407) 566-1200.

Orlando when Celebration first came to their attention.

"Our next-door neighbor was an architect and construction project manager for Celebration," recalls Joe. "He kept us advised what was going on down here.

"We figured that if someone who was on the inside of this project was enthusiastic enough to plan to move here, we would just follow along and see what was going on."

The Storeys visited the preview center and watched a presentation. "We liked what we saw," but that early in development, "it was a leap of faith," says Joe. However, Pat thought so highly of the plans for Celebration that she told her husband, "We should move there even if we have to live in a closet."

Needless to say, they didn't have to live in a closet, and they relied on Disney's longstanding reputation for high quality in making their decision to buy. "We knew about their track record, and judging by that, we thought it would be a beautiful place. And it is. It's a great, great place," Joe says.

Then why are they moving? "We're moving to a CCRC (continuing-care retirement community) because of our health. To get to places you have to visit, such as getting your car repaired, you have to drive down a very busy highway (U.S. Highway 192) for at least five minutes. My wife hates it. As long as you don't leave Celebration, that's no problem. But outside the gates, access gets less convenient as you get older," Joe says.

The Storeys particularly liked the sense of community in Celebration, and they found it easy to make friends. They say they will miss those friends when they move, but they had no trouble selling their home. "Homes only last about two months on the market," Pat says. And some homes have almost doubled in price just within the past couple years, she adds.

That level of appreciation is lamented by friends of the Owenses who considered Celebration but instead retired in Tampa. Now the Owenses say their frequently visiting friends wish they had moved to Celebration. But it's too late — they can no longer afford the prices.

The Ablangs also are thinking of moving again, although they say they love their home. But they'll be staying in Celebration, perhaps moving to a larger home so Ernie can have more space for his hobby, woodworking. Both Ernie and Melie Sue do miss their children, "but they visit a lot because business conferences bring them to the Orlando area. We get to see them often," Melie Sue says.

And that brings up one of the best things about Celebration — its proximity to Walt Disney World. With the theme park just a short drive away, residents who have children and grandchildren say they've never been more popular. "We even have a back road that takes us straight to Disney World without getting on the busy highways," says Melie Sue Ablang. ●

Chapel Hill, North Carolina

This small, historic city in North Carolina grew up around the nation's
first state university

By Jim Kerr

If people are retiring twice to the same place, you know it's got to be good. And that's what Charles and Janet Paddock did — both times for the same reasons. As a career U.S. Navy pilot, Charles was stationed in every far-flung corner of the globe, from Iceland to North Africa, Australia to Europe, the Mediterranean to Hawaii. But when it came time to hang up his wings and touch down to a quieter life, the former Navy captain and aircraft carrier pilot and his wife chose Chapel Hill.

It was the perfect compromise climate from the extremes they had experienced, including Charles' last assignment in Oahu, HI. Chapel Hill, a beautifully preserved 209-year-old city in the rolling hills of central North Carolina, met all their other criteria as well, including a location with superb educational and health facilities. Twenty years later, after Charles' second career in tax consultation with H&R Block, the Paddocks moved less than 10 minutes away from their former home in Chapel Hill to Carol Woods, a continuing-care retirement community.

"We were tired of mostly hot climates where we'd been stationed, but since we had both grown up in Indiana, we also wanted a change of seasons without the severe winters," says Charles, 73.

Chapel Hill, with a population of 51,485, retains a small-town ambiance in a highly cosmopolitan environment. The town is anchored by the University of North Carolina in a region renowned for higher learning. With Duke University just minutes north in Durham, North Carolina State University 30 miles east in the state capital of Raleigh, and an array of high-tech companies in the area, the Research Triangle formed by the three cities boasts more doctorates per capita than anywhere in the country — and perhaps the world.

When the University of North Carolina was chartered in 1789, making it the oldest state university in the United States,

the local terrain and atmosphere contributed heavily to the decision. It is said that a search committee had a pleasant picnic under a shady poplar tree at a crossroads near the New Hope Chapel. Today the same canopy of deciduous trees, including oaks, maples and hickories, shelters many well-heeled neighborhoods of Colonial, Georgian and Victorian homes.

Visitors can get a feel for Chapel Hill's history by stopping at the Horace Williams House, headquarters of the local preservation society, and picking up a map for a self-guided walking tour of downtown. The map highlights homes that date from the early 1800s to the early 1900s, most of them built for UNC professors.

Joan Vanderweert, 67, a former teacher, and husband Garrett, 67, a Toys-R-Us executive, feel energized by the youthful faces and attitudes they encounter here every day.

"That sort of feeling doesn't exist in most places, even New York," says Joan, who still maintains a second home in Wyckoff, NJ. "I've been teaching all my life, and intellectual pursuits interest me. They have shortened courses at Duke and UNC at the masters level for people like us, and it's fun being around students and young people."

She calls their townhouse life at a community called Southern Village "a different kind of retirement" where the Vanderweerts come and go as they like and where most of the residents are students rather than retirees. The Vanderweerts bought their two-story, two-bedroom townhouse more than two years ago in an area near Chapel Hill's southern boundaries. Other similar communities are springing up nearby.

The UNC campus, a square mile of red-brick, Georgian-style buildings amidst a wooded and grassy landscape, is a beehive of activity where 27,000 college students study, socialize and generally dominate the scene during the aca-

demic year. Nearby, busy Franklin Street is an assortment of bookstores, casual clothing outlets and restaurants, from pizza parlors and sandwich shops to moderate and upscale dining. Traffic is heavy, even on quiet days. And following any big Tar Heels football or basketball victory, Franklin Street is not the place to be unless your tastes run toward wild celebrations.

The university offers a vast smorgasbord of opportunities in education and the arts, including campus theater, symphony concerts and other musical events, as well as museums such as the Ackland Art Museum and the Morehead Planetarium. The UNC medical complex includes a top-ranked medical school and hospitals for children, women, neurologic and psychiatric patients, and general adult patient care. Providing some of the most advanced medical care in the Southeast, UNC hospitals are leaders in organ transplants, burn care, cancer treatment, diabetes, gastrointestinal diseases, obstetrics and pediatrics.

Duke University, with its renowned medical facilities and programs for retirees and the aging, is minutes away by car or bus, and Raleigh, an easy drive down Interstate 40, offers symphony concerts, off-Broadway plays, ballet, museums, arts and craft shows and, in mid-October, the popular state fair.

Like most top-rated places to live, Chapel Hill and its environs are rapidly expanding with familiar growing pains. Carrboro, a railroad depot and mill town that attracted blue-collar workers beginning in the 1890s, has grown up adjacent to Chapel Hill with a population of 17,585. Houses, apartments, condos and shopping malls are rapidly filling in farmland and replacing the closed-down flour and cotton mills, and the population is expected to expand dramatically in the next few years.

Meanwhile, the tiny historic towns of Hillsborough and Pittsboro (both with ties to the Revolutionary War and Civil War) are located 15 miles north and south of Chapel Hill, respectively. Both are known today for their antique shops and crafts and have garnered their own share of relocated retirees.

Nearby Jordan Lake is a heavily used recreational area for hiking, picnicking, swimming, camping, boating and fishing. Dr. John Shillito, 78, a retired neuro-surgeon who practiced at Children's Hospital Boston, keeps a small Boston whaler in a slip at the 14,000-acre lake but laments that he doesn't always have much time to use it these days. Six years

Chapel Hill, NC

Population: 51,485 permanent residents, plus 26,000 students during the regular University of North Carolina session, 17,585 in adjacent Carrboro and 120,881 in Orange County.

Location: Rolling, wooded hills in central North Carolina, three hours from the Atlantic coast and three hours from the Blue Ridge Mountains, on the western point of the Research Triangle formed by Chapel Hill, Raleigh (30 miles to the southeast) and Durham (to the immediate northeast).

Climate:

	High	Low
January	51	27
July	89	66

Average relative humidity: 54%
Rain: 41.43 inches annually
Cost of living: Above average.
Average housing cost: $315,172
Sales tax: 7%
Sales tax exemptions: Prescription drugs, eyeglasses, some medical supplies and most services.

State income tax: For married couples filing jointly, the rate is graduated from 6% of taxable income up to $21,250 to 8.25% (plus $14,537.50) on amounts over $200,000. For single filers, it is graduated from 6% of income up to $12,750 to 8.25% (plus $8,772.50) on amounts over $120,000.

Income tax exemptions: Social Security and railroad retirement benefits are exempt. Up to $2,000 of distributions from private retirement benefits and IRAs (up to the amount reported in federal income taxes), or up to $4,000 of government pensions may be exempt. Total deductions may not exceed $4,000 per person.

Estate tax: Applicable to taxable estates above $2 million.

Property tax: The rate is $15.48 per $1,000 assessed market value in Chapel Hill and $16.51 per $1,000 in Carrboro. The tax on a $315,172 home in Chapel Hill would be approximately $4,879.

Homestead exemption: Homeowners age 65 and older or disabled, living in the home and earning $19,700 or less per year, qualify for an exemption of $20,000 or 50% of the value of the home, whichever is greater.

Religion: Churches represent a dozen denominations, with an emphasis on humanitarian issues and community focus.

Education: There are more doctorates per capita in Chapel Hill than any other town in the country. The University of North Carolina was the first state university in the United States and was chartered in 1789. Duke University is located in nearby Durham, and North Carolina State University is located in Raleigh, the state capital.

Transportation: Chapel Hill Transit provides free daily bus service throughout Chapel Hill from about 6 a.m. to 11 p.m. weekdays during the school year, with somewhat less-frequent service on weekends and during the summer. A shared-ride service also is offered, as well as Triangle Transit Authority service between Chapel Hill, UNC Durham and Duke University for $2. I-40 connects Chapel Hill with Raleigh and RDU International Airport, located between the two cities.

Health: UNC Hospitals has more than 900 attending physicians and 500 interns with specialized care for patients with complex medical problems, as well as a complete range of routine services geared for all ages. Outpatient surgery programs also are offered, eliminating costly hospital stays. Nearby Duke University Medical Center in Durham also contributes to an area physician-to-patient ratio that is five times the national average.

Housing options: Many options for single-family houses, apartments, condos and continuing-care retirement communities (CCRCs) are available in Carrboro, Hillsborough and Pittsboro as well as Chapel Hill. **Carol Woods**, (800) 518-9333, a CCRC on the outskirts of Chapel Hill, has both single-family cottages and townhouses in three-unit buildings. **Carolina Meadows**, (919) 942-4014, is another CCRC with 391 apartments and villas on 170 acres. New courtyard, patio homes and single-family homes at **Fearrington Village**, (919) 542-4000 or (800) 277-0130, start in the $350,000s. Resale single-family homes range from $190,000 to $400,000. A guide to a wide range of housing alternatives, from independent-living and assisted-living CCRCs in Orange County, is available by calling Orange County's information line, (919) 968-2087 or www.co.orange.nc.us.

Visitor lodging: There are numerous hotels, inns and bed-and-breakfast facilities, ranging in price from $69 at the Days Inn, (919) 929-3090, to $240 and up at the Fearrington House Inn, (919) 542-2121. Other options include Windy Oaks Inn in Chapel Hill, starting at $135, (919) 942-1001; UNC's Carolina Inn, from $150, (919) 933-2001; Siena, (919) 929-4000, $195 and up; Hampton Inn, $89-$99, (919) 968-3000; and Best Western University Inn, $84-$94, (919) 932-3000.

Information: Chapel Hill-Carrboro Chamber of Commerce, 104 S. Estes Drive, Chapel Hill, NC 27514, (919) 967-7075 or www.chapelhillcarrboro.org. Chapel Hill-Orange County Visitors Bureau, 501 W. Franklin St., Chapel Hill, NC 27516, (919) 968-2060 or www.chocvb.org.

ago, he and his wife, Bunny, 69, a paramedical professional, retired to Fearrington Village, eight miles south of Chapel Hill. Today they seem to be always on the go.

"Most people here are like us — active socially and academically," John says. "Bunny volunteers for anything."

Both work out three times a week at a spa in Chapel Hill and belong to several of the 70 or so clubs available at Fearrington. John's skill with, and passion for, photography has led him to teach courses at two area community colleges and Duke University, while Bunny is involved with several community services, including Meals on Wheels and the Habitat for Humanity Store in Pittsboro. Both get involved in courses at Duke University's Institute for Learning in Retirement, where John is currently studying the U.S. Constitution.

"Such a collection of students you've never seen," he says of the current 800 enrollees. "All you have to be is retired."

Fearrington Village has about 1,800 residents, about 80 percent of them retirees. The development is quiet, pastoral and distinctly upscale, with townhouses and single-family homes spread over 1,100 acres and anchored by a 33-room, five-star inn and restaurant. To preserve both the Scottish heritage and the rural atmosphere, owner-developer R.B. Fitch took an unusual but eye-catching approach when he imported a few rare belted Galloway cows in the 1980s. They have since flourished to 50 head. "We don't eat them, of course," affirms Fitch. "They're just mascots, chosen because they're different." Most

locals refer to the black cows with white bands around the middle as "Oreo cows."

Meanwhile, Carol Woods, where the Paddocks live, also lives up to its name as a pine-forested community in north Chapel Hill. Flowering trees and shrubs like dogwood and azaleas blend with the big blue and white hydrangeas that Janet Paddock tends in her back yard. Spring and fall linger on the 500-foot plateau, with warm summer days reaching into the upper 80s and generally mild winters where cold temperatures and snow are aberrations.

"Everyone laughed when they saw we had brought our blue snow shovel," says Lew Woodham, who, with his wife, Ann, moved to Carol Woods in June 1999 from New York state.

Neighbors weren't laughing, however, when they borrowed the shovel following a freak storm the year the Woodhams moved in, but the occasion was an isolated one. The Woodhams' neat and comfortable cottage is one of 292 townhouses and cottages on 120 wooded acres at Carol Woods.

Comfortable weather aside, Lew and Ann had a long checklist when they left Schenectady, NY, in search of a retirement location. Lew, 67, had been a social worker and youth program coordinator, and Ann, 66, had been a homemaker and community volunteer. Their list of requisites, like that of most retirees drawn to Chapel Hill, included a culturally active community, first-class medical facilities and both local and far-reaching modes of transportation. At least one son still had "itchy feet," and Raleigh-

Durham International Airport connected him with his parents when he was off in Thailand, India and Kosovo.

When Carol Woods became the site of a day camp for 8- to 13-year-olds, Lew jumped in as coordinator. It might have been farmland 20 years ago, but today the area has plenty of facilities for kids to swim, fish, make art objects and listen to storytelling by foster grandparents who, like Lew, thrive on independent thinking in an active community.

"Here, we have 400 activity directors," he says.

Like most Chapel Hill retirees, Charles Paddock is very much involved in the Retired Senior Volunteer Program, and for the past 15 years has helped low- and middle-income families prepare their taxes through the IRS Volunteer Income Tax Assistance Program.

It's hard to imagine that Chapel Hill was once just a remote crossroads with a church and rest stop for the occasional stagecoach. Today it is a lively university town that has attracted retirees from all walks of life. Says John Shillito: "The cross-section of residents here is amazing — top Army brass, big corporate CEOs, doctors, professors, scientists, administrators. And they don't hit you over the head with it. It takes a while to find out what someone did before retirement."

Chapel Hill appeals to the active, intellectually curious retiree, says Lew Woodham. "There are more programs and activities for seniors. Come to Chapel Hill if you're not looking to retire."

"I can't imagine anyone not liking it," says Janet Paddock. ●

Charlottesville, Virginia

Retirees follow Jefferson's lead to Virginia

By Bob Lane

There's nothing like the presence of 20,000 college kids to help keep you young, and Charlottesville, home to the University of Virginia, is a college town with a growing appeal to retirees fleeing the congested, high-priced suburbs of northern Virginia and the Northeast. Escapees from Washington, Philadelphia, New York and other big cities seem delighted to find this central Virginia combination of livability, affordability and sophistication.

"I'm amazed at the people from all over the U.S. and the world who are moving here," says Harold Schrock, 67, who with wife Theodora, 59, came from northern Virginia. "We couldn't be happier," says Harold, a retired homebuilder. Indeed, two of his sisters have followed him to the area.

Those moving to "Thomas Jefferson's Virginia" needn't leave behind the worldly pleasures they've learned to love, either. Supermarkets in Charlottesville sell fresh sushi and organic produce. Restaurants serve Brazilian, Thai, Vietnamese, Indo-Pakistani, Japanese, Szechuan, German and Greek food (not to mention Southern-style fried chicken and cheeseburgers). There are lattes to sip at Starbucks and a dozen other coffee houses. Jazz and Shakespeare weekends are as common as crabgrass. Sports buffs can follow polo, steeplechase racing, lacrosse and mainstream NCAA football and basketball. Nearby are mountains to climb, ski slopes to explore, golf courses to conquer and lakes to fish.

Population: About 39,500 in Charlottesville, 88,400 in Albemarle County.

Location: Charlottesville is in the Piedmont Plateau of Central Virginia. It is 110 miles southwest of Washington, DC, and 70 miles northwest of Richmond. Beginning just west of Charlottesville are the Blue Ridge Mountains. Shenandoah National Park, the Skyline Drive and the Blue Ridge Parkway all are within a short drive of Charlottesville.

Climate: High Low
January 44 26
July 86 65

Average relative humidity: 52%

Rain: 47 inches

Snow: 24 inches

Cost of living: Above average

Housing costs: In Charlottesville the median price of a single-family home is $328,000. However, real estate prices vary greatly, ranging from around $100,000 for a small condo to $1 million and up for a large home in an exclusive development. In early 2006, residential listings with the Charlottesville Area Board of Realtors ranged from $99,000 for a studio condo to $3.5 million for an 8,270-square foot estate. Local real estate agents say retirees moving to the area are likely to spend $300,000 to $400,000 or more for a newer home in a desirable neighborhood. One-bedroom apartments in desirable areas typically rent for $600 to $800 a month, and two-bedroom apartments for $800 to $1,000 and up. Student demand for apartments is high.

Sales tax: 5% (4% state and 1% local)

Sales tax exemptions: Prescription and non-prescription medicine, some medical equipment, utilities and most services. Reduced sales tax rate on groceries.

State income tax: For married couples filing jointly and single filers, the rate is graduated from 2% of taxable income up to $3,000 to 5.75% on amounts over $17,000.

Income tax exemptions: Social Security benefits are exempt. There is a $12,000 deduction per person for residents 65 or older. However, the deduction is reduced dollar for dollar if the adjusted federal gross income exceeds $50,000 for single filers and $75,000 for married couples. There is no deduction for singles with incomes above $62,000 and couples with incomes above $87,000.

Estate tax: On estates over $2 million, Virginia imposes a "pick-up tax" portion of the federal tax. The Virginia estate tax has been repealed for deaths after July 1, 2007.

Property tax: Albemarle County property taxes are $7.40 per $1,000 of assessed value. Charlottesville residents pay $10.50 per $1,000 of assessed value. Homes are assessed at 100% of market value. Annual tax on a $328,000 home in Charlottesville would be about $3,444. Personal property taxes are assessed on automobiles and other vehicles; the rate in Charlottesville is $42.80 per $1,000 of valuation.

Homestead exemption: Low-income persons 65 and older may qualify for reductions in property tax rates.

Religion: The metropolitan area is home to more than 200 churches and synagogues representing most religions and denominations, including Buddhist, Greek Orthodox and Mennonite.

Education: Retirees can take courses at the University of Virginia or at Piedmont Virginia Community College. Virginia's Citizen Scholar Program allows residents age 60 and older who have lived in Virginia at least one year to audit credit courses or enroll in noncredit courses on a space available basis, at no charge. Participants may attend any of Virginia's state institutions of higher learning, including Piedmont Virginia Community College and the University of Virginia through its Division of Continuing Education. Credit classes also are free for those with taxable incomes of $15,000 or less; for others, tuition for credit courses at UVa is $242

All around Charlottesville are the living echoes of history, from the homes of presidents Jefferson, Monroe and Madison to the bedroom of John-Boy Walton. For vinophiles there's another plus: Central Virginia is one of the East Coast's principal wine grape growing regions, with more than 50 vineyards in operation. Thomas Jefferson is considered the father of American wine, as he made his own wines, encouraged Americans to drink wine and selected the first wines to be stocked at the White House.

Most retirees who relocate to Charlottesville say the presence of the University of Virginia was what first attracted them to the area. "I've always been drawn to a university town," says Jeanne Chamales, 58, who first visited Charlottesville on the college tour circuit with her daughter. "The university brings so much to the area, including speakers from around the world," adds Jeanne, who moved to Charlottesville with husband John, 59, from Washington, DC, in 1993.

Bruce Copeland, 75, who with his wife, Carol, also 75, moved to Charlottesville from West Virginia in 1996, agrees. "The university has been a plus, even more so than we expected," he says.

UVa, as it is known, was founded in 1819 by Thomas Jefferson as his last great act of public service. Jefferson spearheaded the legislative initiative to charter the university, chose its location, planned its curriculum, designed its first buildings and served as its first rector. The Rotunda, which Jefferson modeled on the Pantheon in Rome, was designed, with the adjoining two-story Pavilions housing faculty and one-story rooms housing students, to be the heart of Jefferson's "academical village" or community of scholars. Having survived a fire and several redesigns, the neoclassical Rotunda and companion buildings along what Virginians call "the Lawn" remain to this day the focal point of the university. During the United States Bicentennial in 1976, the American Institute of Architects recognized Jefferson's academical village design as the most significant achievement of American architecture in the past 200 years.

Today, the University of Virginia has more than 13,000 undergraduate and 7,000 graduate students, about 30 percent of them from outside Virginia. UVa competes with other top state universities and even with Ivy League colleges for student talent. The university's architecture, law and medical post-graduate

Charlottesville, VA

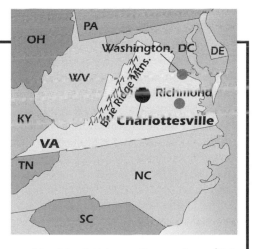

per credit hour, but may very by class.

Transportation: Charlottesville-Albemarle Airport is a small, modern airport with service to Philadelphia, Pittsburgh, Cincinnati, Charlotte, New York and elsewhere on regional commuter carriers Comair/Delta Connection, United Express, US Airways Express and Continental Express. Many Charlottesville residents drive to Washington or Richmond for jet service. Interstate 64 runs east-west through Charlottesville, connecting with I-95 in Richmond, I-81 in Staunton and I-85 in Petersburg. AMTRAK provides passenger rail service with a station in Charlottesville.

Health: The University of Virginia Medical Center, a 552-bed regional acute-care research and teaching hospital, has been rated among the top hospitals in the country. Martha Jefferson is a private 200-bed acute-care hospital.

Housing options: The Charlottesville area offers a wide choice of housing choices. Among them: Forest Lakes is a fully developed community in northern Albemarle County off Highway 29, with townhomes from about $200,000 and resale single-family homes from the high $200,000s, (800) 455-7222. Glenmore, a gated country club community in eastern Albemarle County, has homes from

$679,000 to more than $1 million, (800) 776-5111, and Fontana, near Route 20 and Route 200 East near Charlottesville, offers homes from $450,000 to $600,000, (877) 984-6310. Contact local agents for information about Lake Monticello, a recreation residential area in adjoining Fluvanna County, with homes from $120,000 to $675,000 and higher. Branchlands is a moderately priced retirement village with apartment suites offering housekeeping and meal service, (434) 973-9044. Real Estate III, the largest real estate firm in the area, offers a package of information for those relocating to Charlottesville; contact Linda Oliver, relocation director, at (877) 979-7464. Other real estate professionals who can provide information for prospective residents include Karen Kehoe, RE/MAX Excellence, (800) 818-7629, and Stephen T. McLean, president of McLean Faulconer Realtors, (434) 295-1131.

Visitor lodging: Charlottesville has more than 20 motels and hotels and nearly as many bed-and-breakfast inns, with about 3,000 rooms altogether. Within walking distance of UVa and the Medical Center are several pleasant chain properties, including Hampton Inn, $105-$195 for doubles, (800) 426-7866, and Red Roof Inn, $60-$116, (800) 843-7663. Court-

yard by Marriott is another option, $94-$129, (800) 321-2211. Silver Thatch Inn, (800) 261-0720 or (434) 978-4686, is Charlottesville's oldest country inn, dating from around 1780. The inn has seven rooms, several with fireplaces and canopy beds, with doubles from $145 to $185. Boar's Head Inn, (800) 476-1988, on 573 acres at the University of Virginia, is a resort with Colonial-era furnishings, a restored gristmill, tennis courts, golf, spa, hot-air ballooning and an excellent restaurant. The inn's 171 rooms go for $150 to $575.

Information: Charlottesville Regional Chamber of Commerce, P.O. Box 1564, Charlottesville, VA 22902, (434) 295-3141 or www.cvillechamber.org. It offers a newcomer package for about $10, including shipping and handling.

programs are nationally ranked as among the best in the country.

Retirees say the cultural activities, bookstores, sports and youthful sense of intellectual curiosity that accompany campus life are, for them, the most important aspects of a university town. For example, Charlottesville has more than two dozen bookstores, and the University of Virginia has 14 libraries with more than 4.5 million volumes. UVa has an active drama department, and there are several community theater groups in the area.

For baby boomers who recall their college days in the era of long-haired hippies, flower power and the Rolling Stones, the appearance of University of Virginia students "on Grounds" — UVa-speak for on campus — may be a surprise. While a few sport pierced orifices and tattoos, most seem fresh-scrubbed and refreshingly clean-cut. On a warm spring day, students lounge in small groups on the Lawn or participate in a race for charity. At "The Corner" on Main Street, inexpensive eateries attract hungry young undergrads and older townies alike.

UVa is not the only college in the area. Piedmont Virginia Community College, on a hill across from Monticello, has about 7,000 students. PVCC, in partnership with Mary Baldwin College, also offers a four-year adult degree program.

The availability of superb medical care is another reason for Charlottesville's appeal to retirees. The University of Virginia Health System includes nationally known schools of medicine and nursing, along with the UVa Medical Center, a 552-bed regional acute-care hospital with over 600 board-certified or board-eligible physicians on staff. The Medical Center has been rated one of the top 100 hospitals in the United States by HCIA-Sachs, a health-care information research firm, and the Health Network, a health-oriented cable television network. It has specialty treatment centers for heart disease, cancer, digestive and neurological disorders and other health problems. Also in Charlottesville is Martha Jefferson Hospital, a well-regarded, 200-bed private hospital.

Bob and Pat Zimmer decided to move to Charlottesville from Mobile, AL, in 1997 in part because of a need for specialized medical care. Bob, 76, has

rheumatoid arthritis and needed a knee replacement. "The medical school here keeps a lot of spare knees on hand," Bob jokes. But even retirees who are in good health say that knowing that such good medical care is close at hand is a comfort to them.

Having moved to a college town, many retirees find they develop a new interest in college sports, especially less-well-known sports. Football and men's basketball are the big-time sports at UVa, and the Cavaliers — or Wahoos or just 'Hoos, as they're locally known — have had nationally ranked teams. But the university fields teams in many sports, including swimming, golf, volleyball and crew. Tickets for these events are far cheaper and easier to obtain than for the major events.

Retirees who want to stay active find a lot to do at the Senior Center, a nonprofit community organization open to anyone age 50 or over. The Senior Center, in its own modern building, has more than 90 groups and activities such as investment clubs, lecture series, arts and crafts groups, fitness classes and computer classes, according to executive director Peter Thompson. A travel program through the center offers day trips to Washington, DC, for $30 a person, as well as other travel opportunities.

Shopping options in the Charlottesville area are varied. The area has one enclosed mall, Fashion Square, anchored by JC Penney and Belk department stores. Retirees say they would like to see other national department stores in Charlottesville, but they note that for major shopping expeditions they can go to Richmond or Washington. Charlottesville's Historic Downtown Mall is a gentrified pedestrian-only shopping center with brick streets, flowers and a good selection of restaurants and shops. U.S. Highway 29, a major thoroughfare, sports the usual collection of strip centers and suburban chains. While traffic and congestion don't compare with the situation in northern Virginia and other population centers, suburban sprawl, especially along the Highway 29 corridor, is a growing concern for many residents.

No state in the Union takes a back seat to Virginia in its important role in American history, so exploring the past is a favorite pastime of Charlottesville resi-

dents and visitors. The most famous site, of course, is Monticello, Thomas Jefferson's incomparable plantation home on a hill about two miles southeast of modern-day Charlottesville. "All my wishes end, where I hope my days will end, at Monticello," said Jefferson, and indeed he did die there, on July 4, 1826, precisely on the 50th anniversary of the adoption of the Declaration of Independence. Monticello is open to the public year-round, and local residents get a discount on admission.

Also in the Charlottesville area are the homes of presidents James Madison and James Monroe, both open to visitors. Several museums in the area focus on the history of Virginia, and the Civil War battlefields of Chancellorsville and Fredericksburg are within easy driving distance. One more contemporary attraction is Walton's Mountain Museum, on Route 617 in Schuyler about 20 miles southwest of Charlottesville. Earl Hamner Jr., author of the books that were the basis of the popular TV series, "The Waltons," grew up in Schuyler.

Virginia's long history and Charlottesville's collection of notable FFVs, or First Families of Virginia, have led some prospective retirees to fear that local residents would be snobbish and standoffish, but retirees to Charlottesville generally say that has not been the case. Brian Mandeville, a former senior executive with a medical devices company in Minneapolis who moved here with wife Jean in 1996, says, "The people are wonderful, grand, friendly, good-mannered — trust and a handshake just come with this community."

Agrees Jeanne Chamales, "The people are so friendly and hospitable. There is that Southern hospitality thing that is the real thing — holding the door for you, not cutting you off in traffic."

Not everyone is totally in love with Charlottesville, however. Bob and Pat Zimmer, who moved here in search of good medical care and to be closer to family in Washington, say that while their neighbors at Brookmill condominiums are very nice, they find Charlottesville "kind of boring," according to Pat. They say that compared to other areas where they lived after Bob retired as a plant manager for Anchor Hocking, including Hendersonville, NC, and Mobile, AL, the arts community in Charlottesville seems surprisingly small, especially for a university town, and there's not as much as they'd like in the way of shopping and cultural activities. They also say they feel the University of Virginia doesn't reach out to retirees the way some other colleges do.

But there seldom are complaints about the weather. The moderate four-season climate in Charlottesville appeals to many retirees. In one survey of weather professionals, the American Association of State Climatologists, Charlottesville rated behind only Asheville, NC, as having the "most desirable climate in the Eastern United States." New residents such as Brian and Jean Mandeville, who moved to Charlottesville from Minneapolis, say the four-season climate is one of the things they like best about the area. Both are runners and golfers.

Charlottesville is not for those seeking a consistently warm climate, however. The area gets an average of about two feet of snow a year, and snow skiing is a winter sport at Wintergreen and other ski areas in the mountains just to the west of Charlottesville. The winter of 1995-96 dropped about 55 inches of snow on Charlottesville, making it the snowiest winter in a century, but on average, about one in 10 winters sees no snow at all.

Spring is usually pleasantly mild in Charlottesville, inviting outdoor activities, and fall brings invigorating weather and colorful autumn foliage, especially in the nearby Blue Ridge Mountains. Summers can be hot, with temperatures hitting the 90s. To beat the heat, "we play tennis at 7:30 in the morning," says Bruce Copeland. Humidity, while much higher than in dry Western states, is lower in the Shenandoah Valley area than in most of the rest of the East Coast except parts of New England. The growing season extends to 200 days or more, making it an ideal climate for gardening. In late spring and summer, violent thunderstorms and, on rare occasions, even tornadoes may occur.

Although Charlottesville itself is in Virginia's Piedmont Plateau at an elevation of just 480 feet, it is within shouting distance of some of the East's most beautiful mountain scenery in the Shenandoah Valley and Blue Ridge Mountains. The Chamaleses are typical of retirees who were attracted by the scenery. "We were drawn by the mountains. The landscape here is so beautiful. The mountains are friendly, not so high that they are overpowering," says Jeanne, who previously lived briefly in Washington, DC, and for 13 years in New Jersey.

Richard Worch, 65, a retired civil engineer with the Federal Aviation Administration, who now lives with wife Betty, 64, on a hill overlooking the Blue Ridge Mountains, can't say enough about the natural beauty of the area. "We love the area, the scenery, watching the change of seasons from our house," he says. Richard and Betty moved to Charlottesville from Washington, DC, in 1996.

Those relocating to Charlottesville have a variety of options for housing, from moderately priced downtown condos catering to retirees to gated golf communities to horse farms going for a million dollars and up.

"Some move to golf communities like Farmington Country Club or Glenmore, or subdivision neighborhoods like Ednam Forest, but there are plenty of people who retire to farms out in the county," says Stephen T. McLean, president of McLean Faulconer Realtors.

Says Karen Kehoe, an agent with Re/Max Excellence Realty in Charlottesville, "Many retirees like Branchlands. It is near the Senior Center. They can have dining with other seniors if they desire. Another area retirees like is Brookmill, which is located just adjacent to Senior Center, although this neighborhood has a mix of all ages."

Harold and Theodora Schrock, who moved from northern Virginia, live in a house they built on four acres near the town of Ivy, west of Charlottesville. It's a 4,000-square-foot contemporary designed by a West Coast architect. An unusual feature is the octagon-shaped sunroom, 20 feet across with a 24-foot-high ceiling and two rock walls to absorb heat in winter. The octagonal shape is a nod to the famous architecture of Jefferson's Monticello. The Schrocks' house also has extensive decking — some 2,000 square feet — with mountain views.

Brian and Jean Mandeville say their biggest decision when they moved to Charlottesville in early 1996 was "whether we wanted to buy a lot of acreage and live on an old horse farm in the country, or in a new neighborhood." They decided on Glenmore, a gated golf community with homes from $629,000 to $1 million-plus, because they felt it would be easier to meet people and to get involved. They built a 6,000-square-foot, two-story, Virginia-style brick home with American traditional features. "We can look out our back window and see Monticello," says Brian.

One drawback, or advantage, depending on your point of view, about Albemarle County is that a significant part of the land is tied up in large family owned farms and estates, some of several thousand acres. This keeps the area looking rural in the Jeffersonian gentleman farmer tradition, but it means that land is expensive. In Charlottesville, buildable lots can cost $110,000 to $160,000 or more. The Jefferson Highway area, for example, has been called the area's Millionaire's Row. This is fox hunt country, and working horse farms and estates line the road.

But the Charlottesville area has many middle-class communities as well. For example, Forest Lakes is a planned community of townhomes and single-family homes north of town, with prices starting at around $200,000. Land and housing generally are cheaper in surrounding counties, including Fluvanna to the southeast and Greene to the north. Parts of both counties are less than a half-hour commute from Charlottesville. Says Kehoe, the real estate agent, "Retirees from out of state are looking strongly also at Lake Monticello, a 20-minute ride from Charlottesville. It's a 300-acre lake with boating, golf, dining, swimming, sandy beaches, etc. It's a planned community with something for everyone. Prices start in the $100,000s and go up into the $500,000s. What a mix, eh?"

Housing costs, of course, are relative, and opinions of retirees depend on where they have lived in the past. Bruce Copeland, for instance, says that his home about two miles from Charlottesville is a bargain compared to Evanston, IL, another college town (home to Northwestern University), where he and his wife previously lived. "We have a nicer home here, at one-third of the cost of the house in Evanston, and taxes are a quarter of taxes there," he says. ●

Coeur d'Alene, Idaho

The Idaho Panhandle offers a playground of rivers, mountains and lakes

By Richard L. Fox

Lewis and Clark put it on the map. French-speaking explorers and fur traders named it. Now tourism, retirees and refugees from urban concerns are shaping Coeur d'Alene, the hub of Idaho's panhandle.

In the course of their expedition to find a Northwest Passage in the early 1800s, Meriwether Lewis and William Clark were met by the Nez Perce Indians 100 miles south of present-day Coeur d'Alene. Dispatches to President Thomas Jefferson recounted their explorations and brought new details about this great Western territory to mapmakers, opening the region for exploration and eventual settlement.

The name Coeur d'Alene, roughly translated as "heart like an awl," refers to the keenly sharp negotiating skills of the Schee-Chu-Umsh Indians, whose village occupied the area when French traders arrived several decades after Lewis and Clark.

Today, the Coeur d'Alene Indians are based about 30 miles to the south, where they have achieved economic success with a popular bingo and gaming casino. The rugged wilderness and mystique of which Lewis and Clark wrote still permeate this region.

"When I first came here, the town reminded me of my hometown of Newport Beach, CA, when I was a child," says Shirlee Wandrocke. "The town, the lake, the mountains just overwhelmed me (along with) the warm, congenial, lovely people. I just have a spiritual feeling living here."

Shirlee, 59, made what might be termed a reconnaissance move to the area in 1983, leaving husband Dick, 63, in Newport Beach to manage the family business. She commuted back and forth until 1990, when Dick turned the business over to their son and joined Shirlee in Coeur d'Alene. Their first home sat on a hillside overlooking the Spokane River where it joins Lake Coeur d'Alene, but they recently moved to a new home that sits on one acre of land right in town.

The Wandrockes looked at potential retirement sites in Washington, Oregon and Jackson Hole, WY, before deciding on Coeur d'Alene. "It measured up to all of our requirements. We had to live within an hour's drive of a large city (Spokane) for concerts and symphonies. We also wanted to be near an airport because of our children living in Southern California. We had to be in sight of water . . . and it had to have a decent hospital, because I was bringing my mother with me," Shirlee says.

The desire to live "in sight of water" is shared by natives and newcomers to the area. Rustic cabins, lake villas, condominiums and 10-acre estates all share spectacular views of the lake and surrounding mountains.

With a population greater than 38,000, Coeur d'Alene is the seat of Kootenai County in the northwest Idaho Panhandle. It sits on the north shore of Lake Coeur d'Alene near forests and mountains that beckon climbers, hikers, bikers, skiers and snowmobilers. Some might expect this town to be merely a launch pad for recreational opportunities in the hinterlands.

"Not so," says Dick Compton, 63, who spent 33 years traveling around the country and the world for IBM before retiring to Coeur d'Alene in 1993 with his wife, Janette, a native of the town.

Janette, 64, likes the small-town atmosphere. "It doesn't matter who you are or where you've been — you are accepted," she says.

"Cultural opportunities are good, health-care facilities are good — and getting better — and crime is a minimum issue. There are no gangs and (there is) good law enforcement," says Dick, who finds that civic leaders are more accessible in Coeur d'Alene. "You can know the people who are prominent and influential in the city and become involved much easier than in a large city like Seattle. It's the right size," he says.

Shortly after retiring here, Dick became involved in local politics and was elected chairman of the Board County of Commissioners. He also serves on the board of Jobs Plus, which recruits small businesses to the area.

Coeur d'Alene has experienced a growth spurt in the last few years, creating mixed feelings among residents. "Whether you like it depends on whether you are buying or selling," says Dick. "Prices of real estate have gone up considerably. We're having a tough time absorbing the growth that's going on — the social and economic changes."

He feels that the local economy is good. "When we grew up around here there wasn't a lot of employment… there's more now — more opportunities for young people to go to work in meaningful jobs," he says.

Jim and Margie Porter moved to the area from Diamond Bar, CA, in 1990. "Our home has probably tripled in value since we bought it," says Jim. "Five acres used to run $20,000. Now it runs from $60,000 to $80,000."

The influx of new residents has increased local traffic, as Dick Wandrocke notes. "When Shirlee moved here (in 1983) there were two stoplights. When I moved here (in 1990) I could go anywhere in town from my home in five minutes. Now it takes 20 to 25 minutes. I still haven't adjusted to that, and I'm frequently late for meetings," he says.

Shirlee takes it in stride. "You could not drag me back to California — just too many people," she says. "The traffic is horrendous. I go insane when I drive down there."

With more than 300 businesses, shops and restaurants, downtown Coeur d'Alene is clean, open and tourist-oriented. The trendy, fashionable shops of Coeur d'Alene Resort Plaza spill into the downtown shopping district. Other shopping venues include Silver Lake Mall and, in neighboring Post Falls, a factory outlet mall with 60 stores.

Small, picturesque communities that range in size from 225 to 10,000 residents cozy up to the borders of Coeur d'Alene. Jim and Margie Porter chose Hayden Lake (population about 500), eight miles to the north.

"We found a perfect place in Hayden Lake," says Jim, 67. "A great house… five acres of timber. It's just heaven."

"We built a barn and bought a horse for Jim and a pony for our grandchildren," adds Margie, 63. "We have an acre of grass. When you're out on the patio you feel like you're in the national forest."

Jim's 10 bypasses and a pacemaker were not enough to move the couple from their home in Hayden Lake, though Jim did travel to famed Scripps Institute in California for his most critical surgical needs. He still splits his own firewood, storing up enough for winter. "When I can't chop wood, take care of that acre

of lawn (and) my horse, and put the hay up for the winter, we'll probably have to move," he says.

"But we won't move out of the area," Margie declares.

Lake Coeur d'Alene is the nucleus that binds together the town, a large resort and many recreational areas. Just one of some 60 lakes in a 60-mile radius, this 26-square-mile, huckleberry-hued playground is an outdoor paradise.

Homesites and boat docks line the lake's forested 135-mile shoreline. Standing out on the horizon is the Coeur d'Alene Resort, an expansive complex with a multistoried hotel, marina, boat rentals, private beach, cross-country and downhill skiing and more. The fairways of the resort's championship golf course frame the water's edge, and cruise boats ferry sightseers for a close up view of the nearly five-million-pound, one-of-a-kind floating green on the 14th hole.

The steamboats that moved mining and lumbering supplies in the early 1900s are gone. Now boats take off with parasailers in tow, and sailboats and cabin cruisers barely leave a wake as they lazily ply the calm waters. Heron and osprey circle high above the vessels in summertime, and in January and February avid bird-watchers scan the skies for bald eagles, which fish the lake for kokanee salmon as they migrate to warmer climes.

The Coeur d'Alene, Spokane and St. Joe rivers, flowing in and out of the lake, abound with salmon, trout and bass. In some places, white-water rapids provide a thrill a minute for rafters, canoeists and kayakers.

Mountain peaks are visible to the north, south and east of Coeur d'Alene. National forests and state parks make up more than 50 percent of the Idaho Panhandle.

Coeur d'Alene, ID

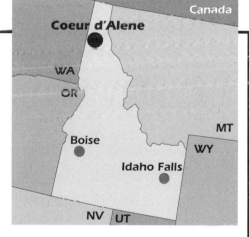

Population: 38,388 in Coeur d'Alene, 122,350 in Kootenai County.

Location: At the edge of scenic Lake Coeur d'Alene in northern Idaho's panhandle. Elevation is 2,187 feet.

Climate:

	High	Low
January	35	22
July	86	52

Average relative humidity: 46%

Rain: 27 inches

Snow: 80 inches

Cost of living: Slightly above average.

Median housing cost: $179,600, according to the Coeur d'Alene Association of Realtors.

Sales tax: 5%

Sales tax exemptions: Prescription drugs and most services are exempt.

State income tax: For married couples filing jointly, the rate is graduated from 1.6% of taxable income up to $2,318 to 7.8% on amounts over $46,356. For single filers, graduated from 1.6% of taxable income up to $1,159 to 7.8% on amounts over $23,178.

Income tax exemptions: Social Security benefits and railroad pensions are exempt. There is an exemption at age 65 or older for federal and some state and local pensions of up to $23,268 for single filers and $34,902 for married couples filing jointly.

The deductions must be reduced by the amount of Social Security benefits received.

Estate tax: None.

Property tax: At the average rate of $15 per $1,000, the annual tax on a $179,600 home would be about $1,944, with $50,000 homestead exemption noted below.

Homestead exemption: State law exempts 50% or $50,000 (whichever is less) of assessed value of the primary residence, exclusive of land value.

Personal property tax: None

Religion: 26 Roman Catholic and Protestant denominations are represented.

Education: Lewis-Clark State College-Coeur d'Alene offers the final two years of a baccalaureate degree program in a number of disciplines. The University of Idaho Coeur d'Alene campus allows students to complete undergraduate and graduate degrees.

Transportation: Spokane International Airport, 35 miles west, is served by nine major carriers.

Health: Kootenai Medical Center has 225 beds and 24-hour emergency care. The North Idaho Immediate Care Center and North Idaho Cancer Center, both in Coeur d'Alene, offer additional health-care facilities. Six major medical centers

and hospitals are less than an hour away in Spokane, offering advanced medical and surgical procedures.

Housing options: Arrow Point Resort offers two-bedroom, two-bath condos on the lake starting at $430,000. Coeur d'Alene Place, with parks and a trail system, has homes priced from $189,000 to the high $200,000s. Lakeview property is expensive, starting at $450,000 in one area minutes from town.

Visitor lodging: The Coeur d'Alene Resort, $139-$199 in winter, $219-$549 in summer, (800) 688-5253. There are more than 50 hotels and motels in the area.

Information: Coeur d'Alene Area Chamber of Commerce, P.O. Box 850, Coeur d'Alene, Idaho 83816, (208) 664-3194 or www.coeurdalenechamber.com.

"Camping is absolutely wonderful up here," says Shirlee Wandrocke. "You can go anywhere and find campgrounds — primitive or with all of the facilities."

There also are opportunities for biking, hiking and climbing, and it's not uncommon to spot a moose, elk, deer or mountain lion in the higher elevations during summer months.

When temperatures dip (the average January low is 22 degrees), boats are put in dry docks, and snowmobiles, skis, snowshoes and ice skates are brought out of storage. Those who enjoy ice fishing break out their ice picks and cold-weather gear to try their luck on area lakes.

Four alpine ski resorts at elevations of 6,000 to 7,000 feet offer trails for downhill skiers, while literally hundreds of miles of cross-country and snowmobile trails crisscross the mountains.

Jim and Margie Foster love the cold and snow. "We don't go south like the snowbirds," Margie says. "We stay here with our two snowmobiles and play."

But she cautions those thinking about moving here to consider the weather. "Everyone can't handle the winters. Some friends tried it for four years, gave up and moved to Arizona," says Margie.

"The good news is there's four seasons. The bad news is there's four seasons," jokes Dick Compton. "We get some snow and we get some winter. If you're concerned about being able to cope with that, you may want to look south." ●

Connecticut River Valley, Connecticut

Retirees find four-season living and pretty waterfront villages in southeastern Connecticut

By Katharine Dyson

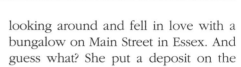

A place of great scenic beauty, southeastern Connecticut's diverse landscape offers beaches, meadows, rivers and forests coveted by those who love the four seasons along with outdoor pleasures like boating, hiking and golf. Encompassing New London and Middlesex counties, the area is bounded by a craggy coastline that runs along Long Island Sound, harboring coves and picturesque seaside towns like Old Saybrook, Westbrook and Niantic as well as the expansive, tawny beaches of Rocky Neck State Park and Ocean Beach Park.

The region is roughly bordered on the west by the Connecticut River Valley that leads from Long Island Sound and Old Saybrook to Essex, East Haddam, Middletown and Portland. To the east, the Thames River runs from New London north to Norwich. It's a slam-dunk for kids whatever the age. In addition to world-class attractions such as Mystic Seaport maritime museum, the Mystic Aquarium, the Carousel Museum, the Mashantucket Pequot Museum and the Olde Mistick Village collection of shops, there is a bevy of wonderful waterfront restaurants, wineries and unlimited opportunities to get out on the water.

Several parks provide hiking, swimming and camping options. For example, the Gillette Castle State Park in East Haddam has extensive hiking trails as well as a fieldstone castle, once William Gillette's home. In Essex you can see the countryside unroll from your seat in a 1920s coach pulled by an authentic steam locomotive, and you can take a riverboat cruise along the Connecticut River.

For golfers there is the dramatic Quarry Ridge golf course in Portland, characterized by massive rock outcroppings as well as stonework, ledges and trees. The stunning new Lake of Isles course adjacent to Foxwoods Casino reveals hole after hole of staggering drama, including huge carries over deep ravines and a 90-acre lake, and the Shennecossett Golf Course in Groton is a rolling links-style course by Donald Ross dating from 1898. There are others worth playing, like the pretty Elmridge Golf Course in Pawcatuck and the feisty Fox Hopyard Golf Club in East Haddam with elevated tees and dramatic shots through tall stands of trees.

Keeping all these things in mind, it is no wonder that Tim and Marie Horan were drawn to the Lower Connecticut River Valley. The Horans' home in Madison, CT, was getting to be more and more like work. It was a large house on more than an acre of land, and there was always the lawn to be mowed and the garden to tend. Madison, where Marie was raised, was growing from a sleepy seaside village into a sprawling, upscale town. Taxes, especially on waterfront property, tripled in just two years.

All these reasons, plus the fact that the couple's two children were grown and living on their own, started the Horans thinking about downsizing. At the time, Tim was helping a friend start a new business northeast of Madison in Essex, a small town on the Connecticut River. In the mid-1700s, Essex was a bustling shipbuilding and seafaring town. Now it harbors trendy small shops and antique stores and is home to the Griswold Inn (locals call it "The Gris"), not just a place to stay, eat and drink, but an institution that has been welcoming guests since 1776. Still, Tim was thinking about heading southwest into Fairfield County, where he had worked. Marie, however, had another idea.

"Actually," Tim says, "I never said anything about moving, but Marie started looking around and fell in love with a bungalow on Main Street in Essex. And guess what? She put a deposit on the house. Once Marie found the bungalow — end of story," he says, laughing.

"We're New Englanders. We love the climate, the change of seasons," says Marie. They also like the access to the sea. "We don't have a boat, but we used to be boaters, so now we hang out around people who have them." The Horans, both in their early 60s, moved to Essex with a retirement lifestyle in mind while they were still working, he as director of dining services at a home for the elderly in Hartford and she at a tanning salon.

With just 980 square feet, their little house "is a perfect alternative to a condo. I have a lawn I can cut, but it takes just 20 minutes with an electric lawnmower. In Madison, cutting the lawn was a big deal. We can walk into town to shop, grab a drink or dinner at the Gris and walk to the harbor and marina," Tim says. "Our daughter, who just got married, is just about 15 minutes away in Old Saybrook."

"I take the train into New York about every six weeks — it takes less than two hours," Marie says. "And there's so much to do around here. New Haven is just a half-hour away, and the Ivoryton Playhouse, the Goodspeed Opera House and many other theaters are close by, as well as Foxwoods and Mohegan Sun casinos."

"We are impressed with the genuine friendliness of the people. Everyone says 'Hi' when we pass on the street. Essex is like Madison used to be. People walk by and ask us what kinds of flowers we have in the garden — it's just that kind of town," Tim says. "And there are all kinds of parades for kids," Marie says. "In February they follow a 12-foot-tall giant papier-mâché groundhog down the street, and there are Halloween parades and a parade at Christmas where everyone carries a lantern and strolls to the river where the boats are all lighted. We love it," she says.

"Here the tax base is pretty good, thanks in part to our regional high school and volunteer fire department," Marie says. "And we are just a stone's throw from an emergency medical clinic and Middlesex Hospital. Really, we have the best of both worlds — the quiet of the country and the river — yet we can easily access I-95 or Route 9, which takes us to New York or Boston."

Comparing housing costs in pricier neighborhoods like Boston, MA; Fairfield County, CT; and Westchester County, NY, where many of the new retirees to this region are coming from, reveals that prices in the Connecticut River Val-

ley are more reasonable. According to Maureen Wiltsie O'Grady, owner and broker at Rachel Thomas Properties in Essex, average home prices in the region run about $550,000, although the closer you get to the center of the villages, the more you'll have to pay. In Westport, CT, or North Salem, NY, a comparable house costs $1 million or more. This means people can sell their homes in Fairfield County, put half or more in the bank and still afford their new home.

But downscaling for economic reasons is only one of the incentives that bring retirees to southeastern Connecticut. When people decide to retire to this area, it's often because they have family in the region, grew up in New England or love four-season living. For Janet Rose, a retired New York salesperson with AT&T, all these factors come into play.

She grew up in Syracuse, NY, and moved to Arizona with her husband when his health deteriorated. When her husband died, Janet decided to move back to the Northeast to be close to her three daughters and her roots.

Janet, who is in her early 70s, has a small apartment in Jacksonville, VT, where she has been living during the summers. "Flying back and forth and carrying double insurance, without having enough time in either place, is not what I want to continue doing," she says. "I want to establish roots in the Northeast. I'm looking for a pretty little place that has mild winters and is near the girls."

Janet wanted "a place off the beaten path within convenient traveling distance of my daughters (who are living in Vermont, New York and Maine), a moderate, sunny climate without heavy-duty

Connecticut River Valley

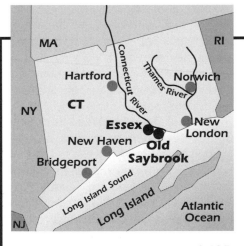

Population: Old Saybrook, 10,535; Essex, 6,500; Old Lyme, 7,480; New London, 26,582.

Location: Essex, at the southern end of the Connecticut River near Long Island Sound, is 38 miles southeast of Hartford and 32 miles east of New Haven. New London, considered the center of the southeastern Connecticut, is 20 miles east of Essex.

Climate: High Low
January 37 23
July 82 66

Average relative humidity: 68%

Rain: 41.5 inches annually

Snow: 25 inches annually

Typically the area gets snow starting in December, and snowfall can be heavy during the months of January and February. Inland areas usually get more snow

as the shoreline is tempered by Long Island Sound. Some winters can be quite mild with little snow.

Cost of living: Above average

Average housing cost: In Essex, the average sales price is $596,832. In Old Lyme, it's $507,264.

Sales tax: 6% state tax

Sales tax exemptions: Most food, prescription and nonprescription drugs.

State income tax: The rate is 3% on the first $10,000 of taxable income for single filers and 3% on the first $20,000 for married couples filing jointly. The remaining income is taxed at 5%.

Income tax exemptions: Social Security is exempt for individual taxpayers with federal adjusted gross incomes of less than $50,000 and for married taxpayers filing jointly with federal adjusted gross incomes below $60,000.

Estate tax: Applicable to taxable estates of more than $2 million.

Property tax: The tax rate in Essex is $15.50 per $1,000 of assessment; Old Lyme is $16.60; Old Saybrook, $14.60; Montville, $29.10; and New London, $28.61. Assessments are 70% of market value. Real estate is subject to county, school district, vocational school district and municipal property taxes. The state offers various tax relief programs for resi-

dents 65 and older and for residents with disabilities.

Homestead exemption: Homeowners 65 and older with an income level below $33,900 for married couples ($27,700 for singles) can receive a tax credit of $250-$1,250 ($150-$1,000 for singles).

Religion: All major religious denominations are represented throughout the region.

Education: Colleges include Three Rivers Community College, Mitchell College, University of Connecticut at Avery Point (graduate and undergraduate study specializing in marine sciences), Connecticut College, U.S. Coast Guard Academy, University of New Haven branch; Yale University; Rensselaer at Hartford-Avery Point branch. Most towns have adult education programs. See www.newlondonadulted.org or www.stoningtonhigh.org.

Transportation: Rail is available via Amtrak from New London and Mystic, (800) 872-7245. Major routes in the area include Interstate 95, Interstate 395, Route 9 and Route 2. Ferry services include the Cross Sound Ferry and the Block Island Ferry leaving from New London. Bus services are available from Greyhound Bus Lines from New London. SEAT (Southeast Area Transit) offers low-

winters, a place that is quiet and not overpopulated, a town that practices good conservation, has a favorable tax structure and is near museums. It doesn't have to be a retirement community."

Essex was among the places that fit Janet's criteria, although she hasn't made her next relocation yet. She plans to eventually sell her Arizona and Vermont homes.

In some cases, a desire for a lifestyle change results in a move. In nearby Westbrook, Christmas comes early each year for Susan and Brett Haddad, who for the past 10 years have worked together in their shop, The Pink Sleigh Christmas and Gift Barn on Route 153, a far cry from the corporate world of New York and the insurance business they left behind. Housed in a 200-year-old barn, the shop is a holiday fantasy filled with every imaginable Christmas orna-ment. "I had come here to shop for several years," Susan says. "When it came up for sale, we bought it. We have been working together here for 10 years and love it."

Going east from Essex to Uncasville north of New London, Fred Gosselin, 64, and his wife, Carole, 62, have found their ideal retirement home at Hillcrest, one of 28 developments operated by Jensen's Residential Communities, which develops and manages manufactured home communities for adults 55 and over in seven eastern states.

"We were living north of Hartford in an old farmhouse surrounded by lots of trees. I didn't look forward to spending the month of November blowing leaves and climbing up on the roof to clean gutters," says Fred, who taught chemistry in Canton, CT, for 37 years. "A lot of older people get trapped in their houses. We didn't want to do that. We wanted more time to ourselves. We wanted a place that didn't require a lot of upkeep, and we were looking for a house all on one floor."

Their search led to Hillcrest, one of Jensen's most progressive and newest communities. With single-family homes ranging from 1,040 to 1,404 square feet selling between $157,000 and $183,000, these ranch-style homes appealed to the Gosselins both because of the quality and value of the homes. It didn't take them long to make up their minds. Carole loved the idea of a new house, and Fred liked the easy lifestyle it promised.

"We came in here knowing no one. Already we've made a lot of friends," says Carole. "Moving into Hillcrest was a piece of cake. It's so easy to make friends here," Fred says.

"There are so many things to do in the

cost transportation to towns in the region and to transfer points for buses outside of the area. Major airports are located in Hartford, CT; Providence, RI; and Boston, MA. Approximate travel time is three hours to Albany, one hour to Hartford, one hour to Newport, one hour to Providence, two hours to Boston, two and a half hours to New York and five hours to Philadelphia.

Health: Options include Lawrence & Memorial Hospital in New London, one of the state's most contemporary health centers; William W. Backus Hospital in Norwich, a 213-bed, acute-care community hospital and the only state-designated trauma center east of the Connecticut River; Middlesex Hospital in Middletown, a full-service hospital operating more than 30 inpatient, outpatient, primary care and emergency facilities throughout Greater Middlesex County; and Hospital of St. Raphael in New Haven, a 511-bed acute-care hospital known for its excellence in cardiovascular care. Yale-New Haven Hospital in New Haven, a 944-bed tertiary care facility that includes the 201-bed Yale-New Haven Children's Hospital and the 76-bed Yale-New Haven Psychiatric Hospital, is the primary teaching hospital for Yale University School of Medicine and ranks among the best hospitals in the United States.

Housing options: There are several planned communities in the area. In East Lyme, **Chapman Farms** and **Chapman Woods**, (860) 691-2401, offer single-family residences with average sales prices in the low $400,000s. Manufactured-home developments are available through **Jensen's Residential Communities**, which has several communities in the southeast Connecticut towns of Westbrook, Old Saybrook and Uncasville. Jensen's has 14 communities throughout the state, (800) 458-6832 or www.jensencommunities.com. Typically residents 55 and over own their homes but lease the land, averaging one-quarter acre. Homes are attractive single-family, single-story manufactured houses, similar in style but customized to the homeowner's taste. Each community is maintained by Jensen's, including the common areas, and for a reasonable fee ($50 a month at Hillcrest, one of the newest communities), Jensen's will also maintain the homeowner's land.

Visitor lodging: Accommodations range from bed-and-breakfast inns to seaside resorts and chain hotels. There are more than 7,600 rooms in New London County, including inns, B&Bs, chain hotels, independent hotels, motels and two resort casinos, (800) 863-6569 or www.mysticmore.com. The Griswold Inn has been in business since 1776, $110-$360, (860) 767-1776. The 285-room Mystic Marriott Hotel has an Elizabeth Arden Red Door Spa, from $209, (860) 446-2600. The 100-room Spa at Norwich Inn overlooks the Norwich Golf Course, from $175, (800) 275-4772. For B&B accommodations, the 1740 Inn at Lower Farm B&B in North Stonington has four guest rooms with private baths, $95-$160, (866) 535-9075. At the nine-room Inn at Harbor Hill Marina, a B&B on the Niantic River, balconies overlook yachts and rooms have fireplaces, from $125, (860) 739-0331.

Information: Mystic Places, Mystic Coast and Country Travel Industry Association Inc., 101 Water St., Suite 102, Norwich, CT 06360, (800) 692-6278 or www.mycoast.com. Connecticut's Heritage River Valley, 31 Pratt St., Fourth Floor, Hartford, CT 06103, (800) 793-4480 or www.chrv.org. Old Saybrook Chamber of Commerce, 148 Main St., Old Saybrook, CT, (860) 388-3266 or www.oldsaybrookct.com. Helpful Web sites include www.essex.com and Rhythm of the River, www.rotr.com, a guide to the Lower Connecticut River Valley.

area, and it's all so accessible," Carole says. "We've been to concerts and have started to research our family history at nearby libraries and the Family History Centers. We also like to travel and visit our daughters, who live in France and Cincinnati. With three airports to choose from (Boston, Providence and Hartford), this makes traveling a lot easier."

Just south of Essex is another wonderful town, Old Saybrook, which lies at the mouth of the Connecticut River. It's bigger than Essex with more restaurants and services, and it appeals to those who want to be near the sea. There is also Old Lyme, another popular seaside town where people come to stay, not just visit.

All who have chosen to retire here agree on one thing: It's the quality of life that draws them, says Diane Moore of the Central Regional Tourism District for Connecticut. "The quality of life in this area is not just an accident of nature. People have been taking good care of their rivers and land here for more than 50 years," she says. "They've practiced good management. The Connecticut River is the largest river in the country without a major port at its mouth. There is very little development where the rivers meet the sea, just lighthouses."

Indeed, the folks who live here are proud of the fact that the Nature Conservancy has named the Tidelands of the Lower Connecticut River Valley as one of the 40 "Last Great Places in the Western Hemisphere."

Some would say that the people here are among the reasons. "Just step out the door and try to take a walk, and someone will stop you every 20 feet to chat," says Carole Gosselin. "I'm still waiting to find someone I can't get along with," laughs husband Fred. ●

Dade City, Florida

Picturesque small town evokes memories of a slower-paced time

By Jay Clarke

A common thread runs through Dade City's retirees — a love of country living. The small-town ambiance is an attribute that all of the retirees here cite, although there are many other attractions. Some relocated retirees even find that Dade City reminds them of their former homes while offering the pleasing retirement lifestyle they were seeking when they moved.

"We had been coming to Florida for a number of years," says Tom Brennan, 72, former chief justice of the Michigan Supreme Court and later a law school professor. "Years ago we sent our middle daughter to St. Leo College (near Dade City) and we had a condo in Innisbrook. As we began spending more time in Florida, we wanted to build, but we weren't crazy about Innisbrook," says Tom, explaining that he and his wife, Polly, decided it had become too crowded for their tastes.

Then, while revisiting the area, they came upon the Lake Jovita Golf and Country Club development, which opened in August 1999 and has homes from $300,000 to more than $1 million. "We fell in love with the place. It had rolling terrain reminiscent of home in Michigan. But what turned out to be the most pleasant surprise was Dade City," Tom says.

"I brought down all these boxes of files and Polly didn't want them in the house, so I rented an office downtown," he says. "That began a love affair with Dade City. I go into the office almost every day, have coffee at the local bakery, take lunch at a table in back with judges and old-timers. I've found the city to be very delightful, a friendly place. A walk around downtown gives you a real high."

Another aspect that pleases the Brennans is meeting home folks. "Where we were in Innisbrook, everybody was from somewhere else. Here we meet people from Dade City," Tom says. So, even though Tom had been active in the pub-

lic life of Michigan, moving from Lansing to Dade City wasn't a difficult choice. Polly, also 72, loves the town as well, Tom says, and both have had no trouble developing a busy social life.

The downtown that Tom loves is dominated by a white-domed courthouse, a regal structure that dates to 1909. But activity revolves around the 30-odd antique shops that line the streets, spawning a tourism industry. "Bus tours from St. Petersburg, Clearwater and Tampa come here on day trips," says Phyllis Smith, executive director of the Dade City Chamber of Commerce. The occupants alight to shop

Another visitor destination is the Pioneer Florida Museum, a grouping of historic buildings brought here from all over the region, as well as a collection of artifacts from the early 20th century. Such structures as a train depot, school, church and country store — even a moonshine still — are spread over several acres.

And just outside of town is Dade Battlefield, where Major Francis Dade was ambushed and killed by Seminole Indians while leading troops from Fort Brooke (Tampa) to Fort King (Ocala) in the 1830s. The incident started the Second Seminole War and immortalized Dade. This city is named after him, as is Miami-Dade County to the south, the most populous in Florida.

The site of the ambush is now a state park whose picnic grounds are busy every weekend the year around. A small museum tells Dade's story, and next to it the park has rebuilt a log redoubt similar to what Dade troops hastily constructed while under attack.

Within a few miles of Dade City are several small towns that are part of the city's outreach. One of them is the village of St. Leo, home of Florida's only abbey, a lovely complex on a lake that was founded by German monks in the 1890s. It's also the site of St. Leo University, a Catholic liberal arts school no

longer run by the Benedictine monks, and a public golf course owned by the abbey. San Antonio, a bedroom community that conducts a popular yearly rattlesnake festival, stands next to St. Leo, and a few miles south of Dade City is Zephyrhills, a city of about 12,000 known internationally for its bottled water and skydiving center.

Like any other small town, Dade City is immensely proud when one of its hometown boys makes good. That's why a large sign at the city limits announces that Dade City is the boyhood home of tennis star Jim Courier. Though he still visits, Courier has moved away, but the Bellamy Brothers, well-known country singers, still return to their farm home here when not traveling the world on tour.

On Dade City's annual calendar are a variety of events from bluegrass festivals and antique shows to Indian powwows and bicycle races. Biggest is the Kumquat Festival in January, centered on the small citrus fruit that is often used to make jellies or decorate dishes. Dade City claims to be the kumquat capital of the world, and this year's fete drew more than 30,000 visitors. San Antonio's Rattlesnake Festival, held every October, is another major hoopla. In the past it has attracted television coverage from as far away as Japan.

And this past March, Dade City inaugurated a new event, the Little Everglades Steeplechase. It's the only steeplechase in the state as well as one of only 21 in the nation — and it was constructed as a labor of love by a new Dade City retiree, Bob Blanchard.

Bob and his wife, Sharon, maintained two homes for many years, one in Cashiers, NC, and another in Tampa. Retiring from a holding company, he sold his home in Tampa and has just built another — his prime residence now — on a 1,775-acre ranch just outside Dade City.

"Both of us like the country. We have

Hanoverian horses and 300 cattle, and we have room. The closest neighbor is a mile away," Bob says. The semi-isolation also is changing their lives in other ways. "We used to be much involved in (community) activities in Tampa, but that's dropping off sharply," Bob says.

Though retired, Bob admits he likes to keep busy. "I have to have projects," he says. The steeplechase track — a not-for-profit operation — is one of them. "It's a world-class track, with jockey quarters, judging towers and ancillary facilities," he says. The facility will be used only once a year, when it opens the nation's steeplechase season in March. Last March, in its first race season at the new track, Little Everglades attracted 3,500 spectators.

The country-town atmosphere of Dade City also is part of what attracted Robert "Smoky" Stoever and his wife, Wilma, to move from their home in Southbridge, MA, after they retired in

1993. "Our kids were shocked when we moved here," Smoky says. "But my best friend lived nearby, and we liked the weather and the country living."

Smoky and Wilma were among the first to move into the then-new South-fork Mobile Home Community here. They have a spacious double-wide home with three bedrooms, dining room, living room with fireplace and a porch on a tree-lined street, and four grapefruit and orange trees in the back yard.

"Senior park living is great," says Smoky, 70. "Nobody (who lives here) is working, so we're able to do things together. We have a lot of dances, potluck suppers, pancake breakfasts. We take bus trips to the dinner theater, to Clearwater or Cape Canaveral."

Before moving to Florida, Smoky also had looked in Kentucky, home of his wife's family, and in southern Illinois. But Dade City won out, and life here

seems to agree with him. "I do what I want to do," he says. He's into flowers and gardening, and his wife, Wilma, calls him the "shuffleboard king of the park."

Wilma, 69, who worked in home-care nursing in Massachusetts before her retirement, still keeps a hand in nursing, working as a volunteer at local hospices. She also is quite active in Southfork community organizations.

And what about their children, who were so surprised about their parents' move to Florida? Six of the eight still live in Massachusetts, but they've mellowed. When winter blows in, they aren't a bit sorry that their parents have a place in Florida they can visit.

Smoky Stoever is one of many retirees who have gravitated to this city from distant states. Some have moved from no farther away than Tampa, 45 miles south. Dennis and Gloria Huffman, for example, moved to Dade City a year ago after many years in Tampa.

Dade City, FL

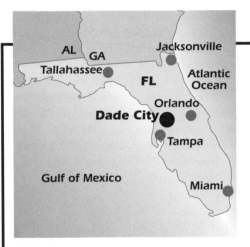

Population: About 7,500 in Dade City, which serves as a commercial center for more than 71,000 area residents.

Location: About 45 miles north of Tampa.

Climate: High Low
January 72 49
July 92 71

Average relative humidity: 60%

Annual rainfall: 49 inches

Cost of living: Below average

Average housing costs: $233,641 for a single-family home.

Sales tax: 7%

Sales tax exemptions: Groceries, medicine and professional services.

State income tax: None

Intangibles tax: None. The tax was

repealed as of Jan. 1, 2007.

Estate tax: None

Inheritance tax: None

Property tax: $24.3566 per $1,000 valuation in Dade City, about $17 per $1,000 in Pasco County, with homes assessed at 100% of market value. The tax on a $233,641 home would be about $5,082 in the city and $3,547 in the county, with homestead exemption noted below.

Homestead exemption: $25,000 off assessed value of primary, permanent residence.

Religion: 64 churches

Education: Nearby are St. Leo University, (800) 334-5532, offering four-year liberal arts degrees, and Pasco Hernando Community College, (352) 567-6701, whose two-year degrees are transferable to the state university system. Three four-year colleges are within 40 miles: Florida Southern College in Lakeland and the University of South Florida and University of Tampa in Tampa.

Transportation: Nearest major airport is Tampa International, about 47 miles. Dade City is Amtrak's only stop in Pasco County.

Health: Two hospitals are within 10

miles. Pasco Regional Medical Center has 120 beds, and East Pasco Medical Center has 139 beds. Both have 24-hour emergency services. Several nursing homes and home health care services are available in the area.

Housing options: Lake Jovita Golf and Country Club, (800) 267-2768, (352) 567-7000 or www.lakejovita.com, has 1,054 acres. It offers single-family homes from the $300,000s to more than $1 million and has a clubhouse, swimming pool and two 18-hole golf courses. Southfork Mobile Home Community, (352) 523-0022, with attractive manufactured homes on tree-lined streets, has a pool, clubhouse and shuffleboard courts. Edwinola, (352) 567-6500, a large congregate living facility, has about 200 units in a renovated landmark structure in town. Tampa Bay Golf and Country Club, (800) 588-2108, has a pool and golf course.

Visitor lodging: The 52-room Best Western of Zephyrhills is seven miles from Dade City, $69-$89, (813) 782-5527.

Information: Greater Dade City Chamber of Commerce, 14112 Eighth St., Dade City, FL 33525, (352) 567-3769 or www.dadecitychamber.org.

That may not sound like much of move, but the Huffmans, both 59, say that despite their proximity, the two cities are vastly different.

"Tampa is flat and palm trees, like most of Florida," Gloria says. "Out here there are hills and live oaks. It looks like North Carolina. We moved here because of that."

Actually, they had lived in quite a few places before settling in Tampa in the 1980s, including Jackson, MS; Hartford, CT; and Jacksonville, FL. So when they began thinking of retirement, they had a pretty good idea of what they wanted. Still, says Gloria, "We looked at the 'best' retirement places — Naples, Sarasota, even the mountains of North and South Carolina. We spent 10 days in a cabin in the mountains, but that was too isolated for me."

In 1999 they visited Lake Jovita Golf and Country Club, liked what they saw, bought a lot and constructed a house there. "We like golf," Gloria says. "In Tampa we lived in a nice place with nice golf and tennis. But there were not enough retirees there. Here you can always find someone to play with."

Another plus, Gloria says, is the plethora of activities available to Lake Jovita residents. She ticks off some of them: "They have a fitness center; we go there two or three times a week. Some ladies have a knitting class. Every Tues-day we meet for lunch and play cards. Wednesday night is family night, with a big dinner buffet. Thursday night is poker night. The Couples Club plays golf every first and third Sunday."

Dade City suits them well, too. "There's not a lot of traffic here, no parking meters. Everybody's real friendly, very laid back. It's easy to make friends and there are no cliques. It's like a little country town," Gloria says.

Bob and Sally Davis also moved from a nearby Florida town, Lutz, a suburb of Tampa that got too big for them. But as Bob had been an executive in the Postal Service, they had lived previously in many other places — Alabama, Mississippi and Tennessee, among them. "We moved every three years," Sally sighs. "We looked around for five years, but we knew we liked the Tampa area. My husband is a big golfer, and he can play golf the year around here."

Like other retirees, the Davises like Dade City's country-town atmosphere. "Everybody's friendly, comfortable. It reminds me of the town I grew up in — Jasper, AL," Sally says. "There's always something going on. Groups meet for suppers, for walking, for sewing. We go to concerts. Anything we want to do, we do," she says.

"And there are younger couples here, too," she says. Though retired, both are still relatively young: Sally is just 60, and Bob is 63.

Retirees say that few who experience Dade City ever express longing to return to urban life, although they do enjoy the big-city amenities in nearby Tampa. "Any kind of entertainment I want is just 25 minutes away," says Sally, echoing the feeling of most others.

The cost of living is another attraction. "It seems a little less in Florida — there's no income tax," says Tom Brennan. "Insurance, taxes, utilities — they're all less," says Sally Davis. "Taxes are less, utilities cheaper," agrees Gloria Huffman. "But food costs about the same."

Smoky Stoever, however, finds his costs considerably less, in part because of the type of home he has. "The insurance is less, the energy costs less, the eating out is cheaper," says Smoky, who worked in security positions both as a career soldier and as a civilian. And because he leases the land his mobile home stands on, and because it is technically a vehicle, he only has to buy a license tag every year. He pays no real estate taxes. "Taxes were high in New England," he notes.

Whatever the cost, though, Dade City's retirees seem to think life in Florida is worth it. As Tom Brennan says, "If I had to choose between Michigan in January and Florida in August, I'd choose Florida."

He did, and thousands of others have done the same. ●

Danville, Kentucky

Amid the horse farms of central Kentucky, this town has an award-winning main street and new arts center

By William Schemmel

Beauty, history and affordable housing are prime reasons retirees consider Danville in central Kentucky's bluegrass country. And some come searching for their roots and find that their ancestors had the right idea when they settled here.

"I retired here because Kentucky is home, it's beautiful and Danville is exceptional and very affordable," declares Eric James, 62, who moved to Danville from Dana Point, CA, between Los Angeles and San Diego. "I came home to family in Kentucky, just like a lot of Californians and others are doing."

Eric says he's had two careers. "The first was a 16-year career in television and stage, followed by 35 years in international real estate brokerage, overlapping with 10 years when I was researching and writing family history, including my distant relatives, Frank and Jesse James and the Daltons," he says.

Eric has roots in Kentucky, so it was natural for him to consider the state for retirement. "My great-grandfather was here before the Civil War to the 1870s, when he moved to Coffeyville, KS. I bought my 1872 Victorian house from a man who had come home from the Fiji Islands, and I discovered that a descendent of the builder was a relative of mine. Her name was Edna Lanier Toliver, and a local elementary school is named for her."

The ability to stretch his retirement dollars was another reason Eric found Danville attractive. "A friend in California, who is about 77, is looking forward to retiring here," he says. "She likes the idea that she can find a modest house near the center of Danville for about the same as a down payment in California."

Eric says the average price of a three- to five-bedroom house on a large lot is about $189,000, and smaller houses "are easy to find" in the $120,000-$150,000 price range. Property taxes, he adds, are comparable to what he paid in California, with most of it going to public schools.

In addition to the James and Dalton gangs, Eric has a connection to the late Archbishop Fulton J. Sheen, host of "Life is Worth Living," a popular 1950s TV program. "As a child, my mother forced me to watch every broadcast of the archbishop's show. Ironically, he married me to his niece. When he sat next to me at the wedding reception, he told me, 'A whole generation has grown up hating me for that (show). I'm sure you would rather have been watching Milton Berle.'"

Eric doesn't have trouble finding things to do to fill his time. In fact, the reverse is the problem. "It's hard to find time not to be busy," he says. "I do research, I write, I lecture and keep my Web site, Stray Leaves, up to date, and if that doesn't fill up my day, I do a little gardening," he says.

"There's always something going on, such as Christmas and fall festivals, arts and crafts, a brass band festival and cultural events at the colleges and the Community Arts Center," Eric says. "When I need to get away, I'm an hour or two from Lexington, Louisville and Cincinnati."

Founded in 1775, Danville was the capital of the Kentucky District of Virginia for a number of years and capital of the new state of Kentucky for three days while the state's constitution was being drafted in what's now known as Constitution Square State Historic Site in the center of town. Log cabins in the square trace Kentucky's path to statehood. A bronze statue with the motto, "United We Stand, Divided We Fall," is in the center of the square, which also includes the oldest post office west of the Alleghenies and replicas of the first courthouse, first jail and a tavern where statehood was debated.

The square steps back to 1780 the third weekend of September for the Historic Constitution Square Festival. Strolling musicians, hundreds of artists and craftspeople, fiddle contests and

hands-on activities from creating corn shuck dolls and brooms to baskets, pottery and candles set the tone for the celebration.

Five districts are on the National Register of Historic Places. Beaten Biscuit Row, downtown on Third Street, is named for a favorite culinary specialty.

"Beaten biscuits are as Southern as grits," explains Mary Quinn Ramer, executive director of the Danville-Boyle County Convention and Visitors Bureau. "The hard and dry, half-dollar size biscuit is often served as a counterpart to a moist, salty slice of country ham. In the 1800s, they say you could walk down Third Street and hear the sound of the cooks making biscuits for breakfast."

Ten historic homes are bed-and-breakfast inns. The Ephraim McDowell House and Apothecary, a national historic landmark, was the home of the 18th-century physician known as "the father of abdominal surgery."

The 600-acre Perryville Battlefield State Historic Site, 10 miles west of Danville, was the Confederacy's last stand in Kentucky. After their defeat in October 1862, Confederates retreated to Tennessee, putting Kentucky firmly in Union hands. Hundreds of Confederate and Union re-enactors bring the battle back to life each October.

Danville was the first Kentucky city to receive the National Trust for Historic Preservation's Great American Main Street Award. Centre College and the Community Arts Center are the linchpins of Danville's thriving cultural and entertainment life. Established in 1819, Centre College is the best known of five higher-learning institutions around the city and Boyle County.

The first law school west of the Alleghenies, the 1,100-student liberal arts college was the scene of the 2000 vice presidential debate between Democratic candidate Sen. Joseph Lieberman and Republican Dick Cheney. Danville is the smallest town to host a nationally televised vice presidential debate.

Centre College's Norton Center for the Arts, where the debate was conducted, gives Danville a diverse mixture of arts and culture, ranging from Shakespeare and ballet to touring Broadway shows, lectures, seminars and appearances by popular musical groups. Designed by a protégé of Frank Lloyd Wright, the ultra-modern center has featured such internationally known artists as violinist Itzhak Perlman, cellist Yo-Yo Ma, ballet superstar Mikhail Baryshnikov and Irish musicians The Chieftains.

The college's grassy lawns are favorite "stages" for the annual Great American Brass Band Festival, which attracts thousands of visitors and bands from around the world in mid-June. "When you have a really outstanding college or university in your town, that institution will bring an array of people in the arts, public policy-makers and others into the community," says Centre president John A. Roush. "We have a performing arts series you would expect to find in a city 25 times our size."

Centre's indoor pool, gymnasium, library, walking tracks and other facilities are available to the public. Other area colleges are the Danville campus of Eastern Kentucky University (EKU-Danville), Central Kentucky Technical College, the Danville extension of Midway College and the National College of Business and Technology.

With about 850 students enrolled in traditional four-year college programs and in continuing-education and dis-

Danville, KY

Population: 15,477 in Danville, 27,697 in Boyle County.

Location: The geographic center of Kentucky, 35 miles south of Lexington, two hours east of Louisville.

Climate:

	High	Low
January	40	23
July	86	68

Average relative humidity: 56%

Rain: 45 inches

Snow: 15 inches

Cost of living: Below average

Average housing cost: $189,000 for a three- to five-bedroom house on a large lot, $120,000-$150,000 for smaller houses.

Sales tax: 6%

Sales tax exemptions: Food, prescription drugs and residential utilities.

State income tax: The tax is graduated in five tiers ranging from 2% on the first $3,000 in taxable income to 6% on taxable income higher than $8,000.

Income tax exemptions: Social Security benefits are exempt. There is an exemption for pensions of up to $41,110 per taxpayer.

Estate tax: The estate tax, or "pickup tax," is a tax on the estate equal to the amount by which the credit for state death taxes allowable under the federal estate tax law exceeds the Kentucky inheritance tax. Legislation was passed under the federal Economic Growth and Tax Reconciliation Act of 2001, which enacted a five-year phaseout of the estate tax for the Commonwealth beginning with dates of death after Jan. 1, 2005.

Inheritance tax: The state imposes a graduated inheritance tax ranging from 4% to 16% on the transfer of real and personal property to certain beneficiaries. All estates passing to parent, spouse, child, grandchild or sibling are exempt.

Property tax: Homes in Kentucky are assessed at 100% of fair market value. In Danville and Boyle County, the rate is $10.33 per $1,000, making the annual property tax on an $189,000 home, taking the $29,400 homestead exemption, $1,649.

Homestead exemption: $29,400 for residents age 65 and older living full-time in the home at the beginning of the calendar year.

Religion: Most faiths are represented; the nearest synagogue is in Lexington.

Education: Centre College, a four-year liberal arts college with 1,100 students, is the largest of five area higher-education institutions, with classes open to retirees.

Transportation: No public transportation system. Lexington, 35 miles away, has the nearest commercial airport. Danville is located on U.S. Highway 27/127, about 25 miles west of Interstate 75, a major north-south highway.

Health: Ephraim McDowell Regional Medical Center, in downtown Danville, has 177 patient beds and 125 physicians in all major fields.

Housing options: All types of housing are available, including single-family homes in established neighborhoods and new subdivisions; also apartments, condos and assisted living and farmland with horse stables. **Old Bridge Golf Club** is a golf community next to Herrington Lake, (859) 236-6051.

Visitor lodging: Golden Lion Bed and Breakfast has three guest rooms with private baths in an 1840 Greek Revival home. Owners Jerry and Nancy Jones have genealogical resources for those with Jones surnames, $89-$95, (866) 453-5466. Old Crow Inn, built in 1780, is the oldest stone house west of the Alleghenies. Three guest rooms on 27 acres, a mile from downtown, have private baths. Property includes a winery and pottery shop, $80-$100, (859) 236-1808. Country Hearth Inn at Old Bridge Golf Club has a package that includes greens fees, golf cart, continental breakfast and dinner card along with accommodations, $89 per person, (859) 236-8601. Hampton Inn has 72 rooms, $69-$149, (859) 236-6200. Super 8 Motel has 47 rooms, $42-$55, (859) 236-8881.

Information: Danville-Boyle County Convention and Visitors Bureau, 304 S. Fourth St., Danville, KY 40422, (800) 755-0076, (859) 236-7794, or www.danvilleken tucky.com. Danville-Boyle County Chamber of Commerce, 304 S. Fourth St., Danville, KY 40422, (859) 236-2361 or www.danvilleboylechamber.com. For a packet of relocation information ($5), (877) 282-2899.

tance-learning classes, EKU-Danville is the area's second-largest college. Retirees can take classes at all the colleges.

An elegant beaux arts-style building in downtown Danville is the city's new home for the arts. The Community Arts Center was dedicated in December 2004 at the conclusion of a $1.1 million program to convert the former federal building and post office. The city's main post office from 1911 to 1916, then a military recruitment center and judges' chambers, the building was vacated in the early 1990s.

"Artists and performers have always been strongly represented in Danville but were forced to display their talents in numerous scattered venues," says Wilma Brown, executive director of the Community Arts Center. "Now there's a central focal point that emphasizes all the arts and allows visitors to view different programs at one location."

The center, she adds, has plenty of gallery space for paintings, sculpture and photography exhibits, as well as the Grand Hall for theatrical performances, dance programs, concerts and receptions. Painting, pottery, weaving, photography and other classes are popular with retirees and other residents.

Pioneer Playhouse is a thriving summer attraction. Founded in 1950 by Danville native and former New York actor Eben Henson, the outdoor theater offers five summer plays, preceded by a barbecued chicken dinner. John Travolta, Jim Varney and Lee Majors are the best known of hundreds of actors who've gone from the Pioneer to careers on bigger stages. Travolta was 14 when he played the title role in "The Ephraim McDowell Story."

Danville, a Kentucky Certified Retirement Community, has a new conference center complex that is also a hit with retirees. Opened in September 2004 in a converted home-improvement warehouse, the complex includes an eight-screen movie theater, a day spa, stores and restaurants.

Danville and Boyle County have abundant natural beauty. The landscape is marked by gently rolling hills, horse farms and fertile fields. Winding, tree-lined roads are a magnet for retirees who enjoy hiking, biking and walking.

Lakes, rivers and streams also offer opportunities for sports and recreation. Herrington Lake, three miles from Danville, is considered one of the state's most rewarding fishing lakes. The lake has marinas, a golf course and some of the area's most high-end residential areas.

Robert and Betty Glover and Jerry and Norma Kennedy live at the lake in the Old Bridge neighborhood, where large homes are in the $250,000-$450,000 range. "When I retired, my wife, Betty, and I started looking for lake property in Kentucky," says Robert, 62, a GM supervisor in Michigan for 34 years. "While we were driving around Danville, we saw a sign for property on Herrington Lake.

"It has a golf course, and I like to play a little, so we built a ranch-type house, with four bedrooms and a full basement in the Old Bridge subdivision," he says. "It's right on the fairway, and I also do some fishing and yardwork. Betty keeps busy with her church group and other activities. We've been blessed. We've been here six years and really enjoy the lifestyle."

Jerry and Norma Kennedy, both 76, moved from Seattle, where Jerry was a computer marketer. "We have a daughter in Perryville, so we decided to move here to be near her," Jerry says. "We're originally from a small town in Illinois and have really fallen in love with Danville. Our house in the Old Bridge neighborhood is a derivative of a Frank Lloyd Wright Prairie-style house. In 1999 it was Life Magazine's 'Dream House of the Year.'"

Residents don't have to travel to a big city to receive quality health care. Ephraim McDowell Regional Medical Center in downtown Danville is capable of meeting the health-care needs of central and south-central Kentucky. One of Kentucky's most up-to-date medical facilities, EMRMC's 125 staff physicians specialize in every major field. The complex has 177 patient beds.

EMRMC's new cancer-care center is one of its most recent advancements. Along with the cancer-care center, the hospital has added open magnetic resonance imaging and introduced capsule endoscopy, or "camera in a pill" technology, in which a patient swallows a pill with a high-tech camera that allows doctors to see the entire lower intestine.

Like Eric James, former Californian Kathy Schaefer, 56, was attracted to Danville's beauty, history and affordable housing. "One of my neighbors in California moved to Kentucky, and I came to Danville because the price of real estate is so reasonable," says the TV producer and real estate agent from Mission Viejo, CA.

"And I read where Danville is one of the nicest towns in the country. I moved out of a 1,300-square-foot condo into an 8,000-square-foot house on 44 acres, with three barns, for about the same amount of money," Kathy says. "A partner and I are planning a retirement home for off-the-track Thoroughbreds."

Robert and Ann McNew, retired teachers, both 66, moved from Bella Vista, AR, to be near their daughter in Lexington, 35 miles north, and son in Dayton, OH, 180 miles north. "We're originally from Iowa and moved to Bella Vista after we retired," Ann says. "We were there four years and decided we wanted to be closer to our children.

"Our daughter in Lexington recommended Danville, and we've been very happy here. People are very friendly, and we've always wanted to live in a small-town college community," she says. "We keep very busy. We love going to events at the Norton Center. We're sports-oriented. We play golf and bowl and enjoy walking in the natural surroundings here."

The McNews purchased a new 2,100-square-foot, open-plan home in Colonial Heights, a subdivision on the north side of Danville.

"I have a quilting room and my husband has a workout room, and we have plenty of room when our children come to visit," Ann says. And for her, that adds up to a perfect retirement situation. ●

DeFuniak Springs, Florida

A renowned cultural and academic program adds to the appeal of an old-fashioned town in northwest Florida

By Jay Clarke

You know a town is beloved when those who once lived there move back for retirement.

"I was born and raised here," says Dr. Dennis Ray, 73, a professor who left DeFuniak Springs in 1950 and didn't return until he retired from Mississippi State in 1993.

When it came time to retire, "we looked in Tennessee and Virginia," says Dennis, whose wife, Brenda, 63, taught music at the same university. "And we even turned down Seaside," a trendy coastal town in Florida's Panhandle. "We weren't coming back to family, but because of the charm and heritage of this town," Dennis says. "Both of us like the cultural atmosphere, the academic life of Chautauqua."

Chautauqua is what sets DeFuniak apart from other small towns. It's a winter offshoot of a renowned cultural program that began in Chautauqua, NY, in the 19th century. A century ago, the Chautauqua program at DeFuniak was at its peak, attracting thousands of visitors to this northwest Florida town for a 37-year span ending in 1922.

In recent years, the Chautauqua program has been revived here, and this past year it encompassed 11 days of enrichment programs, lectures and performances in a wide range of subjects — everything from bioterrorism and the war on drugs to quilting, writing for magazines and grandparenting in the new millennium. Presenters have included Sandy d'Alemberte, former president of the University of Florida; composer Dr. David Ott, a two-time Pulitzer nominee; and Israeli Consul General Miki Arbel. The programs are held in the original lakeside Chautauqua as well as in churches and other venues arounde town.

Not only did Dennis and Brenda Ray settle in DeFuniak, but Dennis also started a couple of businesses to keep busy. Today he operates the Lil' Big Store, an old-time general store chock full of goods reminiscent of yesteryear. For some this might be a hobby, but Dennis, true to his teachings as a business management professor, has made it a money-making enterprise. He also owns an antique shop next door, and he is reopening the Busy Bee Cafe.

Dennis says he misses friends at Mississippi State (as well as at the universities of Florida and Alabama, where he also taught), but while he loved the academic world, he doesn't miss it. "That sounds strange, but I have found so much here that I don't have time" to look back, he says. "I'm a member of everything — president of Partners in Prayer, chair of the music trustees, president of the Walton County Heritage Association. One of the reasons that I have a store, antique shop and cafe is that I saw downtown needed it."

Dennis is not the only retiree who has gone into business after moving here. Pam and Tom Hutchins also jumped into DeFuniak life soon after retiring here. "We moved here from Pensacola three years ago," says Tom, who, like his wife, is 54. "We considered moving west to Colorado or to South Florida, but with seven children between us, we realized the need to be in the Southeast."

On earlier visits, DeFuniak had seemed "like a ghost town," according to Tom, who was a chiropractor. But the return of the Chautauqua programs had changed things by the time they moved here. "I found a sense of community here that I had not felt before," says Pam, who was a schoolteacher and real estate agent. "Every person we met introduced themselves and invited us to their church. They announce weddings, and everybody is invited. It's amazing how old-fashioned this town is," she says.

Tom and Pam, like the Rays, bought one of the great Victorian-era homes that ring Lake DeFuniak, one of two perfectly circular lakes in the United States. All the homes fronting the lake are listed on the National Register of Historic Places.

Then Tom and Pam bought the old Hotel DeFuniak, seeing it as a possible catalyst for reviving the downtown area. "It's our retirement hobby, not our livelihood," declares Tom, who completely redecorated the hotel with antiques and gave each of the 10 rooms a distinctive decor. One, for example, is a safari room with 300-year-old bamboo furniture and African masks mounted on its walls. Another is an art deco room with Prohibition cabinets, and a third room has a romantic theme with paintings of cherubs and lovers.

Don Bodiford is another who lived in DeFuniak Springs as a child and returned later in life. "I moved here to take care of my mother," Don says. He had been living in Greensboro, NC, after retiring from IBM. A year and a half ago, he bought DeFuniak's H&M Hot Dog Shop because its owner thought he would have to close it — and Don didn't think this venerable and well-loved place should shut down. Now Don and his wife, Lora, both 67, cook hotdogs and hamburgers in the friendly hole-in-the-wall restaurant and love every minute of it.

Lloyd and Dara Dobson did not live far from DeFuniak Springs, but when they decided to retire and move away from Fort Walton Beach on the Panhandle coast, it was a major lifestyle change. "Fort Walton was getting too crowded," says Dara, 53, who operated a large day school in Fort Walton. Husband Lloyd, 47, ran an adjacent horse-boarding business.

"We sold the businesses and looked around for a year and a half. Then we learned friends had bought property here in DeFuniak," Lloyd says. So they scouted the area and came across a large spread of 240 acres just north of town. "It fit everything," Dara says. "It was like we were supposed to be there, a kindred feeling. It was heaven."

The property has a couple of lakes on

it, and after he caught a six-pound bass there, Lloyd says that he, too, was hooked. "We don't miss the noise, the loud music, the sirens" at Fort Walton Beach, he says. "Now we see quail, turkey, deer, rabbits and foxes." And there are so many birds, Dara says, that "we had to buy a birding book."

Moving from a busy milieu to a quiet rural town, Dara admits, required a period of adjustment. "We had to go through decompression. You can't be in a hurry," she says. But they've grown to love it here. "DeFuniak has a 'Leave It to Beaver' look. It's like going back in time," says Dara. She says that she and Lloyd found it easy to make new acquaintances here. They also have taken roles in the community.

"Since we're retired, we have time to give back through volunteering," Lloyd says. He's involved in Little League baseball and has been asked to speak several times at state forestry gatherings. Dara, meanwhile, became interested in wildflowers, headed up the local garden club and suddenly found herself wildflower chairwoman for the state federation as well.

Certainly there are more stores and conveniences in Fort Walton Beach, but Dara says there's only one thing they miss from their life there — going to Gold's Gym.

Tom and Pam Hutchins also have found little they miss about their former home in Pensacola. "We don't miss the water. We faced three hurricanes in two years there," Tom says emphatically. And there's no time to get bored. "The hotel keeps both of us busy," says Pam, "and so do clubs and organizations."

Living in DeFuniak, as might be expected, is less expensive than in the popular coastal settlements of the Florida Panhandle. Property costs are less, and so are taxes, according to Tom Hutchins.

Dennis Ray, however, feels the cost of living is about the same as it was in Mississippi, including taxes, but he says insurance is significantly higher. That may be because the Panhandle is vulnerable to Gulf hurricanes.

As far as medical services are concerned, Dennis feels DeFuniak's are limited. Healthmark Regional Medical Center in DeFuniak has 24-hour emergency care and some "really good" practitioners, he says, but he and his wife Brenda go to Pensacola or Fort Walton Beach for most procedures. "Dothan (Alabama) has a good complex, and there's also

DeFuniak Springs, FL

Population: 7,000 in DeFuniak Springs, 49,623 in Walton County.

Location: DeFuniak Springs is located on Interstate 10 in northwest Florida, about a half-hour inland from the tourist center of Destin and between Tallahassee and Pensacola. DeFuniak Springs is the county seat of Walton County.

Climate:

	High	Low
January	63	40
July	92	71

Average relative humidity: 40%

Annual rainfall: 65.5 inches

Cost of living: Below average

Average housing cost: $191,867 in the DeFuniak Springs area. Homes available at press time started at around $200,000 for a three-bedroom, 2,000 square-foot home in DeFuniak Springs, and there are options for well over $1 million.

Sales tax: 7%

Sales tax exemptions: Food and medicine

State income tax: None

Intangibles tax: None. The tax was repealed as of Jan. 1, 2007.

Estate tax: None. The state's "pick-up" portion of the federal tax was eliminated as of January 1, 2005.

Inheritance tax: None

Property tax: $15.2154 per $1,000 (city and county combined). Property is appraised at full value. However, assessments cannot be increased more than 3% per year, so some property held for several years actually may be assessed at less than full value. Tax on a $192,000 home would be about $2,541 with homestead exemption.

Homestead exemption: $25,000 of assessed value of primary, permanent residence.

Religion: About 50 churches are in the city.

Education: Okaloosa-Walton College, (850) 892-8100 or www.owc.edu, offers two-year degree programs in DeFuniak Springs and other locations in Okaloosa and Walton counties.

Transportation: Okaloosa Regional Airport is 45 minutes away, and Pensacola Regional Airport and Panama City-Bay County International Airport

are each one hour away.

Health: Healthmark Regional Medical Center, with 50 beds, has a 24-hour emergency department, specialized critical care, full-service laboratory and diagnostic testing. Elsewhere in the county, Sacred Heart Hospital in Miramar Beach has 75 physicians on staff.

Housing options: Some retirees opt for single-family homes on Lake DeFuniak. Homes also are available on small and large acreages. Another option is **Windswept**, a golf-course community located about 20 miles south of DeFuniak Springs (halfway to the coast). For assisted-living needs, call the **Stanley House**, (850) 951-1880, in DeFuniak Springs.

Visitor lodging: Hotel DeFuniak, $90-$100, including breakfast, (877) 333-8642. Best Western Crossroads Inn, $69-$99, (850) 892-5111. Days Inn, $50-$99, (850) 892-6115. Super 8 Motel, $59-$89, (850) 892-1333.

Information: Walton County Chamber of Commerce, 95 Circle Drive, DeFuniak Springs, FL 32435, (850) 892-3191, www.waltoncountychamber.com. City of DeFuniak Springs, (850) 892-8500, wwwdefuniaksprings-fl.com. Beaches of South Walton, (800) 822-6877 or www.beachesofsouthwalton.com.

pretty good access to Shands (the University of Florida hospital) in Gainesville," he says. For clothing, Dennis says, there's no choice but to drive to Fort Walton, and dining out in DeFuniak is "significantly limited."

But Dennis, like many others here, likes to entertain at home. "We'll have a Victorian evening in our house. Sometimes we dress up," he says. Guests may take turns looking at an old-fashioned stereopticon, a 3-D viewing device from Victorian days. Likewise, Tom and Pam Hutchins say dinner parties and backyard barbecues are popular diversions.

That fits in well with the remarkable homes that face circular Lake DeFuniak. All but one or two were built around the turn of the century. The Thomas House, for instance, is an outstanding example of Queen Anne style, with a three-story round turret and patterned shingles. The folk-Victorian Verandas House owned by the Rays features double wraparound verandas in "steamboat" style. The Magnolia House, so named for its 12 stately magnolias, is an example of Colonial Revival style.

Several other significant structures rest on the lakeshore. The Chautauqua building, when completed in 1909,

boasted porticos supported by 40 columns representing the 40 states existing at that time. Its 4,000-seat auditorium was destroyed years ago by a hurricane, but the remaining structure now houses the chamber of commerce and is rented for social functions. It still serves as a venue for some Chautauqua events.

Nearby is the Walton-DeFuniak Library, founded in 1886 and the oldest continuously operating library in Florida. Across the street stands the old L&N Railroad Depot, built in 1882, where as many as 4,000 passengers arrived daily during DeFuniak's Chautauqua heyday. Today, the depot serves as a regional museum. Miles of trains still rumble through town, but none stops for passengers. Close to the depot is an unusual town meeting spot, the Opinion Place. It's a gazebo where elderly men gather to discuss current events, be it local gossip or international affairs.

An advantage of living in DeFuniak Springs, says Tom, is that residents have easy access to other population and transportation centers. Three airports are within easy reach. Pensacola and Panama City are just over an hour away, and Fort Walton Beach is just 45 minutes away. The coastal tourist city of Destin,

with its hotels, condos, malls, diverse restaurants, outlet shops, Gulf fishing and attractions, is within an hour.

Located directly on Interstate 10, DeFuniak also has convenient access to longer-range destinations — the Florida capital of Tallahassee is about two hours away, New Orleans around four hours. Also on I-10 is the Chautauqua Winery, which produces 15 different wines. It makes six varieties from muscadine grapes grown in its 40 acres of vineyards. Its top seller is its Noble, though the Carlos has won the most awards. The winery also produces chardonnay, merlot, cabernet and zinfandel wines from California grapes.

A few miles away from DeFuniak bubbles Ponce de Leon Springs, where on a summer day dozens of teenagers and young families go to escape the heat of north Florida. Alternatively, pristine beaches caressed by the Gulf of Mexico's clear green waters are less than an hour away. Tom, however, feels there's not enough in DeFuniak for kids and cites the lack of a movie theater as an example.

But for retirees, there's activity enough. As Lloyd Dobson puts it, "I'm not retired. I'm tired." ●

Delray Beach, Florida

Residents in Florida "village by the sea" enjoy a lively cultural arts scene in a revitalized downtown

By Karen Feldman

Retirees who settle in Delray Beach can indulge their inner beach bums and their cravings for culture at the same time. The city's bounty of pristine waterways and a full measure of cultural attractions are drawing ever more baby boomers who want all the arts and entertainment they were accustomed to in their former locales but in a balmier, more laid-back setting.

The "village by the sea," as the city has dubbed itself, boasts award-winning beaches along the Atlantic Ocean and the Intracoastal Waterway, affording water lovers ample opportunities to boat, fish, water ski, snorkel, dive and go sailboarding virtually year-round.

The community has some 250 restaurants, galleries and boutiques as well as theaters, multiple festivals, golf courses and tennis courts. The American Orchid Society has its national headquarters at Delray, and the renowned Morikami Museum and Japanese Gardens adds unique splendor in the subtropics.

The revitalized downtown shows off brick sidewalks, statuesque royal palms and live oaks. The district has garnered awards from the American Society of Landscape Architects for its historic preservation with an emphasis on pedestrian access. (Other award recipients included New York's Central Park and San Francisco's Ghirardelli Square.)

Delray's sophistication in the sunshine won the hearts of Karen and Roger O'Neill during their three-year quest to find the ideal retirement spot. They both worked in the computer industry, primarily at Hewlett-Packard in Cupertino, CA, though Karen later ventured out with a startup company. After more than 18 years in a demanding industry, they decided they'd had enough and set their sights on retirement.

They loved the San Francisco area where they'd spent their working lives, but they agreed it was a colder climate than suited them for retirement. They met while attending college in the Virgin Islands and both wanted to return to a similar balmy setting.

"We made charts — why did we want to move to certain places, and really determining precisely what we wanted, the home we chose, what sort of location it had to be," says Karen, 51. They plotted the criteria for their retirement haven: a place near the ocean, warm weather and a home on the water with a swimming pool already in the back yard and plenty of bathrooms.

They considered North Carolina, but it was a bit too northerly for them. They thought about San Diego but eventually ruled out all of California. "It's stunningly beautiful, but it is so overcrowded and absurdly expensive," Karen says of the Golden State. "We really wanted a tropical climate. That was probably our No. 1 reason for moving here."

At first, Roger, 55, resisted the idea of a Florida retirement. Then the couple visited Miami and the Keys. To his surprise, he discovered he loved the area. They also found the prices appealingly low compared to the wildly expensive California real estate market.

There were plenty of Florida communities they could have chosen. During a series of vacations in the Sunshine State, they visited towns on both coasts and explored southward to the Keys. But, because they had longtime friends in Boca Raton, they always wound up there during their sojourns. Eventually, they realized that Delray Beach, neighboring Boca Raton to the north, had everything they wanted.

"We fell in love with Delray and it was nowhere near as pretty as it is now," Karen says. "We've been here 11 years and we absolutely love it."

Once considered a sleepy community best suited to the older "early-bird special" crowd, Delray Beach now attracts a sizeable number of 50-somethings intent on leading active lives in retirement.

Randy Welker, director of business recruitment for the Greater Delray Beach Chamber of Commerce, says, "It's an exciting time to be down here. For people who want to retire, they have a chance to move and experience the excitement of creating something new and special."

The downtown area is undergoing a renaissance as new restaurants, shops and nightclubs have opened over the past decade or so. Like many downtowns in the 1960s and '70s, the town's center of commerce shifted as the population grew and developments sprung up farther away. The once-thriving downtown became a downtrodden district of empty storefronts and crumbling sidewalks, and people went elsewhere to shop, dine and dance.

But when word spread that Atlantic Avenue through the downtown was going to be widened to four lanes to improve the hurricane evacuation route from the beach, "people rose up in righteous indignation," Welker says. They insisted on keeping it two lanes and worked to make it more pedestrian-friendly.

They realized the value of the tired old buildings and, in the late 1980s, launched a long-range restoration effort that brought the district back to life. At the core of the revitalization, three buildings that were once the city's first elementary, high school and gymnasium have been transformed into the Old School Square Cultural Arts Center. The buildings, dating from 1913 to 1926, were saved from demolition and now are on the National Register of Historic Places.

The arts venue now boasts the Cornell Museum of Art and History, the 323-seat Crest Theatre for live productions and a new outdoor entertainment pavilion for films, concerts and festivals. The center provides a powerful incentive for people to venture downtown now and is complemented with galleries and numerous dining and shopping spots within easy walking distance.

While many people like living within walking or bicycling distance to downtown, others prefer master-planned communities and the activities they offer in outlying areas. Still others settle on the waterfront.

Karen Rose, an agent with Nestler-Poletto Realty in Boca Raton, says that while housing prices skyrocketed over the past three years, they have leveled off and, in some cases, dropped a bit.

"There's a lot of inventory right now," she says. "The buyer now has a lot to choose from. The better communities still aren't giving anything away, but buyers have way more choices than they did a year ago."

At the 500-home development called Vizcaya, single-family homes range from $350,000 to $599,000. Rose describes it as "camp for grown-ups. It's got everything except golf in a nice gated community."

Golfers might want to look at Boca Delray Golf and Country Club, where there are condos and single-family homes, and it's not mandatory that resi-

Delray Beach, FL

Population: 64,757 in Delray Beach, about 1.27 million in Palm Beach County.

Location: The city occupies about 16 square miles south of Palm Beach on the state's east coast, neighboring Boca Raton. It's about 28 miles north of Fort Lauderdale.

Climate: High Low
January 75 57
July 90 75

Average relative humidity: 73%

Rain: 61 inches annually

Cost of living: Slightly above average

Housing cost: For Delray Beach, median prices were $479,000 for a single-family home and $205,000 for a townhouse or condominium for the first quarter of 2006, according to data from the Housing Leadership Council of Palm Beach County. The countywide average price was $451,100.

Sales tax: 6.5%

Sales tax exemptions: Groceries and prescription drugs

State income tax: None

Intangibles tax: None. The tax was repealed as of Jan. 1, 2007.

Estate tax: None

Property tax: $21.97 per $1,000 of assessed value. On a $479,000 home with a $25,000 homestead exemption, annual taxes would be about $9,974. On a $205,000 townhouse or condominium, with the homestead exemption, annual taxes would amount to $3,955. Homes are assessed at 100% of market value. However, the Save Our Homes constitutional amendment caps increases in taxable value at 3% a year or the rate of inflation, whichever is lower, for as long as you own the home. Once it's sold, the house is reappraised at market price for taxes.

Homestead exemption: $25,000 off assessed value of primary, permanent residence.

Religion: There are about a dozen houses of worship in Delray Beach, with more in adjoining towns.

Education: Palm Beach County's Adult Education Center and 25 community schools provide programs to some 300,000 county residents each year. Florida Atlantic University and Lynn University in Boca Raton and Palm Beach Community College, with campuses in Boca Raton and Palm Beach, offer various degree programs and some noncredit courses.

Transportation: Palm Beach International Airport is 16 miles north of Delray Beach, and the Fort Lauderdale/Hollywood International Airport is 33 miles south. Interstate 95 provides a major north-south route and Florida's Turnpike connects South Florida with Orlando and farther north with Interstate 75. The South Florida Regional Transportation Authority's Tri-Rail commuter service, (800) 874-7245, operates in Palm Beach, Broward and Miami-Dade counties. Palm Tran, (877) 930-4287, the county's public transit provider, offers both fixed-route public bus service and door-to-door service for people with disabilities. Greyhound Lines bus service and Amtrak operate in the area.

Health care: Delray Medical Center is a 403-bed acute-care hospital that offers services including emergency, psychiatric, neurological, outpatient, orthopedic, sleep disorders, surgical weight reduction, urology and women's health. Bethesda Heart Institute, a $50 million specialty hospital, is scheduled to open in 2007 inside Bethesda Memorial Hospital, a not-for-profit establishment in nearby Boynton Beach.

Housing: Stone Creek Ranch, (800) 477-9651, is a 187-acre community offering 37 lakefront estate homes, each on a minimum of 2.5 acres. Homes start above $4 million and range in size from 6,500 to 14,000 square feet. **Lakes of Delray,** (877) 264-5909, is a 55-plus community with condos that range from $125,000 to $230,000 and run 940 square feet to about 1,500 square feet. In downtown, a townhouse in **Mallory Square** ranges from the low $500,000s to the mid-$600,000s, offering upward of 2,026 square feet, three bedrooms and three-and-a-half baths. **Monterey Lake** is an all-ages gated community with townhouses, villas and single-family homes ranging from 1,650 square feet to 3,000 square feet and priced from the mid-$300,000s to $550,000 (contact a real estate agent for resales).

Visitor lodging: The Delray Beach Marriott is a 264-room hotel overlooking Ocean Boulevard, $209-$374, (877) 389-0169. The Colony Hotel and Cabana Club is a historic hotel on the Atlantic waterfront with 70 rooms, $185-$215, (561) 276-4123. Wright by the Sea is a 29-room suite hotel on the oceanfront, $115-$450, (877) 234-3355.

Information: The Greater Delray Beach Chamber of Commerce, 64-A S.E. Fifth Ave., Delray Beach, FL 33483, (561) 279-1380 or www.delraybeach.com.

dents join the golf club. A two-bedroom condo with fireplace runs in the mid- to high $200,000s, Rose says.

Monterey Lake is an all-ages gated community with townhouses, villas and single-family homes ranging from 1,650 square feet to 3,000 square feet and priced from the mid-$300,000s to $550,000. In the condo market, older complexes such as Kings Point start at about $100,000 for a two-bedroom, two-bath unit, while other developments, such as Lakes of Delray, range from $125,000 to $230,000 and run 940 square feet to about 1,500 square feet.

A townhouse in Mallory Square downtown ranges from the low $500,000s to the mid-$600,000s, Rose says. Small, older homes in the downtown area command high prices because of their location. She says a 916-square-foot home recently sold for $450,000.

Those with their hearts set on a condo on the slender span of land between the Intracoastal Waterway and the Atlantic Ocean can expect to pay from the low $400,000s up to about $3 million. On the high end, a house will cost somewhere between $1.2 million and about $19 million — the latter the purchase price of a 13,000-square-foot home with six bedrooms built in 2005.

The O'Neills looked at big, new houses around town but chose a more modest three-bedroom, three-bath home situated on a cove along the Intracoastal Waterway. At 1,700 square feet, it's about a third the size of houses they could have bought for the same price away from the water, but living on the waterfront was important to them.

The couple moved in 1995 but wound up working from a distance for a year for their California employers before calling it quits for good. For the past decade, they have reveled in their retirement lifestyle.

They bought a 22-foot motorboat and enrolled in boating classes. With the boat docked behind the house, it was easy to go cruising on the Intracoastal Waterway and into the Atlantic whenever they wanted. "We used it like crazy the first three or four years," Karen says. "Then it got to be we were using it a few times a year and, in the last few years, hardly at all." They sold the boat this past summer.

Photography occupies much of Karen's time these days. Her hobby has become a small business that now involves Roger, too. Because of her background in computers, digital cameras sparked her interest.

"I was never interested in traditional film," she says. "But once all the digital equipment came out, I was like a kid in a candy store. I loved it." Her computer acumen and her love of all things tropical converged as she began photographing South Florida flora.

A couple of years ago, on a walk along Atlantic Avenue, they stopped at an outdoor art show in the park near where they live. The show intrigued Karen and she wound up joining the sponsoring group, the Delray Art League. In the group, she found some 250 like-minded souls with whom she enjoys spending time. She also takes part in 10 sidewalk sales the league holds each year.

Roger's role is that of frame maker. Karen couldn't find a commercial framer whose work really satisfied her, so Roger stepped in to help. He makes regular forays to find exotic woods, such as purpleheart and bubinga, then fashions frames from them.

"It's been a wonderful collaboration for the two of us," she says. "We end up creating pieces together. That's what I sell."

Recognizing that property prices were on the rise, Liz and Frank Longo, both certified public accountants from Yonkers, NY, bought a Delray Beach condo in 1999. "We were trying to get in before all of the other baby boomers," says Liz, 55.

They had visited the area regularly for several years because Liz's mother lived in nearby Lantana. They decided to buy a waterfront condo in preparation for their retirement and found a two-bedroom, two-bath unit in Delray Summit. The fourth-floor unit is one of 67 in the eight-story building and, Liz says, "I can see the Intracoastal (Waterway) from every window."

The 1,463-square-foot condo was built in 1968 and hadn't been updated much before the Longos bought it. They pulled up the shag carpeting, repainted the pink bedroom in neutral tones, installed a stackable washer and dryer and dispensed with the outdoor carpeting on the deck. They also installed hurricane-resistant windows.

Last year they renovated the kitchen, refinishing the solid-wood cabinets and installing a tray ceiling, under-counter lighting and new countertops. The color scheme is black and white. "It's a very clean look and it works for us," Liz says. Both of the Longos love to cook, and Frank, 57, has become their condo building's official cook at the annual spring barbecue.

They found they quickly made friends with their neighbors, particularly those on the same floor. "It's sort of informal," Liz says. "Everybody is in and out of each other's apartments."

To offset the calories from their cooking, they work out regularly at a nearby gym and are avid walkers and bikers. At first they were among the youngest in their complex. Now, Liz says, "we've started seeing people our age or even younger coming in."

The Longos are happy that they bought when they did. "If we hadn't had the foresight, we couldn't afford it now," she says. "It's tripled in value." They still spend the summer months at their house in Long Island, NY, and try to schedule vacations when the heat and hurricane threats are greatest. They also make an effort to visit Europe once a year and travel frequently to San Francisco.

Charlie and Fran Cannone left Yorktown Heights in Westchester County, NY, a decade ago after Charlie took a buyout from Reader's Digest at age 49. "The day after I retired, my wife put the house on the market and said, 'We're moving south,'" says Charlie, 59.

One of their sons had moved to Delray Beach about a year earlier, so they had visited frequently. "We really liked the area," Charlie says. "It's a very active, very social, very friendly area. We never really looked at anything else."

Well, not for long, anyway. They first bought a house in nearby Boca Raton in a country club community but quickly realized they had made a mistake. "We didn't like it," Charlie says. "It wasn't our type of area. We don't golf. We're not country-club type of people."

After six months, they started looking for a new place and found Ocean Ridge Yacht Club, a townhouse community that's a block-and-a-half from the beach on the east side of the Intracoastal Waterway. They specifically looked for a townhouse, he says, "because I was tired of doing things around the house, taking care of everything. If I'm going to be partly retired, I might as well act like it."

Their 2,500-square-foot home has three bedrooms, two-and-a-half baths, a one-car garage, decks on both floors and a view of the development's pool.

Charlie says he has no hobbies but keeps busy with the accounting firm he started shortly after moving south. Fran, 56, plays tennis, takes care of the house and runs errands for Charlie's business. It all adds up to a lifestyle that suits them both. "We have good friends and we're very comfortable here," he says.

The Longos and the O'Neills feel much the same way and have no plans to make another move anytime soon. "I don't want to say never," Liz Longo says. "Once you're retired, your whole world changes. You start realizing you're not really confined. I can do whatever I want. We don't have to worry about a job. We don't have children, we don't have pets. We're very footloose and fancy-free."

However, she says, "I don't think I would go anywhere else in Florida." If they were to move, Liz says they would probably rent for a while before buying, something she recommends others do, too, before investing in a new community that might not be a good fit.

As for the O'Neills, "every few years, Roger and I think about checking out other places," Karen says. "We even considered moving back to the Caribbean, but we keep coming back here and nothing even comes close to this. It's been three or four years since we even thought about bothering to test the waters." ●

Door County, Wisconsin

This wooded Wisconsin peninsula is rich in arts, culture, scenery and recreation

By Bill and Edie Hibbard

Door County, Wisconsin's limestone "thumb" that juts north eastward into Lake Michigan, often is compared to Cape Cod, but with an upper Midwest flavor. A variety of scenic villages are nestled at water's edge, with fascinating islands to explore and recreational and cultural activities galore. And like Cape Cod, Door County counts legions of vacationers, more than 2 million each year.

The same things that appeal to vacationers also convince an increasing number of people to retire here. The continuously changing scenery of the 80-mile-long peninsula, the abundance of recreational activities and the flowering of the arts make it a prime place to live. To these advantages, add a vitality in the air, friendly locals, excellent medical services and good roads.

For retirement, Door County is particularly attractive to couples who want to interact with their neighbors, stay active in community affairs and desire four well-defined seasons, including — yes — snow and ice in winter. But winter here is milder than in many other areas at this latitude. The Door peninsula is only six to 20 miles wide, and the water on each side moderates both the cold in winter and the heat in summer. When snow comes, roads are plowed quickly and residents get around easily,

"Winter is my favorite season," says Ted Kubicz, who with wife Agnes has lived in Baileys Harbor in Door County for 16 years. "You can sleep longer, you get fewer visitors and it's quiet. I like to read, so it's the perfect time to finish a good book."

And life doesn't end when the tourists go home. "Even in winter, there's plenty to be doing," says Agnes, who is involved in a multitude of activities.

George and Barbara Larsen, who have lived near Sister Bay for 14 years, concur. "We just love winter here — it's beautiful and quiet," says George, who adds that winter gives him more time for genealogical research on his computer. "In summer, you're often busy with guests," says Barbara. "In winter, there's lots more activity with your Door County friends."

Harvey and Alice Kroboth, who recently completed their second Door County retirement home near Carlsville, take a different tack. They also own a home in Arizona and spend five months or so there in winter to be near a daughter and grandchildren. But, as their grandchildren grow older, the Kroboths expect to be spending winters in Door County and have no qualms about it.

Harvey, 75, and Alice, 71, retired to Door County from the Milwaukee area, where Harvey, whose career started in art and advertising, had been assistant manager of the Milwaukee Journal promotions department. After 30 years at the newspaper, he took early retirement and joined Kohl's department stores, setting up photo and production sections of the company's advertising department.

After about four years with Kohl's, he retired permanently to Door County, where he and Alice had built a cottage in 1974 near Juddville on a bluff overlooking Green Bay. They had visited other parts of the state, but "this area appealed to us more than the others. It is so different from the rest of the state. It has some truly unique features — the shoreline, the little villages, the small-town atmosphere," he says. The art community and the artistic opportunities in Door County also played a part in their decision, adds Alice.

"We came here by chance in 1962 and loved it," says Harvey. "In addition, it was the right distance from Milwaukee," about three hours by car. After retirement in 1984, they built a larger year-round home on the property and used the cottage as a guest house. A few years ago, they decided that they didn't want the upkeep of two houses, so they bought another bluff-top lot overlooking the bay about 10 miles to the south and had a sleek contemporary home built there.

They bought at the right time. "We bought the lot for $79,000, and now they're going for $138,000," Harvey says.

In 16 years in Door County, Harvey has melded in smoothly, serving on the county's board of adjustment, Scandia Retirement Center's board of directors, Miller Fine Arts Center committees, Peninsula Music Festival's publicity committee and St. Peter's Lutheran Church's planning committee. He also found time to teach basic drawing at the Peninsula Art School in Fish Creek and The Clearing in Ellison Bay, a 70-year-old school that teaches arts, crafts, humanities and other courses in the Danish Folk School tradition. He's a member of the Door County Art League, the Nor-Door Bird Carving Club, which sprang from a seminar at The Clearing, and the Peninsula Golf Association, which operates the 18-hole course in Peninsula State Park. He works two or three days a week as a starter at the course. "The pay is minimal, but I can play free on my days off," says Harvey.

One of his most memorable experiences was helping to prepare for publication a biography of Door County's dean of watercolorists, Gerhard Miller. Miller acknowledged Harvey's help in the book and presented an original watercolor to him in appreciation.

Alice Kroboth is an accomplished quilter and has continued this avocation in retirement. She has taught classes in quilting at The Clearing and produced quilts to harmonize with and be displayed with pottery at the prestigious Hardy Gallery. One of her quilts gleaned $2,000 for a church fund-raiser.

Harvey believes that the cost of living is slightly higher in Door County than in Milwaukee because of high real estate valuations and consequent taxes, but he finds groceries, gasoline and restaurant meal prices about the same as elsewhere. He also notes that younger retirees seem to be buying lots and building along their road, "people who are able to do it at 50 or 55."

When the inevitable vacationing houseguests arrive at the homes of Door County retirees, active options include sailing, powerboating, water-skiing, wind surfing and fishing for king salmon, steelhead, brown and lake trout, bass and walleye in the waters of Lake Michigan to the east and its Green Bay arm to the west. Each waterfront village in Door County boasts its own marina.

Snorkeling and diving abound, too. Door County took its name from Death's Door Strait at the northern tip of the peninsula, a graveyard — along with the rest of peninsula's 250 miles of rugged shoreline — for sailing ships and other vessels. Divers visit some of the wrecks when the water is clear.

Visitors also haunt gift shops and art galleries that carry an amazing array of paintings, sculpture, carvings and pottery. Seminars on photography, music, nature and other topics are conducted at

Lawrence University's Bjorklunden (a 425-acre estate that offers weeklong seminars), The Clearing, Birch Creek Music Center and the Peninsula Art Center. Concerts are held at Birch Creek Music Center and the Door Community Auditorium, with an annual Peninsula Music Festival each August offering appearances by such performers as Willie Nelson, Joan Baez and Debbie Reynolds.

Museums dot the peninsula, including a few stately lighthouses and the new

Door County, WI

Population: 29,114 in Door County; 9,696 in Sturgeon Bay, the county's only city.

Location: Door County sits on a peninsula jutting into Lake Michigan in the eastern part of Wisconsin. Sturgeon Bay is about 40 miles northeast of the city of Green Bay and about 140 miles north of Milwaukee.

Climate:

	High	Low
January	23	9
July	81	63

Average relative humidity: 73%

Rain: 27 inches

Snow: 40 inches

Cost of living: About average.

Average housing cost: $180,000

Sales tax: 5.5% (5% state, 0.5% county)

Sales tax exemptions: Prescription drugs and most groceries.

State income tax: For single filers, graduated from 4.6% on taxable income up to $8,610 to 6.75% plus $8,201.03 on income of $129,150 or more. For married couples filing jointly, from 4.6% on taxable income up to $11,480 to 6.75% plus $10,934.70 on income of $172,200 or more.

Income tax exemptions: There is a personal exemption of $700 for taxpayer, spouse and each dependent. Those age 65 and older are allowed an additional personal exemption of $250. Military, uniformed services and railroad retirement benefits are exempt. Private pensions are taxable. Most federal, state and local pensions are taxable, although some may be exempt for taxpayers who retired before 1964 or who receive benefits from accounts established before 1964. No more than 50% of Social Security benefits

are included in Wisconsin taxable income.

Intangibles tax: None

Estate tax: Tax is pegged to federal rates on estates worth more than $675,000. Wisconsin has capped the exemption at $675,000, even though the federal tax is charged only on estates of $2 million or more.

Inheritance tax: None

Property tax: The rate in the city of Sturgeon Bay ranges from $16-$20 per $1,000 in valuation, depending on the school district. Outside the city limits the rate ranges from $10-$13 per $1,000. The annual tax on a home valued at $180,000 in Sturgeon Bay would range from $2,880-$3,600.

Homestead exemption: For homeowners with a gross income of up to $24,500, the state allows a homestead credit of up to $1,160.

Religion: 50 churches are maintained by 18 denominations, including Baptist, Catholic, Episcopal, Lutheran, Methodist and Moravian. Nearest Jewish synagogue is in the city of Green Bay.

Transportation: Cherryland Airport at Sturgeon Bay offers charter service, and there are small airports at Ephraim and Washington Island. The regional airline hub is Green Bay, with limousine service available. Senior transportation assistance is available in Door County.

Health: Door County Memorial Hospital in Sturgeon Bay has 89 beds. Additional specialists are available in Green Bay, an hour by car or ambulance. There also are seven clinics in the county.

Housing options: Single-family homes,

townhouses, condominium units and apartments are available as year-round or part-time residences. Assisted-living facilities are available in Sturgeon Bay and Sister Bay.

Visitor lodging: The county has 4,200 rooms for visitors, according to the Door County Chamber of Commerce. They range from cabins to bed-and-breakfast inns, condominium resorts and hotels to campgrounds. Some are timeshares. Check www.doorcountyvacations.com for rate ranges, information and online inspections or call (800) 527-3529 for a free vacation guide. At New Yardley Inn in Baileys Harbor, a bed-and-breakfast inn, rates are $95-135 in peak season, lower in the off-season, (888) 492-7353. At Inn at Baileys Harbor, rates range from $99-$109, (920) 839-2345. At Cherry Hills Lodge, a small resort in Sturgeon Bay, rates are $115-$155 in peak season and $97-$135 off-season, (800) 545-2307.

Information: Door County Chamber of Commerce and Visitor Information Center, 1015 Green Bay Road, Box 406, Sturgeon Bay, WI 54235, (920) 743-4456 or www.doorcountyvacations.com.

Door County Maritime Museum at Sturgeon Bay. Peninsula Players Theatre is the oldest professional resident summer theater in the nation. In addition, theatergoers can chose from options at the Door Community Center, American Folklore Theatre in Peninsula State Park, Door Off Broadway and Door Shakespeare at Bjorklunden.

Hiking and biking are popular in the five state parks in the county, including Peninsula State Park, the state's largest. Birding and ecological walks are held in the parks and at The Ridges Sanctuary, a privately held wildflower sanctuary in Baileys Harbor. Golfers can tee off at nine full-size courses, and cross-country skiing, snowmobiling and ice fishing are popular in winter.

George and Barbara Larsen had rented vacation places in Door County since 1957, and they knew they would retire to Door County. "We were among six couples that came here each summer," says Barbara, 73. "All six built homes here and three of us have retired here."

"When we moved here, we were so familiar with things that it was like moving from one end of town to the other," says George, 76. "I hadn't been here a week and I felt I was at home."

"There's a small-town feel," says Barbara. "Tradespeople get to know you; they help you out when needed. People here really care about one another."

When the Larsens were retiring from their jobs as faculty members in the Sheboygan, WI, school system — George as a high school choral music teacher, Barbara as an elementary school librarian — they found a piece of land they liked inland. Before they ended negotiations, however, the owner suggested they also look at a lot her brother owned nearby on a bluff overlooking Green Bay.

"The sun was setting as we came up on it," George recalls, "and we agreed this was it." They had their seven-room ranch house built there in 1986 and have enjoyed the often-spectacular sunsets ever since.

The Larsens' activities since retiring equal whole new careers. Barbara has written and published four books of poetry and teaches poetry writing and appreciation and life-history writing at The Clearing. She is regional vice president of the Wisconsin Fellowship of Poets, a 400-member organization. She takes regular dance-fitness classes, and when they are not scheduled, she does yoga on her own.

Besides acting as hosts at open houses at Bjorklunden, Barbara and George regularly take one to four of the seminars scheduled there each summer. They live at Bjorklunden's lodge for one of the seminars "as a vacation," Barbara says. They also are active in fundraising for Scandia Retirement Village in Sister Bay and are avid supporters of the Peninsula Music Festival.

When the Door Community Auditorium was being built, George served as liaison between the board and the architect. He also directed the Peninsula Chamber Singers, a 100-voice choir, for 10 years. Now he's assembling historical archives for Bjorklunden. Many of the archives that dated back to 1980 were lost in a fire that destroyed the old lodge in 1993.

Both Alice Kroboth and George Larsen have had positive experiences with local medical facilities. Alice says, "I had to have rotator-cuff surgery at Door County Memorial Hospital in Sturgeon Bay (the county's largest community, about 20 miles from her home) and I was impressed with the quality of the doctors and the treatment. It was a good job and I'm back to normal. All reports we've had from others who've gone there have been good, too."

George, who uses a wheelchair as a result of polio he contracted in 1956, also praises Door County Memorial Hospital and local paramedics who, he says, have been quick to respond when needed.

Another local couple, Ted and Agnes Kubicz of northern Illinois, discovered Door County separately — Ted with his first wife and Agnes as a guest of her employer. Once they'd discovered it, each continued to visit year after year. After they married 24 years ago, they spent all their summer vacations here. Each took early retirement — Ted, now 81, from the advertising department of a GTE (now Verizon) subsidiary, and Agnes, 72, as secretary to the senior vice president for government affairs of United Airlines.

During their visits they often walked along Lake Shore Drive in Baileys Harbor, stopping occasionally to admire their "dream house." One day in 1977 they found a sign in front of it and realized it was for sale. They made an appointment, liked what they saw on a quick tour, and made an earnest-money payment then and there for the 50-year-old, natural limestone home.

"When we moved in we found we had a septic system and a crawl space," says Ted. "We had no idea about some of the basics. But we lucked out and we've never regretted the way we did it." They retired to Door County seven years after purchasing the home.

Although Agnes says you can be as busy or as lazy as you like in Door County, the Kubiczs choose to be busy. They have volunteered at Bjorklunden, which lies just south of their home, and at The Ridges wildflower sanctuary, and they take classes at The Clearing. Season ticket holders for the Peninsula Music Festival, they also are members of its sustaining committee, picking up artists in Green Bay, sometimes providing housing for them, preparing lunch on rehearsal days and distributing posters and brochures. They also find time to attend performances by the Peninsula Players, the Birch Creek musicians and the American Folklore Theatre.

Agnes is president of Immanuel Lutheran Church's women's group and sings in the choir. She also sings with the Peninsula Chamber Singers, which has performed in Germany, Austria and New York City's Carnegie Hall.

In what has become a morning ritual, the Kubiczs meet friends for breakfast on the western side of the peninsula, then drive through Peninsula State Park. "We like to see the cross-peninsula scenery and how it changes," explains Ted. "We often see our favorite kingfisher at Kangaroo Lake, and we've seen blue herons along the road and sandhill cranes in the fields." As their property backs up against a wooded bluff, they often host deer, foxes, wild turkeys and groundhogs in the yard.

They enjoy watching a trio of mute swans that paddle by just offshore in summer and trumpeter swans that stop for a rest in March on their migration. "There may be more beautiful areas of the world, but I'm not sure they have as much activity," Agnes says.

"Each year we have to make a list of things we haven't done, so we can do them the next year," Ted adds. "We think it's a great place to retire," Agnes concludes. ●

Dothan, Alabama

This southeast Alabama town is a budget-friendly retiree haven

By Lynn Grisard Fullman

After 34 years in the Air Force, a dozen years working with Swiss Bank Corp. (now UBS AG) and a stint as president of United Technologies' Sikorsky Support Services, Roger Peterson and his wife, Sally, had seen the world.

"We've had 38 addresses in 52 years," notes the retired major general, who, before his retirement from the Air Force, worked at the Pentagon as deputy chief of staff for logistics and engineering. "We could have lived anywhere," observes the Southern California native. And when it came time to retire, he and Sally packed their worldly goods and headed to the southeast corner of Alabama. "How we got here is very fortuitous," Roger says.

The couple had spent some time in Montgomery, but they did not venture the 103 miles southeast of the state capital to Dothan until several years later when they were beckoned there from Switzerland to present the eulogy at a friend's funeral. From that day forward, thoughts of Dothan never left their minds.

It was as though the Biblical verse that had inspired the city's name had stayed with them. When the Civil War ravaged most of the Deep South, the area that would become Dothan lost all of its inhabitants. Originally called Poplar Head, the region did an about-face with the arrival of the Pony Express. Then, just before Thanksgiving in 1885, Houston County's largest town was incorporated. It took its name from Genesis 37:17, "For I heard them say, 'Let us go to Dothan.'"

Prosperity followed, especially after Dothan outbid other Alabama towns for a railroad. As Dothan positioned itself to become the thriving city that couples like the Petersons one day would want to call home, cotton was king and fueling the economy. However, the hungry appetite of the boll weevil replaced cotton with peanuts as Houston County's major crop.

Today, the peanuts harvested within a 100-mile radius of Dothan equal one-half of the entire U.S. peanut crop, prompting the area to dub itself "Peanut Capital of the World" and to scatter dozens of four-foot-tall, whimsical peanuts around the city. The "Peanuts Around Town" family members include Sports Nut in front of the Quality Inn on Ross Clark Circle, Elvis Nut in front of the Days Inn on Ross Clark Circle and History Nut outside Landmark Park, an early 1900s farmstead with buildings, animals and a boardwalk.

Dirt fields laden with peanuts might have seemed a world away from the Petersons, who, at one point, were living in Switzerland and owned a condominium in downtown Chicago. But their hearts were tugged toward Dothan, and they moved in the spring of 1999. The cost of living, real estate prices, cultural options and warm hospitality drew them here.

Natives of Los Angeles, the Petersons initially rented a house in Dothan and were impressed by how far their housing dollars stretched. Committed to putting down roots in the city, the couple bought a 6,200-square-foot, four-bedroom, three-bath, two-story brick house. Not far from the hub of Dothan, the house has a swimming pool, front porch, stately columns and extra space tucked above a carport where the retired major general keeps an office.

"We love the house, the town and the people," Sally says. Her family feared that, after a lifetime of trotting the globe, Sally might not be satisfied living in a small Southern town. But with all that Dothan offers, it took only days to assuage their concerns.

"I didn't have one bit of trouble," she says, citing her involvement in church, water aerobics, bridge and a wives club for retired officers.

Dothan's mild, tropical climate makes being outdoors possible almost year-round, which especially appeals to Roger, 75, who puffs his cigar next to his swimming pool all year long.

The Wiregrass Region, a nickname that refers to grass that has long, wirelike blades and spikes, offers plenty of places to play: 20 parks, six public swimming pools, 40 public tennis courts and a 16-court tennis facility, four recreation centers, a five-diamond softball complex and several organized team sports, including soccer, which is increasingly popular in the South.

The city also has a theme park with a giant wave pool and water slides, two skating rinks, two bowling centers, five golf courses, and racquetball and handball facilities. Lakes, rivers and an 80-mile drive to the Gulf of Mexico appeal to many who have retired to Dothan and enjoy wetting a line or cooling off in balmy waters.

"We're on the go all the time," says Sally, 73, the mother of three sons who live in Colorado, Illinois and Florida. "Our sons love it here; they think it is wonderful," she adds.

Dothan is not a town where pedigree is equated to acceptance by locals with deep roots in the community, she notes. "There is none of that in Dothan; they don't exclude you," she says of newcomers. "We were made to feel so welcome when we came. The people are absolutely wonderful."

She attributes their openness to the city's beginnings. Founded in the late 1800s, Dothan did not come into its own until the opening of nearby Fort Rucker — a late start, compared to many Southern towns. There are no antebellum houses, but the restored Dothan Opera House is a landmark in the historic downtown district, often the setting for professional and community theater productions, concerts, ballet performances and other cultural events.

The Wiregrass Museum of Art, where the Petersons went one night for a wine tasting, holds changing exhibits, including pieces from permanent collections and historic and contemporary decorative art. An area for children focuses on interactive art and discovery.

Describing her husband as having a "Type A" personality, Sally lists his involvement with several boards, including the Wiregrass Museum of Art, the Boys Club and Boy Scouts of America. Tall and ramrod straight, a testimony to his years in the military, the former officer continues to fly his own airplane.

Although retired, Roger can't relinquish the habit of waking each morning before dawn. His plunge back into yet

Dothan, AL

Population: Dothan's population is 58,435, with 14.6% age 65 or older. Population in the metropolitan statistical area is 133,332.

Location: Dothan is in the southeast corner of Alabama, 20 miles from the Florida and Georgia borders.

Climate:

	High	Low
January	60	38
July	92	69

Average relative humidity: 74%

Annual rainfall: 63.4 inches

Snow: Rare

Cost of living: Below average

Average housing cost: The median sale price for a single-family home in Dothan is $127,250.

Sales tax: 8% (state, 4%; city, 3%; county, 1%)

Sales tax exemptions: Services and labor are exempt.

State income tax: For a married couple filing jointly, the state taxes the first $1,000 of income at 2%, the next $5,000 at 4% and the amount over $6,000 at 5%. Single head-of-family or married filing separately rate is: 2% of the first $500, 4% of the next $2,500 and 5% over $3,000.

Income tax exemptions: Social Security benefits are exempt. Federal, state of Alabama and Alabama teachers retirement benefits are exempt. Private and public pensions that qualify as a "defined benefit plan" are exempt.

Estate tax: None.

Property tax: Alabama's property taxes are among the lowest in the nation. If homesteaded, residential property within the city of Dothan is taxed at a rate of $31 per $1,000 assessed at 10% of market value, less a state exemption of $6.50 per $1,000 on up to $4,000 of value and a county exemption of $11.50 per $1,000 on up to $2,000 of value. If not homesteaded, residential property is taxed at a rate of $31 per $1,000 assessed at 20% of market value. Taxes on a home valued at $127,250 would be $345 if homesteaded, $789 if not homesteaded. For information on a specific property, call (334) 677-4714.

Homestead exemptions: Applicable to persons over 65 or totally disabled, all are exempt from the state portion of the property tax; those with incomes of less than $12,000 can also receive an exemption of up to $5,000 from the county portion, and those with incomes of less than $7,500 receive a total exemption from property taxes.

Religion: The Dothan area has more than 140 churches representing 25 denominations including Roman Catholic, Jewish, Mormon and Protestant faiths. Among them are Baptist, Episcopal, Presbyterian, Lutheran, Methodist, Church of Christ and Assembly of God.

Education: Wallace State Community College is a two-year associate degree institution; Troy State University Dothan is a four-year university offering undergraduate and graduate degrees in many disciplines. Vocational education is available in Dothan Technology Center, Houston County Career and Technical Center, and Wallace Community College. Many offer courses of interest to retirees.

Transportation: Dothan Regional Airport is served by Atlantic Southeast Airlines/Delta Connection. Greyhound Bus service and rail service are available. Wiregrass Transit Authority operates a public bus service.

Health: The area has two acute-care hospitals (400-bed Southeast Alabama Medical Center and 235-bed private Flowers Hospital), three immediate-care facilities, three outpatient surgery clinics, two mental health centers, two rehabilitation centers and one center for the sensory impaired. More than 250 physicians and 50 dentists serve the area.

Housing options: Neighborhoods are quiet, close-knit and well-maintained and offer as many choices as a large city. In both urban and rural settings, homes range in size and style, including brick, frame, single or multistory, stately and modern, townhouse or estate. The rental market also is strong with a typical two-bedroom apartment renting for $495 a month and a two-bedroom townhouse from $400 to $500. There are no specific retirement communities. Since opening in 1999, **Grove Park,** (334) 712-9692, has drawn retirees — along with families and singles — who favor its single entrance, parks and public areas. Convenient to Flowers Hospital, Grove Park offers a combination of housing options, including Craftsman- and bungalow-style homes, cottages, duplexes, triplexes and an assisted-living facility.

Visitor lodging: Dothan has more than 2,000 rooms (in a range of prices, typically from under $30 to $85), extended-stay accommodations, RV parks and campgrounds. Holiday Inn Express, $65-$69, (334) 671-3700. Quality Inn, from $61, (334) 794-6601.

Information: Dothan Area Chamber of Commerce, P.O. Box 638, Dothan, AL 36302, (800) 221-1027 or www.dothan.com. Dothan Area Convention and Visitors Bureau, 3311 Ross Clark Circle, (P.O. Box 8765), Dothan, AL 36304, (888) 449-0212, (334) 794-6622 or www.dothanalcvb.com. City of Dothan, P.O. Box 2128, Dothan, AL 36302, (334) 615-3000 or www.dothan.org. Southeast Alabama Trails, P.O. Box 519, Andalusia, AL 36420, (334) 222-1125 or www.southeastalabamatrails.com.

another career was spurred when locally owned SunSouth Bank discovered his expertise within their shadow, and he was brought aboard as managing director of marketing. Having tripled in size since opening in Dothan, the bank started a women's advisory board, working to help women achieve the financial skills needed to make independent judgments in their lives.

For a man who knows the value of a dollar, Dothan is a logical choice for retirement. The Petersons acquired their home at a fraction of the cost of similar housing in Beverly Hills, Chicago or New York. Taxes on their house in Dothan are far below anything they previously had experienced. "We own a 758-square-foot condo in downtown Chicago, and the taxes on it are four-and-a-half to five times more than on our house here," Sally reports.

Their decision to retire to Dothan was affirmed by Roger's high school classmates. Some 30 fellow graduates from University High School in Los Angeles converged in Dothan a few years ago for a reunion hosted by the Petersons. They visited in early November, attended the city's annual peanut festival, played golf, went swimming and had a ball, the couple reports, recalling the friendly reception Roger's former schoolmates received in Dothan.

"Dothan doesn't have much crime," Sally notes, adding that she and her husband regularly attend weekly city council meetings, where they discovered that "the biggest concern for citizens is whether there should be a charge for garbage pickup service."

Their only dilemma is finding the city's best barbecue. "We like Larry's Barbecue," Sally says, admitting that Dobbs Famous Bar-B-Que is a favorite, among others. If Dothan lacks anything, Sally suggests, it is a fancy restaurant with white tablecloths and crystal. However, she says, "We are one and a half hours from Montgomery, Destin and Panama City, and not far from Atlanta."

Delighted with its ever-growing retiree population, Dothan offers special services, such as a chamber of commerce Web site (www.dothan.com) with links to relocation and retiree information, including real estate, mortgages, developers and builders. In addition, the Department of Leisure Services provides a seniors-only facility at Rose Hill Senior Adult Center that has game rooms, a sewing room, craft rooms and occasional speakers. Here seniors find instruction on computers, exercise, golf and tennis, and the chance to enjoy bingo, dominoes, cards, quilting, art and crafts.

Sally has been pleased with the area's shopping options, which include abundant choices, ranging from a popular mom-and-pop shop for women to three regional malls, factory outlet centers and antique malls. Anchored by Dillard's and JCPenney, among other stores, Wiregrass Commons Mall contains a food court and more than 100 specialty shops. Area malls and shopping centers often offer special promotions, fashion shows, educational and cultural displays, health fairs and live entertainment.

Food and shopping are not all that lured the Petersons to Dothan, an attractive city with well-maintained roads and virtually no litter, evidence of citizens' pride in their community. Dothan's "very good medical community and good hospitals" also were important to the Petersons, who wanted assurance they would have access to high-quality medical care and facilities.

In Dothan there are more than 250 physicians and 50 dentists, two hospitals, three immediate-care facilities, three outpatient surgery clinics, two mental health centers, two rehabilitation centers and one center for the sensory impaired. Two acute-care hospitals — Southeast Alabama Medical Center and Flowers Hospital — mean that retirees have access to services such as open-heart surgery, cancer treatments and magnetic resonance imaging.

The town's medical facilities were also a priority for Larry and Kathryn Castleman, who several years ago decided the time had come to slow down. Following his 20-year stint in the military and another 20 years working for the federal government, and her career also with the federal government, the couple was ready for a pace slower than what they had experienced in the nation's capital.

With one child still at home and two out of the nest, Larry, a 64-year-old Missouri native, researched communities that interested them and reconsidered towns and cities they had visited during their careers.

Raised in the Panama Canal Zone, where her American-born father worked, Kathryn says she wanted to move to a city with a population of about 50,000 and with proximity to a military base and good medical facilities. After visiting Dothan, the decision to move came quickly.

The city's low cost of living was a deciding factor. In the Washington, DC, area, they had been paying $6,000 to $8,000 in property taxes. When they found a two-level, 3,200-square-foot house they liked in Dothan, they inquired about property taxes and were delighted to learn that taxes were only about $500.

With the frenzy of Washington, DC, traffic a fading memory, the couple knew they had made the right decision to move to Dothan. They both work several hours a day, two days a week, in administration with a company that certifies nurses. He also volunteers at a local hospital, at the city's botanical gardens and food bank, and at the police department, where he enters evidence into a computer. Both volunteer with the city's convention and visitors bureau.

Enticements that drew the Castlemans likewise attracted a couple from Idaho. In the market for a retirement town, Kay and Bob Springer happened one day to be watching a golf tournament televised from Dothan's Robert Trent Jones-designed golf course, Highland Oaks. The 36-hole course is part of a statewide golfing trail that has become a major tourist attraction, offering public play on well-maintained greens.

Bob recalls that, at that time, "we were interested in moving from Idaho, where we lived 24 years in the mountains in a little town where we had met," Bob recalls. With a population of some 3,000 residents, the Idaho town provided spectacular views of the Rocky Mountains and places to hunt, fish and ranch.

"But as you get older, those mountains get higher and the snow gets deeper," laughs Bob, 71, who traveled 48 states during his working years. "We looked at other towns, but they all had their problems. The only problem here is traffic on Ross Clark Circle," he says, referring to the busy road that loops the city, which is known for its downtown murals detailing significant events from the area's earlier days.

"We knew we wanted to come south,"

recalls Bob, a retired Revlon executive. Having already eliminated several possible places to retire, the Springers had never been to Dothan. The televised golf tournament and knowledge of the state's low tax rates prompted their visit.

Adding Dothan to areas to be visited on an upcoming trip south turned out to be a life-changing decision. Although they later inspected other possible places to retire, the two knew right away that "this was the place; there was no question," Bob says. "The cost of living is absolutely minimal," he says, describing real estate values as "unbelievable. The house you can buy for the money is absolutely fantastic," says Bob, who was born in Oklahoma and grew up in Minneapolis. He and Kay have been married for 23 years.

During their visit, they toured medical facilities and discovered that Dothan is "just absolutely vibrant, (and) the people are very gracious." Following their whirlwind journey, the Springers returned to Idaho, sold their house and in July 2001 moved to Dothan, where they purchased a one-story brick home with four bedrooms, two bathrooms and a two-car garage.

"The home, for what we paid, is absolutely unbelievable," he reports, adding that annual taxes on the house, which they purchased in 2001 for $131,000, total $336.

Retired in 1999 from hospital administration, Kay, 66 and a native of England, has learned to like the city's ever-present boiled peanuts. "Like liver, boiled peanuts are an acquired taste," Bob laughs, referring to an appreciation he has yet to value.

Other major selling points were the city's athletic venues, all suited to Kay's weekly regime of aquacize and gym workouts, which she couples with daily walks in their neighborhood. Bob now golfs three times a week on the same course he saw on television before they moved to Dothan.

"Most people don't appreciate how beautiful this course is," he speculates, explaining that by buying an annual pass, he can play without limit at this course or any of the other Robert Trent Jones courses in the state. (While he prefers to walk, cart fees are additional.)

Bob remains convinced that he and Kay made the right choice. "This is the place," he says. For those considering retiring to Dothan, he suggests a visit.

"It's a great little town," he says. "It has lots of good restaurants, the people are fantastic, the cost of living is great, (there are) recreational facilities of all kinds. It's not missing a thing," he says. "It's true. Dothan is the ideal area to retire."

His sentiments are echoed by other retirees. "Not one nanosecond" has Sally Peterson regretted her decision to move to Dothan. "It is fabulous here," she says.

A billboard hovering above busy Ross Clark Circle confirms in bold letters what these retirees have discovered: "A great place to live: Dothan, Alabama." ●

Easton, Maryland

Maryland's rural Eastern Shore brims with "pleasant living"

By Mary Lu Abbott

John and Fran Wolfe are sailors and nature lovers. From their home in Gaithersburg, MD, a northwest suburb of Washington, DC, they would drive an hour and a half in heavy weekend traffic to their boat in Annapolis, where they encountered more congestion in the harbor.

They would sail the Chesapeake Bay, exploring its many inlets, and often anchor in the small towns of St. Michaels and Oxford on Maryland's Eastern Shore.

"Our dream was to retire and do some sailing, go south in the winter. We knew we wanted to retire early when we were still able to handle a sailboat and fulfill our dream," says Fran, noting that their goal was to leave the work world by the time John turned 55. They had dismissed Florida as a destination because they preferred four seasons.

"I refused to retire until we found a house on the water," Fran says. Waterfront property can be hard to find and extremely pricey, but before they even were seriously hunting, they stumbled upon the right place.

Several years ago, John was invited to play in a golf tournament at the Easton Club, a planned community of 342 homes on the edge of Easton, a small Eastern Shore town dating to 1710. It's the Talbot County seat and business center.

"I fell in love with the community and the development. I wasn't even looking for a house, really, but I found this place for sale and thought it was a perfect house for us. I brought her over and we bought it on the spur of the moment," John says.

Out the front door is a golf course and out back is a river where Fran enjoys studying a wide array of waterfowl, from swans to Canada geese, heron, kingfisher and an abundance of migratory birds.

Part of the headwaters of the Tred Avon River, which flows into the Chesapeake Bay, the water behind the Wolfes' home is shallow but deep enough to keep small craft, including a kayak, there. Their large boat is in the deeper water at Oxford, only a 10-mile drive. "We could ride our bikes down to the boat," Fran says.

They bought the house in 2000, enjoying it on weekends until they retired in August 2001. John, a commercial real estate broker, was 54 and Fran, in marketing, was 58 at retirement.

"We love the 'land of pleasant living.' That's what they call it here, and that's exactly what we believe it is. When we first moved here, once we crossed the Chesapeake Bay Bridge, which connects the Eastern Shore and the Western Shore, we felt the weight of the world lifted off our shoulders. We were away from the Beltway traffic and driving through farmland — we saw barns and farm animals. It's wonderful," says Fran, noting that the rural landscape triggers memories of growing up on a farm in Indiana.

Going to and from Oxford, they frequently stop at a farmer's produce stand and buy whatever fresh pickings are available that day.

The Eastern Shore, a reference to its location on the Chesapeake Bay, is Maryland's slice of the Delmarva Peninsula, so called because it also includes Delaware and a strip of northern Virginia. The Eastern Shore is an expanse of flat land, a patchwork of farms with crops of wheat, corn, soybeans and tomatoes, small historic towns, twisting rivers and creeks, groves of tall trees, marshes, bay shoreline and beaches on the Atlantic Ocean.

With scores of little coves and inlets leading to Chesapeake Bay, Talbot County alone has 602 miles of shoreline. Its waters are rich with blue crab, oysters, clams, rockfish (striped bass) and a wide range of waterfowl. Its towns tantalize artists and photographers with their beauty and brim with amenities that appeal to city sophisticates.

It's a haven for those who enjoy boating, fishing, hunting, bird-watching and biking — and for those who like fine dining, a lively arts scene with theater, music, galleries and museums, active communities and historic sights. "It's a nice blend of necessary amenities and pleasant living," John says.

"Lower and slower" is another slogan about the Eastern Shore, say Carolyn and Jack Batty, who retired here from Connecticut. Also boat people, they had looked seriously at Annapolis but found it "entirely too hectic and overbuilt."

The Eastern Shore is "flat, flat and slower because it's away from the population center, but it's close enough to get to the center easily," says Jack, 66, noting it's about 45 minutes from Annapolis and less than 90 minutes from Baltimore or Washington, DC. The Eastern Shore is slower paced in part because it was somewhat isolated before the early 1950s when the bridge was built outside Annapolis to connect to the Eastern Shore. Until then, residents had to drive up to the northeastern corner of the state and down the other side.

"We think we have a perfect situation, with a very active, attractive little town where there's a volunteer or interest group for anything you think of. There's plenty to do around here, including good music. But we also have a country life. We can look up and watch the geese fly overhead. It's very idyllic, the best of all worlds," says Carolyn, 66.

"For a town of a little over 12,000, Easton and its cultural opportunities are amazing," Jack says. "It has a vibrant downtown. You don't see any boarded-up stores like so many downtowns in small-town America today. There are some very good restaurants in Easton and surrounding towns, and a cultural life. We have a restored theater that has been brought back to life and is home for concerts, entertainers and musical groups. The Mid-Atlantic Symphony plays regularly."

In downtown Easton, the Avalon Theatre, a 1920s art deco movie and vaudeville playhouse, now is a performing arts center seating 400. A couple of blocks from it, the Academy Art Museum, a merger of historic buildings including an 1820s schoolhouse, hosts both permanent and visiting exhibits, concerts, numerous classes, workshops, programs and arts-oriented trips. The Historical Society of Talbot County preserves late 1700s and early 1800s buildings and a reconstructed 1680s home and gardens. The society offers twice-monthly walking tours of historic Easton among its programs.

The town has a farmers market twice weekly from spring through fall, offering

Easton, MD

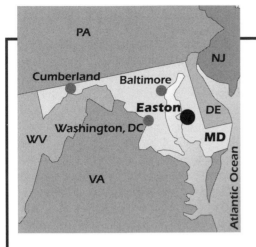

Population: About 12,000 in Easton, about 35,500 in Talbot County. Easton is the county seat and business center.

Location: On Maryland's Eastern Shore, a reference to its location on the Chesapeake Bay. Maryland shares the Delmarva Peninsula with Delaware and part of Virginia. Easton is 40 miles from Annapolis, 59 miles from Baltimore and 73 miles from Washington, DC.

Climate: High Low

	High	Low
January	44	28
July	88	69

Average relative humidity: 54%

Rain: 43 inches

Snow: 15 inches

Cost of living: Above average

Average housing cost: The median sales price is $395,000. New homes range from $325,000 to several million dollars.

Sales tax: 5%

Sales tax exemptions: Prescription drugs and some groceries.

Income tax: The state has a graduated tax peaking at 4.75% on income above $3,000. In addition, Talbot County imposes a 2.25% tax rate.

Income tax exemptions: Social Security benefits are exempt. Those 65 and older may exclude up to $22,600 each in pension income, and there's an exemption of up to $5,000 on military retirement for those who are eligible. Personal exemption is $2,400, with an additional $1,000 if the taxpayer is 65 or older, or blind. For a more complete list of exemptions, visit www.marylandtaxes.com.

Estate tax: The Maryland estate tax return is required if the decedent's federal gross estate plus adjusted taxable gifts equaled or exceeded $1 million and the decedent was either a resident of Maryland at the time of death or a nonresident who owned real or tangible personal property in Maryland.

Property tax: Easton residents pay a combined city-county-state rate of $1.082 per $100 of assessed value, with homes assessed at about 100% of market value. Residents in unincorporated areas of the county pay a combined county (.52) and state (.132) rate of $.652 per $100 in valuation. Easton taxes on a $395,000 home would be about $4,274, while taxes on a home in an unincorporated area would be about $2,575.

Homestead exemption: Homeowners' and homestead property tax credits may apply depending on income.

Religion: Easton has more than 30 places of worship, including a number of historic sites. Among them: the nation's oldest religious building still in use and earliest dated building in the state, the Third Haven Friends Meeting House built in 1682.

Education: Chesapeake College in nearby Wye Mills has the Institute for Adult Learning with classes for seniors, and programs are offered by the Academy Art Museum and Historical Society of Talbot County, both in Easton, and the Chesapeake Bay Maritime Museum in nearby St. Michaels.

Transportation: Maryland Upper Shore Transit (MUST) runs regular bus service in Easton and to other shore communities.

Health: The 137-bed Memorial Hospital in Easton provides a broad range of medical services for the entire area and is expanding. The world-renowned Johns Hopkins Hospital, considered one of the nation's best, is in Baltimore, slightly more than an hour's drive.

Housing options: Chesapeake by Del Webb at Easton Club East, (866) 444-0246, an active-adult community, has a recreational clubhouse, outdoor pool, tennis courts, putting green and walking trail. The adjacent Easton Club community has a public golf course. About 420 homes are planned and about 285 sold; prices run $335,000-$380,000. **Cooke's Hope**, (410) 822-1335, blends homes with a pastoral setting that includes a herd of Belted Galloway cattle. The community has an exercise facility, indoor pool, nature path, five miles of trails and a small-boat marina. Homes currently start at $650,000, and townhomes are available in the $600,000s. The golf-course community of **Easton Club** is built out but may have resales available, townhomes from the mid-$300,000 and houses from the $600,000, (410) 820-9800.

Visitor lodging: The area is noted for inns and historic homes turned into B&B lodging. In downtown Easton, The Tidewater Inn and Conference Center has rooms from $70, including breakfast (low season), (800) 237-8775. The Inn at Easton, an 1800s Federal mansion, offers rates from $195, including breakfast (ask about special rates and packages), (410) 822-4910. The Bishop's House is an 1880 Victorian mansion with rooms from $140, including breakfast, (800) 223-7290. St. Michaels and Tilghman Island also have a good selection, and there are chain accommodations in the area.

Information: Talbot County Chamber of Commerce, P.O. Box 1366, Easton Plaza Suite 53, Easton, MD 21601, (410) 822-4653 or www.talbotchamber.org, and Talbot County Office of Tourism, 11 S. Harrison St., Easton, MD 21601, (410) 770-8000 or www.tourtalbot.org.

arts and crafts as well as vegetables, fruits and other foodstuffs and live music at the Saturday market.

While not on a harbor, Easton is within a few minutes of rivers and creeks feeding into Chesapeake Bay and less than 10 minutes from two notable smaller waterfront towns. St. Michaels and Oxford enrich the cultural scene. St. Michaels, a trading port from the 1670s with about 1,200 residents today, fronts the Miles River. Its narrow streets have restaurants, gift and antiques shops and white picket fences bordering Victorian homes. On the harborfront, the Chesapeake Bay Maritime Museum, a collection of buildings with exhibits, boats, a wharf and a lighthouse, lets visitors experience the history of the region. Famed author James Michener spent time at the museum researching the region for his novel "Chesapeake."

Oxford existed about 20 years before its official founding as a port in 1683 and for more than a century was a major international shipping center for tobacco plantations. It was the home of a number of noted statesmen of the Revolutionary period and in the late 1800s was a major canning and packing center for Maryland's oysters. It has fewer than 1,000 residents today but attracts many tourists to its restaurants, B&Bs, shops and harbor, where yachts and sailboats mix with fishing boats.

Carolyn and Jack were familiar with the Eastern Shore, frequently visiting her brother in Oxford from their home in Trumbull, CT, close to metropolitan New York City. In 1999, Jack retired from General Electric and she wound up a career in education. Originally from the Midwest, they had lived in New England most of their careers.

"We agreed we'd stay put two years before we moved so we'd be sure we wanted to move," she says. They had looked around the Northeast, including Cape Cod, but since their children were in the Philadelphia and Washington, DC, areas, they decided to go south.

They wanted to be near saltwater — they had sailed for years in Long Island Sound off the Connecticut coast — and they liked Easton. "Finding Cooke's Hope really decided it for us," says Carolyn. On the edge of town, Cooke's Hope is part of a 1659 land grant, now a small planned community surrounded

by a split-rail fence. Half its land is green space, including large pastures for its small herd of Belted Galloway cattle, nicknamed "Oreo" cows for their black body with white center band.

"We call them our decorator cows," says Carolyn, who likes that the community maintains the rural nature of the area. The community has five miles of walking paths through woods and around ponds and a tidal creek with a marina for small boats. Cooke's Hope has clusters of townhomes, a village of traditional single-family homes on smaller lots with brick sidewalks, and two-acre lots for larger homes. In 2001, the Battys moved into one of the townhomes, which now are nearly sold out. The community plans about 360 homes, and about half are built.

The Battys enjoy canoeing and kayaking in the tidal waters and watching the wildlife. "Canada geese are a trademark of the area because it's on the migratory route. A lot of the geese spend the winter here. We also see egrets, osprey, heron, occasionally eagles, hawks and all kinds of small birds. Deer are everywhere — too much so," Jack says.

The Battys sold their sailboat and bought a powerboat. "There are so many backwaters to explore, and a powerboat lets us explore the beautiful little creeks better," Carolyn says.

While they were boaters, Stewart and Sandra Darrow had other priorities in choosing a place to retire. They wanted to live in a 55-plus community with a clubhouse and activities, and proximity to golf was important.

"I used to fish a lot, and then I got into golf. You can't be a boater and a golfer at the same time, I decided," says Stewart, noting they sold their boat.

They had lived in a small town near the bay south of Annapolis. He was an attorney with the government, commuting to Fort Meade between Baltimore and Washington, DC, and she was in real estate. They retired in 1998 when he was 55.

They looked at 55-plus communities throughout the mid-Atlantic region, from Hilton Head, SC, to Virginia and over into Delaware. They liked the Del Webb community close to Hilton Head and "might have gone there but for the fact that we had family in Maryland," says Stewart, 61.

They knew of Easton and visited it. "It turned out even better than we thought. There's always something going on — art shows, music," says Stewart, noting they also like the proximity of Oxford and St. Michaels, with attractions of their own. "Part of the beauty of this area is things are so close and it's still not as crowded as the Western Shore. The pace is different here, even though the Eastern Shore is trying to catch up, but we hope it doesn't."

They like the area's combination of "feeling like you're out in the boonies" yet being convenient to everything desirable. "On one hand, it's very rural. On the other, we're five minutes from all the grocery shopping you want, golf — everything is very close but not impinging on you," Stewart says.

They discovered Easton Club East — now Chesapeake by Del Webb — which had the clubhouse and activities Sandra wanted and offered golf privileges at the adjacent Easton Club community. They moved in July 2003 and enjoy such community activities as social hours, Friday night movies and outings to New York City for special events.

Rated among the nation's best small towns and arts-oriented communities, Easton exudes a charm reminiscent of an English village. Once known as the "Colonial capital of the Eastern Shore," its county courthouse from the 1700s remains the center of town, where narrow streets are lined with brick storefronts. A toy store, rare-book purveyor, paint-your-own pottery shop, library, church and banks mix with art galleries, antique shops and other businesses along brick sidewalks.

Among numerous events, Easton hosts a summer chamber music festival, an antiques fair, a major arts and crafts show, a family-oriented First Night Talbot celebration on New Year's Eve and an internationally acclaimed Waterfowl Festival featuring wildlife art, which brings about 20,000 people in November.

"There are the friendliest people over here — the shop owners, people who work in stores, the people in the art galleries, the whole gamut. It's incredible, and it's uniformly that way. It's very casual. Everyone seems to be just genuinely friendly," Stewart says.

"It's a small community where everybody gets to know everybody else. You go in one boutique or another and you see someone you saw two days before," says Sandra, 57.

Its quality of life is helping fuel growth, particularly in people retiring here or buying second homes for later retirement. With politicians, government officials and retirees coming from higher-priced metropolitan areas, housing prices in Talbot County have escalated, with the median house price at $395,000 in June 2005. There are new homes in the $300,000s, but there also are many properties above $1 million.

"You definitely get value for your money. You get more house for your money on the Eastern Shore than the Western Shore," Stewart says.

Jack Batty says, "There's ongoing debate on growth, with the two extremes — the preservationists who want to pull up the drawbridge and not let any growth occur except for commercial, and the other side that wants growth for jobs. Somewhere in between is the answer. You don't want to destroy the beauty and the things that brought people to the Eastern Shore, but you can't stick your head in the sand and ignore growth. We need to grow gracefully rather than unbridled."

Easton has adopted a comprehensive town plan focused on building in currently available areas rather than expanding now, says Matthew Davis, assistant town planner in 2004. "We have a no-annexation policy for six years. We have enough land to develop now," he says. While there are new developments, he adds that the town has restrictions on the growth of housing because its sewage capacity currently is limited, but a new plant is scheduled to open in 2006.

"We don't want to grow too fast. We want to retain the small-town charm — that's why people come here," he says.

Permits for "big-box" superstores have been turned down, though major chain retailers such as Wal-Mart have regular-size stores in the area.

A number of new housing developments are started or planned, including some at St. Michaels and other nearby towns. Most development is within town limits rather than in unincorporated areas of the county, as there is no county water-sewer system, says George Kinney, Talbot County planning officer. The county has a low-density policy. "Our vision is to keep the developments in the towns," Kinney says.

The Wolfes support "smart growth," as John notes that without development to help create jobs, it's hard to keep young people in the area. "I've lived in areas before that have had rampant development and lived through some of those problems. I've not seen that here and don't think I will," John says.

The Wolfes last year realized their dream, sailing south in the fall and spending about seven months on their boat. With a daughter getting married this past fall, they decided to stay home this winter.

"In Maryland we have early springs, late falls, mild winters," Fran says. "Spring is beautiful, fall is beautiful, it's a wonderful four seasons." Because they like the area so much, the Wolfes are rethinking their game plan and may alternate years staying here and sailing south.

The couples say it's easy to get into activities and volunteer work and that there are numerous leisure learning opportunities in area museums, at the historical society and at Chesapeake College about 15 miles away in Wye Mills. The couples praise the local hospital, which serves the entire upper shore area, but Easton also is within easy driving distance of Johns Hopkins Hospital in Baltimore, considered one of the best in the country.

The couples say the area attracts an interesting variety of newcomers from all over the country. While many are retired, others still work, often telecommuting and consulting from their homes.

Carolyn Batty says she thought she missed some elements of their life in Connecticut — until she went back and found it more congested and hectic. "Every time I go back, I'm really glad to get home to Easton. I've adapted nicely to the Eastern Shore way of life. We have wonderful friends, wonderful neighbors and everything we could possibly think of to do."

"It's a perfect retirement spot," says Jack Batty. ●

Edenton, North Carolina

Lovely bayfront town takes pride in its Colonial past

By Jim Kerr

On the Fourth of July, the folks of Edenton, a 300-year-old town that knows something about American history, gather in the park fronting Edenton Bay to celebrate with games, food and fireworks. Brick buildings from the 19th and 20th centuries line Broad Street, the main downtown thoroughfare, as kids and adults amble southwest toward the park. And as they approach the waterfront, the buildings grow more historic until they reach the oldest, a Jacobean-style structure known as Cupola House, built in 1725.

Crape myrtle trees, brimming with bright purple and white flowers, decorate the town, and well-groomed magnolias and oaks shade carefully restored Federal, Georgian, Greek Revival and Victorian homes. A breeze off the bay tempers the warm July afternoon as hundreds of Edenton's 5,000 residents gather in a scene Norman Rockwell might have conceived.

But while broad strokes of Americana characterize the event and give it a New England flavor, Edenton is a bona fide Southern town, laid out in 1712 along the north bank of Albemarle Sound at the mouth of the Chowan River in the northeastern corner of the state. It is North Carolina's second-oldest town and its first Colonial capital, and Cupola House was its first customs house. For several decades leading up to the American Revolution, goods were cleared here and distributed from perhaps 100 ships anchored in the same bay that now overlooks the annual Independence Day picnic.

Winds of change have swept over Edenton, but through good times and bad, the little town has persevered as a functioning community. English settlers ventured south from Virginia beginning in the 1650s, and while the town still is closely linked with immigrants from the former Northern colonies, most today come as tourists and retirees attracted by the town's historic ambiance, sense of community and progressive, if laid-back, pace.

"We wanted our kids to grow up in a small town where we could also retire," Mary Jo Sellers says. "It's a move we have never regretted."

Their children, now 14 and 18, were just youngsters when Mary Jo and Larry Sellers moved to Edenton in 1992 from the Washington, DC, area where Larry and his partners owned a string of Ben Franklin stores. The couple had seen an ad in The Washington Post for waterfront property outside town, but they were captivated by Edenton's historic character, and instead bought a large 1920s-era house in town. A year later they sold it and bought their double-porched, Georgian-style house on Blount Street. Located two blocks north from the Cupola House, it was built in 1772 and had been Edenton's second customs house.

Being on the daily historic walking tours, the pilgrimage tour in April and Edenton's Christmas candlelight tours every December doesn't bother the Sellerses in the least. "People make you feel so good about your home and where you live," Mary Jo says, "and we like to talk to people from our front porch. We feel we have bragging rights."

Each morning Larry and Mary Jo stroll under the oaks and crape myrtles to the Lovin' Oven downtown for coffee and socializing with friends. Later in the day, the local hardware store clerk doesn't mind spending a few minutes with Larry to find a 15-cent item. Everyone in Edenton seems to have time to be helpful and neighborly.

Community spirit doesn't arise only on the Fourth of July, either. It has been bred here beginning with the actions of men and women who were in the forefront of American history, including a signer of the Declaration of Independence and a signer of the U.S. Constitution. The restored Chowan County Courthouse on East King Street, a national historic landmark, dates to 1767, making it the oldest continually operated government building in the state.

And the degree of cooperation between elected officials and volunteer organizations today has led many newcomers to believe Edenton embodies the best qualities to be found in small-town America. Located in a convenient, yet out-of-the-mainstream corridor of the state along U.S. Highway 17, the town is 75 miles southwest of Norfolk, VA, 140 miles southeast of Richmond and 135 miles east of Raleigh. "People like to say it's an hour and a half from everything," Mary Jo says. "And that includes the beach at the Outer Banks, an easy and pleasant drive."

Edenton is the county seat of Chowan County, the smallest county in the state with 181 square miles and a population of 15,000. Lumber, cotton and peanuts are the long-time staples of the area's agribusiness, and while Edenton is no longer a commercial port, pleasure boating is a substantial "industry," with three marinas and two recreational boat manufacturers. There are waterfront condominiums along one marina, and many residents are boating and fishing enthusiasts. Larry and Mary Jo keep a jet ski at the ready behind a friend's house.

Carolina boaters enjoy wide-open sailing on Albemarle Sound and have long known about historic and boater-friendly Edenton, where visiting craft are offered two free nights at the town-operated, nine-slip marina. But anyone driving along U.S. Highway 17 between Hampton Roads and Raleigh could easily miss the town. Such was the case with Steve and DeAnn O'Neil, a couple researching retirement locations a few years ago from their home in Chantilly, VA, just west of Washington, DC.

"Every two years we went to real estate expos in DC looking around," remembers Steve, who retired three years ago as a full colonel after 29 years of service in the Army. "We planned a schedule of visits no farther south than North Carolina, and to places close enough to our daughter in Maryland. We looked first in Maryland and Virginia, then mapped out routes for two separate trips to North Carolina."

The first was to the Asheville-Hendersonville area in the western mountains. The second was to the Triangle area of Raleigh-Durham-Chapel Hill in the central Piedmont, which also included a swing east to the historic town of New Bern, which succeeded Edenton as the state's Colonial capital. But while Edenton was on their list of stops as they headed home, the long trip began to weigh on them, and when they reached the U.S. Highway 17 bypass around the little town, DeAnn suggested they skip it. "I said, 'If we do, we'll never know,'" Steve recalls.

That was seven years ago. It was February and snowing. The real estate agent they talked to apologized for the coldest day of the year, but the O'Neils were undaunted.

"We drove down Broad Street and saw St. Anne's Catholic Church right in town," Steve says. "We wanted something near the water, something historic. We saw all the beautiful homes. I was impressed."

While they liked the idea of living in a historic town, the O'Neils did not want an older home. Steve had grown up in an old 900-square-foot house, and he wanted something with space and a view. They selected a large lot at the Edenton Bay development, a large finger of land on the sound connected to the town by a single-lane wooden bridge. The residential property is part of a huge family-owned peanut and cotton plantation considered the oldest continually operating plantation in the state.

The O'Neils rented a house in town for 10 months in 1996 while their Cape Cod-style house was being built. While approximately 600 homesites are on the plantation, only a few lots are still available in Phase I along the Albemarle Sound. Many face southwest, where the expansive waterway extends to the Lowcountry horizon, affording remarkable views.

"There's not a night that goes by when the sunsets aren't more spectacular than in Hawaii, where we lived for five and a half years," Steve says. "The sky turns the most gorgeous of colors, and no two are ever the same."

In Steve's long military career, the O'Neils had moved 28 times. Now it was time to settle in, but they had no intention of becoming disconnected recluses. They joined the 250-member St. Anne's Church as well as Edenton's active arts council. The town was getting artsy with the influx of new talent. There were art lessons, sewing and cooking classes. Steve, who served two years as the homeowners association president in his neighborhood, also unlimbered his clubs at the nearby Chowan Golf Club, a pastime interspersed "with that other old standby, yard work."

Soon after their arrival there was an influx of new entrepreneurs in town, opening shops and restaurants, and the choices increased from one barbecue place to half a dozen eateries specializing in various cuisines. Together the O'Neils began making lots of new friends. "One thing I learned about living in a small town," DeAnn says. "It's always social time. A 15-minute trip to town takes an hour or more, stopping to talk to people."

Just a mile or so down the road, Dave and Peggy Blomquist enjoy the same

Edenton, NC

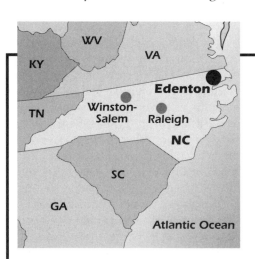

Population: 5,000 in Edenton, 15,000 in Chowan County.

Location: In Chowan County along Edenton Bay on the north shore of Albemarle Sound, approximately 135 miles northeast of Raleigh, NC, 90 miles southwest of Norfolk, VA, 140 miles south of Richmond, VA, and 60 miles from the Atlantic Coast and Outer Banks.

Climate: High Low
January 52 31
July 85 72

Average relative humidity: 76%

Rain: 47.9 inches

Snow: 4.6 inches

Cost of living: Below average

Average housing cost: $145,000 for older homes in town but outside the historic district and not on the water, to $600,000 for historic, waterfront homes in town, and $250,000 to $450,000 in new waterfront or country club developments.

Sales tax: 7%

Sales tax exemptions: Prescription drugs, eyeglasses, some medical supplies and most services.

State income tax: For married couples filing jointly, the rate is graduated from 6% of taxable income up to $21,250 to 8.25% (plus $14,537.50) on amounts over $200,000. For single filers, it is graduated from 6% of income up to $12,750 to 8.25% (plus $8,722.50) on amounts over $120,000.

Income tax exemptions: Social Security and railroad retirement benefits are exempt. Up to $2,000 of private retirement benefits and distributions from IRAs and up to $4,000 of government pen-

sions may be exempt. Total deductions may not exceed $4,000 per person.

Estate tax: Applicable to taxable estates of more than $2 million.

Property tax: $1.21 per $100 of assessed value in the city, $0.83 per $100 in the county. Homes are assessed at 100% of market value. Tax on a $145,000 home would be about $1,755 in the city and $1,204 in the county.

Homestead exemption: Residents 65 and older, with combined incomes of $19,700 or less, are exempt from the first $20,000 or 50% of assessed value, whichever is greater.

Religion: 35 Protestant churches of various denominations, but primarily Baptist, and one Roman Catholic church, St. Anne's.

Education: College of the Albemarle is a public, two-year community college serving the seven-county Albemarle region with locations in Chowan County, Dare County and Elizabeth City, home of Elizabeth City State University, 30 miles from Edenton. East Carolina University in

sunsets from the living room or veranda of the home they built at Edenton Bay in 1995. Dave often travels to Atlanta and the Midwest as a freelance writer and industrial consultant, and he finds easy access from both the Norfolk and Raleigh airports. The couple had lived outside Frederick, MD, but an article dubbing Edenton as the "prettiest small town in America" drew them down U.S. Highway 17 in 1994.

"It was charming," Dave says. "It's a real, working town with a functioning and thriving downtown. At 13 feet above sea level, we're the highest point in our neighborhood of Hardy's Hill." He calls their 2,900-square-foot East Hampton/Cape Cod-style house "our boat on the water."

Despite the convenience of living in town, many retirees find prices lower and life just as enjoyable on the outskirts of town and in rural settings. When Arch and Jane Edwards first moved here in 1980 from a rural area outside Richmond, they found similar country living in an 1800s-era house five miles outside Edenton. Today they own the 18-room Lords Proprietors' Inn, one of seven bed-and-breakfast hostelries in town.

"I was 44 years old when we came here," Arch says, "and I've seen no change in the nature of the population. I was charmed when I first saw it. I had never seen a town as lovely and well-maintained and as prosperous. Attracting and keeping civic-minded people has been a key to Edenton's success."

Instead of tearing them down, Edenton restores and uses older structures. Part of an old brick school was converted into an auditorium for theater performances, while another portion was made into 30 apartments for senior citizens. The Edenton Cotton Mill, founded by locals as a regional marketplace in 1898, formed the nucleus of a village that operated until 1995 when it was donated to Preservation North Carolina, a statewide nonprofit organization that promotes the preservation of heritage sites.

Several homes and empty lots have been sold at low prices to residents or newcomers willing to invest in restoration or construction. A tranquil courthouse green, laid out on the waterfront in 1712, is anchored at the north end by the Chowan County Courthouse, built in 1767 and considered the finest Georgian courthouse in the state. It was recently restored by the Department of the Interior as a national historic landmark.

Life here is almost like being suspended in another time, but with instant access to a modern outside world. Although major shopping malls are miles away, and there are times when a trip is necessary, most products that can't be purchased in town can be ordered by mail or found on the Internet. Larry Blomquist, who telecommutes from his waterfront home, says, "Living is easy here. Even though we do drive a lot to DC to visit our son, I've done entire projects from home without ever leaving."

When Larry Sellers needed a new vehicle, he knew what he wanted. But instead of roaming big-city dealers, he bought the exact model and color he was looking for on eBay and had the car trucked to Edenton from a dealer in Kansas. Edenton may not be a major port of the Americas as it once was in the 1700s, but as Larry's experience proves, goods get here a lot faster. ●

Greenville, NC, is 65 miles away.

Transportation: Four-lane U.S. Highway 64 and Highway 17 connect Edenton with Raleigh-Durham-Chapel Hill. State Highway 32 runs north to Virginia's Hampton Roads area and Norfolk. Closest international airports are Norfolk, VA, and Raleigh-Durham, NC, located 70 and 140 miles from Edenton, respectively.

Health: Chowan Hospital, part of the University Health Systems of Eastern Carolina, provides state-of-the-art services by an academic medical center with 111 beds. Albemarle Hospital, a 182-bed regional medical center, has more than 100 resident physicians representing various medical specialties. Emergency helicopter service is available through Nightingale for specialized treatment in the Hampton Roads area. EastCare Emergency Helicopter is also available from Pitt County Memorial Hospital. Edenton-Chowan County operates three strategically located rescue squad units. There is one nursing home with 160 beds.

Housing options: Homes in Edenton's historic district are frequently for sale and range from $250,000 to $800,000, but there is rarely waterfront property available in town. Waterfront lots are being sold at Phase II of nearby Edenton Bay, where new houses cost $400,000 and up. Waterfront homes outside town on the Chowan River, Albemarle Sound and other waterways, as well as those near Edenton Country Club, also start around $400,000. Home sites a few minutes from downtown but not on the water start at $25,000, and resales in the area are $100,000 and up. Completed homes are available at the Preservation North Carolina-controlled Cotton Mill Village in Edenton for around $300,000. At **E. A. Swain Apartments**, (252) 482-5211, a restored school building in town that shares space with the Arts Council, there are 30 comfortable apartments for seniors. Houses can be rented in town for $1,000 to $1,300 a month. **Britthaven** is Edenton's only long-term care facility, (252) 482-7481.

At **Albemarle Plantation**, (800) 523-5958, a large, waterfront golf course and marina real estate development on Albemarle Sound 17 miles from Edenton off U.S. Highway 17, home sites range from $69,500 to $800,000.

Visitor lodging: There are half a dozen area motels and hotels, including Hampton Inn, (252) 482-3500, and Super 8, (252) 482-2017, both located at Exit 227 off Highway 17, with rooms ranging from $65 to $85, depending on season. More conveniently located in the heart of the historic district are half-a-dozen bed-and-breakfast inns, all in restored houses, including the elegant Lords Proprietors' Inn, $170 per night, (252) 482-3641; Granville Queen, $105-$125, (252) 482-5296; Captain's Quarters, $110, (252) 482-8945; and The Trestle House, $95, (800) 645-8466.

Information: Edenton-Chowan Chamber of Commerce, 116 E. King St., Edenton, NC 27932, (252) 482-3400, (800) 775-0111 or http://chowancounty-nc.gov. See also www.edenton.com.

Eufaula, Alabama

Enjoy life on a lake in this historic, affordable Alabama town

By Jay Clarke

Ask retirees how they selected the town of their dreams and you'll get a variety of reasons. Bill Fleming's answer, however, is one of the best. "There's one Sunday and six Saturdays every week when you live in Eufaula," he says.

Bill and his wife, Abie, moved to Eufaula in 1998 after scouting several other locales. Eufaula, which lies on the high bluffs of the Chattahoochee River, is known for its wealth of antebellum homes and the recreational opportunities offered by dam-created Lake Eufaula.

"We started thinking about a retirement place about five years before I retired in 1996. It had to be on the water, had to be in the South, had to be a small town. We had enough of big towns," says Bill, 62, who moved to Eufaula from Germantown, TN, in 1998. President of a managed health-care administration, he and Abie had lived in Germantown for 15 years.

Before deciding on Eufaula, they looked at Destin, FL, and Hot Springs Village and Hebrew Springs, AR. Eufaula seemed to fit the bill best. It was on water (Lake Eufaula and the Chattahoochee River), it was a small town in the South, and the cost of living was reasonable. "An added value was its antebellum heritage and strong feelings about ancestry. This town really feels very strongly about where they came from," Bill says.

So they bought a lot on the lake. Bill drew the house plans and acted as his own general contractor in its construction. They moved into the house in 1998, but Bill says he's still working on the property. "I built a dock, but I'm working on a boat, a 23-foot classic mahogany runabout," he says. His next project will be a biplane. "We love to do aerobatics and water sports," explains Abie.

Eufaula's small-town ambiance also impressed retirees Hank and Joy Bryan,

who had lived in many cities during his career in upper management of General Electric. Another attraction was the low cost of living. "You get twice as much here for half the price," says Hank, 77. He estimates that living costs in Eufaula are 30 to 40 percent less than in Atlanta, where he spent some of his last active years at GE before retirement.

Like the Flemings, the Bryans looked at several prospective retirement sites, among them San Antonio, TX; Hot Springs, AR; and Naples, FL. "We both wanted to live on the water," Hank says of Naples, "but my wife didn't want to be on the Gulf." In Eufaula, they found a house under construction on the lake. "It was 90 percent completed, so we bought it and finished it off," he says.

That was back in 1984. In the years since, the Bryans have taken integral roles in the town. "We founded the Humane Society here, and I built the animal shelter. I'm on the board of the church and county chairman of the Republican Committee of Barbour County. My wife was the first and only woman ever to serve on the city council. She's now on the city's parks and recreation board, the vestry of the church and is a director of the Humane Society."

The Bryans lived on the lake for 12 years, moved to a smaller house closer to town and then back into a larger house on the country club golf course "because we found we couldn't accommodate all our children and grandchildren when they came to visit," Hank says. Joy, 65, is an excellent golfer and tests her skills on the course behind their house. Hank, meanwhile, breeds show dogs as a sideline.

Hank admits that moving to Eufaula has taken some adjustment. The town doesn't have the dining and medical facilities of the larger cities where the couple had lived, he says, nor the cultural resources. "And I wish we had a movie house," he adds. "But there's so

much else in our sense of values that compensates for that."

High among these is Eufaula's remarkable cache of 19th-century structures, many of which were built before the Civil War. While many buildings in the South were razed by Union troops, notably during Gen. William T. Sherman's notorious "march to the sea," Eufaula escaped destruction when the war ended just as the Union troops under Gen. Benjamin H. Grierson were advancing on the town.

Today more than 700 structures in Eufaula are listed on the National Register of Historic Places. Most renowned is the 17-columned Shorter Mansion, built in 1884 and an outstanding example of Neoclassical Revival architecture. Since 1965 it has been the headquarters of the Eufaula Heritage Association, which sponsors the town's biggest event, the annual Eufaula Pilgrimage. Alabama's oldest tour of homes, it takes place in April when the azaleas and dogwood trees are in full bloom, providing a colorful backdrop for the stately homes on view.

Another notable Greek Revival home is the 1854 Couric-Smith house, the homestead of Charles M. Couric, great-grandfather of NBC Today Show anchor Katie Couric. The home and the city received national attention in 1999 when Couric traced her family's roots to Eufaula.

Fendall Hall, an 1860s-era Italianate home, contains three rooms with fine Victorian-era murals painted by a French artist. Owned by the Alabama Historical Commission, it is open to the public the year around. Also built in Italianate style in the same era is Kendall Manor, whose interior has Waterford chandeliers, hand-stenciled walls and a carved walnut staircase. It is now an elegant bed-and-breakfast inn.

The 1850 Dean-Page Hall is topped with a belvedere, built so a servant could keep a lookout for river steamboats.

Eufaula's oldest frame building is the 1836 Tavern, which served as an inn and a Confederate hospital before becoming a private residence.

This plethora of historic structures is what attracted Dr. Calvin Wingo and his wife, Pat, to Eufaula when they retired from their university teaching positions in northern Alabama. "We have an interest in old houses and have done some renovations," says Pat, 60. "So we bought an old house and are constantly working on it — a labor of love." The Italianate-style home they purchased here was started in the late 1850s, but the Civil War interrupted its construction and it was not completed until after hostilities ceased.

But old homes are not the only reason the Wingos came to Eufaula. "The people are so delightful, so warm and receptive," Pat says. "It's just a grand place to live." The Wingos also participate in community groups like Eufaula Pride, whose members pick up litter and clean abandoned lots, and are active in their church and the home preservation movement.

Eufaula fulfills their desires in another way as well. It's a small town close to larger cities that have better facilities for medical care, shopping and travel. Columbus, GA, and Dothan, AL, each are less than an hour away, and the Gulf beaches are only three hours by car, Pat notes.

"We have a hospital in town that is certainly adequate, and we have some fine doctors," she says. "But we would go to Birmingham for major medical needs."

And though big cities have much wider choices in dining, Pat says Eufaula has some interesting restaurants that are not part of chains, like Cajun Corner and Old Mexico, "and we have caterers who do fancy meals. Those of us who live here all the time enjoy the local restaurants." Eufaula has 35 restaurants, about half of which are fast-food outlets.

Her husband, Calvin, 61, likes to fish, and Lake Eufaula is one of the best places in the South, if not the country, to dip a line. Considered by many to be the

Eufaula, AL

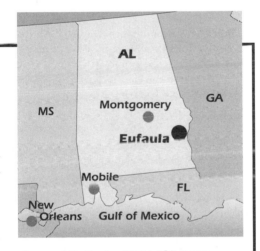

Population: 13,908. Some 2,262 of the city's residents are age 62 or older.
Location: Eufaula lies in southeastern Alabama on the banks of the Chattahoochee River, which forms the border between Alabama and Georgia. It is 50 miles from both Dothan, AL, and Columbus, GA, 88 miles from Montgomery, AL and 168 miles from Atlanta, GA.
Climate: High Low
January 58 37
July 91 71
Average relative humidity: 72%
Annual rainfall: 68 inches
Cost of living: Below average
Average housing cost: Approximate cost of a new 1,800-square-foot home is $135,000. A 5- to 10-year-old, 1,800-square-foot home costs about $100,000.
Sales tax: 8%
Sales tax exemptions: Prescription drugs
State income tax: For married couples filing jointly, graduated from 2% of taxable income up to $1,000 to 5% on amounts over $6,000. For single filers, graduated from 2% of taxable income up to $500 to 5% on amounts over $3,000.
Income tax exemptions: Social Security benefits and most private and government retirement pensions are exempt.
Estate tax: None. Alabama's federal estate tax credit was phased out as of Jan. 1, 2005.
Inheritance tax: None

Property tax: Eufaula has an ad valorem tax rate of 44 mills, or .044, with homes assessed at 10 percent of market value. The tax on a $135,000 house, without the homestead exemption, is $594.
Homestead exemptions: Those over 65 are exempt from the state portion of the tax with a county tax exemption of up to $2,000 (up to $5,000 for those with incomes less than $12,000), and those with incomes of less than $7,500 receive a total exemption from property taxes.
Religion: More than 50 churches serve Eufaula residents, the majority of them Baptist.
Education: Vocational subjects are taught at Wallace Community College, (800) 543-2426 or www.wallace.edu.
Transportation: Nearest commercial airports are in Dothan, AL, and Columbus, GA, each 50 miles from Eufaula. Dannelly Field in Montgomery, AL, is 88 miles away. Hartsfield-Jackson International in Atlanta is 164 miles.
Health: Lakeview Community Hospital has 74 beds and a 24-hour emergency department. It also offers home health and senior circle programs.
Housing options: There are no planned developments for seniors. The home sites most popular among retirees are along the lake and in historic homes. Assisted-living residences include **River Oaks East**, (334) 687-3089; **River Oaks West**, (334) 687-6089; and the **Gar-**

dens of Eufaula, (334) 687-0430.
Visitor lodging: The Eufaula area has 11 hotels and motels, including such chains as Best Western, Comfort Suites, Days Inn and Econo Lodge, as well as 101 rooms and 29 cabins in Lakepoint Resort State Park. Sample minimum rates (plus taxes but less such discounts as those offered through AAA and AARP) are: America's Best Value Inn, $55, (334) 687-2021; Best Western Eufaula Inn, $45-$49, (334) 687-3900; Jameson Inn, $68, (334) 687-7747; and Lakepoint Resort State Park, $49-$59 for rooms or $90-$175 for cabins, (800) 544-5253.
Information: Eufaula/Barbour County Chamber of Commerce and Tourism Council, 102 N. Orange Ave., P.O. Box 697, Eufaula, AL 36072, (800) 524-7529, (334) 687-6664 or www.eufaula-barbourchamber.com. For more information on retiring to Alabama, contact Alabama Advantage, (800)235-4757or www.alabamaadvantage.com.

"Bass Capital of the World," Lake Eufaula is a year-round fishery. In the past two years, the 85-mile-long lake has experienced an explosion in its number of bass, according to Tom Mann, one of America's most renowned fishermen and the owner of Mann's Fish World in Eufaula. "It's the best fishing in 10 years," he says.

Mann, also famed for the fishing lures he has designed, displays freshwater fish native to the area in a 38,000-gallon tank and in 10 smaller ones at his attraction. He also has built what is possibly the only memorial anywhere to a fish. It's a $4,000 marble monument that commemorates Leroy Brown, a legendary bass that Mann trained to jump through a hoop and whose funeral was attended by 700 people.

Lake Eufaula also was the lure for Johnny Tweddle, 66, a pilot for a major airline who retired here in 1995. "I had old military friends who had a place on the lake," he says. "So I had bought a home on the lake in 1982 and leased it out."

In 1992 he regained the home and started commuting back and forth to his main residence in Fairfax, VA. When retirement neared, he and his wife, Carolyn, considered moving to Florida. "But we like rolling hills and the four seasons. And I like living on the lake," he says. So they settled in Eufaula.

Like many other retirees here, the Tweddles like being busy. Johnny sings in a choral group that gives benefit concerts at Christmas and in spring to help finance scholarships for music majors. Carolyn, 65, belongs to a garden club and sings in the church choir. "We stay busy all the time," he says.

Especially attractive to retirees here is the Eufaula Community Center, which has a swimming pool, sauna, two racquetball courts, a fitness room, three meeting rooms, a community room with a two-level walking and running track, an activity room, concession area and child-care playroom. Annual membership is $150 for a single senior, $200 for senior couples. The daily charge for nonmembers is $4, and a 15-visit coupon book can be had for $30.

The region also is popular with bird-watchers and nature lovers who converge on the Eufaula National Wildlife Refuge on the eastern edge of the Mississippi Flyway. Covering 11,184 acres on both sides of the Chattahoochee River, the refuge is a habitat for such endangered species as the bald eagle, wood stork and peregrine falcon.

Johnny and Carolyn do miss some of the options available to them in their former Virginia home. "There's a definite limitation here. We miss the Kennedy Center (in Washington), the plays, the concerts," he says. "We do try to do the bulk of our shopping here, but occasionally we go to Columbus (GA) or Dothan (AL)."

Aside from taxes and real estate, which he says run considerably less, Johnny says the cost of living in Eufaula is "pretty much on a par" with Fairfax. In comparison with other parts of the country, Eufaula boasts lower living costs overall.

"People aren't afraid to speak out, as they are in some other towns," Johnny Tweddle says. "It's a nice small town, very friendly." ●

Fairhope, Alabama

Retirees find friendly neighbors and affordable living in this bayfront Alabama town

By William Schemmel

Stan Grubin doesn't really need anybody to tell him how fortunate he is to be retired in Fairhope. But he loves to hear it, all the same.

"My brother-in-law is a judge who lives in one of the nicest areas of Denver," Stan says. "When he and my sister come down to visit us, he always says, 'You people are getting away with something. This place is too nice.' He can't believe how clean and pretty our town is and how friendly people are."

Stan, 71, and his companion, Joyce, 61, relocated to the Mobile Bay city of 14,106 from Mission Viejo, CA, in 1997.

"Joyce was born in Pascagoula (MS) and grew up in Pensacola (FL), so we'd been coming to the Alabama Gulf Coast for several years," Stan says. "Every time we came, we'd look for a place to retire. We finally hit Fairhope, and it was so pretty. There were flowers everywhere, nice shops and restaurants, and beautiful, well-kept residential neighborhoods. And the people were so friendly and welcoming. It reminded us of Monterey and Carmel in California."

It's no coincidence that Fairhope seems like utopia to Stan Grubin and other retirees. In 1894, Midwestern followers of economist George Henry's single-tax theory chose the site on Mobile Bay for an experimental colony. They named it Fairhope, in the "fair hope" it would succeed — and it did.

Under the single-tax theory, land was owned by a corporation and leased to individuals for the good of the community. Those who used the land paid rent to the corporation, which enabled the corporation to combine property taxes, city taxes and sales taxes into a single tax on the land. Lasting legacies of the colony include the bayfront municipal pier and park, which was donated to the town in the 1930s. The municipality was established in 1908.

The city's progressive climate has attracted many writers, craftspeople and artists who lend their talents to the annu-al Fairhope Arts and Crafts Festival and other cultural activities. Alabama native Fannie Flagg wrote her best-selling novel, "Fried Green Tomatoes at the Whistle Stop Cafe," while living in Fairhope.

One of the first Alabama communities with a horticulturalist on the municipal payroll, Fairhope has an attractive downtown with wide streets and brick-edged sidewalks lined with art galleries, boutiques and good restaurants. Flower baskets adorn streetlights and utility poles, and every year more than 200 new trees are planted on city streets and in parks.

Large single-family homes, many with cedar shake roofs and lovely gardens, patios and swimming pools, fill residential neighborhoods. Spacious lots, many with waterfront views, are beautified by live oak trees, Spanish moss and lush stands of azaleas, camellias and other flowering plants. Planned communities such as Rock Creek, Quail Creek and Fairfield Place have a variety of housing styles with easy access to golf, tennis and social activities. Rental apartments and condos also are available. Homestead Village and the Hamlet at Carroll Place have independent and assisted-living apartments and cottages.

Retirees like Stan Grubin were attracted by the low cost of living in Fairhope. "Our home is a 2,000-square-foot patio house, called a villa, in Quail Creek," Stan says. "It's on the 18th fairway of the municipal golf course. We've done a lot of improvements, including a screened back porch, which Joyce just loves. We can sit out there and it's like looking at a movie set. Compared to where we lived in California, where we could hear the hum of a freeway day and night, it's so quiet that we can hear the crickets."

Stan and Joyce are enthusiastically involved in their adopted hometown. Stan, who worked in management for churches in California before his retirement, plays golf two or three times a week. He volunteers for the mayor's Christmas Parade, coordinates a weekly seniors golf tournament and helps his neighbors set up computers. Joyce is part of a tai chi aerobics group, volunteers at a hospital wellness center and spends much of her free time in her garden.

True to its Midwestern roots, Fairhope continues to attract many retirees from Iowa, Michigan, Wisconsin, Indiana and other Midwestern states. Almost 25 percent of the population is 65 or older. Gary and Jean Wilson made the move from Wisconsin in January 1999.

"If you can't find something to do in Fairhope, you simply aren't looking," says Jean, who left a law partnership in Baraboo, WI, to move to Fairhope, "The James P Nix Center has something going on all the time."

A club for seniors, the Nix Center's weekly calendar includes video exercises, billiards and table tennis, board games, golf and tennis tournaments, tai chi exercises, health screenings, nutritional lectures, arts and crafts, line dancing, financial advice, grief support, travel talks and many other programs.

Retirees are invited to volunteer at the Nix Center, local hospitals and annual festivals like the Christmas Parade as well as a huge arts and crafts festival in spring. Volunteers staff the Eastern Shore Art Center, a 12,000-square-foot privately supported gallery that displays works by local, regional and national artists and sponsors concert, film and lecture series and art education classes.

In whatever free time remains, Fairhope residents can enjoy the single-tax colony's best-loved legacy, the beautiful bayfront park with a municipal pier extended by a quarter mile into Mobile Bay. Around the pier are duck ponds and seasonal plantings by the town's accomplished gardeners. Fairhope's 2.5 miles of beach are the stage for boating and fishing tournaments and the yearly Jubilee. One of Fairhope's most eagerly anticipated happenings, Jubilee is a natural late summer phenomenon when bottom-dwelling fish, shrimp, crabs and other sea creatures, delirious from a sudden lack of oxygen in the water, rush en masse to shore. Waiting are hundreds of seafood lovers, armed with every bucket, scoop, net and cooking pot they can get their hands on.

Fairhope protects its beauty and enviable character with some of Alabama's most stringent zoning laws. And it has won national recognition for its dedication to preserving trees in its parks and along streets, both in commercial and residential areas, every year since the National Arbor Day Foundation created its Tree City USA award in 1983.

Alabama and Florida Gulf Coast beaches are about 40 minutes by car from Fairhope. Gulf Shores and Orange Beach, on the Alabama Gulf, are vaca-

Fairhope, AL

Population: 14,106 in Fairhope, 18,115 in Daphne, 5,611 in Spanish Fort, 1,876 in Point Clear and 156,701 in Baldwin County.

Location: On the eastern shore of Alabama's Mobile Bay, a half-hour by car from Mobile, 45 minutes from the Gulf of Mexico beaches and Pensacola, FL.

Climate: High Low
January 62 42
July 91 72

Average relative humidity: 73%

Rain: 67 inches

Subtropical climate with mild winters, balmy springs and delightful autumns. Summers are long, hot and muggy with frequent thunderstorms. Occasional hurricane threats in September and October.

Average housing cost: $184,000 for Fairhope, $193,000 for Spanish Fort and $157,000 for Daphne.

Cost of living: Below average

Sales tax: 6% (2% county, 4% state)

Sales tax exemptions: Prescription drugs.

State income tax: For married couples filing jointly, graduated from 2% of taxable income up to $1,000 to 5% on amounts over $6,000. For single filers, graduated from 2% of taxable income up to $500 to 5% on amounts over $3,000.

Income tax exemptions: Social Security benefits and most private and government retirement pensions are exempt.

Intangibles tax: None

Inheritance tax: None

Estate tax: None

Property tax: $43 per $1,000 of assessed value, with homes assessed at 10% of market value. Taxes on a $190,000 home are $817 per year, not including homestead exemption.

Homestead exemption: Homeowners under age 65 are entitled to a $4,000 homestead exemption. Homeowners 65 and older who have an annual adjusted gross income of less than $12,000, and those homeowners retired due to disability, are entitled to an exemption up to $5,000 of assessed value.

Religion: More than 100 churches and synagogues represent all major faiths.

Health: Thomas Hospital in Fairhope is a 150-bed facility that offers acute care with a 24-hour emergency department, surgery and nuclear medical expertise. Mercy Medical, a Sisters of Mercy facility in Daphne, has a rehabilitation center, subacute care, long-term and Alzheimer's care, hospice and home health services. Baldwin County Mental Health provides a 24-hour crisis line, rape crisis center, family and group counseling, and alcohol and drug abuse treatment. There are five nursing homes and seven assisted-living facilities in the area. Helicopters can transfer patients to hospitals in Mobile and Pensacola.

Transportation: There is no regularly scheduled public transportation system. The Baldwin Rural Area Transport System (BRATS) transports the handicapped and indigent to doctors, shopping centers and other areas. The state-operated Mobile Bay Ferry connects Dauphin Island and Gulf Shores. Mobile and Pensacola airports are an hour away.

Education: Continuing-education courses in business, education and liberal arts are offered at the University of South Alabama at Baldwin County, an accredited branch of the main campus in Mobile.

Most courses meet once a week at the Fairhope campus downtown. The Eastern Shore Art Center and Bay Rivers Art Guild offer continuing-education courses in painting, pottery, photography and other media.

Housing options: Quail Creek and Rock Creek, planned communities in Fairhope, have 1,800- to 2,000-square-foot patio homes as well as larger homes of 2,400 to 3,000 square feet. Quail Creek homes start at about $225,000, and Rock Creek homes start at $350,000. Built around the 18-hole Fairhope Municipal Golf Course, Quail Creek has its own tennis courts, pool and clubhouse. **Rock Creek**, (251) 928-2223, has a semiprivate 18-hole course, tennis, pool and clubhouse. **Fairfield Place**, (800) 625-8330, is a new subdivision five minutes from downtown with homes from the $200,000s. **Arbor Gates**, (251) 928-2002, is an upscale one- to three-bedroom apartment development with monthly rental from $565 to $840. **The Hamlet at Carroll Place**, (251) 928-5413, and **Homestead Village**, (251) 929-0250, have independent and assisted-living cottages and apartments.

Visitor lodging: Fairhope Inn and Restaurant, a bed-and-breakfast inn in the center of town, has three guest rooms and a carriage house with private baths, $120-$170 including full breakfast, (251) 928-6226. Marriott's Grand Hotel, a resort on Mobile Bay, has seasonal rates of $179-$319, (800) 544-9933. Gulf State Park, on the beach at Gulf Shores, has seasonal rates of $84-$139 for furnished cabins and $19-$23 for camping; call (251) 948-7275.

Information: Eastern Shore Chamber of Commerce, 327 Fairhope Ave., Fairhope, AL 36532, (251) 621-8222 or www.eschamber.com. City of Fairhope, (251) 928-2136 or www.cofairhope.com.

tion destinations with hotels, condos, seafood restaurants and championship-caliber golf courses. Urban attractions also are within easy reach. Mobile, Alabama's second-largest city, is about a half-hour across Mobile Bay. Pensacola and Florida's Gulf Coast are about 45 minutes away.

Baldwin County, which includes Fairhope, is Alabama's largest in area and the fastest-growing in population. The South Alabama Regional Planning Commission projects that the county's current population of 156,701 will increase by 20 to 30 percent during the next 10 years.

Other Baldwin County communities include Point Clear, a resort and residential community of 1,876 residents on Mobile Bay. An attraction there is Marriott's Grand Hotel, a resort with golf, tennis and boating facilities. Nearby communities also include the 19th-century resort town of Daphne, population 18,115; Bay Minette, the county seat with about 7,820 residents; and Spanish Fort, population 5,611.

The Gulf Coast was Jean and Gary Wilson's introduction to Fairhope. "It wasn't a major decision for us," Jean recalls. "We had a condo at Gulf Shores and had been coming down here for several years. My husband is originally from Birmingham, and when he retired from Rayovac in Madison (WI), we decided to move down here full time."

The Wilsons purchased a 2,400-square-foot home in Quail Creek. "I'm in my 40s and my husband is in his 50s, so we say we're only partly retired," Jean says. "I was appointed by the mayor to the zoning and planning committee and the Fairhope First Civic Association, which plans various events. We play a lot of golf and my husband works part time at the golf pro shop."

The Wilsons say the cost of living is one of Fairhope's many tangible pluses. "You can really stretch your money here," Jean says. "Home prices may be a little high by Alabama standards, but you can get a lot more house for the money here than in Wisconsin. And taxes and utilities are much lower. I'd recommend it to retirees or anyone else looking for a less-stressful place to live. Other than the summer heat and humidity, I can't think of any real drawbacks to living here."

Helen and Bob Rudy, who moved from Michigan in 1997, second that endorsement. "We didn't look at any other areas. When we saw Fairhope, it was a gut feeling. I guess you could call it love at first sight," Helen says. "It's such a beautiful area, and the people are so friendly."

The Rudys, both in their 70s, moved into a custom-built, 1,800-square-foot villa in the Quail Creek community, where they found a social network ready to make them feel at home. "My husband plays golf several times a week. He belongs to Kiwanis and volunteers for local events," Helen says. "We get together with friends for lunch and dinner, we play bridge and tennis and enjoy the pool and the art galleries and activities in town. If you can't find enough to do, it's your own fault.

"Taxes and utilities are definitely less expensive," she adds. "Here we get one utility bill. In Michigan we'd get three or four."

Barbara Lawson began visiting the Alabama Gulf Coast in the 1950s, but when she retired from teaching in Columbia, TN, 11 years ago, she looked all over south Florida before coming back to the Alabama coast and settling in Fairhope.

"I love golf and the Gulf, and they drew me back here," Barbara says. "I can't say that I've really retired. If you're able-bodied, they won't let you do that. They want to put your expertise to work. I've worked for the chamber of commerce for a while, then the mayor got me involved with all kinds of activities."

Barbara now is a senior specialist for ERA Suncoast Real Estate. "The city is growing, but we're not losing the small-town charm and quality of life that makes this such a wonderful place to live," she says. "I can help people find what they're looking for — and be as happy here as I am." ●

Ferndale, California

This small California farming community captivates with Victorian spirit

By Mary Lu Abbott

North of San Francisco, beyond the hills and vineyards of Napa, Sonoma and Mendocino, the traffic thins on U.S. Highway 101 and the stress gives way to a much slower-paced California. It is a land defined by mountains, rivers, redwoods and ocean, rather than the steel, glass, freeways and frenzy of cities.

The inland highway snakes into a forest of redwoods so tall and thick that only slivers of light penetrate. The trees seem to hug you, then allow you to pass into their protected kingdom where, even today, the Pacific coastline is so rugged and wild that there is no through road or development along the water for almost 100 miles. It is a pristine coast, rocky and often cloaked in fog, much the same as when spotted by explorers of the 1500s.

The farthest west point of the mainland, it's known as the Lost Coast. Here, retirees have found a haven in a small Victorian town called Ferndale about five miles inland. It's a wonder the town wasn't lost after U.S. Highway 101 and the railroad bypassed it to the east as they pushed through to Eureka. The transportation and commercial hub of the late 1800s and early 1900s, Ferndale watched development move about 17 miles north to Eureka, which had a deep-water port. Perhaps it was best, though, for Ferndale retains a rural small-town lifestyle where retirees find an embracing warmth that cities often lack today.

Peggy and Mike Bailey celebrated their 40th wedding anniversary when they moved here in 2000. "We said it was like wandering 40 years in the wilderness and coming into the promised land here. It is a super little town," Peggy says.

Disney can't match Ferndale for setting, looks and personality. It's about five miles off U.S. Highway 101, at the end of a pastoral valley with a checkerboard landscape of dairy farms, where egrets roam with Holsteins, Jerseys and Guernseys. Farmers still fuel the economy here, taking their milk to the local co-op, Humboldt Creamery, and coming to Ferndale to shop, visit, eat and partake in the full calendar of parades, concerts, plays and other entertainment.

The highway becomes Main Street, and it's a good bet that no one drives into town without using the terms "cute" and "charming" about the colorful Victorian buildings in mint green with chocolate trim, robin's egg blue, warm orange and golden yellow, burgundy and beige. Main Street is on the National Register of Historic Places, and the entire town is California Historic Landmark No. 883. But its beauty extends beyond the facades.

The Baileys were a bit skeptical before they came on the recommendation of their daughter. They'd had previous experiences of people extolling a town, only to find it "a tiny piece of junk in the middle of no place," says Peggy, 64. Not so with Ferndale — they were sold on it for retirement in one day.

"It wasn't just the appearance of the town," says Mike, also 64. "You can have a really pretty town and a bunch of cold people, and you feel you couldn't adjust to it. This town, everybody on the street smiled at you and said hello. They took time to explain things to you. It's a very cordial town, and that wasn't something we were used to."

They lived in Fremont in the San Francisco Bay Area, a large metropolitan area where the Baileys rarely encountered anyone they knew when they went out. Both Peggy and Mike were from Southern California, though Mike's 20-year career in the Navy had taken them all over the country. After retiring from the military in missile technology, Mike worked with Lockheed in the Bay Area for 20 years. About seven years before retiring, they began looking for a retirement town, searching the West from New Mexico to Oregon and all over California.

They found most places either too hot, too far from their children or too isolated. Peggy really wanted to be near the coast. They had nearly settled on Fort Bragg, farther south on the coast, but they were concerned because it was at least 35 miles over the mountains to a larger town for shopping and hospitals. They were taking vacation to give it one more look when they decided to tack on a few days to visit Ferndale in 1998 — and immediately started making plans to retire here.

For Dan and Martha Tubbs, Ferndale fulfilled their retirement dreams. They lived in Laguna Hills, in Orange County in Southern California. Martha taught elementary school for 38 years and was divorced and a single parent for many years. Dan was in the printing and graphic design business for 38 years.

One day in 1993, the two briefly met in a grocery store, and at the insistence of her daughter, Martha gave Dan her name on a coupon. He called her, explained he was going through a difficult time with his marriage and said if it didn't work out, he would "search to the ends of the earth to find you." When his marriage broke up, he retrieved the coupon with her name on it and called her. It turned out they lived in the same condo complex. They married in 1997.

"We shared a dream about retirement, and I think it's what drew us together," says Martha, 63. She wanted to buy and restore a Victorian home. He had that in mind, too, and wanted a rural area. "I wanted a quieter, more laid-back place to live, someplace that was a natural beauty," says Dan, 62. An amateur photographer and writer, he wanted to nurture both hobbies.

They looked at rural areas of Southern California, up into the Gold Country, north and west of San Francisco and along the Mendocino coast. Everywhere seemed to be growing so quickly that they feared it would become as crowded as where they lived. Then Dan recalled that in 1975, he had been to Eureka on business and visited Ferndale. "I saw this beautiful valley, and the sign said, 'To Ferndale.' It looked like time had stood still. I talked to some people and thought, 'Golly, I'd sure like to live here some day,'" he recalls.

So they came to see Ferndale — and discovered it hadn't changed much, save for normal freshening of paint.

"I fell in love with it. It's such a beautiful area and matched so closely with what we were looking for. There was a college (nearby) and the people were so friendly," Martha says. "We were able to find the perfect Victorian home here and belong to a restoration group and do some gardening." All had been part of her dream.

But she was hesitant about being farther away from family, and they visited the town several times between 1996 and 2000. They decided on Ferndale as they saw the price of housing start to increase. They told their real estate agent in late 2000 that they wanted to buy and got a call in May 2001 about a four-bedroom 1899 Victorian home for sale.

"I could just tell it was going to be our home. It had wonderful old woodwork and moldings. I used to go visit my grandmother in Los Angeles in a house almost like this," Martha says. Their

Ferndale, CA

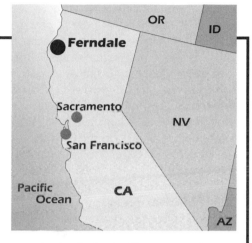

Population: About 1,400 in Ferndale. About 11,000 in nearby Fortuna and 26,100 in Eureka, the seat of Humboldt County, with about 128,000 residents.

Location: On the Redwood Coast, about 265 miles north of San Francisco and 125 miles south of the Oregon border. Ferndale is about five miles from U.S. Highway 101, seven miles from Fortuna and 17 miles south of Eureka, a seaport on Humboldt Bay. Ferndale is about five miles inland.

Climate:

	High	Low
January	57	40
July	70	52

The opposite of sunny Southern California, Ferndale has a mild, cool climate with an average temperature only in the 50s. About half the days each month are cloudy; sunniest periods are April-July. Winters are rainy, summers often foggy.

Average relative humidity: 77%

Rain: 36-40 inches a year

Snow: Rare

Cost of living: Average to above average (low for California)

Median housing cost: About $444,250 in Ferndale; the median in the mid-county area, including Ferndale, Fortuna and several smaller towns, is $305,000. Housing availability in Ferndale is limited.

Sales tax: 7.25%

Sales tax exemptions: Groceries, prescription drugs and most services.

State income tax: For married couples filing jointly, the rates range from 1% on the first $12,638 to 9.3% (plus $3,652) on amounts above $82,952. For single filers, rates run from 1% on the first $6,319 to 9.3% (plus $1,826) on amounts above $41,476.

Income tax exemptions: Social Security and railroad retirement benefits are exempt.

Estate tax: None. The state's "pick-up" portion of federal tax was eliminated Jan. 1, 2005.

Property tax: The base tax is 1% of the market value, which is the price you pay for the home with the value increased 2% percent or less each year thereafter. Local assessments are added, and Ferndale has additions for school bonds, sewer and fire department. Tax on a $444,250 home would be about $4,837 without exemption, $4,766 with exemption.

Homestead exemption: There is a homeowner's exemption of $7,000 off the value of owner-occupied homes. The state's homeowner assistance program reimburses up to $473 to those who are 62 or older, blind or disabled, with incomes under $39,699.

Religion: Ferndale has about a half dozen churches, most built before 1900. Other worship centers are in Fortuna and Eureka.

Education: The two-year College of the Redwoods is between Eureka and Fortuna. The four-year Humboldt State University in Arcata, five miles north of Eureka, has Elderhostel programs and continuing-education classes.

Transportation: Eureka-Humboldt Transit Authority runs buses along U.S. Highway 101 with stops in Fortuna and Fernbridge, about four miles from Ferndale.

Health: The nearest hospital is about eight miles away in Fortuna, and Eureka has larger medical facilities. Ferndale has doctors' services, and the fire department's trained paramedics have quick response times.

Housing options: Choices range from historic homes to new construction but supply is limited. The town is not expanding, but occasionally some parcels of land open for development of new, small neighborhoods. There are no large planned developments in the area. Note: Leave your name with a real estate agent to call when something goes on sale.

Visitor lodging: The town has several historic lodgings. Among them: Gingerbread Mansion Inn, an 1899 Queen Anne-Eastlake design, 11 rooms from $160, (800) 952-4136. Collingwood Inn, an 1885 Italianate, four rooms from $120, (800) 469-1632. Shaw House Inn, oldest house in town, from the 1850s, eight rooms, $115-$275, (800) 557-7429. The Victorian Inn is an 1890s hotel with a restaurant and period rooms for $95-$225, (888) 589-1808. All these lodgings include breakfast. There is other lodging in Ferndale and Fortuna and a bigger variety in Eureka.

Information: Ferndale Chamber of Commerce, P.O. Box 325, Ferndale, CA 95536, (707) 786-4477 or www.victorianferndale.org/chamber. Humboldt County Convention and Visitors Bureau, 1034 Second St., Eureka, CA 95501, (800) 346-3482 or www.redwoodvisitor.org.

condo sold the day the Victorian home went on the market. They both retired on June 15, 2001, moved in July, then started renovations.

Dan and Martha have painted their gingerbread Queen Anne home two shades of sage green with trims in creamy beige and dark chocolate. It has original stained-glass windows, some of them solid red, considered the most expensive of the period. On the small lot, Martha found room for a "wonderful cottage garden with herbs and a rose garden." Dan counts the Carnegie Library across the street as an extra asset.

It was a Victorian beauty that Ken Torbert fell for, also. A financial analyst in San Francisco, he had been visiting small towns all over California and enjoyed staying in bed-and-breakfast inns, particularly in the country. In the early 1980s, he came for a weekend in Ferndale.

"I thought, 'Boy, this would be a beautiful place to retire," he recalls. "I was thinking it'd be a nice town to have an inn, and I turned the corner and saw the Gingerbread Mansion with a 'For Sale' sign on it. I made an offer the next day and it was accepted. To me, it was the idyllic town to live in."

Talking to merchants and residents as he walked on Main Street, he was impressed that each person was excited about the town, showing more enthusiasm and commitment than he had encountered anywhere else.

Ken worked on the home on weekends and in the mid-1980s retired from his corporate job — before he was 40 — and moved to Ferndale to start a second career as innkeeper. "If it hadn't been for my passion for the town, I wouldn't have done it," he says. He helped put Ferndale on the national map with his Gingerbread Mansion Inn, vividly painted and set amid tall palm trees and gardens with topiaries. It was frequently photographed, and with hospitality that included great breakfasts, it was the first inn in California to earn a four-diamond rating by AAA.

Ferndale and the Gingerbread Mansion Inn linked Ken to his wife, Sharon. She was living in Southern California when she saw a newspaper article about the town and came to visit in the mid-1980s.

"Everyone seemed to have beautiful gardens, and there were so many unique stores on Main Street that I said, 'I need to live here,'" she recalls. An assistant manager at The Ritz-Carlton, Laguna Niguel, she had been thinking of relocating to a part of the state less harried than Southern California. She didn't find property she wanted in Ferndale but bought a Victorian home in nearby Eureka. It was owned by the couple who founded Restoration Hardware, the company created out of frustration after trying to find items to restore their house. Sharon opened the home as a B&B and, on her time off, often visited Ferndale.

Married to different people in the 1980s, Ken and Sharon went through divorces at different times in the 1990s. As members of innkeeper associations, their paths had crossed and they began dating in the mid-1990s, marrying in 1998. She sold her inn, moved to Ferndale and became director of the conference center at Humboldt State University in Arcata, a few miles north of Eureka. She retired in 2001, and Ken sold the inn and retired in 2002. For them, there was no better place to retire than Ferndale.

Beyond its eye-catching appeal, Sharon was drawn by Ferndale's visual and performing arts, including a repertory theater and art galleries, "and how everyone embraces the arts." Schoolchildren's artwork is displayed by businesses on Main Street. Ethnic festivities celebrate the area's Scandinavian, Swiss-Italian and Portuguese heritage. The restored 1920s theater schedules a full calendar of live productions, including plays by local teenagers.

"It's a great theater for such a small town," says Mike Bailey. "In the Bay Area, we went to the theater and never saw anything as good as Ferndale."

Peggy Bailey praises the community choir, which she joined, and Martha Tubbs says the choir's performances at Christmas and Easter "are phenomenal, some of the best music you will ever hear." Martha takes watercolor classes at Valley Arts, a studio and shop on Main Street.

Ferndale is small — only one mile in any direction from the center of town, and beyond that is farmland. About 1,400 people live in town, about 3,000 across the valley. There are no stoplights, and Main Street has no stop signs, though cross streets do. Historic buildings stretch along nearly six blocks of Main Street, and many of the businesses have catered to the needs of the community for years. Among them are a pharmacy and a meat shop, both in business for more than 100 years. The town was the setting for the 2001 movie, "The Majestic" with Jim Carrey, though special facades were built and other sites changed to give it a 1950s look.

Sharon ticks off a variety of stores. "My favorite is the Golden Gait Mercantile. It has everything imaginable — soaps, clothing, cooking utensils, everything from candies to buttons, anything you would find at the turn of the century — and a museum upstairs about life then. We have the best hardware store (Nilsen Co.) you can find. It looks like a small space but they pack so much into it — cat food, appliances, gardening tools." The hardware store dates to 1896 and advertises everything from feed and seed to a bridal registry. The mercantile opened about 30 years ago in an 1893 building.

Hospitals are in nearby Fortuna and Eureka. The couples say they've been pleased with the medical care and the quick response by the Ferndale paramedics.

Settlers came into the area in the 1850s during California's gold rush, and Humboldt County became a major agricultural center. Many of the redwoods were lost to logging. Ferndale attracted a large number of Danes, who found the surrounding Eel River Valley grasses perfect for dairy cattle.

"Before I moved here, history was only in the history books, but here I've talked to people who were raised by grandparents who had come on the Oregon Trail. There is so much oral history here," says Ken, 57. "The families stayed and intermarried. The richness of the community and the traditions are all intact and ongoing. The Humboldt County Fair, an old-fashioned fair, is really like going back in time, like you might imagine a middle-America small town might have been in the early 1900s. The town has people of all ages, and you see families together at fairs and festivals. In the neighborhood where I first lived, there were, within a couple of blocks, brothers and sisters living next door to each other, or fathers and sons, and around the corner a cousin."

The town has a fun, whimsical side. An annual Kinetic Sculpture Race from Arcata to Ferndale draws crowds to watch people-powered crazy contraptions navigate through sand, water and the streets. As a fundraiser for the theater, Mike Bailey engineered an event to liven up the winter — a flamingo flocking month. He explains: Friends honor (surprise is a better word) friends by sending a flock of pink plastic flamingos to their yard, and the friends have to pay to get rid of them (usually sending them to flock at another friend's home). It's all done in good fun to help the theater. A committee delivers and picks up the flock.

All three couples have been welcomed as volunteers in the community, helping the Ferndale Museum, which showcases the history of the area, the theater, schools, events and other civic projects.

The three couples say the old, small-town tradition of stopping to visit when you see someone holds true today here — and contributes to the great community spirit. The post office, in particular, is a common meeting place, as everyone must come to get the mail. "You go to the post office and meet half the town, and everybody you see, you know, and they know your name," says Peggy Bailey. It doesn't hurt that next door the Sweetness & Light shop sells handmade chocolates.

"You have to allow two hours to walk downtown because you're stopped by all your friends and have to talk to them. You don't want to insult anyone by not taking time to talk," adds Mike Bailey.

There are some caveats about Ferndale. Housing is in tight supply. The town's boundaries are defined, and it's not annexing. Historic houses and other homes do come on the market, but in limited numbers, and small neighborhoods of new homes sometimes are developed on parcels of land.

When the Torberts sold the inn, they bought a new house in a small development of about 18 homes.

"If you love the town, you buy what's on the market. The community is more important than a specific house. There aren't many parcels for sale. Part of the reason people come here is the small town, and it would be paradoxical to come here and want a subdivision with 300 lots," says Ken Torbert.

The Baileys had a difficult time finding an existing house that fit their needs, so in 1999, they reserved one of the first lots in the new neighborhood that later attracted the Torberts. The Baileys knew what they wanted so Mike drew up their house plans on the computer — and launched a retirement career. The builder was so impressed with his plans that Mike went to the College of the Redwoods in nearby Eureka to study computer-aided design and now has a booming business.

The weather is, well, not for everyone. It's cool, cloudy and rainy, and fog slips in from the coast and wraps the town in a blanket. "It's a little tough at first," says Martha Tubbs after living in sunny Southern California. "In two to three years, you make up your mind (whether you like it), and we've turned the corner. It's a trade-off — we don't have that traffic and congestion."

Summers are cool and foggy, but a short way inland the sun breaks through faster. Falls are warmer and sunnier. It never gets really hot, say the Baileys, noting that when it got above 70 degrees for 19 or 20 days, it was considered a heat wave, and records were broken when it reached the mid- to upper 80s in Eureka. Peggy Bailey doesn't handle heat well and has loved Ferndale, while Mike was "kind of cold the first year or two."

Mike and Peggy caution that professional sports fanatics won't find live action here, though there is a semipro baseball team in Arcata and high school and college sports. There are no large malls in the area, though major stores are in Eureka. "People joked with us, 'You have to remember you're behind the Redwood Curtain.' You sometimes have to travel a distance to get what you're looking for," says Martha Tubbs.

The president of the chamber of commerce, Karen Pingitore, is an early retiree who said goodbye to Hollywood and traded the movie sets of Warner Bros. for the real Victorian Ferndale. In the late 1980s, Karen's husband, Carl, retired from a career in motion pictures and suggested they explore Northern California since she hadn't taken a vacation in 10 years. They liked Victorian architecture, fell in love with Ferndale, joked about retiring here and then bought a Victorian home in the early 1990s. She commuted back to work until 1993 and then retired and moved full time to Ferndale, where she launched a second career, opening Ferndale Clothing Co., a women's shop on Main Street.

"When you live here, you want to be involved in the community," she says. The chamber is run by volunteers who handle calls, but there is no visitor center. "The town is the visitor center," she says.

She points to the many things to do in the area — a beautiful, rugged undeveloped stretch of beach over the hills, state parks with recreation, wildlife refuges with thousands of migrating birds and gray whales along the coast in winter, hiking in the mountains and forests. Martha and Dan Tubbs enjoy driving the narrow road outside Ferndale to the ocean bluffs and hiking down to the windswept beach.

Karen says Ferndale probably won't change much — "and that's a plus. That's what makes it so enticing," she says.

Dan and Martha Tubbs agree. "We saw so much change in the last 15 years in Southern California. We watched all the agricultural areas go to asphalt and cement buildings. So for us it's a real boon that there isn't that growth here," Martha says.

"I like stepping back in time," Dan says.

The Baileys say it's important to respect the nature of a small town. "If you're retiring to a small town, you have to realize you can't move into town and make it what you want it to be. You have to take it as it is," says Peggy Bailey.

"We realized from the beginning that you have to go with the flow — and we like the flow here. It's our kind of flow," Peggy says. ●

Fort Collins, Colorado

Active retirees enjoy a host of outdoor activities in this Colorado college town

By Doris Kennedy

When Phyllis and Bill Dean, long-time residents of Michigan, began searching for a location in which to retire, the opportunity for continuing education was high on their list. According to Bill, "When you stop learning, you stop living."

One important thing they learned was that they wanted to retire to Fort Collins. After Bill's many years as a control systems engineer, the couple set out on a one-year adventure in a fifth-wheeler to check out the most appealing communities they had researched. They sought pleasant weather that included four distinctly different seasons, ample outdoor activities in a college or university town, and opportunities to volunteer in various ways as a useful means of making new friends.

"Fort Collins seemed to be the perfect fit for us," Phyllis says. "I wasn't ready to just sit around in a rocking chair. I wanted to be where there was always something going on." She says that if retirees can't find things to do to keep them happy in Fort Collins, "they can't be looking very hard."

"Fort Collins is just the right size city," Bill concurs. "It's not so small that everyone knows everyone else's business, and yet it's small enough so neighbors make friends with one another and strangers are likely to greet you with a cheery 'good morning.' The crime rate is low, and the cost of living isn't prohibitive. And it's not so big that you have to drive 30 miles to buy a loaf of bread."

Located in north-central Colorado, 63 miles north of Denver and 43 miles south of Cheyenne, WY, Fort Collins lies on the eastern slope of the Continental Divide in the shadow of the spectacular peaks of the Rocky Mountains. The Cache la Poudre River vigorously tumbles through Poudre Canyon until it reaches Fort Collins, where it lazily meanders through the city. Farther east, the Pawnee National Grassland and the history-packed plains and prairies occa-

sionally reveal a deteriorating "soddy" and ruts left behind by covered wagons. Grain-producing farms and cattle ranches encircle the perimeter of the city.

What was first known as Camp Collins, named for highly respected Lt. Col. William O. Collins, leader of the 11th Ohio Volunteer Cavalry, was established in 1862 to protect travelers heading west on the Overland Trail. A disastrous flood demolished the camp in June 1864, but within two months, a new post, this time called Fort Collins, was built five miles downstream from the original structure. Three years later, the fort was abandoned.

Ranchers struggled to cultivate dry land while settlers moved onto the former fort site and built a post office, livery stables, small hotel, brickyard and general store. Times were tough. In 1877 an infestation of grasshoppers destroyed an entire year's grain crop, the bank failed, and the town became nearly deserted.

Fortunately, the Colorado Central Railroad decided to provide a vital link to Fort Collins from its transcontinental route, and the subsequent shipping and travel opportunities saved the settlement from becoming just one more ghost town. With the influx of train traffic, a new vitality emerged. Irrigation canals were built, a flourishing sugar beet industry developed, and sheep were introduced to the area.

Education has always been a driving force in Fort Collins. The first schoolroom was opened in "Auntie Stone's" tiny cabin in 1866. An agricultural college was founded in 1870, and nine years later the Remington Street School earned the distinction of being the first school west of the Mississippi River to operate a kindergarten. The agricultural college continued to grow and now, as Colorado State University (CSU), it is the state's second-largest university with an enrollment of nearly 25,000 students.

Phyllis and Bill Dean chose to pur-

chase a townhouse in a small subdivision with biking and hiking trails right outside their door. A short walk reveals a variety of wildlife, including deer, raccoons, fox and many species of birds.

Phyllis had volunteered hundreds of hours in the Troy, MI, area where she served on the League of Women Voters of Michigan and was a trustee for the local library. "I'm now doing the things that I've always wanted to do but kept putting off," she says. At the senior center, she is learning to crochet ponchos for their two 3-year-old granddaughters. She hasn't been able to shake off the volunteering habit, however. She helps sew quilts for Project Linus, a nonprofit organization that makes comfort blankets for children and adults in need.

Bill, who retired in 1993, hikes and bikes many of the 25 miles of maintained trails within the city limits. He is involved in a senior center program to help those who need assistance with filling out their income tax forms, and he supervises the center's woodshop three days a week.

Unlike many senior centers that operate without sufficient funds and aren't able to do much more than provide a place to enjoy a hot meal and play a hand of cards, the Fort Collins Senior Center is often used by planners of other communities as a model. The facility includes an indoor swimming pool, an indoor running track, woodshop, full-size gym, billiards room, small theater, several classrooms and a park with walking paths.

Eric and Carolyn Biedermann retired in Fort Collins 10 years ago. Eric is a former Lutheran clergyman with a master's degree in theology, and Carolyn has a degree in teaching with a substantial background in piano and organ music. Iowa natives who experienced many winters when the snowfall didn't melt for weeks at a time, they were attracted to Colorado's milder climate, where more than 300 days of sunshine do not allow the snow to stay on the ground for more than a few days.

Eric's parents lived in Colorado, and he and Carolyn visited them often, so they were well acquainted with the state when they decided to retire in Fort Collins. Eric, 72, rides his recumbent-style bicycle to the senior center each morning to spend several hours playing badminton, tossing basketballs through

Fort Collins, CO

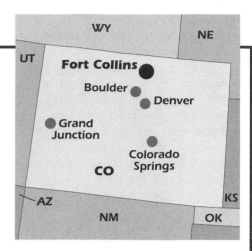

Population: 128,000

Location: 63 miles north of Denver and 43 miles south of Cheyenne, WY, in north-central Colorado five miles west of Interstate 25. Elevation is 5,000 feet. The city is within easy access to Rocky Mountain National Park, Arapaho and Roosevelt national forests, and Pawnee National Grassland.

Climate: High Low
January   42   15
July   85   56
Fort Collins enjoys relatively comfortable evenings during the summer months.

Average relative humidity: 57%

Rain: 9 inches per year

Snow: 50 inches per year

Cost of living: Above average

Average housing cost: The average selling price for a home is about $220,000. Rent is about $500-$600 on a one-bedroom apartment, $600-$800 for a two-bedroom apartment.

Sales tax: 6.7%

Sales tax exemptions: Groceries and food are subject to a 2.25% city tax only. There is no tax on prescription drugs.

State income tax: 4.63% of income as reported on federal income tax filings.

Income tax exemptions: The first $20,000 of pension or annuity income is exempt from tax for individuals ages 55 to 64, and for individuals receiving the pension as the result of the death of the individual who earned the pension. The first $24,000 of pension or annuity is exempt from tax for individuals age 65 and over.

Estate tax: Colorado's estate tax was phased out after Dec. 31, 2004.

Property tax: Approximately $9 per $1,000 of assessed value. Tax on a $220,000 home would be about $1,980.

Homestead exemption: Rent is about $500-$600 on a one-bedroom apartment, $600-$800 for a two-bedroom apartment.

Education: In Fort Collins, Colorado State University, the state's second-largest university (approximately 25,000 students) offers a variety of undergraduate degrees

as well as master's and doctorate degrees. Front Range and Aims community colleges offer many two-year degrees.

Transportation: Four exits lead from Interstate 25 into the city. The Loveland/Fort Collins Municipal Airport serves both corporate and general aviation aircraft. A commuter service is offered five days a week to Las Vegas. Shamrock Airport Express provides door-to-door airport shuttle, taxi, luxury limousine and courier service. Shuttle service to Denver International Airport also is available. Express Charters offers transportation to a variety of Colorado attractions. Transfort is the city's public transportation system operating Monday through Saturday. All buses are wheelchair accessible. Dial-A-Ride provides door-to-door transportation for those eligible under the Americans With Disabilities Act and for those age 60 and older. Both Advantage and Enterprise have rental car service offices in the city.

Health: Poudre Valley Hospital Health Care System is Fort Collins' full-service medical center offering 37 specialties with nearly 3,000 health-care professionals. U.S. News and World Report magazine awarded it a "Top 50 Hospital" designation in July 2004 for excellence in patient care and orthopedic surgery. Solucient, an independent monitoring company, recently named the Poudre Valley Hospital one of the nation's top 100 hospitals. Major services include the Heart Center of the Rockies, the Regional Neurosciences Center, the Regional Orthopedic Center and the Regional Trauma Center. The Aspen Club is a free membership organization for people age 50 and above providing streamlined hospital admission, discounts on health screening procedures, hospital cafeteria discounts and a variety of other medical and social programs.

Housing options: Several small, private lakes in the area offer lakefront homes in the premium price range of $500,000 to $1.5 million. Recent housing developments have spread southward toward the neighboring community of Loveland.

Here you will find an assortment of home styles including condominiums, patio homes and townhouses ranging in price from $150,000 to $600,000. **Observatory Village Community**, (970) 226-1560 or www.observatoryvillage.com, offers a variety of styles starting at $227,000 to $275,000. Other attractive options include homes near open space, parks, trails and Fort Collins' historic Old Town, where a variety of cultural events take place. Apartments are abundant. Among local real estate agents, Dawn Mathis of Realty Executives is a senior real estate specialist, (800) 472-8580.

Visitor lodging: Fort Collins, as a university town as well as an outdoor recreation destination, offers a wide range of bed-and-breakfast inns, motels, hotels, cabins and RV parks. The Edwards House Bed and Breakfast Inn is a completely refurbished, eight-bedroom, luxurious 1904 Victorian. Rates range from $95 to $165 per couple and include a full breakfast and evening refreshments, (800) 281-9190. Located downtown, the 38-room Armstrong Hotel has rates that range from $89 to $150, (866) 384-3883. The 72-room Best Western University Inn is convenient to CSU and starts at $85 per couple, (888) 484-2984. The Super 8 Motel's 71 rooms start at $59, (800) 800-8000.

Information: Fort Collins Area Chamber of Commerce, 225 S. Meldrum, Fort Collins, CO 80521, (970) 482-3746 or www.fcchamber.org. Fort Collins Convention and Visitors Bureau, 3745 E. Prospect Road, No. 200, Fort Collins, CO 80525, (800) 274-3678 or www.ftcollins.com.

the hoops, swimming and keeping in shape for the annual Rocky Mountain Senior Games, where he already has earned a gold medal in badminton. It is no small matter to win a medal at these games because the level of competition is exceptionally high.

Carolyn, 69, who was an organist at the church over which Eric presided, still substitutes for local church organists and volunteers at the senior center. The Biedermanns wholeheartedly agree that the best thing about retirement in Fort Collins is having the choice of so many activities in which to participate. According to Eric, "Relief is spelled R-E-T-I-R-E-M-E-N-T."

"It seems we've always been performers," Eric says, "first in the ministry and now as volunteer actors at the local Cemetery Crawl, where we dress in costumes, play the parts of local historic figures from the 1880s, and relate their pasts while standing beside their headstones in one of the region's cemeteries. We also volunteer as docents at the Lincoln Center of Performing Arts."

The Biedermanns' reasons for choosing Fort Collins for their retirement location includes the miles of bike paths they can share together, the pleasant climate, friendliness of the people, easy access to the mountains, abundance of quality cultural events, and the outstanding senior center, where it is easy to make new friends.

Tom and Shirley Dandy have known many communities by way of comparison. Both born in Toronto, Canada, they did a lot of traveling during his 25 years as a U.S. Air Force officer. "In our opinion, Fort Collins is the best city to retire to," says Shirley, 79. "We have lived here for two and one-half years and think it is one of the most active cities you could hope to find. Nearly everyone, without interfering, seems to be concerned about others."

The Dandys live in Mira Mont Village, a complex of upscale homes with covenants that keep the neighborhood picture perfect. They have a self-appointed "mayor" who has voluntarily taken on the responsibility of making new residents feel welcome, and his neighborliness has caught on. If help is needed, it's immediately available.

Married for 48 years, the Dandys say their relationship began with "love at first sight." Their son and daughter-in-law are both professors of chemical engineering at Colorado State University, and their 3-year-old grandson is a frequent visitor.

Former residents of Atwater, CA, where Tom, 75, was a certified public accountant and the Red Cross manager for Merced and Mariposa counties, the Dandys say they made so many family visits to Fort Collins that it almost became cheaper to move here.

Tom Dandy's advice to those seeking a retirement location is to "rent a house or apartment at the place of their choice for at least six months before making a final decision. And if you think you'd like to return to the place of your youth, check it out carefully first. You can be sure that a lot has changed since you once lived there and, remember, you probably have changed, too."

The Dandys' advocacy for Fort Collins extends beyond their friendly neighborhood. The numerous parks, walking trails, playgrounds, cultural activities, climate, good restaurants and ease of making friends contribute to their appreciation of their chosen retirement city.

They particularly like Fort Collins' historic Old Town, a triangle of impeccably restored buildings from the 1800s that provide one-of-a-kind shops, including the Ten Thousand Villages store, an international nonprofit organization that ensures that artisans in need worldwide are paid a fair price for their handicrafts.

Shirley says shopkeepers are in the habit of greeting all customers upon arrival and often walk them to the door to say goodbye, as though they were houseguests. Summertime visitors to Old Town can ride a restored 1919 streetcar and people-watch from the sidewalk cafes. The handsome fire hall at Disney World is an exact replica of Fort Collins' circa-1800s fire station, and Disneyland's Main Street was fashioned after Fort Collins' Old Town.

For retirees Bill and Evie Weddel, music, entertaining and education are important aspects of their lifestyle, and they say they can get their cultural fix in Fort Collins. Together and individually, they are members of several performing groups that sing on the radio and at nursing homes and churches. Bill is one of the facilitators of the Front Range Forum, a learning program similar to Elderhostel that offers classes in a variety of subjects, including theater, physics, history and music, tapping former CSU faculty as participants.

Bill, 76, retired from CSU, where he held the positions of student counselor and activities manager, dean of men, director of financial aid and director of the Lory Student Center. Evie, also 76, retired from CSU, as well, where she worked as secretary for the Department of Fishery and Wildlife Biology.

"Spend at least a week, longer if possible, at your choice of retirement communities before you actually move there," Bill advises. "Make a list of your priorities and a list of the regions that provide resources that interest you. Go to convention and visitor bureaus and chambers of commerce with a long list of questions. Put yourselves into the 'what would living here be like' mode. Be realistic about decision making."

For the Weddels and other retirees, the decision was Fort Collins. And it wasn't a hard decision to reach. ●

Fort Myers, Florida

This southwest Florida city has a flourishing cultural scene and affordable housing

By Karen Feldman

If the fact that Thomas Edison obtained close to 1,000 patents in his lifetime isn't proof enough of his ingenuity, his choice of Fort Myers as his winter home is a clear sign of his visionary gift. In 1886 the inventor and his bride, Mina, arrived by steamer for their honeymoon. Thus began their lifelong love affair with Fort Myers, where they built a winter home along with a laboratory and botanical garden on the banks of the Caloosahatchee River.

Edison's good friend, Henry Ford, created his own estate next door. Together they entertained such luminaries as Harvey Firestone and Charles Lindbergh at a time when Fort Myers had fewer than 900 residents and lacked both air conditioning and mosquito control.

Today, their estates have become the most popular attractions in a city that boasts 57,585 full-time residents, a number that almost doubles during the balmy winters when so-called snowbirds flock south. Like their famous predecessors, many winter visitors come for a brief respite from the cold but wind up putting down roots in this thriving city on Florida's southwest coast.

"Many people are drawn to the area for the first time on vacation," says Marietta Mudgett, executive director of the Greater Fort Myers Chamber of Commerce. "They go to the Edison Home and the beaches and they keep it in their memory banks when they think of retiring."

Fort Myers has been dubbed the City of Palms after the mile of towering royal palms planted along both sides of McGregor Boulevard, which runs from downtown past the Edison and Ford estates and on toward the county's barrier islands. It is the seat of county, state and federal government offices and a cultural center in Lee County.

Although the city itself has no beaches, it is situated just miles from the Gulf of Mexico and the beaches on Sanibel and Captiva islands and Fort Myers

Beach. A mild climate, an abundance of golf courses and other natural attractions make it a popular choice among retirees, Marietta Mudgett says.

Yet another draw is the range and value of real estate. "The market is good. Median home prices have increased by 45 percent in the past year. The county as a whole is appreciating by more than 20 percent inland, and waterfront homes are appreciating at rates up to 40 or 50 percent," says Denny Sharma, a broker associate with Coldwell Bankers Residential Real Estate in Fort Myers.

Among that latter group are homes along canals and the Caloosahatchee River, which snakes along the edge of downtown and on toward the Gulf and barrier islands. Single-family homes and condos in the Fort Myers area fall in the $200,000 to $600,000 range, from a basic three-bedroom home at the low end to 3,000 square feet with modern amenities at the high end.

Few homes in Fort Myers date much before the early 1920s, Sharma says, with smaller houses in the older, centrally located Edison Park and Dean Park running $250,000 to $275,000 and larger homes costing about $450,000. Some homes priced at the lower end may need renovations. Condos start at about $200,000, and golf-course communities offer a mix of condos and single-family homes starting at about $275,000.

Anyone wanting to build a home can choose from a wealth of builders and lots that run $50,000 to $150,000 and more, $400,000 on the water, utilities included. Downtown apartments and condos provide another option of late, the result of efforts by entrepreneurs who are renovating old buildings and turning them into living space.

The downtown area, largely abandoned a decade ago as malls lured consumers away, is undergoing a renaissance as an arts-and-entertainment district, with boutique shopping, bars and restaurants and a resident theater com-

pany in a historic theater. All combine to encourage people to live and play as well as work downtown. The whole region has undergone a cultural awakening in the past two decades, with the opening of new theaters, art galleries, restaurants, shops and movie theaters as the county more than doubled in size from 205,266 residents in 1980 to 521,253 today.

The Barbara B. Mann Performing Arts Hall is the home of the Southwest Florida Symphony Orchestra and Chorus and the venue for concerts and shows like "Miss Saigon" and "Phantom of the Opera." The Broadway Palm Dinner Theater presents musicals and other productions year around.

For sports fans, there's spring training with the Boston Red Sox at the City of Palms Park downtown and the Minnesota Twins at the Lee County Sports Complex. From April through August, the Twins' farm club, the Miracle, plays ball at the complex. There's hockey with the Florida Everblades and basketball with the Sea Dragons at nearby Estero's TECO Arena, which also offers ice and in-line skating to the public at designated times.

Tee and Gene Lawrence have lived in Fort Myers long enough to remember the way things used to be and to appreciate how far the city has come. The couple moved to Fort Myers from Piqua, OH, in 1976. "We were in our 50s," remembers Tee, now 74. "We didn't really have enough money to retire, but we were bored where we were."

Although they had long spent vacations in Fort Lauderdale, "by the time we wanted to move, Fort Lauderdale wasn't the place I wanted to be," she says. "It was entirely too hectic." Then they visited retired friends in Fort Myers. They liked it so much that they bought a little stone cottage.

"We knew we were going to retire in Florida somewhere," says Gene, 79. "We liked the casual atmosphere of Fort

Myers. It was an easygoing place where I could throw away my ties."

They returned to Ohio, but as the temperature plummeted, so did their attitude about the place in which they'd raised their children. So they sold Gene's credit business and headed south. Once they settled into their new home, Gene began dabbling in real estate, while Tee took a

Fort Myers, FL

Population: 57,585

Location: On the southwest Florida coast, about 120 miles south of Tampa and 130 miles northeast of Miami.

Climate: High Low
January 74 53
July 91 74

Average relative humidity: 54%

Rain: 53 inches

Cost of living: Slightly below average

Median housing cost: $300,000

Sales tax: 6%

Sales tax exemptions: Groceries, prescription drugs and some professional services.

State income tax: None

Intangibles tax: None. The tax was repealed as of Jan. 1, 2007.

Estate tax: None

Inheritance tax: None

Property tax: Fort Myers residents pay $17.5004-$21.6343 per $1,000 of assessed value, with homes assessed at 100% of market value. Yearly tax on a $300,000 home with homestead exemption below is about $4,813-$5,949, depending on location.

Homestead exemption: $25,000 off the assessed value of a permanent, primary residence.

Religion: Fort Myers has churches representing all major religions as well as some less common ones, including Reform, Conservative and Orthodox synagogues. Additional houses of worship operate in nearby Cape Coral, North Fort Myers and Sanibel Island.

Education: A variety of adult education classes are taught at high schools in and around Fort Myers. Edison Community College offers continuing-education programs and several two-year degree programs and soon will offer four-year degrees in several disciplines via the Internet. Florida Gulf Coast University is a four-year state institution offering 20 graduate and 37 undergraduate programs as well as seminars and special programs.

Transportation: Southwest Florida International Airport offers a variety of domestic and international flights, adding more each year. Public bus transportation is provided by Lee County Transit with year-round routes and trolley shuttles. Greyhound buses also operate from Fort Myers, connecting to its nationwide system. Interstate 75 connects Fort Myers to Tampa and points north, and U.S. Highway 41 is the main thoroughfare through the area.

Health: Because of the large number of retirees in the area, Fort Myers abounds with medical options. Lee Memorial Health System is a not-for-profit, full-service, acute-care hospital system that includes two Fort Myers hospitals, the 360-bed HealthPark Medical Center and the 367-bed Lee Memorial Hospital Cleveland Avenue campus, a number of medical practices and other services, such as the Diabetic Treatment Center and the Neuroscience and Stroke Center. The for-profit HCA health care. also has two Fort Myers hospitals. The 400-bed Southwest Florida Regional Medical Center is a full-service hospital that includes the Heart Institute, a chest pain unit and a kidney transplant program. The 120-bed Gulf Coast Hospital is an osteopathic facility that offers a full range of services. Family Health Centers of Southwest Florida provide basic medical care to clients with limited incomes, including the Senior Outreach Center designed to offer lower-cost medical care to older clients. The Senior Friendship Centers are staffed entirely by retired medical professionals who volunteer their time. Seniors receive basic medical care for little or no money, depending upon ability to pay.

Housing options: A full range of housing options is available in Fort Myers, both within the city limits and in the surrounding unincorporated areas. Manufactured homes start in the 150,000s. Condominiums start at $200,000, depending on amenities. At a golf community, two-bedroom condos run $275,000 to $350,000, and on the river they can run $400,000 and up. For single-family homes, prices range from about the mid-$200,000s for a smaller, older home in a residential neighborhood and $400,000 and up for a three-bedroom home in a golf community. Most homes range from $400,000 to $600,000, though on the river prices reach up to $3 million. The following master-planned communities offer amenities such as golf, tennis, a clubhouse, social clubs and planned activities: **Heritage Palms Country Club**, (800) 883-9876; **Hampton Park at Gateway** and **Pelican Preserve**, (800) 924-2290; **Lexington Country Club**, (800) 390-9334; and **Herons Glen** in North Fort Myers, (800) 521-9557. **Shell Point Village**, (800) 780-1131, is a continuing-care community with independent living in apartments ranging from studios to three-bedroom suites and on-site assisted living and skilled nursing care.

Visitor lodging: The Hibiscus House B&B is within walking distance of the Edison-Ford Winter Estates as well as the downtown arts and entertainment district, $119-$159, double occupancy, (941) 332-2651. The Hilton Garden Inn, offering rooms packed with amenities, is convenient to the airport, downtown Fort Myers, and Sanibel and Captiva Islands, $99-$279, (239) 790-3500. Best Western Coral Bridge Inn & Suites at the southern end of town offers suites with full kitchen, $99-$159 for a one-bedroom suite, (239) 454-6363.

Information: Greater Fort Myers Chamber of Commerce, 2310 Edwards Drive, Fort Myers, FL 33902, (800) 366-3622, (239) 332-3624 or www.fortmyers.org. Lee County Visitor and Convention Bureau, 2180 W. First St., Fort Myers, FL 33901, (941) 338-3500 or www.LeeIslandCoast.com.

job in property management. But it wasn't long before she discovered a major problem with her adopted hometown.

"My interests were in arts and theater, and this was a wasteland," she says. She joined a group of like-minded residents to found the Lee County Alliance of the Arts. Today the alliance is an umbrella organization for a wealth of local arts groups, occupying the 12,000-square-foot William R. Frizzell Cultural Centre, which houses three art galleries, an outdoor amphitheater and a 175-seat indoor theater. The Theatre Conspiracy performs innovative shows there, as does the Edison Community College drama department.

She also took part in preserving and restoring the historic Arcade Theater, built in 1908 as a vaudeville playhouse in downtown Fort Myers. After a rousing fund-raising campaign that included a local performance by Mikhail Baryshnikov and his dance troupe, it was painstakingly refurbished in 1991 and today houses a professional theater group, the Florida Repertory Theater.

In 1978, the Lawrences moved to their current three-bedroom, three-bath house. Built in the mid-1950s, it's in a quiet residential area just two miles from the Edison-Ford Winter Estates. They paid $40,000 for the 1,800-square-foot home, which has more than doubled in value since then, Tee says. While the prospect of moving into a more modern house appeals to them, they like their neighborhood and its central location, so they plan to stay put.

Gene continues to buy and sell homes, offering mortgages to people who might otherwise be unable to get them from conventional banks. Tee, who finally retired in 1995, keeps busy with the arts alliance and has begun taking tap-dance lessons. They attend exercise classes twice a week through the Senior Friends program at Southwest Florida Regional Medical Center. Both find the city a good choice for retirement.

"Fort Myers has more oldsters than many cities, so it has more facilities for us," Gene says. "There are a lot of good

doctors here, the restaurants give you a discount, and there are programs like Senior Friends," which offers health seminars, exercise and computer classes, among other things.

Bill and Mary Barbour, who lived in northern New Jersey for most of their married life, never considered retiring anywhere else. Bill, 78, retired as chairman of Fleming H. Revell, a publisher of inspirational and religious books, after a 39-year career. Mary, 76, worked as an executive secretary at Vick Chemical Co. for several years and spent many more as "a professional unpaid volunteer," as she describes it.

They'd been vacationing for about five years in their condo on Sanibel Island, but when they decided to retire, there was only one choice: Shell Point Village, in southern Fort Myers not far from the Sanibel causeway.

Owned by the Christian and Missionary Alliance, the not-for-profit life-care community on the shores of the Caloosahatchee River offers homes and apartments as well as assisted living, skilled nursing and rehabilitative care and a full range of activities and services. Upon moving in, single residents pay an entrance fee of $89,000 to $480,000, depending upon the housing unit selected, then a monthly fee of $1,077 to $3,915, which covers utilities, basic housekeeping, nursing and assisted-living care as needed. Additional fees apply for couples.

Bill Barbour's parents had retired to a similar type of community on the state's East Coast years before. "We knew the concept and it was a fabulous place where we wanted to be," he says.

The Barbours had made friends by attending church at Shell Point when they were vacationing on Sanibel, so their social life started up quickly. Now they add to their list of friends as new people move into their 105-unit building — "Bill makes a loaf of bread for each new person," Mary says — and as newcomers join their church or get active in community events.

Companionship without the yard work but with plenty of golf was what

drew John and Doris Lynch to their current home, a condominium at Heritage Palms, a new U.S. Home development in Fort Myers. Like the Barbours, John and Doris had vacationed on Sanibel since the 1970s when they bought a time-share unit there.

John drove a tractor-trailer for a Newark, NJ, plastics company, and Doris worked in personnel at AT&T until they retired in 1992 and moved from their home of 40 years in Old Bridge, NJ, to a mobile home in south Fort Myers. "We knew where we were going," says John, 73. "We knew the area, liked the climate and the convenience of everything, like stores and doctors."

They thought the mobile home would be their permanent residence, but they started having second thoughts after they were twice ordered to evacuate as hurricanes threatened the area. Besides that, "staying there all year was too lonesome," says Doris, 68. "Everyone went home each spring."

So they found Heritage Palms, which was centrally located and has 36 holes of golf. They bought a two-bedroom, two-bath condo that overlooks a large lake and clubhouse and moved in January 1999. The change suits them both.

"There's a lot more room, the clubhouse is open all year and we're not lonesome," says Doris, who with her husband likes to play golf, visit the beach on Sanibel, shop and entertain. "Everybody here is very friendly," says Doris. "Everybody's anxious to make friends. We're all in the same boat because it's a new community."

Ask any of these retirees what they like least about the area and they all have the same answer. It's the heavy traffic of the winter tourist season. But they also say the weather and lifestyle make the traffic worth enduring.

For those considering retirement in Fort Myers, Doris Lynch advises: "Do it, because it opens up another world. It opens up a more outdoor type of life." Adds her husband, John: "If we were up in New Jersey, we'd be in the house most of the time. Down here, we're out all the time. The weather is beautiful." ●

Gainesville, Florida

Residents of this University of Florida town have access
to superb cultural, educational and medical facilities

By Jay Clarke

Over the years, former Navy pilot Carter Nute and his wife, Barbara, moved more than two dozen times — an inescapable corollary of career military life. But they always wanted to live in Florida, so when the time came to make their retirement move two years ago, it was a happy moment for them.

"When we left Pennsylvania, I left the snow shovel in the garage for the next owner of the house," says Carter, 64. Today the Nutes are among retirees enjoying life in the college town of Gainesville.

Gainesville is the home of the University of Florida and thus offers more activities and a richer lifestyle than many other towns of its size (population 117,000). It also has won national acclaim as a very livable city. In such surroundings, the Nutes have found plenty to keep them occupied.

They are volunteer ushers at the university's performing arts center and thoroughly enjoy that role. They help out at Bible school at their church. Carter teaches an AARP driver safety course.

They attend performances at downtown's Hippodrome State Theatre and other Gainesville venues. "We're living a cultural life," says Barbara, 59. Travel is important, too. "We love to travel and go on cruises," Barbara says. And while they have a network of Navy friends, "we have met some great people here," says Carter, who retired as a Navy captain.

To keep in good shape, the Nutes joined the Heart and Fitness Center and go there three times a week. "She does water aerobics; I do a power walk," Carter says. "And the doctors here are absolutely marvelous," adds Barbara.

"Most important, though, is being full-time grandparents," Barbara says. Their daughter also lives in Gainesville (one reason they chose this city for retirement) and has four children age 6 and younger. The Nutes also have a son in

Colorado who has two children. "Four grandsons, two granddaughters," Barbara says happily.

Though the Nutes have moved many times, the Gainesville house is only the fourth one they've owned. "We owned our home in Pensacola, where the kids were born," Carter says, "and we still own a summer home in Maine." They also owned a home in Valley Forge, PA, their last stop before they moved to Gainesville. The Nutes say the cost of living here is about the same as in Pennsylvania, but Carter notes that property taxes on their Gainesville home are "not quite double" that in Valley Forge. And while they have no regrets about leaving Pennsylvania and its winter snow, Barbara fondly remembers shopping at the King of Prussia Mall there. "It's the one thing I really miss," she says.

For Carl and Gina Carlson, retiring to Gainesville was a homecoming. Carl, 72, attended the University of Florida, but his work in the insurance business took the couple to a number of cities during his career, among them Hartford, CT; Charlotte, NC; Atlanta, GA; and Sacramento, CA. During those years, though, the Carlsons never lost touch with Gainesville.

"We're big (University of Florida) Gator fans and used to catch planes to go to games," Carl says. "We never got our roots down."

His last stop in business life before retiring seven years ago was Jacksonville. That city isn't too far from Gainesville — less than two hours by car — and the Carlsons found themselves making the trip quite often to attend Gator games. So they decided Gainesville was where they should retire and made the move in 1997.

Carl is an avid Gator fan. "We belong to all the athletic clubs, like Tipoff, Touchdown and Dugout," notes Gina, 71. But they have another life as well. "I like opera and plays and going to the Hippodrome," she says. She works out

daily, loves her choir and enjoys lunching with friends.

"You have to have something to do, and the university has so many things to do," Carl says. "We've never been bored."

Indeed, many cultural opportunities are offered by the university, including plays, concerts and other events at the Phillips Center for the Performing Arts and art exhibits at the Harn Museum. One of the state's best museums, the university's Florida Museum of Natural History opened two new exhibit halls in 2004. The Hall of Florida Fossils displays skeletons of prehistoric creatures in active poses and illuminated in dramatic fashion. The new Butterfly Rainforest, the second-largest exhibit of its kind in the world, showcases the delicate winged creatures in indoor and outdoor exhibits.

In addition to university-operated attractions, the city offers other cultural and recreational opportunities. The Hippodrome, one of four state-supported theaters in Florida, produces eight contemporary productions yearly in its Palladium classical revival building. The Gainesville Community Playhouse offers six works annually, plus a holiday show. Regular concerts are performed by such groups as the Gainesville Chamber Orchestra and University Symphony.

Within the community, too, are such attractions as the unique Fred Bear Museum, which showcases a vast collection of archery and bow-hunting artifacts. Kanapaha Botanical Gardens has a hummingbird garden and an extensive collection of bamboo, and a wooden walkway takes visitors to the bottom of the Devil's Millhopper, an enormous sinkhole that is a state geological site.

Those are some of the attractions that appeal to retirees like the Carlsons. Another, Carl points out, is that Gainesville isn't primarily a retirement community. "It's a young person's town," he says. The University of Florida alone has nearly 49,000 students, and they have a tremendous impact on the city. "They keep prices down," he says, noting that most live on a budget. "They dictate restaurant menus. You won't find a lot of gourmet restaurants here." But students also lend the city a lively outlook. "It's a young, vibrant community," he says.

Living in a university city with a medical school has still another advantage.

"There's tremendous medical help here. Our closest neighbors are all doctors," Carl says. Shands Hospital, affiliated with the University of Florida's medical school, is the major medical facility here, but the city has three other hospitals as well.

While cheering for his beloved Gator teams is his avocation, Carl says his main goal in retirement is just that: retirement. "My job in insurance was stressful. I

want to lessen stress. Now, every day belongs to me. I don't want to be burdened."

Another couple for whom moving to Gainesville meant coming full circle is Mary Ann and Bill Frederick. They came here from Miami, where he had been president of Jordan Marsh and in charge of all the department store's Florida branches. Both grew up in St. Petersburg, though, and knew each other

Gainesville, FL

Population: About 117,000
Location: Gainesville is in north-central Florida about midway between the Atlantic Ocean and the Gulf of Mexico. Jacksonville is 70 miles away, Orlando 109 miles and Tampa 128 miles.
Climate: High Low
January 69 42
July 91 71
Average relative humidity: 72%
Annual rainfall: 51.5 inches
Cost of living: Below average
Average housing costs: $178,800 for a single family home. Rent on a two-bedroom, two-bath apartment averages $775.
Sales tax: 6.25%
Sales tax exemptions: Food and medicine
State income tax: None
Estate tax: None. The state's "pick-up" portion of the federal tax was eliminated January 1, 2005.
Inheritance tax: None
Property tax: $25.32 or $25.35 per $1,000 of assessed valuation, depending on location. All property in Florida is to be appraised at 100% of market value every Jan. 1, but state law limits property tax increases (and hence appraisal increases) to 3% per year on homestead properties. Property values have been rising more than that, so as the years go by, many properties are taxed substantially below market value. However, the year when you buy an existing home or build a new home, you will be assessed and taxed at its full market value. Property tax on a $178,800 home in Gainesville is $3,894-$3,899 depending on location, with exemption noted below.
Homestead exemption: $25,000

Intangibles tax: None. The tax was repealed as of Jan. 1, 2007.
Religion: More than 35 denominations have churches in Gainesville.
Education: The University of Florida, (352) 392-3261 or www.ufl.edu, is a state university with more than 48,000 students, one of the five largest in the country. Santa Fe Community College, (352) 395-5000 or www.santafe.cc.fl.us, is a two-year state college with over 16,000 students. City College, (352) 335-4000 or www.citycollege.edu, is a private junior college with 350 students.
Transportation: Gainesville Regional Airport, five miles from downtown, offers several daily flights by ASA (Delta Connection), US Airways, Continental Connection and Northwest Airlink. Amtrak and Greyhound serve major U.S. cities out of Gainesville.
Health: Gainesville has four hospitals with a total of more than 1,700 beds, and more than 1,200 physicians practice in the county. Shands Hospital at UF, affiliated with the University of Florida's medical school, is the top facility with 570 beds. North Florida Regional Medical Center has 287 beds, Malcolm Randall Veterans Administration Hospital has 239 beds and Shands/AGH has 367 beds. All have 24-hour emergency departments.
Housing options: Housing ranges from historic homes in the city's 63-square-block historic district to gated communities of new homes popular with retirees. Among the latter is **Savanna Pointe**, which sits on the northern rim of Payne's Prairie State Preserve. Lots range from $50,000 to $150,000 for a half-acre estate lot, and homes are true to Florida architecture from the 1880s to the 1920s, (352) 376-8033. At **Oak Hammock**, affil-

iated with the University of Florida, occupants can choose from 21 floor plans with one to three bedrooms and up to 2,530 square feet on a 136-acre site. Entrance fees range from $106,000 to $489,000 and are 50% or 95% refundable, (888) 311-6483 or www.oakhammock.org. Twice a year the 500-member Builders Association of North Central Florida conducts a Parade of Homes to showcase area properties, (352) 372-5649 or www.bancf.com. For more information about local properties, contact the Gainesville-Alachua County Association of Realtors, (352) 332-8850 or www.gacar.com.
Visitor lodging: Many chains have motels in Gainesville: Holiday Inn West, from $94, (800) 465-4329 or (352) 332-7500; Cabot Lodge, from $79, (800) 843-8735 or (352) 375-2400; and Econo Lodge, from $53, (800) 446-6900 or (352) 373-7816.
Information: Gainesville Area Chamber of Commerce, P.O. Box 1187, Gainesville, FL 32602, (352) 334-7100 or www.gainesvillechamber.com. Alachua County Visitors and Convention Bureau, 30 E. University Ave., Gainesville, FL 32601, (866) 778-5002, (352) 374-5260 or www.visitgainesville.net.

through 12 years of school there. And both attended the University of Florida, where they began dating.

When Jordan Marsh was sold and then went bankrupt in the 1980s, the Fredericks began thinking seriously of where to retire. About the same time, the University of Florida offered Bill a position in development (fund raising), and he leaped at the chance.

"We always loved Gainesville," says Mary Ann, 66, so they moved here in 1988. They built a house on a 4.5-acre wooded tract six miles west of town, and with Bill, now 67, no longer working regularly, Gainesville has become their retirement home. "It's met our expectations in every way," she says.

"There's a lot that goes on in a university town," she says. Both the Fredericks keep busy. "I do a lot in our church, and I went back to school and got a master's degree in religion. It took a lot longer than just the normal two years — about five years," Mary Ann says. Bill also is active in the church and still does some consulting. "He likes to fish and goes to Cedar Key," a funky community on the Gulf of Mexico about an hour away, Mary Ann says.

One of the couple's three children lives in Gainesville, so they see him frequently. "The others come to visit as often as possible. They love it here," Mary Ann says.

As for the climate, "There's little change of seasons here, but it's not as tropical as Miami. We have different trees, different flowers," she says of Gainesville, which bills itself as the "city of trees."

Though they spent quite a few years in South Florida, Mary Ann says, "I don't miss Miami. I miss our friends. If there's anything I miss there, it's the water — just seeing the water. Still, I wouldn't trade our trees for the water."

While the Nutes, Carlsons and Fredericks all own single-family homes, Frank and Jan Covington have moved into an apartment that is part of an innovative new retirement community associated with the university. Residents at the $132 million Oak Hammock complex are given access to campus facilities similar to those accorded university staff and faculty, including health care through the university's doctors and Shands Hospital, and admission to most cultural and sports events, museums and classes. University experts are brought in to lecture to Oak Hammock residents.

"It's a life-care (facility) with prepaid medical," says Frank, 72, adding that he and his wife, Jan, 63, wanted to make this move while both were still in good health. Residents can graduate from their apartment or villa to assisted living and private skilled nursing rooms as their health dictates. Oak Hammock has 212 apartments and 57 villas, as well as a commons building, tennis courts and pool.

The Covingtons moved to Florida from Denver, where both worked for — and retired from — the Environmental Protection Agency. They moved in the late 1990s to Crescent City on Florida's Atlantic coast, where Frank had a brother.

"Both of us are Type A's," Frank says. "I was active in the Lions Club and Rotary Club, did tutoring, community projects and church, and the first thing you know, I ran for mayor." Unopposed, he won a three-year term that ended last year.

But the Covingtons knew they weren't going to stay in Crescent City. They had visited other retirement communities before settling in Gainesville, among them Jacksonville. "We also looked in California and Chicago and visited seven (cities) in all," Frank says. He had worked in California, and Jan had worked in Chicago.

"No place is perfect. We loved something at every place," says Frank, but Gainesville won out. "We like Florida for its climate, taxes and ambiance." He says taxes and the cost of living are less than in Chicago, California or Denver, but also notes that Florida offers fewer state services.

To be sure, there are things they will miss. "We'll never get over (not having) the change of seasons. And skiing, we'll miss that," he says. Their children — he has three, she two — are scattered, so they make several trips every year to visit them.

Another potential resident at Oak Hammock is Matilda, a full-sized mannequin who resides in a test "smart home" in the university's Computer and Information Science and Engineering Department. Matilda plays the role of an 85-year-old widow in an unusual project aimed at helping seniors live alone longer if they desire.

A new and larger smart home for the project is now open at Oak Hammock, and Matilda may make "guest appearances" there. Normally, though, human volunteers will live in the 2,500-square-foot home for a week at a time to test computerized devices intended to make living easier for the elderly. Among them are mobile phones that can turn on lights and television and open and close curtains, a sensor that notifies when mail arrives and whether the resident has missed taking a pill, a refrigerator sensor that tells when milk is out of date, and a "magic" bathroom mirror with a hidden monitor that prints out messages to the resident.

In the future, such smart homes may make living easier for people in their later years. In the meantime, retirees will have to enjoy life as best they can without all the computerized comforts of home.

That shouldn't be a problem for active seniors like Carter and Barbara Nute. As Carter puts it, "We're not retired. We're rewired." ●

Galena, Illinois

Historic architecture and scenic countryside lend
a timeless beauty to this charming Illinois town

Catherine Watson

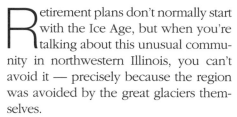

Retirement plans don't normally start with the Ice Age, but when you're talking about this unusual community in northwestern Illinois, you can't avoid it — precisely because the region was avoided by the great glaciers themselves.

That geological oversight is why the hills and valleys of Jo Daviess County are so lovely and why the little city of Galena, its county seat, is a treasure chest of 19th-century architecture and Civil War history. The combination makes Galena one of the prettiest and most popular destinations in the Midwest, as well as an increasingly popular place to retire.

"It's so beautiful, so different from the rest of Illinois," says Ellen Wittenbrink, who retired to the Galena area with her husband, Boniface (Boni), 10 years ago. "I think it's the most beautiful spot in the country."

It would have been a different story if glacial ice sheets had flattened the landscape and scraped away or covered up the region's rich deposits of "gray gold" — a nearly pure form of lead ore called "galena" in Latin. Instead, the shiny, pewter-colored mineral lay close to the surface, where early French explorers discovered it.

Miners and entrepreneurs started flowing into the region as early as the 1820s from England, Ireland, Germany and other parts of the young United States. Among those attracted to Galena was Ulysses S. Grant, who moved to the bustling community with his family the year before the Civil War broke out. The town is still intensely proud to have sent not only Grant but eight other generals into the Union ranks.

Many Galenians got rich from lead mining and steamboating on the Mississippi and its once-wide tributary, the Galena River. By the 1840s, in fact, Galena was the most important town between St. Louis, MO, and St. Paul, MN. The town still reflects that prosperity and prominence.

Though the population has shrunk from its 19th-century peak of nearly 15,000 to 3,400 today, Galena's red-brick mansions, historic neighborhoods and long, regal Main Street are still intact. In fact, when Galena was named a historic district on the National Register of Historic Places in the late 1960s, 85 percent of the town was included.

But it wasn't heirloom architecture that attracted Ellen and Boni Wittenbrink to Galena from Chicago. They came for the New England-like scenery and quiet charm of the surrounding countryside. The couple's Chicago roots are typical of many immigrants to the area because the big city is only a three-hour drive from the little one, and many Chicagoland residents have visited as tourists. Most other incoming retirees hail from elsewhere in the Midwest, chiefly outstate Illinois, Iowa, Wisconsin and Minnesota.

One of the first things potential residents notice about the area — besides all that beauty and history — is the diversity of the Galena area housing market. First, there is the original city of Galena, which preserves every type of American architecture from hand-hewn log cabins to tidy Federal-style red-brick row houses to grand Victorian painted ladies.

Then there's the surrounding county, whose rolling pastures and woodlands include several smaller towns, with working farms, hobby farms and a sprinkling of new houses in between. Finally, there's the Galena Territory, a planned community about six miles east of Galena proper, with single-family homes, townhouses and condominiums (many available for vacation rental), a resort complex, a man-made lake, four fine golf courses and great cross-country skiing.

The Wittenbrinks bought land in the Territory and began building a second home in the late 1970s, when both were still working, she as an elementary school teacher and he in social services for a large city hospital. They finished the house in 1980. "It was close enough to

get away for the weekend," Ellen recalls, and for the next decade, "that's all we did — we basically came up and escaped."

In 1992, when Ellen was 52 and Boni 55, they retired and moved permanently to their weekend home, bringing Ellen's elderly mother with them. Although they knew people in the area, thanks to years of weekend visits, they didn't know the historic city very well. They were happily surprised. "There's so much to do," Ellen says, "and not just in Galena, but in the whole county. I've never been bored."

Ellen is active in the League of Women Voters, serves as an election judge and a board member of the Galena Territory Association, and spends a lot of time at the Territory's Shenandoah Riding Center, where she stables Taj, her 20-year-old Arabian horse. (She took up riding at age 42.)

Her husband's "whole orientation is service," Ellen says, so it's no surprise that Boni is an emergency medical technician and a volunteer fireman for two communities. He also takes frequent advantage of the Territory's well-designed golf courses.

Like Ellen Wittenbrink, Charlotte Kennedy brought her mother along when she and husband George decided to retire to the historic town of Galena eight years ago. The Kennedys had loved the Galena area for years but worried that local health services wouldn't measure up to what they'd had in Chicago. Amazingly, for a town this small, "it has met and exceeded that," Charlotte says.

Galena boasts its own medical center, which combines a small hospital, nursing home, clinic, physical therapy and fitness center and an assisted-living facility. There are two top-notch hospital complexes in Dubuque, IA, barely 15 minutes away across the Mississippi River.

Charlotte, now 63, retired from teaching home economics in a junior high school on Chicago's North Shore. George — "I've seen my 65th birthday," he laughs — is a retired dentist who practiced in Chicago's western suburbs. Friends for 30 years, they have been married for 13. Both have children from first marriages who are spread out across the country, from Illinois to California.

"We have never had any intention of following our kids," Charlotte says. "And we don't hang around with people who do," George adds. Like so many of today's active retirees, the couple is drawn to people "who are stimulating, who are creative, who are involved," Charlotte says — exactly the kind of people who seem to seek out Galena.

"There are a lot of quality people out here," she says. There's also a surprising amount for them to do: the historical society, the Friends of the Library, theater groups and the art guild, just for starters. "You can get involved," says Charlotte, who spent several years coordinating local programming for Elderhostel. "If you have some talents, you can show

Galena, IL

Population: 3,405 in Galena, 22,580 in Jo Daviess County.

Location: Jo Daviess County forms the extreme northwestern corner of Illinois. Galena, the county seat, is about eight miles south of the Wisconsin border and about 15 miles east of the Mississippi River at Dubuque, IA. Galena also is about 180 miles northwest of Chicago.

Climate:

	High	Low
January	24	7
July	82	62

Rain: 46.3 inches
Snow: 43.5 inches
Average relative humidity: 62%
Cost of living: Average

Housing cost: The county median, $180,000, can be misleading because there are three different housing markets in the area: historic Galena, Galena Territory six miles east of the old city, and the surrounding county.

Sales tax: 6.75% on general merchandise. Groceries, prescription and nonprescription drugs, and other medical items are taxed at 1%.

State income tax: The rate is 3% of taxable income.

Income tax exemptions: Social Security benefits, federal, state, local and private pensions are exempt.

Estate tax: Applicable to taxable estates above $2 million.

Property tax: Ranges from $55.0268 to $72.9339 per $1,000 of assessed value, depending on location. Homes are assessed at 33.3% of market value. Taxes on a $180,000 home would range from $3,026 to $4,011 with exemption noted below.

Homestead exemption: $5,000 off assessed value.

Religion: There are seven Protestant churches and two Catholic churches within 10 miles of Galena.

Education: Three colleges within 30 miles of Galena, a vocational school 14 miles to the east, and some adult-education extension classes in town. Some of Galena's resident artists also give lessons.

Transportation: Jo Daviess County Transit offers an in-town bus route most weekdays, free for seniors over 65 and 50 cents each way for all others. Special service is available for those with disabilities, as well as curb-to-curb service and transport to medical appointments for seniors. Reservations are required, (815) 777-8088. The nearest airport is a regional airport in Dubuque, IA, 21 miles west of Galena.

Health care: Galena has four doctors and four dentists, as well as chiropractic care and the Galena-Stauss Hospital complex, which includes a 25-bed hospital wing, nursing home, clinic, a fitness center and assisted-living units. The Midwest Regional Medical Center, a 35-acre campus about three miles west of the current hospital, is scheduled to open late 2007. The state-of-the-art facility will offer senior care, emergency medicine and physician services, among others.

Housing options: In the Galena historic district, homes range from about $60,000 to $749,000, depending on size and state of restoration. Other options in town include a few condos and townhouse units for sale, rental apartments in restored commercial buildings, and new houses that are going up on the edges of town. In the Galena Territory, housing options include condos and townhouses as well as individual homes on lots of one-half acre to 25 acres. Prices start at $133,500 for townhomes and $189,000 for condos. Houses run from $164,900 to $1.38 million. Jo Daviess County and the City of Galena have zoning ordinances, and the Galena Territory development requires new structures to meet its design standards. The City of Galena requires that all external changes to properties within the historic district be approved by the Historic District Advisory Board and the building inspector in advance. The city also monitors the uses of historic district buildings. For example, if you plan to convert a large home into a bed-and-breakfast inn or start an in-home business in a residential neighborhood, find out before you buy whether the city will allow it.

Visitor lodging: There are 51 lodging establishments within 10 miles of Galena. Lodging options include bed-and-breakfast inns, hotels and motels, and many require a two-night stay on weekends. Many properties in the Galena Territory are available for short-term vacation rentals. Call (888) 842-5362 for assistance. Stoney Creek Inn, $79-$99, (800) 659-2220. Eagle Ridge Resort and Spa, from $129 for rooms at the inn to $169 and up for villa stays, (800) 892-2269. Abbey's High Street B&B, in a historic estate, $89-$189, (815) 777-4847.

Information: Galena Area Chamber of Commerce, 101 Bouthillier St., Galena, IL 61036, (815) 777-9050 or www. galena chamber.com. The Galena-Jo Daviess County Convention and Visitors Bureau, (877) 464-2536 or www.galena.org. Galena Territory, (815) 777-2000 or www.thegalenaterritory.com. The City of Galena, (815) 777-1050 or www.cityof galena.org.

them off here. You can find a niche."

You can also work, and not just in the region's booming tourist industry. Telecommuting from home is also an option, thanks to a successful effort by the City of Galena to bring in wireless broadband access.

"Especially after Sept. 11, we have seen an increase in people wanting to get away from the rat race of large cities," says Cindy Pepple, the city's economic development director. "Galena is unique because we offer small-town life with more sophisticated amenities . . . so we are working to capitalize on this. It would also help us to diversify our economy and make us less dependent on tourism."

Its own history taught Galena what happens when a community depends too long on one industry or one economic boom. After the Civil War, first lead mining, then steamboating faded away. By the start of the 20th century, Galena was just another sleepy little country town. Its once-busy river silted in, and a long series of disastrous floods began. Today the city rightfully calls itself "a gated community," a tongue-in-cheek reference to the tall green floodgates framing the entrance to Main Street.

The distinctive gates and the town's long economic sleep are what preserved so much of its fine architecture. The economy wasn't growing, so there was no need — and no money — to tear the old buildings down.

Then, starting in the 1960s, Galena slowly began to come back to life. Artists found the picturesque town first, partly because it made great subject matter, partly because its old buildings offered cheap housing and bargain studio spaces. Charlotte Kennedy fell in love with Galena while visiting an artist friend who eventually sold her a parcel of land in town. Charlotte relocated a small antique log cabin to the site and used it as a summer and weekend home while she was still teaching.

For the first six years of their retirement, Charlotte and George lived in the cabin, but with its tiny rooms, steep stairs and lack of garage, it wasn't ideal for long-term living. Two years ago, the couple moved to a brand-new, more comfortable white frame house on one and a half acres farther out in Jo Daviess County, about 10 minutes from town. Their new property has great views and space enough for extensive gardening and for Charlotte's latest passion: creating large-scale metal sculptures. She and George comb the region for scrap metal and cast-off farm implements for Charlotte to weld, a skill she picked up in an auto-body course at a local vocational school — just one more Galena-area amenity.

Whereas the Kennedys moved from a log cabin in the historic district to a bigger house outside town, retirees Patricia and Joe Terry did just the opposite. In 1993, the couple moved from a stately five-bedroom, three-floor Victorian gem in Wilmette, on Chicago's North Shore, to a small — make that tiny — 150-year-old cottage in old Galena. The Terrys now live happily, though snugly, in a mere 840 square feet.

"Sometimes it gets pretty small," Patricia says. "Then the dog and I take a walk, and it helps," says Joe with a laugh.

Like the Wittenbrinks, the Terrys used their cozy home as a weekend getaway long before they retired. And like the Kennedys, they connected with it through friends. The Terrys' friends owned a minuscule 19th-century house — known as a "miner's cottage" — in Goat Hollow, a deep, narrow valley in the middle of town. It's so secluded that you might live in Galena for years and not know it's there.

"We so loved this little valley," Patricia says, but when the house next door to their friends' home came up for sale in 1981, the first thing they thought was, "we can't really do this." She was teaching drama full time at a private girls' school, and Joe was putting in long hours as a veterinarian. They bought it anyway.

"This is our 'house in the country' — in town," Joe jokes. Small though it is, there's still room for their musical instruments — he plays cello, she plays violin — and a big rambunctious dog named Dolly that they rescued from the Dubuque, IA, humane society where Joe is on the board of directors. Patricia sings in a chorale in Dubuque and directs a church choir in Galena. "I just feel as if I've fallen into a pot of gold," she says.

The emotional scale-down to their miner's cottage was easier because their big Victorian, where they'd raised their three children, stayed in the family. Their daughter, her husband and their six youngsters moved into it when the elder Terrys moved out.

But the material transition was a different matter, since the Terrys had to pare down even more dramatically than most retirees. Joe gave away half his library, for example — about 2,500 books. But there were a few things they couldn't part with — things that couldn't fit in the miner's cottage.

The Terrys' solution is a good example of the kinds of compromises new Galenians make to live in their chosen community. They got themselves a getaway from their getaway.

They're renting an efficiency apartment in one of downtown Galena's commercial buildings. It functions as an annex, holding the remainder of Joe's books, some heirloom furniture, Patricia's antique doll collection, their VCR and a kitchenette with just enough room to make popcorn when they decide to rent a movie and spend an evening "in town."

The town and county are both different now from what they were when these retired couples first encountered them. The three aspects of the area — old Galena, Jo Daviess County and the Galena Territory — now form a remarkable community, startlingly sophisticated but comfortably down-home.

Today's tourists can enjoy elegant bed-and-breakfast inns, good restaurants, art galleries, gift and antique shops, good golf and skiing, and spend time touring what Galena is famous for — historic houses on the hills above the Galena River (including the U.S. Grant Home, a gift to the victorious general from grateful citizens).

But the really important thing is that those activities benefit lifelong Galena residents as well. The whole area remains a living, breathing community. As proof, just look at the changes in the Galena Territory. It can no longer be called a resort community, says Ellen Wittenbrink, nor is it just a retirement community. It's both, and "it's more than that," she says.

Granted, part-timers with second homes still predominate, but there are also close to 500 full-time residents, and they aren't all retirees. Some young families and even some young singles have moved in. Ellen describes the result in terms that fit the entire Galena area: "I think," she concludes, "we're getting a nice mix." ●

Grand Junction, Colorado

Hiking, fishing and biking make this Colorado town a hit with outdoors enthusiasts

By Steve Cohen

You can't ask much more of a comunity that makes relocating retirees feel like they are getting younger rather than older. And that's what retirees say about Grand Junction, perhaps known best for the nearby natural wonders of the Colorado National Monument. The town of 45,000 on the western slope of the Rocky Mountains is becoming home to retirees seeking an energetic outdoor lifestyle.

Grand Junction is cradled in the fertile Grand Valley, which lies between three natural barriers. The Little Bookcliffs cut across the northeastern skyline. The world's largest flat-topped mountain, Grand Mesa, covers the southeast. And the incredible, monolithic rocks and plunging canyons of the Colorado National Monument create a western wall.

"The thing I like best about this town is the beautiful valley," says Dick Gerhardt, 57, a retired traffic manager from Philadelphia who moved to Grand Junction in 1997 with his wife, Aylene, 60, a retired schoolteacher. "We're a day trip from the Grand Canyon, Albuquerque or Yellowstone National Park. We have mountains all around us where we can hike, ski or snowmobile. The town next to us is known for its fruit, so we have lots of fresh fruit," he says.

The Gerhardts seriously considered other retirement sites but also liked Grand Junction's friendly residents and moderate weather. "We used to go down to Pine Isle, GA, about 80 miles northwest of Atlanta, but discounted it because of high humidity. My wife's first choice was Maui, HI. We used to go there every summer for a couple of weeks," he says.

Colorado was Dick's preference. "We used to come out to Colorado every Christmas to ski, beginning in 1986," Dick says. When he suggested Colorado, Aylene was receptive but didn't want to live in an area where winters were long and hard. "That's when we started look-ing around the state and discovered this area that's known as the banana belt," Dick says.

Eight local vineyards and abundant cherry, peach and apple orchards around Grand Junction attest to the moderate climate. With above-freezing low temperatures averaging 35 degrees in January, and with only 25 inches of snow a year, winter in Grand Junction is not exactly the roughest in the Rockies.

The Grand Valley was carved from rugged geography by the Colorado and Gunnison rivers and was one of the last settled regions in the lower 48 states. Grand Junction takes its name from its location at the confluence of the two great rivers. And it's not far from some of the West's most fabulous sites.

Another couple, Bill and Jane Stewart, both 78, discovered Grand Junction the second time around during their retirement. Originally from Topeka, KS, where Bill sold insurance and Jane was a homemaker, they spent their first 16 years of retirement in Vero Beach, FL, and had a second home in Vail, CO. Now they spend much of their winters at a second home in the Phoenix area. "But we still come back to Grand Junction," Jane says.

The winters here are colder than Jane would like, and she's not much of a fan of the occasional snow, but Bill likes to be in or near the mountains. "The winters are quite mild," he says. "I like to do a lot of hiking. I come back in the winter from Phoenix to ski."

Their son lived in Grand Junction, and they had visited three or four times over a period of about a year before deciding to move here. They knew at the time that their son would be leaving, but they moved anyway. Their home backs up to the public golf course at the Seasons at Tiara Rado, a master-planned community.

"The primary reason we left Florida was allergies I picked up while living there," Bill says. "And we sure don't miss the humidity and the bugs," adds Jane. Solid health care provided by two regional hospitals, as well as a growing list of senior-oriented services in the Grand Valley, add to the reasons people like the Stewarts feel comfortable here.

"We find people of all ages, including a growing number of retirees, moving here from all over to enjoy and partici-pate in the outdoor Western lifestyle Grand Junction offers," says Karin Mast, promotions coordinator for the Grand Junction Visitor and Convention Bureau. "While we don't have retirement com-munities that are exclusively for retirees, we do have several beautiful master-planned communities," she says.

"What people tell us is that the biggest reason for choosing to relocate to Grand Junction is because there's just so much to do around here," she says. "The Grand Valley is home to eight wineries. The Colorado National Monument, which is practically right next door, con-tains 20,000 acres of incredible rocks and canyons. You can hike the canyons, visit Indian ruins, spot bald eagles and deer. And we have access to seven raftable rivers, from mild float trips to exciting whitewater."

The Grand Valley also is located with-in the famed "Dinosaur Diamond" of western Colorado and eastern Utah. The area is internationally known for its wealth of dinosaur excavation sites, exhibits, fossil trails and hands-on pale-ontological activities. There are several historic and scientific museums, a sym-phony orchestra and live theater at ven-ues that include Mesa State College.

"We're getting bigger and better all the time, culturally," says Karin Mast. "And how many places are there where you can ride on 1,000 miles of mountain bike trails ranging from paved roads to chal-lenging single tracks, or glimpse a herd of 100 wild horses in the Little Bookcliffs Wild Horse Area, a 30,000-acre recre-ation area north of Grand Junction? You can rock climb or hike in the monument in the morning, play golf on the Grand Mesa in the afternoon, and sip a terrific Merlot or Chardonnay from the valley at night."

Attractions like these are why Grand Junction was really the only place that Pete Dickes, 57, and his wife, Karen, 53, considered for retirement. Pete, a banker, and Karen, a data processor, moved from Aurora, IL, 40 miles outside Chicago. Beginning in 1984, they visited every year, in different seasons, and always found it to their liking. They bought a lot in 1997, built a home and

moved in on the last day of 1999.

"The town is extremely friendly," Karen says. Pete recalls a helpful store clerk who impressed him soon after he moved to Grand Junction. "I went to the Sears store to purchase a Skil saw," Pete says. "We weren't able to find one, and I purchased another item on my Visa card and left. The next day I had a phone call from the clerk, who had located the saw I was looking for, had gone to the office to get my name from the Visa transaction, looked up my telephone number, and left a message that she had the Skil

saw if I still wanted it. That wouldn't happen in Chicago."

They're happy here, according to Pete. They're also happy with their home in the Seasons at Tiara Rado. A small drawback is that the development doesn't have a clubhouse, but they belong to the Bookcliff Country Club nearby, where they play a lot of golf.

"I'm sitting here at home looking at the Colorado National Monument," Karen says. "It's absolutely beautiful." She also appreciates the area's four seasons and moderate climate. "The weath-

Grand Junction, CO

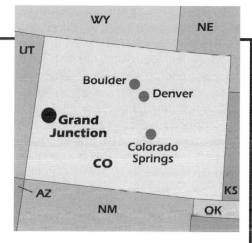

Population: Approximately 45,000 in Grand Junction, 123,000 in Mesa County.

Location: On Interstate 70, 258 miles west of Denver. Grand Junction lies in a fertile high desert mountain valley at an elevation of 4,586 feet.

Climate:

	High	Low
January	36	15
July	94	64

The weather is very dry and relatively warm for Colorado's western slope.

Average relative humidity: 8%-18%

Rain: 8.64 inches

Snow: 25.4 inches

Cost of living: About average

Average housing cost: $177,045

Sales tax: 7.65%

Sales tax exemptions: Prescriptions, groceries and residential energy.

State income tax: For married couples filing jointly and single filers, taxable income is taxed at 4.63%.

Income tax exemptions: There is an exemption from taxable pension and Social Security benefits of up to $20,000 for each person age 55-64 and up to $24,000 for each person age 65 and older.

Intangibles tax: None

Estate tax: None

Property tax: Mill levies vary depending on location. For a home in downtown Grand Junction, the rate is about 75 mills. The assessment rate on residential properties is estimated at 7.96%. A $177,045 home with an assessed value of $14,093 ($177,045 multiplied by .0796) would have a tax due of approximately $1,057 ($14,093 multiplied by .075).

Homestead exemption: The homestead exemption for senior citizens provides an actual-value reduction to a maximum of $100,000. This applies only to a primary residence for citizens over the age of 65. Also, this exemption is applicable only to a primary residence that has been owner-occupied for the 10 years immediately preceding the subject tax year.

Religion: There are more than 100 churches of varying denominations, as well as two synagogues.

Education: Mesa State College offers programs for adults.

Transportation: I-70, U.S. Highway 6 and U.S. Highway 50 pass through the area. Walker Field is an airport served by United Express, America West and Sky-West/Delta, as well as charter services. Bus and train service is available from Greyhound and Amtrak, respectively. Rental cars are provided by Avis, Budget, Enterprise, National, Sears and Thrifty. Shuttle and taxi services are available from several local firms.

Health: There are three hospitals in Grand Junction with a total of 395 beds. An assisted-care facility, Grand Villa Assisted Living Community, (970) 241-9706, offers one-bedroom apartments for $2,960 monthly. Another assisted-care facility, offering 72 one-bedroom apartments in three buildings, is located in Fruita, five miles west of Grand Junction. There are 14 nursing homes in the Grand Junction area, with a total of 1,000 beds.

Housing options: Redlands Mesa golf course community is newer, combining golf and outdoor recreation in a 500-acre

development featuring a world-class golf course designed by Jim Engh, with more than a third of the community dedicated to natural open space, and home sites priced from $170,000 to $450,000. For information, call (877) 501-6372 or visit www.redlandsmesa.com.

Visitor lodging: Grand Junction Visitor and Convention Bureau recommends about 30 motels and hotels. About half of those are national chains. The largest motel is a 292-room Holiday Inn, with indoor and outdoor pools, a hot tub, restaurant and lounge, $84-$94, double occupancy, (888) 489-9796. The Grand Vista Hotel carries a AAA three-diamond rating. It features an indoor pool and hot tub open 24 hours, restaurant and lounge, $69-$79, some including breakfast, (800) 800-7796.

Information: Grand Junction Area Chamber of Commerce, 360 Grand Ave., Grand Junction, CO 81501, (970) 242-3214 or www.gjchamber.org. Grand Junction Visitor and Convention Bureau, 740 Horizon Drive, Grand Junction, CO 81506, (800) 962-2547 or www.visitgrandjunction.com.

er out here is just very, very good," she says. "It has very low humidity, around 15 percent," Pete adds. "It's perfect for golf."

"Every time we go away to Aurora, I miss being here," Karen says. "When I get about 50 miles outside of Denver I feel like I'm coming home. And that's amazing, considering I left a place I've lived all my life. It felt like home here immediately."

Part of the attraction is the opportunity for recreation. "Within two hours we can be in the mountains, we can be in a snow resort, we can be in a desert. It's amazing the variety of places we can get to from this central location," Karen says. "Active seniors would enjoy living in this town. People are always out walking or hiking or biking. It's the most active area I've ever seen. People get out and go.

"You would think we're going back in age instead of aging," Karen says.

In part because of their active lifestyle, the Dickes have found that their tastes in autos have changed from a Pontiac Grand Prix and Mazda RX-7 to a four-wheel-drive Honda Sierra and a Jeep Wrangler. "Pete and I have gotten into off-roading," Karen says.

For Bill and Jane Stewart, the activity of choice is golf. The Stewarts eat dinner at their country club every day, then play nine holes of golf. They like it here so much that they are building a bigger house just a block and a half away in the Seasons at Tiara Rado.

"We're moving from the 14th tee to the 17th tee," Bill says. "We love the Seasons and we decided we need a larger home. It's a wonderful place for almost anyone who has grown up in a small town or for those looking for a little slower lifestyle."

Bill does note that it's an overnight trip to a large city — Denver or Salt Lake City — for cultural activities. Jane acknowledges a challenging fact of life far from Florida's malls. "I'm here, I'm adjusted to this life," sighs Jane, "but I can't spend all the money I want!"

Dick Gerhardt doesn't particularly care for summer heat that averages 93 degrees in July. It's a dry heat, but in summer he's learned to do his outdoor chores early, getting them done before midmorning. Otherwise he waits until late in the evening.

And there were a few surprises. "We paid $24 to register a car in Pennsylvania, old or new," he says. "Here, it cost me $650 to register a new car. A friend bought a new motor home, and the tax was $5,000."

Overall, though, he finds the cost of living lower. Dick had several requirements on his relocation wish list, "a lower cost of living, and decent year-round weather being the most important." He and his wife researched and traveled quite a bit in the year before they retired, and yet the place they chose was not found in any of the books they read.

"We came out here first in 1996 to ski. After skiing, we drove to this area, looked around, liked what we saw, went home and put our house up for sale," he says. "When we had a firm buyer, we flew out, spent a week and a half, picked out a house and bought it," says Dick, who selected a home in a new subdivision that was under construction. "The next time we came we were following a moving van."

For those who enjoy hiking, downhill skiing, snow-shoeing, or target and trap shooting, Dick feels the Grand Valley is really special. "You don't need a target range here — you just go out into the desert," Dick says, noting that 65 percent of the 3,400-acre county is federally owned forest or desert and also prime recreation space. There also are six area golf courses.

"Anyone who likes fishing, hunting, snow-skiing, hiking, mountain biking — any kind of outdoor activity — would enjoy living here," he says. ●

Grand Lake/Grove, Oklahoma

Easy living draws retirees to Grand Lake O' the Cherokees
in the Ozark foothills of northeast Oklahoma

By Mary Lu Abbott

Jim and Jan Gottardi lived in Chicago, St. Louis, Houston and as far away as Milan, Italy, during Jim's career. But when it came time to choose where they wanted to enjoy life after work, they packed up and headed to Oklahoma.

Oklahoma for retirement? The state doesn't make Top 10 lists — but the place the Gottardis chose regularly pops up among choice sites for retirement: Grand Lake O' the Cherokees.

It's a huge lake, about 65 miles long with 1,300 or so miles of shoreline in the green, wooded, hilly country of northeastern Oklahoma.

A recreational haven, it's in a mainly rural area but easily accessible to the Will Rogers Turnpike (Interstate 44). Several small towns on or near the lake provide plenty of activities and amenities, and it's only about an hour from Tulsa and even less from Joplin, MO.

The Gottardis, who grew up in Pennsylvania and met in college, discovered Grand Lake when Jim was with Phillips Petroleum Co., now ConocoPhillips, in Bartlesville, about 60 miles northwest of the lake.

"In northeastern Oklahoma, there are a ton of lakes. On this one, you can have waterfront property and a dock. We bought a cabin in 1988, and that convinced us we were lake people," says Jim, noting that they enjoy boating and other water sports.

Being able to live on the water is a major attraction at Grand Lake, a project of the state of Oklahoma. The Gottardis enjoyed the lake cabin so much that in 1993 they built a larger home on 225 feet of waterfront with a dock in a 662-acre gated, golf-course community called The Coves at Bird Island.

Jim, 63, took early retirement from Phillips in 1993 and began working with an Italian oil company, so they moved to Milan for two years and then were transferred to Houston. They had sold their home in Bartlesville but kept the lake home, which they used for vacation getaways when they lived in Texas.

Jim retired again in 1999. "We stayed in Houston one year to see what we wanted to do. We didn't really know where we wanted to live," says Jan, 59. They looked at Lake Conroe outside Houston, dismissed the Lake of the Ozarks in Missouri because they felt it was too crowded, and thought about Arizona, Florida and Rockport, TX, where they have friends.

"We definitely wanted on the water — and on freshwater, not saltwater," Jim says. They soon decided there was no better place than Grand Lake. Beyond the water sports and good fishing, Jim says, "we have a very active community. It's predominantly retirees."

Another couple who found their way to The Coves was Matt and Judy Starcevich, who came for a weekend on the lake with friends who had a sailboat. They liked it so much that they bought a summer cabin in 1988. They both grew up in the Chicago area and first lived in Oklahoma when Matt earned a graduate degree at the University of Oklahoma. He later taught at Notre Dame, joined Phillips in Bartlesville and then started his own management training business in Bartlesville. Judy taught in elementary school for a number of years.

In the late 1990s, they began to think about retiring, as Matt wanted to ease out of his consulting business and travel less. "We love Oklahoma. We love the climate. We really have seasons here," says Judy, noting that the redbud and dogwood trees splashed the woods with colorful blossoms this spring. "We like where we're located. We didn't want to go farther north or south." They found a larger home more suited to full-time living on a point of Duck Creek.

"We love getting on the lake. In fact, we don't mention 'boat' in front of the dogs," says Judy, 61, noting that their dogs want to go immediately if they hear the word.

"We enjoy going out in the boat to eat at places on the lake," adds Matt, 61, who says that they often cruise at sunset and go for brunch on Sundays.

A vibrant blue body of water with many coves, Grand Lake is clean and not overcrowded, the Starceviches say. Matt is involved with a group monitoring water quality, drainage into the lake and development around the shores. There has been concern about drainage from septic tanks and runoff from poultry farms in the area. "We want to be sure this resource is going to be here for our children," Matt says.

To many people, the area is unknown. "We have friends from a suburb of Detroit who came to visit us, and they could not believe it. They never thought of places like this in Oklahoma — because it's hilly, it's green and there's lots of trees. It's not like western Oklahoma, where it's flat," Judy says.

For Carol and Mike Langley, their decision was to trade retirement in the Arizona desert for life on Grand Lake. Mike had relatives in this area, but they really hadn't thought of Oklahoma for retirement. They spent most of their careers in Denver, CO, and San Diego, CA — Mike as a systems analyst and Carol in human resources. Mike, 64, took early retirement in the '90s, and they moved from Denver back to San Diego, where they had kept a home. He went into consulting, and she continued her career.

"We really liked San Diego. It's the best weather year-round, but the price of homes is so expensive there," he says. Then they visited friends who lived in a gated golf community in the Phoenix area. "Mike plays golf, and that was appealing. It was much more reasonable in Phoenix," says Carol, 63.

They moved to the Phoenix area in the mid-1990s, living in two different active-adult communities. She liked all the amenities of the communities, friendship with others of the same age and easy access to urban facilities. While he

Grand Lake/Grove, OK

Population: About 5,670 in Grove, about 39,100 in Delaware County, and an estimated 150,000 around the entire lake.

Location: In the foothills of the Ozarks in northeastern Oklahoma, Grand Lake is about 65 miles long and has about 1,300 miles of shoreline, with housing developments scattered around it. Grove, 76 miles from Tulsa, is the business hub on the eastern shore. Langley, with about 680 residents, and Disney, even smaller, are the main towns on the south end of the lake at Pensacola Dam.

Climate: High Low
January   46   26
July   94   73

Average relative humidity: About 60%

Rain: 42 inches

Snow: 9 inches

Cost of living: Below average to average

Average housing cost: $139,005. New housing averages about $150,000, but you're more likely to pay $175,000 and up off the lake and from $250,000 up on the waterfront. Homes go above $1 million.

Sales tax: Varies from 5.5% in the county to 8.9% in Grove and other towns.

Sales tax exemptions: Prescription drugs, electric or natural gas utility bills for residential use.

State income tax: Rates range from .5% to 6.25%.

Income tax exemptions: Social Security benefits are exempt. There is an exemption for private pensions of up to

$10,000 for each taxpayer with an adjusted gross income of up to $37,500 for single taxpayers and $75,000 for couples filing joint returns. There is an exemption for federal, state and local pensions of up to $10,000. The total pension exemption cannot exceed $10,000 per person. Military retirees may exclude the greater of 50% of their retirement income or $10,000.

Estate tax: None for spouses. For lineal heirs, there is no estate tax for the first $1 million in 2006 and succeeding years. For estates above the exemption amounts, rates range from .5% for a taxable estate below $10,000 to $838,850 plus 10% of the amount over $10 million. For all other beneficiaries, there is no exemption. Rates range from 1% to $115,200 plus 15% of the amount over $1 million.

Property tax: From $71.91 to $80.86 per $1,000 assessed value, with homes assessed at 11.5% of market value. Taxes on a $150,000 home with homestead exemption noted below would range from about $1,169 to $1,314 a year.

Homestead exemption: If it's their main residence, owners can exempt $1,000 off the assessed value.

Religion: The Grove area has about 30 places of worship for varying denominations. More options are available elsewhere around the lake and in nearby towns.

Education: A branch of Northeastern Oklahoma A&M College offers credit and enrichment classes in Grove. The main college is in Miami, 24 miles northwest.

Transportation: Residents can call a van for door-to-door transportation to services around Grove. A trolley runs throughout the Grove area in summers.

Health: INTEGRIS Grove General Hospital serves the region with an expanding medical complex, which will include a new hospital, offering a wide range of care, including specialties. Craig General Hospital is in nearby Vinita, within a half hour or so from most points around the

lake. More extensive health services are available in Joplin, MO, 43 miles northeast.

Housing options: There are numerous developments and individual lots and acreages around the lake with everything from cabins to custom homes. In Grove, **Melody Point**, (800) 527-4406 or (918) 786-2438, is a small, gated community in a wooded lakeside setting with homes starting around $200,000. In Grove, **Patricia Island Estates and Golf Club**, (800) 495-5253, has an 18-hole championship golf course and lakefront and golf course homes from the $180,000s. On the western shore of the lake, **Vintage on Grand Lake**, (877) 664-7263, is a gated community with pool, tennis, boat slips, nature trails and homes from the $215,000s; the neighboring **Dogwood Hollow** development has new homes from about $70,000. **The Coves at Bird Island**, (918) 782-3269, has a staffed security gate, a private championship golf course, clubhouse with planned activities, and waterfront and wooded home sites in the Duck Creek area toward the south end of the lake; homes start at about $200,000. **St. Andrews Harbor** on Monkey Island, a peninsula in the central part of the lake, (918) 257-8484, has homes from about $253,000 and golf villas from $139,000.

Visitor lodging: Shangri-La Resort on Monkey Island has a spa, two golf courses, pool, tennis and varying accommodations starting around $75 a night, (800) 331-4060. In Grove, Best Western TimberRidge Inn has rooms from about $70 a night, (877) 785-6725.

Information: Grove Area Chamber of Commerce, 9630 Highway 59 N., Suite A, Grove, OK 74344, (918) 786-9079 or www.groveok.org. Grand Lake Association, 9630 Highway 59 N., Suite B, Grove, OK 74344, (866) 588-4726 or www.grandlakefun.com. South Grand Lake Area Chamber of Commerce, P.O. Box 215, Langley, OK 74350, (918) 782-3214 or www.grandlakechamber.org.

enjoyed the golf, he says all the regulations for homeowners "took a little getting used to," as he'd not been accustomed to so many guidelines, including restrictions on exterior colors of homes.

On a trip to see family in Oklahoma last year, they decided to look for possible retirement sites. "The hot weather in Phoenix burned us out," Mike says.

They toured around Tenkiller Lake and Tahlequah, farther south, but did not see any houses they liked. When they returned to Arizona, Carol began checking more places, including the town of Grove on Grand Lake, which had been recommended by the innkeeper where they stayed in Oklahoma.

On the Internet, she found a house at Grove that looked promising, with the front of the house across the street from the lake and the back of it on the Patricia Island golf course. "We liked the inside from what we could see. It was new," she says.

They returned to Grand Lake in the fall, located a real estate agent, saw the house they'd found on the Internet and, at the agent's insistence, looked at others around the lake for comparison. But the house they saw on the Internet won their hearts. Back in Arizona, two hours after they signed papers to put their home on the market, it was sold. So they scurried to arrange purchase of the home on Grand Lake and moved in December 2003.

They live in Patricia Island Estates & Golf Club, which has an 18-hole championship course. "The houses are not all alike. Even though there are not a lot of rules, the houses are kept up. People care," says Carol. They're only 10 minutes from downtown Grove, but deer frequently roam their neighborhood.

On the eastern shore of the lake, Grove is the business hub and the address for a number of communities built on the shoreline. Its 2004 population is about 5,670. Grove has been the fastest-growing town in the fastest-growing county in Oklahoma for most of the last half-dozen years, and retirees are fueling most of that growth. The median age in Grove is 49.9.

A trading center dating to the early 1800s, Grove has a mixture of American Indian, cowboy and pioneer history. As the Indians were forced to move west from the Appalachians, many settled in eastern Oklahoma, known as Indian Territory, in the 1860s. After the Civil War, settlers moved into the valley, and Grove was incorporated in 1888. It covers 11 square miles.

To bring electricity to the area, the state in 1940 built Pensacola Dam across the Grand River between Langley and Disney, about 30 miles south of Grove. The resulting lake grew as a recreational center for weekend escapes and summer vacations, attracting people mainly from Oklahoma City, Tulsa, Wichita and the greater Kansas City area.

Today small fishing boats, big cruisers and all types of craft ply the waters. There are 110 marinas and an estimated 6,000 private docks, according to the South Grand Lake Area Chamber of Commerce in Langley. With the size of the lake and so many arms and inlets, it doesn't feel crowded, residents say. The Duck Creek area toward the south end of the lake is reportedly the second-most-affluent area in the state and has more than 2,000 boats that are more than 35 feet long.

Lori Gray, a real estate broker at The Coves, has watched the area develop since the mid-1970s. The Coves is on the western shoreline in the Duck Creek area with a mailing address at Afton, a small town inland. When The Coves first opened in the 1980s, waterfront lots were about $50,000, and now the limited number remaining run around $200,000, she says. Interior wooded lots average $20,000. Most lots are a half-acre.

"Where we are is more rural," Judy Starcevich says of The Coves. The Starceviches and Gottardis shop and do business in both Langley and Grove or in Vinita, a slightly larger town to the west. "Everything takes 20 minutes or a half hour to get to. The roads are curvy," Judy says.

Grove and the areas around it are more developed, with major stores such as Wal-Mart and Lowe's, boutiques and restaurants, and it's busier on weekends and during summer vacations. Grove has an expanding medical complex. Among attractions are five state parks around the lake and Har-Ber Village, a turn-of-the-century collection of 100 cabins, homes and buildings with period furnishings and implements, a nature trail and gardens.

A community theater group in Grove stages and hosts live productions, and an amphitheater at Disney has outdoor biblical-themed shows in the summer. Tulsa, slightly more than an hour away, offers more extensive cultural attractions.

"The people here are the friendliest," says Carol Langley. "It's overwhelming. If you go into the Lowe's or Wal-Mart, you have so many people ask to help you. They don't just point to something. They physically take you there. Part of it is that Southern hospitality."

The other couples echo the warmth and outreach of the area. When one of their neighbors had a medical problem and needed to go daily to Joplin, a group of residents in The Coves community organized a driving pool for him. "We had 25 guys (helping). It's a group of seniors called the Romeos — Retired Old Men Eating Out. We have breakfast every Wednesday," says Jim Gottardi.

The Starceviches and Gottardis find plenty of action in their community, with potluck meals monthly, a large Fourth of July catered barbecue to accompany fireworks on the lake, golfing tournaments, bridge groups and more on the calendar. The community has an 18-hole championship golf course, the only private one on the lake. There are four other courses, including two at the Shangri-La Resort on Monkey Island and one at Patricia Island Estates.

Numerous regattas challenge boaters, and fishermen compete for the big catch in more than 300 tournaments celebrating the abundance of bass and crappie here. Enrichment classes are available locally at a branch of Northeastern Oklahoma A&M College. "Fun things are happening all the time," says Matt Starcevich.

Carol Langley had sung in a Sweet Adelines women's barbershop chorus previously and found one in nearby Joplin, with members from four adjoining states. She and a group carpool once a week for rehearsals and recently came in fourth in regional competitions.

Both Matt Starcevich and Jim Gottardi have been volunteers with the men's golf association at The Coves, and Jim now is director of the property owners association. Jan Gottardi, who was a teacher for a few years, is active with a philanthropic educational organization. Matt, who still does some consulting work, serves on the board of directors for the Northeast Oklahoma Electric Cooperative and the executive committee of the Grand Lake Sail and Power Squadron, which promotes water safety. He and Judy are active in their church, assisting with a new building program.

The Gottardis say their property taxes are much lower here than in Houston. Even with Oklahoma's income tax, they're paying less in taxes overall than they did in Houston, where there is no state income tax. The Langleys feel their costs are less here than in Arizona.

Grand Lake has fairly moderate seasons, although Judy Starcevich warns about occasional heat. "It's hot in summer, after the Fourth of July. September cools down and is beautiful," she says. "We jump in the lake to beat the heat when it's hot." The Starceviches also have a condo retreat in southern Colorado.

Mike Langley was concerned that it might be too cold for Carol, and although it snowed the day they moved into their home, he says four winter storms brought only about five inches of total snow, which didn't stay long on the ground. For her part, Carol is waiting to see how she fares with the summer humidity. "I've already enjoyed watching the seasons, because you don't have seasons in Phoenix. I enjoyed seeing the pear trees bloom and all the birds playing outside," Carol says.

While the lake area attracts thousands of retirees, the lifestyle may not be for everybody, the couples note. "If an individual really wants a lot of cultural activities, they would find it inconvenient here. But if you're active, like the outdoors, want near or on the water and golfing and fishing, this is an ideal place," says Jan Gottardi.

Judy Starcevich says that while it's an active area, it's comparatively quiet. "If you want the hustle and bustle, you won't like it. It's more laid-back," Judy says. She suggests living in or close to Grove if you want to be near most amenities.

"I'm absolutely happy here," says Matt Starcevich, who enjoys looking out on the lake from their home. "We enjoy traveling but always like coming home here. It's relaxing to sit on the deck," Judy adds.

"One thing never changes: People come here for enjoyment," says Lori Gray, the real estate broker. ●

Grants Pass, Oregon

Retirees forge new paths in this Rogue River town in southern Oregon

By Stanton H. Patty

Roy and Camille Lindsay were driving home to California on Interstate 5 after a few days of house shopping in Grants Pass. It was the peak of the commute hour when they reached Medford, 30 miles south of Grants Pass. "Yes, yes!" Roy Lindsay exclaimed.

"We were able to drive the freeway speed limit all the way through Medford. No rush-hour traffic. Wonderful."

And so, in September 2000, the Lindsays moved from fast-paced Livermore, in northern California, to Grants Pass and the serene surroundings of southwestern Oregon. "We are greatly at peace here," Camille says.

"And now I have the shortest commute there is — from the bedroom to the study," Roy adds.

Roy, 67, a retired computer scientist, and Camille, a nurse, are among active retirees who make up almost half of the population in this city of 25,000 or so. "There are a lot of young families, too," Camille says. "It's a nice balance."

Grants Pass was not the site of a Civil War battle. But pioneer settlers did name the community in honor of Gen. U.S. Grant when they learned of Grant's victory in the 1863 Civil War battle for Vicksburg in faraway Mississippi. Grants Pass is the seat of Josephine County, named for the first Anglo woman to reach the area. That was in 1851, when prospectors roamed the creeks here in search of gold. Josephine Rollins didn't stay long, but her name lives on.

What's the main attraction here for the Lindsays and other retired couples? "It's the climate," says Dwight Ellis, executive director of the Grants Pass/Josephine County Chamber of Commerce. That climate: mild, sunny weather most of the year, moderate rainfall, light winds and rare snowfalls.

And then there's the scenery. The Rogue River, a favorite with rafters, kayakers, campers and sport fishers, races right through the heart of Grants Pass. The snow-crowned Siskiyou Mountains are in view from most neighborhoods. Sapphire-blue Crater Lake, Oregon's only national park, is about 100 highway miles to the northeast. The rugged Oregon coast and redwoods of California's coast are about the same distance to the west via U.S. Highway 199.

It's a small city, yes, but certainly not culturally deprived. Grants Pass has theater, a symphony, a galaxy of galleries, a community college with adult-education courses and more. The celebrated Oregon Shakespeare Festival is in Ashland, only 40 miles to the south by Interstate 5. Jacksonville, a historic gold-rush town 35 miles south, is the site of the Britt Festivals, where audiences picnic under the stars while enjoying programs ranging from jazz to classics performed by top-rated artists.

Grants Pass retirees have exciting stories to share when they get together. Roy Lindsay is an example. The former computer scientist, now managing his investments as a day trader, was an Air Force pilot for more than seven years, often in air-sea rescue work. He flew several missions in support of early astronauts, "in case anything happened."

He remembers a spectacular flight in Alaska when he flew a C-124 Globemaster transport from Elmendorf Air Force Base on the outskirts of Anchorage. "We broke through the clouds, and there was Mount McKinley, totally clear," Roy says. "It was a marvelous sight." Roy and his crew were fortunate. Statistically, North America's highest mountain — at 20,320 feet — is in full view only about 20 percent of the time, and much of that is during frigid winters.

Travels have taken the Lindsays from London to Tokyo. "But it is the Pacific Northwest that we enjoy now," Camille says.

Ditto for Dr. David Trump and his wife, Elaine, who moved to Grants Pass in 1993 from Washington, DC. David, 70, a pediatric surgeon and a retired major general in the Air Force Reserve, formerly was deputy surgeon general of the Air Force. He also served as dean of the Uniformed Services University of the Health Sciences, a medical school for armed forces officers in Bethesda, MD.

Elaine, 58, a retired surgical nurse, was a volunteer at the White House and the Smithsonian Institution during David's military service in Washington. In Grants Pass, the Trumps tend to three acres of Syrah and Zinfandel wine grapes on their 25-acre property in the historic Applegate Valley. Oregon Trail pioneers etched covered wagon ruts through the verdant valley during their arduous westward journey.

"We wanted something meaningful to do in retirement, so we decided to grow grapes," David says. "We sell the grapes to wineries — we don't plan on having a winery of our own."

After the grape harvests in late September and October, the Trumps go traveling — mostly to provide polio immunizations for children in India, China and other countries. Their next immunization destination is Niger in West Africa. David serves as a Rotary International volunteer for the medical missions. He also has volunteered at a medical clinic in a remote section of the Amazon, 500 miles from the Amazon's mouth.

Two other local retirees also have seen much of the world. Joe and Wilma Henner, both World War II refugees from Soviet-occupied Poland and Germany, met in Toronto, Canada, in 1952, married and moved to San Jose, CA, in 1963. They settled in Grants Pass in 1975.

Austrian-born Joe, 72, owned an automobile-mechanics business in California, sold the company 25 years later and semiretired. Later, in Grants Pass he bought a service station-equipment business, sold it four years later and retired again. Now the Henners have a Christmas-tree farm here.

They spend most of the winter seasons in the Palm Springs area, where

Joe, an avid golfer, says he has counted at least 128 golf courses. Wilma, 68, sometimes golfs with her husband but prefers tennis.

It is difficult for any of the Grants Pass retirees to find something negative to report about life in this contented corner of Oregon. If there is one across-the-board complaint, it is the lack of big-city-

Grants Pass, OR

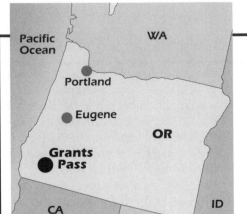

Population: About 25,000 in the city of Grants Pass, 78,350 in Josephine County.

Location: Grants Pass is located on the Rogue River in southwestern Oregon, adjacent to the north-south Interstate 5 freeway. Grants Pass is the seat of Josephine County. It is about 245 highway miles south of Portland, OR, and 412 miles north of San Francisco. The California state line is 57 miles to the south via I-5. Driving distance to Brookings, on the Oregon Coast, is 104 miles. Distance to Crescent City, on the California coast, is 86 miles.

Climate: High Low
January 47 33
July 90 52

Rain: Annual average is 32.6 inches.

Snow: Annual average is 2.3 inches.

Average relative humidity: 67%

Cost of living: Generally comparable to prices in Portland for housing, groceries and utilities.

Average housing cost: About $200,000 to $210,000 for an existing three-bedroom home.

Sales tax: None

State income tax: For single filers, it ranges from 5% of taxable income up to $2,650 to $413 plus 9% of the excess over $6,650. For married couples filing jointly, it ranges from 5% of taxable income up to $5,300 to $825 plus 9% of the excess over $13,300.

Income tax exemptions: Social Security benefits are exempt, as is all federal pension income based on service performed before Oct. 1, 1991. For federal pension income based on service before and after

Oct. 1, 1991, the pension subtraction is prorated. Federal pensions for service on or after Oct. 1, 1991, and state and private pensions are not exempt.

Estate tax: Applicable to estates of $1 million or more. For estates exceeding this amount, an Oregon Inheritance return must be filed.

Intangibles tax: None

Property tax: $13.54 per $1,000 of assessed valuation in the city. Outside the city, most of the county is taxed at $6.19 per $1,000 valuation. The tax on a home valued at $200,000 in the city would be about $2,708.

Homestead exemption: The homestead deferral program exempts from property taxes those 62 and older or disabled who meet certain income requirements. There is a 6% interest on the deferred amount, payable at death or upon selling the home.

Religion: More than 100 local churches serve about 30 denominations.

Education: Rogue Community College, with full-time enrollment of about 4,650 students, has its main campus about three miles west of Grants Pass. There is a branch campus in Medford, 30 miles south of Grants Pass. Southern Oregon University, a four-year college, is in Ashland, 40 miles south of Grants Pass.

Transportation: The nearest major airport for Grants Pass-area residents is the Rogue Valley International Airport in Medford. Carriers serving the Medford airport are United Express, Delta Connection, Horizon Air and America West. Josephine Community Transit is the public-transit system for Grants Pass and Josephine County. Full fare is $1; 50 cents for seniors. There also is curb-to-curb service, with wheelchair lifts, for seniors with disabilities. Curb-to-curb fares start at $2 in-town, and vary, depending on distance traveled.

Health care: Three Rivers Community Hospital, with 100 beds, opened in Grants Pass in 2001. It offers 24-hour emergency service, a family birthing cen-

ter, critical-care units and other facilities. Three Rivers, part of Asante Health System, is affiliated with Rogue Valley Hospital in neighboring Medford. About 180 medical and osteopathic physicians, 75 dentists and 23 chiropractors serve Grants Pass and Josephine County.

Housing options: Grants Pass is composed mostly of single-family homes. Some residential acreage is available in rural areas of the county. However, residential acreage is becoming scarce because much of Josephine County is controlled by the U.S. Forest Service, the Bureau of Land Management and other government agencies. Housing for seniors includes the new **Horizon Village** retirement community for residents age 55 or older. Horizon Village, about 2.5 miles west of the city center, offers rental duplexes and single-family homes designed for seniors. Rentals range from $1,250 a month for a 813-square-foot duplex to $2,100-$2,600 for single-family homes with about 1,800 square feet, (541) 955-0777 or www.horizonvillage.com.

Visitor lodging: Grants Pass offers a wide variety of lodging options, with about two dozen motels and six bed-and-breakfast inns. Motels range from establishments such as the Riverside Inn Resort, (800) 334-4567, with double rates for seniors from $80 to $107 a night, depending on season, to the Best Western Grants Pass Inn, (800) 553-7666, with senior rates from $73 to $87. B&B choices include the five-unit Ivy House, (541) 474-7363, for $65 a night, including a full breakfast.

Information: Grants Pass/Josephine County Chamber of Commerce, P.O. Box 970, Grants Pass, OR 97528-0290, (800) 547-5927 or www.grantspasschamber.org. City of Grants Pass Economic Development Department, (541) 474-6360 or www.ci.grants-pass.or.us. Josephine County Economic Development Department, (541) 474-5210. Southern Oregon Regional Economic Development Inc., (800) 805-8740 or www.soredi.org.

style airline service. The closest airport is the Rogue Valley International Airport down in Medford, and it is served only by four smaller airlines. To board major airlines for long-distance flights, Grants Pass residents must travel either to Portland (almost 250 miles north of Grants Pass) or to the San Francisco area (about 400 miles to the south).

"That adds to the cost, so we often opt to drive," says Wilma Henner.

Medical care in Grants Pass wins plaudits from retirees. Almost new is the 100-bed Three Rivers Hospital in Grants Pass. Three Rivers is associated with the larger Rogue Valley Medical Center in Medford. "And there are lots of good doctors here," Wilma says.

As was the case with many seniors planning ahead for their retirement years, the Lindsays considered other communities before choosing Grants Pass. One possibility was Oakhurst, CA, near the southern entrance of Yosemite National Park. But the Lindsays had friends in Grants Pass, came for a visit, found the slower pace here to their liking and decided, "This is it."

The Henners also looked around California for possible retirement sites before choosing Grants Pass. Then one day Joe Henner came across a real-estate advertisement in their hometown San Jose newspaper listing property in Grants Pass. He decided to visit Grants Pass and have a look.

"How would you like to move to Grants Pass?" he asked Wilma after returning from his solo trip. "No way,"

she replied. "But then I fell in love with Grants Pass," Wilma recalls. "The scenery is lovely, and the people are wonderful."

Joe and Wilma bought four acres of hillside property — room enough for their Christmas tree farm, as things turned out — with a two-bedroom, 1,600-square-foot home in the south end of Grants Pass. As for Roy and Camille Lindsay, they have a three-bedroom home with 2,100 square feet in the northern section of the city — "a nice, 15-minute walk to town," Camille says.

The Trumps considered several areas, including Sedona, AZ, where they owned property, as well as the Washington, DC, area and East Coast communities. "But this is where we wanted to be," says David. Their 5,000-square-foot home in the Applegate Valley is at an elevation of 1,200 feet, with a dynamite view of 6,500-foot Grayback Mountain in the Siski-yous. The house was built with plan-ahead senior features, including extra-wide doors "in case there ever is a need for wheelchairs," Elaine says.

Maybe it's something in the water or the invigorating Northwest weather, but few towns boast more energetic folk than the Grants Pass retirees. In addition to growing grapes and conducting overseas medical missions, David Trump lectures occasionally at the Uniformed Services University and teaches military-trauma courses to physicians at Fort Sam Houston in San Antonio. He is chairman of the board of education for the Rogue

Valley Community College System and is on the board of the Southern Oregon Adolescent Study and Treatment Center.

Elaine Trump is active with the PEO Sisterhood, a philanthropic organization that raises money for scholarships to help women achieve their educational goals. The Trumps also find time to go touring with a Grants Pass-area RV club.

Roy Lindsay is a baritone with the Rogue Community College Chorus and serves as president of the Rogue Valley Symphony. "It's a very good symphony, with 75 to 90 musicians," he says.

The orchestra's roster includes doctors, lawyers, teachers and other professionals. Camille Lindsay is hospitality chairperson for symphony concerts. She also volunteers at a Grants Pass elementary school and at the library of the Christian Science Reading Room in Grants Pass. Hiking with friends is one of her favorite activities. She walks most days for 30 to 40 minutes.

Joe Henner volunteers with a public-safety unit that patrols parking areas set aside for disabled drivers in law-abiding Grants Pass. "We used to issue a number of citations (for parking violations), but now it's hard to find cars illegally parked in this town," he says.

Wilma Henner is a longtime volunteer at the Grants Pass/Josephine County Chamber of Commerce. Wilma, the one who responded, "No way," when her husband suggested they move to Grants Pass back in 1975, is a full-time Grants Pass booster now. "I'm never moving again," she says. "It's beautiful here." ●

Green Valley, Arizona

A tiny Arizona desert retirement community finally comes of age

By Ron Butler

In 2006, Tucson, AZ, celebrated its 331st anniversary. At precisely the same time, Green Valley, the upscale, age-restricted retirement community to its south, marked the 31st anniversary of its founding. Nothing really separates the two communities except 25 miles of Interstate 19 and 200 years.

Ah, but the differences couldn't be more spectacular. Sprawling Tucson, with a population of about 532,000, somehow manages to retain a sense of Wild West spaces and dusty bravado, while Green Valley, population 29,000, couldn't be more neat, trim and refined.

That's why the people who live in Green Valley like it so much. Cradled in the Santa Cruz Valley, a happy mixture of the oldest of Arizona's history (it was part of a 16th-century Spanish land grant) and the most modern of its times, Green Valley has one of the best climates in the country. At an elevation of 2,900 feet, it's consistently seven to 10 degrees cooler — averaging 80 degrees in the day and 50 at night — than Tucson. Laced with mountain ranges east and west, wild cholla (jumping cactus) and towering saguaros, the scenery couldn't be more stunning.

Elements such as these are what motivated Charles and Mary Townsend, 70 and 68 respectively, to settle into Green Valley's Espinoza Estates nine years ago. Chuck, a retired Air Force major originally from Wilkesboro, PA, and his wife, a former medical assistant, weighed all the pros and cons as any seasoned, world-traveling couple would.

It wasn't a quick decision. They initially moved to Colorado Springs, but eventually Green Valley's clean, safe, quiet appeal won them over. Crime is so unusual in Green Valley that when a trio of masked gunmen robbed a local fast-food restaurant several months ago, it made television and newspaper headlines throughout the state. (Attempting a similar robbery in neighboring Sahuarita two nights later, the trio was apprehended by police.)

"Green Valley has no gangs, no graffiti, no blazing streetlights," says Mary Townsend, whose trim good looks defy the fact that she and Chuck are great-grandparents twice over. Their two children have given them five grandchildren.

Lighting in Green Valley is kept at a low — some say romantic — glow so as not to impede nocturnal gazing at several nearby observatories, the Fred Lawrence Whipple Observatory and those at nearby Kitt Peak. Eight and a half miles long, the town of Green Valley is unincorporated, functioning with a quasi-governing board called the Green Valley Community Coordinating Council. Proposals to incorporate repeatedly appear on the ballot in local elections but are always defeated. "The last thing we need," says Chuck Townsend, "is another layer of government."

Like most of his fellow Green Valley embajadores (ambassadors), Chuck participates in many volunteer projects in and out of town. An avid horseman (former president of the Santa Cruz Valley Horseman's Club), he's particularly active in a group dedicated to the preservation and promotion of the Anza Trail, the 4.5-mile stretch along the Santa Cruz River from Tumacacori to Tubac, part of the National Historic Trail that runs from Nogales to San Francisco, set down in 1775 by Spanish explorer Juan Bautista de Anza. Participation includes a re-enactment of the early trail ride with costumed riders and the area's finest horses. Townsend looks as imposing in a conquistador's outfit as he does in Air Force blues.

Volunteerism also is a high priority with Charley Stevenson, 79, and Berta Humphrey, 73, who share a home and life in Green Valley. Both Charley and Berta hail from the Midwest — Waterville, KS, and Iowa City, IA, respectively.

"When I came here 20 years ago, everything struck me as ugly," says Berta, a former high school teacher. "But I quickly began to appreciate the beauty of the deserts, the pecan groves, the mountains."

Both Berta and Charley are devoted to desert walks where squirrels, rabbits, coyotes and javelinas (wild pigs) often scurry across their path. "I wake up and the sky is sunny. It's always sunny," Charley says. "I feel warm and safe." And to help ensure that safety, Charley is a member of SAV (Sheriff's Auxiliary Volunteers).

Charley, who has a real-estate background, points to affordable housing as a real advantage in Green Valley. "You can get a furnished villa with one bedroom and one bath for less than $35,000. Freestanding homes can be had for $80,000 to $100,000. There's a barbecue outside, patio and no bugs. Not even flies," he says. An amateur astronomer, Charley also appreciates the clear night skies. "Arizona is geology by day, astronomy by night," he says, quoting famed British author J.B. Priestley.

Proving that golf and the desert are made for one another, Green Valley has four public courses and three private. Initiation fees at the popular Green Valley Country Club vary, with packages starting at $2,400 and monthly fees of $370 for a family of two. Guests are welcome but must pay nominal greens fee charges. Members are required to spend a minimum of $60 a month in food and beverage charges.

Golf is a priority throughout the area, and for many, golf carts are the transportation of choice. Several major streets have special golf cart lanes. The Kevin Costner hit golfing movie "Tin Cup" was filmed 20 minutes away at the golf and country club in Tubac.

While most of Green Valley is age-restricted, there are a few areas where families with children live. There's also a section on the outskirts of town devoted to high-end motor homes, those in the $200,000 range.

There is no regular bus service in Green Valley, but there is plenty of van, shuttle and charter service. Green Valley residents like to travel in groups, and charter buses are always taking them to theatrical performances in Tucson or the nearby Casino of the Sun and Desert Diamond Casino, or to square dances, professional and University of Arizona ball games, restaurants and special museum openings and gallery exhibits. Before several major supermarkets came to town (Safeway, Wal-Mart, Bashas'), busloads of Green Valley residents were a common sight hunkering down the aisles at Tucson's many markets.

James and Rosemary Long, 71 and 68 respectively, came to Green Valley via Wilkesboro, PA, in 1978 and settled into a four-bedroom townhouse in what is now one of the older, classier sections of town. They liked the idea of being in the center of things where they could walk everywhere. James is a former securities trader for a major corporation.

The Longs enjoy the good life — the theater, symphony and classy restaurants, citing the Agave Restaurant in the Desert Diamond Casino, just north of Green Valley, as one of their favorites. Several local restaurants also get high marks, namely China Vic's, Manuel's Mexican Restaurant, the Old Firehouse (occupying the former fire station) and the nearby Burro Inn, built on the site of a former Titan Missile silo, one of 18 that

Green Valley, AZ

Population: About 29,000, dropping to about 17,000 in the summer.
Location: In Southern Arizona, midway (about 30 miles) between Tucson and the border town of Nogales.
Climate: High Low
January   67   31
July   101 61
Annual temperatures average 80 degrees during the daytime and 50 degrees at night.
Average relative humidity: 25%
Rain: 10.86 inches annually
Cost of living: About average
Average housing cost: Prices for homes in Green Valley generally range from around $125,000 for the smaller and older residences to the mid-$500,000s for homes in the Acres Foothills or in Madera Reserve, a development near Madera Canyon. Home ownership in Arizona has been booming for several years thanks to interest rate cuts and low-cost mortgages. Property values have remained strong.
Sales tax: There is a 5.6% state sales tax.
Sales tax exemptions: Groceries and prescription drugs.
State income tax: For married couples filing jointly, graduated from 2.87% of taxable income up to $20,000 to 5.04% minus $2,276 on amounts over $300,000. For single filers, graduated from 2.87% of taxable income up to $10,000 to 5.04% minus $1,138 on amounts over $150,000.
Income tax exemptions: Social Security benefits and up to $2,500 on federal, state and local government pensions are exempt.
Estate tax: None

Inheritance tax: None
Property tax: About $14 to $16 per $1,000 of assessed valuation. Tax on a $100,000 home would be about $1,000 to $1,200.
Homestead exemption: None
Religion: Many denominations are represented in Green Valley. A guide to places of worship is available through the chamber of commerce office.
Education: Off-campus extension classes are frequently offered by Tucson's Pima College and the University of Arizona.
Transportation: Oddly, there are bus stops in Green Valley, but no buses. Taxi service also is nonexistent. Although several attempts have been made in the past to provide a volunteer taxi service, none is currently in operation. Greyhound, on its route between Tucson and Nogales, stops in Green Valley, and the Arizona Stagecoach Co. offers door-to-door service to and from Tucson International Airport.
Health: Nearby Tucson offers 15 hospitals and a number of specialty clinics. Green Valley has nearly two-dozen adult-care homes, two nursing homes, three assisted-living centers, affiliated medical clinics, dental offices and ambulances with trained emergency medical technicians and paramedics.
Housing options: Medium-priced and luxury condominiums, townhouses, patio homes and ranch-style homes are all available, as are mobile homes. Numerous agencies handle rentals, including Long Realty, (520) 625-5000; Green Valley Rentals, (520) 625-6608; Tower Rentals, (800) 461-5093; and Premier Properties, (800) 507-9217. Meritage Homes is developing three active-adult communities in Green Valley: **Canoa Ranch**, with homes from the mid-$200,000s to the mid-$300,000s, (800) 528-4930; **Las Campanas**, where homes start in the $220,000s, (877) 658-5444. Visit www. meritageactiveadult. com. Robson Communities has developed **Quail Creek**, (888) 648-0332 or www.robson.com, an active-adult community with championship golf, pro shop, lighted tennis courts, fitness center, pool and social center. Home prices start at $304,000.
Visitor lodging: There are three motels in Green Valley. Nearby are resort hotels, lodges and bed-and-breakfast inns, RV parks and guest ranches. Best Western has 110 rooms at $74.95 per double, (520) 625-2250. The Holiday Inn Express has 60 rooms at $69 to $119 per double with free breakfast, (520) 625-0900.
Information: Green Valley Chamber of Commerce, 270 W. Continental Road, Suite 100, Green Valley, AZ 85614, (800) 858-5872 or www.greenvalleyazchamber.com. The chamber's executive director, Jim DiGiacomo, heads a staff of about 35 volunteers.

ringed the city of Tucson during Cold War days. Another such site is now the Titan Missile Museum in Green Valley, where guided tours are offered through the only partially dismantled re- minder of serious international tension.

The Longs are quick to point out Green Valley's many acting, drama and reading groups. "If I had known Green Valley was so intellectual, I would have never moved here," jokes James.

Because of its newness, Green Valley has no fading homes or ancient forts and temples to crow about, but if you continue a few miles south on I-19, you'll find Tubac, the state's first settlement. It boasts Tubac Presidio State Park, which contains the ruins of an 18th-century Spanish colonial fort, and some 80 shops and art galleries. Mount Wrightson and Mount Hopkins, the highest peaks in the Santa Rita Mountains east of Green Valley, were named for U.S. Cavalry officers killed by raiding Apaches. And some 30 miles south of Green Valley is the Mexican border town of Nogales, where you can shop and buy low-priced prescriptions, eat great Mexican food (Elvira's at Obregon 1 is tops) or just practice your Spanish.

Green Valley's wealth of facilities includes 12 recreational centers, tennis courts, three major shopping plazas, top-notch medical facilities, including four affiliated medical clinics, two highly rated nursing homes, dental offices and emergency services. More than 300 clubs and organizations are represented, including one that at first glance always causes eyebrows to raise — the Green Valley Rug Hookers.

With its clean, wide, palm-lined streets and towering saguaros popping up all over the place (the multilimbed giant cactus plants are protected; it virtually takes an act of Congress to relocate them), Green Valley is a remarkably pretty town. The architecture is a fusion of Spanish and Western styles, sprawling houses with arches and tiled roofs and mud-brick walls. Nothing is out of place. Swimming pools sparkle in the sun.

Off in the distance, in any direction, you can hear the swat of a golf ball or the thunk of a tennis racquet. The local radio station plays Golden Oldies. All seems right with the world. For many, it's the town at the end of the rainbow. ●

Hattiesburg, Mississippi

Newcomers quickly feel at home in Mississippi university town

By Richard L. Fox

In the early 1990s, Tom and Jane Moseley were looking for a town where they could spend their retirement years — "just a nice place where we could be integrated into the community," Tom recalls.

They left their home near Atlanta in 1992 and settled into Hattiesburg, a city of about 46,000 residents in southern Mississippi. Now Tom, 60, a retired IBM engineer, and his wife, Jane, 58, a homemaker, are so well integrated into their new community that Tom is the featured commentator on a retiree-attraction videotape produced by the Hattiesburg Area Development Partnership.

"The first and foremost attraction for us was its friendly people," says Tom. "This is a thriving town . . . the leaders have a great 'can-do' attitude."

This also is a town that rolls out the red carpet for retirees. In January 1995 the Mississippi Department of Economic and Community Development named Hattiesburg the first "certified retirement city" of its Hometown Mississippi Retirement program. The statewide mission promotes Mississippi as a retirement haven and helps city leaders market their communities to relocating retirees. Cities must meet a long list of criteria in order to be certified, including good healthcare facilities, available housing, educational and cultural opportunities and a retiree-attraction committee.

An integral part of Hattiesburg's retiree-attraction effort is the Retirement Connection. A division of the Area Development Partnership, this organization is staffed by senior volunteers — called "connectors" — who contact prospective new residents and share information about Hattiesburg as well as their own experiences.

Charles and Helen Short received a phone call from a Hattiesburg connector shortly after visiting the town. "The information and assistance we received from that group was vital in our decision to move to Hattiesburg," says Helen, 67.

The Shorts moved in June 1995 after 35 years in Rochester, NY.

"When we moved down here, we were the 100th retired couple," recalls Charles, 69. "So we got a little publicity from that." They also got a reception, a key to the city from the mayor and a basket of goodies.

"A few months later we sat down and wrote a letter saying, 'Thank you, Hattiesburg,' for all of the things Hattiesburg had done to make us feel so warmly received. We got quite a bit of press from that and made even more new friends as a result. We had about 20 calls from people saying, 'We're so glad you're here,'" says Charles.

Bill and Nancy Litwiller, 68 and 65, moved to Hattiesburg from Hampstead, NC, where they had lived for 10 years after a long career in overseas government service. They found the Retirement Connection to be a tremendous help to their relocation. "We had friends we didn't even know — before we arrived here," says Nancy, who along with her husband now is active in the group herself.

Recently Hattiesburg has been cited in a number of national publications for its "livability," low cost of living and retiree-oriented programs. The U.S. Conference of Mayors awarded the city the Livability Award for communities of less than 100,000 residents.

If there's one thing upon which everyone in Hattiesburg agrees, it is that 12,000-student University of Southern Mississippi and 2,300-student William Carey College are largely responsible for the town's growing reputation as a great place to live.

Prominently situated on a pretty, oak-shaded campus just west of downtown, USM is credited for bringing a youthful exuberance and vitality to Hattiesburg, along with social, cultural and educational opportunities generally found in much larger cities. William Carey College is a private, Baptist-affiliated, four-year

liberal arts college.

For many retirees, the university's Institute for Learning in Retirement (ILR) is the ultimate example of the community's outreach to its retired population. Established under the auspices of the university and Mississippi Hometown Retirement, the organization is run by retirees for retirees and offers dozens of courses year-round, with retirees often serving as instructors.

Seminars and a luncheon lecture series bring large numbers of people to its off-campus location. Members attend ILR classes for about $15 each and a $50 "listener's license" is available to audit regular university classes on a noncredit basis. Other perquisites include discounts on all continuing-education courses at USM and honorary University Club membership.

The Litwillers have taught and taken courses at the institute and rank it high among their reasons for retiring to Hattiesburg. Helen Short, who was a microbiologist at the University of Rochester in New York, lectures at ILR, and she and Charles, a former marketing executive, regularly attend classes there.

Helen credits what she calls the "centrality" of Hatticsburg for its special qualities. "It has a small-town environment and yet all of the amenities," she says. "At Christmastime, people come from 100 miles away to do their shopping and participate in festivities."

Heavily traveled Hardy Street is Hattiesburg's primary east-west artery. It is named for founder Capt. William H. Hardy, who first recognized the area's potential when surveying a new railroad route; the city itself is named for his wife, Hattie. Hardy Street connects a busy, attractive downtown to the university, hospitals, restaurants and shopping malls that extend to the west.

Hattiesburg boasts a number of restored late 19th- and early 20th-century homes, churches and commercial buildings listed on the National Register of Historic Places. A 1985 historic conservation ordinance encourages the restoration of homes and buildings in six separate historic districts. The largest is 23-block Hattiesburg Historic Neighborhood District, which features Victorian, Queen Anne and Greek Revival-style homes. During a Victorian Christmas celebration each December, the district becomes a holiday wonderland.

A striking 53,000-square-foot public library near downtown features a circular 167-foot mural in its atrium. Painted on sandblasted stainless steel by local artist William Baggett, the mural depicts life in Mississippi before a 16th-century visit by explorer Hernando de Soto, and scenes extend all the way to contemporary times. Other library highlights include a 100,000-volume collection, computer lab, books by mail and a growing collection of large-print books. At Lunch With Books sessions held at the library, university professors and writers host lunchtime discussions on such topics as rare book collecting and famous authors.

Hattiesburg was settled just south of the confluence of the Bouie and Leaf rivers, and the gently undulating terrain is marked by lakes, great oaks and towering pines. An exploration of recreational resources reveals an exceptional array of golf courses, public tennis courts, miles of landscaped walking and jogging trails, and water parks for swimming, fishing, boating, camping and hiking. South of town off U.S. Highway 49, Paul B. Johnson State Park has a 300-acre lake, cabins, nature trail, canoe and boat rentals, and fishing and picnic areas.

Hattiesburg's convenient hub location at the intersection of several highways means easy access to Jackson, New Orleans and popular Gulf Coast beaches, all within a two-hour drive.

Hattiesburg serves as southeast Mississippi's regional medical center and has won notice for the quality of its health care. Forrest General Hospital and Wes-

Hattiesburg, MS

Population: 46,103 in Hattiesburg (not including 19,000 college and university students).

Location: In southeastern Mississippi, 115 miles northeast of New Orleans.

Climate:

	High	Low
January	59	39
July	91	70

Average relative humidity: 74%

Rain: 60 inches

Cost of living: Below average

Average housing cost: $139,500

Sales tax: 7%

Sales tax exemptions: Prescription drugs.

State income tax: For married couples filing jointly and single filers, the rate is graduated from 3% of taxable income up to $5,000 to 5% on amounts over $10,000.

Income tax exemptions: Social Security benefits, public and private pensions, IRAs and annuities are exempt. There is an additional $1,500 personal exemption for residents age 65 and older.

Intangibles tax: None

Estate tax: None

Property tax: In Hattiesburg, $165.53 per $1,000 of assessed value, with homes assessed at 10% of appraised value. With exemptions noted below, annual property tax on a home in Hattiesburg appraised at $139,500 is about $2,009 for homeowners under age 65 and about $768 for homeowners age 65 or older.

Homestead exemption: There is a $300 tax credit for all homeowners. For those age 65 and older, the first $75,000 of appraised value is exempt from taxation.

Personal property tax: For automobiles, there is a tax of $165.53 per $1,000 based on 30% of the depreciated value, less a tax credit of 5% of the assessed value.

Religion: There are more than 150 places of worship, including churches and synagogues.

Education: The University of Southern Mississippi offers undergraduate and graduate degree programs. William Carey College is a four-year private liberal arts school. USM's Institute for Learning in Retirement is a self-run, self-directed association of retirees offering a variety of courses.

Transportation: Amtrak offers direct service from Hattiesburg east as far as Atlanta and west as far as Los Angeles. Hattiesburg-Laurel Regional Airport has connecting flights to Memphis. Jackson International Airport is 90 miles away, and New Orleans International is 105 miles away.

Health: Forrest General Hospital is a 537-bed, full-service regional medical center serving 17 counties. Wesley Medical Center has 211 beds. More than 300 medical professionals in Hattiesburg practice 32 specialties.

Housing options: Prices for condominiums and townhomes in older developments start around $93,000. Currently, a limited number of condominiums and townhouses are available, but more are planned. **Timber Ridge** has homes with underground utilities from $128,000. There are several manufactured-home parks in the city and rural areas with new homes from the $60,000s. Homes in historic districts go on the market for about $120,000-$300,000. Master-planned developments include **Canebrake**, (601) 264-0403, a lakeside golf-course community with homes for $239,000 to over $1 million; **Timberton**, a popular golf community just minutes from downtown with homes for $237,000-$350,000; and **Lake Serene**, which has homes on large, wooded lakeside lots with resale prices of $215,000-$567,500.

Visitor lodging: Comfort Suites, from $98, (601) 261-5555. Hampton Inn, $86-$93, (601) 264-8080.

Information: Area Development Partnership, 1 Convention Center Plaza, Hattiesburg, MS 39401, (800) 238-4288 or www.theadp.org.

ley Medical Center have a total of 748 beds and 550 medical professionals. Hattiesburg Clinic has 180 physicians and health care professionals, making it the largest multispecialty group practice in the state. Both hospitals have programs that provide seniors with 100 percent of Medicare-approved hospital costs, plus health education, paperwork assistance and various cafeteria and gift-shop discounts.

A stellar array of museums, art galleries, parks and gardens promote interest in the visual arts, and performing arts forums present plays and musical performances to enthusiastic audiences. The 1,000-seat Saenger Theatre hosts a variety of events; the restored art deco movie palace is a local landmark on the National Register of Historic Places. At noon on Thursdays in October, the Hattiesburg Arts Council sponsors brown-bag concerts in Fountain Park.

As expected in a college town, the university is a source of diverse cultural happenings. The music school features concerts by bands, choirs, a symphony orchestra and vocal artists, while the theater and dance departments perform each spring and fall. The C.W. Woods Art Gallery hosts major traveling shows as well as solo and group exhibitions. For sports fans, USM has an NCAA Division I athletic program.

Affordability figures prominently in Hattiesburg's increasing popularity with retirees. Retirement income such as Social Security benefits, pensions and IRAs are exempt from state income tax, and a generous $75,000 homestead exemption for homeowners age 65 and older helps ease property tax burdens.

When Tom Moseley compared taxes and household expenses such as insurance and utilities between his former home in Dunwoody, GA, and Hattiesburg, he found that living costs were reduced by more than $9,000 a year in Hattiesburg. Charles and Helen Short

also noticed a substantial decrease in their cost of living. "Our property tax went from $5,000 to $1,000, and we went from 1,700 square feet in Rochester to 2,700 square feet here," says Helen.

Bob James, chairman of the Retirement Connection and a Coldwell Banker real estate agent, says newcomers can find a variety of housing at very reasonable prices.

"There are several manufactured-home parks in the area with new homes selling for $50,000 to $75,000. Historic districts have a half-dozen homes on the market at any time, most priced from $120,000 to $250,000."

Hattiesburg's condo and townhome inventory is low (only four such properties on the market at press time), but the few that are available can start in the $90,000s. Older, well-maintained subdivisions, such as the Avenues downtown, have homes priced from the $90,000s, as well. Homes in rural areas around Hattiesburg start in the $60,000s, but most are priced over $80,000.

Lake Serene, a master-planned development outside the city, has homes on large wooded lots situated around several lakes for $215,000 to $568,000. Timberton, south of town with an 18-hole golf course and clubhouse, offers new homes for $237,000 to $350,000.

The Moseleys live in Canebrake, an upscale lakeside community located six miles from town. Amenities here include security guards, walking trails, tennis courts and a golf course. "About 20 retired couples live here," says Tom Moseley. "It's a nicer house, with tremendous amenities, in a nicer neighborhood than Dunwoody, and we paid one-third less for our house here.

"It also has 92 doctors living there," Tom continues. "I tell people (that) if I don't feel well, I stand out in my front yard and just yell out my symptoms and get advice from a dozen specialists."

The Litwillers also bought a house in

Canebrake. Bill describes it as a two-story Arcadian-style home, similar to a Cape Cod with deep porches at the front and back. When they aren't playing golf, their favorite pastime, the Litwillers enjoy reading, computers, gardening and traveling.

Charles and Helen Short bought a one-year-old house in Bent Creek, a subdivision eight miles from town. "It's a young community. We are the old geezers, surrounded by young people. You can count the number of retirees on one hand," says Charles, who enjoys living among younger residents.

Hattiesburg was the recipient of 10 additional police officers via a federal grant under President Clinton's community-oriented policing initiative. Neighborhood enhancement teams patrol higher-crime areas by foot and bicycle, getting to know residents on a first-name basis and leading to a greater degree of cooperation and willingness to report criminal activity.

All three couples — the Moseleys, Litwillers and Shorts — were hard-pressed to come up with drawbacks to living in Hattiesburg. "If you get down to brass tacks," Charles Short says, "there's really not a thing we don't like."

For some, the heat may take some adjustment, though. "The first summer we were here it just about wiped us out," says Helen Short, "but now that we're accustomed to it we have no problem with it."

"We were attracted by a small city that literally has everything," says Nancy Litwiller. "The university is an integral part of the city. The Institute for Learning in Retirement is just wonderful. Medical facilities are outstanding. I think, bottom line, (it's) the people… so kind and so generous and so caring."

"Get connected!" advises Bill Litwiller. "Listen to what the connector has to say. He's a volunteer. He's not selling anything. He'll tell you what's here." ●

Healdsburg, California

Retire among the vines of Northern California

By Fred Gebhart

It's easy to become infatuated with a small town that calls itself the hub of the wine country. Vineyards roll across small river valleys and up the hillsides in all directions. More than 60 wineries lie within a 10-minute drive of Healdsburg's classic Spanish-style central plaza. Hundreds of elegant Victorian-era homes dot quiet streets shaded by century-old trees.

Dotty and Jim Walters don't wonder why they retired to Healdsburg in 1991. "We fell in love with the plaza and the agricultural side of the community," Dotty says. "We still wake up every morning and think we've gone to heaven."

The relaxed country atmosphere lured Dotty, now 67, and Jim, 68, from the upscale San Francisco suburb of Lafayette. When they first saw Healdsburg in 1985, Jim says, they hadn't even started thinking about retirement. He was still advancing his successful career marketing food products to corporate accounts nationwide. Dotty had a thriving dental hygiene practice.

"We came up to Healdsburg with a friend who was scouting for property," Jim says. "We got hooked on the spot. When an old Victorian came up for sale just outside of town, we bought it in 30 minutes, sight unseen."

What they got was a late 19th-century farm near Dry Creek, just beyond the Healdsburg city limits. Originally built without indoor plumbing or running water, the house required substantial interior work to add all the modern necessities as well as a few conveniences. Dotty and Jim also created an extensive garden that has become a favorite place to hold fund-raising events for the Healdsburg hospital and other local groups.

What was originally a small sheep barn has become their guest cottage. And wine grapes were planted in the original pastures decades before they moved in.

"We have what may be the smallest winery in California," Jim says. Grapes from their Big Eleven Vineyards, a mix of Zinfandel, Carignane and other red varietals, provide enough juice to fill two or three 55-gallon aging barrels every year.

"This is winemaking for fun, not profit," he adds.

"We didn't fall in love with Healdsburg just because it's wine country, but it didn't hurt, either."

Love at first sight isn't an unusual story in Healdsburg. Werner Buechy didn't even need to see Healdsburg to be enticed. The Swiss attorney found a photograph of a home surrounded by vineyards in a throwaway real estate magazine. His wife, Dorothy, a human genetics researcher at the University of California at San Francisco, drove to Healdsburg and gave the home a thumbs-up. The purchase closed a week later.

That was 1982. The couple used Healdsburg as a weekend escape for a decade. In 1993, they retired from Mill Valley, a suburban town north of San Francisco. "We moved to Healdsburg to get away from the crowds," explains Dorothy, now 77. Werner recently turned 80.

"It was the relaxed, quiet feeling — the feeling that here was an established town, an integrated community that knew what it was and where it was going," Dorothy says. "Healdsburg wasn't a suburb, and it didn't depend on the big city for its identity. Ten years later, people still recognize the specialness of this town."

Healdsburg's instant appeal is no accident. In a state known for creating and embracing the latest social and technological trends, Healdsburg is a throwback. It is one of California's few surviving examples of 19th-century town planning. It has always been too far from San Francisco to become a bedroom community, has too little easily buildable land to encourage urban sprawl, and has yet to succumb to the social whirl of the wine country.

The town was designed in the 1860s by Harmon Heald, an Ohio entrepreneur who drifted west in the 1850s. Heald was one of dozens of squatters who settled on what had been Rancho Sotoyome, a vast 48,800-acre land grant given to sea captain Henry Delano Fitch in 1841 when California was still part of Mexico.

During the confusing years after California became a U.S. territory and then a state, gold miners, farmers and merchants flocked to the fertile lands surrounding the Russian River, which meanders west to the Pacific Ocean. Heald ended up with a townsite nestled beneath Fitch Mountain near the river. He built a store and post office, laid out a town grid surrounding a central Spanish-style plaza, and sold building lots for the unheard-of price of $15 each.

Grape growers and winemakers have been the economic pillars of the community for more than a century, Jim Walters explains. Healdsburg sits in Sonoma County at the junction of three of America's most decorated wine regions — the Alexander Valley, the Dry Creek Valley and the Russian River Valley.

Just east is Napa County, where California's wine industry was reborn in the 1950s and 1960s and mushroomed amidst a well-publicized shower of gold medals in the 1970s. Healdsburg-area wineries have taken home more than their share of awards, too. But they take more pride in their product than in their gold medals, famous-name winery owners and high-profile wine auctions.

Jim Walters takes a tongue-in-cheek approach to the differences between wine country, Healdsburg style, and wine country à la Napa, where Francis Ford Coppola and other Hollywood movers and shakers have settled. Walters' wine labels are adorned with vintage cars and the slogan, "Napa makes auto parts... Sonoma makes great wines!"

Dotty is more practical about the different approaches to life in the wine country. "Sonoma doesn't court the society pages like Napa does," she explains. "We're more down-home about wine. I don't have to worry about getting dressed up to go to a winery here."

New retiree Warren Watkins doesn't dress up to visit wineries, either. At 63, the retired teacher is more likely to arrive hot, sweaty and grinning after a 20-mile bike ride than to cruise up in his air-conditioned car. If he gets bored biking, there is always something to be done on his 1897 home.

"I've always wanted an older house to work with and to work on," Warren says. "Now I've got it, complete with a brick-lined well in the basement. One of the great things about Healdsburg is that you can find anything from a genuine Victorian to a contemporary building that was finished last week."

Warren enjoys tinkering with his well-preserved historic home almost as much as he likes making wine in the basement. And when he has had enough of

Healdsburg, CA

Population: 11,700 in Healdsburg, 50,000 in the area.

Location: Healdsburg is a major population center in Sonoma County. The 3.5-square-mile town lies 75 miles north of San Francisco off Highway 101 near the Russian River between Fitch Mountain (east) and a low range of mountains (west).

Climate:

	High	Low
January	57	39
July	90	54

Weather is typical California/Mediterranean, warm and dry in summer, cooler and rainy in winter with occasional frosty nights. Snow is all but unknown.

Rain: 40 inches annually, most falling between November and March.

Cost of living: Well above average

Average housing costs: Single-family homes start at $550,000 and condos average $325,000. Rental prices start at $700 for a one-bedroom apartment to $1,500 for a single-family home with 1,200 square feet.

Sales tax: 7.75%

Sales tax exemptions: Groceries, prescription drugs and most services.

State income tax: For married couples filing jointly, state tax rates run from 1% on the first $12,638 to 9.3% (plus $3,652) on amounts above $82,952. For single filers, rates run from 1% on the first $6,319 to 9.3% (plus $1,826) on amounts above $41,476.

State income tax exemptions: Social Security benefits and railroad retirement pensions are exempt.

Estate tax: None. The state's "pick-up" portion of the federal tax was eliminated January 1, 2005.

Property tax: The property tax rate ranges from $11.25 to $11.70 per $1,000 of assessed value, depending on location, plus several hundred dollars in special district fees that also vary by location. Special district fees are higher in newer developments on the outskirts of town. There is a $150 North Coast Hospital fee charged to every parcel. The tax on a $550,000 home with homestead exemption would range from about $6,259 to $6,503. Without homestead exemption, from $6,338 to $6,585.

Homestead exemption: There is a homeowner's exemption of $7,000 off the value of owner-occupied homes. The state's homeowner assistance program reimburses up to $473 to those who are 62 and older, blind or disabled, with incomes under $39,699.

Religion: Healdsburg has some two-dozen houses of worship, with additional churches, temples, synagogues and other places of worship in surrounding communities.

Education: Santa Rosa Junior College is 15 miles south in the city of Santa Rosa, with many courses offered at Healdsburg High School. Sonoma State University, a four-year public institution, is 22 miles south in Rohnert Park. Healdsburg also has three public elementary schools, a junior high school and several private schools.

Transportation: Domestic and international air service is available from Oakland International Airport and San Francisco International Airport, about 90 miles south. Sonoma County Airport has feeder flights to both gateways, and regular airport bus service is available. Healdsburg Transit runs city buses Monday through Saturday, with connections to Sonoma County Transit, which connects cities and towns countywide seven days a week. Bicycling and walking are popular in Healdsburg itself.

Health: Healdsburg District Hospital is a full-service, 49-bed acute care facility with 24-hour emergency services. There are several private medical clinics and medical service providers in Healdsburg with additional hospitals, clinics and providers in Santa Rosa, 15 miles south.

Housing options: Healdsburg has an excellent stock of vintage homes near the downtown area, newer single-family dwellings on the outskirts, and apartments throughout the city. Most new construction is on the outskirts of town, in Santa Rosa and nearby communities, or in unincorporated parts of Sonoma County outside the city limits.

Visitor lodging: Rates are seasonal and tied to wine country tourism, which peaks May to late September. Bed-and-breakfast inns average $125 to $350 per night, depending on location and wine country activities. Hotels and motels start at $69 midweek and run to $400 nightly for high-demand weekends. Accommodations near the plaza (downtown) are generally more expensive. Less expensive motels are located near Highway 101 from Santa Rosa south to Rohnert Park.

Information: Healdsburg Chamber of Commerce and Visitors Bureau, 217 Healdsburg Ave., Healdsburg, CA 95448, (707) 433-6935 or (800) 648-9922 (California only), or www.healdsburg.org. Ask for a free relocation guide.

home improvements, there is hiking, riding, boating, fishing, golf, tennis and floating down the calm, shady reaches of the Russian River as it curves past Healdsburg toward the Pacific Ocean.

"I'm a small-town guy," Warren explains. "I left the city sprawl of Santa Rosa, 15 miles south, because I can walk anywhere in the commercial area in Healdsburg. I prefer local vendors to the 'big box' stores in shopping centers. There's a friendly feeling here."

There is also plenty of open space nearby. Santa Rosa is the edge of suburban sprawl extending north from San Francisco. East, north and west is a mix of vineyards, steep mountain slopes and public parklands that has largely stymied development.

"Healdsburg is really the end of the line in terms of development," Warren says. "There is lots of open space every direction except south, and every reason to expect it to stay open space."

There are also plenty of local activities. Healdsburg supports a long list of dance, music, theater and art groups. In the summer, local musicians stage free concerts in the plaza. The focus is American music, which includes everything from bluegrass and Dixieland to mariachi and marching bands.

Outdoor antique markets draw buyers and sellers from all over the West. And a twice-weekly farmers market brings local buyers the same premium-quality fruit, vegetables, cheeses and meats that command sky-high prices at the most expensive restaurants in San Francisco.

Top-quality local ingredients are also good for the local restaurant scene. The allure and upscale tourist traffic of the wine country has spawned cutting-edge restaurants that would be at home in any major urban area. But the tourist business is seasonal. Financial success depends on steady business from local residents who expect local prices.

"Restaurants have multiplied faster than the population," Jim Walters says. "But the locals have to carry them during the winter. We get tremendous value that you can't touch in the city."

There's another advantage to small-town life: political control. With about 12,000 residents, it is relatively easy to be heard. "Quality of life is what people want here," Warren Watkins says. "The city council is listening, and people are acting on their own. There is a real opportunity to stay small because of our physical location and our city council."

Limits on building permits and restrictions on noise and signs have slowed development. Citizen groups help keep official attention focused. One of the more influential groups is the informal Bench Bunch — residents, mostly retired, who meet over coffee on benches in front of the Downtown Bakery on Center Street. Dotty Walters is one of the original Bunch.

"We got tired of things like the plaza looking run-down, so we did things ourselves, like donating barrels for flower planters," she says. "The city noticed."

The entire plaza area has been refurbished, she says, with new gardens, new landscaping and a restored bandstand. The 1990s plaza renovation helped reinforce a winery-based tourism boom that was already under way.

Tourism is good for the local economy, Dorothy Buechy says, but it also changes the character of the community. The stationer, drugstore, soda fountain and other local businesses that once surrounded the plaza have been replaced by wine country souvenir shops, wine-tasting rooms, new restaurants and a hotel. Artists who once exhibited on the sidewalks or in community centers now have their own galleries.

"Parking is harder now," Dorothy says. "There are a lot of stores in which I don't buy because I'm not a tourist. But it wasn't that long ago that 60 percent of the plaza storefronts were empty. Now they're filled and business is booming. And the variety of local merchants is better than ever before."

That's good news for those who already live in Healdsburg. But prices for housing and retail space have been rising steadily for the past decade. The most expensive areas are downtown near the plaza, Warren Watkins says. Central neighborhoods offer the largest concentrations of older homes, especially the Victorian buildings that have become so popular in recent years.

"You can see prices drop by the block as you move away from the plaza," he says. "Older and bigger houses are in greater demand. It's getting pricey because the word is out that Healdsburg is a great place to live." ●

Hendersonville, North Carolina

This North Carolina town shines in its scenic setting of mountains, rivers and forests

By Richard L. Fox

Not long ago, Hendersonville was considered an undiscovered haven by many retirees. But with a 58 percent increase in population in the last 15 years, it can no longer claim to be undiscovered, although the descriptive word "haven" still applies to this scenic retreat nestled on a Blue Ridge mountain plateau in the southern highlands.

"The growth rate is a plus," says Bill Johnson, a retired bank president who moved here in 1997 from Rockville, MD. "Hendersonville is a nice small town that is growing very rapidly but has a long way to grow before becoming a large metropolitan-type place."

Bill, 61, and his wife, Barbara, 59, feel that the town's growth — much of it generated by relocating retirees — provides an opportunity to help shape the direction in which it moves. "We enjoy being involved in that growth," says Bill. He is not shy about explaining his philosophy of how a town should work. "If you want to become involved in politics you can," he says. "But you don't have to have government-run agencies to get things done. People all over this town are volunteering their services to make it a better place. That's why our taxes are so low."

The Johnsons didn't know anyone when they moved to Hendersonville, but Bill says that, too, is a plus. "That's one of the common bonds everyone has," he says. "You really strike up new acquaintanceships quite easily." In fact, he warns, residents quickly can become socially overextended. "We don't have any spare time anymore," he says. "It's not a popularity thing — people here are just so amenable to meeting new people."

"It's nice to move into a community where everyone is open to meeting new people," Barbara adds. "It's a great place

to grow old because it's not a real glitzy place."

The town's founding is attributed to William Mills, a Revolutionary War soldier, in the 1780s. Chartered in 1847, the struggling backwoods town got a shot in the arm with the completion of a railroad line from Charleston, SC, in 1879. Sweltering Carolina lowlanders and Floridians flocked to this easily accessible, cool mountain retreat for relief from summertime heat and humidity.

For years summer tourism kept merchants busy and smiling. But downtown traffic dwindled after World War II when new suburban shopping malls began springing up in small towns across the country. Hendersonville took steps to ensure the survival of its downtown and in 1986 became a federally designated Main Street city. Today, the fruits of that decision can be seen in the restored historic buildings, wide sidewalks, colorful planters, comfortable benches and free parking along tree-lined Main Street. Antique shops, galleries, boutiques and trendy restaurants now occupy once-empty storefronts, enticing tourists and residents back to the town center.

Only on a late summer weekend in early September, when some 250,000 people descend on downtown Hendersonville for the annual North Carolina Apple Festival, does the town take on the semblance of a major metropolitan area. Then its broad main street fills with apple-munching shoppers, browsers and sightseers in a carnival atmosphere.

"We came, saw it and said, 'this is it,'" recalls Jim Finch about the move he and wife Joan made in 1990. After living 32 years in the hectic northern Virginia suburbs of Washington, DC, the Finches

were ready for the slower pace promised by this small highlands community. As they experienced the scenic beauty of the surrounding Blue Ridge and Great Smoky mountains, discovered the recreational possibilities of the nearby French Broad and Nantahala rivers, and found a new — and affordable — condominium under construction in a master-planned community, the decision was sealed.

Jim, a two-career Navy commander and former principal of Annandale High School in Fairfax County, VA, and Joan, a home economist, say they loved living in northern Virginia, "but Hendersonville is the place to retire," says Jim. "The first year you are here, you are the Club Med," he says. "Everyone wants to come down for a visit and see the beautiful mountains. We have six granddaughters and they love this place. I take them white-water rafting, kayaking, canoeing and hiking."

The Oaks, a 200-unit condominium complex within minutes of downtown, provides everything the Finches were looking for in housing, and at an affordable price. "We bought down," Jim says happily. "We spent less for a new house here — with more square footage — than we got for our old house in Virginia."

He now serves on the homeowners' board at The Oaks and is responsible for building maintenance and upkeep of common grounds. "We had a condo at Cocoa Beach and sold it," Jim says. "If you want to be part of a community, you can't live half a year here and half a year there."

Another couple at The Oaks, Robert and Amy Foster, discovered Hendersonville 10 years ago while visiting her brother, who had retired to Lake Lure, a small resort community 20 miles east.

Amy noticed there was little commercial activity around Lake Lure and asked her brother where he shopped, bought groceries and went to the library. When the answer kept coming up Hendersonville, she told her husband that they should take a look at the town.

They did and liked what they saw. "The Oaks was new, and we found a very spacious condominium — over 2,000 square feet — at a very good price," Amy remembers. "With annual property taxes of $1,700 versus $5,000 in Syracuse," Robert adds.

"We were sick of the snow. I didn't want to shovel anymore," Amy says of Syracuse. "We liked the mountains and scenic beauty of the area — the small town, the four seasons," she says of Hendersonville.

The Fosters immediately became active, joining a church, the Welcome Wagon and Opportunity House, a non-profit arts, crafts and cultural center with more than 1,400 members. Robert, a former television executive for an ABC affiliate in Syracuse, had district oversight responsibility for 41 Rotary clubs in upstate New York and quickly assumed fund-raising and leadership activities for the local club. Amy, who taught high school Spanish, volunteers her language skills and participates in Habitat for Humanity projects.

The Fosters, Finches and Johnsons all were surprised by the array of cultural organizations supported by the small populations of Hendersonville and Flat Rock, a tiny, historic village four miles south. The Henderson County Arts Council and Art League of Henderson County promote visual art programs

Hendersonville, NC

Population: About 11,500 in the city, 98,000 in Henderson County.

Location: On a plateau 2,200 to 3,000 feet above sea level, between the Blue Ridge and Great Smoky mountains, 25 miles south of Asheville and 15 miles north of the South Carolina border.

Climate: High Low
January 47 25
July 84 62

Average relative humidity: 60%

Rain: 52 inches annually

Cost of living: Average

Average housing cost: $243,543

Sales tax: 7%

Sales tax exemptions: Prescription medicine, eyeglasses, some medical supplies and most services.

State income tax: For married couples filing jointly, the rate is graduated from 6% of taxable income up to $21,250 to 8.25% (plus $14,537.50) on amounts over $200,000. For single filers, it is graduated from 6% of income up to $12,750 to 8.25% (plus $8,722.50) on amounts over $120,000.

Income tax exemptions: Social Security and railroad retirement benefits are exempt. Up to $2,000 of distributions from private retirement benefits and IRAs (up to the amount reported in federal income taxes), or up to $4,000 of government pensions may be exempt. Total deductions may not exceed $4,000 per person. Intangibles tax: None.

Estate tax: Applicable to taxable estates above $2 million.

Property tax: In Hendersonville the rate is $9.45 per $1,000 of assessed (market) value. The rate increases for downtown and Seventh Avenue homes by $3.00 and $1 per $1,000, respectively. In unincorporated Henderson County the rate is $5.15 per $1,000. The annual tax on a $243,543 home is $2,301 in Hendersonville, $1,254 outside the city.

Homestead exemption: The first $20,000 or 50% in appraised value (whichever is greater) is exempt for North Carolina residents age 65 and older with incomes of $19,700 or less.

Religion: More than 135 churches and a Jewish synagogue.

Education: Blue Ridge Community College enrolls more than 2,000 students. Its Center for Lifelong Learning is member-directed and offers popular workshops, seminars and lectures for over-50 members.

Transportation: Apple County Transit provides regular public bus service throughout Hendersonville weekdays from 6:30 a.m. to 6:30 p.m. Fare is 75 cents ($15 for a monthly pass) and dial-a-ride service is also available, (828) 698-8571. Interstates 26 and 40, U.S. highways 25, 64 and 176, and the Blue Ridge Parkway serve the area. Asheville Regional Airport, 10 miles north of the city, provides air service to national and international destinations.

Health: Margaret R. Pardee Memorial Hospital is a 222-bed full-service facility with 204 physicians on staff. Park Ridge Hospital has 103 beds and 150 physicians on staff.

Housing options: Carriage Park is a gated community on 399 acres offering such amenities as tennis courts, walking trails and a heated indoor pool. Homesites are priced from $87,000, homes from the low $300,000s and patio homes from the low $200,000s, (800) 639-8721. **Highland Lake**, a 100-acre resort with hiking trails and golf course, has single-family homes from the mid-$300,000s, (828) 692-1359. **Lake Pointe Landing**, a retirement community, has villas, rental apartments, assisted-living services and a life-care center with skilled nursing, (800) 693-7801 or (828) 693-7800.

Visitor lodging: The area boasts 17 motels and a dozen lodges and inns, including Hampton Inn, $82-$96, (828) 697-2333; Holiday Inn Express, $67-$119, (828) 698-8899; Woodfield Inn, $89-$244, (800) 533-6016; Waverly Inn, $169-$269, (800) 537-8195; and Highland Lake Inn, $99-$239, (800) 762-1376 or (828) 693-6812.

Information: Contact the Hendersonville Chamber of Commerce, 330 N. King St., Hendersonville, NC 28792, (828)692-1413 or www.hendersonvillechamber.org. Henderson County Travel and Tourism, (800) 828-4244 or www.historichendersonville.org. Hendersonville Board of Realtors, (828) 693-9642.

throughout the year, including monthly art shows and an annual Sidewalk Art Show in which 110 artists from 16 states display and sell their works.

For music lovers, the 50-voice Carolina Concert Choir, 100-voice Hendersonville Chorale, 70-piece Symphony Orchestra and swing band perform for enthusiastic audiences in all seasons. The renowned Brevard Music Center is a scenic 20-minute drive southwest of town.

Flat Rock Playhouse, designated the state theater of North Carolina in 1961, has been open since 1940, with a brief hiatus during World War II. The Playhouse stages about 10 professional sell-out productions between April and December, performed by local and summer stock actors and actresses from across the nation. Three smaller acting companies, including the all-volunteer Little Theater group, founded in 1966, entertain audiences with performances by local artists.

Carl Sandburg, America's poet laureate, historian, author and lecturer, lived in Flat Rock at his home, Connemara, for 22 years. Built in 1838, the home houses his 10,000-piece collection of books and papers and hosts thousands of visitors annually. Other popular tourism sites include St. John in the Wilderness Episcopal Church (1836), historic Woodfield Inn, the 1879 Hendersonville Depot, the Singleton Centre Art Studios, the 19th-century Johnson Farm, and Bonclarken, the Associate Reformed Presbyterian Church camp that features the 1886 Heidelberg House.

With an elevation of 2,200 to 2,800 feet above sea level, Hendersonville avoids the extreme summer temperatures of Piedmont cities and towns only a few miles south and east. Cooler temperatures and an average annual 52-inch rainfall foster the growth of hemlock, spruce, rhododendron and towering Carolina white pines reminiscent of the giant redwoods of California. Winter temperatures sometimes dipping into the 20s and low 30s bring occasional light snow to the area.

Spring, summer and colorful fall beckon residents to lush green golfing fairways, white-water rivers, dark blue mountain lakes, verdant forests and inviting mountain trails that punctuate the landscape within a 10-mile radius of Hendersonville. Popular outdoor retreats include Great Smoky Mountains National Park and the Pisgah, Nantahala and Cherokee national forests west and northwest of the city; the 390-acre Foothills Equestrian Nature Center in Tryon, a few miles southeast; and the 426-acre gardens of the North Carolina Arboretum near Asheville. Breathtaking scenic vistas, natural habitats for wildlife viewing, and miles of hiking, biking and equestrian trails surround Hendersonville.

The Mills and French Broad rivers just north of town are popular venues for fishing, boating, kayaking and canoeing. Farther west, the white waters of the Nantahala offer excitement and adventure for more daring outdoorsmen.

One statistic that illustrates the impact of retiree migration to Henderson County is the dramatic increase in Social Security payments to county residents. In 1980, Social Security benefits totaled about $47.5 million. By 1990 that figure had grown to $117 million, and in 1998 to almost $200 million, according to Hendersonville Magazine, which estimated that $16.5 million in Social Security benefits was distributed monthly to county residents.

A growing population and greater disposable income have attracted new shopping facilities, including numerous shops and department stores in the Blue Ridge Mall, the World of Clothing, and other discount and factory outlets. "Some people go to Greenville (SC) or Asheville for more upscale shopping," Bill Johnson says. "We're getting a new Super Wal-Mart. That's the big news around here."

The Fosters and Finches have used local medical facilities and rate them "very good" for a small community. Two hospitals, Margaret R. Pardee Memorial and Park Ridge, provide 24-hour emergency services, advanced diagnostic equipment, a certified cancer care center and excellent medical, surgical and intensive care services. Asheville, 25 miles away by interstate highway, is a regional medical center with five hospitals and more than 500 doctors. It provides big-city health care facilities, including heart and cancer centers, trauma services and emergency air transport.

The fast growth of Henderson County's population has put pressure on the home-building industry to keep up with demand, and new housing developments are popping up all over the county. Riverwind and White Oak Park are attractive manufactured-home communities favored by retirees on a budget. Heritage Hills and Heritage Lodge have single-family homes with housekeeping, maintenance, transportation, some meals and personal care options. Lake Pointe Landing and Carolina Village both offer independent-living quarters, assisted-living apartments and long-term care.

Kenmure, Carriage Park, Wildwood Heights, Champion Hills, Cummings Cove, Highland Lake and Etowah's Reach are some of the neighborhoods attracting retirees with a variety of amenities, including great mountain views, clubhouses, pools, golf courses and hiking trails. Demand for resales in The Oaks is strong, according to the Fosters, with "word of mouth" selling most properties before "for sale" signs can be erected.

Danny and Donna (Oz) Ogletree migrated to the area in 1998 after highly successful careers in environmental-process systems and real estate sales and marketing, respectively, in the Piedmont area of the state. Oz's family has lived in the tiny community of Centre Friends (also known as Pole Cat Creek), birthplace of two famous Carolinians, O. Henry and Edward R. Murrow, since 1750, so the move from the familiar rolling foothills of midstate to the mountainous southern highlands was a major relocation decision. History, art and music aficionados, they were lured by the opportunity to pursue these interests, and they bought a home in Flat Rock, the historical-cultural center of the area.

Now working as a real estate sales team in the Hendersonville office of Beverly-Hanks and Associates — "Maybe she and I will retire in the year 3000," Danny says — they have helped hundreds of retirees find their dream homes in one or another of the 154 subdivisions in the area. Continuing-care retirement communities, including Carolina Village, Givens Estate, Tryon Estates and Deerfield, usually are fully occupied, Danny says.

"There are at least nine assisted-living

facilities in the area," Oz adds, but she believes the area needs "more and better transitional homes for seniors between home ownership and assisted living."

The Johnsons found just what they were looking for, but Barbara suggests potential newcomers "vacation here to check out the area." Her husband, Bill, believes visitors who like small-town ambiance will find that there's no better place.

"You can go to Hilton Head and live in a strictly resort environment, but one of the great aspects of this place is that it has resort features, beautiful developments and homes all around the mountain," he says. "You can live in remote scenic areas, but you can get into town in a matter of minutes. It is very convenient, and you feel more connected to the town because you live so close in." ●

Hilton Head, South Carolina

This South Carolina barrier island blends a pristine natural environment
with the amenities of a small city

By Jim Kerr

There are many surprises hidden in the woods as you motor along U.S. Highway 278 on Hilton Head Island, SC. The road is a four-lane divide, fringed on both sides by a thin forest of pines and palmettos. Birds and animals native to the semitropical Lowcountry — blue herons, dwarf deer, alligators — lurk beyond the road, and wide beaches hosting seagulls and sandpipers stretch along the coast of this 12-mile-long barrier island.

But the biggest surprise on this island refuge of birds and animals is the ever-growing presence of man and all his trappings. Only on close examination, behind the veil of woods, does Hilton Head reveal the attributes of a city — shopping malls, restaurants, theaters, offices and a dozen burgeoning resort and residential complexes.

To a large degree, the primordial wetlands and ancient ecosystem that has sustained the flora and fauna on Hilton Head for thousands of years is still here, co-existing with a human urban environment of 34,000 permanent residents who interact and co-habit the island with 2.5 million annual vacationers. Yet no neon signs disturb the night. Only subtle signage reveals the whereabouts of all these people.

"The first time we saw the island, we knew it was the place for us," says Bob Houlihan, who, with his wife, Pat, retired here permanently in January 2001. "We wanted walks on the beach, golf and wildlife. But Pat grew up in Manhattan and we were both used to cities, and we didn't want a retirement community."

Atop a wooden bridge railing, which crosses a tidal lagoon behind the Houlihans' townhouse, sits a great blue heron. He comes here every day at the same time, perching above fishing grounds in this section of an 11-mile lagoon network that meanders through the community. Extending about a mile from the Atlantic beach to just past Highway 278,

the residential complex is called Palmetto Dunes. It's one of 11 so-called "plantations" on Hilton Head — gated communities with golf courses, a variety of housing choices and a large slice of nature's salt-marsh environment.

"The birds alone are beyond beautiful," Bob says. "Our blue heron comes twice a day to feed and stalk the lagoon. There are 50 turtles and a 6-foot resident alligator we call Charlie who suns himself on the bank."

Like many who retire to Hilton Head, the Houlihans traveled along a figurative line of connecting real estate dots. For the first 26 years of his career, Bob, now 66, was a New York City police officer, working his way up to inspector. From a security post at New York's Chemical Bank, he went on to the credit card division and a job with MasterCard before retiring as a consultant for foreign banks.

The couple first came to Hilton Head in 1984 as vacationers on the recommendation of Bob's boss at Chemical Bank. They bought two time-share units in the Shipyard Plantation adjacent to Palmetto Dunes, then found their townhouse in 1995, renting it out for two years while Bob continued to work in New York. But when a debilitating stroke forced him into permanent retirement in 1997, they sold their New York house and began dividing their time between a rented townhouse there and Hilton Head.

"It became clearer and clearer with each trip that this was where we wanted to retire for good," says Bob, now almost fully recovered from the stroke. "We never seriously considered anywhere else."

The growing attachment to the island felt by the Houlihans, and the progression from vacation to retirement, was exactly what the founders of Hilton Head's now formidable resort and real estate empire had in mind. It was in 1956 that Charles E. Fraser bought out his father's interest in the Hilton Head

Co. and began developing Sea Pines, the island's largest and most prestigious plantation.

That same year a two-lane swing bridge was opened, connecting Hilton Head Island, the largest barrier island on the East Coast, with the mainland. Some 48,000 cars traveled across it that first year, but by the time a new four-lane bridge replaced it in 1982, the number of annual visitors had increased to half a million, with a full-time island population of 12,500.

Except for a brief period in the 1970s, when real estate and development slumped, modern-day Hilton Head Island has never looked back. Although ancient Indians hunted prehistoric mammals here 10,000 years ago and the Spanish discovered it in 1521, it was an English sea captain named William Hilton who established the English presence here and gave the island its name in 1663.

Charleston, located 90 miles north, was established a few years later, and Savannah, GA, 45 miles south, came into being in 1733. The closest city, historic Beaufort, founded in 1711, is only 30 miles away. The Civil War and its aftermath altered Hilton Head and isolated it for almost 100 years before it found its present-day niche as a resort and burgeoning island community.

"It's perfectly located midway between New York and Miami," notes David Warren, director of marketing for Sea Pines Co. "Someone's first contact here may be in a group setting — a corporate meeting, business seminar or golf tournament. Then they vacation here with the family. After five visits they buy a condo to rent out or a time-share to use or trade. Then they retire, find the condo too small and buy a house."

The "guest for life" concept envisioned by Charles Fraser sometimes begins with the game of golf. There are 23 golf courses on Hilton Head Island, most of them public, with an overflow of another dozen or so that have spawned in the immediate vicinity of Bluffton, a small but rapidly expanding town across the Intracoastal Waterway. Most of these golf-course communities are mirror images of Hilton Head's gated plantations, with links designed by noted architects like Arthur Hills, Robert Trent Jones II, Jack Nicklaus, George Fazio and others. Real estate on the Bluffton side, however, is considerably less expensive than on the island, and

Hilton Head, SC

Population: Hilton Head Island has approximately 34,000 permanent residents with 2.5 million annual visitors. Nearby Bluffton Township, which includes the town and Daufuskie Island, has 21,000 residents. Beaufort County, the fastest-growing county in the state, has a total population of 135,725.

Location: A foot-shaped barrier island off the Atlantic coast of South Carolina, Hilton Head is about 45 miles north of Savannah, GA, 90 miles south of Charleston, SC, and 30 miles south of historic Beaufort, SC. The island is 12 miles long and three to five miles wide.

Climate: High Low
January 58 48
July 88 75
Average relative humidity: 79%
Rain: 47 inches
Cost of living: Slightly above average
Average housing cost: A wide range of real estate prices from $100,000 for a condo to $6 million for a waterfront home gives Hilton Head Island an average close to $400,000.

Sales tax: 5%. Persons 85 and older pay a reduced sales tax of 4%.

Sales tax exemptions: Prescriptions, dental prosthetics and hearing aids.

State income tax: For married couples filing jointly and single filers, the rates are graduated in six tiers from 2.5% on the first $2,530 of taxable income to 7% (minus $367) on taxable income above $12,650.

Income tax exemptions: Social Security benefits are exempt from state income

taxes, and that portion of benefits taxed at the federal level is deductible from South Carolina taxable income. There is an exemption of up to $3,000 in any pensions if under age 65 and up to $10,000 in pensions if 65 or older. Each person age 65 and older receives an age deduction of $15,000 off any income, although that's reduced by the amount of retirement exemption taken.

Intangibles tax: None
Estate tax: None
Property tax: 4% of appraised value for residents and 6% for nonresident property owners is multiplied by various millage rates of Hilton Head's four districts. Rates range from $165.10 to $175.10 per $1,000. The taxes on a $400,000 primary residence would range from about $2,642 to $2,802, without homestead exemption. The state imposes a personal property tax of 10.5% on the assessed value of boats, recreational vehicles and airplanes, based on their purchase price. The rate is 6.75% for automobiles.

Homestead exemptions: The first $50,000 of the fair market value of a home is exempt from property taxes for citizens age 65 or older.

Education: The University of South Carolina has a campus in nearby Beaufort with about 1,300 students, as well as a 200-acre south campus in adjacent Bluffton. The Technical College of the Lowcountry offers classes at Bluffton High School.

Transportation: Hilton Head Island regional airport has daily service from Charlotte, NC, and Atlanta. Savannah-Hilton Head International, 45 minutes away, offers many additional flights. Taxis and private vehicles are the only way around the island.

Health: Hilton Head Regional Medical Center, a privately owned acute-care hospital, has 93 acute beds with more than 100 board-certified or board-eligible physicians in more than 30 specialties. The hospital is fully certified for Medicare, Medicaid, Blue Cross/Blue Shield and Tricare. The Bluffton-Okatie Outpatient Cen-

ter also provides outpatient services and procedures. A primary care center and physicians offices are located at the facility. Savannah and Charleston hospitals and medical centers provide more extensive care and treatment facilities.

Housing options: Real estate values have sky-rocketed on Hilton Head Island. Today, waterfront homes can range from $1 million to $6 million. Residential property at **Sea Pines**, (800) 846-7829, ranges from $285,000 for condos to $500,000 and up for single-family homes to $5.5-$8 million for oceanfront homes. Prices are not much lower in other plantations, although there is an occasional condo under $200,000. Homes at **Tide-Pointe**, (800) 386-8433, an assisted-living complex of villas and homes, start at $239,000. Off the island, single-family homes in several Bluffton-area communities start at $170,000, including **Del Webb's Sun City Hilton Head**, (800) 978-9781, a 5,100-acre development nine miles west of Hilton Head Island.

Visitor lodging: An array of accommodations ranging from luxury beachfront villas with private swimming pools to motels and bed-and-breakfast inns are available. More than 7,000 villas and time-shares are geared to families with about 3,000 hotel and motel rooms, plus two RV resorts and one off-island campground. The Marriott Hilton Head, (843) 686-8400, located at Palmetto Dunes, has 500-plus rooms, starting at around $119 a night during the off-season. The nearby Hilton Oceanfront Resort, (800) 845-8001, with 323 rooms, starts at $120 off season. Both resorts are on the beach. Rooms at the Main Street Inn, located on the north end of the island, (800) 471-3001, range from $189 to $289 per night, and $20 less per night during the off-season.

Information: Hilton Head Island-Bluffton Chamber of Commerce, P.O. Box 5647, Hilton Head Island,SC 29938, (800) 523-3373, (843) 785-3673 or www.hilton headisland.org.

Bluffton's once modest population has swelled over the past 10 years.

Like Pinehurst and Myrtle Beach, golf is king on Hilton Head Island.

"It takes a lot of our time," says Bill Bury, 64, a retired American Airlines pilot who plays four or five days a week. He and his wife, Susan, 59, live in Leamington, a single-family neighborhood within Palmetto Dunes. Their golf and social associates at the club are a diverse and interesting lot — retired couples from South Africa, London, Spain and "every walk of life." Susan is a professional photographer who has converted a studio business in Bethel, CT, into a beach operation at Hilton Head.

"The beach is a mile away and I ride my bike there everyday," she says. "I'm not working as much as I used to, but through word of mouth I've developed a visiting family portrait business in a kind of beach party atmosphere."

Bill, a certified public accountant before he was a commercial pilot, worried about being disconnected from a thriving freelance tax consulting business. His 28-year career with American produced a lot of pilot and flight attendant clients, and while he lost a few in the move, he employs electronic communication technology to do the job today, spending long hours during tax time and a couple of hours a day the rest of the year poring over returns and providing retirement planning.

While Hilton Head's median age is 46, 24 percent of residents are 65 or older. Most retirees, like Bill and Susan Bury, spend a tranquil life tucked away in the forest and manicured marshland of well-maintained plantation neighborhoods where the architecture and earth tones of residences blend with the natural setting. But even though gated privacy ensures a slow pace inside, the community is an active one.

"We met a lot of people right away," Bill says. "They were more interested in volunteer work than keeping up with the Joneses. Many teach English, sell things for charity, do student mentoring.

There's something for every interest."

The town of Hilton Head Island, incorporated as a municipality in 1983, offers up cultural and commercial amenities similar to any big city. There are more than 250 restaurants on the island, many providing the kind of fine dining made possible by the patronage of 2.5 million tourists a year. The arts are also alive, with exhibits, galleries, a Coastal Discovery Museum, live theater and a symphony orchestra.

"We were active theater-goers when we lived in New York," says Bob Houlihan, "and the Self Family Arts Center located just outside Palmetto Dunes does some very creditable productions. Savannah is 40 minutes away with a symphony and similarly good productions, and Charleston isn't that far, either."

Pat, 64, a homemaker, likes to read on the beach, take yoga classes, work at the church thrift store and play golf three times a week. She spent a year helping her husband, who had been an English major at Long Island University, learn to read, write and speak again after his stroke. Now he's doing something he always wished he could do: teach adult literacy.

Stew and Judy Brown of Chagrin Falls, OH, outside Cleveland, also began connecting the dots to a new life here beginning in the 1990s. They first came to play golf in 1992 on the recommendation of a friend and wound up buying a timeshare unit from Marriott. In 1998 they found their dream home in the Long Cove Plantation.

The fabulous tidal marsh view from the living room window was the clincher. Stew, 61, a former regional vice president for Dow Chemical, occasionally shoos away the island deer nibbling in his back yard, but more often than not they're left on their own while he's working in Beaufort as a volunteer in the Service Corps of Retired Executives (SCORE) program. Judy, 57, volunteers her time with the Junior League and the orchestra.

While golf on Long Cove's private Pete

Dye-designed course was a big plus for the Browns, it was secondary to the island's water and salt-marsh environment. The couple keeps a 23-foot boat nearby on Broad Creek, which they use for recreation and sojourns to Savannah and Beaufort.

Water travel to Savannah is shorter and less congested than by road, and if there is one major drawback to Hilton Head Island, many residents agree, it's the traffic. When the six-mile, $81 million Cross Island Parkway opened in January 1998, slicing across the north end of the sneaker-shaped island, it considerably reduced the load on Highway 278.

But traffic on this major thoroughfare, which connects most of the larger plantations, is always heavy, especially during spring when school break periods run into the April golf tournament. The wide public beaches offer solace, however, as does the 4,000-acre Pinckney Island National Wildlife Refuge in Port Royal Sound, with its miles of bike paths and hiking trails, thousands of birds and no human inhabitants.

Hilton Head Island includes an eclectic mix of nationalities, with residents at various income levels. Descendants of Civil War-era slaves, who developed a folk culture and language known as Gullah, live and work on the island where annual festivals highlight Gullah crafts and folklore. The island also has the largest population of Hispanics, about 4,000, of any municipality in the state.

The likelihood of visits from family and friends was a consideration for many retirees to Hilton Head Island. But the island's family-friendly atmosphere and accessibility has proven to be a magnet. The Burys' grandchildren visit every summer, delighting in golf cart rides to the beach. And last year, the Browns spent 24 weekends entertaining out-of-town guests.

"The permanent residents attract a lot of out-of-towners," Judy Brown says. "We share the beaches and roads, but the infrastructure handles it all quite well." ●

Hot Springs, Arkansas

This historic Arkansas spa town sits amid gently rolling mountains and sparkling lakes

By Marcia Schnedler

From time immemorial, the Hot Springs region of Arkansas' Ouachita Mountains has been a place where strangers meet, make friends and do business.

Here, where 47 healing springs bubbled from the rolling hills and steep-sided hollows, Native Americans found it a place of peace even in times of strife. Tradition has it that the Spanish expedition led by Hernando de Soto stopped here in 1541, fatigued and sick after struggling through the swampy Mississippi River delta ridden with mosquitoes, poisonous snakes and other hazards. The explorers stayed for several weeks of recuperation.

The first settlers arrived in 1807. Hot Springs grew fast into a ramshackle, sometimes rowdy spa town. To preserve both the springs and the scenic beauty surrounding them, Hot Springs was named the nation's first national reservation in 1832 and a national park in 1921.

Today Hot Springs still features springs, streams and wooded mountainsides. Now five sparkling man-made lakes lap its edges or lie within an easy drive — including Lake Ouachita, Arkansas' largest body of water and among the cleanest in the nation. The town, and the national park's historic Bathhouse Row within it, is perched at

Population: About 37,000 in the town of Hot Springs, 88,068 in Garland County. In Hot Springs Village, there are 34,044 property owners and a resident population of 15,000.

Location: Hot Springs lies slightly southwest of the geographic center of Arkansas amid the gently rolling Ouachita Mountains.

Climate:

	High	Low
January	51	30
July	94	70

Average relative humidity: 55%

Rain: 54 inches annually

Snow: 4.5 inches annually

Cost of living: Below average

Average housing costs: In Hot Springs, $182,333 for a new three-bedroom home with two baths and attached garage. Average rental is $532 per month. In Hot Springs Village, prices for homes and townhomes range from $60,000 to $1.5 million.

Sales tax: 8.5% in Garland County, 7.875% in Saline County. (A portion of Hot Springs Village is in Saline County.)

Sales tax exemptions: Prescription drugs and some medical equipment.

State income tax: Graduated in six brackets from 1% on the first $3,399 of taxable income to 7% (minus $763.45) on taxable amounts greater than $28,500.

Income tax exemptions: Social Security, railroad retirement, veteran's benefits and the first $6,000 of pension income is exempt.

Estate tax: There is no Arkansas estate tax for deaths on Jan. 1, 2005 and thereafter.

Property tax: Property is assessed at 20% of appraised valuation. Taxes range from $34.60 to $41.60 per $1,000 of assessed valuation, depending on school district.

Homestead exemption: $300

Religion: Dozens of houses of worship are in Hot Springs; 21 are within Hot Springs Village. Denominations include Assembly of God, Southern Baptist, Missionary Baptist, Church of God, Christian, Christian Science, Episcopal, Evangelical Free Church, Jewish, Lutheran, Methodist, Church of the Nazarene, Presbyterian, Roman Catholic, Unitarian and nondenominational.

Education: The nearest colleges and universities include National Park Community College in Hot Springs, which offers a wide range of courses and associate degrees in the arts, applied science (such as accounting, early childhood education, computer information, graphic design, health information technology) and science (including lab technology and nursing). The University of Arkansas at Little Rock, with bachelor's, master's and Ph.D. programs, is 54 miles away, as is the University of Arkansas for Medical Sciences. Both Henderson State University and Ouachita Baptist University are 44 miles south in Arkadelphia. Continuing education for seniors is available at the Shepherd's Center and senior centers in Hot Springs and the McAuley Center in Hot Springs Village.

Transportation: A full range of ground services includes Hot Springs Intracity Transit and a major bus line. Hot Springs Shuttle serves Amtrak stations in Malvern and Little Rock, as well as Little Rock National Airport/Adams Field, about 55 miles away. A commercial service airport, Memorial Field, is 15 miles from Hot Springs. Little Rock Air Force Base is in Jacksonville, about 62 miles distant. Hot Springs Village's west gate is 12 miles north of Hot Springs on Arkansas Scenic 7 Byway, while its east gate is 31 miles from the intersection of Interstate 30 and Interstate 430 in southern Little Rock.

Health: National Park Medical Center is a full-service acute-care hospital with 166 private beds. It is a referral center for a five-county area and includes a total heart-care center plus a breast-care center among its specialties. St. Joseph's Mercy Health Center includes cancer, women's, heart and diabetes centers, plus home health services, senior centers and a mobile mammography unit. Levi Hospital provides inpatient rehabilitative service at St. Joseph's following stroke, surgery, acci-

the edge of a national forest that extends west into Oklahoma and north to the Arkansas River and the Ozark Mountains beyond. Thanks to its mild winters, boaters, anglers, hunters, hikers, canoeists, bird watchers, golfers and others who love the outdoors can enjoy the region year-round.

Residents and visitors also find a growing district of fine arts, crafts and antiques galleries, family attractions, shopping and dining spots. The town's calendar is packed with festivals and events, from the Arkansas Senior Olympics to an internationally recognized documentary film festival, an Oktoberfest, music festival, jazz and blues fest and an extravaganza of Christmas lights.

That's why the Hot Springs region

remains a place for relaxation and rejuvenation as well as a haven for people who seek a retirement as vibrant as its spring wildflowers and flaming fall foliage.

They find a choice of a myriad of housing styles and prices: Craftsman-era cottages in snug neighborhoods, stately Victorian homes and newly constructed houses. There are condominiums, rental apartments and even prefabricated places with views of lakes, forests, mountainsides and golf courses.

And 12 miles north lies a planned community with nine golf courses and eight lakes of its own.

Bob Honzik had never heard much about Hot Springs or the gated Hot Springs Village until a morning coffee break at work — even though he and

his wife, Mary Anne, had already begun thinking seriously about where to move after retirement.

"A guy was talking so enthusiastically about someplace in Arkansas that I asked my secretary to see what she could dig up on her computer on 'Cooper,' or 'the village,'" says Bob, then marketing manager for John Deere & Co. in Minneapolis.

"Cooper" turned out to be Cooper Communities, the 50-year-old builder and developer of planned communities, commercial property and timeshares. "The village" turned out to be Hot Springs Village.

"The idea of a planned community was off our mental road map," Bob says. "We had gone to Albuquerque, Tucson, Phoenix and other areas, but they

Hot Springs, AR

dents and other injuries or diseases. It also offers psychiatric counseling and assists in day respite care. HealthPark Hospital, which opened in 2002, is owned and was designed by more than 100 local physicians. It is gaining a reputation for convenience and comfortable care. Surgical services include diagnostics, general and orthopedic surgery, gastroenterology, pain management, eye surgery, plastic surgery, podiatry, otolaryngology and urology. It also houses a walk-in clinic with extended hours and nonemergency services, and it has a hyperbaric oxygen therapy unit and physical therapy department. Hot Springs Rehabilitation Center Hospital is a 72-bed nonprofit hospital associated with the University of Arkansas medical school. People from across the state come for treatment of injuries and illness involving the spinal cord and brain and for stroke and orthopedic injuries. Complete inpatient and outpatient services include physical and occupational therapy, speech pathology, recreational therapy, psychological services and acupuncture. It is one of nine such facilities in the nation.

Housing options: There is a full range of housing types available in Hot Springs. In **Hot Springs Village**, lots, houses and townhomes are available on the resale market. Of the village's 35,000 lots, about 8,000 have homes on them in some 287

subdivisions built by Cooper communities, but none with "cookie-cutter" styles. Some 200-250 new homes are built annually. Property owners may build homes using a local builder or their own architect, as long as plans meet village regulations and guidelines required for permits. Permits also are required to construct fences, walls and other such structures like boat docks. Tree-cutting and other building-related activities also require permits. Hot Springs Village is run by a nonprofit property owners association established in 1970. A seven-member board is elected by the membership. The board employs a professional staff headed by a general manager to oversee day-to-day affairs. The monthly assessment of $32 covers roads; emergency services (police, fire); lakes and golf courses; and other common property such as the community and arts centers. An annual fee is charged for water, sewer and sanitation services, and golf and other amenities are self-supporting through user fees. The Good Samaritan Campus within Hot Springs Village offers 85 apartments, 25 assisted-care apartments and a 50-bed nursing-care facility, all within easy walking distance of one another. Other such facilities are found throughout the greater Hot Springs area.

Lodging: Options include chain motels, hotels, condos, timeshares and apart-

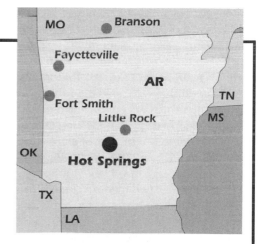

ments. Arlington Resort Hotel and Spa has a funky ambiance with a bathhouse in the downtown Hot Springs historic district, from $78, (800) 643-1502. North of the west entrance to Hot Springs Village is Mountain Thyme Bed and Breakfast Inn, $105-$175, (888) 820-5424. Just outside Hot Springs Village is Village Inn, $74.95, (888) 922-9601, and several property management companies, including Village Villas Vacation Rentals, (800) 738-7368, and Century 21 HSV Realty, (800) 643-1554, offer rentals.

Information: Greater Hot Springs Chamber of Commerce, 659 Ouachita, P.O. Box 6090, Hot Springs, AR 71902, (800) 467-4636 or www.hotspringschamber. com. Hot Springs Village Area Chamber of Commerce, 4585 Highway 7 N., Suite 9, P.O. Box 8575, Hot Springs Village, AR 71910, (877) 915-9940 or www.hot springsvillagechamber.com.

weren't for us. They were too crowded." The Honziks had similar feelings about other spots like the Pacific Northwest, however much they'd enjoyed them when Bob's job took them there.

Then they checked out Hot Springs Village.

"The beauty! The scenery! The peace and quiet!" Bob says. "The density of population is so low, and the village is designed to stay that way."

The village's 26,000 acres make it the largest planned community in the country. While Cooper sold all of its 35,000 lots, only 7,500 to 8,000 homes have been built, and the town's resident population is about 15,000. (A selection of golf-course, lakeside, ridge-top and forest lots, as well as existing homes, are available for purchase.)

The village also encompasses nine 18-hole golf courses, 12 man-made lakes with over 2,000 acres of water (three with swimming beaches), a tennis complex, a performing arts center and other activities and recreational facilities. Small shopping locations and service buildings for the village's infrastructure, police and fire stations and ambulances — even an animal control center — are also operated and maintained by the nonprofit Property Owners Association (POA). Hot Springs Village also has two medical centers and a nonprofit residential, assisted living and nursing facility. Like the homes, these buildings are tucked in and among mountains and ridges in a way that generally hides them from view.

The POA has guidelines and codes in place that ensure all buildings adhere to architectural policies. Codes also minimize tree cutting. About 25 percent of the land in the community will always be green space, complete with trails.

The Honziks chose a lot atop a ridge with long views over the undulating landscape, built their home and moved there in 1997. Richard and Karen Meyers, lifelong residents of Racine, WI, made a different choice — an existing house on a golf course.

"Rick was hoping to retire at age 58 1/2 and had begun to read up on places," Karen says. "We knew we didn't want to move to Florida or Arizona because we like to have seasons. He suggested North Carolina or Hot Springs Village.

"When we got here, I wondered where all the people were," Karen says.

"We expected rows of houses, but this was so rural, even in August when it should have seemed busier."

Rick and Karen were acquainted with people who had lived in the village for 10 years and were also in real estate. Their friends offered to show them a number of houses.

"We knew we wanted a place on a golf course, and of a certain type and square footage," Karen says. "When I walked into the third house we visited, I took one look around and said that this was it. This was the house I wanted."

While Rick became an avid tennis player again after retirement, the village's nine outstanding golf courses proved a special lure.

"This place is an amusement park for golfers," Karen says. Hot Springs Village has nine courses, and Rick plays four or five times a week. He's also on the senior golfers team. All the courses have golf shops and full-service restaurants with meeting space, or snack bars and delis. (Including the golf courses, the village has 25 restaurants and delis.) Several courses have driving ranges and putting and chipping greens. One of the courses within the village is part of a private country club.

Bob Honzik learned how to golf after retirement and plays twice a week. Mary Anne prefers to bowl and is a gardener. They enjoy boating on Lake Ouachita, where friends also have boats. "The lake is so big and so beautiful, with no homes along the shoreline," she says. "We can park on an island and let the dogs run and splash. I never thought I'd have a boat."

But over the long run, it hasn't been the recreational opportunities that have proven the most important to Hot Springs area retirees.

"It wasn't until we actually moved here that we realized how really fortunate we were because of the people," Bob says. "They come from all walks of life. The educational level is quite high, and with it an enormous variety of backgrounds and interests. For example, one neighbor lives here part of the year and the rest in Cognac, France. They're teachers there."

Karen and Rick feel the same way. "We almost have more friends than we can handle," Karen says. "Maybe it's because we've all moved here. It doesn't

seem to matter what you used to do. If you feel lonely, it's maybe because you're not reaching out."

A friendly resident convinced Dolores Quade and her recently retired husband, now deceased, to move from northern Illinois to Hot Springs, a city with about 37,000 residents. Her parents had owned a winter home in town, "so I knew it well," she says. Toward the end of a road trip to check out potential retirement places, they visited Hot Springs. A chance encounter at a sightseeing stop convinced them to move there 12 years ago.

"I met someone going down some steps when I was and we chatted," Dolores says. "I told her why we were here. She told me that there was a house for sale at the end of her street and invited me to come with her for coffee while she called her realtor girlfriend so I could see it."

They sold their properties in Illinois and Wisconsin and moved in. "It's right on Lake Hamilton," Dolores says. "Thirty steps and I'm in the water. It's a clean, deep channel so I swim out there all the time. This spring, I'm going to swim across it."

Dolores also maintains a whirlwind schedule of volunteer activities. She assists in women's welcome activities at the Hot Springs Village Area Chamber of Commerce. As a master gardener, she works on projects with Alzheimer's patients. She was a charter member of the award-winning Garvan Woodland Gardens, one of only eight U.S. gardens set within natural forests.

She spends some weekends and weeknights as a live-in house parent at the Hot Springs Rehabilitation Center, which trains people who have physical disabilities due to strokes, accidents and other causes in skills that will allow them to work independently. Dolores goes to the monthly Friday night gallery walk in downtown Hot Springs when she can and plays pinochle and bridge with friends.

In Hot Springs Village, recreational activities are abundant — from golf and tennis to woodcarving, fishing, needlepoint, herb growing, photography and basketball. The village boasts the largest bridge club in the United States. Karen Meyers tones up twice a week at the village's well-appointed fitness center and is delighted at the number of dancing groups, from line to ballroom. She has taken art courses at a local college, and she's active in a Christian women's organization. Rick volunteers as a marshal on the golf courses and at the tennis complex, and he has been active in Habitat for Humanity.

Bob Honzik has given time to the POA and volunteers through his church. He also developed a fund to assist a Honduran girl who was born missing an arm and a leg. The fund also paid for projects to bring fresh water to the girl's mountain village.

Three times a year, an active Arkansas Symphony Guild brings the orchestra to the village's performing arts center, noted for its outstanding acoustics, while the Village Players give five performances annually.

When Mary Anne and Bob Honzik were leaving after their first visit to Hot Springs Village and neighboring Hot Springs, Mary Anne told her husband, "I feel like I'm leaving home." And that may be the region's main appeal. ●

Jackson Hole, Wyoming

Open spaces and spectacular mountains inspire retirees
to enjoy the great outdoors in Wyoming

By Everett Potter

Jackson Hole has long been a haven for ranchers, ski bums and fly fishermen. But now their ranks have been joined by savvy retirees who've pegged Jackson as one of the top retirement destinations in the Rockies.

The Jackson Hole area offers one of the most breathtaking mountain settings in the United States, along with world-class skiing at Jackson Hole Mountain Resort. Grand Teton and Yellowstone national parks are within an hour's drive. And despite an influx of tourists in summertime, Jackson manages to retain its small-town feel.

"We've always liked the mountains, and Wyoming seemed like it had more to offer," says Doyle Vaughan, 72, who moved to Jackson from Dallas in 1984 with his wife, Diana, 60. "I was a pilot for Southwest and I was very, very fortunate. I started with Southwest when they had just three aircraft and I flew with them for 23 years. What we like about Jackson is that the area really has not changed that much. And we like the low population numbers. That brought us up here. We love the wide open spaces."

And those wide open spaces will stay wide open forever. Ninety-seven percent of Teton County is owned by the government. That leaves 3 percent for the rest of us. "We're an island within a public entity," says Clayton Andrews of Sotheby's International Realty.

Jackson Hole actually refers to the 80-mile valley, or "hole," that lies at 6,200 feet between two mountain ranges, the Tetons to the west and the Gros Ventres to the east, with the Snake River flowing between them. It is in the heart of Teton County, which encompasses 2.7 million acres of largely mountainous terrain but has a population of just 19,000.

Jackson Hole became a base for trappers starting in 1807, when John Colter, one of the members of the Lewis and Clark Expedition, was returning eastward to scout for a fur trading company. Later in the 19th century, after the cre-ation of Yellowstone, big game hunters and the first "dudes" visited the area. Cattle ranching followed, then skiing and mass tourism in the nearby parks.

The town of Jackson is situated on the eastern edge of the valley near its southern end. Adjoining town to the north is the National Elk Refuge, a 25,000-acre reserve created in 1912 that's home to the world's largest elk herd during the winter months. Take Highway 22 west across the Snake River five miles from town and you'll see the road to Jackson Hole Mountain Resort. Along the way, you'll pass gated communities such as Teton Pines, home to Vice President Dick Cheney.

Carry on west on Highway 22 and you'll go through the town of Wilson, population 1,294, before climbing over Teton Pass to eastern Idaho and the western side of the Tetons. Here are the towns of Victor and Driggs, ID, as well as Alta, WY.

All of them are a short drive from Grand Targhee, a low-key paradise for skiers who love powder. Long the domain of locals who commute over the pass to work in Jackson, these towns have started to attract retirees fleeing Jackson's high real estate prices. Properties on this side of the Tetons boast considerably lower prices, and larger parcels of land are still available.

Given this incredible beauty and range of territory, it's easy to see why the area lures retirees who love the outdoors. After Doyle and Diana Vaughan moved here, he commuted for a number of years before retiring here. But like many retirees, he manages to keep on working. In Doyle's case, he started a synthetic lubricant business and is an independent distributor for a product called Amsoil, which he describes as a "true synthetic motor oil." Diana acts as his secretary.

"But Diana's also very active in the Republican Party," Doyle explains. "She was county chairman for six years and also served on the state executive com-mittee. Wyoming's a conservative state and moving here suited us."

But work and politics are only part of why the Vaughans moved here. "We love the outdoors," Doyle says. "We love snowmobiling. If you take a guided tour of Yellowstone on a snowmobile, it's one of the best experiences you'll ever have. And we love the boating on the lakes. Just being outside and enjoying the mountains is great. I'm not as avid a skier as my kids are. My three sons are all captains for Southwest and they're all skiers and love to visit us."

Doyle, who has a house on a "two-acre piece on Snake River eight miles south of town," also cites another factor in moving to Wyoming. "There's no state income tax," Doyle says. "That's one big advantage to living here."

Indeed, Wyoming is arguably the most tax-friendly state in the Union. Wyoming also has no gift tax, no inheritance tax and no corporate tax. And Wyoming is the only state that has a dynasty trust, which can be set up for as long as 1,000 years.

This tax situation is why many affluent individuals designate their home here as their primary residence. Besides Vice President Cheney, actor Harrison Ford lives quietly on an 800-acre spread on the Snake River just south of Jackson. Other notable residents include James Wolfensohn, president of World Bank, and the Walton family, who own Wal-Mart. And it explains why Teton County is, per capita, the wealthiest county in the United States.

"In some cases, you can buy or build a phenomenal home and offset the purchase by the reduction in your taxes," Clayton Andrews states. But apart from taxes, "people come here for the space and privacy they wouldn't otherwise have in other parts of the country."

Wyoming has other advantages for retirees, including the third-lowest gasoline tax in the nation. Health care costs are 22 percent below the national average, while electricity is 35 percent below the rest of the country. As for the town of Jackson, you'll find sophisticated shops but you won't find Aspen-like attitude. There are exceptional restaurants like Snake River Grill and Old Yellowstone Garage that satisfy epicures from the coast. And there's easy air access.

Bill Wesley, 55, and his wife, Virginia, 48, are among those who've staked a claim on the other, more affordable side of the Tetons. They live in Victor, ID, which has become a bedroom community for the town of Jackson. There are some solid reasons to consider living on their side of the Tetons.

"The lifestyle is a little more relaxed on this side of the mountain," Bill explains. "We've got 50 acres over here. When we bought the land 15 years ago, we knew we wanted to have lots of elbow room."

They bought the property before Bill retired from Lockheed Martin in Orlando, FL, where he worked as an aero-

Jackson Hole, WY

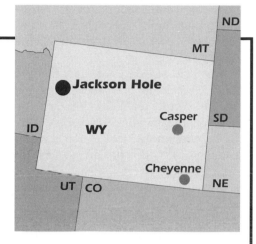

Population: 9,000 in the town of Jackson, 19,000 in Teton County.

Location: Jackson Hole is an 80-mile-long valley or "hole" in northwestern Wyoming with the dramatic Teton mountains on the west side bordering Idaho. The town of Jackson is near the southern end of the valley. To the north lie Grand Teton and Yellowstone national parks.

Climate: High   Low
January   25   2
July   81   41
Jackson has long, cold, snowy winters, relatively short springs and dry summers with low humidity and lots of sunshine. Fall is beautiful but short, as snow can begin to fall in October.

Average relative humidity: 50%

Rain: 12 inches annually

Snow: About 190 inches in the valley, but 459 inches at Jackson Hole Mountain Resort.

Cost of living: Above average

Average housing cost: Properties in the Jackson Hole area range from $450,000 to $20 million. While the average real estate transaction, which includes land and houses, was $1.1 million in 2005, the median housing cost is $750,000 for a single-family house and $600,000 for a condo in greater Jackson. On the other side of the Tetons, $80,000 to $100,000 is the cost of three- to five-acre parcels of land with a view in Idaho. In Alta, WY, prices start at $100,000 and rise to $600,000 for the same size land parcels. The rarest and best properties are adjacent to the national forest and offer spectacular views for $1.5 million to $3 million.

Sales tax: 6% (4% state, 2% in Jackson)

Sales tax exemption: Prescription drugs

State income tax: None

Estate tax: None

Inheritance tax: None

Property tax: The tax rates vary slightly for homes in town and homes in the county, but both are about $59 per $1,000 of assessed value. Homes are assessed at 9.5 percent of market value. Tax on a $750,000 home would be about $4,200.

Homestead exemption: None

Religion: There are 19 houses of worship in Jackson Hole.

Education: Central Wyoming College provides educational opportunities through its Jackson Outreach Center.

Transportation: The Jackson Hole Airport is eight miles north of town and has daily service. The next closest air service is Idaho Falls Regional Airport, 70 miles west on the other side of the Tetons. Alltrans Inc. operates a shuttle between Jackson and Idaho Falls, Pocatello and Salt Lake City (www.jacksonholealltrans. com). The Southern Teton Area Rapid Transit is funded by the Town of Jackson, Teton County and the federal government. It serves Jackson and Teton Village (www.start bus.com).

Health care: St John's Medical Center, in the town of Jackson, has 109 beds and annually handles about 35,000 people through its outpatient and emergency departments. St. John's medical staff is comprised of more than 145 providers, including 100 physicians.

Housing: There are single-family dwellings primarily, with some condo developments available. Subdivisions have become popular, all sold through real estate agents. Well-heeled CEOs live in luxury subdivisions such as **John Dodge Homestead**, **Tucker Ranch** and **Teton Pines Resort**, where many homes run above $10 million. In Teton Village, the ski community at the base of Jackson Hole Mountain Resort, high-end townhouses are available at **Granite Ridge**, where ski-in, ski-out duplexes run $2.2

million to $4 million; two-bedroom cabins are in the $1.2 million range. Near the village core, three-bedroom townhouses at **Moose Creek**, which has a private lift, are in the $1 million range. At the **Jackson Hole Golf and Tennis Club**, located north of town near the airport, three-quarter-acre home sites (land only) are in the $500,000 range. In the neighboring town of Wilson, there are small historic cabins, funky condos and new homes in subdivisions such as **HHR Ranches**, where a 4.8-acre plot costs $785,000. On the other side of the Tetons, in the town of Victor, a three-bedroom log home on a 1,600-square-foot lot was selling for $325,000 recently.

Visitor lodging: Jackson Hole has a wide range of accommodations as it's a major gateway for visitors bound for Yellowstone and Grand Teton national parks. At the top end is Amangani, a member of Aman Resorts, where rates begin at $565 a night, (877) 734-7333. At Four Seasons Jackson Hole, doubles start at $180 off-season, (800) 295-5281. But there are charming, modestly priced inns, such as The Alpine House, where doubles start at $95, (800) 753-1421.

Information: Jackson Hole Chamber of Commerce, P.O. Box 550, 990 W. Broadway, Jackson, WY 83001, (307) 733-3316 or www.jacksonholechamber.com.

space engineer. Virginia also worked at Lockheed. Now they have an enviable lifestyle. They live in Victor from about Aug. 1 to mid-April and spend summers in Florida.

"We have three bird dogs and there's good local bird hunting here," Bill reports. "We love to work with our dogs and we go after grouse here and then go up to North and South Dakota for pheasant throughout the fall. When the snow flies, we ski 80 or 90 days a season at Grand Targhee."

When ski season ends, they load up their Winnebago with their dogs and head to Fort Pierce, FL, where they also own a home. "We like to go down there for boating on the ocean," Bill says. "In summertime, the ocean waters are calm."

The lion's share of their time is spent in the Jackson area. "Living over here is a little more to our liking, but we drive into Jackson for dinner at least once a week, sometimes more," Bill says. "And we socialize a lot with a group of people who ski as much as we do. Age isn't a factor. The young people are very friendly here and we've got plenty of young friends as well as older ones. The common bond is being out of doors."

If there's a downside to living in Jackson, it's the long, cold winters, which most retirees here embrace. But there's also the high price of real estate. If you're planning to retire to Jackson, it helps to have deep pockets. In 2005, the average MLS sale price was $1.1 million in Teton County, says Andrews of Sotheby's. Scarcity of buildable land is the prime factor in high prices.

The younger face of retirement in Jackson Hole is embodied by Devra Lee Davis, 59, who owns a townhouse in Teton Village with her husband, Richard Morgenstern, 61. They have one foot in Jackson and one foot in their careers, part of the generation that has recognized how important it is to make retirement plans early.

"We have our retirement place in Jackson but we're both still working," Devra says. "I commute between Pittsburgh and Washington, DC. But being away from Jackson Hole is the bane of my existence. And we certainly don't have a trophy home. We live in Eagle's Nest Village."

Devra is an environmental health expert, a professor of epidemiology at the University of Pittsburgh Graduate School of Public Health, a visiting professor at Carnegie Mellon University's Heinz School of Public Policy and Management, and a National Book Award finalist for her book, "When Smoke Ran Like Water." Her husband is an environmental economist at a think tank.

"Why Jackson? Because it's God's country," Devra says. "It's one of the most beautiful places on Earth and I've traveled all over the world. And its beauty is hard to put in words even though I'm a writer. The physical beauty creates a spiritual beauty. We now have some really wonderful friends in Jackson and they're the kind of friendships that are different from urban friendships."

Underlying that beauty and the special relationships is the outdoors. Everyone who lives in Jackson is there, in large part, because of the outdoor opportunities and the healthy and vigorous lifestyle that the town offers. "My daughter and I went to a cross-country trail recently and other skiers were whizzing by on skate skis," she says with a laugh. "Not a single one of them was under 70. There are a lot of good role models for aging in Jackson."

Many are retirees who Devra terms "aging jocks. In winter, we cross-country ski right out the back yard. Or, we hit Trail Creek Ranch in Wilson, or head up to Ski Lake. And we snowshoe on back trails on the mountain. We go downhill skiing at the resort and love the Hobacks when they are full of fluff, or even light 'chowder,' which is what the locals call chopped-up powder. There's also Dick's Ditch, which can be daunting but lets you know you are alive in ways that few other things can," she says.

Summertime brings its own pleasures.

Devra and her husband "hike out our back yard and head up Rendezvous Mountain to the saddle, or go two miles across to Granite Canyon Trail. If you hike up you get to ride the tram down, which is much smarter for older knees. We might bike on the great new trail to Wilson and go out Fish Creek Road," she says.

Beyond the great outdoors, social life in Jackson for Devra and her husband means extraordinary chamber music and symphonies in summer and a Monday night folk song group. They love dinner with their friends and attending "occasional lectures at the terrific local library."

In a town where the restaurant scene seems to get better each year, Devra cites the Alpenhof Bistro, Old Yellowstone Garage and Masa Sushi among the best. She likes the Mangy Moose, the most famous ski bar in Teton Village, for the local color. And Nora's Fish Creek in Wilson is a roadhouse with a world-class breakfast.

"The friends we've met here share a reverence for the place that is rarely articulated but always there," Devra says. "They're some of the most talented medical, legal and other professionals you can imagine who have elected to get off the treadmill. One of my favorites is a fellow now in his 70s who teaches country swing dancing and guides rafting and skiing. He left a senior position at the University of Chicago 25 years ago."

With real estate prices continuing to escalate, there's even more urgency on the part of those who love the outdoors to act upon their passion and consider living in Jackson.

"I've got friends who moved to more conventional retirement places and they seem to be sort of bored," Bill Wesley says. "But I'd tell people who are thinking about moving to Jackson not to wait any longer than they have to. Sure, real estate prices are increasing. But it's more of an age thing. The Jackson area is a really outdoorsy place and you should get into the skiing and outdoors life while you're still fit and active." ●

Jupiter, Florida

Retirees give high marks to this Florida Gold Coast town

By Molly Arost Staub

In some respects, Jupiter is typical of Florida's lure for retirees — it enjoys warm weather and sunshine, it boasts lower costs of living than many other areas of the country, and it has the opportunities and facilities for year-round golfing, tennis and boating. But Jupiter has its own special charm that makes it one of the last outposts of rural ambiance and unhurried lifestyles before you hit the hustle and bustle of South Florida's larger cities.

Ideally situated for aficionados of water sports, Jupiter basks on the Intracoastal Waterway south of the federally designated "wild and scenic" Loxahatchee River. Parks provide ramps for waterway access, and boats and skis can be rented at a variety of marinas. And for some retirees, Jupiter's superior healthcare facilities provide icing for the cake.

Typical are Bob and Annamarie Broeder, who were lured by the winter climate and good weather for golf. Before moving here in 1993, they began visiting Annamarie's brother in Jupiter in 1985, then rented a condo before buying their current unit in Indian Creek, a development boasting an 18-hole golf course and clubhouse.

Previously they had lived in Grass Valley, CA, for 17 years. "We visited Phoenix but found it too hot," says Bob, 72, machine shop supervisor at Stanford University before he retired. Besides playing golf, he walks two miles daily and has become active in the Elks Club. He also helps provide transportation for seniors who need rides to their medical appointments.

Annamarie, 67, likes the social scene in Jupiter. "It's really easy making friends here in a condominium development," she says. "We meet people at the pool and in golf club events."

Avid travelers, they like to cruise from Miami — easily accessible to South Floridians — aboard Carnival, Royal Caribbean and Holland America vessels. They also travel on Jupiter Parks and Recreation Department-sponsored trips to Walt Disney World, Cypress Gardens, Universal Studios and Branson, MO. "There are nice activities and trips for seniors," Annamarie says.

She and Bob love the winter climate, and they return to California in the summer when South Florida gets hot and muggy. Bob suggests that anyone considering retiring to Florida's Atlantic coast "rent for three months during the summer to see if you can handle the heat." As for expenses, he says, "utilities and taxes are less here, and real estate is much less expensive."

Both are impressed with the area's medical facilities, which Bob says are "better equipped to handle seniors" than most hospitals. "We live a 10-minute trip to the hospital. What I miss least about where we formerly lived was the one-hour drive to the hospital," he says.

Besides the lack of snow skiing, which was nearby when they lived in California, about the only thing the Broeders miss is not having a garage and garden in their condo lifestyle. "We like to putter in the lawn and can't do that here," says Annamarie.

Another activity Bob loves is fishing, and opportunities are plentiful along the Gold Coast and its Atlantic beaches. Although fishing licenses are required for fresh- and saltwater fishing, he appreciates that they are free to residents over 65. Year-round boating lures many here, and numerous marinas cater to their needs.

Fishermen, nature lovers and beach aficionados enjoy the nearby John D. MacArthur Beach State Park, a sea turtle nesting area from May through August, where ocean swimming and diving are available, and Jonathan Dickinson State Park featuring campgrounds, canoe rentals and boat ramps.

The fishing and good weather are products of the Gulf Stream, which runs close to shore in this area. A long maritime association is illustrated by the signature red-brick Jupiter Lighthouse, built in 1860, which boasts a museum of lighthouse memorabilia and local artifacts.

Another couple pleased with the myriad activities here is Tom and Mary Kirby. "You almost never find us home because we're always so busy," says Tom, 75.

When he and Mary, 73, aren't doing volunteer work at the parks and recreation department in Jupiter — such as working in the art gallery or helping organize five-kilometer runs and an annual beach cleanup — they're liable to be at the new Roger Dean Stadium watching spring training games of the Florida Marlins and St. Louis Cardinals or farm teams in the summer. They've made many friends through their volunteer work, "and my wife is an excellent cook," Tom says of Mary, who also enjoys painting.

Those interested in the arts find many opportunities in nearby West Palm Beach at the Norton Museum of Art and Palm Beach's galleries — not to mention the legendary shopping along tony Worth Avenue. Broadway shows and concerts are held regularly at the Kravis Center for the Performing Arts, and more theater is available at Palm Beach's Royal Poinciana Playhouse.

The couple's choice of Jupiter also was influenced by family concerns. After living 25 years in Farmingdale, NY, they moved to Jupiter in 1985, primarily because their daughter lived here. Tom had worked as a bookbinder at McGraw-Hill for 19 years, then in construction and at the Cedar Creek Water Treatment Plant on Long Island. Mary was an assistant manager at Chemical Bank.

"I would never move back," Mary says. "And we have two grandchildren here."

Nearby attractions to lure the grandchildren (whether they're residents or visitors) beyond the ocean and pool include the expanding Dreher Park Zoo and Lion Country Safari. The Burt Reynolds Ranch and Film Studios includes a museum exhibiting movie memorabilia from the native son's films, plus a small petting farm for little ones.

Two county parks, Burt Reynolds East and Burt Reynolds West (reflecting the actor's many contributions to the area and the pride Jupiter has in him), offer boat ramps, picnic areas and the Florida History Center and Museum, spotlighting prehistoric, Seminole Indian and Spanish colonial influences.

The Kirbys previously considered Ocala, FL, and bought property there, but the section where it was located was never developed. They visited the Jupiter area many times over an eight-year period but unfortunately found themselves victims of crime soon after they moved. "Someone broke into our car before the plates were off the car," Tom says.

"Then we built the house of our dreams in Jupiter Farms, but I got sick and panicked, so we bought a condominium in the Indian Creek development nine years ago," says Tom. "It has an 18-hole golf course, a clubhouse and tennis courts. We feel safe here."

Health care is another powerful draw for the Kirbys. "I rave about the medical facilities, which are great, especially for the elderly," says Tom. "I've been in the emergency room about 15 times at the hospital at the Jupiter Medical Center. And the Comprehensive Cancer Care Center is wonderful."

He admits he misses the change of seasons "and visiting places with nice trees and hills. But at my age, I wouldn't like the cold." The summer season also can be a drawback, "muggy and buggy," he says. The thing he misses least, though, is New York traffic. "People don't know what a traffic jam is until they've been in one in New York City," he says.

And he also doesn't miss the higher cost of living in New York. "There's no comparison between the cost of living here and up north, and housing costs over 20 percent less here," says Tom, noting that heating expenses and real estate taxes also are lower. Their condo has appreciated in value since they bought it, he says.

Jupiter, FL

Population: About 45,000
Location: On the east coast of Palm Beach County north of West Palm Beach.
Climate: High Low
January 74 54
July 90 73
Average relative humidity: 76%
Rain: 58.5 inches
Cost of living: About average
Median housing cost: $602,000
Sales tax: 6.5%, and there's a 4% Palm Beach County tourist development tax required of any person who rents or leases accommodations for a period of six months or less.
Sales tax exemptions: Groceries, medicine and most professional services.
State income tax: None
Intangibles tax: None. The tax was repealed as of Jan.1, 2007.
Estate tax: None
Inheritance tax: None
Property tax: $20.5977 per $1,000 of

assessed value, with property assessed at 100 percent of market value. The annual tax for a home assessed at $602,000 would be about $11,885, with the homestead exemption noted below.
Homestead exemption: $25,000 off the assessed value of a permanent, primary residence.
Religion: There are 29 churches and one synagogue in Jupiter.
Education: Florida Atlantic University offers courses at its convenient Northern Palm Beach Campus in Palm Beach Gardens. Palm Beach Community College's Edward M. Eissey campus in Palm Beach Gardens offers academic courses and continuing education for retirees at its Etta Ress Institute of New Dimensions.
Transportation: Palm Beach International Airport is a major airport 20 minutes from Jupiter. North County Airport in West Palm Beach opened in 1994. Amtrak serves major U.S. destinations from West Palm Beach, and Tri-Rail is a commuter rail service running between West Palm Beach and Miami, with special trains added for major events. Palm Tran is a countywide bus system.
Health: The 156-bed Jupiter Medical Center is totally comprised of private rooms. Its highly regarded departments include the Comprehensive Cancer Care Center, Women's Diagnostics, Diabetes Education, Health and Rehabilitation, Sleep Disorders Center and Pain Man-

agement Clinic.
Housing options: The following are mixed-dwelling communities, including condominiums, villas (semidetached homes) and single-family homes. **Indian Creek** is a community with resales ranging from $335,000 to $469,000 for single-family homes and $210,000 to $298,000 for condominiums. **Jonathan's Landing** offers 27 villages with homes ranging from $355,000 to $4 million. All are resales. Monthly maintenance fees average $475. For information on both communities, contact Jonathan's Resales & Rentals Inc., (561) 747-2977. **Admiral's Cove**, (561) 744-8800, is an upscale community with most homes located on the Intracoastal Waterway. They range from $500,000 to more than $15 million with an average monthly maintenance fee of $700.
Visitor lodging: The only oceanfront property, the Jupiter Beach Resort, offers several packages and specials, $199-$1,000, (800) 228-8810. Numerous motels and campgrounds include the Best Western Intracoastal Inn, $129-$169 with AAA and AARP discounts, (561) 575-2936, and Wellesley Inn at Jupiter, $89-$149, including continental breakfast, (561) 575-7201.
Information: Jupiter-Tequesta-Juno Beach Chamber of Commerce, 800 N. U.S. Highway 1, Jupiter, FL 33477, (800) 616-7402 or www.jupiterfl.org.

But another couple, Sophie and Charlie Dineen, found the cost of living in Jupiter higher than they experienced in their preretirement communities in Alabama and New York. Charlie, 70, a former regional president for Manufacturers Hanover Trust, lived in Olean, NY, about 80 miles south of Buffalo, and Sophie, 60, moved to Jupiter from Tuscaloosa, AL.

Charlie considers South Florida an expensive place to live, although he notes that lower real estate taxes and the lack of a state income tax reduce costs. But he says it costs more to dine at restaurants than in upstate New York, and "dry-cleaning costs are unbelievable here."

Still, they're happy they chose Jupiter. "I had a seasonal place at PGA (in Palm Beach Gardens) and had always planned to move to Florida," says Charlie, who retired and moved to Jupiter in 1987. "I didn't consider any other place. I didn't want any part of the winter weather any longer. I love to play golf, and there's only a 10- to 12-week window when you can golf in western New York. Now I play golf five days a week."

After his wife died, he met and married Sophie 10 years ago. But she owned a horse and wanted to live in an area where her equine companion could be boarded nearby. "Jupiter had places to board a horse — there's a big community of horses in Jupiter Farms," she says, explaining their decision to buy in the Ranch Colony development of The Links. "Jupiter was a small town 10 years ago," Sophie says, "and it's still kind of rural."

What Charlie misses most are his four children and seven grandchildren, who all live in New York. He also misses having a basement, and he has had difficulty finding reliable workmen for chores around the house. "I think we were taken the first few years," he says.

"Another mistake I made, based on the seasonal community I lived in, was that I envisioned that everything had to be in pastel colors," he adds. "I gave away some beautiful wood furniture and antiques to my kids. Now I'm sorry I didn't keep it."

But he rates Jupiter's hospitals and medical care very highly. "I'm very pleased with the excellent care by the doctors and nurses and the Jupiter Medical Center, where I've been three times," he says. It's a refrain echoed by many seniors in these parts. ●

Kerrville, Texas

Friendly folks welcome newcomers to the heart of the Texas Hill Country

By Tracy Hobson Lehmann

From any direction, the drive into Kerrville is downhill. This peaceful community nestles comfortably in the Guadalupe River Valley. Travelers arriving from the northwest cross vast ranchlands on the Edwards Plateau, where sheep, goats and cattle outnumber people, before the road begins to twist and turn, climb and descend into the town that is the major population center of the Texas Hill Country.

From the west, the road follows the crooks and bends of the Guadalupe (the locals say GWAH-da-LOOP). Along this route, limestone cliffs loom like magnificent monuments above green water, and trees form a canopy of green over the roadways. Herds of exotic game animals populate pastures west of Kerrville, introducing a safari element to the drive.

From the southeast, verdant limestone hills rise up along Interstate 10. Live oaks and wildflowers color the scene in spring and summer. In fall, gold and red leaves of red oaks and other trees daub autumn hues on hillsides that fade from green to blue to purple in the distance as they stack against the horizon.

It's the welcoming embrace of the Texas Hill Country landscape that lures tourists and retirees to Kerrville, and it's the warmth of the community that makes them stay in the town of about 21,477 located an hour northwest of San Antonio and two hours west of Austin.

On their first visit to Kerrville, Butch and Carol White were expecting the same pancake-flat metropolitan scenery they had found when visiting their son in Dallas. The hills that rose in the distance caught them by surprise. "We came up Interstate 10 from San Antonio," Carol recalls. "The view was spectacular."

If it wasn't love at first sight in Kerrville, the get-acquainted date sold the Whites. Turns out more than the view was spectacular.

Climate was a top priority for Butch, 65, and Carol, 63, when they chose a retirement community in 1994. As he wrapped up a 32-year career as a junior high school teacher and she retired from teaching kindergarten and first grade, they considered retiring in Tennessee or North Carolina. On visits there, they found both the weather and the people cool.

Next on their list was Arizona. Because Butch has Parkinson's disease, they wanted to live where the weather was mild year-round so he could remain active to stave off the effects of the degenerative illness. Before they moved from Alton, IL, outside St. Louis, MO, their son in Dallas convinced them to visit the Texas Hill Country.

During their January visit, the Whites marveled at 73-degree temperatures. "I said, 'No question, this is it,'" Butch recalls. The decision was cemented when they flew home to Illinois and had to chip ice off their car doors.

The climate and healthy environment long have been a draw to the Kerrville area. The picturesque community became renowned for its healthy climate during the nation's tuberculosis epidemic in the 1920s. Patients from all over the country converged on the town — formerly known for producing cattle, sheep and cypress shingles — to breathe the clean air. In 1921, the U.S. Department of Health deemed Kerr County the healthiest place in the nation. The hamlet, perched 1,645 feet above sea level, boasts pleasant temperatures, low humidity and moderate rainfall year-round. The city remains clean with non-polluting industry such as health care, jewelry manufacturing, aircraft production, tourism, ranching and summer youth camps.

In November 1994, the Whites moved into Windmill Ridge, an adult community of manufactured homes west of Kerrville. When they settled into their triple-wide mobile home, they were among the first residents in the restricted neighborhood. As the Whites became acquainted with Kerrville and as more neighbors moved in, they discovered the people were as warm as the climate. "Down here, everybody talks to you like they've known you all your life," Butch says.

Neighbors helped each other lay sod in the new development, and friendships began to grow with the budding landscapes. "It's the warmest group of people I've ever been associated with," Carol says. "We're from all walks of life and from all different parts of the country, but we've become friends."

Last year at Thanksgiving, the Whites opened their home to any Windmill Ridge resident without holiday plans. Carol set a formal lunch table with china and silver, and 25 people gathered for a potluck feast. They spent the afternoon watching football on television and talking on the back deck that overlooks a greenbelt. That night, the crowd reconvened for leftovers. "It's like an extended family," Carol says of her neighborhood. "Nobody bugs you, but they are there when you need them."

Neighbors offer transportation for shopping, medical appointments or trips to San Antonio. They also volunteer to watch houses, water plants and gather mail for people who are away. Groups of Windmill Ridge residents sometimes load up RVs for out-of-state treks with their neighbors or for daylong shopping excursions to San Antonio or a major outlet mall in nearby San Marcos.

With good friends and good weather, the Whites stay active. On the days he doesn't play golf, Butch hits golf balls at the driving range in Windmill Ridge. The member-owned Riverhill Country Club offers an 18-hole course with bentgrass greens and a 16-acre lake, and the Comanche Trace master-planned community features a Tom Kite-designed championship course and a 15-acre practice facility. The refurbished municipal golf course in town and the links in nearby Fredericksburg and Comfort offer additional options for golfers.

Golf isn't Butch's only game. The former physical education teacher earned a silver medal in the basketball free-throw competition at the Senior Games, an annual spring rite that draws about 1,000 participants to Kerrville. The event is a qualifying site for the Texas Senior Games State Championships.

Carol gets exercise on the walking trails that meander over the rocky hills in the community's country setting. The mild climate also allows the couple to watch wildlife from their deck. Deer cross the greenbelt regularly, as do wild turkeys and rabbits. A roadrunner makes a daily pilgrimage across their front yard, and wilder species such as a fox, coyote and cougar also have been spotted.

They also like to take in the scenery in surrounding areas. "When you go out in

Kerrville, TX

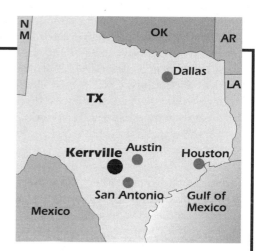

Population: About 21,477 residents in the city and 45,675 in Kerr County. About one-third of the residents are retirees.

Location: Set on the Guadalupe River in the Texas Hill Country, Kerrville is about 60 miles northwest of San Antonio and 105 miles west of Austin, the state capital.

Climate:

	High	Low
January	60	32
July	94	68

The area averages 275 days of sunshine each year, and the altitude is 1,645 feet.

Average relative humidity: 55%

Rainfall: 31.5 inches

Cost of living: Below average

Average housing cost: $134,175 for the first half of 2005, according to the Kerrville Board of Realtors.

Sales tax: 8.25%

Sales tax exemptions: Groceries, pharmaceuticals and some agricultural products and equipment.

State income tax: None

Intangibles tax: None

Estate tax: The state eliminated its "pick-up" portion of the federal tax as of Jan. 1, 2005.

Inheritance tax: None

Property tax: Paid to the city, county, school districts and other special taxing entities. Taxes are assessed at 100% of valuation. Rates in the city of Kerrville are $2.6575 per $100 valuation. The tax on a $134,000 home in the city is about $3,561, without exemptions.

Homestead exemption: Each taxing entity offers different homestead exemptions. Kerr County reduces the appraised value of a qualifying homestead by $3,000, and school districts offer a $15,000 homestead exemption in accordance with state-mandated minimums. Residents over 65 who qualify for homestead exemption receive an additional $10,000 reduction from the school district and another $3,000 from the city of Kerrville. Additionally, the Kerr County Appraisal District freezes property taxes for residents over 65.

Religion: Some 90 churches represent 20 denominations. The nearest Jewish synagogues are in San Antonio.

Education: Schreiner University, a four-year private liberal arts university with an enrollment of about 800, offers classes for area residents. San Antonio College has online classes (www.accd.edu/sac/online), and Kerrville Independent School District provides adult education classes. Art and drama classes are available through the Hill Country Arts Foundation. The Dietert Senior Center, (830) 792-4044, has volunteer-led classes on topics ranging from computers to dance.

Transportation: There is no local transportation system. The Alamo Area Council of Governments, (830) 896-2755, offers wheelchair-accessible van and bus service in town by appointment for $5, round trip. Round-trip service to San Antonio is available weekdays, $35-$70, depending on the day of the week. Charter flight service is available from San Antonio to Louis Schreiner Field, the city-county airport. Commercial airline service is available in San Antonio, a one-hour drive from Kerrville. Limousine service is available to and from San Antonio International Airport.

Health: Kerrville's three major hospitals are a 145-bed regional referral center, a 177-bed Veterans Administration hospital, and a 210-bed state psychiatric hospital. A local radiation therapy center offers care for cancer patients, and residents have access to a 15-station dialysis center. Emergency helicopter and ambulance services are available from San Antonio.

Housing options: Single-family houses, condominiums, townhouses, duplexes and apartments all are options. **Windmill Ridge**, (830) 895-3003, is a manufactured-home community west of Kerrville. The land-lease community, which is restricted to adults, features a clubhouse, golf driving range, walking trails, RV storage and homes priced at $65,000-$120,000. South of town, **Riverhill Country Club**, (830) 257-1400, offers garden homes, townhouses and single-family homes priced at $150,000-$1.6 million. Country club members have access to tennis, golf, swimming and dining, but residency does not require club membership. **Comanche Trace**, (877) 467-6282, is a new, upscale golf course community with garden homes and duplexes from about $250,000 and homesites from $69,000. Retirement communities, assisted living and nursing homes also are available.

Visitor lodging: A popular tourist spot, Kerrville has a variety of lodging options, from more than 1,000 hotel and motel rooms to bed-and-breakfast inns to cabins and RV parks. Hotels include Inn of the Hills Resort, $89-$125, (800) 292-5690; Y.O. Ranch Resort Hotel, $109, (877) 967-3767; and Best Western Sunday House Inn, $79, (800) 677-9477. Riverhill Country Club, (830) 896-1400, offers nightly rental cottages.

Information: Kerrville Area Chamber of Commerce, 1700 Sidney Baker, Suite 100, Kerrville, TX 78028, (830) 896-1155 or www.kerrvilletx.com. Kerrville Convention and Visitors Bureau, 2108 Sidney Baker, Kerrville, TX 78028, (800) 221-7958 or www.kerrvilletexascvb.com

any direction, you see something different," including cliffs, waterfalls and pastoral settings, says Carol. Butch is captivated by the clean streams, the waterways that drew settlers to the area in the 1840s. "We're used to the muddy Mississippi," he says. "Every stream here, you can see to the bottom."

Outdoor activity and community involvement also keep retirement hopping for Harvey and Marsha Fritter, who spend time most days on the golf course at Riverhill Country Club. "Our friends said we would go crazy when we retired because we would have nothing to do," says Harvey, 82. "Truth is, we find more to do."

Marsha, 77, is president of the board at the member-owned country club. They golf and play bridge and enjoy the company of friends in dinner clubs. Harvey is active in a Bible study group, served as president of the library auxiliary and has taken art classes through the Hill Country Arts Foundation.

"One of the reasons our retirement has been great is because it has been very active with an active circle of friends," Harvey says.

The Fritters moved to Kerrville from Maryland in 1987 and immediately felt comfortable. "It took about two hours to feel at home," Harvey says, noting that many people move from out of state without knowing anyone in the community. "The people are interesting and are also interested in meeting people and getting acquainted," Marsha adds.

Like the Whites, the Fritters explored the Texas Hill Country on the advice of a family member. Marsha, a West Texas native who grew up in the flatlands, had never visited the south-central part of the state. Her brother suggested the area, and they planned to spend a month exploring Kerrville and surrounding towns.

They rented a house at Riverhill Country Club, and their Kerrville stay stretched to three months. "It's just a beautiful little town. It had everything," Marsha says. After their three-month familiarization visit, the Fritters decided to call Kerrville home. That was in 1987, and they haven't had a twinge of homesickness for Maryland.

Though Marsha had lived in the Baltimore-Washington, DC, area for more than 40 years, where she first worked for the FBI during World War II and retired as a branch manager for a bank, she was ready to come home. "I was glad to get back to Texas," she says.

"When you marry a Texas girl, part of the vows are, 'I promise to take you home again,'" adds Harvey, who retired from a petroleum servicing business started by his father. Harvey and Marsha built a house at the country club on the south end of town, where they enjoy the proximity to golf, tennis, swimming and a restaurant at the clubhouse. "We knew when we got older we wouldn't want to drive so much," Harvey says. "Here we can take the golf cart and be at the clubhouse in five minutes. We can eat there, or they will bring meals to us."

When their children and grandchildren visit from Maryland, they revel in outdoor activities in Kerrville and the surrounding area. Whether hiking at nearby Lost Maples State Natural Area, hiking at the Kerrville-Schreiner State Park, swimming in the Guadalupe River or climbing the granite dome of Enchanted Rock in Fredericksburg, outdoor enthusiasts have plenty of options for soaking up the fresh air.

The Fritters appreciate the arts offerings of the small town. Though they held season tickets to the Majestic Theater in San Antonio for many years, they find the local roster satisfying. The Smith-Ritch Point Theatre in Ingram offers outdoor performances on the banks of the Guadalupe River in spring and summer and indoor performances in fall and winter. The Kerrville Performing Arts Society sponsors symphony performances each year. The Fritters look forward to the annual Harvest Moon dance, which turns the pedestrian-oriented Main Street into an outdoor ballroom for one autumn evening.

It is that type of small-town living that appeals to Ruth and Randall Nyman, who settled into the adult community of Vicksburg Village three years ago. "I love the way everybody waves at everyone here," says Ruth, 81. "We moved here and didn't know a soul. Everybody we would meet would say 'howdy,' 'good morning' or 'how are you.' They didn't know us from Adam, but they were friendly."

Kerrville is the second retirement home for the Nymans, who relocated to Kerrville from Sarasota, FL. "We moved from Fort Worth to Florida like you're supposed to," says Randall, 82. "We had a boat and a swimming pool." Then a doctor admonished the retired pediatrician and his wife to get out of the sun.

They had visited Kerrville with Ruth's sewing club and liked the proximity to their daughters in Dallas, Denver and Los Angeles. With one call to the chamber of commerce, Randall was flooded with informational brochures. In investigating the community, they liked the location on Interstate 10 and found the medical facilities outstanding.

"At this stage in life, you need lots of doctors," Randall says. "Sid Peterson (Memorial Hospital) is one of the top hospitals in the state." The Fritters and the Whites echo his praise of the city's medical care, and all three couples report low utility bills and a strong sense of security.

After renting an apartment, the Nymans found a lot in Vicksburg Village, a community geared to over-55 residents. Its clubhouse includes an indoor pool and a meeting place for the residents' weekly coffee klatch. A monthly fee to the homeowners association covers maintenance of front yards, freeing residents who don't want the hassles of yard work or who want to leave town for extended periods.

While the Nymans enjoy the friendly community, they are less enthusiastic about increasing congestion in the area, which reports annual growth of about 3 percent. They also would like to see a grocery store on the north side of town, near where they live. But the inconvenience of going to the nearest store is minor, Ruth admits, since it's only seven minutes from their house. It's a small complaint about the town they call home.

"We had a choice," Randall says. "We could have gone anywhere we wanted, and we chose Kerrville." ●

Lake Geneva, Wisconsin

This community in southeast Wisconsin is rich in history and recreation

By Bill and Edie Hibbard

Along the shoreline of Geneva Lake in southern Wisconsin, Chicago millionaires competed for more than half a century, starting in the 1870s, to construct magnificent country mansions that outdid those of their contemporaries. Today, the surviving flamboyant mansions form a collage with antebellum Main Street buildings and architectural treasures from the 1920s to give this lake community the feeling that you are stepping back in time.

The lake itself was formed by giant glaciers that inched through this area eons ago. Geneva Lake and the surrounding countryside have long been a summer haven and regional playground for residents of northern Illinois and southern Wisconsin and an increasingly popular retirement area.

Though plunked down in low, rolling countryside, Geneva Lake is considered a mountain lake, as it is mainly spring-fed with no major inlets. Nearly eight miles long and more than two miles wide, the lake has a single outlet and depths that bottom out at 140 to 160 feet. Though officially called Geneva Lake, many people — and some maps — call it Lake Geneva. And that's the name by which the area, which includes the lakeside villages of Williams Bay and Fontana, is known today.

Typical retiree newcomers move from northern Illinois after weekending and vacationing here for years. "It's a very friendly community," says Joan Eklund, who with husband Charles lives just outside Fontana at the southwestern corner of the lake. "It's diverse and interesting. And there's a lot to do."

One popular activity takes advantage of a bequest of the American Indians who developed an advanced civilization here about 3,000 years ago. They were the mound-building Oneotas, part of the Hopewell culture, who flourished until they were driven out by eastern forest tribes who were hunters and warriors forced westward by British and American settlers. The last American Indians here were the Potawatomi, led by Chief Big Foot. After signing a treaty following the Blackhawk Indian War, the tribe was resettled in Kansas in 1836.

The American Indians left a legacy — a 21-mile trail around the lakeshore that is still open to all who want to hike it. It's a free scenic walk that takes you alongside the remaining mansions and their gardens. You'll walk on grass, gravel, brick, planks, wood chips — each property owner does his own thing with the trail. Most maintain some sort of path to encourage walkers not to stray. The path, originally with connections to the southern end of Lake Michigan and to the Four Lakes area at Madison, WI, reputedly was part of an American Indian trail that spanned much of the continent.

The earliest Anglos to see the lake came by in 1831. A government surveyor, John Brink, followed them, and returned in 1835 to claim land along the lake outlet, the White River. There he built a log cabin and set up a sawmill. Soon others flocked in to take advantage of the consistent lake water that cascaded 14 feet to power grist and woolen mills as well as lumber mills.

Settlers from New York and New England were pouring into the Wisconsin Territory through the Erie Canal and the Great Lakes, and many of them ended up in Lake Geneva. By 1840, the burgeoning little city boasted a distillery, three churches, two hotels and two general stores. Milling continued strong and was joined by furniture, wagon and typewriter manufacture.

The area has had a symbiotic relationship with Chicago since just after the Civil War. The railroad arrived in 1871, carrying in wealthy Chicagoans who wanted to vacation and to build lake homes. Some of those homes were already built when the Great Chicago Fire occurred in October 1871, so families moved to Lake Geneva while their Chicago homes were being rebuilt. All the building and maintenance of these households created booming employment. And, from 1871 to the beginning of World War II, tons of ice were cut from the lake each winter to be shipped to Chicago.

Though Dan and Sandra Barker claim Williams Bay as home, their passion for travel and outdoor sports takes them all over the world. Sandra, 65, who worked for a travel agency in northern Illinois, continues to work out of her lakefront home here for Geneva Lakes Travel, so she has a handle on interesting places to go and gets some discounts as a perquisite of her job. The Barkers moved here from Barrington Hills, a Chicago suburb, four years ago when Dan, 71, a salesman, retired from Smurfit-Stone Container Corp. He had been vice president of sales, but the job was eliminated in a merger and he returned to the road before retiring.

Both the Barkers are outdoor enthusiasts. Dan dives, swims, sails, hikes and snow skis. Sandra also skis but she says her days of crewing a sailboat are over, and she now judges sail races. Her work doesn't allow her much time away, though the couple does slip out West to ski. Both also cross-country ski on a nearby golf course and on trails in Kettle Moraine State Forest, about 20 miles to the north. They've hiked around the lake — Dan all the way around in seven hours, Sandra taking it in easier segments.

They own a 22-foot water-ski boat and a 23-foot sailboat, which Dan races. He's on the board of directors of the Lake Geneva Yacht Club. Dan celebrated his 70th birthday by climbing 19,000 foot Kilimanjaro in Tanzania, "really more of a hike than a climb," he says. He also hiked the trail to Machu Picchu in Peru with his daughter Kim, who manages a restaurant in nearby Fontana. And he recently returned from skiing at Aspen, CO, with a group of buddies, despite bypass surgery last summer. In March, Dan and Sandra plan a ski trip to the Salt Lake City area.

"In the past, major trips have taken us to Egypt, Italy, New Zealand and Australia, Thailand and Bali," Sandra says.

"But Lake Geneva is home and it's always good to be back. We've made many good friends here, so we go to

Lake Geneva, WI

Population: 7,276 in Lake Geneva, 98,334 in Walworth County.

Location: Lake Geneva is located in southeastern Wisconsin 10 miles north of the Illinois state line, 75 miles north of Chicago and 45 miles southwest of Milwaukee. Interstate 43 is six miles to the north, and Interstate 94 is 27 miles to the east.

Climate: High Low
January 28 12
July 86 63
Rain: 35 inches
Snow: 48 inches
Average relative humidity: 70%
Cost of living: Average

Average housing cost: For older homes within walking distance to downtown, the median is $220,000. Newer homes or those that are close to the water run $350,000-$500,000. Homes on Geneva Lake start at $2 million. Condos with a water view run about $300,000. The median home price in greater Walworth County is $184,400.

Sales tax: 5.5%

Sales tax exemptions: Most groceries and prescription drugs.

State income tax: For single filers, graduated from 4.6% on taxable income up to $8,610 to 6.75% plus $8,201.03 on income of $129,150 or more. For married couples filing jointly, from 4.6% on taxable income up to $11,480 to 6.75% plus $10,934.70 on income of $172,200 or more.

Income tax exemptions: There is a personal exemption of $700 for taxpayer, spouse and each dependent. Those age

65 and older are allowed an additional personal exemption of $250. Private pensions are taxable. Most federal, state and local pensions also are taxable, although some may be exempt for taxpayers who retired before 1964 or receive benefits from accounts established before 1964. No more than 50% of Social Security benefits are included in Wisconsin taxable income.

Estate tax: Tax is pegged to federal rates on estates worth more than $675,000. Wisconsin has capped the exemption at $675,000, even though the federal tax now is charged only on estates of $2 million or more.

Intangibles tax: None

Property tax: $25.52 per $1,000 in equalized assessed valuation. Taxes on a $200,000 home would be $5,104.

Homestead exemption: For homeowners with a gross income of up to $24,500, the state allows a homestead credit of up to $1,160.

Religion: Local churches serve Baptist, Lutheran, Roman Catholic, Christian Science, Episcopal, Congregational, Methodist, Presbyterian, Wesleyan, nondenominational and interdenominational congregations.

Education: Gateway Technical College is 10 miles north at Elkhorn, and the University of Wisconsin-Whitewater is 40 miles northwest.

Transportation: General Mitchell International Airport is 45 miles away in Milwaukee. O'Hare International Airport is 75 miles away in Chicago. Small aircraft can land at Grand Geneva Resort and Spa (Lake Geneva) or Lake Lawn Resort (Delavan). Two airport limousine services, two taxi services and vans for the handicapped are available locally.

Health care: A wide range of health professionals are in Lake Geneva, with primary medical care provided locally by Aurora Health Center. The nearest large hospitals are located in Elkhorn (10 miles) and Burlington (12 miles).

Housing options: Lake Geneva has a broad range of housing units available,

mostly resales, and an equally broad price range for those units. Housing in the $100,000-$300,000 range can be found throughout the city, particularly in the older, more established neighborhoods. Condos, apartment houses and duplexes are intermingled with single-family homes. All Lake Geneva property owners are entitled to free beach passes, downtown parking and boat launching and are eligible to rent any of the lakefront boat buoy and boat slips. Geneva National Resort at Williams Bay offers the largest cluster of homes for sale, with current asking prices ranging from $200,000 for a condo to $1.2 million for an opulent single-family home. Styles vary widely, and local real estate agents can provide listings, including **Resort Realty**, (262) 245-8000.

Visitor lodging: Lake Geneva offers a wide variety of lodging options, ranging from romantic bed-and-breakfast inns to full-service resorts. Rentals in the area include suites, condos, townhouses and extended-stay facilities at $50-$350 per night. Short- and long-term rentals are available at Geneva National Resort, with rates for a one-bedroom condo unit $200 on weeknights April through August, higher on weekends and lower the rest of the year, (262) 245-4000. Monthly summer rates range from $1,100 for a one-bedroom condo to $2,000 for two bedrooms, lower in winter season, (262) 245-8000. Grand Geneva Resort and Spa, from $289 per night for a double room May through October, lower the rest of the year and through special promotions, (800) 558-3417 or www.grandgeneva.com. T.C. Smith Historic Inn Bed & Breakfast (1865), $165-$225 on summer weeknights, higher on weekends and lower in winter and for extended stays, (800) 423-0233.

Information: Geneva Lake Area Chamber of Commerce, 201 Wrigley Drive, Lake Geneva, WI 53147, (800) 345-1020 or www.lakegenevawi.com. The City of Lake Geneva, 626 Geneva St., Lake Geneva, WI 53147, (262) 248-3673.

lots of luncheons and parties."

The Barkers had vacationed here since they started sailing on Geneva Lake in 1985, mainly weekending with friends. "We decided we wanted a cottage and we looked at many," Dan says. "Finally we found what we wanted and we made an offer — then we couldn't sell our home and we had to withdraw the offer. After we sold ours, this was off the market. Then it came back on — and we grabbed it."

It's a 1920s cottage that started modestly, evolving over the years into an Alpine chalet, and it now boasts six bedrooms. The Barkers did extensive remodeling, particularly to open views toward the lake. The home, which perches roughly 60 feet above the lake, offers a gorgeous view over the water and of some spectacular sunsets, the Barkers say.

In winter, when the lake freezes over and the ice is smooth, it also offers a view of iceboats skimming the surface at speeds up to 70 miles an hour. Ice fishermen's shanties dot the frozen landscape. The home frequently serves as a gathering place for daughter Kim and their two sons, Peter and Mike, and their families. Holidays, particularly the Fourth of July, are a special magnet.

Also initially drawn here by the water activities were Charles and Joan Eklund, who worked their way into retirement by increments. They bought a cabin cruiser in 1989 and used the Abbey Resort at Fontana as a base, docking there and living there on weekends.

In 1991 they moved into a condo unit. Later, after a two-year search, they bought the spacious contemporary home they now occupy on three wooded, ravine-laced acres outside Fontana. It's rural enough that they frequently have four-footed visitors, and recently they saw two bucks fighting in their yard.

Charles, 75, retired about six years ago as a civil trial attorney in downtown Chicago. Joan, 70, finished her teaching career in special education in the Chicago suburbs. They take the train frequently to Chicago for shopping, concerts, theater and visits to the Art Institute. They say the train is quick and easy — and much cheaper than driving and paying for parking in downtown Chicago.

The Eklunds break up their winters by spending 10 days or more in Palm Springs, CA, and on the east coast of Florida. Joan is on the board of directors of the Lake Geneva chapter of the Lyric Opera of Chicago, active in the American Association of University Women, helps organize the benefit ball for Aurora Lakeland Medical Center in nearby Elkhorn and is a member of Questers, a national preservation and restoration society. She also enjoys golfing.

Charles is president of the Lyric Opera chapter, a board member and secretary of the Big Foot Country Club, active in the local Rotary Club and a member of the Walworth County Bar Association. He's a golfer and boater, frequently taking friends out on his 21-foot runabout. The Eklunds' son, Jonathan, a Chicago stockbroker, shares their love of the area and spends summer weekends with them frequently.

Another couple, Lloyd and Vivian Smith, chose the city of Lake Geneva rather than settling in one of the smaller villages. Lloyd's ambition is to make retirement profitable. He and Vivian moved here about three years ago from the Chicago suburban area and, with no retail experience, opened a shop called Lure of the Lake that specializes in gifts from his two favorite pastimes, boating and golf. Ironically, he works so many hours now that he has little time for either.

"For years I worked 30 hours a week and made a lot of money," Lloyd says. "Now I work 70 hours a week and hope to make a profit. But I'm enjoying it — though it does get rather boring January through April, when there's not that much traffic." The shop stays open seven days a week with the assistance of Vivian, who attends merchandise shows, does the buying, sets up creative displays, "does the paperwork" and tends the store once or twice a week.

"It's a busy schedule and we don't see as much as we'd like of each other," Lloyd says. "But Tuesday night is always 'date night' with dinner and a movie."

Before moving here, Lloyd, 66, packed in a nearly 40-year career as a traveling salesman of billing envelopes to large companies such as Sears and Playboy. Vivian, 55, had been a hair stylist and worked in the human relations department of a suburban daily newspaper. "I commuted for a while," she says, "but it got to be too much driving and I quit."

Though his family had a summer home in Ely, MN, Lloyd began coming to the Lake Geneva area nearly 50 years ago. A major lure at the beginning was the fact that, at that time, the legal age for drinking was only 18 in Wisconsin. Later the scenery and the wide variety of activities available in the area, particularly boating, drew him back.

Lloyd and Vivian met and married in Massachusetts, her home territory, 23 years ago. Back in the Chicago area, he introduced her to Lake Geneva and they often made visits here for antiquing and other shopping. About six years ago they bought a downtown condo unit and spent three or four days a week here, returning the rest of the week to their home in the Chicago suburbs. "But it was too much like the hotels I'd been living in when I was on the road," Lloyd says. So a year later, they bought a ranch home just over a mile away from their shop so they can walk to work.

Both allow that they don't have much time for leisure activities. "We love to walk and luckily there are lots of places to do it here," Vivian says, "and we hope to take more time off in the future for day trips."

Summer residents about double the population around the lake, while day-trippers, weekenders and vacationers push total visits upward of 2.5 million each year. Due largely to more than a dozen bed-and-breakfast inns — one dating back to 1865 and another said to have been a hideaway for Chicago gangster Bugs Moran in the 1930s — Lake Geneva rates highly as a honeymoon retreat.

The area also boasts some noted resorts: Grand Geneva at Lake Geneva, Geneva National at Williams Bay (a golf resort with a wide variety of condos), The Abbey at Fontana and Lake Lawn at Delavan. Grand Geneva offers the most amenities, with a spa, an indoor water park and skiing in winter.

All the resorts offer challenging golf courses, adding to the mix of good golf throughout the area. Grand Geneva includes the Brute, designed by Robert Bruce Harris, and the Highlands, designed by Pete Dye and Jack Nicklaus. Geneva National has three championship courses designed by Arnold Palmer, Lee Trevino and Gary Player.

In summer, Lake Geneva offers horseback riding, tennis, hiking, biking, swimming, boating and fishing, in addition to golf. Geneva Lake grows a wide variety of fish for the angler: largemouth, smallmouth and rock bass, northern pike, walleyes and panfish — primarily bluegills, crappies and perch.

Racing fans can find their niche at the Geneva Lakes Greyhound Track at Delavan. Then there are exotic activities such as hot-air balloon rides and powered parachute flights. And for the truly fit, there's an annual early summer marathon and a yearly fall triathlon. In addition to scenic cruises, Lake Geneva offers rides on what is believed to be the only regularly scheduled passenger-carrying mail boat in the United States.

Along with downhill and cross-country skiing, ice fishing and ice boating, winter recreation includes snowmobiling, sledding and ice-skating. One of the featured winter attractions is the annual Winterfest and National Snow Sculpting Competition scheduled late January into the first weekend in February. About 30,000 spectators usually turn out for the snow sculpting by 15 top teams from across the country.

In any season, some residents make a pastime of tracing the history of the lakeside estates. Among prominent Chicagoans who boasted opulent mansions here, William Wrigley, who founded the chewing gum company and once owned the Chicago Cubs, probably has the most recognizable name. Other family mansions included those of the Searses and Wards (both department store and mail-order titans), Swifts (meat packers), Pinkertons (security providers), Seipps (brewers), Bartletts (hardware dealers), Maytags (washing machine manufacturers) and Youngs (real estate brokers).

On the south side of the lake, Black Point, a 20-room Queen Anne-style mansion built in 1888, has gained National Historic Register status and is scheduled to be turned into a museum. In the city of Lake Geneva, developers converted the largest mansion of the lot, Stone Manor, an Italianate Renaissance palace built in 1901 by Otto Young, into six deluxe condo units. Some of the historic mansions are open to the public occasionally when local groups sponsor home tours.

Couples like the Barkers, Eklunds and Smiths agree: All the activities available in Lake Geneva combine with the history and beauty of the area to enable retirees to find what they are seeking in retirement. ●

Las Cruces, New Mexico

A university, vibrant cultural scene and mountain vistas enhance this oasis in New Mexico

By Ellen Barone

When Gabriel Fusco, a 69-year-old retired traveling salesman, and his wife, Katharine, traded the congestion, earthquakes and high taxes of the San Francisco Bay Area for retired life in 1995, they hightailed it straight to Las Cruces, NM. "Our friends and family thought we were crazy," Gabriel recalls. "They'd barely even heard of Las Cruces."

But those days of relative obscurity are quickly changing. Framed by the lush banks of the Rio Grande and the dry, jagged Organ Mountains, Las Cruces is New Mexico's second-largest city and one of the fastest-growing in the United States. An economic, agricultural, tourist and cultural mecca in southern New Mexico, the city is the seat of Doña Ana County. Situated in the heart of the fertile Mesilla Valley, Las Cruces is a thriving metropolis surrounded by desert and conveniently located less than an hour from El Paso International Airport.

Talk to a few retirees and you'll see that they haven't ended up in Las Cruces by accident. Drawn by a reasonable cost of living, a warm and sunny climate, beautiful scenery, cultural diversity and educational opportunities, a growing number of retirees are choosing to call Las Cruces home. Las Cruces offers all the benefits of New Mexico without the expense of Santa Fe, the traffic of Albuquerque or the remoteness of more secluded havens like Ruidoso or Silver City.

"With its colorful mix of Hispanic, Native American and Anglo cultures, Las Cruces is a community with personality and history," says Mike Hand, a 57-year-old retired veterinarian. He and his 48-year-old wife, Ruth, relocated to Las Cruces from a ranch in Kansas in April 2000. "We wanted to live in a university town, not overly large, with the cultural amenities of a city and the charm and seclusion of a rural area," Ruth explains.

After nearly two years of searching throughout the Rocky Mountain states, they chose Las Cruces.

For retired schoolteachers Jim and Mary Pierce, sunshine — and lots of it — was an important factor in their decision to replace Wisconsin's frigid winters with Las Cruces' 350 annual days of sunshine. But it wasn't just the mild high-desert climate that attracted the Pierces. "I always dreamed of seeing the mountains every day, and now I do," says Mary, glancing at the jagged peaks of the Organ Mountains that dominate the view no matter where you are in the valley. "It's the view that sold us," she says.

For Gabriel and Katharine Fusco, the 16,000 students who attend New Mexico State University (NMSU) add a youthful balance to Las Cruces. "The presence of a university was an important factor when we considered a place to retire. And the influx of retirees brings a lot of experience and talent to both the university and the community," Gabriel says. "NMSU's Retired Executives Adjunct Program makes good use of retirees' real-world business experience by bringing students, faculty and retirees together," adds Gabriel, an active volunteer in the program.

As career educators and impassioned lifelong learners, the Pierces also wanted to retire to a college town. "For the past 20 years we've spent our summers taking classes at different universities across the nation — always on the lookout for the perfect place to live," Jim says. "At first we bought land in Mesa, AZ, but something just didn't feel right. As it turns out, Las Cruces is our perfect place."

For the new wave of boomers who mix retirement relocation with second or continuing careers, Las Cruces continues to surpass job growth for any other metro area in the state outside of Albuquerque. Seven years ago, Sam Ritchey relocated his marketing and communications business from Denver to Las Cruces. "This is the biggest bargain in the country," says Sam. "The city has great weather and it's the perfect size."

After passing through Las Cruces on business in 1994, Sam and his wife, Nancy, began researching the possibility of relocating their business here. "The taxes were reasonable, we got more house for our money and, best of all, we left Denver's horrendous traffic problems and poor air quality behind. A traffic jam here only slows you down five minutes," Sam says.

As the Ritcheys discovered, housing in Las Cruces is very affordable. The average cost for a new three-bedroom home is $195,000 compared to the national median of $224,900. For retirees looking to stretch their retirement dollars, that, plus property taxes that are half the national average, makes Las Cruces a real paradise. Plus, health care is good and getting even better. The city's second full-service medical facility, Mountain View Regional Medical Center, opened its doors in 2002.

Because retirement dollars go a long way in Las Cruces, retirees can spend their newly acquired time contributing to the community rather than searching for a second income. Just a glance at the long list of volunteer organizations in the Las Cruces daily newspaper, the Sun-News, confirms that volunteers are needed and welcomed. "You can't dry up and die just because you retire," Gabriel Fusco says. "It's an ideal time to give back to the community."

Shortly after arriving, Mary Pierce

Las Cruces, NM

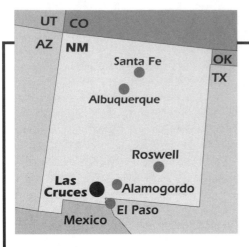

Population: 82,671 permanent residents plus approximately 16,000 New Mexico State University students during the school year. Population in Doña Ana County is 189,444.

Location: At an average elevation of 4,210 feet, Las Cruces, the county seat, is located in the verdant Mesilla Valley in south-central New Mexico. It is located 45 miles from El Paso, TX, 220 miles from Albuquerque, NM, and 275 miles from Tucson, AZ.

Climate:

	High	Low
January	57	21
July	96	62

Average relative humidity: 27%

Rain: 9 inches

Snow: 3 inches

Cost of living: Below average

Average housing cost: $195,000 for a new three-bedroom home.

Sales tax: The gross receipts tax is 7.125% in Las Cruces and ranges from 5.9375% to 7.375% in surrounding Doña Ana County.

Sales tax exemptions: Prescription drugs, groceries and most services.

State income tax: New Mexico uses a four-bracket, graduated-rate table. For single filers, ranges from 1.7% of taxable income of $5,500 or less to 6% of taxable income over $16,000. For married couples filing jointly, ranges from 1.7% of taxable income of $8,000 or less to 6% of taxable income over $24,000.

Income tax exemptions: Depending on income level, taxpayers who are 65 and older may be eligible for a deduction from taxable income of up to $8,000 each. Social Security benefits are not exempt. Unreimbursed and uncompensated medical expenses not already itemized on the federal 1040A schedule for the same year may be eligible for a tax deduction.

Estate tax: None

Property tax: In Las Cruces, the tax rate is $26.985 per $1,000 of assessed value; in Mesilla, it's $22.937 per $1,000 of assessed value. Homes are assessed at 33.3% of the market value. Tax on a $195,000 home, minus the $2,000 exemption below, would be about $1,700 in Las Cruces and about $1,445 in Mesilla.

Homestead exemption: $2,000 of assessed value for heads of family and a $4,000 exemption for veterans. Homeowners age 65 or older or disabled, who have a modified gross income of $21,000 or less, qualify for a valuation limitation, which freezes the assessed value of a home beginning with the first year one qualifies. Homeowners must reapply yearly.

Religion: Las Cruces reports 159 houses of worship representing a wide variety of denominations and faiths.

Education: The city enjoys substantial education opportunities with Doña Ana Branch Community College and New Mexico State University. Approximately 21,000 students are enrolled in higher education. Both NMSU, (505) 646-0111, and Doña Ana Community College, (505) 527-7500, are known for their adult and continuing-education programs.

Transportation: The city's RoadRUNNER Transit offers a citywide public bus system. Adult fares are 50 cents (25 cents for senior citizens, students and the disabled.) Door-to-door services are also available through the city's Dial-A-Ride, (505) 541-2777. El Paso International Airport is located approximately 45 miles southeast of Las Cruces via Interstate 10. Interstate 25 connects Las Cruces to Albuquerque, 220 miles north.

Health: Las Cruces offers several major medical centers. Mountain View Regional Medical Center provides a full-service emergency room, specialized women's center, comprehensive intensive-care services, surgical care and a specialized cardiology center. Memorial Medical Center is a full-service hospital and serves as the acute-care facility for the county. PromptCare, First Step Women's Health and Pediatrics, the Family Practice Center, UNM Cancer Center and Memorial Ikard Cancer Treatment Center also offer quality services.

Housing options: In Las Cruces, options range from restored or fixer-upper homes to large custom-built homes with acreage. Country club master-planned communities such as **Picacho Hills**, (505) 526-3818, offer a wide range of housing options. Home sites run $95,000 for a patio-home lot on the fairway to $225,000 for a one-acre-plus site with valley views. Homes are priced from the low $200,000s for 1,500 square feet to the $500,000s and up for homes with over 2,500 square feet. Homes in **Sonoma Ranch**, (877) 700-7210, a golf-course community, range from the low $200,000s to $450,000 and up, depending on customization. Less expensive is the **Country Club Estates** subdivision with homes starting in the $150,000s. **The Village at Northrise**, (888) 218-4013, offers independent living to complete 24-hour care. For those seeking a unique, energy-efficient New Mexican home, **Soledad Canyon Earth Builders**, (505) 527-9897, builds rammed-earth (adobe) custom homes.

Visitor lodging: Visitors can choose from 37 hotels, motels, bed-and-breakfast inns or RV parks. Hotels include Fairfield Inn Las Cruces, with a year-round outdoor heated swimming pool, $65-$90, (505) 522-6840; Hotel Encanto with 203 guest rooms, $99-$149, (505) 522-4300; and Comfort Suites, $90-$120, (505) 522-1300. B&B options include the 22-room Lundeen Inn of the Arts in the downtown historic district, $58-$105, (888) 526-3326, and Happy Trails B&B in Old Mesilla, $85-$100, (505) 527-8471.

Information: Greater Las Cruces Chamber of Commerce, 760 W. Pichaco Ave., Las Cruces, NM 88005, (505) 524-1968 or www.lascruces.org. Other helpful Web sites: Las Cruces Convention and Visitors Bureau, www.lascrucescvb.org; City of Las Cruces, www.las-cruces.org; Las Cruces Home Builders Association, www.lchba.com; Living in Las Cruces (a relocation guide), www.lascrucesrelocation.com; New Mexico State University, www.nmsu.edu; and Mesilla Valley Economic Development Alliance, www.mveda.com.

offered to escort visiting school groups at New Mexico Farm and Ranch Heritage Museum. Katharine Fusco has become involved with the Memorial Medical Center Auxiliary. Mike Hand is an active board member of Jardin de los Niños, a center for homeless children. Ruth Hand, a certified nurse practitioner, donates one day a week to a medical clinic's indigent program. "Volunteering is a great way to be a part of the community," Ruth says.

Not that Las Cruces doesn't already have a developed sense of community. The city's historic areas are filled with restaurants and a variety of museums and galleries. Any Wednesday or Saturday, stroll the downtown pedestrian mall and you'll find local growers and artisans offering fresh produce and handcrafted wares at Las Cruces Farmers and Crafts Market.

The strong cultural presence of NMSU is the driving force behind a robust selection of performing arts theaters, chamber music and symphony concerts, and presentations of ballet, drama, comedies and musicals. There's lots to do outdoors as well. Golf, tennis, bicycling and miles of hiking trails can be enjoyed year-round.

Agricultural abundance, spectacular landscapes and stunning displays of sunlight have long been attractions. In 1598, Don Juan Oñate led hundreds of colonists along the Camino Real from El Paso through Las Cruces and the Mesilla Valley to Santa Fe. The name Las Cruces means "the crosses" in Spanish, harking back to an 1830 massacre of travelers by Apaches that left approximately 40 dead. The city takes its name from crosses left to mark the graves, and subsequent travelers referred to the spot as "La Placita de las Cruces," the Place of the Crosses.

In time, a community developed in the fertile valley, and with the arrival of the railroad, the small settlement grew to become a thriving town. Today, with a population of 82,671, Las Cruces is the nation's 11th-fastest-growing city. Las Cruces has managed its growth well, retaining the charm and flavor of the Old West and preserving its Spanish heritage.

The flavor of Old Mexico wraps around Las Cruces like a tasty tortilla. If you like Mexican and Southwestern cuisine, Las Cruces and the neighboring town of Mesilla probably have more excellent restaurants that specialize in tantalizing chile dishes than any area in the state. The hottest event in town is the Whole Enchilada Fiesta, an annual celebration held during each fall's chile harvest. The centerpiece of this festival is the world's largest enchilada, boasting 750 pounds of corn, 75 gallons of chile sauce, 75 pounds of grated cheese and 50 pounds of chopped onions. After this monster has been prepared, it's parceled out to the waiting crowd.

The famed New Mexico green chile is grown here in abundance. Just 30 miles northwest of Las Cruces is the village of Hatch, which cultivates more than 30,000 acres of the hot pod. The fiery plant has played a passionate role in New Mexico's culture and cuisine since the early 1600s when the Spanish first planted chiles along the fertile Rio Grande valley.

It was also the Spanish who founded the tiny village of Mesilla, the best-known and most-visited historic community in southern New Mexico, located just minutes from downtown Las Cruces. Mesilla was once a stop on the infamous Butterfield Overland Stage. The dusty old plaza was the scene of many a gunfight and a favorite watering hole for

Billy the Kid and other outlaws who frequented its gambling halls and saloons. It was here that Billy the Kid was jailed in 1881 and found guilty of the murder of Lincoln County Sheriff William Brady. Today the only evidence of its lawless past is found in the names of boutiques and restaurants that line the historic plaza.

Following state Highway 28 south from Mesilla, the road passes beneath a three-mile-long canopy created by thick groves of pecan trees. Newcomers to Las Cruces are surprised to learn that they're in one of the world's most prolific pecan-producing regions. More than 20,000 acres are dedicated to growing pecans in Doña Ana County, with a total of 733 orchards producing 36,000 pounds of nuts annually.

Retirees accustomed to the workings of farms and ranches find Las Cruces an ideal retirement location. Leaving a ranch in Kansas, Ruth and Mike Hand knew they still wanted to live in a rural environment. They purchased a picturesque five acre parcel near Mesilla only minutes from Las Cruces' bustling city center. Following strict covenants written to balance the region's agricultural and residential demands, the Hands grown alfalfa, sharecropping their land with a local farmer.

Fortunately for the Hands, Las Cruces offers a diversity of housing options. "As it turns out, farming ties us down a bit more than we want," Ruth explains, "so we've bought a smaller house with less acreage on the city's west side." Even though Ruth and Mike are giving up farming, they're not giving up Las Cruces.

Others feel the same way about Las Cruces. Says Jim Pierce, "It took us 30 years to get here. We're planning to stay." ●

Las Vegas, Nevada

From affordable living to plentiful recreation, retirees find that this desert city has it all

By Adele R. Malott

Las Vegas Valley at night is a soup bowl of stars, an oasis of lights hugged up close by the Spring Mountains. For several decades this view has welcomed millions of vacationers arriving from throughout the world.

But for newcomers moving to the Las Vegas area each month, it now says "welcome home" to people like Ken and Marlene Rengert, who came to Las Vegas after Ken retired from the Air Force in Rantoul, IL. The Rengerts are great travelers — gone as much as 75 percent of the time some years — so the view of their new hometown from an airplane window when they return is one they know well.

Marlene Rengert says that when the plane crests the mountains, she likes to see the lights laid out beneath her. And when she's home, she tells her friends, "It's like having Christmas lights in the back yard all year long." The Rengerts chose a three-bedroom ranch home on Sunrise Mountain with views of the city lights for their retirement oasis.

Las Vegas did begin as an oasis for the Spanish and Mexicans who used the Old Spanish Trail to travel between Santa Fe and Southern California. These travelers named the area "Las Vegas," meaning "the meadows" — an image difficult to imagine when looking at the towers of neon and construction gantries that now dominate the skyline.

Las Vegas started to take shape in 1905 when the San Pedro, Los Angeles and Salt Lake Railroad (Union Pacific) auctioned off building sites for the spot it had chosen to change crews and get water for its trains. Another growth spurt pumped the city in the early 1930s when construction of Hoover Dam began, and again in the '40s when Bugsy Siegel built the Flamingo Hotel as a gaming spa for the mob, then in the 1960s when Howard Hughes came to town, and the '70s when the mammoth MGM Grand was built. Now, every third or fourth year a new wave of construction adds to the skyline.

All the superlatives to describe Las Vegas have been used up as a tightening time-line spiral of boom and boom and boom has thrust the city repeatedly to the top of many different kinds of "fastest-growing" lists. So it is no surprise that people from all backgrounds, occupations and parts of the United States in search of a retirement home find what they want in Las Vegas. Retirees comprise the fastest-growing segment of Las Vegas' population, and the National Association of Home Builders predicts the city will be the most popular seniors housing market in the coming decade.

Many, like Terry and Claudia Culp, who moved to Las Vegas in 1998 from Buffalo, NY, are quick to emphasize that the Las Vegas in which they live is not the Las Vegas they were accustomed to reading about. Terry explains that the typical Easterner's view of Las Vegas "is a misinterpretation that assumes that all there is to do is to lay out in the sun or gamble. As it turns out, Las Vegas is totally different than what I envisioned," he says as he describes his discoveries. "Valley of Fire is absolutely gorgeous. I had heard about Lake Mead, but it is much bigger than I thought. Another surprise is Lake Powell — it's not that far away. And Hoover Dam is a little touristy, but you have to do it once, right?"

Perhaps one reason the Las Vegas Strip works so hard for the attention of visitors is that its glitter and glitz must compete with vast natural spectacles like Valley of Fire and Red Rock Canyon, places that could serve as God's own statuary gardens filled with sandstone creations named Elephant Rock and the Seven Sisters. These two geological parks are the east and west bookends for Las Vegas, and both draw millions of visitors annually.

Lake Mead National Recreation Area is the massive playground that resulted from creating a needed flood- and drought-control project. With 822 miles of shoreline, Lake Mead offers a bonanza of water sports, as does Lake Mohave, created by the construction of Davis Dam nearly 50 years after Hoover Dam. Hoover was built to rein in the Colorado River's rampages and supply electrical power for much of the Southwest.

The enormous Hoover Dam construction project jump-started southern Nevada's economy in post-Depression years and today offers tourists a chance to take river rafting and excursion boat trips through Black Canyon at the base of the dam, which towers 726 feet overhead. River rafters are intrigued with often-told ghost stories that describe the moans and cries of construction workers trapped in the dam wall.

The Culps undertook methodical research to find their new home after they sold a family business in Buffalo and left 70-hour work weeks behind. They believed they would prefer the Southwest and began buying books and retirement publications to research their choices. Then they chose eight cities to look at critically during a 3,000-mile trek across the country: Lake Havasu City, Page, Phoenix and Tucson in Arizona, Santa Fe and Albuquerque in New Mexico, and Reno/Sparks and Las Vegas in Nevada. Each stop included visits with chamber of commerce officials and real estate agents. And once they decided on Las Vegas, they moved into an apartment to give themselves time to get a feel for the area until they found their 2,600-square-foot home in Henderson, southeast of downtown.

"There were a lot of pluses for each city we looked at, but when we boiled it all down, Las Vegas was the most attractive," says Terry Culp. "The small-town feel was a big advantage and, because Las Vegas is so easy and inexpensive to get in and out of, it was a good choice so our family and friends could visit." Terry laughs when he admits their decision was "sort of scientific" but also involved "our gut feelings."

Many of his views are seconded by Gail Imazaki, a nurse who retired to Las Vegas from Southern California in 1997. "You can live as quietly as you want, or you can get out and go to the clubs and shows," says Gail, who also researched a variety of locations, including Port Ludlow, WA, and Palm Desert and Roseville, CA.

Gail earned the crown of Ms. Senior Nevada in 1998 and was fourth runner-up in the national pageant, partly because of her dancing skills. A single senior, she now lives in a duplex on the eighth hole of Eagle Crest Golf Course in

Las Vegas, NV

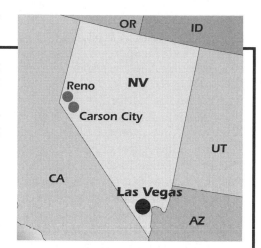

Population: 559,824

Location: In a broad desert valley in the southern tip of Nevada surrounded by mountains. The valley's elevation is about 1,200 feet, with surrounding mountains rising from 2,000 to 12,000 feet. Las Vegas is at the crossroads of I-15 (connecting southern California, Arizona and Utah), I-95 (from the northwest) and I-93/95 from the southeast.

Climate: High Low
January 57 34
July 108 76

Average relative humidity: 31%

Rain: 3.8 inches

Cost of living: Above average

Median housing costs: $313,000 for a single-family home. The average monthly rent for a two-bedroom apartment starts at $700.

Sales tax: 7.75%

Sales tax exemptions: Prescriptions and groceries.

State income tax: None

Intangibles tax: None

Estate tax: None, except the state's "pick-up" portion of the federal tax, applicable to taxable estates of more than $2 million.

Property tax: All property tax is assessed at 35% of appraised or market value. The state limits the rate of property tax to $3.64 for each $100 of assessed value. The rate is $3.2812 per $100 in Las Vegas; tax on a $313,000 home would be $3,595.

Homestead exemption: There is a property tax/rent rebate program for those 62 and older who meet specific income limits as well as property tax exemptions for veterans and widows.

Religion: Las Vegas has nearly 600 churches, temples and synagogues representing more than 63 faiths.

Education: Two two-year colleges, Community College of Southern Nevada and Las Vegas College, and one four-year college, University of Nevada at Las Vegas. Those who are 62 or older can attend fall and spring semester credit classes at UNLV on a space-available basis without paying credit or tuition fees. Summer credit courses are offered at half-price. The Clark County School District offers a large number of adult education programs, as do area park and recreation departments.

Transportation: McCarran International Airport, 10 minutes south of the business district, is ranked in the top 10 busiest national airports with daily traffic of about 840 flights. Public bus transportation is provided by CAT (Citizens Area Transit). Trolleys also run along the Strip and from downtown to a mall and the Stratosphere Hotel. A monorail covers four miles in the resort corridor. A recent project, the Senior Neighborhood Trolley Routes, stops at various senior centers and shops.

Health: About 10 hospitals boast a combined staff of 13,000 and specialized care centers such as a bone marrow transplant facility, diabetes treatment center, coronary heart disease reversal program and a burn-care center. There are 2,578 licensed active physicians in Clark County.

Housing options: There is a vast array of housing choices available from townhouses, condominiums and apartment complexes to single-family homes (many of them on new golf courses). Nearby cities such as Henderson and Boulder City also are claiming their share of new residents. There are a number of active-adult housing developments. In Henderson, **Anthem** incorporates three types of neighborhoods: a gated country club community, an active-adult community for residents 55 and older, and a traditional neighborhood geared to families; call (888) 349-2595 for information. On the western rim of Las Vegas Valley, **Summerlin**, (800) 295-4554, is a 22,500-acre master-planned community currently comprised of about 17 villages in various stages of development and covering a broad range of housing styles and prices, including the age-restricted Sun City Sum-

merlin. Plans call for a total of 30 villages. **Siena**, (800) 856-7661, is a guard-gated community designed for people 55 and older with an 18-hole golf course and a health and fitness center. Homes range from 1,040 square feet to about 3,200 square feet and are priced from the $400,000s to over $1 million for premium golf-course home sites.

Visitor lodging: Las Vegas has a huge inventory of hotels and motels with more than 100,000 rooms, including some of the largest hotels in the world. In addition, the city offers long-term stay and corporate apartment facilities for those needing more than casual or vacation accommodations. Space can be at a premium during high-traffic conventions. For more information, call the hotel reservations hot line of the Las Vegas Convention and Visitors Authority, (800) 332-5333.

Information: Las Vegas Chamber of Commerce, 3720 Howard Hughes Parkway, Las Vegas, NV 89109, (702) 735-1616 or www.lvchamber.com. Ask for the biannual Las Vegas Relocation Guide. Las Vegas Convention and Visitors Authority, 3150 Paradise Road, Las Vegas, NV 89109, (702) 892-0711 or www.lasvegas24hours.com. Clark County Department of Comprehensive Planning, 500 S. Grand Central Parkway, No. 3012, Las Vegas, NV 89155-1741, (702) 455-4314. Aging Senior Division, Department of Human Resources, 3100 W. Sahara Ave., Suite 103, Las Vegas, NV 89102, (702) 486-3545.

Sun City Summerlin, "with a spectacular view of the mountains that amazes me every morning when I wake up. I could never have afforded to live on the golf course in Los Angeles," she adds, noting that it is a location she enjoys even though she is not a player.

Gail ticks off the city's "pluses" in rapid order: "First, cheaper auto insurance; second, utilities much cheaper; third, no state (income) taxes." And then she laughs, "Another factor that swayed me were the inexpensive buffets. I rarely cook now, only microwave." But while Gail lists many good things about her choice, she admits Las Vegas is not perfect and worries that city amenities and services may not be able to keep up with rapid growth, especially in the area of health care.

The chance to spend more time dancing was one reason she decided to retire at age 60. As a registered nurse working on the open-heart surgery team at Good Samaritan Hospital in Los Angeles, Gail "was so busy I couldn't do my dancing." Now she practices in her dining room as well as attending recreation classes and serving as president of the Nevada chapter of the Cameo Club of Ms. Senior America, an alumni group.

Gail was persuaded to enter the Ms. Senior Nevada competition by Lori Sanchez, another Summerlin resident who claimed the Ms. Senior America title a few years earlier. The two met as performers putting on talent showcases at convalescent homes. Gail entered the Ms. Senior Nevada competition "with an attitude of meeting new ladies and for the experience — not to win," she says.

Representing Nevada also gave Gail a chance to "do some PR with senior citizens, to make sure they're well cared for. I can also help with referrals since a lot of seniors may not know about everything that's available to them in the way of services."

And there are many. Each Sunday's newspaper is filled with activities at dozens of senior facilities throughout the Las Vegas Valley, as well as news of health and financial assistance, discounts, volunteer opportunities, special continuing-education studies and seminars at the University of Nevada at Las Vegas. Terry Culp is enrolled in Spanish classes at the University of Nevada at Las Vegas and a computer class at the Community College of Southern Nevada.

Volunteering is part of what the Rengerts do, now that they are no longer in the military. Marlene Rengert helps at the hospital at Nellis Air Force Base, her church and as an AARP recruiter, while husband Ken is a tax aide volunteer for AARP.

When the Rengerts were moving from base to base during Ken's 30-year Air Force career, they learned about many areas in the United States. But Marlene Rengert says, "We fell in love with the desert and its warm, dry climate, which seems to make my rheumatoid arthritis less painful." While the weather was the top reason Las Vegas was right for the Rengerts, they also liked being close to a Veterans Administration hospital and connected to military roots at nearby Nellis Air Force Base.

Las Vegas is the kind of city that attracts more than the usual number of visitors, both friends and relatives of residents. But the Rengerts always look forward to visits from their grandchildren and say Las Vegas' many parks and libraries help them entertain their young guests. Other favorite stops are attractions like the Wet 'n' Wild water park and the highly interactive Lied (pronounced "leed") Children's Museum. Here kids of all ages can try out gadgets, work at solving problems and enjoy the performances and workshops of artists-in-residence who showcase arts from photography to puppetry and creative writing to sculpture.

If the man-made attractions weren't enough, the Rengerts point out that the Grand Canyon is nearby, and residents can ski on Mount Charleston and explore historic mining towns. "We could have chosen anywhere. But we often say, 'Didn't we make a good decision?' and pat each other on the back," says Marlene. "We think we did a really good job choosing." ●

Longboat Key, Florida

Retirees bask in the casual lifestyle of this Florida isle

By Jay Clarke

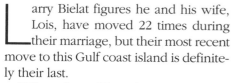

Larry Bielat figures he and his wife, Lois, have moved 22 times during their marriage, but their most recent move to this Gulf coast island is definitely their last.

"What do I like about Longboat? Everything," says Lois, 60. "I like the hot weather. I like the water. I like the people."

Larry, whose work as a college football coach took him to several Midwest schools during his career, agrees. "A friend got me interested in the area — said he figured living here would add 10 years to his life. So we vacationed here and really enjoyed it," says Larry, 62. The trip convinced the couple that this was where they wanted to spend their retirement years.

"The next summer we rented a place here and drove up and down the island, looking where we might want to buy," Larry says. They settled on the condominium complex where they now live, but it had no vacancies at the time. Two years later they learned that a couple living in the complex was thinking about moving into an assisted-living facility.

"I made a deal that they'd give me the first opportunity to buy when they were ready to go. A few months later, we moved in," Larry says.

Though retired, Larry still leads an active life. He maintains his contacts with Michigan State University, where he spent 10 years as a coach and alumni director. Every fall he returns to Lansing on weekends as a broadcast commentator for Michigan State home football games.

When he's not cruising the bay off Longboat Key in his 20-foot boat or dealing with problems as a member of the condominium board, he works with a neighbor on a new motivational book (he's written six others) that he says will be published soon.

"We love the area," he says. "We love boating and golf — there are 50 golf courses within a 45-minute drive. We have access to airports in Sarasota and Tampa."

Another factor in the couple's decision to move to Longboat Key is its proximity to good medical facilities. Longboat is just a bridge removed from Sarasota and less than an hour from Tampa. "I have a cancer problem," Larry says, "but we have one of the top cancer centers at Moffitt Cancer Center in Tampa."

For other retirees like Art Golden, 77, it's the top-notch cultural scene in nearby Sarasota that convinces them to move to Longboat Key. "It's extremely good — amazing for a small town," says Art, who moved to Florida from Great Neck, NY. "We have the West Coast Symphony, the Asolo State Theater — there's just a lot going on. We wouldn't have come here without it."

A retired management consultant and corporate executive, Art says he doesn't miss New York. "We go north every year. What we do miss is the distance from our children. One is in Washington, one in Allentown (PA)."

But with the cultural connection cemented, making the decision to move to this elegant island was easy. "We'd been coming to Longboat for 10 or 15 years. And we wanted to be on the water," he says.

Longboat Key fit that criterion as well. Art and his wife, Eleanor, enjoyed boating in Great Neck, and they also have a boat here. And moving from the large house they maintained in Great Neck to the much smaller condo they occupy in Longboat also was no problem. "My wife wanted to downsize. Living here suits her fine."

Another relocated retiree, Annette Grishman, moved from Philadelphia to Longboat Key to satisfy a longtime dream of her husband's. "He loved Florida — always wanted to live in Florida," she says.

Planning retirement, they had looked at other Florida sites, notably Palm Beach and Boca Raton on the state's east coast. "But I didn't like either one," Annette said. "When we came to Longboat, though, I said, 'Let's buy here.' And we did."

Like many others who have moved to Florida's west coast, she likes the friendliness of the people and the ease of living. "One thing I observed in this community is the openness to newcomers. People here are far more open, more receptive," she says.

Though she lived on Philadelphia's Society Hill for 35 years, she doesn't miss it. "I never felt rooted there," says the Chicago native. "When I go back to Philadelphia, I see great fear in the city. They (Philadelphians) are closed-off, not eager to meet new people."

To be fair, however, she does remember with some fondness the beat of the city in Philadelphia — its vitality and shopping. "It isn't a thing I miss much, though," she says. And while she likes cold weather, she doesn't miss that either, she says.

The Grishmans moved to Longboat Key seven years ago but, sadly, their idyll together lasted only a few years. Her husband died three years ago.

Nevertheless, Annette stays plugged into the pulse of the city. "I like to keep busy," she says. Annette serves on the board of Sarasota's symphony and opera, both of which she and her husband enjoyed. "Culturally, this is a marvelous community," she says.

She also plays golf and tennis and keeps in touch with her close-knit family. Her three children come en masse to visit her every June, "and each comes once during the winter," she notes.

While much of the growth of Longboat Key has come in recent years, another retiree, Dr. Robert Garber, 89, can remember when the island was far less populated. He first visited in 1961. "My wife and I loved it, so we kept coming back," he says.

When it came time to retire, the psychiatrist and his wife looked at a number of other sites, among them Phoenix, Tucson, Dallas, Mexico and San Diego. But they settled on familiar Longboat Key.

Like many other retirees, Robert found it easy to make friends here. Those friends sustained him when his wife died in 1987, and now, because an eye problem prevents him from driving, he relies on them to take him to his appointments. And after a lifetime of caring for people's minds, Robert has turned to caring for plants in retirement. At his condo complex, he has created and maintains a lovely garden with 27 rose bushes and 60 orchids.

At the opposite end of the age spectrum are Leo and Debbie Russo, who are unusual because they, too, are retired, but at a much younger age than most others. Leo, a New Jersey accountant, is just 45, and his wife is 43. They have no children.

The Russos vacationed in Longboat Key in 1995. "Once we crossed over the bridge, we fell in love with Longboat," Leo says.

They bought a condo two years later, and Leo says that "every day is paradise." He also praises the island's casual lifestyle. "I've had a suit on only twice in the past five years," Leo says. He and Debbie walk the beach, do a little fishing and "wind down." He still does some accounting work for an old client.

Though Longboat Key is an elegant island, Leo says he finds the cost of living about the same as in New Jersey. The property taxes are a lot less, he says, but that is partly because he has downscaled his lifestyle.

Longboat Key, FL

Population: 8,000 permanent, 22,000 during peak season (February through April).

Location: On Florida's Gulf Coast, directly offshore from Sarasota. Longboat Key is 10.8 miles long and one-half to 1 mile wide, with elevation ranging from 3 to 18 feet.

Climate:

	High	Low
January	72	49
July	90	74

Average relative humidity: 88% in the morning, 58% in the afternoon

Rain: 53 inches per year

Cost of living: Above average

Average housing cost: Longboat Key is an upscale island. The average sale price for a single-family home is $1.3 million. The average cost of a condominium is $832,641.

Sales tax: Longboat Key lies in two counties whose tax rates differ. The southern half of the island is in Sarasota County, where the sales tax is 7% and tax on transient rentals is 10%. The northern half of the island is in Manatee County, whose sales tax is 6.5% and tax on transient rentals is 10.5%.

Sales tax exemptions: Prescription drugs, groceries and medical services.

State income tax: None

Intangibles tax: None. The tax was repealed as of Jan. 1, 2007.

Estate tax: None

Inheritance tax: None

Property tax: The town of Longboat Key's millage rate depends on which side of the island you live. In Manatee County, beachside property owners pay $18.5592 per $1,000 of valuation while bayside owners pay $18.1256. In Sarasota County, beachside owners pay $15.5399 per $1,000, and bayside owners pay $15.1063 per $1,000.

Homestead exemption: $25,000 off assessed value of primary, permanent residence.

Religion: Longboat Key has seven houses of worship, including an interfaith chapel, a Jewish synagogue and Roman Catholic, Lutheran and Episcopal churches.

Education: There are no schools on the key. Nearby is the University of South Florida (main campus in Tampa, New College campus in Sarasota). Community education courses are available at Longboat Center for the Arts and The Education Center.

Transportation: Longboat Key is connected to the mainland at the south end by New Pass Bridge to Sarasota, on the north by Longboat Pass Bridge to Bradenton. Public bus service connects the island to Sarasota. Sarasota/Bradenton International Airport is served by 13 airlines, some of them seasonally. Tampa International Airport, less than an hour away, is served by all major airlines year-round.

Health: The island has one medical center and a cardiology center and there are several hospitals in adjacent Bradenton and Sarasota: Blake Medical Center and Manatee Memorial Hospital in Bradenton, and Sarasota Memorial and Doctors Hospitals in Sarasota. Nearby Tampa has excellent medical facilities.

Housing options: Longboat Key has 1,778 single-family homes, 6,058 condos, 286 manufactured homes and 1,446 tourist units. Recent listings ranged from $549,900 to $13.9 million for single-family homes, and $349,000 to $6.5 million for condos. The Longboat Key Chamber of Commerce lists 22 member real estate agencies on the island with several more in Sarasota.

Visitor lodging: Major resorts are the Resort at Longboat Key Club, $215-$1,160, (888) 237-5545; The Colony, $280-$1,475, (800)426-5669; and the Longboat Key Hilton, $195-$495, (941) 383-2451 or (800) 282-3046. There are also a number of smaller properties, among them the Sea Grape Inn, a resort condominium $995-$1,850 weekly, (941) 383-2105. Vacation homes and condos also are available; one rental agent is Florida Vacation Connection, (877) 702-9981. Many lodgings can be rented by the week or month, and some properties impose minimum stays in season.

Information: Longboat Key Chamber of Commerce, 6960 Gulf of Mexico Drive, Longboat Key, FL 34228, (941) 383-2466 or www.longboatkeychamber.com.

Larry Bielat also finds no difference in the cost of living relative to his former home. "In a good restaurant, dinner for four may cost $125, the same as in Michigan," he says. Art Golden has found property taxes less here but, again, that's because of downsizing. "We had a big house in Great Neck," he says. The lack of a state income tax in Florida also helps, he says.

The island's popularity can cause some problems, though. Robert Garber can remember when Longboat Key was quiet and pristine. With the array of luxury condominiums and designer mansions that have risen in recent years, he admits, the island today is "pretty crowded — but that comes with growth. You learn to tolerate it."

Larry agrees. "From December to Easter, the traffic is extremely heavy. So you learn when to shop and when to get a haircut, and you stay off the road from 4 to 6 p.m.," he says.

But what makes living on Longboat Key easy is that it is remarkably self-contained. Residents seldom need to leave the island. "We have just about all the facilities you need on the island — a grocery, two drug stores, a liquor store, plenty of golf and tennis," Robert says. The cultural venues are off-island, as are the movie theaters.

And island shoppers have money-saving options: They can make their big purchases in Bradenton near the north end of the island, where the sales tax is less because it is in Manatee County. Or they can hang it all and head south to adjacent St. Armands Key, home of elegant boutiques taxed at Sarasota County's higher rate.

Another attraction is that crime is minimal on Longboat Key. "The funniest reading we have every week is Cop's Corner, the police blotter report in the local newspaper," Larry says. The paper also keeps a running tally of police reports, among which are such gems as "dead turtles, 1; golf cart joyrides, 1; rude in restaurant, 1; picking toenails, 1; strange noises, 2; bizarre messages, 2; and loose iguanas, 0."

With problems rarely more serious than these, it's no wonder that many retirees consider life on Longboat a dream fulfilled. ●

Maryville, Tennessee

Smoky Mountains town in eastern Tennessee attracts nature-loving retirees

By Richard L. Fox

Tucked in the foothills of eastern Tennessee's Smoky Mountains, Maryville's greatest asset is its enviable location.

Far from busy interstate highways and crowded urban centers, modern-day worries are forgotten — at least temporarily — when one is greeted daily by panoramic vistas of rolling, velvety slopes. A slower pace, small liberal arts college and abundance of outdoor recreation further add to the appeal of this quiet town of 25,000.

Maryville, the seat and geographical center of Blount County, cherishes its Smoky Mountains connection. Spring festivals celebrate regional heritage, wildlife and crafts, and in fall, residents and tourists alike take delight in a spectacular show of colorful foliage.

Many retirees, primarily attracted by the beauty of the mountains and lakes, live in rural planned developments outside Maryville and rely on the town for cultural, educational and social amenities.

"We love the isolation. We have bears, wild turkeys, deer and foxes roaming the area, and we live within walking distance of some wonderful hiking trails in the Great Smokies," says Bob Tiebout (pronounced Te-BOO). He and his wife, Lil, moved 22 times during his military career before settling in a gated community near Maryville in June 1994.

The Tiebouts began their search for a retirement town with a long list of requirements. "We wanted a planned community with plenty of space and facilities for outdoor recreation. We wanted a college town, quick access to air travel, and proximity to a military PX and medical facility. We got all of that — and a lot more," says Bob, 58.

The area's low cost of living and taxes that are among the lowest in the country were big incentives in their choice. "After spending our last two service years in Washington, DC, we were looking for economy," says Bob. "It's very economical here. Property taxes and utilities are very, very reasonable."

The Tiebouts found a home at Laurel Valley Country Club in Townsend. A scenic 16-mile drive south of Maryville, the 1,600-acre planned residential development backs up to Great Smoky Mountains National Park. There are approximately 360-370 homesites ranging in size from quarter-acre lots to 12-acre tracts. To date, nearly 250 homes have been constructed, with prices ranging from $120,000 to $1 million.

Laurel Valley offers a clubhouse, pool, restaurant and 18-hole golf course. Residents joke that the manned security gates are in place to keep out bears rather than criminals.

Opportunities for recreational activities abound throughout Blount County. Bicycling along lightly traveled roads is such a popular sport that the chamber of commerce offers a brochure with detailed descriptions of routes covering more than 100 miles.

For hiking, there are more than 125 miles of designated trails, including Greenbelt Park's two-mile lighted fitness trail and exercise course in the heart of Maryville.

Lakes Fort Loudoun, Tellico and Chilhowee and the Tennessee and Little Tennessee rivers form a semicircle to the west of Maryville. Sailboats, canoes, houseboats and cruisers ply these waters in search of fish, waterfowl and spectacular scenery.

To the south there is white-water rafting on the Nantahala and Ocoee rivers, and about 40 miles to the east is the Ober Gatlinburg Ski Resort.

Dr. Chuck and Jane Gariety vacationed in the Smoky Mountains for 15 years before moving permanently in 1992. "The mountains, climate and relaxed lifestyle that brought us here as vacationers keep us here as residents," says Jane, 64.

Formerly residents of Piqua, OH, the Garietys first bought property on Cherokee Lake northeast of Knoxville. After two years, the Garietys felt they had not formed strong attachments to that area. They also found that the glistening lake waters of summer nearly disappeared in winter when the Tennessee Valley Authority, which manages the lake, lowered the water level by 40 feet.

"If we had it to do over we would have moved here first," says Jane.

Like the Tiebouts, the Garietys moved to Laurel Oaks and appreciate its proximity to the national park. Chuck, 68, is a self-described do-it-yourselfer who enjoys woodworking and gardening. He took up golf after retirement and now lists it as his favorite recreational activity. Both Chuck and Jane love the mountainous landscape and the easy accessibility to area lakes.

As a bonus to Maryville's natural abundance, the urban trappings of several major cities are readily available. Travel from downtown Maryville to Knoxville is a quick 20 miles on the Pellissippi Parkway. Chattanooga is about 100 miles to the southwest, and Nashville is 194 miles west. McGhee Tyson Airport, the metropolitan Knoxville facility with more than 100 scheduled daily flights, is minutes away by car.

Maryville is off the major interstate highways, preventing heavy traffic from flowing through town. (From downtown Maryville, it is 17 miles to Interstate 40 and 22 miles to Interstate 75.) This has helped Maryville retain a peaceful and safe atmosphere, something retirees often cite as a factor in their decision to move here.

"We wanted to be close to a large city, but far enough away not to be caught up in the traffic, crowds and crime," says Ed Crick.

Originally from Fort Washington, MD, Ed and his wife, Faye, ended a 10-year search for the right retirement town when they discovered Maryville. "We had looked all the way from Florida to Pennsylvania but couldn't find what we were looking for," explains Ed, 65, a retired federal auditor. "We visited Maryville for the first time in January 1993, left for two weeks, and came back and bought a lot. We've never second-guessed our decision."

Ed and Faye settled in Royal Oaks Country Club, a gatehouse-secure golf community within Maryville city limits. "It was a fairly new community with just 50 or 60 families at the time. We had an opportunity to get in on the ground floor and meet people as they came in. It now has around 160 households — mostly retired — and we know everyone who lives here," Ed says.

Faye, a former schoolteacher, serves on the official welcoming committee for Royal Oaks, and Ed is treasurer and on the board of directors for the property owners association. Ed also serves as a counselor for SCORE (Service Corps of Retired Executives), which advises small businesses. He does not plan to take on more activities any time soon: "I don't want to get so involved I don't have time for golf."

Ed and Faye both took up golf soon after moving to Royal Oaks and say it is their favorite hobby. The community boasts two of the county's seven 18-hole golf courses and has single-family homes and golf villas situated around the greens. Villas start at 1,600 square feet and are priced from approximately $150,000. Custom homes on a lake, in

Maryville, TN

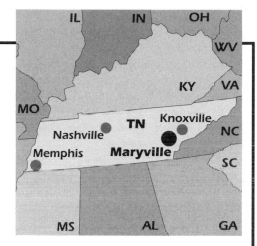

Population: 25,000 in Maryville, 113,000 in Blount County.
Location: In southeast Tennessee at an elevation of about 1,000 feet, within view of the Appalachian Mountains and Great Smoky Mountains National Park.
Climate:

	High	Low
January	47	30
July	87	68

Average relative humidity: 59%
Rain: 47 inches
Snow: 12 inches
Cost of living: Below average
Median housing cost: $200,000 in the city; $155,000 in the county.
Sales tax: 7.25% on groceries, 8.25% on all other tangible personal property unless specifically exempted.
Sales tax exemptions: Prescription drugs, professional services, hearing aids, prosthetic devices.
State income tax: None on earned income, but there is a state tax of 6% on interest and dividend income from certain stocks, bonds and long-term notes and mortgages. Interest from CDs, savings accounts, obligations of the federal government and Tennessee government is exempt.
Income tax exemptions: Social Security benefits and private and government retirement pensions are exempt. The first $1,250 ($2,500 on a joint return) of taxable income is exempt, and individuals 65 or older with total annual income of $16,200 or less ($27,000 for joint filers) are exempt from the tax.
Intangibles tax: None
Estate tax: None
Inheritance tax: From 5.5% to 9.5%, based on amount of inheritance; spouse normally exempt. If value of estate is

under $700,000, there is no tax.
Property tax: $2.27 per $100 of assessed value in Maryville, $2.43 per $100 in Blount County, with homes assessed at 25% of market value. Yearly tax on a $200,000 home in the city is about $1,135. Yearly tax on a $155,000 home in the county is about $942.
Homestead exemption: A reduced rate is available to homeowners are 65 and older.
Religion: There are 219 Protestant and two Catholic churches in Blount County.
Education: Maryville College is a liberal arts institution offering baccalaureate degrees in over 35 majors. Pellissippi State Technical Community College has a campus in Blount County, and the University of Tennessee in Knoxville is about 30 minutes away.
Transportation: McGhee Tyson Airport (also called Metropolitan Knoxville Airport), only minutes from downtown Maryville, is served by eight major carriers and five commuter airlines with 120 scheduled flights daily.
Health: Blount Memorial Hospital is a 334-bed, acute-care facility with a trauma center equipped for all medical emergencies except neurological surgery. Eight hospitals and medical centers in Knoxville include the University of Tennessee Medical Center, a full-service facility with a trauma center and complete range of specialties.
Housing options: The **Laurel Valley Country Club** offers nightly rentals as well as mountain homes for sale. Homes range from the $120,000s to $1 million, with most homes in the $250,000 to $400,000 range. Most homes in **Grand Vista**, a subdivision just outside city limits,

are priced in the $130,000s to $140,000s. **Royal Oaks Country Club** offers golf villas and custom single-family homes starting at $150,000 and up, with most homes priced in the mid-$200,000s. For information on these communities, contact Realty III at (865) 984-1111. **Rarity Bay**, (423) 884-3000, a 960-acre gated community southwest of Maryville on Lake Tellico, wooded homesites start at $98,000, golf course lots start at $125,000, and homesites on the water are priced up to $350,000.
Visitor lodging: Rates at Airport Hilton-Alcoa are $99-$169, depending on season, (865) 970-4300. Rates at Comfort Inn-Townsend are $39-$179 with continental breakfast, (865) 448-9000. The Inn at Blackberry Farm, a 1,100-acre retreat, provides three meals daily and use of all amenities for $745-$1,195, depending on season, per couple, per day, (865) 984-8166. Rustic cabins in secluded mountain settings are available in a wide range of prices; call the Smoky Mountains Visitors Bureau, (800) 525-6834.
Information: Blount County Chamber of Commerce, 201 S. Washington St., Maryville, TN 37804-5728, (865) 983-2241 or www.blountchamber.com.

the woods or on the golf course run about $250,000 to $700,000.

There are housing options in Maryville for those not looking for gated, planned communities. Smaller homes in town, around 1,200 square feet, range from about $89,000 to $129,000, or $79,000 to $119,000 in the county. Five-acre tracts in the suburbs can be purchased for about $150,000 up to $675,000 for a mountain or lake-view site. Slightly smaller four-acre tracts start at $30,000 to $150,000 with most available in the $70,000s.

A good hospital was high on the list of amenities Ed Crick sought in a retirement town. Health-care needs are met by 128 medical doctors and 464 registered nurses practicing in 334-bed Blount County Memorial Hospital. The hospital is equipped for all medical emergencies except neurological and cardiac surgery. In Knoxville there are more than 2,500 practitioners of every medical specialty and subspecialty.

Bob Tiebout, who used the facilities at famed Bethesda Naval Hospital while stationed in Washington, DC, is content with the local services. "We live within 20 minutes of Blount County Memorial and have access to Fort Sanders Regional Medical Center in Knoxville. We are more than satisfied with the health-care options in this area."

In the center of town stands the quiet, tree-lined campus of Maryville College. The liberal arts school with a Presbyterian Church connection was founded in 1819 and provided a way out of the mountains for many young people. Now it's one of the beacons attracting retirees to these mountains.

The 370-acre campus has 20 major buildings, including several listed on the National Register of Historic Places. With an enrollment of 1,150, this small college contributes to the town's quality of life without dominating its pace and rhythms. The doors of its library are open to residents for study and browsing. Beautiful campus paths and serene wooded trails, easily accessible from downtown, are favorites among residents for walking, hiking and running.

The college's 1,200-seat Wilson Chapel and 400-seat Maryville College Playhouse theater offer orchestral and choral concerts and theatrical productions. Art gallery exhibits, the school's Appalachian Ballet Company and Division III NCAA athletic events add to the mix of activities available to the community through the college. There's also a series of non-credit courses designed for seniors.

The musically talented can toot their own horns by trying out for the Maryville-Alcoa College Community Orchestra. Made up of college musicians and residents of Maryville and nearby Alcoa, the orchestra performs six concerts a year.

Festivals are among the favorite rites of spring and fall in Maryville, and all conspire to foster an appreciation of the great outdoors. In April, the Appalachian Wildflower Celebration features garden tours, bird-watching walks, wildflower hikes and wildlife programs. At the end of the month, the eight-day Townsend in the Smokies Spring Festival offers food, music and the natural beauty of the Great Smoky Mountains. The Autumn Harvest Crafts Fair in October entertains the crowds who come to see the changing of colors that ushers in the fall season.

Civic organizations, many sponsored by the chamber of commerce, make an impact on the social, cultural and economic life of Maryville. Beautiful Blount, a group involved in beautification projects, recycling and litter education, and Blount County Partnership, a cooperative effort of four organizations, are among two dozen groups in town that work toward community improvement. Retirees work alongside civic leaders to recruit new industry, promote tourism, support education and develop cultural and philanthropic projects.

Maryville retirees find little to complain about. A few wish for better shopping and dining options, adding that Blount County is a "dry" county.

And though Bob Tiebout still misses the "camaraderie, and fervor of political drama" of military life in Washington, DC, he plans to stay in east Tennessee for the nature and the outdoor lifestyle he's come to enjoy.

"Every season has its own character, and all are beautiful," says Bob. ●

Mountain Home, Arkansas

City escapees happily take refuge in this Arkansas town
surrounded by beautiful lakes and rivers

By Olin Chism

There's no quick way for outsiders to get to Mountain Home. The closest interstate is 115 miles away, the nearest scheduled airline service is two hours away, and the community is blockaded by two large lakes and three rivers, not to mention the hills of the Ozarks.

All this is just fine with many of the retirees who live there. A common thread in their discussions of Mountain Home is the benefits of small-town life and the frustrations of the congested areas from whence many of them came.

"People say, 'How can you move away? This is your hometown.' But it's easy when what you want is not there anymore. The peace and quiet are gone. The town you grew up in no longer exists. If they came up and saw what we have here, they would be jealous, because this is what they had when they were growing up. This is how life should be. A small town, and not the hustle and bustle of a big city."

That's the opinion of Paula Theriot, 56, who moved to Mountain Home with her husband, Jim, 58, when the overflow from New Orleans began to transform their Gulf Coast hometown of Houma, LA.

A retiree from Chicago is even more emphatic. "I wouldn't go back up North for all the money in China. Ever, ever, ever. I don't like to go visit now, except to see my grandchildren. I'd much rather have them come here," says Kathleen De Groot, 62, who wasn't so convinced at first. "In the beginning she thought I was going to put her in a trailer out in the boondocks," says her husband, Michael, 65.

Instead of a trailer in the boondocks, Michael and Kathleen De Groot have a comfortable house on a wooded ridge above Norfork Lake, which twists through the hills from southeast of Mountain Home well up into nearby Missouri. Michael and Kathleen live about 10 miles from the center of Moun-

tain Home, which is due north of Little Rock and about 15 miles from the Missouri line. The community has been a retiree haven for years, once earning the nickname "Little Chicago" because of the number of Chicagoans — many of them retired police and fire officers — who settled in the area.

More recently retirees have come from a wider area, though upper Midwestern states such as Illinois, Wisconsin, Minnesota and the Dakotas remain heavily represented.

Mountain Home itself is pleasant but not scenically remarkable, though its trees are a plus. The name is a little puzzling since the town is relatively low and flat. But drive out of the center of town and within minutes the scenic wonders manifest themselves.

Water and the pleasures it brings dominate the area. To the west of town is Bull Shoals Lake, which winds in a southeasterly-northwesterly direction and, like Norfork Lake, stretches for miles into Missouri. Norfork Lake is to the east. The North Fork River flows into it. Cutting across the south is the White River, which, not far from Mountain Home, connects to the Buffalo National River, the first river in America to receive the "national" designation. The Buffalo stretches to the west halfway to Oklahoma.

You could spend a lifetime in a fishing boat and never explore every nook and cranny of this vast expanse of waterways. It would be a pleasant quest, however. Because of the area's rocky geology and the lack (so far) of pollution, the waters are remarkably clear. Paula Theriot exclaims, "I told my girlfriend, 'You won't believe it when you come up here. You can actually see the bottom of the rivers.' This is what we would call drinking water down there, it's so clear."

The waterways are enhanced by the heavily wooded hills that loom above them, often fronting the rivers and lakes with high rocky cliffs. Visitors can get a good sample of this by approaching

Mountain Home from the south on State Highway 5. At the charming village of Calico Rock, ask one of the local residents how to get to the scenic overlook by the water tower. From there, high above the surrounding countryside, you get a spectacular view of the White River and environs.

Another convenient place to see river and bluffs is at Buffalo City, a few miles south-southwest of Mountain Home. You don't have to ask directions to the river; just drive to the end of State Highway 126. Be prepared to share the experience with platoons of boaters and others who appreciate water and scenery.

Denny Penticoff, 53, compares the area favorably with the American West, where he has also lived. "If you want to get off the beaten path and enjoy nature, the Ozarks is the spot, more so than the West. The West has much more wide-open spaces, but where the real beauty is (in the West), there's a concentration of people. Here you can take any trail that you see going off into the Ozarks, and you're by yourself as long as you want to be by yourself."

Denny moved to Mountain Home in 2002 with his wife, JoAnn, 57, after big-city life in Las Vegas, Houston and Dallas. An enthusiastic outdoorsman, he extols the area's wildlife. "Thousands of people float the Buffalo. There's wildlife — elk and bear, mountain lions, wolves, mink, beaver." He's had frequent deer and at least one bear show up in his back yard a short distance from Michael and Kathleen De Groot's house.

Naturally, water activities abound. There are 21 Corps of Engineers campgrounds on the two lakes, plus eight leased to public and quasi-public groups to operate. These offer access to boating, water-skiing, sailing and swimming. The rivers are favored sites for floating and canoeing.

Communal life often centers on the water. Michael De Groot has a pontoon boat, as do many of his neighbors. He describes what he calls "float and boat." "We all get our pontoon boats, go out in the cove and tie them all together. Everybody brings a dish. We go from boat to boat to boat. We go swimming first, then we eat, then we go swimming again. It's just like being in heaven — you can't beat it."

All of this is just a sidelight to what many in the area see as its major attraction: fishing. Bull Shoals and Norfork are favored sites for several species of bass, as well as catfish, crappie and walleye, among other species. Bull Shoals is a magnet for professional fishing tournaments. Fishermen head to the area's three rivers for trout, which the Arkansas Game and Fish Commission stocks throughout the year.

Guided fishing trips can be arranged through resorts and marinas on the

Mountain Home, AR

Population: 11,012 in Mountain Home (with 48.2% age 55 or older), and 38,386 in Baxter County.

Location: Mountain Home is located in Baxter County in north-central Arkansas, north of Little Rock and about 15 miles from the Missouri border.

Climate: High Low
January 45 23
July 91 67
There are four distinct seasons. Winter snows tend to melt quickly.

Average relative humidity: 55%

Rain: 44 inches

Snow: 7.4 inches

Cost of living: Slightly below average

Median housing cost: $144,625

Sales tax: Arkansas has a 6% tax on sales of tangible personal property. Mountain Home levies an additional 1% and Baxter County another 1%.

Sales tax exemptions: Prescription medicine, medical equipment for use by persons enrolled in or eligible for Medicare or other federally established medical aid programs, food purchased with federal food stamps, electricity usage by taxpayers with household incomes less than $12,000.

State income tax: Graduated in six brackets from 1% on the first $3,399 of taxable income to 7% (minus $763.45) on taxable amounts greater than $28,499.

Income tax exemptions: Social Security

benefits and up to $6,000 of private, federal, state and local pension income are exempt.

Estate tax: None

Property tax: In Mountain Home, $37.71 per $1,000 of assessed value, with houses assessed at 20% of market value. Yearly tax on a $144,625 home is $1,091, without homestead credit mentioned below.

Homestead exemption: For the principal place of residence, a taxpayer is allowed a credit of up to $300. For taxpayers 65 or over, the assessed value of the principal place of residence is frozen.

Personal property tax: The formula is the same as for the property tax: assessment at 20% of market value, tax of $37.71 per $1,000 of assessed value.

Religion: There are about 50 churches representing a wide range of denominations.

Education: Arkansas State University Mountain Home, a two-year branch campus of Arkansas State University, (870) 508-6100 or www.asumh.edu, has more than 1,300 students taking courses on its 130-acre campus. It offers adult and continuing-education courses.

Transportation: There is no local bus service. There's long-distance bus service, and there are plans for commuter flights to St. Louis starting in 2006 from Ozark Regional Airport.

Health: Baxter Regional Medical Center has 268 beds, 24-hour emergency-room service, 10 surgical suites including two dedicated to open-heart surgery, and an array of facilities dedicated to cardiovascular care, treatment of stroke and spinal cord injuries, cancer care and diabetes care, among other services. There is a center devoted to women's cardiac care. More than 100 physicians are on staff, representing 23 specialties.

Housing options: A variety of housing is available in town, in nearby communities and on the lakes and rivers. Areas in Mountain Home that are popular with retirees include Village Green (average price of houses sold during the past year there is $110,500), Northern Hills ($124,253), Indian Creek ($152,993) and Southern Meadows ($126,279). Assisted-living communities include **Good Samaritan Village**, (870) 425-2494 or www.gsvmh.org; **Outlook Pointe**, (870) 425-6868; and the **Monroe House**, (870) 425-7878. **Park West Condominiums**, (870) 424-7460 or www.leisurehomes.us, has condominiums for sale. Professional Property Management, (870) 425-6076, has listings of apartments for rent throughout the area. **Park West Senior Apartments**, (870) 508-6675, has new one- and two-bedroom apartments for rent to persons 55 and older. The following realty companies can provide further information on the area's real estate scene: Gilbert Realty, (800) 562-7893 or www.gilbertrealty.com; Larry Black and Associates, (877) 425-9898 or www.larryblackrealestate.com; and Countrywood Realty, (800) 624-6366 or www.countrywoodrealty.com.

Visitor lodging: Baxter Inn, $39.95-$49.95, (888) 644-6555. Best Western Carriage Inn, $50-$85, (877) 425-6001. Comfort Inn, $60-$145, (870) 424-9000. Days Inn, $62-$68, (870) 425-1010. Executive Inn, $40-$85, (870) 425-2300. Holiday Inn Express, $71.10-$99, (870) 425-6200. Mountain Home Motel, $40-$50, (870) 425-2171. Ramada Inn, $58-$119, (870) 425-9191. Super 8 Motel, $49.99-$69.99, (800) 800-8000 or (870) 424-5600. Town & Country Motor Inn, $35-$70, (870) 425-9525.

Information: Mountain Home Area Chamber of Commerce (Where to Retire magazine), P.O. Box 488, Mountain Home, AR 72654, (800) 822-3536 or www.enjoymountainhome.com.

lakes. Denny Penticoff has high respect for the expertise of local fishermen. "When I first came here I got involved with the Norfork bass club — local boys," he says. "They know how to fish, believe me!"

As appealing as the scenery is, that's not Mountain Home's prime attraction for some retirees. For Bob and Jan Wacha, who came down from Wisconsin, the weather was the deciding factor. Both 66, they live in Mountain Home proper, not in the hills.

"We still have winter here, but nowhere near as severe as the Dakotas or Minnesota, where most of my family lives, and not as bad as Wisconsin," Bob says. "The older we got, the harder it was to cope. I was, like, three miles out of the city. I had five acres — a nice little place — but moving the snow was starting to become a problem. Your mind might tell you, 'You can do it,' but the body says, 'No, you can't.'"

The weather was also a factor in Jim and Paula Theriot's decision to move to Mountain Home. They weren't fleeing snow, of course — not in southern Louisiana — but they were fleeing hurricanes. They can reel off their names like those of old friends: Andrew, Camille, Betsy, Hugo. Andrew was the worst, says Paula. "It took off three-quarters of our roof, and it stayed off from August to the following February." The Theriots had to make do with makeshift protection. The damage was so widespread that it took repair crews months to get around to everybody.

"They do have tornadoes around here," Jim grants. "But they are a lot more selective than hurricanes."

Like the Wachas, the Theriots live in the town proper, not up in the hills. But their place, in a western subdivision, has almost a rural feel to it. There's plenty of space between houses, the topography is grassy and rolling, and a large pond 100 yards or so away has serenely floating swans and ducks.

Like other newcomers, the Theriots are impressed by the friendliness of the town's residents. "Once we moved in, the neighbors started to come. People would show up on our doorsteps with cookies and cake. It was amazing," Jim says.

Paula agrees. "We've been here not quite two years, and we've lived all the rest of our lives in Louisiana. We could walk into the Wal-Mart down there and never see a soul we knew. We move up here, and there are no strangers. Once you get located into the church, you begin meeting people, and it just blossoms from there. We've made a lot of good friends up here."

One attraction of Mountain Home, a factor cited by several retirees, is safety. "The crime rate here is very, very low, very low," says Bob Wacha. "There's many times that I have forgotten to lock up my home. I've got my little workshop out here, and I've got band saws, skill saws and cable saws and things of that nature, and I've never been bothered."

Denny Penticoff says, "You have adolescent meth problems, like you do anywhere in America today, but I've heard of no violent crimes. We don't even lock our doors. People still take checks here."

In fact, so casual is everybody in Mountain Home about security that an outsider begins to feel a little embarrassed at his longtime habit of locking the car doors before stepping away for even a few minutes.

Mountain Home does have some negatives. One of them is the lack of cultural activity. Those whose lives must include opera, symphony, ballet, great art or professional theater won't find them in Mountain Home or any other place within a reasonable drive. Those who thrive in a diverse cultural setting also won't find that stimulation in Mountain Home. Less than 2 percent of the residents are members of minority groups.

Although the basics are available in Mountain Home — there's a Wal-Mart superstore, a Home Depot and Lowe's will soon move in — for high-end shopping, residents have to drive to Springfield, MO, which is a two-hour drive, or Little Rock, three and a half hours away.

Those same two cities also offer the closest access to airline flights, which even those residents who love Mountain Home's relative isolation find inconvenient at times. That may soon change, however. Eddie Majeste, executive director of the Mountain Home Area Chamber of Commerce, says that RegionsAir is planning to inaugurate flights from Mountain Home to St. Louis in 2006.

One of the big surprises of Mountain Home is Baxter Regional Medical Center, which is a far more elaborate complex with a much larger staff of physicians than you would expect in a town of about 11,000. The "regional" in its name explains much. The center serves 14 counties in Arkansas and Missouri.

Advertising "big-city health care with a hometown touch," the center has 268 beds, more than 100 doctors on staff, and 10 surgical suites, two of which are dedicated to open-heart surgery. It has experience to go along with its facilities: More than 1,000 open-heart surgeries have been performed at the center. Especially significant for retirees is Baxter's Hensley Behavioral Health Center, which serves patients 55 and older.

Despite all the scenic attractions, residents of the Mountain Home area occasionally want to get away. One favored trip is to country-and-western concerts in Branson, MO, which is about 75 minutes away by car. Another is to quaint Eureka Springs, AR, which doesn't take much longer.

But those are just quick side trips. Mountain Home residents tend to want to stay close to home. As Michael De Groot says, "It's just like being in heaven," and who would want to leave that? ●

Mount Dora, Florida

A century-old Florida town evokes New England charm

By Richard L. Fox

Scenic meandering pathways lead from downtown Mount Dora to the calm, blue waters of beautiful six-mile-long Lake Dora. For boat owners, the lake offers pleasant cruising waters as well as a popular shortcut to the city center from lakeside homes. It is connected by the Dora Canal to a chain of lakes leading to the St. Johns River and ultimately to the Atlantic Ocean, providing seagoing access that few inland towns can offer.

Bob and Mary Anderson had lived in rural Virginia 25 years when they discovered the small-town charm, convenience and historical legacy of Mount Dora. "We had built a room and porch on our house and planned to stay in Rockville," says Bob, 70. But then the couple planned a trip to Florida to help a neighbor who was moving in retirement, and Mary happened to see a newspaper article about Mount Dora.

"So we stopped by just for the fun of it, checked into Lakeside Inn, ordered a cocktail and watched the sunset over Lake Dora," says Bob, who retired from the office supplies industry. "The next day we drove home, sold our house and moved to Mount Dora."

Mount Dora — named for its 184-foot elevation in the generally flat Florida terrain — is an enchanting lakeside town of about 10,000 residents, located 25 miles northwest of Orlando. It is characterized by its wide brick sidewalks, colorful outdoor cafes, and crafts and antique shops. Six pretty tree-shaded parks dot the town's landscape, and they are especially attractive to seniors who enjoy tennis, shuffleboard and lawn bowling. The Mount Dora Lawn Bowling Club is one of the largest in the United States, with more than 300 members hosting local and regional competitions.

"We moved here because it was small, 'antiquish,' and we liked the preservation, old houses, the historical aspects," says Mary, 68. Mount Dora predates a rail line that opened in 1887,

bringing passengers and freight to a town that had two general stores, three hotels, two churches, a drug store and a carriage factory.

"It has a nice, relaxed atmosphere and provides great access to the beaches, Disney World and Miami," adds Mary, who worked for Signet Bank in Richmond. Bob also likes the convenience of living in town, even a small one like Mount Dora. "We had never lived in a city and were tired of going 15 miles to buy groceries, attend church and enjoy city amenities," he says.

They wasted no time getting actively involved in the social and civic opportunities of their new home. "We joined everything in sight," Mary laughs. Bob joined the chamber of commerce and serves on the membership committee, and he was appointed to the city's historic preservation board. He also is on the board of trustees of the United Methodist Church. "You have to be active in civic affairs to enjoy retirement here," he says.

The relatively recent discovery by retirees and young working families of this quiet haven just minutes from Greater Orlando has had its impact on Mount Dora's population and real estate prices. The 1990 census recorded an 11 percent increase in population in the 1980s, from 6,483 to 7,196 residents. Today's count is approaching 10,000, roughly a 25 percent increase in the last 10 years. Like many retirees who were drawn to the town by its small-town atmosphere, newcomer Ed Jones says in resignation, "I hate to see it grow."

Ed and Betty Jones, from Wilmington, DE, had lived in Vero Beach and Clearwater during their working lives but sought something smaller for their retirement. "The towns had grown so much that they had lost the small-town atmosphere we were looking for," says Betty, who was in sales prior to retirement. "We found it in Mount Dora, a place where we felt we could belong. It has lots of clubs and organizations, a nice

library and very friendly people."

Waterfront housing is available along Lake Dora and on smaller lakes within a mile of the city. The quiet, tree-lined streets adjacent to downtown, resplendent with beautifully restored Victorian homes, churches and landmark commercial buildings, are popular with those who savor the history of this century-old town and the convenience of living within walking distance of the village center. Several master-planned developments offer affordable, active lifestyles just a few minutes from downtown.

In the early 1990s, Mount Dora's homes sold for $50,000 to $300,000, with a median price of $80,400, according to local appraisers. The current median price of homes sold is $225,000. Several attractive condominium and townhouse developments recently offered homes from the $100,000s to the $300,000s. Most lakeshore homes are priced from the $300,000s to $1 million and up.

The Andersons chose a home built in 1955 on one of the smaller lakes in northwest Mount Dora, about a mile from downtown. Neighbors include residents in their 70s and 80s and young couples with children. Extensive renovations to the Andersons' home have paid off in substantial appreciation of their investment, but Bob doesn't like paying both city and county taxes — something he didn't have to do while living in rural Virginia. However, Mary claims that Virginia "had as many hidden taxes and 'gotchas' as Florida."

Though she wouldn't move "unless we win the lottery," Mary says she sometimes misses the peace and quiet of their home in rural Virginia. "Young people with loud car stereos can be a real nuisance," she says of life in Florida.

The Joneses also found a neighborhood they liked. "One reason we built in the Country Club of Mount Dora was its excellent tennis facilities," says Ed, 65, a retired engineering designer and one-time avid tennis player. Betty, also 65, enjoys the quiet, safe environment of her neighborhood, walks five days a week and spends her spare time volunteering at the chamber of commerce and the arts festival.

"There's always something going on downtown," adds Ed. Two dozen restaurants, mostly located within a six-block downtown area, range from casual sidewalk cafes and English-style tearooms to cozy, candlelit dining rooms with an international flair. These same streets harbor a dozen antiques and collectibles shops, and there's an annual Downtown Antique Extravaganza. Renninger's Twin Markets, just outside town on U.S. Highway 441, sponsors the Antique Extravaganza in January, February and November, with more than 1,500 dealers participating.

In fact, Mount Dora leads the state as the home of major festivals. The 24th annual February Fine Arts Festival attracted almost 300,000 visitors, and the April Spring Festival, a celebration of music and literature, always packs the 300-seat Ice House Theatre, the 700-seat community building and every hotel in the area. A bicycle festival is the largest and oldest cycling event in the state, bringing hundreds of cyclists from across the nation in early October. Later that month, an annual juried craft fair displays the talents of some 350 skilled artisans, drawing about 250,000 visitors.

John and Billie Keenon visited popular retirement towns in six states before settling on Mount Dora. Both in their mid-60s, they had lived in Little Rock, AR, for six years when they read about Mount Dora in Where to Retire magazine and decided to pay it a visit.

"Neither of us ever expected we would retire to Florida, but we fell in love with Mount Dora at first sight," Billie says. "And the people — real quality people — are so interested in the betterment of the community."

John, who spent his working years in the financial services industry, says he likes the wide assortment of activities and opportunities for participating in the community. He has served on the board of the Center for the Arts, the Mount Dora Chamber of Commerce and the Country Club of Mount Dora homeowners' association. "And I enjoy the concerts, Ice House Theatre performances and volunteering at the chamber of commerce," he says. His favorite recreational activities include golfing, boating and surfing the Internet.

"I play bridge, volunteer at the chamber, attend city council meetings and walk the dog," his wife, Billie, says. They describe their 2,200-square-foot contemporary home as light and airy with high ceilings. John feels it is appreciating in value. "They are still building and selling

Mount Dora, FL

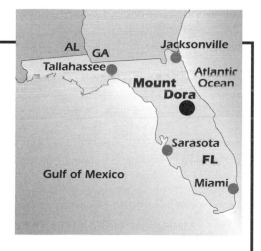

Population: About 10,000

Location: In central Florida, 25 miles northwest of Orlando.

Climate:

	High	Low
January	72	49
July	92	73

Average relative humidity: 85%

Rain: 54 inches

Cost of living: Below average

Median housing cost: $225,000

Sales tax: 7%

Sales tax exemptions: Prescription drugs, groceries and most services.

State income tax: None.

Intangibles tax: None. The tax was repealed as of Jan. 1, 2007.

Estate tax: None

Property tax: The combined city-county tax rate is $22.2109 per $1,000 of assessed value, with homes assessed at 100% of market value. The annual tax on a $225,000 home, with exemption noted below, is $4,442.

Homestead exemption: First $25,000 of assessed value on a primary, permanent residence.

Religion: One Roman Catholic and 27 Protestant churches.

Education: There are no college or university campuses in Mount Dora. Lake Sumter Community College in nearby Leesburg offers two-year associate of arts and sciences degrees, plus many continuing-education and noncredit courses. Lake Technical Center in nearby Eustis offers vocational training and a school of cosmetology.

Transportation: Orlando International and Daytona Beach Regional airports are approximately 60 minutes from Mount Dora. Amtrak's East Coast auto-train stops in Sanford, 20 miles east of Mount Dora.

Health: Florida Hospital Waterman, five miles north in Eustis, is a full-service facility with 204 beds, 24-hour emergency room and 200 physicians on staff. Leesburg Regional Medical Center, 25 miles away, has 429 beds and serves a three-county area.

Housing options: Newcomers have a choice of lakeside and lake-view single-family homes, condominiums and townhouses, many within a short walking distance of downtown, ranging from the $100,000s for a small condo to $1 million and up for a luxury townhome. Rental retirement community **Waterman Village**, (352) 383-0051, offers independent living at the Villas, with a yearly lease and $2,400-$3,300 monthly, and at the Manors, with a life-lease fee of about $200,000 and $1,600-$1,850 monthly. Assisted living at the **Bridgewater** is $2,315-$4,990 monthly. Its Edgewater Health Care and Rehabilitation Center costs $183-$210 daily and provides long-term nursing care. Prices include one to three meals daily, weekly housekeeping, security, scheduled transportation, emergency response system and events in their activities center.

Visitor lodging: Options include Lakeside Inn, $79-$289, (800) 556-5016 or (352) 383-4101, and Mount Dora Historic Inn, a restored 19th-century bed-and-breakfast inn downtown, $125-$165, (800) 927-6344.

Information: Mount Dora Area Chamber of Commerce, 341 N. Alexander St., Mount Dora, FL 32757, (352) 383-2165 or www.mountdora.com.

new homes, so it is likely prices are going up," he says.

Cost of living has not been a problem, all three couples say, agreeing that taxes in general are lower than in their previous home states. But there are plenty of opportunities to spend money, they say, citing the multitude of shopping, dining and entertainment outlets in the Greater Orlando area.

"In reality, the cost of living here is very reasonable," John Keenon says. "We still live the same lifestyle but eat out a lot more now." As for the Andersons, they credit financial planning with providing adequate income for their carefree retirement, along with one additional step taken some years ago. "We

quit feeding our children money," Bob says with a laugh.

Although Mount Dora is sometimes called "New England of the South," thanks in part to some Victorian mansions near the downtown antiques district, the town is quintessential Florida when it comes to weather. Summers are hot and humid, with temperatures reaching into the 90s and humidity averaging 85 percent. Electrical storms are prevalent in late summer and early fall and winters are mild, with temperatures generally in the 50s to 70s.

Betty Jones misses the changing of seasons, but says, "Up North, there were a lot of gray, cloudy, rainy days. We don't get that much here." However, Bil-

lie Keenon doesn't like July and August in Mount Dora. "We try to go to Virginia to see our grandchildren in the summer," she says, "but sometimes it gets as hot there as here."

The Andersons are glad to put behind them the winter snowfalls back in Virginia. "Bob stood at the window and watched me shovel snow," Mary says of Virginia winters. "From November to April I hibernated," admits Bob.

Despite some misgivings about the hot summer temperatures, all three couples are glad they made the move and have no plans to relocate again. As John Keenon says, anyone considering Mount Dora as a retirement site "should put it on the top of their list." ●

Myrtle Beach, South Carolina

Retirees find life on South Carolina's Grand Strand is a year-round vacation

By Jim Kerr

Throughout its half-dozen or so mini seasons, Myrtle Beach never sleeps. Traffic rolls north and south along Route 17, ebbing and flowing through a 60-mile-long coastal corridor known as the Grand Strand, not so much in concert with the climate as with the habits and lifestyles of residents and visitors.

"Summer brings families, and in fall the golf season starts," says Patrick Walsh, a former fire department officer in Washington, DC, who moved here eight years ago. "We don't go into downtown Myrtle Beach very much between June and September when traffic is heaviest, but we've never stopped going to the beach whenever we want."

Pat, 61, and his wife, Cathy, 51, live just west of Route 17 in a golf community called Indigo Creek. It's south of the main Myrtle Beach action, but only two miles west of their favorite fishing pier and outdoor cafe at Garden City Beach. Like many retirees now settled on the Strand, they made the transition from vacationers to residents over a period of years, and they've adapted to myriad seasonal changes signaled by many things, including no less than 10 different golf course green fee rates throughout the year.

"The week we retired we drove here from Maryland on a golf vacation," remembers Pat. "A friend had seen Indigo Creek in a magazine, and the second day here we bought a lot. Later we switched to a larger one, built a house selected from 15 different models, and moved down for good in 1995."

Everything accelerated like a four-alarm fire after that. In 1996 he took a Horry County job as a fire department battalion chief, but the 600 square miles he covered burned him out. "It definitely wasn't retirement," he says. So while he is still on call as a volunteer, he now spends more time teaching and consulting on his specialty — emergency response management and planning. It's satisfying self-employment that takes him far and wide, from the North Carolina capital of Raleigh down to Louisiana State University in Baton Rouge, and the travel has taught him how to negotiate the increasingly complex regional road system that links several distinctly different social and economic segments of two counties.

In the early 1900s, farmers from across the Waccamaw River brought their families by wagon to the cooling breezes along the white sands of Atlantic beaches. In the southern portion of what is now the Grand Strand, wealthy rice plantation owners in Georgetown County gathered at rambling beach houses on Pawleys Island as early as the 1840s. Timber and turpentine production occupied the less affluent farmers in Horry County to the north, and today tobacco still reigns as the primary cash crop in western environs of the county.

Myrtle Beach, with its inexpensive and available land, surged into a golf course building boom in the 1960s, but it wasn't until the 1980s and '90s that the various towns along the coast melded and consolidated into one long linear resort and residential mecca. The stream of tourists became a flood, which in recent years has reached almost 14 million. Meanwhile, the resident population has grown by 36.5 percent in the last decade, making it the 13th-fastest-growing area in the United States.

Myrtle Beach, the largest and most developed of the Strand's dozen or so municipalities, has a population of 25,000. In World War II, an air base was established and remained the town's largest employer until it was closed during military base cuts in 1992. Now the former base is an international airport with nine commercial airlines.

Even so, the vast majority of visitors arrive by car, primarily from the Carolinas, Ohio, Pennsylvania, Virginia, Maryland and New York. They come for the informal beach atmosphere, family entertainment and outdoor recreation, including fishing, boating and, above all, golf. The first course opened in 1927, and by 1992 there were 80. Today the count is up to 120 public courses, and while competition is heated, there appears to be no saturation point in sight.

Active retirees like Pat Walsh, who plays at least three days a week when he's in town, are targets for numerous special deals. Package rates and senior memberships can generally get them on 30 to 40 different courses for an average of $26 a round with cart. With rates like that, few retirees restrict themselves to one club, although Pat and Cathy Walsh's three-bedroom, 1,900-square-foot house conveniently backs up to a pond across from the white tees of Number 14 at Indigo Creek.

Al and Carolyn Montanaro live in somewhat similar circumstances at Blackmoor Golf Club just a couple of miles west of Indigo Creek. The couple moved here two years ago from Montgomery County, MD, where Al, now 62, specialized in international banking with a Washington, DC, financial institution. Carolyn, 59, worked 36 years with the federal government until she retired as a management analyst with the Department of the Army. They vacationed here almost every year for 20 years before relocating, and the transition has been flawless.

"It was a bustling place even 20 years ago," says Carolyn, a South Carolina native who works 10 hours a week at a part-time job and as a volunteer for her church and the local chamber of commerce. "We're still only six minutes away from the beach at Garden City, a family place where people rent homes and beach cottages. We go there for walks and the sunsets. Meanwhile, we've made so many good friends here — and feel blessed that we've ended up in an area with such great people. All the growth around us has only added things to do."

Carolyn's mother and younger brother, who attended college here, also live nearby in Myrtle Beach. Her own son now attends Coastal Carolina University, while her two daughters and "three and a half grandchildren" live in Maryland. "We go to Maryland an average of once every six weeks, and they come down here on holidays," Carolyn says.

The couple's new four-bedroom, 2,800-square-foot house, while smaller than the 3,300-square-foot home they had on two acres in Maryland, is plenty big to accommodate visiting family — and has a lot less lawn to mow. The kids love the seashore, and their grandparents especially like to take them to Huntington Beach State Park, a 2,500-acre retreat of tidal creeks, salt marshes and long stretches of beach that offer a bit more solitude than the more crowded resort beaches.

Al, an avid golfer who launched his game only six years ago while on vacation here, now balances his own playing time with coaching football at a local middle school. Next year he graduates to a volunteer coaching position at a new high school.

Myrtle Beach and North Myrtle Beach, a consolidation of several smaller townships, are in Horry County, the fastest-growing area of South Carolina. The county covers more than 1,000 square miles and holds nearly 211,000 people.

At the southern end of the Strand, smaller Georgetown County, with 815 square miles and less than a third of Horry's population, retains a more pastoral and affluent atmosphere reminiscent of the old plantation days prior to the Civil War. Some historic beach houses on Pawleys Island date to 19th-century Scottish and English settlers. However, most of today's retirees in this area reside in gated golf communities like Pawleys Plantation, a former rice plantation whose 582 acres include lakes, salt marshes, moss-covered oaks and a Jack Nicklaus golf course.

Chick and Gene Ferrell, a couple from West Virginia, picked the less-expensive northern fringe of the Strand to retire. Little River, the unincorporated community where they live in a trim duplex development, borders the North Carolina state line and is home to the area's fishing fleet. The Ferrells have known this region well for more than 40 years, having vacationed here since 1959. Yet they always figured they would wind up

Myrtle Beach, SC

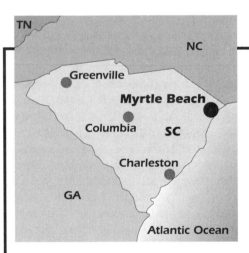

Population: Approximately 25,000 within Myrtle Beach, 211,000 in Horry County, 55,797 in Georgetown County.

Location: Myrtle Beach and its environs cover a 60-mile stretch along the northeast coast of South Carolina known as the Grand Strand. The area is 360 miles east of Atlanta, GA, 437 miles north of Daytona Beach, FL, and 175 miles southeast of Raleigh, NC.

Climate: High Low
January   56   38
July   91   75

Average relative humidity: 78%

Rain: 41.39 inches

Snow: 0.5 inches

Cost of living: Below average

Average housing cost: The median price of a residential home in Horry and Georgetown counties is $166,000.

Sales tax: 5% state tax on the sale of goods and certain services.

Sales tax exemptions: Persons 85 and older pay 1% less sales tax on food and services.

State income tax: Six income tax brackets are adjusted annually for inflation. Rates range from 2.5% on taxable income of $2,530 to 7% on taxable income above $12,650 (minus $367).

Income tax exemptions: Social Security benefits are exempt from state income taxes, and that portion of benefits taxed at the federal level is deductible from South Carolina taxable income. There is an exemption of up to $3,000 in any pensions if under age 65 and up to $10,000 in pensions if 65 or older. Each person age 65 and older receives an age deduction of $15,000 off any income, although that's reduced by the amount of retirement exemption taken.

Estate tax: None

Property tax: Appraised value of a personal, legal residence is assessed by both Horry and Georgetown counties and cities at 4% minus a state tax relief deduction on the first $100,000 and any applicable homestead exemption. A wide variety of municipal rates are factored in, along with any special taxing district rates. Real property taxes on a Myrtle Beach home assessed at $166,000 would be about $1,279 based on the formula as calculated in that city. The area has the lowest tax base in the state.

Homestead exemptions: The first $50,000 of the fair market value of a home is exempt from property taxes for citizens over 65.

Religion: There are nearly 500 houses of worship in the area, representing every denomination.

Education: Coastal Carolina University is a state-supported, four-year college with a variety of programs and about 7,000 students. Webster University offers MBAs and other higher-education programs with an enrollment of about 475 students. Horry-Georgetown Technical College has three campuses, 60 certificate and associate degree programs and more than 4,000 students.

Transportation: Interstate 95, the main north-south connector between the Northeast and Florida, is about an hour and a half west of Myrtle Beach. Myrtle

retired in Florida.

"After seeing Florida, we realized what a different atmosphere this was," Gene recalls. "This place was young and active. It's interesting and exciting to live here with all this growth and development." Instead of hanging up his work clothes, Gene leaped into the economic opportunities he saw for himself, buying a few empty lots and building some houses.

"All my life, working was hard," says Gene, 69, who had an electrical heating business. "It was never fun like it is here. I tell my friends that when I moved here I was 80. Now I'm 50. I can't wait for daylight to get going. I have enough projects now to cover me until age 74."

"I've never been bored here," adds Chick Ferrell, 68, who helps Gene with his new building projects. "We found you stay younger when you work and socialize with younger friends. We discovered a great little church where we

go for Bible studies and to play cards." They downsized from a 6,000-square-foot home in Madison, WV, to their 1,700-square-foot townhouse in Little River. "We had a lot of garage sales," Chick says. "But I don't regret it or miss it at all."

In the seven years he's lived here, Gene has played at least 40 different golf courses, but a highlight of living in the area, he says, remains the couple's enjoyment in watching the Little River fishing fleet unload its catch at the inlet a few blocks away. When their two grandchildren visit, which is often, Gene entertains them by taking them fishing. They also keep a small house in Pocahontas, WV, an eight-hour trip from Little River.

Meanwhile, a faster pace is always available to those willing to face the traffic in Myrtle Beach. There are hundreds of restaurants, a dozen shopping malls, movie theaters and numerous live entertainment venues. Most of them, like

Dixie Stampede, Carolina Opry, Alabama Theatre and Legends in Concert, are more in tune with places like Branson or Dollywood than Broadway and Washington, but that's just fine with folks like Pat and Cathy Walsh, who lived for years in the DC area.

"I never went to the Kennedy Center unless it was on fire," jokes former fireman Pat. He adds that while golfers, college students and motorcycle enthusiasts still seek out the beach bars and clubs for entertainment, the area has undergone changes in recent years. "The atmosphere in Myrtle Beach was pretty honky-tonk," he says. "But now it's been redirected much more toward family entertainment." This includes amusement parks, arcades, boardwalks and almost 50 miniature golf courses.

With plenty of housing options on the Strand, you can be as close or as far removed from all this as you want. When Nita and Donald Bolton first

Beach has an international airport with daily flights to cities primarily in the Midwest and Northeast, as well as service to Europe. Greyhound has bus service to and from Myrtle Beach, and Amtrak has train service out of Florence, SC. Nearly $1 billion is being spent on road construction projects in the area and another $100 million on airport improvements.

Health: A medical facilities building boom is under way on the Grand Strand as a result of the population explosion. The 219-bed Grand Strand Regional Medical Center underwent a $33 million expansion completed in 2002 that included a third intensive-care unit, additional surgical areas and other patient facilities. It has a trauma center and cardiac surgery program. Georgetown Memorial Hospital is a 131-bed acute-care facility, and 40-bed Waccamaw Community Hospital opened in 2002 with 24-hour emergency services and medical/surgery units. Two other facilities, Conway Hospital and Loris Healthcare System, are also available.

Housing options: There is a wide range of choices on the Grand Strand, from condos, apartments and townhouses to single-family homes, mainly in new residential developments and gated golf communities. Prices can range from the $170,000s for golf villas to $900,000 for single-family homes on larger lots $170,000 to $400,000. Most gated golf community homes, however, are located on small lots sold separately with a choice of model home styles ranging from $170,000 to $400,000. **Barefoot Resort**, (888) 996-4100, on the Intracoastal Waterway in North Myrtle Beach, has more than a dozen neighborhoods with townhomes and resort and golf villas, priced from the $170,000s. **EdgeWater**, a gated community of waterway villas at Barefoot Resort, is scheduled to open July 2006. Prices start in the $390,000s. **Lakeside Crossing**, (800) 679-4155, is a new active-adult community of one-story, single-family homes ranging from $87,800 to $136,200. At **Indigo Creek Golf Club**, (800) 277-7704, several models are available for resale, (Prudential Burroughs & Chapin Realty) from $175,000 to $400,000s. **Grande Dunes**, (877) 347-2633, is an upscale community embracing both sides of the Intracoastal Waterway.

Homes start in the $600,000s.

Visitor lodging: A major family beach and golf resort region, the Grand Strand has more than 72,000 rooms. At the Atlantic Coast Resorts, (800) 248-0003, rooms range from $32 a night in January and February to $142 in late May for an oceanfront balcony room. Dozens of rental agents include Seaside Rentals, (866) 252-9930, and Rose Real Estate, (800) 845-6706. Bed-and-breakfast inns are located throughout the region. Evans Pelican Inn on Pawleys Island is a rambling beach home built for a Southern planter in the 1840s. Double rooms are $170 for two adults and include breakfast, (843) 237-2298. Golf packages abound. One of the best is the "Island Package" at Pawleys Plantation Golf and Country Club, (877) 763-7341, which offers four nights of accommodations ranging from $344 to $629, depending on season, with four rounds of golf at your choice of four outstanding courses.

Information: Newcomer Information, Myrtle Beach Area Chamber of Commerce, 1200 N. Oak St., Myrtle Beach, SC 29577, (843) 626-7444 or www.myrtle beachinfo.com.

moved here from Macon, GA, three years ago, they tried condominium life but discovered "we weren't condo people." They moved to a duplex development called Rivergate, became friends with the Ferrells, and got part-time jobs as ushers at the Celebrity Theater, a family musical venue in North Myrtle Beach.

"We have so many things to do in this area," says Donald, 67. "Yet it's not the hustle and bustle of Myrtle Beach." Like his friend Gene Ferrell, golf is a favorite pastime for Donald, but what both couples enjoy most is the sea, and the bounty that comes with it. Calabash, NC, home of another fishing fleet and a virtual "restaurant row" for seafood, is only minutes away.

For two couples with a landlocked past, that's a year-round gift with no seasonal limitation. ●

Naples, Florida

With beaches, golf, culture and shopping, this chic town on Florida's southwest coast proves irresistible to retirees

By Karen Feldman

Palm Beach may have a higher profile, but the diminutive city of Naples holds its own in attracting the well-known and the well-to-do. Oozing savoir-faire, overflowing with sophisticated boutiques, restaurants and golf courses, and bounded by pristine beaches, Naples has plenty to attract visitors, swelling the town's population of 27,000 to twice that during the winter high season.

Its tony hotels — most notably the Ritz-Carlton Naples, frequently ranked among the world's 10 best resorts — attract celebrities seeking time in the sun without the glare of the limelight, including Tony Bennett, the Rolling Stones and Steve Forbes. Authors Robin Cook and Ben Bova call Naples home, as did the late Robert Ludlum.

Many area residents start by vacationing there. Then they buy a condo or house for the winters, hesitant to commit to staying through the hot and rainy summers. Finally, many settle in full time.

"It's the quality of life here that attracts them," says Mark Gianquitti, former vice president of member services for the Naples Area Chamber of Commerce. "With the gorgeous beaches, the entertainment opportunities, the arts, some great restaurants and some first-class shopping, all of those tied in together make it irresistible."

Donald and Mary Moon lived in Kettering, OH, for many years before buying a condo in Naples in March 2001. The couple, whose spouses died several years ago, got married on the lanai of that condo three months after buying it.

"Florida is now our primary residence," says Donald, 70, a retired chiropractic physician. "We will probably spend the summers in Ohio. We're keeping our home there until we really see how we like spending the whole year in Florida."

Before buying their North Naples condo, the couple visited the area three times over six years, staying at a different condominium each time. "Every time we came down we loved the place," Donald says.

Bob and Christa Lederer lived in Leavenworth, KS, when they bought a condo in Naples in 1988. They vacationed in Naples four times a year until 1996, when they moved south full time.

Bob, 70, dreamed of retiring in Las Vegas during the 20 years the couple lived in Leavenworth, where he had an orthodontic dental practice. Meanwhile, 50-something Christa worked in her husband's office and envisioned life in Florida.

Bob's parents lived in Miami Beach, but Christa disliked the area. "We looked at the entire east coast (of Florida), but I told my husband, 'If we have to live on the east coast, I'll stay in Leavenworth.' The traffic was just awful."

Then they visited one of Christa's cousins in Naples on Florida's southwest coast. "The minute I drove into Naples, I said, 'This is it. We're buying a condo now,'" she says.

They bought one on the spot at Bay Colony, using it for five years. They put it on the market in early 2001. They have since moved to a luxury high-rise at The Seasons at Naples Cay.

"Activity has been steady," says Phil Wood, broker for John R. Wood Realtors in Naples. "It's been strong since the start of the year," he says. "There's a good inventory and a nice selection in a variety of price ranges."

Bob and Jo Ann Wasylenko lived in Naples for five years before selling their home and moving to neighboring Bonita Springs to live among a somewhat younger crowd (he's 64, she's 60). It took them only three weeks to sell their Naples property. It was Naples' cultural climate that attracted them in the first place.

There aren't quite as many cultural opportunities as there were in their hometown of St. Louis. But "the Philharmonic (Center for the Arts) is top-notch. Art galleries and exhibits are abundant and it isn't difficult to get to St. Petersburg or Sarasota for cultural events," Jo Ann says.

Culture notwithstanding, retirees considering a purchase in the Naples area "are mostly looking for one of two things — golf or gulf," John Wood says.

It's small wonder, considering that Naples boasts 11 miles of well-tended beach, including two beaches named to the annual top 20 list by Stephen Leatherman, also known as Dr. Beach, director of the Laboratory for Coastal Research and International Hurricane Center at Florida International University.

The city has more than 110 golf courses and more under construction. Its courses attract not only amateurs but also the pros that compete at the Senior PGA Tour's ACE Group Classic and the Dodge Celebrity Invitational, among others. Even people who never picked up a club before quickly seem to get into the swing.

"When we moved here my husband didn't have a hobby and he was getting in my way," says Christa Lederer with a laugh. "Then I decided we were going to play golf. Neither of us had ever been on a golf course. We're playing now six or seven days a week. The people we meet on the golf course are now our best friends."

That's not the only thing that's changed since they left Leavenworth. "What's amazing to me is the wealth," she says. "It's mind-boggling to me: the size of homes and cost of homes. Coming from Kansas, I am shocked every day. When you ask someone here, 'How much is it?' they say 2.0, 5.9, 10, and that's always millions. It's something I can't comprehend."

Naples' reputation for style and sophistication is relatively new, but it's long been a haven for wealthy Northerners looking for respite from long, bleak winters. The city got its start in

1887, when the land on which it now sits was first surveyed, plotted and put on the market. It began as a small fishing village and beachside getaway for the affluent, which it remained for almost 80 years.

Millionaire Barron Gift Collier eventually acquired much of the land and was responsible for some of the area's early economic growth. He brought electric power, paved roads, telegraphs and other vital infrastructure improvements to the area. Among his most important projects was the Tamiami Trail (U.S. Highway 41), completed in 1928, running from the state's more developed east coast to Naples and north along the west coast. The county, of which Naples is the seat, is named Collier in his honor.

Development began in earnest in the 1960s and has ramped up steadily ever since. Collier County has seen a serious boom in growth in recent years. "We had a 65 percent growth in population from 1990 to 2000," Mark Gianquitti says. "From 2000 to 2001, it grew at about a 5 or 6 percent clip, about eight times faster than the national average."

Mary Moon, 65, is impressed by how the city is coping with its burgeoning population. "Take downtown Naples — Old Naples — as an example. They have decided not to tear down the low buildings and put up high rises. It's a delicate balance they're trying to achieve, accommodating an influx of people, but at the same time keeping the characteristics that have been so attractive," she says.

A cornucopia of upscale housing options, as well as golf and water-related activities, provides much of the draw, but so do the entertainment options. Annual festivals and events run the gamut. There's the twice-yearly swamp buggy races in which the souped-up swamp buggies battle their way over the Mile O' Mud. The affair concludes with the winner tossing the swamp buggy queen in the mud.

Local residents also value the arts. The Philharmonic Center for the Arts, built in 1989 for cash, regularly hosts big-name shows, with performers such as Itzhak Perlman, Lyle Lovett and Mandy Patinkin appearing there. It's the west coast home of the Miami City Ballet and the home of the Naples Philharmonic Orchestra.

Smack in the middle of the tony shopping and entertainment district along Fifth Avenue South in Old Naples is the Sugden Community Theatre, home of the Naples Players, an accomplished amateur troupe. The Naples Dinner Theatre produces musicals such as "Carousel" and "The King and I," as well as musical revues.

The city also boasts an impressive and diverse assortment of museums. The Naples Museum of Art hosts world-class traveling exhibitions. The Collier County Museum affords modern-day visitors a glimpse back at 10,000 years of the region's history. The Teddy Bear Museum is home to an international collection of 5,000 stuffed bears.

Bordered by three bodies of water — the Gulf of Mexico, Naples Bay and the Gordon River — Naples offers

Naples, FL

Population: About 27,000 in the city, 350,000 in Collier County.

Location: Naples is the Collier County seat, located in southwest Florida about 110 miles west of Miami, 134 miles south of Tampa and about 35 miles south of Fort Myers.

Climate:

	High	Low
January	74	53
July	91	75

Average relative humidity: 89% in the morning, 56% in the afternoon

Rain: About 52 inches

Cost of living: Above average

Median housing cost: $480,000

Sales tax: 6%

Sales tax exemptions: Groceries, medicine and some professional services.

State income tax: None

Intangibles tax: None. The tax was repealed as of Jan. 1, 2007.

Estate tax: None

Inheritance tax: None

Property tax: All city residents pay $12.7013 to $15.6183 per $1,000 of assessed value. Some also are situated in special taxing districts for services such as street lighting. With a $25,000 homestead exemption, the annual tax on a $480,000 home would range from $5,779 to $7,106.

Homestead exemption: $25,000 off assessed value of primary, permanent residence.

Religion: Dozens of houses of worship are located in and around Naples, representing all major denominations as well as many other faiths.

Education: Edison Community College, based in Fort Myers to the north, has a branch campus in Naples that offers a wide range of courses for credit as well as continuing education. Among continuing-education courses available recently were music and creative writing, art appreciation, Shakespeare and computer use. Florida Gulf Coast University, situated midway between Naples and Fort Myers, also offers a mix of programs that lead to degrees and a variety of continuing-education classes.

Transportation: Southwest Florida International Airport in southern Lee County is served by more than two dozen major air carriers and is the region's primary airport. Naples Municipal Airport offers private charters, some commuter flights and some regularly scheduled flights. Naples Trolley Tours operates within the city, making many stops along the route and conducting guided tours. Taxi and limousine services are available from Southwest Florida International Airport. U.S. Highway 41 (also known as Tamiami Trail) is the main commercial route through the area, while Interstate 75 to the east of the city connects the region to Miami to the east and most of the state's west coast.

plenty of water-related activities, from a relaxing sunbath on the beach to the always popular fishing off the Naples Pier to boating, water-skiing and swamp buggies.

While the city doesn't have a resident baseball team for spring training, it's less than an hour's drive to Fort Myers, where the Minnesota Twins and Boston Red Sox work out each February and March.

And the city still retains some of the classic attractions that amused visitors decades back. Caribbean Gardens is a prime example of an old-time attraction that has kept pace with the times. Its 52 acres include tropical gardens and an animal preserve. There are boat rides near islands with monkeys in a natural habitat and a variety of animal shows daily. On some Sundays during the winter, visitors can have brunch in the gardens.

As the population grows, so do the shopping opportunities. All the usual chains can be found in Naples, including most of the upscale ones, such as Saks Fifth Avenue, Williams-Sonoma and Talbots. But one of the city's enduring charms is its wealth of boutique shopping along well-groomed streets that draw visitors and residents alike. Third Street South and Fifth Avenue South in Old Naples — the city's historic district — are favorites of those seeking one-of-a-kind stores, art galleries and trendy restaurants.

Several of Naples' private art galleries include the works of big-name artists, including Robert Rauschenberg (who lives on Captiva, about an hour north of Naples), David Hockney and Pablo Picasso. During the winter, up-and-coming artists get a chance to show their works at monthly Art in the Park exhibitions sponsored by the Naples Art Association as well as at juried art shows.

The drawbacks of living in Naples are few, say the Moons and Lederers. Donald Moon hates the bugs, which include mosquitoes, gnats and beefy cockroaches, some of which fly. "We don't like the drinking water, either," he says, and traffic during the winter months seems to get worse every year.

Bob and Christa Lederer find the traffic annoying at times but say it's offset by the area's beauty and the quality of life they have there. To others considering a move to Naples, Christa says they should love to be outdoors. "A person who likes seasons cannot live in Naples."

Donald Moon cautions that newcomers should "make sure they have a decent income. It's a very expensive town." Before making a permanent commitment, Christa Lederer says, "the most important advice I can give is move here and rent for one or two years. Get familiar with the area, get familiar with the prices, get familiar with the different housing areas. Then you can make an educated decision."

For her, there's no going back to Kansas. "Bob wants to be buried in Leavenworth because his parents are buried there," Christa says. "I told him, 'Bob, I'm not going to your funeral. I'm not going back to Leavenworth!'" ●

Health: Naples Community Hospital is a private, not-for-profit, acute-care hospital with 390 beds in the heart of the city. North Collier Hospital is an 88-bed, not-for-profit hospital also offering acute-care services. The prestigious Cleveland Clinic has an 83-bed not-for-profit, acute-care hospital, surgery center and clinic in north Naples. The David Lawrence Center offers psychiatric services for children and adults.

Housing options: Naples has a broad range of housing, starting at about $200,000 and rising to $30 million. Golf-course homes vary according to the exclusivity of the course. Small condominiums may still be found from the high $100,000s, but most are priced in the $300,000s to $400,000s, which is the low-end range of single-family homes. Waterfront homes start at about $2.5 million. In the **Port Royal** neighborhood, a long-established upscale area in which most homes are situated along lush waterways, seven-figure sales prices are the rule. There is no development office (individual builders construct custom homes), but the Port Royal Property Owners Association can be reached at (239) 261-6472. A sampling of the many housing options: **Bridgewater Bay** in North Naples, (877) 596-2619 or (239) 596-7020, offers homes from the $200,000s to over $400,000, which includes membership in the residents club. **Tiburon**, (800) 924-2290 or (239) 593-9199, offers a 27-hole championship golf course designed by Greg Norman, with condos and homes from the high $400,000s to about $4 million. **Pelican Marsh**, (239) 597-5277, another golf-course community, has condos and homes starting in the high $200,000s to $6.9 million. The **Estates at TwinEagles**, (800) 281-9245, has estate sites starting in the high $500,000s, with homes starting at $2.2 million. **Green-Links**, (239) 732-5532, is a condominium community with units priced from $379,000 to $429,000; it has a Robert Trent Jones Sr. signature golf course, lighted tennis courts, fitness room and concierge service. The **Colony Golf and Bay Club** in nearby Bonita Springs has single-family homes, villas and luxury high-rise condos from $639,000 to $5.5 million, (800) 683-9997.

Visitor lodging: Regularly awarded five diamonds by AAA and five stars by Mobil Travel Guide, the Ritz-Carlton Naples has a prime gulf-front location, a spa, fine dining and a full range of services, $179-$4,500, (239) 598-3300 or (888) 856-4372. Just a few miles away is the Ritz-Carlton Golf Resort with 295 rooms and a Greg Norman-designed golf course, $129-$2,000, (239) 593-2000. The gulf-front Edgewater Beach Resort offers one- and two-bedroom suites, $129-$1,300, (239) 403-2000. Staybridge Suites Hotel by Holiday Inn has spacious studios as well as one- and two-bedroom suites at the northern end of the city, $180-$229, (239) 643-8002.

Information: Naples Tourism Alliance, 3050 N. Horseshoe Drive, Suite 218, Naples, FL 34104, (800) 688-3600 or www.classicflorida.com. Naples Area Chamber of Commerce, 2390 Tamiami Trail N., Naples, FL 34103, (239) 262-6141 or www.napleschamber.org.

Natchez, Mississippi

Retirees find a welcoming town on a bluff overlooking the Mississippi River

By Lynn Grisard Fullman

Winter was lingering in Michigan in 1982 when Sue Ann and Carl Wilt read a newspaper article about an upcoming pilgrimage in Natchez, MS, a town noted for its moss-draped trees, slow pace and columned homes.

The two made plans for a quick trip south. What they didn't expect was that their lives would be changed forever. "We both like history, cemeteries and old things," says Sue Ann, who retired in 2002 after working 32 years with Michigan State University, first as a librarian and later as a fleet manager.

When that spring pilgrimage was over, the Wilts returned home, leaving a bit of their hearts in Natchez, which originally was occupied by the French, then the English and later by the Spanish, who in 1798 relinquished the area to the United States.

"We pretty well knew in the early 1990s that we wanted to retire here," she remembers. Some people wear their hearts on their sleeves; the Wilts wore theirs on their car's bumper, with a personalized Michigan car tag that read "NATCHEZ."

"We were head over heels in love after our first visit," she recalls, explaining that after that initial visit they "were 85 percent sure that we would retire to Natchez."

The couple returned once a year — sometimes twice — intending to see different places and different seasons, explains Sue Ann, a Wisconsin native who at age 57 is three years younger than her husband. He retired after 37 years of selling life insurance and restaurant and food equipment.

"We checked the tax situation versus Michigan (and found that) because the cost of living here is much lower, we could retire five years earlier. Property taxes here are less than one-third of what we paid in Michigan," Sue Ann says.

"Natchez has many wonderful qualities of life not available in your typical

---

Population: 19,460 in Natchez with 15.6% age 65 or older, and 35,356 in Adams County.

Location: Natchez is in southwest Mississippi, 200 feet above the Mississippi River on the highest promontory north of the Gulf of Mexico. It is the oldest continuous settlement on the river, two years older than New Orleans.

Climate:

	High	Low
January	58	39
July	91	72

The area enjoys complete seasonal cycles with pleasant spring and fall seasons. Winter months are usually mild with cold spells of short duration.

Average relative humidity: 59%

Rain: 59 inches

Snow: Rare

Cost of living: Lower than average

Average housing costs: In 2005 the average sale price of a home was $101,984. Resale homes average about $50 to $70 per square foot. Typical cost of a new 1,800-square-foot house with two-car garage is $180,000.

Sales tax: Mississippi has a 7% sales tax on retail purchases. There is an added 3% tax on lodging and a 1.5% tax on restaurants.

Sales tax exemptions: Prescription drugs, residential utilities, motor fuel, newspapers, health-care services and payments made by Medicare and Medicaid.

State income tax: The first $5,000 of taxable income is taxed at 3%, the second $5,000 at 4%, and amounts above $10,000 are taxed at 5%.

Income tax exemptions: Social Security benefits, public and private pensions, IRAs and annuities are exempt. For taxpayers age 65 and older, there is an additional exemption of $1,500.

Estate tax: None for decedents after January 1, 2005.

Property tax: Current combined county and city tax on residential homes located in Natchez is $145.92 per $1,000 of assessed value set at approximately 10% of real value. With exemptions noted below, a home worth $100,000 would be taxed at $1,159, or $365 after age 65.

Homestead exemption: Residential property used as a primary residence has a homestead credit up to $300. Those age 65 and older or those who are disabled are exempt from ad valorem taxes up to $75,000 of the market value on homesteaded property.

Personal property tax: Automobiles are assessed at 30% of market value, and the tax is reduced by a percentage assigned by the legislature.

Religion: The Natchez area has more than 100 churches representing 30 denominations including Catholic, Jewish, Mormon and Protestant faiths (Baptist, Episcopal, Presbyterian, Lutheran, Metho-dist, Church of Christ and Assembly of God).

Education: Natchez is home to campuses of both Copiah-Lincoln Community College and Alcorn State University's School of Nursing and a new business school that includes an MBA program. Course work is available in a wide range of academic, technical and vocational areas. The Institute for Learning in Retirement is located at Co-Lin and is affiliated with the International Elderhostel Program. The institute provides noncredit, college-level course work in addition to noncourse offerings such as luncheon lectures, seminars and out-of-town trips for members.

Transportation: Air service is available

---

retirement community," confirms Roy Winkworth, director of Natchez Retiree Partnership. The city "is not a typical retirement town," adds Winkworth, a Toronto native who remained in Natchez after being transferred there in the early 1980s. "The history of Natchez is a major contributor to the reasons I love living here," he says, citing antebellum and Victorian-style homes, excellent restaurants, "amazing" gardening and the availability of great hunting, golf and other sports.

With more than 500 structures built before the Civil War era, Natchez is a virtual museum. One of the most visited sites is Melrose, an elaborate estate with Doric columns and delicate iron railings. Built from 1842 to 1848, Melrose today is part of the Natchez National Historical Park.

While Roy Winkworth already was in Natchez when his retirement rolled around, the Wilts had to pack up to head south following their retirement. When they moved, their Mississippi home was waiting. On a visit in 1996, they bought an all-brick, ranch-style house with attached garage. The 1,800-square-foot home, which sold for $110,000, is on three country acres once part of an indigo plantation. To offset the home's costs, the couple, married 28 years, rented it for several years.

Before moving in the summer of 2002, they sold their Cape Cod-style, 1,200-square-foot house where they had lived for 26 years. Situated on a small city lot in Lansing, it sold for a bit more than they had paid for their home in Natchez.

"Overall the cost of living in Natchez is quite low compared to the rest of the country," Winkworth notes, adding that housing costs on older homes are about $50 per square foot.

Before they moved, the Wilts checked out the town's medical offerings. "We have two hospitals — not monster hospitals, but good ones," Sue Ann says, explaining that the state capital of Jackson is 100 miles away and Baton Rouge is 90 miles away should they need additional medical care. But with "no huge department stores, no Target or Home Depot but a Wal-Mart Supercenter, shopping can be a challenge," she reports. "A lot of people go out of town to shop, but I'm not much for shopping, so for me it hasn't been a problem," she adds.

The town, with a mall and several shopping strips, is known for antiques, collectibles, prints, estate jewelry and gift items. "Restaurants are wonderful," Sue Ann says, citing Biscuits & Blues and Mammy's Cupboard as favorites. Busy with volunteer work and gardening on their land, the Wilts have not been bored. Nor have they looked back. When they arrived, they were "welcomed most warmly. This town is welcoming, very friendly, not boring, and there is always something to do," Sue Ann says.

A focal point for services, activities and programs, a senior citizens center offers indoor swimming in a heated pool, arts and crafts and day care facilities for seniors. "I was a city kid all my life (but) I'm

Natchez, MS

through American, Continental and Delta airlines to Baton Rouge Metropolitan Airport some 90 minutes away. Bus service to Natchez is provided through Delta Bus Lines (Greyhound). The city's transportation network includes downtown trolleys and a citywide bus system run by the Natchez Transit System, with buses that are wheelchair-equipped providing needed transportation to the senior citizens center, doctors, grocery store, pharmacy and other places. Cost is 50 cents for those older than 65.

Health: Two modern hospitals serve Adams County/Natchez: Natchez Community Hospital and Natchez Regional Medical Center, with a combined total of 306 beds. The county is also served by a personal care home, three nursing homes, four home-health agencies and a pain-treatment center. Approximately 100 licensed medical professionals work in the area, including the specialties of anesthesiology, cardiology, dentistry, dermatology, ear/nose/throat, family practice, gastroenterology, general surgery, internal medicine, obstetrics/gynecology, oncology, ophthalmology, orthopedics, patholo-

gy, pediatrics, pulmonary medicine, radiology and urology.

Housing options: Natchez offers a variety of homes, diverse in cost, style and location. Those preferring newer homes will find moderately priced subdivisions offering wooded lots, convenient shopping and easy access to the downtown business district. Historic antebellum and Victorian homes are also available, either for renovation or already complete with modern amenities priced far below replacement cost. Custom-built homes on a championship golf course also are available. Home and apartment rentals are available with a two-bedroom apartment renting for about $450-$600 per month. There are no retiree-only communities.

Visitor lodging: With more than 1,100 rooms ranging from luxury suites to economy motels, Natchez offers accommodations in antebellum mansions, historic homes, cozy cottages, rustic cabins and modern hotels and motels. Campsites and RV parks are available. Dunleith Historic Inn, a stately white colonnaded structure with 26 rooms and suites and surrounded by 40 acres, is $135-$225, (800) 433-2445. Natchez Eola Hotel, built in 1927 and renovated in 1998, is $101-$415, (866) 445-3652. Isle of Capri Casino Hotel, with river views, is $79-$99, (800) 722-5825.

Information: Natchez Retiree Partnership, P.O. Box 700, Natchez, MS 39121, (800) 762-8243 or www3.bkbank.com/nrp. Natchez Convention and Visitors Bureau , 640 S. Canal St., Box C, Natchez, MS 39120, (800) 647-6724 or www.visitnatchez.com. Natchez-Adams County Chamber of Commerce, 211 Main St., Natchez, MS 39120, (601) 445-4611 or www.natchezchamber.com.

learning about living in the country," Sue Ann says. "Without all the intrusion of city lights, we can see the Milky Way at nights," Carl adds.

Sue Ann and Carl, who used to travel with Michigan State's sports teams, especially during basketball playoffs, are seldom on the road anymore. "Now that we're in Natchez, we're on vacation all the time," Carl says. Asked what they would advise those considering retiring to Natchez, Carl is quick to say, "Come ahead."

Come ahead is exactly what Andre Taylor did after an exhaustive search for a place to retire. Single and without children, the Philadelphia native had delved into books about how to prepare for retirement, doubled her mortgage payments and worked toward a pension. At age 27, she had begun her career as a patrol officer. She retired as a lieutenant overseeing a nine-person unit that investigated harassment claims within the nation's fourth-largest police department, whose 7,500 officers far outnumber the 59 members of the police department in Natchez.

Before undertaking her search, Andre "had never heard of Natchez." Having read books on ideal places for retirement, she called for information and scheduled a meeting with Roy Winkworth on Good Friday of 2004. Before visiting, she explored housing options on www.realtor.com and found a Natchez house that intrigued her. Ultimately, though, she bought another house, a 1,900-square-foot hybrid of Queen Anne and Colonial Revival styles. Built in 1895, the house has tall ceilings, crown molding, some original hand-blown windows and a wraparound porch. Needing only cosmetic work, the house sold for $115,000; its taxes are $600.

Before buying the house, Andre returned to Philadelphia and sold the 950-square-foot house where she had lived for five years. Built in 1810, the house had hardwood floors and ceilings so low she could reach up and touch them. Taxes on the house, which sold for $295,000, were $2,700. "Philadelphia is wonderful, but I couldn't afford to retire there," she says. "Mississippi reeled me in because of its retiree partnership group that is so clear-cut on how it works."

Mississippi is noted for its positive tax breaks for seniors. Among the appeals is that Mississippi does not tax pensions earned out of state. Andre also was impressed with the city's medical facilities, low crime rate and moderate year-round temperatures. "I wanted to get away from the snow," she says, adding that educational opportunities were other deciding factors. At Copiah-Lincoln Community College, course work and vocational training is available to students of all ages. Located at Co-Lin and affiliated with the International Elderhostel Program, the Institute for Learning in Retirement offers noncredit, college-level course work plus luncheon lectures, seminars and tours. Classes also are available through Alcorn State University.

"They offer a lot down here. I see so much happening in Natchez," Andre says, citing variety in restaurants, with Biscuits & Blues, the Castle Restaurant at Dunleith Plantation and the restaurant at the Natchez Eola Hotel as favorites. Weekly she walks the short distance to the Mississippi River, which is known for spectacular sunsets, especially when viewed from a bluff that oversees the bridge linking the city to Louisiana. "I just look at the river, and it is so beautiful," she says.

The river is not all that draws a second look. Columned homes remain as monuments to earlier prosperity and the men who owned plantations across the river in Louisiana and lived lavishly in Natchez. During its early years, the town prospered primarily because of its strategic river location, but that changed with the coming of railroads. While other cities were tearing down to make way for change, Natchez, short on funds, could only afford repairs, inadvertently preserving mansions that now draw spring and fall pilgrims seeking closer looks. (The spring pilgrimage occurs in March of each year, and the fall pilgrimage is in October.)

Andre, who is black, considered whether or not there would be problems with stereotyping, but says, "I have not faced that. People have welcomed me and brought me the most wonderful cakes and dinners, even loaned me furniture until mine arrived." Referring to the town's racial mix, she reports that the demographics in Philadelphia, where some 40 percent of the population is black, are the same as in Natchez, "and that was a factor. I didn't want to feel uncomfortable here — and I don't feel that."

For those considering retirement, she says, "If you want a slower pace, a lower cost of living and nice, friendly, trusting people, then this is it."

But "not in a million years" did Mike Gemmell suspect that he and his wife, Elaine, would retire to Natchez, a town so quaint that downtown has no parking meters. Yet the signs were there, including when a former Natchez mayor visited the couple in their Alexandria, VA, home and asked when they planned to move back to Elaine's hometown.

"My generation left for employment opportunities. There wasn't a whole lot to bring us back (after college)," explains Mike, 61, who hails from Guatemala and attended Jefferson Military College just outside of Natchez.

While several industries had driven the town's economy, they have left in recent years, leaving tourism as the No. 1 industry. What kept the Gemmells connected with Natchez was a lake house that had been in Elaine's family for decades. A couple dozen miles from town, the house had been a haven for the Gemmells and their two children, both now grown.

During family vacations, the pair, married 37 years, rarely drove into Natchez, preferring instead to embrace the allure of lake living as a retreat from Mike's Washington, DC, job as an association executive. Toward the end of his 25-year tenure, the association asked him to write a corporate history. Needing a writing sanctuary, the couple headed to their lake house in the summer of 2001. While in Mississippi, the Gemmells ventured occasionally into town, remembering the old days and seeing the history-shrouded town in a new light.

Two years after arriving, they bought a Natchez-style cottage just like Elaine, 60, always wanted. In the town's historic district and five minutes from restaurants and the river, the one-story, 2,800-square-foot cottage sold for $165,000. "We put a good bit into it," Mike says, explaining that the house dates to 1790.

"They are giving stuff away here," he says of low prices. "I didn't believe the prices and the ease of finding things. Living in Natchez is like living in a college town — you meet interesting people and see interesting things." In fact, new friends often foil the couple's goal of walking to raise their heart rates. They tread a few feet and encounter a friend. The walk stops, the heart rate falls and conversation flows. A few more feet, a few more friends. "That's my only complaint about living here," Mike laughs.

"There is no excuse to be bored in this town," says Mike, who volunteers with the Festival of Music and the Retired and Senior Volunteer Program, is a Rotary Club member and president of his high school alumni association, has performed with the Natchez Little Theatre and, is an instructor at Alcorn State University. Elaine, too, has been immersed,

volunteering with the National Park Service and Trinity Episcopal Church where they are members, as well as pruning camellia bushes to help restore historic gardens. "You automatically get involved and can be acclimated in a very short time," she says.

They also like the weather. "The weather is better here (than back home)," Mike says, adding that moderate temperatures mean lower heating bills and golf that is playable year-round. With a private course at Beau Pré Country Club and a public course at Duncan Park, "there is no problem getting a tee time," notes Mike, who golfs twice a

week.

Explaining what brought them to Natchez, Mike mentions "excellent banks, high-speed Internet, a wonderful blues festival, opera, musical events, excellent hospitals, outstanding physicians with all specialties covered — and you can get an appointment the same day you call."

"People here are so hospitable and everything is so convenient," Mike says. "We have been welcomed with open arms," adds Elaine, who spent most of her married life as a homemaker. "Natchez is a great place to retire (and) a very pleasant place to live," Mike says. ●

New Hope, Pennsylvania

Country meets cosmopolitan in this eastern Pennsylvania village

By Mary Lu Abbott

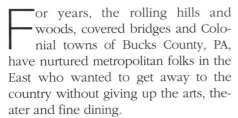

For years, the rolling hills and woods, covered bridges and Colonial towns of Bucks County, PA, have nurtured metropolitan folks in the East who wanted to get away to the country without giving up the arts, theater and fine dining.

Here visitors step back in time to a gentler lifestyle that's only a short drive from Philadelphia and New York City. It's scenic, with the greens of spring rich and dense, rivaling the beauty of fall's vibrant golds, reds and purples. It's steeped in history, dating to the days of William Penn in the 1600s and George Washington crossing the Delaware River in the Revolutionary War. And it's as noted for its outdoor recreation as for its art galleries and the Bucks County Playhouse, which for years attracted top actors and was the testing ground for pre-Broadway shows.

On the eastern edge of Bucks County, the village of New Hope faces the Delaware River separating Pennsylvania and New Jersey. It has only four main streets, interlaced with smaller side streets and alleys. Some of the walkways are still cobblestone, passing old homes and buildings that now house art galleries, crafts and antique shops, restaurants, inns and other businesses in a thriving historic district. A steam train huffs and puffs its way through town, stopping traffic on the main street crossing to New Jersey.

Gordon and Libby Nieburg recall places they vacationed that piqued their interest as possible retirement sites: Jackson Hole in Wyoming, Sausalito in California, Lahaina on Maui, Taos in New Mexico. "We'd say, 'Gee, this is really pretty,' and then we'd always say, 'But we like New Hope better,'" Gordon recalls.

"It's like the 'Little Apple' — ballet, theater, museums, and you can walk to all these places," Libby says, drawing a comparison to New York City, the "Big Apple." Libby had been coming to New Hope since childhood, and after she met Gordon, they came here on dates.

"I came antiquing as a child, and I still have some of those antiques my parents bought. We spent many dates here, going to the music theater and the playhouse. We always said we'd like to live here some day," Libby remembers. Adds Gordon, "It was a cheap date. We'd go kayaking on the canal or the river and bike riding along the canal."

The Nieburgs lived in suburban Philadelphia, where he was an engineer and teacher, and she also taught. They retired in 1997, did some traveling to look at possible places to retire, and considered the southwest coast of Florida, where Gordon's brother lives. But nothing topped New Hope. They wanted a new home, and on one visit they noticed a new neighborhood on the edge of downtown.

"I wanted a walking community. I didn't want to have to drive everywhere. In Florida, everything seemed to be on those fast highways — at least, the developments we looked at. It also felt sort of redundant there. The models were different, but so much seemed the same," says Libby, 63. "This is diverse. People are all different, the houses different. There are no chain stores, no fast-food places. Only thing that's a chain is a Starbucks, and it's in an old building," she says.

In 1999, they moved into their new home on a hill above Main Street. "We back up to the woods. I can't grow anything. We have deer, birds, wild turkey, owls, fox. I used to think it was cute until they ate everything. I made a buffet for them with my plantings," she says with a laugh.

They can walk to the bottom of their street to the Delaware Canal and cross a bridge into town or hike and bike along the old towpath where mules once pulled barges. Beyond the canal is the Delaware River, a prime recreational haven in this area. The Nieburgs have kayaks and often put into the canal or the river. Canals run on both the Pennsylvania and New Jersey sides of the river, and the towpaths have become popular recreational trails.

A river of commerce from the Philadelphia area into Chesapeake Bay and the Atlantic Ocean, the Delaware River in Bucks County and northward runs clean and clear, an often-shaded waterway enjoyed by kayakers and canoeists. Only a short distance downstream from New Hope, Gen. George Washington made his famous crossing of the Delaware River to the Battle of Trenton during the Revolutionary War.

Main Street is part of River Road, Route 32, which is one of the most scenic routes in the entire country as it winds northward from New Hope. Paralleling the river and canal, sometimes beneath bluffs and other times atop the hills, the road is narrow and twisting in places that you're slowed to 15 mph. It's reminiscent of driving in England, with old stone homes hugging the roadside, mansions set behind stone fences, farms with horses, and fields of orchards. Canopies of trees sometimes blot out the sky.

Fred and Diane Burmeister love exploring the attractions of New Hope and the countryside. "There's so much history and so many museums," says Diane, noting that they've visited the nearby country home of the late author Pearl S. Buck, the first American woman to win the Nobel Prize in literature.

New Hope now has a satellite of the area's most notable museum, the James A. Michener Art Museum in nearby Doylestown, Michener's hometown and the county seat about 10 miles from New Hope. Michener, a Pulitzer Prize winner, was an avid collector and supporter of the arts. Like the main museum, the Michener in New Hope showcases the wealth of regional art and culture.

The Burmeisters lived in New Jersey, overlooking the skyline of New York

City. Fred was a chemist in cosmetic product development, and Diane was active in volunteer work. About five years ago, they set off in their motor home, vacationing up and down the East Coast to see where they might want to retire. They liked the picturesque towns of Maine but felt it was too cold in winter, and they thought Florida was too hot in the summer. Fred took early retirement several years ago and started a consulting business.

"We decided we wanted a house in the country," says Diane, 60. They discovered Bucks County when their son went to college in the Philadelphia area. "It's very country — rolling hills, cornfields, horses — yet we're only an hour and 10 minutes back to the New York area."

They particularly liked the New Hope area. "It's a little more laid back across the Delaware. I feel like the people are a little more relaxed than in the New York area. It's the most beautiful spot here," she says.

They started looking at communities and kept coming back to Fox Run Preserve, an active-adult development by DeLuca Homes a few miles outside the village of New Hope, which itself is only one square mile.

"Nothing compared to it, and we said, 'Before they sell out, maybe we should invest in a house and make it our country home for weekends,'" Diane says. "It has an old stone farmhouse at the entrance. It's warm and inviting." The farmhouse now serves as a gathering place for residents after undergoing renovation. The community has about 130 homes, and all are sold now.

New Hope, PA

Population: About 2,300 in New Hope, about 7,800 in surrounding Solebury Township and about 613,000 in Bucks County.

Location: In scenic Bucks County about 40 miles northeast of Philadelphia and 65 miles from New York City. It's on the Delaware River, the Pennsylvania-New Jersey border, close to the site of the historic crossing by Gen. George Washington in the Revolutionary War

Climate:

	High	Low
January	39	21
July	87	63

Average relative humidity: About 56%

Rain: 49 inches annually

Snow: About 32 inches annually

Cost of living: Above average

Average housing cost: $553,130 in New Hope, $680,875 in Solebury Township, and $334,325 in Bucks County for the first half of 2005, according to TREND. There's limited property in New Hope and Solebury Township, and prices continue to rise in 2005, real estate agents say.

Sales tax: 6%

Sales tax exemptions: Groceries, drugs, most wearing apparel.

State income tax: The state income tax rate is 3.07%. In the New Hope area, a local tax of 1% applies to earned income.

Income tax exemptions: Pennsylvania is one of the most retiree-friendly states on income taxes, allowing exemption of Social Security benefits and private and public pensions.

Estate tax: None, except the state's "pick-up" portion of the federal tax, applicable to estates above $1.5 million. Pennsylvania has an inheritance tax. The rate is 4.5% for lineal descendants, 12% for siblings and 15% for other heirs; spouses are exempt.

Property tax: In New Hope, residents currently pay a borough, county and school tax rate of .0975 and in Solebury they pay a township, county and school tax rate of .0976. Currently assessments set at 100% of the 1972 market value, calculated on new homes in 2005 by taking 12.4% of the price. On a new $500,000 home, the estimated tax is about $6,050.

Homestead exemption: None

Religion: About 30 places of worship serve the New Hope area, with an even greater selection in the rest of Bucks County.

Education: Bucks County Community College has enrichment classes in New Hope and about 10 miles south at its main campus outside Newtown.

Transportation: There is no local transit system. Buses run regularly to New York City, or residents can catch the train from nearby Trenton, NJ.

Health: St. Mary Medical Center, a regional full-service facility with 500 physicians, is about 14 miles away between Newtown and Langhorne. It has trauma care, and its services include both heart and cancer centers. Doylestown Hospital, about 10 miles from New Hope, is a full-service medical facility with doctors in 40 specialties and a heart center. Also, there are major medical centers in Princeton and Trenton, NJ, each about 20 miles away, and in Philadelphia.

Housing options: The village of New Hope is only about one square mile. New housing is limited, though there are older homes and newer resales available in neighborhoods within walking distance of downtown. Outside the village, Solebury Township has some new construction, and there's more in outlying areas within minutes of New Hope. Farther out in Bucks County, housing is available in the $300,000-$400,000 range.

Visitor lodging: The area is known for bed-and-breakfast accommodations, many in historic properties. For a choice, contact Bucks County B&B Association of Pennsylvania at www.visitbucks.com. There also are historic inns and modern motels throughout the area. Golden Plough Inn is in popular Peddler's Village, a collection of shops and restaurants outside New Hope. Rooms start at $140 a night, (215) 794-4004.

Information: New Hope Chamber of Commerce and Visitor Center, 1 Mechanic St., New Hope, PA 18938, (215) 862-5880, (215) 862-5030 or www.newhopepa.com. Bucks County Conference and Visitors Bureau, 3207 Street Road, Bensalem, PA 19020, (800) 836-2825 or www.bccvb.org.

They bought in 2003. Even though the Burmeisters didn't live here full time, they found it easy to meet residents when they came on weekends. All homeowners were invited to community events, such as the Christmas party. "They have all kinds of social activities, whatever you're interested in," Diane says, noting that residents meet in homes or go to restaurants together.

In the spring of 2004, they sold their New Jersey home and moved permanently to the community. They have subscriptions to the Bucks County Playhouse, the designated state theater, in New Hope, where they especially enjoy the musicals. The theater has staged live drama and musical productions since 1939, attracting such stars as Hume Cronyn, Jessica Tandy, Lillian Gish, Walter Matthau, Linda Darnell and Kim Hunter.

Every two weeks the Burmeisters go to the theater, sampling different dining venues before the performances. "New Hope has the best restaurants. We went to one the other night with only five tables. It was charming, with tiny candlelights, and the food was out of this world," Diane says.

The location and the mix of country setting and cosmopolitan lifestyle attract many to the New Hope area. The location was ideal for Nancy and Jim Hilgendorf, who had lived overseas much of their lives. She grew up in Japan and Taiwan, and Jim called a variety of places home as his father moved with an oil company. They both went to college in New York. Then his career with Exxon-Mobil took them to Hong Kong, New York City, Buenos Aires and Japan, where he was at retirement in 2001.

They came back to the States looking for places to retire. They briefly considered the Pacific Northwest, checked out the Carolinas and also visited Nancy's sister, who lives in the New Hope area. The Hilgendorfs' daughter was engaged, and Nancy was scouting places around New Hope for the wedding one fall.

"September and October are absolutely glorious here. There's every color. As I was looking around, I thought this was as beautiful or more beautiful than in the Carolinas," says Nancy, 58. And it was a lot closer to their children in Manhattan.

"When she suggested settling in Pennsylvania, I wasn't quite sure. It never occurred to me to retire in Pennsylvania,

but over the 18 months we talked about it, it came to make more sense. Nancy likes a rural setting, and I like being near big cities. So I saw the benefits," says Jim, 58.

They settled in a home in the countryside outside New Hope in 2002. While they enjoy attractions in the area, Jim also frequently goes into New York City for the day to museums and to take photography courses. He may drive into Manhattan or catch a bus from New Hope or the train from nearby Trenton, NJ.

Long known as an artists' colony, New Hope in recent years has become more tourist-oriented, attracting large weekend crowds who stroll the narrow streets and cross the short bridge into Lambertville, NJ. Also a historic town, Lambertville is considered prime antiquing territory. Residents say as the weather warms, the town gets crowded with visitors.

"We have thousands coming in, oohing and aahing at our town. It's very exciting on a summer evening on the weekend to see all those people flowing down the main street, in and out of cafes. It's alive and exciting," says Libby Nieburg.

New Hope's narrow streets get congested, however. When Bob and Jo-Ann Lambert were looking around Bucks County for a retirement home, they fell in love with an active-adult community in Washington Crossing, about seven miles south of New Hope.

"It's a more rural area," says Bob, 65. "It's a village of about 1,500 people and has far less traffic and congestion, yet New Hope is only a 10-minute drive." Washington Crossing has a state park commemorating the Revolutionary War troop crossing that led to victory over the British, but it does not get as many tourists as the quaint historic area of New Hope.

The Lamberts are from West Chester, PA, where Bob was a bank executive. When he retired in 1997, they bought a home in Estero, FL, but decided they wanted to come back to eastern Pennsylvania to be closer to family. They considered Montgomery and Bucks counties, both bordering greater Philadelphia.

After looking at about a dozen communities, they chose Traditions at Washington Crossing, a Pulte Homes development. "It's a very active community, with numer-

ous clubs, trips to New York City and theaters, classes in Spanish and French — so many things," says Jo-Ann, 63.

Bob, who is active in organizing community activities, estimates that about two-thirds of the residents come from the region and the other third come from all over the country, from as far away as California, Colorado and Florida.

"We can walk into the village in five minutes and do light shopping and go to the bank, and we can be at the Delaware River in 10 minutes," he says. The Lamberts enjoy tubing — floating in big inner tubes — on the Delaware with their family and grandchildren. On the river, often you can't see anything commercial — "just trees and water and the beautiful hills," Bob says.

The Nieburgs immerse themselves in community projects. "If you're willing to volunteer, you're accepted. All you have to have is a passion for New Hope," Libby says. She works with the garden club on plants for the town and serves on several committees that sponsor festivals. She's on the board of a chamber music society, which puts on concerts, and was a volunteer with the chamber of commerce, planning the community holiday party for three years. She also serves with Partners in Progress, a group that works "to maintain the cultural and historical significance and beauty of the area."

Gordon, 70, serves on the State Civil Service Commission, is a volunteer firefighter, and does photography for the police and fire departments and for civic projects.

Diane Burmeister was on a number of volunteer boards at their former home and is already considering where she would like to get active in the area. Nancy Hilgendorf volunteers with a library in Doylestown, at a wildflower preserve and with a program that teaches English to immigrants.

Because of its popularity, the price of housing in Bucks County has been climbing steadily, with New Hope and Solebury Township among the highest. The influx of people from higher-priced metropolitan areas and the limited space for new development have contributed to spiraling prices. A survey by the Philadelphia Inquirer compared the median price of homes from 1998 to 2003, rising in Bucks County from

$179,708 to $234,900, in New Hope from $255,376 to $360,000 and in surrounding Solebury Township from $276,500 to $417,700. Real estate agents say it is difficult to find housing in New Hope and Solebury Township under $300,000.

"Our home has tripled in value in the five years we've been here," says Gordon Nieburg.

When the Lamberts bought in early 2003, they got a townhouse-style carriage home at Traditions in the low $300,000s, but now the community is entirely sold out, with the last-available single-family homes selling for around $400,000.

For the Burmeisters, taxes on their home represent a savings. "Our taxes in New Jersey were about $17,000 a year. It was a big house, but the square footage wasn't much bigger, and here we pay less than half that," says Diane Burmeister.

The Hilgendorfs say they have a friend who retired to a 55-plus community in the Princeton, NJ, area only minutes away, and she pays as much in taxes for her small house as they do for a home on four acres here.

All the couples note that the area is strongly oriented toward the arts and is an eclectic community that includes a gay population.

Despite its cultural amenities and fine dining, Diane Burmeister says a die-hard city dweller might think it was a lovely place to visit but would not want to live here. "They might say it's too quiet, too green," agrees Fred, 59.

Diane enjoys "one delightful thing after another" here. She recalls a visit by their grandson. "We heard the steam train and its whistle. It gives me chills when I hear it. My grandson said, 'Oh, that must be the Thomas train,'" she says, referring to a popular children's toy. ●

Ocala, Florida

Amid the hills and horse farms of central Florida, retirees find a warm welcome and variety of real estate options

By Karen Feldman

Ocala is a city that loves to run fast and live slow. While it has deep roots in both horse and car racing, residents like it for the relaxed pace they find there.

The city of about 47,000 people is ideally situated for those who want proximity to Florida's main draws — the ocean and Orlando's many attractions — without having to live smack in the middle of them and the crowds they attract. And, unlike most of the state, Ocala and surrounding Marion County are richly endowed with rolling hills, sprawling horse farms and towering oaks reminiscent of Kentucky or points even farther north.

"There's a lot to be said for a slower pace, a Southern lifestyle," says Ocala native Jaye Baillie, who is president and chief executive officer of the Ocala/Marion County Chamber of Commerce. "It's very genteel; there's less stress. What makes Ocala a great place, besides the climate, is the friendly, welcoming attitude, whether you're a newcomer or have been here all your life."

There are many opportunities to get involved in the community and plenty of natural attractions to explore. The region's rolling hills and year-round pastures were important factors in making it the horse capital of the world, a title approved by the U.S. Department of Agriculture in 1999 after its Census of Agriculture determined that Marion led all counties in the number of horses and ponies in residence. Between 45 and 50 breeds are represented in the area, with hundreds of horse farms and about 17,000 people who are employed in the county's horse industry.

Among the equine luminaries to emerge from the region is Affirmed, the last horse to win the Triple Crown (in 1978). Silver Charm and Real Quiet are Marion County-bred horses, each winning two-thirds of the Triple Crown in the late 1990s. Driving along the winding roads of the area, visitors can see horses frolicking in pastures or mares nursing their foals.

Most of the 380,000-acre Ocala National Forest lies within Marion County. It

---

Population: About 47,000 in Ocala, with 293,000 in Marion County.

Location: The city is in north-central Florida, 35 miles south of Gainesville, 75 miles north of Orlando, 64 miles west of the Atlantic Ocean and 45 miles east of the Gulf of Mexico.

Climate: High Low
January 70 46
July 92 71

Average relative humidity: 74%

Rain: About 55 inches annually

Cost of living: Below average

Median housing cost: $169,500

Sales tax: 6.5%

Sales tax exemptions: Food and medicine

State income tax: None

Intangibles tax: None. The tax was repealed as of Jan. 1, 2007.

Estate tax: None

Inheritance tax: None

Property tax: $19.97-$21.84 per $1,000 of assessed value, depending on location. With a $25,000 homestead exemption, the annual tax on a $169,500 home would be $2,886-

$3,156. Property in Florida is appraised at 100% of market value, although increases after purchase are limited to 3% per year.

Homestead exemption: $25,000 off assessed value of primary, permanent residence.

Religion: There are 275 churches representing all major denominations and three synagogues in Ocala and surrounding Marion County.

Education: An adult-education center run by the county school board offers an array of recreational and leisure courses. Central Florida Community College conducts associate-degree programs while Saint Leo University offers four-year degrees on the community college's campus. Florida Southern College also has bachelor's programs, and Webster University has night and weekend classes for those seeking master's degrees. In addition, Pathways, a program operated by the community college, provides seniors the chance to learn about volunteer opportunities available in the community.

Transportation: A number of highways run through the Ocala area, including U.S. highways 27, 41, 301 and 441, making it easy to get to either Florida coast and nearby cities. Interstate 75, which traverses the country, brings travelers from the north and south into Marion County, and the Florida Turnpike connects to I-75 just south of the Marion County line. Greyhound bus lines provides daily passenger and package express service, (352) 732-2677. The Ocala International Airport is a general aviation facility that offers private and charter flight services, as well as a business aircraft terminal, (352) 629-8377. Amtrak provides daily passenger train services, (352) 629-9863. SunTran is the local bus service, providing low-cost transportation throughout the area, (352) 401-6999. Orlando International is about 75 miles south of Ocala.

Health: The city has three hospitals, several walk-in centers and more than 350 licensed physicians covering a wide range of specialties. Ocala Regional Medical Center has 200 beds and a full range

draws an estimated 2 million visitors annually. It contains four designated wilderness areas, a number of lakes, walking and bicycling trails, and snorkeling, diving and swimming spots. There also are recreational areas set aside for horseback riding, bird watching and off-road vehicles.

For even more outdoor enjoyment, the county boasts 41 parks that offer a variety of recreational opportunities, including horseback riding, picnicking, camping, boating, swimming and wildlife observation.

Silver Springs is believed to be the world's largest formation of clear artesian springs. Visitors can board a glass-bottom boat for a great view of underwater life as far as 40 feet below the surface. And Jeep Safari provides a four-wheel excursion through 35 acres of primeval forests where emus, deer and sloths, among other creatures, roam free. Other exhibits allow visitors to see rare bears, Florida panthers, western cougars, alligators, crocodiles, turtles and waterfowl.

Another big local draw is Don Garlits' auto museum complex. The longtime dragster, also known as Big Daddy, has put Ocala on the map with the Museum of Drag Racing and the Museum of Classic Automobiles. Garlits and his wife, Pat, live on the grounds of the popular museum that attracts car enthusiasts from around the world. Cultural draws also include the Appleton Museum of Art, the Silver River Museum, the Ocala Civic Theatre, the Discovery Science and Outdoor Center, four historic districts and a multitude of antique stores.

Besides its physical and cultural attractions, Ocala appeals to many retirees because of the range of real estate options available. From 2004 to 2005, median housing prices in the Ocala area soared by 27 percent, making it the tenth-hottest housing market in the country, according to the National Association of Realtors. Yet while prices are on the rise, the region remains quite affordable compared with the rest of the country. Says Donna Johnson-Phillips, an agent with Foxfire Realty in Ocala: "It

just boomed."

The reason? "We've been discovered," she says. "We're catching up with every other place in Florida." Residential lots that previously went for $25,000 to $30,000 had jumped to $40,000 to $50,000 within eight months. There are relatively few condos in town, but some retirement communities have patio homes available, starting at $150,000 for about 1,350 square feet of living area, three bedrooms, two baths and a garage, says Johnson-Phillips.

It is difficult to find a three-bedroom, two-bath home with double garage in Ocala for under $150,000, regardless of the home's age or condition. A three-bedroom, two-bath home with 1,500 square feet of living area runs about $160,000 and up. In the downtown historic district, what little there is to be had ranges widely, depending on whether it has been renovated. Johnson-Phillips says that many homes needing renovation often start at $250,000, while remodeled homes can easily be $350,000 to well over $600,000.

Ocala, FL

of services including 24 hour emergency services and departments specializing in bariatrics, cancer, cardiac care, diabetes, orthopedic services, wound care and women's health, (352) 401-1000 or www.ocalaregional.com. West Marion Community Hospital has 70 beds, emergency services, all private rooms and is affiliated with Ocala Regional Medical Center, (352) 291-3000 or www.westmarion.com. Munroe Regional Medical Center is a private, not-for-profit hospital with 421 beds. It offers a wide range of services including cardiac care, neurology, orthopedic services, pulmonary care, obstetrics and emergency care, (800) 575-3975 or www.munroeregional.com. In addition, both the University of Florida's Shands Hospital and the Veterans Administration Hospital are about 35 miles north of Ocala in Gainesville.

Housing options: SummerGlen, (800) 277-8707, an active-adult community, is under development just south of Ocala. There are 17 single-family models from which to choose. They range from 1,485 square feet to 2,576 square feet and sell

for $180,900 to $257,900. This Florida Leisure Communities development features an 18-hole championship golf course and a town center, which includes a pool and spa, residents' club, sports complex, golf club and grand hall.
On Top of the World Communities, (800) 421-4162, has a variety of gated, active-adult neighborhoods with homes ranging from 1,120 square feet to 3,203 square feet and prices from $126,000 to $303,000. The community features golf, pools, walking trails and other amenities.
Devonshire, (888) 247-0877, a Bradford Homes development, has lots starting at $79,000, homes on your lot starting at $325,000, and home-and-lot packages that start at $400,000. The private, gated community is designed with European architectural styles, with lots ranging from one-third to one acre.

Visitor lodging: Courtyard by Marriott has 166 one-bedroom units and eight one-bedroom suites, $94-$179, (800) 821-8272. The Hilton Ocala is a pet-friendly hotel with 193 one-bedroom units and six one-bedroom suites, some

with whirlpool, $104-$779, (800) 916-2221 or (352) 854-1400. Howard Johnson Inn is a motel with 125 rooms, some with whirlpools, that welcomes pets (for a fee), $70-$130, (800) 262-8358 or (352) 629-7021. Seven Sisters Inn is a historic bed-and-breakfast inn built in 1888 in Queen Anne style and set in Ocala's downtown historic district, with one- and two-bedroom units, $139-$279, (800) 250-3496.

Information: Ocala/Marion County Chamber of Commerce, 110 E. Silver Springs Blvd., Ocala, FL 34470, (352) 629-8051 or www.ocalacc.com.

Custom-built homes in gated golf-course communities, on average, are in the $600,000 to $700,000 range, with prices quickly rising into the millions. A home with two to five acres of land, where someone could keep horses, runs well above $600,000, but these homes are not often on the market.

But despite the rise in prices, Johnson says Ocala remains popular with retirees, some of whom choose to live in active-adult communities. One of the newest communities for adults age 55 or older is SummerGlen, which is being developed by Florida Leisure Communities just south of Ocala. About 150 homes have been completed in SummerGlen, which eventually will have 950-1,000 homes. Residents can play the 18-hole, Scottish-links style course and a residents' club with fitness center, pool and spa, sport facilities and a crafts center. Prices start at $180,900.

For Gary and Linda Uhley, who spent a decade researching active-adult communities around the country, Ocala's beauty and location, as well as the opportunities they found at On Top of the World Communities, sealed their decision to move there. The couple lived in Michigan much of their lives and then headed to New Castle, IN, where Gary, 62, was Chrysler Corp.'s chief of security. They spent many vacations visiting Linda's parents, who lived in an active-adult community in Sun City, AZ.

"We generally fell in love with the concept of the 55-and-over retirement idea once we saw the golf, the club, the lifestyles, the tremendous range of activities — everything in the alphabet from athletics all the way to zoology," says Linda, 61. "We'd go out for 10-day vacations and come home exhausted."

So they set out to explore as many such communities as they could, checking out possibilities in Nevada, Arizona, Illinois, North Carolina and Florida. Then some friends discovered On Top of the World and urged the Uhleys to visit. They made a few trips and kept comparing it to other places they'd been.

"This one kept standing out for us," Linda says. She and Gary sat down and made a chart, listing the pros and cons of On Top of the World versus a community in Arizona they liked a lot. The deciding factor was its appeal to their children.

"Would the kids visit us in Arizona?" Linda says. "Not likely. We didn't get a chance to visit (my) folks out there until later in life." With two daughters, one son and five grandchildren all in the Detroit area, they decided it would be far more likely that the family would visit if they could get direct, relatively short flights to the Orlando or Tampa airports, both of which are about an hour away.

The city's proximity to Interstate 75 also meant that the Uhleys could drive north to visit relatives in a fairly short time. They bought a lot, had a house built, and moved in December 2003, making six trips between New Castle and Ocala, each time unloading piles of belongings into a storage unit and spending time vacationing between trips.

The Uhleys built a single-family home with just slightly less than 2,000 square feet. They wanted to make some modifications to the standard floor plan, and the company was happy to work with them, Linda says. The house has two bedrooms and a large computer room that could be turned into a bedroom. Instead of a den or another bedroom, they opted for a large master closet that's big enough to hold Linda's sewing machine and supplies as well as clothes. There are two bathrooms, a two-car garage and a large concrete slab that will eventually become an enclosed sunroom overlooking the 16th hole of the golf course.

The Uhleys find plenty to do within their gated community. Gary plays golf at least twice a week. Linda participates in a walking group and takes pilates, aerobics and water aerobics classes. They spend a lot of time with the many friends they've made.

"We've never had such fun neighbors in our entire lives," Gary says. "We're all in the same boat. The kids have all grown and moved away. Nobody's working full time so everybody's pretty much doing the same activities. My son wrapped it up nicely. He says it sounds like a senior college town."

Linda feels the same way. "It seems like this group is so different from what we've run into before. We all come from different parts of the country, and they just don't really care what you did before or where you lived before. They're just out to have a good time. If you want to

do things, fine. If you don't for whatever reason, that's fine, too. It's a wonderful neighborhood."

The fact that everyone is relatively new makes for some lively social gatherings. Last Christmas, for example, the Uhleys started what they called the On Top of the World First Annual Orphans Dinner. "Linda invited everybody she could find to the house for dinner," says Gary, who loves to cook and needs little excuse to hit the kitchen. "About 30 people came. It was a ball. It looks like it will be bigger next year."

Like the Uhleys, Chris and Gert Ziegler put a lot of time and effort into choosing a place to retire. The Zieglers, both 71, grew up and met in Cincinnati but moved about every two years throughout the four decades Chris worked in the steam generating business as a new equipment sales engineer. From Cincinnati, they moved to Wilmington, DE; Fredericksburg, Prince George and Richmond, VA; Philadelphia, PA; Birmingham, AL; and Charlotte, NC, where Chris retired at 53.

Although Gert liked the area, Chris wanted to go elsewhere to live out his retirement. They considered Charleston, SC; Tallahassee, FL; and Columbus and Savannah, GA. Meanwhile, Gert's aging parents were in Jensen Beach, FL, between Melbourne and West Palm Beach, and the couple thought they ought to be closer to them.

They'd been looking for a place that was smaller and quieter than Charlotte and happened upon Ocala. This was it, they decided. They bought a lot and headed back to Charlotte to sell their house. Then Hurricane Hugo swept through North Carolina, causing a lot of damage to their heavily wooded, two-acre property. They took the house off the market and spent a year cleaning up. When they put the Charlotte house back up for sale, it went quickly and they found themselves without a place to live.

They headed back to Ocala and rented a place while their house was being constructed. The home they built was 3,000 square feet, which sounds big until you consider that their Charlotte home was 5,200 square feet. "Whenever the kids came down, we said we'd downsized too much," Gert says.

So they searched for a more suitable house and found one with 4,200 square feet in the Fort King Forest neighborhood in southeast Ocala. It was built in 1991 and has four bedrooms, one of which Chris uses as an office. There are three and a half baths, a pool, a game room over the garage and another downstairs.

While both of their homes were in standard subdivisions rather than master-planned communities, the Zieglers found it easy to make friends. Shortly after moving to Ocala, Chris started up a men's bowling league while Gert volunteered at the Ocala Civic Theatre. Both activities allowed them to quickly form friendships with people who had similar interests.

Chris eventually swapped bowling for the theater as well. He's a member of the ACT IV group, which raises money to support the theater, and he landed a lead role last year in the theater's production of "Bleacher Bums." Gert helps out wherever she's needed, working the box office two days a week, lending the marketing director a hand with mailings and recently putting together a cookbook to raise money for the theater.

They both like to dress up and represent the theater at community functions. They recently attended a fair for seniors looking to get involved in the theater. Chris had on a zoot suit, while Gert went in what Chris describes as "a flapperish type of easy woman" costume. Neither is shy about making a bit of a public scene.

Chris has long been a car fanatic. While up in Charlotte, he had a collection of 26 classic Mustangs and was president of the local Mustang Club. As with their home, he scaled down when they moved south. These days he has a Corvette Indy Pace Car that he drives in parades and to car shows. In 1998, the couple took part in a Corvette caravan that traveled from Nashville, TN, to Bowling Green, KY, where the annual convention attracted some 8,000 Corvettes and their owners.

But when the Zieglers hit the road now, they are virtually impossible to miss. The 1998 pace car is purple with yellow seats and wheels and graphics in yellow, orange and red. "The Corvette matches my personality," he says. Gert maintains her sense of humor about it all. "It's eye-catching," she says. "Everybody knows that it's us."

What caught Shirley Risoldi's eye in Ocala was the architectural splendor of the Appleton Museum of Art. An elegant neoclassical design, the exterior is as beautiful as much of the artwork it contains.

Shirley, 69, retired from a public relations job with Bell Atlantic in Pittsburgh, PA, and moved to Ocala full time in 1997, joining her husband, Matthew, who had retired two years earlier. He died of cancer two years later, and her Northern friends urged her to return to Pittsburgh. She wouldn't consider it.

"I was totally sold on this area and location," she says. She decided that with her marketing skills, she could offer help to any number of organizations. She picked the art museum, which she'd long admired. She spends many mornings there behind the greeter's desk, answering phones, directing people into the museum, taking admission and doing whatever else needs to be done. The look of the Ocala/Marion County Chamber of Commerce attracted her, too.

"I was taken by the beautiful structure," she says. "I happened to be strolling around downtown and went in and met some of the people. They make you feel so wonderfully needed. They're so appreciative. Sometimes I come away from both places thinking I should really pay them," she says, for the enjoyment she gets from being there.

In her spare time, Shirley sings in the choir at her Catholic church, spends a lot of time on her home computer, and makes frequent trips to the Paddock Mall, the city's main shopping complex. She also has dinner out every Monday night with three women she met at a widows' support group several years ago.

Besides the weekly dinners, the four women have taken a couple of cruises together. Shirley, who says she's "gotten addicted to cruising," takes still more on her own. "I'm enjoying a very happy retirement," she says. "A lot of pleasure comes from the fact that I have met so many nice people here. They've added some substance to my life."

The friends they've made will keep the Uhleys in place as well. "We can't anticipate moving," Gary says.

"At least not until we get to the point that we can't take care of ourselves," adds Linda. "We could stay here for 20 years." ●

Ocean County, New Jersey

Find your haven amid the sandy beaches, picturesque
seaside towns, pine forests and bays of this New Jersey county

By Katharine Dyson

Roger A. Adams, now a resident of Surf City in Ocean County, NJ, has retired and gone back to work so many times in various capacities with the United Nations, even he has lost count. When he retired as director of marketing for UNICEF about 10 years ago, it wasn't long before he was asked to go to Croatia as director of procurement for the United Nations.

In the past few years his responsibilities for the United Nations have taken him to Zagreb, Croatia; Brindisi, Italy; and Kosovo. Between various assignments, he would retire, be called back, retire again, and be called back for yet another assignment, including heading up auctions to sell U.N. assets in several nations.

With all this traveling, Roger, a divorced dad with four grown children, found having two homes, one in Florham Park, NJ, and one in Surf City on Long Beach Island in Ocean County,

made less and less sense. So Roger, 68, a man on the move, decided to consolidate, sell his home up north and move permanently to his second home just minutes from the beach. In order to accommodate visiting children and grandchildren, he increased the size of the small vacation house to a five-bedroom home.

For Roger, deciding to make his permanent home in Surf City was a no-brainer. "I love the climate, the beach

---

Population: About 564,000. The largest municipality is Dover Township with a population of about 95,000. With one of every four people aged 50 or older, Ocean County is the most densely senior-populated county in New Jersey.

Location: Bordering the Atlantic Ocean in central New Jersey about 70 miles south of New York City and 50 miles east of Philadelphia. A line of islands just offshore includes Long Beach Island. County seat is Toms River (part of Dover Township), population 10,000.

Climate:

	High	Low
January	39	22
July	85	63

Average relative humidity: 73%

Rain: 41 inches.

Snow: Typically the area gets little snow and it rarely sticks on the ground for more than 24 hours.

Cost of living: Above average

Housing cost: Median home value is about $275,000. Average price of a new home is about $550,000.

Sales tax: 6%

Sales tax exemptions: Clothing, food purchased in grocery stores and prescription and over-the-counter drugs.

State income tax: Graduated from 1.4% of taxable income up to $20,000 to 6.37% on incomes up to $500,000, and 8.97% on incomes of $500,000 or more.

Income tax exemptions: Residents over 65 receive an additional $1,000. Those 62 or older or disabled with incomes less than $100,000 can qualify for a pension exclusion of up to $20,000 for married couples filing jointly ($15,000 for single or head-of-household, $10,000 for married filing separately). An "other retirement income" exclusion is also available for the unclaimed portion of the pension exclusion.

Inheritance tax: New Jersey imposes a transfer inheritance tax at graduated rates from 11% to 16% on property having a total value of $500 or more that passes from a decedent to a beneficiary. All estates passing to parent, spouse, child, grandparent or grandchild are exempt.

Estate tax: Applicable to taxable estates above $675,000.

Property tax: In Toms River/Dover Township, $3.088 per $100 of assessed value for county, library, health, municipal, regional school and fire district taxes. Houses are assessed at 51.43% of market value. Tax on a $275,000 home in Toms River is $4,367 a year. There are slight variations in taxes from one township to another.

Homestead exemption: For homeowners age 65 or older or disabled, $1,000-$1,200 rebate for those with gross incomes up to $70,000; $600-

$800 rebate for incomes from $70,001 to $125,000; and a $500 rebate for incomes from $125,001 to $200,000. For homeowners under age 65 and not disabled, $350 rebate on incomes up to $125,000 and $300 rebate on incomes $125,001 to $200,000. There is also a $250 annual property tax deduction for qualified veterans and homeowners age 65 or older or disabled who meet certain income and residency requirements. There is a full exemption for 100% disabled veterans.

Religion: More than 200 houses of worship represent all major religious denominations.

Education: Ocean County College welcomes seniors at a nominal enrollment fee on a space-available basis. County high schools offer adult-education programs throughout the year. The Academy for Lifelong Learning, in partnership with Sovereign Bank, provides quality educational programs and resources for people 55 and older in a flexible and accessible educational environment. Programs are offered on computers, health and wellness, law and humanities. Annual yearly membership is $10, (732) 255-0404.

Transportation: There is countywide bus transportation plus free door-to-door service for seniors and handicapped resi-

---

and the community," he says. "To stay in shape, I run almost every day year-round when I'm home."

Long Beach Island, just across Barnegat Inlet, is a virtual playground filled with fun. Barnegat Lighthouse ("Old Barney") sits on the northern tip, a historic landmark that has been restored and invites visitors to climb the 172 feet up its spiral staircase. A portion of the Edwin B. Forsythe National Wildlife Refuge anchors the south end of the island, and between the lighthouse and refuge are miles of great beaches.

People who come here love to be near the water. "They are living within minutes of places that (tourists) pay thousands of dollars to enjoy," says Barbara Steele of the Toms River-Ocean County Chamber of Commerce. Indeed, with long stretches of white sandy beaches, Ocean County has long been a vacation haven for people of all income levels.

Accessible airports and commuter bus services are as important to those who live here as to those who visit. "Obviously, with so much travel, being close to Newark International Airport is a big plus. I have the best of all worlds down here," says Roger Adams, who is currently working for Daher, a French logistics company, as a liaison to the United Nations. Since his job requires frequent travel into New York City, Roger also finds the commuter bus, which leaves from Toms River, extremely convenient. "It's nonstop into the city, just a one-and-a-half-hour trip," he says.

Like Roger, Donna and George Ventz had been coming to Long Beach Island on vacation for years — in their case, since 1986. When George retired, the couple decided to make their Surf City summer home their permanent residence, and they moved from Clifton, NJ. Although Donna, 60, continues to drive an hour and a half to work — she is purchasing director for Revlon — George says he is happy taking care of his "Honey Do" list as well as fishing and maintaining their home.

"He's even beginning to start having dinner ready when I come home," Donna says. "It's a whole different world down here. We watch the sun rise and set, ride our bikes, go out in our boat (a 24-foot Sea Ray), enjoy our neighbors. It's casual, easy."

George likes the fact that he doesn't have to worry about locking his doors. "It feels very safe here," he says. And although they have been on the move a

Ocean County, NJ

dents for shopping, medical appointments and other essential trips. Cities have their own transit systems, and there are two deep seaports. Several major highways run through the area from north to south, including the Garden State Parkway and U.S. Route 9. There are three public airfields, including the Robert J. Miller Air Park, also known as the Ocean County Airpark, and one military airfield.

Health: Ocean County has eight hospitals with 1,661 beds. There are 28 long-term-care facilities. The Senior Gold Prescription Program provides prescription drugs, insulin and other medicines to qualifying New Jersey residents 65 years or older. The Senior Gold participants pay $15 plus 50% of the remaining cost of the drug. When the out-of-pocket costs exceed $2,000 per year if single, or $3,000 per year if married, all costs are covered after a $15 co-pay.

Housing options: There are more than 88 planned adult communities with 60,994 units ranging from one-bedroom apartments to three-bedroom houses. Developer K. Hovnanian offers four active-adult communities in Ocean County for residents age 55 and older. **Four Seasons at South Knolls** is in Jackson Township, (732) 928-8044. The gated development will have 831 homes start-ing at 1,546 square feet. Other communities include **Four Seasons at Metedeconk Lakes**, also in Jackson, (800) 471-1273; **Four Seasons at Mirage** in Barnegat Township, (800) 982-0152; and **Four Seasons at Sea Oaks** in Little Egg Harbor, (888) 294-4096. Residents can expect such amenities as tennis, pools, a fitness center and an attractive, well-outfitted clubhouse. For more information, visit the company's Web site at www.khov.com. Also for residents age 55 and better, **Enclave at the Fairways** in Lakewood has a clubhouse complex featuring indoor and outdoor pools, tennis, billiards, a library, fitness center, arts and crafts studio and more. Residents receive a reduced membership fee at the nearby 18-hole championship Eagle Ridge Golf Club. The Kokes Family community will have 349 homes. For information, call (800) 215-5253 or visit www.lakeridge.com. In Jackson, **Riviera at Westlake** is an active-adult community by developer Toll Brothers. It offers 18 holes of golf, a 35,000-square-foot clubhouse, tennis, fitness, aerobics classes, and indoor and outdoor pools. For information, call (732) 928-7440 or visit www.rivieraatwestlake.com. **Renaissance**, a Centex Homes community for active adults, is located in Manchester Township and boasts an 18-hole golf

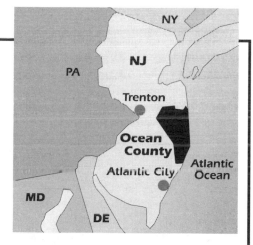

course, tennis courts, 25,000-square-foot clubhouse and playground for visiting grandkids. Call (888) 552-3858 or visit www.centexhomes.com for information. Generally, prices for homes in these communities start in the $300,000s.

Visitor lodging: Accommodations range from B&Bs to seaside resorts and chain hotels. In Toms River: Holiday Inn, from $110, (800) 465-4329, and Howard Johnson Hotel, from $95, (800) 446-4656. In Seaside Heights: Aztec Ocean Resort, from $50 (closed November through the beginning of March), (888) 976-9277.

Information: Toms River-Ocean County Chamber of Commerce, 1200 Hooper Ave., Toms River, NJ 08753, (732) 349-0220 or www.oc-chamber.com. For an information kit on the resort communities, call (800) 365-6933.

lot — they have moved 21 times and have visited almost every state — it appears they are here to stay. In fact, George says that because he has traveled so much in the past, "I stay away from airports. I've been there, slept there. I like it right here where there are a bunch of crazy nice people. We have a good time and enjoy frequent visits from our three daughters and five grandchildren."

For visiting grandchildren, there is plenty to do on the island, which is home to Viking Village, an odd combination of a commercial fishing port and boutique shops that have taken over the fishing shacks. And the island offers high-powered shopping, art galleries, a water park, Fantasy Island amusement park, museums and theater.

But the beach is not the only reason people come to Ocean County. Many older adults who move here are drawn by opportunities to continue to be professionally active. Take Julie Mattsson, 55, a resident of Fairways at Lake Ridge in Lakewood. Three years ago, following the death of her husband and devastated over her loss, she relocated to Ocean County from a condominium community in northern New Jersey. "The first step was to find a new home base, a challenge because of the strict criteria I imposed," says Julie, who wanted to start a new life and redirect her energies.

She says she looked for a community that offered maintenance-free living along with residents on the younger side of retirement age. The Fairways, restricted to adults 48 years or older, was an obvious choice. "After I toured the Fairways, I knew that I had found my new home," she says. "Many people around here are grandparents, but young grandparents. Like me, they got married just out of school and are still in their 40s, 50s and 60s."

Once she moved in, Julie, who has a daughter, son and five grandchildren, was not about to stand still. "I knew I wanted to work, but not for an established company. I wanted my own business," says Julie, a former medical secretary. "Out of the blue, the sales counselor who helped me buy my new Fairways home called to tell me about available space in The Shoppes at Lake Ridge just a mile from my home. I took the space and everything fell right into place."

Word of Julie's new shop, Remember Me Gifts (named in memory of her husband), spread and in three years she has expanded from gifts to clothing and even furniture.

Her personal life has also changed dramatically. This spring she married Robert Ziemak, 53, an old friend who also had lost his spouse. "Never in a million years would I have thought it would work out this way," she says. But after two and a half years of dating, Bob, an engineer in Edison, NJ, moved to Ocean County to be near Julie. When another retail space became available next to Julie's shop, the couple decided to open an ice cream store, Shakes to Cakes.

Julie's home is in the first phase of 900 homes of the Fairways at Lake Ridge, a Kokes Family community adjacent to Eagle Ridge Golf Club, a semi-private 18-hole golf course with a 17,000-square-foot clubhouse. The clubhouse has an indoor pool, state-of-the-art fitness center, billiards and other recreational facilities.

When Fairways, located in the northern part of the county, first came on the market, it sold out quickly. Sales are closing out for another Kokes community, The Enclave, which will have 349 homes located across the street from Fairways. A third Kokes community, Country Walk offers 300 homes with six house models.

The golf course and leisure facilities are an obvious draw, and residents get a break on golf membership, which is $3,800 annually for singles, and $5,600 for couples, both a savings of $700. Preferred tee times and other perquisites also go along with a resident membership.

With close to 90 retirement communities in the county, people have a lot of choices. In Manchester Township, for example, Crestwood Village — the largest retirement community in the state — has 6,494 homes. Renaissance has 1,031 homes.

Sheila and James English, both 74, moved to Renaissance from Monmouth County, where they had been living in a two-story townhouse. "We decided to look for a home all on one level," Sheila says. "We kept seeing ads for Renaissance in the paper, so we decided to check it out. We liked the amenities and the facilities and decided to

make the move."

Sheila says she loves her home, a one-level, 2,400-square-foot house with a two-car garage. To keep busy, she volunteers at Kimball Medical Center and co-chairs teaching Ceilidh, an Irish dance group. James plays golf, has joined a men's club and likes bridge.

K. Hovnanian, a major homebuilder in the East, has developed four active-adult communities in Ocean County. They include the intimate 375-home Four Seasons at Sea Oaks in Little Egg Harbor, where buyers can choose from a dozen floor plans and enjoy a clubhouse, tennis and pool. Another K. Hovnanian active-adult option in Ocean County is Four Seasons at South Knolls. Centrally located in Jackson Township, it eventually will have 831 homes starting at 1,550 square feet. Amenities include indoor and outdoor pools, putting green, tennis, and a clubhouse with fitness facilities, billiards and a fireside lounge.

At Four Seasons at Metedeconk Lakes, also in Jackson, homebuyers can choose a floor plan with lofts, adding extra space for a home office or hobby room. Close to the coast in Barnegat Township, Four Seasons at Mirage also features lofts among its floor plans, which range up to a spacious 3,450 square feet. Both communities also offer an array of recreational and social amenities.

Many retirees particularly enjoy the region's physical beauty. Although it's the fastest-growing county in the state, Ocean County contains vast areas of protected open space, with the Pine Barrens home to virgin forests, streams and ponds. West of the Garden State Parkway are large tracts of state parkland, forests and wildlife management areas, and approximately 20,000 acres east of the parkway are protected under the Edwin B. Forsythe National Wildlife Refuge.

Barnegat Bay and Little Egg Harbor, which stretch nearly the entire north-south length of the county, are protected under the National Estuary Program, and active farmland is being preserved through the County Farmland Preservation Program. Much of the natural assets that drew vacationers here in Victorian times still exist today. New to the scene are extensive shopping and entertainment facilities.

Ocean County has three state parks

and more than 20 small parks, some with more than 500 acres. Point Pleasant Beach in the north, the end of the line for commuter rail service from New York, has a boardwalk, aquarium, games of chance, miniature golf, and plenty of beach bars and nightlife as well as deep-sea fishing facilities. Art galleries, gourmet restaurants and B&Bs are found in the seashore village of Bay Head.

In the central part of the county there is Seaside Heights and Island Beach State Park, the largest stretch of natural beach in New England. Located in the Pinelands, Island Beach is home to cranberry bogs and a reconstructed sawmill. In the south are Forsythe National Wildlife Refuge, Long Beach and Tuckertown.

Ocean County activities include free summer concerts, fairs and art shows. Inexpensive tours, cruises, dancing and theaters — such as the Surflight Theatre, offering Broadway shows and children's theater — are popular. And for just $6 to $9 you can take in the action of the Lakewood BlueClaws, a Class A baseball team affiliated with the Philadelphia Phillies.

The Garden State Philharmonic performs at the Ocean County Carousel, and there's country, folk and bluegrass music every Saturday night at the Albert Music Hall in Waretown. Among the area's more interesting museums are the Toms River Seaport Society Maritime Museum, Long Beach Island Museum, Barnegat Light Museum, Giffordtown Schoolhouse Museum and the Ocean County Historical Society Museum, a 15-room Victorian wood clapboard house.

Tuckerton Seaport, a 40-acre reconstructed historic maritime village, includes displays of buoys and old boats, including shallow-draft boats used for oystering and clamming. A walking trail for the visually impaired can be found in Wells Mills County Park, and there is a boardwalk at Cattus Island County Park that accommodates wheelchairs.

Originally constructed to keep sand out of hotel lobbies, the boardwalks hugging the coastline in Point Pleasant Beach and Seaside Heights/Seaside Park today are lined with rides, games of chance, arcades, miniature golf courses, restaurants, nightclubs, snack bars, boutique shops, gourmet candy shops, an aquarium, a beach train, a water park and an antique carousel. A less hectic boardwalk is found in Lavallette and the southern mile of Seaside Park, where ocean views mesmerize.

Three Mississippi-style riverboats ply the rivers of Ocean County: The River Lady cruises Toms River, the Crystal Queen cruises Little Egg Harbor with daily excursions to Atlantic City by boat via the inland waterway, and the River Belle cruises Metedeconk River.

Among area golf courses are the George Fazio-designed Ocean County Golf Course at Atlantis, one of the top 100 public courses in the country, and Forge Pond in the northeastern region of Ocean County, a par-60 executive course tucked into a 300-acre conservation area. The good news is that for resident seniors who purchase an I.D. card for $25, greens fees are a bargain at either course with rates from $10 to $16 depending on when seniors 62 and older play.

Visiting grandchildren can build sandcastles on the beach, walk along the boardwalks, visit historic Hangar 1 at the Lakehurst Naval Air Engineering Station, and take in the thrills at Six Flags Great Adventure amusement park along with Wild Safari drive-thru animal park. Hurricane Harbor water park provides wet-and-wild fun with a massive wave pool and plenty of water slides. Listen to a 1923 Wurlitzer organ, catch a ride on the antique carousel in Seaside Heights, and play miniature golf. Fantasy Island Amusement Park in Beach Haven offers rides for all ages, an arcade and food stands.

Julie Mattsson extols the business opportunities in Ocean County, especially in Lakewood where she and husband Bob live and work. "There is so much growth taking place here. The area has so much going for it. We're close to the beaches, the major highways, restaurants, parks," she says.

Apparently Julie's enthusiasm was contagious. "After I moved here, my best friend and her husband moved down from northern New Jersey and live right next door, and my brother and sister-in-law relocated here as well," she says. ●

Ormond Beach, Florida

This east Florida town was the winter playground of American royalty

By Karen Feldman

Many Florida towns lay claim to well-known winter residents. Palm Beach touts its ties to railroad magnate Henry Flagler. Thomas Edison put Fort Myers on the map. And in Ormond Beach, modern-day residents reckon that since this was the place John D. Rockefeller chose to stay warm, it's just fine for them, too.

Ormond Beach enjoys a much lower profile than its flashier neighbor to the south, Daytona Beach. But it's that modest size and a well-developed sense of community that attract people to the city on the state's northeastern coast.

As frequently happens in Florida, those who wind up living in Ormond Beach frequently start as vacationers visiting family or friends who already made the move. Donna and Dan Ruttan retired from their jobs as elementary school teachers in Chappaqua, NY, in 1999 and 2000, respectively, and looked around Florida for a suitable place to live.

They considered spots where they had friends. Stuart had too much traffic for their tastes; Homosassa was a little too quiet. They wound up in Ormond Beach, where Donna's parents had lived for 35 years.

"We preferred the northern part of Florida over the southern part," says Dan, 59. "We did want to have the small amount of climate changes you get here. We didn't want it to be tropical all of the time, as much as we love it."

Donna, 60, says there's plenty to do, and it has been easy fitting in. "It's a very diverse, wide-ranging community," she says.

Martin and Rita Press chose Ormond Beach 13 years ago when they left Baldwin, NY, behind. "We had relatives down here," says Martin, 73. "One bunch lived in the Boca Raton area, and one bunch lived in the Ormond area. We checked out both and decided we loved Ormond Beach."

Like the Ruttans, they preferred the moderate size and abundant natural endowments they found in Ormond Beach. "And the pace," says Rita Press, 67. "Although the population is about 37,000, you still get that small-town atmosphere, yet you have all the amenities you find other places."

A civic-minded populace helps create a lively, appealing community. "One thing everyone in Ormond Beach has in common is that they all love the town," says Martin Press. "We have about 18 advisory committees that help steer the government, and getting on one of those is considered quite a plum." That's a distinct departure from the norm in many cities that have trouble filling such volunteer positions.

The Presses are prime examples of the participatory nature of the citizenry. Rita is the vice chair of the city's planning board. Both serve as volunteer advisers to small businesses through SCORE, the Service Corps of Retired Executives, and both are active in local politics.

"We've worked hard to put an honest and competent group of people on the city commission. We have an excellent board," Martin says. Rita concurs. "Anyone who lives in Ormond Beach gets a fair shake. They are listened to with courtesy," she says.

Janet Landis, 71, found a new home and a new life when she left Lewistown, PA, and moved to St. Augustine in January 1998. The domestic violence and assault counselor wasn't quite ready to retire, but she found on visits to relatives that there was much more for a single woman to do than in her hometown of 10,000.

Not long after moving south, she met a man at a singles dance in Ormond Beach and they began dating. She moved to Ormond Beach three years ago, and they still enjoy dancing as well as canoeing and traveling.

"If you're going to be on your own, there are things to do here, people to meet," she says.

Like the Presses, she feels motivated to give something back to her adoptive community. She volunteers at the Ormond Memorial Art Museum as well as at a local charitable thrift shop and serves as a volunteer court advocate for the Domestic Abuse Council.

Ormond Beach residents have lots of strictly recreational opportunities as well. Smack in the middle of town is Central Park, a verdant 145-acre spread that was once a coquina shell mine. Today it's the city's largest park, offering residents a place to hike, fish and boat.

Tomoka State Park, just north of downtown, sits at the meeting point of the Tomoka and Halifax rivers. There residents have easy access to walking trails, picnic areas and lush vegetation that attracts some 200 bird species.

One stretch of road within the city limits is known as The Loop. It's a circular route that takes travelers through areas shaded by lush tree canopies and a stretch of open wetlands with nary a man-made structure to be seen.

"When people visit from out of town, we take them for a ride around this road. It's so unique, with so much that's overbuilt and overcrowded, to see a large section that looks like old-time Florida," Martin Press says.

Not long ago there was talk of developing property along the road, but several thousand residents plastered "Save the Loop" bumper stickers to their cars. The county council took the hint and is working on a plan to preserve much of the route in its natural state.

As befits the adopted home of a Rockefeller, the city's recreation division has the grand title of Department of Leisure Services. Named one of the nation's top four departments in 2002, it spends about $3 million a year maintaining a wide-ranging assortment of recreational facilities that offer all sorts of activities and programs.

"It could be called the city of parks," Martin says. "There's recreation for seniors, kids, adults. Just about anything you can think of."

Rita, an avid tennis player, adds that although the city's millage rate is among the lowest in the region, Ormond Beach is one of the few cities to offer Hard-Tru public tennis courts as well as a performing arts center, a senior center with lots of activities, and places to launch boats, fish and bird watch.

Longtime city resident Ruth Horan had a hand in creating this bounty. She helped found the Friends of Recreation, a nonprofit group that raises money for the leisure services department and offers scholarships to youngsters who might not otherwise be able to afford dance lessons or art classes. At 81, she's taught judo professionally for 53 years, first in New York and New Jersey and now in Ormond Beach, turning all the money raised from her weekly Monday night classes to Friends of Recreation.

"Everybody should know how to protect themselves," she says, adding that judo workouts keep her and her students limber and active. She also serves on the city's recreation advisory board and is active in the city's Senior Theater Workshop.

The myriad recreational options as well as a goodly assortment of cultural opportunities were among the qualities that attracted the Ruttans. They enjoy driving around the region and exploring parks and other inviting sites they happen upon. Often they take a picnic lunch to enjoy.

One of their favorite outings is to load up the car and head to the beach. This is the one area of Florida in which driving on the beach is still permitted (in specified areas). They drive to a location they like and spend time enjoying the sun and surf without having to drag their belongings from a parking lot to the waterfront.

Culturally, the Ruttans find plenty to satisfy them. Having lived so close to New York City for many years, they are discerning fans and find that profession-al theaters in the area offer shows that are often comparable in quality to those they saw on Broadway.

"And it's so inexpensive to get tickets here," Donna says. They also frequent Daytona Beach's community playhouse, as well as concerts, shows and art exhibits at Daytona Beach Community College and Stetson University in nearby DeLand.

The Ruttans are a little more than an hour away from Orlando and Jacksonville, and, as retirees, they have time to make the trip to either city if ever there's something they want to see.

Ormond Beach has been a retirement haven since the late 1800s. Although a group of British men and their slaves settled the area in 1765, crop failures and the Seminole Wars drove all but the most stalwart away. When Florida became a state in 1845, there were only 20 families living in Volusia County.

Some years later, a group of former employees of the Corbin Lock Co. in

Ormond Beach, FL

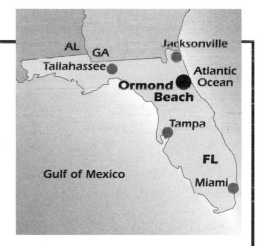

Population: 39,009

Location: The city encompasses 30.74 square miles in east-central Florida, just north of Daytona Beach in Volusia County. It's 80 miles south of Jacksonville, 50 miles south of St. Augustine and 60 miles east of Orlando.

Climate:

	High	Low
January	73	51
July	91	74

Average relative humidity: 74%

Rainfall: 50 inches annually

Cost of living: Below average

Median housing cost: $202,000 in the Ormond Beach area.

Sales tax: 6.5%

Sales tax exemptions: Food and medicine

State income tax: None

Intangibles tax: None. The tax was repealed as of Jan. 1, 2007.

Estate tax: None

Inheritance tax: None

Property tax: $22.84 per $1,000 of assessed value. The annual tax due on a $202,000 home, minus the $25,000 homestead exemption, would be $4,043.

Homestead exemption: $25,000 off assessed value of primary, permanent residence.

Religion: There are 37 houses of worship in Ormond Beach, representing all of the major religions as well as some smaller ones.

Transportation: The closest commercial airport is Daytona Beach International, which is served by most major airlines. Smaller craft use Ormond Beach Municipal Airport. The city is bisected by Interstate 95, which runs north to Maine and south to Miami. Nearby Interstate 4 connects the region to Orlando and Tampa on the state's west coast. The Florida East Coast Railway runs trains through the area daily.

Health: Florida Hospital has two campuses in Ormond Beach that offer a full range of inpatient and outpatient services.

Housing options: Fisherman's Landing, (386) 672-7600, is a rental community with one- and two-bedroom units. **Il Villaggio**, (386) 673-6058, is a gated, patio-home community of 53 home sites with home-and-lot packages starting in the $400,000s. **Plantation Bay**, (800) 779-4164, is an ICI Homes gated golf development with homes priced from the $200,000s into the millions.

Visitor lodging: Best Western Mainsail Inn and Suites, $77-$149, double occupancy, with rooms, apartments and suites available at this oceanfront motel, (800) 843-5142 or (386) 677-2131. The Villa Coral Beach Motel, located directly on the beach, offers spacious rooms with full kitchens and views of the Atlantic Ocean as well as an oceanfront outdoor pool deck, (800) 553-4712. Comfort Inn on the Beach, $86-$176, offers 50 units in a central location and allows small pets, (800) 456-8550 or (386) 677-8550.

Information: Ormond Beach Chamber of Commerce, 165 W. Granada Blvd., Ormond Beach, FL 32174, (386) 677-3454 or www.ormondchamber.com.

Connecticut moved their families to the west bank of the Halifax River and called their fledgling town New Britain. It became Ormond Beach when it was incorporated in 1880.

A pair of enterprising settlers opened the first hotel in 1888 and, two years later, Henry Flagler bought it, along with the railroad and a bridge that allowed trains to cross the Halifax River and pull up to the hotel's entrance.

Motorcars soon played a role in the town's development after car races on the beach were established in 1903. The competition endured for many years as race drivers zipped along 20-plus miles of beachfront. The annual competition earned the town the nickname, "Birthplace of Speed." That moniker is celebrated each year with a parade and other events that celebrate classic cars and racing. There's even an antique auto beach race that re-enacts the 1903 competition.

While the races in Daytona Beach eventually drew fans south, Ormond Beach's climate, proximity to the beach and lush beauty captured the attention of the rich and famous, including Rockefeller, who bought a house known as The Casements, named for its casement windows. Rockefeller made the rambling, three-story place his winter home from 1914 until his death in 1937, inviting the whole town in for his annual Christmas celebration. Residents still visit frequently, as Rockefeller's former residence is now owned by the city, which uses it as a cultural and community center.

As is happening in most of the Sunshine State, real estate is moving briskly in Ormond Beach. Over 2,000 homes, condos, and townhomes were sold in the first half of 2005 alone, says Brad Yelvington, a realtor with Century 21 A.H. Stone & Associates in Ormond Beach.

The $100,000 to $200,000 market is hottest right now, "the biggest selling area by far," he says. Additionally, the Ormond Beach area is seeing more home sales than anything else, with the number of condos sold coming in at a distant second.

The city has a lot of housing choices to fit a variety of budgets and tastes. After years of maintaining a house in New York, the Presses decided to rent instead. They have a two-bedroom, two-bath apartment with its own washer and dryer.

"If anything needs attention they have a great maintenance crew that's on the scene within minutes," Rita says. "We're not having to fuss with things like a leaky roof or broken-down washing machine or garbage disposal. We don't even think about those things."

The Ruttans rented for a year so they could shop for a house at their leisure and, after choosing to build in Ormond Lakes, could be close by as it went up. They didn't play golf and therefore didn't want a golf course community. Gated communities weren't their style, either. Nor did they want to live in a 55-and-older community.

Ormond Lakes won them over, Donna says, because it's only a few minutes to the beach. The all-ages development just minutes from the Atlantic Ocean seemed ideal. On periodic visits to Donna's parents in the area, they had watched the community rise and liked what they saw.

They purchased a 2,500-square-foot home with three bedrooms, a den and two-and-a-half baths. There's a screened-in pool with a full roof extending from the house over much of it, giving the Ruttans a veranda and covered bar. This is essentially another large room that becomes part of the house during the temperate months when they can slide open all the glass doors that separate the indoors from the pool.

The split plan allows for guests to have their own bedroom, sitting room and bathroom with a separate entrance. With such a set-up, they encourage family and friends to visit often.

The well-maintained community has good roads and lush landscaping, making walking for exercise easy and enjoyable. It's something Donna does daily and Dan does on occasion, when not working out on his Nordic Track.

Donna says she meets people just by walking around the neighborhood and has come to know still more people through a continuing-education course she takes at her church. "Everybody is from somewhere else, so people are very friendly," she says. ●

Oxford, Mississippi

A cultural and literary tradition enriches this unique Mississippi town

By Linda Herbst

If you ever tour the Deep South, make time to visit one of its jewels — Oxford, home of the University of Mississippi. Located on the picturesque route through the Mississippi Delta from Memphis to Natchez and New Orleans, Oxford has long been a favorite stopover for travelers meandering through the historic South.

Just an hour south of Memphis, the gracious curves of the area's rolling hills slope to level stretches of grassy valleys and pastureland. On the way into town, travelers often stop at the gates of one of the farmhouses that line the road. This particular one belongs to one of the nation's most popular writers, John Grisham, and is just one of Oxford's many literary landmarks. Beginning with Pulitzer and Nobel Prize winner William Faulkner, Oxford was the home and inspiration of nationally renowned novelists, poets, photographers, artists and musicians for the greater part of the 20th century.

It is its literary tradition, however, that sets Oxford apart from other arts meccas. Writers as diverse as Faulkner, Willie Morris, Larry Brown, Barry Hannah, Cynthia Shearer, John Grisham, Donna Tartt and Mary Hood have lived and worked in Oxford. Nearly every week world-renowned writers and poets visit Oxford and the university to read from their work and revel in what nearly all have called its "literary mystique." Residents and visitors alike have a hard time pinning down exactly what that mystique is all about, but one thing is for sure: The creative atmosphere here is intoxicating.

Once a year, usually in April, Oxford and the University of Mississippi host the Oxford Conference for the Book, a weeklong conference attended by the nation's foremost publishers, novelists, short story writers and journalists. The nonacademic conference is generally free and open to the Oxford community, and the whole town gets into the spirit of celebrating books. In August, the university hosts one of the most respected and longest-running literary conferences in the world, the Faulkner and Yoknapatawpha Conference.

Despite the Southern summer sun, the town seems to burst at its seams with distinguished Faulkner scholars from around the world, and once again the city revels in the excitement of being part of this important tradition. In many ways, Oxford is the manifestation of Faulkner's words: "The past is never dead. It's not even past." This is true of both the city of Oxford and the University of Mississippi, known as "Ole Miss," whose homes and public buildings house the sorrows and joys of the people who lived here during its frontier days, through the Civil War and the turbulent '60s. In its own way, Oxford's heritage is a story about the South from a perspective unparalleled in Southern history.

Aside from its literary traditions and historical value, Oxford's charms are so numerous that it is hard to choose the singular aspect that has placed it at the top of great places to settle for retirement. The overwhelming majority of retirees living in Oxford, however, are quick to point out that while Oxford is a great place to retire, it's not a retirement community.

"By that, I mean Oxford's a real place with a multigenerational population. It's not a controlled environment at all," says Bill Gurley, who with his wife, Clair, retired to Oxford several years ago from Greenwood, MS. Bill, a former bank president, maintains that the word "retirement" has great latitude. "For us, it doesn't necessarily mean strictly a time of leisure. Just because you don't have a job anymore doesn't mean you don't work," points out Bill, who has become a sales associate with a local real estate firm.

Bill and Clair's raised Louisiana cottage was completed in 1996. They were lucky to have found a lovely lot in an older, established neighborhood within easy walking distance of the town square. One of the most charming features of their three-bedroom home is its wraparound porch, which the Gurleys have decorated with ceiling fans and small groupings of easy chairs and cocktail tables. Bill and Clair can be seen nearly every nice afternoon enjoying the ease of this wonderful porch, and neighbors and friends are likely to join them.

Several years ago Clair Gurley was diagnosed with a heart problem, so quality of health care was a primary concern when it came time to decide on a retirement location. Baptist Memorial Hospital-North Mississippi, a 217-bed acute-care facility, has more than 80 medical and surgical physicians representing more than 30 specialty areas. It is one of the region's fastest-growing hospitals, serving a population of 200,000 in an eight-county area. Their facilities include an outpatient surgery center, cancer center and wellness and rehabilitation center.

The Gurleys also wanted to live in a college town. "The university and all that it offers — open-mindedness, continuing education, performing arts — were very important to us," says Clair. And with two daughters and two grandchildren living out of state, the Gurleys were pleased that Memphis International Airport was only 70 miles north of Oxford. The airport is located in the southernmost area of Memphis, so driving there doesn't require big-city traffic nerves.

Most of Oxford's retirees share Bill's energetic attitude toward retirement. The Rev. Frank Poole and his wife, Mary, retired to Oxford in the summer of 1999 from Baton Rouge, LA. As part of the Methodist tradition, Frank and Mary have made a lifelong commitment to ministry through music. They joined the Oxford-University Methodist Church and immediately became involved in its music traditions.

Frank and Mary love the atmosphere of small towns. In Oxford, they feel safe and independent from the constraints a larger place would put on them in terms of safety. Traffic can be hectic at times, but Mary says that because the weather is mostly nice, she and Frank feel safe enough to walk at any time of the day or night. Frank and Mary have moved into their newly constructed home but continue to add the finishing touches, and they also appreciate the level of trust they have with their contractor and the workmen who come and go at their home.

Mary's mother and father, Dr. and Mrs. A.B. Lewis, live directly behind them. The Lewises, both in their late 90s, have full-time sitters and house-keepers, and Mary says it is a joy and a privilege to spend these last years with her parents.

Oxford, MS

Population: The population of the city is 14,000, and enrollment at the University of Mississippi is about 14,000.

Location: Oxford is located in the hilly section of north Mississippi, 75 miles from Memphis, TN, and 165 miles from Jackson, MS, the state capital. Elevation is 380 feet.

Climate:

	High	Low
January	55	36
July	91	72

Average rainfall: 54 inches

Average snowfall: 3 to 4 inches

Cost of living: Below average

Average housing cost: $193,549 for a single-family home.

Sales tax: 7%

Sales tax exemptions: Prescription drugs

State income tax: For married couples filing jointly and single filers, the rate is graduated from 3% of taxable income up to $5,000 to 5% on amounts over $10,000.

Income tax exemptions: Social Security benefits, public and private pensions, IRAs and annuities are exempt. There is an additional $1,500 personal exemption for residents age 65 and older.

Intangibles tax: None

Estate tax: None for decedents after Jan. 1, 2005.

Property tax: Property and automobiles are subject to ad valorem taxes. Automobiles are assessed at 30% of market value,

and 5% of the assessed value is used as a tax credit. Homestead property in Mississippi is assessed at 10% of its market value. A house valued at $193,549 would be assessed at $19,355. Based on the combined city and county tax rate of $110.12 per $1,000, the yearly tax would be $2,131, without the exemption noted below.

Homestead exemption: There is a homestead exemption in the form of a tax credit of up to $300 for all homeowners. Residents age 65 and above can claim the first $75,000 of market value as exempt from all ad valorem taxes.

Religion: The Oxford area represents, supports and conducts services for a wide variety of beliefs including Protestant, Roman Catholic and Jewish faiths.

Education: The University of Mississippi focuses on seven major schools of study: liberal arts, engineering, education, law, pharmacy, business and medicine. Masters and doctoral degrees are offered. Ole Miss is a participant in the Elderhostel program and has a program for lifelong learning.

Transportation: Memphis International Airport is 70 miles north of Oxford and provides service to all major cities.

Health: Baptist Memorial Hospital is a 217-bed acute-care facility. It has more than 80 medical and surgical physicians representing more than 30 specialty areas. Leased by one of the largest not-for-profit health care systems in the country, Baptist Memorial Health Care System of Memphis, the hospital provides a full range of comprehensive medical care to all ages.

Housing options: Housing sites in the historic neighborhood are few, and houses generally cost more in that neighborhood. However, housing sites are available in newer housing developments that dot the county. At St. Charles Place, one mile south of Oxford Square, most

homes have three bedrooms and two baths and range in price from $215,000 to $272,000. For more information, call Kessinger Real Estate, (662) 234-5555. Grand Oaks is set among rolling hills, with family homes that range from $450,000 to $800,000 on one side of the golf course development and condos and garden homes ranging from $272,000 to $335,000 on the other side. For more information, contact Kessinger Real Estate, (662) 234-5555. At Azalea Gardens, an independent and assisted-living facility, services include transportation, activities, dining, housekeeping, beauty shop, massage therapist, exercise rooms, performances, arts and crafts, a full-time nurse and personal emergency response system. These services are available both to residents of the main facility as well as homeowners on the property. Popular cottages for sale on the grounds have two bedrooms and range from $160,000 to $180,000. For a monthly fee, the management also takes care of 24-hour security, trash pickup and yard maintenance. For more information about Azalea Gardens, call (662) 234-9600.

Visitor lodging: There are eight hotels with more than 400 rooms, including three bed-and-breakfast inns. A sampling includes the Downtown Inn, $84-$119, (800) 606-1497; Oxford Days Inn, $59-$69, (662) 234-9500; Comfort Inn, from $55, (662) 234-6000; and Oliver-Britt House, $65-$93, (662) 234-8043.

Information: Oxford-Lafayette County Chamber of Commerce, 299 W. Jackson Ave., P.O. Box 147, Oxford, MS 38655, (800) 880-6967, (662) 234-4651 or www.oxfordms.com. The chamber has a retiree attraction program director. Oxford Tourism Council, 102 Ed Perry Blvd., Oxford, MS 38655, (662) 234-4680. For information about Hometown Mississippi Retirement, call (800) 350-3323.

Dr. Lewis is the retired dean of liberal arts at the University of Mississippi. He and his wife have lived in Oxford for 40 years, so Oxford has been a second home to Frank and Mary in many ways.

One of the many aspects of Oxford and the university that the Pooles enjoy is the frequency and quality of concerts and theater performances on campus each season. From opera and Shakespeare to visiting symphonies and dance companies, the university's "artist series" is an affordable entertainment option.

"I was made for retirement," says Frank. "I have so much time now to concentrate on music."

"Some of the nicest evenings we've had here in Oxford have been those in which we've had a light supper, then walked to campus to a performance or concert," adds Mary. The Pooles live less than a quarter-mile from the university, which isn't necessarily a rarity in Oxford. Many retirees have chosen to live near the university and historic Oxford Square, and one can see the over-60 crowd walking side-by-side with coeds on any nice afternoon.

Aside from concerts and theater performances, the university offers an array of continuing-education classes, including wine tastings, music lessons, language classes, computer workshops, painting and sculpture lessons and cultural excursions to the Mississippi Delta and Memphis.

Usually, when asked, Oxford retirees either claim the wealth of cultural opportunities, the presence of the University of Mississippi, the literary heritage or the overwhelming sense of history as Oxford's biggest draws. "But don't forget the shopping and dining," says Clair Gurley.

Oxford's historic town square has a lively year-round festive atmosphere. The community boasts more than 50 restaurants, many of them unique to Oxford — gourmet coffeehouses, fine dining, Memphis-style barbecue and down-home cafes. In the spring and fall, students and residents dine on balconies overlooking the square, shop in the multitude of boutiques, gift and antique shops, or just pause for a neighborly chat on one of the square's strategically placed park benches. Oxford's centrally

located department store, Neilson's, is privately owned by an Oxford family and is considered the South's oldest store, established in 1848.

"Let's just say it fits every criteria for a retirement choice," says Shirley Perry, one of Oxford's happy retirees. "In doing my research, I found that Oxford was literally the only place that actually fit every criteria I had on my list — and the list was long, I can tell you."

Shirley retired to Oxford in September 1999, making the move from her long-time home in Boston, where she was a consultant to pharmaceutical and biotech industries in business development. "I had been thinking of where to retire for quite some time," says Shirley. "I literally subscribed to every magazine about the subject. I went to the library, I made calls and attended conferences. My criteria were very specific.

"It had to be a town versus a city, for one — someplace easy to negotiate, as well as one with a defined sense of community," she says. "It had to have regularly organized cultural events, since I've always loved community theater. It also had to have a sense of history and achievement. When I discovered that Oxford had all that and more — a university, a great health-care community and a low cost of living — my decision was made."

Shirley's traditional brick house is in a lovely new neighborhood called South Oaks. Just three miles from the charm of the town square, South Oaks features spacious, wooded lots. Shirley's new four-bedroom home is built in what Shirley calls "Mississippi modern" style and sits on a half-acre corner lot. The one-story home has an imposing gabled roof, and the rooms are light and airy with high ceilings.

Writing and bicycling are two of Shirley's favorite hobbies. Despite the hills, Shirley finds cycling in Oxford a pleasure. The streets are safe and bicycle-friendly, she says, and there are many cyclists, young and old, on the streets. Plans are underway to create a bike path along the old railroad track that runs through town.

For most of her professional life, Shirley worked for the CIA in Europe. She plans to begin work on her memoirs

as soon as her house is completed, and she finds the literary community and the many writers' groups and classes stimulating.

Small, safe, friendly, beautiful and cultural usually add up to expensive, but that's not necessarily true in Oxford. While the real estate market has boomed in the last few years, with values on some properties growing 100 percent or more, deals are still available. The average single-family home is about $194,000. Generally, properties at this price won't be located in the historic district, but Oxford has many welcoming neighborhoods, new and old. There are virtually no empty lots for sale in the historic part of town.

Occasionally there are houses for sale that can be remodeled or demolished and rebuilt. Homes in the historic area range from $400,000 and up.

New housing developments are abundant, however. These include St. Charles Place, designed in the mode of a small harbor town or New Orleans neighborhood; Grand Oaks, an upscale neighborhood on a lovely 18-hole golf course; and Azalea Gardens, an independent and assisted-living retirement community.

The average cost of living in Mississippi is 10 percent below the national average, and Mississippi residents benefit from the lowest per capita tax burden in the nation. In addition to low taxes in general, retirees living in Mississippi benefit from additional tax breaks. Social Security is not taxed, regardless of total income. Retirement income from IRAs, 401(k)s, Keoghs and qualified public and private pension plans are not taxable. The state welcomes, and even recruits, relocating retirees.

"I actually received an invitation to retire in Mississippi," says Shirley Perry, referring to the state's active retiree recruitment program, Hometown Mississippi Retirement. "I'd always heard about Southern hospitality, but now I'm experiencing it first-hand."

"We love the mixture of young and old, as well as the mixture of cultures here," says Frank Poole. "It's a small, but cosmopolitan, town — all the benefits of a city without the negative side. We're having a great time enjoying our freedom together here." ●

Palm Desert, California

A warm, dry climate and casual lifestyle draw retirees to this Southern California valley

By Mary Lu Abbott

Beyond San Gorgonio Pass, the sky becomes bluer, the air fresher, the mountain views clearer and the lifestyle more relaxed as Interstate 10 descends into broad Coachella Valley east of Los Angeles.

State Highway 111 veers off the fast lanes and angles its way through communities that blend one into another for more than 30 miles. At the heart sits Palm Desert, the cultural and retail hub of a growing resort complex that began with Palm Springs and has carpeted the desert eastward to Indio.

Hollywood couldn't improve on the setting — thousands of tall, skinny palm trees standing like sentinels and a half-dozen mountain ranges guarding the desert floor in all directions. The jagged San Jacinto Mountains, topping 10,000 feet, form a protective ridge to the west and southwest and may wear a cape of snow in winter. A defining presence, the mountains continually attract your eyes, whether you're playing golf, shopping, dining al fresco or simply sitting on your patio. In the light of predawn and in late evening, the peaks take on a velvety blue hue, and during the day, shadows add tone and color.

"The view of the mountains is impressive," says Rich Davidson, 58, who retired to the Sun City Palm Desert community in 2000 with his wife, Dianne, 56. Ticking off what she likes best in the Palm Desert area, Dianne cites "the mountains, the blue sky, the colors, the red sunsets." Dawn's illumination of the mountains and valley is so pretty that, she says, "I get up just to watch the sunrise."

Andy and JoAnn Macek, who lived in Simi Valley in the Los Angeles area and used Where to Retire magazine in their search for a retirement spot, agree on the beauty of Palm Desert. "The mountains sometimes look like a painting," says Andy, 66, who retired in 1999.

JoAnn, 65, adds, "Every place we went, we compared to Coachella Valley.

No place is as pretty." Its attractions are far more than what first meets the eyes, she says, noting that it has all the shopping, dining and cultural amenities that active retirees want and all the health facilities that might be needed later.

For the Davidsons, the climate was a major factor in their decision to move here from San Jose in Northern California. Turned by man into an oasis with 100 golf courses where waterfalls and lakes accent expansive greens, the Coachella Valley nonetheless is part of the Colorado Desert, with the great Mojave Desert bordering to the north. It is sunny, warm — perhaps hot is the better word — and very dry here, with an average annual rainfall of less than 5 inches.

Dianne has arthritis and allergies, particularly to ragweed and pine. "I need to be in a dry, dry climate — the drier the better. We used to come here every August for many years and it would dry out my allergies. My allergies have improved immensely being here," says Dianne, who has met others who moved to the area from Northern California to escape the damper climate.

The decision to move south wasn't easy, despite Southern California being her childhood home. A daughter and grandson live in Northern California, so Rich and Dianne began looking for retirement sites closer to San Jose. They discovered the Del Webb communities at Roseville and Lincoln Hills, both near Sacramento. They liked the active-adult lifestyle that Del Webb provides with its golf courses, clubhouses, fitness centers and group activities.

They looked in Nevada and Arizona and visited other active-adult communities, but they found themselves returning to the Del Webb communities and finally settled on the one in Palm Desert.

"We did a lot of research. For the money, the best buy is here. We needed to stretch our dollars. I like the accessibility, too. You get off the freeway and

you're here," Dianne says. Because Sun City Palm Desert is a large community with about 8,000 residents, the monthly association fees are comparatively low, at $177 a month.

Rich says they found similar homes for $50,000 to $70,000 less in Arizona, but they didn't want to move there. They feel that for California residents who want to stay in the state when they retire, Palm Desert is one of the less-expensive options.

"We fell in love with this community," Rich says. Unlike some retirees, they didn't downsize and chose one of the largest home plans, with nearly 3,000 square feet and three bedrooms with a den. They wanted space for their family, including a son in college, to visit.

They decided on a lot and model in the fall of 1999, although Rich wasn't retiring until the following summer. He told the builder he didn't want to start construction until April, "and they held off driving the first nail," says Rich, noting that allowed him to get everything in order for retirement from TRW, the automotive, aerospace and information technology giant, where he was an engineer.

Their best-laid plans went awry, though, when they put their San Jose home on the market and a buyer wanted it before their planned moving date in August. The buyer offered an extra $10,000 if the Davidsons could be out by June 27.

They took the deal and rented a house in Palm Desert until their home was ready. "We spent two months buying furniture and having an eight-week vacation," Rich says.

Originally from Cleveland, OH, the Maceks yearned to live in Southern California, where they had visited friends. When his company offered a transfer in the 1970s, they happily moved to Simi Valley, and Andy later started his own tool business.

The Maceks fell in love with the Coachella Valley on a visit about 30 years ago and bought a second home in Palm Desert in the early 1990s. They weren't sure they wanted to retire here, though, and they considered other places in the Southwest, including Pahrump, outside Las Vegas, NV, where they have property, and Carlsbad, NM.

"Every time we looked elsewhere, we said we would have to give up this or that. Down the line we don't want to have to drive 45 minutes to find a decent medical center. Yes, you have Nevada where you don't have a state (income) tax, but there are trade-offs. I sort of planted my feet and said, 'I really like this area.' It's a beautiful, well-taken-care-of city and has all the services you might need. It's so geared for seniors," JoAnn says.

They decided that for retirement they needed a larger place than their second home. They wanted extra space for Andy's mother to live with them and a garage where he could pursue his hobby of restoring old cars. Andy found his dream place, but it took awhile to convince his wife. "JoAnn said, 'I don't like

Palm Desert, CA

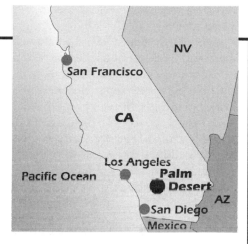

Population: About 48,000 permanent residents and an additional 20,000 in winter. About 330,000 people live year-round in the Coachella Valley communities, increasing to more than 500,000 in winter.

Location: About 125 miles east of Los Angeles (about three hours) and 15 miles southeast of Palm Springs, adjacent to I-10. It's in the Coachella Valley, which extends about 40 miles in desert terrain surrounded by mountains. Palm Desert is the cultural and retail hub of several desert communities lining the valley, including Cathedral City, Rancho Mirage, Indian Wells, La Quinta and Indio.

Climate: High Low
January 70 41
July 107 74
The valley has a sunny, dry climate with warm days and cold nights in winter and hot days with pleasant evenings in summer. Daytime temperatures often top 100 degrees from June into September and can exceed 110 degrees, but low humidity makes the heat more tolerable. The rainy season is usually mid-October to mid-February. Elevation ranges from about 250 feet in Palm Desert to 8,516 feet at the Mountain Station of the Palm Springs Aerial Tramway in the San Jacinto Mountains.

Average relative humidity: 26.5%
Rain: 3.38 inches
Snow: Rare in the valley, but mountain peaks are snowcapped in winter.
Cost of living: Above average
Average housing cost: $519,600
Sales tax: 7.75%
Sales tax exemptions: Food products, prescription medicines and services.
State income tax: For married couples filing jointly, the rates range from 1% on the first $12,638 to 9.3% (plus $3,652)

on amounts above $82,952. For single filers, rates run from 1% on the first $6,319 to 9.3% (plus $1,826) on amounts above $41,476.

Income tax exemptions: Social Security benefits and railroad pensions are exempt.
Estate tax: None. The state's "pick-up" portion of the federal tax was eliminated Jan. 1, 2005.
Inheritance tax: None
Property tax: Homes are assessed at either 100% of market value or purchase price plus 2% per year, whichever is lower. The rate varies by area, and there may be special assessments added by various taxing jurisdictions. Basic tax on a $500,000 home with the exemption noted below would be about $6,163 at a rate of 1.25%. The state's homeowner assistance program reimburses up to $473 to those who are 62 or older (or blind or disabled) and have an income of no more than $39,699.
Homestead exemptions: $7,000 off the value for owner-occupied homes.
Religion: The city has about 30 churches, synagogues and temples, augmented by places of worship in adjoining communities. All faiths are represented.
Education: Adult education classes are available at the two-year College of the Desert, and California State University at San Bernardino has a Coachella Valley campus in Palm Desert.
Transportation: From Palm Desert, Palm Springs International Airport is about 25 minutes away. Of the Los Angeles airports, Ontario and John Wayne are closest, at slightly under two hours by car. Los Angeles International Airport is about 2.5 hours away. Palm Desert runs a free Shopper Hopper bus to major shopping areas, and the SunLine Transit Agency has a SunBus serving towns throughout

the valley at low fares.
Health: The valley has outstanding medical facilities and physicians in all specialties. The three major facilities are the Eisenhower Medical Center in neighboring Rancho Mirage, the Desert Regional Medical Center in Palm Springs and the JFK Memorial Hospital in Indio.
Housing options: Palm Desert has a number of gated and country-club communities with resale homes available, and there are new developments in neighboring Rancho Mirage and La Quinta. The desert communities meld together.
Visitor lodging: The town has 15 resort hotels and other accommodations, including Marriott's Desert Springs Resort and Spa, from $329 nightly in high season and $119 in low season, (800) 331-3112, and Best Western Palm Desert, from $149 in high season and $89 in low season, (800) 231-8675.
Information: Palm Desert Visitor Information Center, 72-990 Highway 111, Palm Desert, CA 92260, (800) 873-2428 or www.palmdesert.org. Palm Desert Chamber of Commerce, 73-710 Fred Waring Drive, Suite 114, Palm Desert, CA 92260, (760) 346-6111 or www.pdcc. org. Joslyn Senior Center of the Cove Communities, 73-750 Catalina Way, Palm Desert, CA 92260, (760) 340-3220.

this,' and I said, 'Isn't this great?'" recalls Andy, who particularly liked the large workshop out back.

The house and garage occupied a quarter of an acre of land — and "in California, that's big. Out here you usually walk out your door and shake hands with somebody," Andy says, noting that homes normally are built quite close to lot lines. The house also had a bedroom and bath that would afford privacy for his mother, 88.

JoAnn finally agreed to the purchase if she could have the house remodeled to her specifications. "I said, 'Not a problem.' So now she says we bought a workshop with a house attached to it," Andy says. They tore out the entire front of the home and redid it. She now has her favored butterfly motif everywhere, and he has room for seven cars.

The Maceks did not want to live in an all-adult community. "I do like a mix in my neighborhood. I like the young, the middle-aged and the seniors together. I enjoy seeing the kids," says JoAnn, who has not retired yet. She's executive director of the Specialty Advertising Association of California and works from her condo in the West Hills area of Los Angeles. She commutes to Palm Desert most weekends, leaving her office on Thursdays, and stays extended periods during holidays.

On the other hand, the Davidsons wanted an active-adult community for several reasons. "I didn't want to move to a community not knowing that there were 12 teenagers in the next house or something like that. The quiet serenity here is just fantastic," Rich says of their home at Sun City Palm Desert. "I can sit outside on the chaise longue at night, especially in summertime, and it's so peaceful and quiet. I like that."

They also wanted activities available. Dianne notes that her husband was worried that she might get bored. "I can kick back, but Dianne needs activity," Rich says. "You can be active all day here if you want, or you can be contemplative." He's trying to write a novel, something he had always wanted to do. While he works on his book, Dianne can go her own way.

While Sun City Palm Desert has about 80 clubs and a large roster of activities, Dianne says she had some trouble finding her niche. Because of her arthritis,

Dianne, 46, retired early from teaching. While the community has a large number of people who are in their 50s, many of them still work.

Friendly and outgoing, Dianne says she went through a lonely period because she had not made friends among her age group. "I didn't know anybody. Everyone sort of has their attachments and you have to work your way in," she says.

At a first-time luncheon for baby boomers in the community, she met 19 other residents and was off and running "with a new project." She has organized the group, which now has more than 150 members in the Sun City community. "We had a '50s-'60s dance and 190 people showed up," she says. "I was surprised at how fast the boomer group came together and how many nice friends I've met."

Both Dianne and Rich have taken their time about getting into groups rather than rushing to try a host of activities. Rich says he's not a club joiner but has no problem partnering for golf a couple of times a week. If he doesn't find someone to play with by phone, he can join threesomes at the course.

"The community is very friendly," says Rich, noting that residents walking or driving their cars or golf carts greet each other with a wave. He meets people playing bocce and ping-pong, and such associations have led to couples meeting for dinner or a glass of wine.

JoAnn says town residents also are quite friendly, noting that it's easy to strike up conversations at the grocery store. "People in California tend to stay to themselves, but here people are more open, maybe because the pace is slower. We've developed a circle of friends and socialize," she says.

Her husband has made friends through his car restoration hobby, joining clubs for Thunderbird, Crosley and Buick owners. "I'm working on a '56 Thunderbird, and have a '52 Crosley Super Sport convertible and a '65 Buick Riviera that I bought from a man at the senior center. He was the original owner," Andy says.

Andy is active at the Joslyn Senior Center of the Cove Communities in Palm Desert. He started bringing his mother to the center on Thursdays for potluck and bingo. When the center needed some-

one to run bingo, he volunteered. He's now on the board of directors of the center, which serves Palm Desert, Rancho Mirage and Indian Wells residents.

A social, recreational, education and health center, Joslyn bustles with activities, attracting about 400 people daily to programs that run the gamut from salsa dancing to Tibetan meditation. About 140 volunteers assist with operations.

"Everything you need is in Palm Desert — all the retail shopping from Target to Macy's to Home Depot, to high-end jewelers, galleries and shops at El Paseo, and plenty of restaurants and theater," says Michael Barnard, executive director of the Joslyn Senior Center. "It's a very stable city with strong civic leadership. It puts a lot of money back into the community. We have a huge park with an amphitheater and baseball fields. It's the nicest in the valley."

He says Palm Desert has attracted all ages, with young families as well as retirees. According to visitor bureau statistics, the average age is 48. It's an easy city to navigate, with broad streets, clear signage and many roadways marked with lanes for electric golf carts. To be driven in traffic, the carts have to be street-legal, with mirrors and horns on them. Andy says he sees many handicapped retirees using the golf-cart lanes to go all over town.

Throughout the valley, Gerald Ford Drive, Ginger Rogers Road, Gene Autry Trail, the Bob Hope Chrysler Classic golf tournament and the Frank Sinatra Countywide Celebrity Invitational pay homage to the many celebrities who have frequented or lived in the area and contributed to its growth.

Palm Desert itself has 150 tennis courts and 32 golf courses, including the city-owned Desert Willow Golf Resort, which has two championship courses recognized for both their play and their environmental design using desert vegetation and reclaimed water to keep fairways green.

The city's McCallum Theatre for the Performing Arts hosts touring musicals and other cultural attractions, and free movies and concerts are staged throughout the summer in the Civic Center Park, where the valley scenery adds to the show. The city's innovative Art in Public Places program has brought 96 artworks to parks, street medians, public facilities and business buildings, with 19 sculptures displayed in the upscale El Paseo shopping district.

El Paseo, with its landscaped median, al fresco cafes and classy boutiques, evokes a promenade ambiance and serves as a downtown. The city has a dozen more shopping centers, and on the western edge of the valley along I-10, the large Desert Hills Premium Outlets has good buys from such retailers as Anne Klein, Ralph Lauren, Giorgio Armani, Barneys New York, Gucci and Tommy Hilfiger.

The Davidsons like the casual lifestyle. "To be able to go to a nice restaurant and not have to wear a coat and tie is really good," Rich says.

When family and visitors come, there's no shortage of things to see and do. The city adjoins the Santa Rosa Mountains National Scenic Area with wilderness hiking. The Living Desert Wildlife and Botanical Park showcases area plants, animals and history. Scenic Highway 74 will take you from the desert into the mountain pines in less than an hour.

The valley is noted for its health-care facilities, including the major Eisenhower Medical Center in neighboring Rancho Mirage. While the Maceks don't need all the medical services now, the proximity of care and the focus of facilities on the older generation were important in their decision to retire here.

"If it's good enough for Bob Hope, it's good enough for me," Rich says of the valley's medical care. The beloved star lived in the valley.

The hot summers, though, are a drawback. Daytime temperatures usually top 100 degrees from June into September and may exceed 110 degrees in July and August. Low humidity is a mitigating factor.

Neither the Davidsons nor the Maceks mind the heat. In fact, both couples cite the weather as a major attraction for them. "We love the dry heat. That's why we moved here," Dianne says. Rich adds, "Eight months, we have perfect weather. Four months, it's hot, but we don't worry about it."

Andy says it's really hot only about two months, in August and parts of July and maybe September. "What people don't realize is that 120 degrees in dry heat here is like 70 or 80 degrees back East with humidity," he says.

Andy does caution that hot summer temperatures raise the monthly electric bills because of air conditioning. "Our high bill was $450, but in the winter it's down to $70 or $80. We're looking into a new air-conditioning system with better efficiency that could save up to 50 percent," he says.

"The only thing we don't like is the growth, which is almost every place, though," Andy says. "They keep building golf courses and gated communities with lakes, and the more lakes, the more humidity."

Highway 111, the main route through the towns, can get congested at peak times and has some ongoing widening projects that slow traffic. Rich doesn't complain, though, because he escaped congestion in San Jose that made his 25-mile commute take about 90 minutes each way.

Rich wishes he knew more Spanish because there are so many Spanish-speaking residents, and he's learning the language. Dianne misses seeing her daughter and grandson in Monterey and experiencing the change of seasons.

Andy thinks the area is especially well-suited for those who enjoy sports, particularly golf.

"The whole city is well-planned and has wonderful services, very in tune to seniors' needs," JoAnn says. "We have friends who just can't handle living without changes of season, but for people who love the desert, keep an active lifestyle and want to have everything close by, this is a wonderful place to live."

"I think this is the place to live," says Andy. ●

Pensacola, Florida

Sugar-white beaches and a flourishing cultural scene sweeten life in this Florida Panhandle city

By Karen Feldman

Living on the edge is a way of life for residents of Pensacola, in the far west of Florida's broad panhandle. Although it's part of the sprawling Sunshine State, the region operates on central time and is closer in distance and mindset to Mobile than Miami.

In addition to its position near the state's western border, the region lies along the northern edge of the Gulf of Mexico, boasting more than 40 miles of beach. Gulf Islands National Seashore, covering 100,000 acres of land and water, was specifically established to preserve resources for the enjoyment of generations to come.

The beaches are renowned for their fine white sand and aquamarine surf. The area's residents are known for their easy hospitality and genteel Southern charm. Pensacola encompasses the best of two worlds, located sufficiently south to avoid blizzards, ice storms and other winter discomforts, but northerly enough that summers aren't swelteringly tropical.

All of those qualities make it a major contender among Northern retirees seeking a gentler climate and more laid-back lifestyle. "It has a small-town vibe with big-city amenities," says Misty Johnson, relocation coordinator for the Pensacola Area Chamber of Commerce. "It has an airport and nice restaurants and a very vibrant downtown area. In comparison with other cities in Florida, it does have that slower pace."

A relatively low cost of living, a mild climate and a cornucopia of cultural and entertainment options combine to attract people of all ages, including ever more retirees.

Count Kathleen and Lamarr Seader among them. The pair of retired Navy master chief petty officers met by phone when he was stationed in Macon, GA, and she was stationed in Arlington, VA. They married 18 months later, and Lamarr moved north to join his new wife. From there they moved to Orlando, where Lamarr retired in 1987, then to a new post

for Kathleen in Naples, Italy. When she retired in 1990, they returned to Orlando.

As many Florida retirees do, Lamarr got into real estate. But by 2001, the Seaders wanted a less frenzied lifestyle than is possible in one of the world's most-visited cities. They headed northwest to Milton, a suburb of Pensacola.

"We retired from the rat race — all the traffic, hustle and bustle," says Lamarr, 64, of their main reason for choosing Pensacola. "And we wanted something that had a little bit of the Navy."

There's a whole lot of Navy here. It's the home of the Pensacola Naval Complex, with its annual payroll of $907 million and an estimated economic impact of about $1.5 million. The relationship between the city and the Navy dates back to the early 1800s, when area brickyards supplied the raw materials used to build forts.

Today the area attracts military retirees because of the easy access it provides to a military commissary, Navy exchange and hospital, not to mention the presence of plenty of kindred spirits.

The Navy's presence is palpable throughout town. It gleams in the granite of the Wall South, a half-size replica of the Vietnam Veterans Memorial in Washington, DC, which stands in Pensacola's Veterans Memorial Park. It's on display at the Civil War Soldiers Museum. And it soars through the skies from the Naval Air Station, home of the Blue Angels, among the best-known stunt aviator teams in the country.

The city's premier attraction is the National Museum of Naval Aviation at the Naval Air Station. The 40-year-old museum has grown to 300,000 square feet filled with exhibits that trace the history of American naval aviation from its start to the present. There are many restored aircraft on display and visitors can work the controls of aircraft trainers and simulators. There's also an IMAX theater that shows films such as "The Magic of Flight" on its seven-story-tall screen. A fund-raising campaign is under

way to raise $30 million to add another 200,000 square feet for, among other things, a national flight academy for youngsters in grades seven through 12.

At the helm of this expanding enterprise is retired Admiral Jack Fetterman, 71, who has served as president and CEO of the Naval Aviation Museum Foundation for a decade. During 38 years in the military, his jobs included commander of the naval forces' Pacific fleet and, just before retiring, he was stationed in Pensacola, where he served as chief of the Naval Education and Training Command. Although he and his wife, Nancy, 54, considered returning to other cities they'd lived in over the years, such as Virginia Beach and San Diego, Pensacola won out.

"We've been all over the world, and felt that Pensacola's quality of life is good, the cost of living is good but, more important, the people are good," he says. "It's a very welcoming place."

In recent years, Pensacola's population has grown slowly but steadily. In the early days, though, development came in fits and starts. Pensacola was founded in 1559 by Don Tristan de Luna for Spain. That was six years before St. Augustine got its first settlement. Pensacola's original pioneers disbanded in 1561, reportedly because they didn't get along well with one another.

The Spanish resettled the city 137 years later and it's been expanding ever since. Over 450 years, it's changed hands 13 times. France, Britain and the Confederate governments also claimed it at various times. During the Civil War, the Confederate government abandoned the city to Union forces and it became United States territory.

The city's cultural credentials include museums dedicated to art, commerce, industry, history and hands-on discovery, plus a zoo, a wildlife sanctuary and a science and space theater. Some of the museums are clustered within Historic Pensacola Village, which also includes houses and other buildings dating to the late 1700s.

Its performing arts community includes the 70-year-old Pensacola Little Theatre (a community theater), the professional Pensacola Opera, Pensacola Symphony Orchestra, Choral Society of Pensacola, the Pensacola Children's Chorus and barbershop groups for men and women.

The region's beaches are consistently rated among the best in the world, and there are bays and lakes suitable for canoeing and boating. Golf courses, bike paths and tennis courts abound.

When it comes to real estate, the choices are broad and affordable. Compared with other Florida cities, Pensacola's prices are below average, yet property values are on the rise.

However, broker Joe Endry, owner of Coldwell Banker JME Realty in Pensaco-

Pensacola, FL

Population: 414,000 in the metropolitan statistical area, which includes Escambia and Santa Rosa counties.

Location: Pensacola is the seat of Escambia County in northwest Florida on the Upper Gulf coast.

Climate: High Low
January 60 42
July 90 74

Average relative humidity: Ranges from 51 percent in the morning to 64 percent in the evening in January, and from 82 in the morning to 63 at night in July.

Rain: 61 inches annually

Cost of living: Slightly below average

Median housing cost: $163,600

Sales tax: There is no sales tax on groceries or medication. Other retail sale and rental of tangible personal property is assessed at 7.5 percent.

State income tax: None

Intangibles tax: None. The tax was repealed as of Jan. 1, 2007.

Estate tax: None

Inheritance tax: None

Property tax: Property owners within the city limits of Pensacola pay $21.896 per $1,000 assessed value. In the unincorporated portions of Escambia County, the rate is $17.586. With a $25,000 homestead exemption, the annual tax on a $163,600 home would be $3,035 within the city limits and $2,437 in unincorporated parts of Escambia County.

Homestead exemption: $25,000 off assessed value of primary, permanent residence.

Religion: A range of churches is represented in the Pensacola area, including most Christian denominations. There's also a Jewish congregation.

Education: University of West Florida, (850) 474-2000 or www.uwf.edu, is one of the state's 10 colleges. The accredited school offers a variety of degrees, including a doctorate in education. Pensacola Junior College, (850) 484-1000 or www.pjc.

cc.fl.us, offers associate of arts degrees, vocational and technical training and many lifelong-learning programs. Pensacola Christian College, (850) 478-8480 or www.pcci.edu, is a private college offering bachelor's, master's and doctoral degrees.

Transportation: Pensacola Regional Airport serves more than a million people annually, with more than 40 flights daily and direct connections to many major cities. Airlines servicing the region include AirTran, Delta, Continental, Northwest and US Airways. The region is easily accessible from Interstate 10 and north-south routes such as Interstate 65. The Port of Pensacola offers easy access to the Gulf of Mexico and is the origination point of several cruise ships.

Health: The region is served by four hospitals. Baptist Health Care, (850) 434-4011 or www.ebaptisthealthcare.org, includes Baptist Hospital, a 492-bed tertiary hospital; Gulf Breeze Hospital, with 60 beds; and Baptist Medical Park, a comprehensive collection of outpatient services and physicians' offices. The hospital provides medical, surgical, psychiatric and obstetrical services, an emergency room and state-designated trauma center, and cancer, open-heart and cardiology care. West Florida Hospital, (850) 494-4000 or www.westfloridahospital.com, includes a 400-bed tertiary-care facility offering a full range of medical and surgical services, including cardiology and cardiovascular surgery, orthopedics, neurology and neurosurgery, oncology, senior care, emergency and trauma, and women's services. It also includes the 58-bed Rehabilitation Institute, an accredited rehabilitation hospital, and The Pavilion, a 73-bed mental health facility. The Sacred Heart Health System, (850) 416-1600 or www.sacredheart.org, includes Sacred Heart Hospital, a 449-bed acute care facility with children's and women's centers and cancer, heart and other forms of care. Pensacola Naval

Hospital, (850) 505-6601 or http://psaweb.med.navy.mil, cares for active and retired military personnel in the region.

Housing options: Area real estate covers the gamut, from basic starter homes to waterfront condominiums and palatial estates as well as gated communities, rural homesteads and the Victorian mansions of the historic downtown district. Basic, single-family homes and townhouses start at less than $100,000. Waterfront homes can run from $365,000 on up, with Gulf-front properties priced from $700,000. Retirees should keep in mind that Pensacola suffered extensive damage due to Hurricane Ivan in 2004, and many homes are being sold "as is" for a lower price. **Coldwell Banker JME Realty** offers "Seniors on the Go" relocation services to newcomers age 55 and older, (800) 422-0004 or www.jmerealty.com.

Visitor lodging: Courtyard by Marriott offers one-bedroom units and a few one-bedroom suites not far from Interstate 10, $99-$149, (850) 857-7744. Noble Manor is a bed-and-breakfast inn operated in a 1905 Tudor Revival style home in the Pensacola North Hill Historic District, $85-$105, (877) 598-4634.

Information: Pensacola Bay Area Chamber of Commerce, 117 W. Garden St., P.O. Box 550, Pensacola, FL 32502, (800) 608-3479, (850) 438-4081, www.pensacolachamber.com and www.visitpensacola.com.

la, says real estate is a relative bargain compared with other Florida cities. Not only that, it has features more Southern locales don't.

"It's a different kind of beauty than a lot of parts of Florida," he says. "There are heritage oaks, tall pines and magnolias here. We have a lot of woodsy areas and magnificent beaches, the waterways are spectacular, with the Gulf, the Intracoastal Waterway and five large bays just near Pensacola."

A basic 1,200-square-foot home or townhouse in a good neighborhood can be had for less than $100,000, but many of these homes are being sold "as is" due to damage sustained from Hurricane Ivan in 2004. The historic downtown has become quite popular, too, with a wide range of prices, depending on the home's condition.

Existing homes bordering a river or bay start at about $150,000. A growing number of residents are building large homes on less-populated parts of the bays. Lots run about an acre and homes can cost between $365,000 and $600,000. Gulf-front property is the most expensive, with prices ranging from about $700,000 to over $1 million.

There aren't a lot of master-planned communities in the area, Endry says, but golf-course communities such as Tiger Point and Stonebrook Village offer golf memberships for $125 to $200 a month plus initiation fees.

The Fettermans purchased a two-story home on almost an acre of land bounded on three sides by Star Lake in Pensacola. It's a two-story structure, with three bedrooms upstairs and one on the first floor. Jack has a home office upstairs and what he calls his "ready room" downstairs, which is filled with his Navy memorabilia. It's in this room decked out in nautical aviation splendor that he likes to relax.

Because they love the city so much, the Fettermans feel obliged to give back to the community. While Jack is heavily involved with the museum, Nancy is finishing her master's degree in history and spearheading a campaign to restore St. Michael's Cemetery. The national historic site with some 3,000 graves fell into disrepair many years ago. She also serves on the board of Sacred Heart Hospital and works 20 hours a week at the University of West Florida.

In their spare time, they get away to the 39-foot trawler they keep at a downtown marina. Sometimes they stay on it at the dock, using it as a condo that affords them easy access to the whole downtown area.

While the Fettermans like being close to the action, the Seaders want just the opposite. They looked for a quiet gated development and found it in Windsor Villas, an active-adult community in nearby Milton.

Kathleen, 58, liked the community amenities, which include a clubhouse and pool. The prospect of peaceful, gated living so close to Pensacola (nine miles west) was another selling point. Within Windsor Villas, "there are lots of planned activities with people about your age, and there are no screaming kids, no loud boom boxes and no cars on concrete blocks," Lamarr says.

They built a 2,150-square-foot brick house with three bedrooms and two baths. Taking a basic model, they had the builders move some of the walls out about four feet. The house has a large sunroom and plenty of space for Kathleen to create needlecraft and art.

They also love the camaraderie within their development. "They have something going on at the community center every day," Kathleen says. "There are crafts classes, like knitting and cross-stitching, game night, coffees, breakfasts and dinners." Residents help one another out, picking up mail for those who are out of town, tending to sick neighbors and teaming up to move heavy loads or help with home-improvement projects.

One event that lures the Seaders away from their cozy community is cruise night at a Pensacola Burger King. On Saturday nights, they climb into the 1965 blue-and-white Mustang that Lamarr restored and join hundreds of other classic car enthusiasts in an evening of good-natured competition and mutual auto admiration.

Another couple, Benny and Millie Klock, took about 10 years to find just the right retirement spot. Over that decade, they considered Arizona, South Carolina, south Florida and Savannah, GA, before moving to Milton in December 1989.

The couple lived in Bowie, MD, where Benny, 68, worked at the Defense Mapping Agency of the U.S. Department of Defense. He made his first visit to western Florida when he was sent to Eglin Air Force Base in Fort Walton Beach to deliver a scientific paper. He was so impressed that he wanted Millie to see it, too.

Two months later, they returned, bought a lot, contracted to have a house built and returned to Maryland, where Benny promptly retired. Just hours after his retirement luncheon, they were headed south.

"We liked the beautiful beaches and the fact that it wasn't congested like some of the places we saw," Benny says.

They built their first home on stilts overlooking Escambia Bay. A decade later, they moved to a one-story home to accommodate Benny's 90-year-old mother, who lived with them and found the steps too taxing. Their current 3,000-square-foot house has four bedrooms and three baths. It isn't on the water, but it's close to Interstate 10, making travel easier.

Benny, 68, plays tennis three times a week, and both work out with weights three times weekly. They also volunteer at Baptist Medical Park, working with an eye surgeon who videotapes his procedures. The Klocks narrate the operations and patients get copies of the videotapes. Their other pastimes include corresponding by e-mail with their six children and 14 grandchildren, who are spread out across the country. They also use their computer for genealogy, playing solitaire and researching all manner of subjects.

None of the three couples plans to move anytime soon. "It's like stepping back in time," says Millie, 70. "People are so nice. No one blows their horn at you. We just got back from California and couldn't go anywhere without hearing honks from impatient drivers. We've been very happy here."

Are there any negatives to living in the area? Millie isn't wild about the six-month hurricane season but reasons that hurricanes are preferable to the tornadoes and earthquakes that occur elsewhere. She also says the mass transit system isn't great (especially in Milton) and people who don't drive may have difficulty getting around.

Other than that, they find it hard to think up any drawbacks, but it's not the first time they've been asked the question.

"We were told by the natives that whenever people from the North ask, to say living here is terrible and it's too hot, because we don't want it to grow anymore," Benny says. But, he admits, "It's really great." ●

Pinehurst, North Carolina

This 105-year-old town in the North Carolina Sandhills is closely linked to the game of golf

By Lan Sluder

If golf, golf and more golf is your idea of paradise, Pinehurst may be your cup of, er, tee. The area has more than 40 golf courses, all playable virtually year-round in this mild climate, and a plethora of golfing communities, gated and otherwise. Yet unlike faster-growing golfing neighbors such as Myrtle Beach in South Carolina, Pinehurst retains a true small-town ambiance. The local newspaper is published only three times a week, and the airport has an honor system for parking.

"The pace of life, running in low gear rather than flat out in high gear, attracted us," says Paul Kauffman, 63, a retired IBM engineer who, with his wife, Amy, moved to Pinehurst from northern Virginia in 1992. Golf also was a deciding factor for the Kauffmans. A 14-handicap golfer, Paul plays four or five times a week.

"There are a lot of things for the non-golfer, but many, many people's lives revolve around golf," says Bill Graning, an employee of Ford Motor Co. for 33 years. Bill took early retirement and moved here in 1996 from Plymouth, MI, and now lives on the 11th hole of the Holly course at Pinewild Country Club, a gated community in Pinehurst. Bill, 62, has a 15 handicap, and his wife, Barbara, a 36. "We have had no second thoughts about moving here and couldn't be happier," he says.

Pinehurst is in southern Moore County, about 70 miles, or 90 minutes by car, southwest of Raleigh. With other towns in the area, including Southern Pines and Aberdeen, Pinehurst is part of the Sandhills region of North Carolina.

The Sandhills take their name from the region's sandy soil, which results from a prehistoric seashore, although the Atlantic Ocean now is about 100 miles away. The sandy soil isn't ideal for most farm crops, aside from peaches, but there are three benefits. First, the sand absorbs water quickly, reducing breeding places for mosquitoes and other noxious bugs, so you'll spend less time slapping and swatting than in most other parts of the eastern Carolinas. Second, the soil, along with the 500-foot elevation, contributes to a lower-than-average humidity for the Southeast, making even hot Southern summer days a little more bearable. Finally, for those with a yen for gentleperson farming, the soft earth is kind to the hooves of horses, so the Sandhills area, like Aiken, SC, has horse farms, riding events and stables. Pinehurst is also home to a newly renovated harness racing track.

Pinehurst owes its existence to a New England drug store entrepreneur named James Walker Tufts, after whom Tufts University in Boston is named. Exhausted from his job as head of the American Soda Fountain Co., Tufts left Boston in 1893 on a trip to Florida in search of a place with fresh air and a healthy environment. He didn't much care for Florida, finding the hotels of the time overpriced and of poor quality, but in the Sandhills he came upon 6,000 acres of pine-barren land, recently cut for its timber. Tufts bought the land for less than $1 an acre and soon undertook to build a resort that he hoped would become "America's winter playground."

Beginning in 1895, Tufts turned over his Boston business interests to his son so he could concentrate on developing the resort first called Tuftstown and later Pinehurst after a planned development on Martha's Vineyard where Tufts had a cottage. He hired Frederick Law Olmsted, the landscape architect of New York's Central Park and fresh from the grounds of the grand Biltmore estate in Asheville, NC, to develop a plan for the new resort.

Olmsted came up with a plan patterned after a New England village, right down to the village green and rambling narrow side streets. He planted nearly 250,000 cedars, hollies, pin oaks, sycamores, maples and other trees and shrubs to go along with the remaining native longleaf and loblolly pines. For his part, Tufts moved swiftly to build first the Holly Inn, a small jewel of a hotel still in business today in the Village of Pinehurst, and then the Carolina, at the time the largest frame hotel in North Carolina. It also is still in existence, part of the Pinehurst Resort. He called the Carolina hotel the "queen of the South."

The story goes that Tufts was introduced to golf when dairy farmers in the area complained to him that his hotel guests were hitting their cows with little white balls. However true that may be, a Scottish golf pro named Donald Ross, who came to be regarded as one of the world's greatest golf course designers with some 600 courses to his credit, was brought in to design and build the first courses at Pinehurst. His second local effort, Pinehurst No. 2, was destined to become one of the most famous of all courses, home to myriad golf tournaments over the years, including the 2005 U.S. Open.

Ross eventually made his home in Pinehurst and died there in 1948. His golf course designs emphasize tricky greens and strategic layouts that test even the best of golfers. His early courses had sand greens and few water hazards, and one of his guiding principles was that Mother Nature should direct the design, with the golf course following the natural lay of the land. That's true of the three courses he designed at Pinehurst from 1898 to 1910, and in some ways also true of the other five courses at Pinehurst Resort. Tom Fazio designed three of them (4, 6 and 8), and the No. 7, a Rees Jones par-72 that was renovated in 2003, has been rated as among the top courses in America along with No. 2.

Pinehurst — that is, the golf courses and hotels in the Village of Pinehurst — was operated as a resort by the Tufts family from 1895 to 1970, then for several years as a real estate development company owned by Diamondhead Corp. After financial problems in the late

1970s, the resort was purchased by Dallas-based ClubCorp, which still operates it today. Though it paid only about $15 million for the property, ClubCorp has invested a reported $100 million or more in restoring and improving the hotels and golf courses. A ninth course, on land off Highway 5 between Pinehurst and Aberdeen, with the design by Rees Jones, is under way.

But retirees who have moved to Pinehurst say they were attracted by the small-town atmosphere as much as by the golf. They like the lack of traffic, the slower pace of life and the fact that they quickly get to know their neighbors.

Most people in Pinehurst are "very gracious, friendly and outgoing," says Arvilla Sheron, who moved here in 1998 with husband Dick from Newport Beach, CA. Trained as a psychologist,

Arvilla was a real estate agent in Newport Beach, and Dick was a regional sales manager for several national companies.

"It's incredible the amount of friends we've made here in a short time — we've been to more parties here in one year than in 10 years in California," she says. Dick, a 9-handicap golfer until a hip replacement slowed him down a little, discovered Pinehurst while entertaining clients on a golf trip. Arvilla says she "tries to stay 39 years old" and has a 32 handicap. The Sherons, like the Kauffmans, ended up at Pinewild, which is predominantly but not exclusively occupied by retirees. Their house, a 3,000-square-foot rancher on the fourth green of the Holly course, cost about $350,000 and has appreciated, according to Arvilla.

Thanks to the fact that Pinehurst and Southern Pines get hundreds of thousands of golf vacationers each year, the area also has more than its fair share of good restaurants. "We like the small-town atmosphere and lack of traffic and congestion, but we also like the larger city amenities such as good restaurants," says Bill Graning, the former Ford employee.

Of course, the area also has a few drawbacks. Residents point to a lack of "big shopping" opportunities. The Pinehurst/Southern Pines area has upscale grocery stores along with a 24-hour Wal-Mart and Kmart, a Belk department store, a Talbots and a number of boutiques. But for mall shopping, residents usually drive 90 minutes to Raleigh or 45 minutes to Fayetteville, where Fort Bragg Army base and Pope Air Force Base, one

Pinehurst, NC

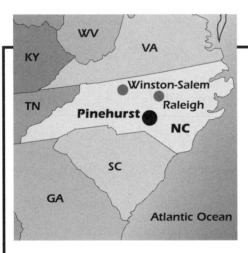

Population: 9,706 in Pinehurst, 74,769 in Moore County.

Location: Pinehurst is located in the Sandhills region of south-central North Carolina, about 70 miles southwest of Raleigh.

Climate: High Low
January 55 44
July 91 68
Pinehurst has a moderate four-season climate.

Rain: 51 inches

Snow: 6 inches

Cost of living: About average

Average housing cost: The average residential sale in Pinehurst is $259,065. However, real estate prices vary greatly, ranging from under $100,000 for a small condo to more than $500,000 for a large home in an exclusive golf community or in the Village of Pinehurst. Homes on an

interior lot in a golf community range start around $125,000. Homes fronting golf courses start in the $400,000s. Local real estate agents say retirees moving to the area typically spend $250,000-$500,000. Building costs average about $150 per square foot. Two-bedroom apartments average about $750 a month.

Sales tax: 6.5%

Sales tax exemptions: Prescription medicine, eyeglasses, some medical supplies and most services are exempt.

State income tax: For married couples filing jointly, the rate is graduated from 6% of taxable income up to $21,250 to 8.25% (plus $14,537.50) on amounts over $200,000. For single filers, it is graduated from 6% of income up to $12,750 to 8.25% (plus $8,722.50) on amounts over $120,000.

Income tax exemptions: Social Security and railroad retirement benefits are exempt. Up to $2,000 of distributions from private retirement benefits and IRAs (up to the amount reported in federal income taxes), or up to $4,000 of government pensions may be exempt. Total deductions may not exceed $4,000 per person.

Intangibles tax: None

Estate tax: Applicable to taxable estates above $2 million.

Property tax: The basic tax rate for Moore County is 49.5 cents per $100 valuation, including 4 cents for paramedic services. Property is assessed at market value. Municipalities in the county levy taxes at varying rates, with Pinehurst being among the lowest at 31 cents per $100. A $260,000 home would be taxed at about $1,610 annually.

Homestead exemption: Homeowners age 65 and older or disabled, living in the home and earning $19,700 or less per year qualify for an exemption of $20,000 or 50% of the value of the home, whichever is greater.

Religion: The area is home to several dozen churches and synagogues representing most religions and denominations.

Education: Over 10,000 students take courses through the Division for Continuing Education at the two-year Sandhills Community College, located on a 250-acre campus near Pinehurst. Within a two-hour drive are four top-rated national universities: Duke University in Durham, the University of North Carolina at Chapel Hill, North Carolina State in Raleigh and Wake Forest University in Winston-Salem.

Transportation: Pinehurst has a small, modern airport for private aviation. Many Pinehurst residents drive 90 minutes to

of the largest military complexes in the world, are located.

Many residents who travel frequently drive to the Raleigh-Durham airport or to Greensboro or Charlotte. But Moore County does have a first-rate regional hospital. Moore Regional Hospital serves 15 counties with state-of-the-art care. A cancer center offers comprehensive cancer care, and retirees say the presence of quality medical care was a chief factor in their decision to come here. "Good medical care and the weather were probably our two main criteria for choosing Pinehurst," says Bill Graning.

The prospective Pinehurst retiree will find plenty of choices in homes, lots and retirement communities. Many of the golf courses were developed as a way to generate sales for the real estate around the courses, and there are dozens of choices in golf communities. Real estate agents say as much as one-half of their buyer clients are people considering retirement in the area.

Real estate choices range from homes and lots on Pinehurst Resort's eight courses to upscale private developments such as the National Golf Club to mid-priced golf developments such as Talamore and Seven Lakes. In rural areas of the county, options include smaller single-family homes and mobile homes.

The Pinehurst area offers some "real bargains," according to George McManus, a broker who sells Pinewild Country Club and other properties. Pinewild has around 650 completed homes starting from around $330,000.

Golf is undeniably a big deal here. But if you're into horses and hounds, you'll also feel at home in the Sandhills. Each fall, owners from the North and Midwest bring their jumpers, hunters and dressage horses to the Pinehurst/Southern Pines area to take advantage of the mild winter climate and soft sand footing. Thanksgiving Day traditionally marks the opening day of the local hunt season, which culminates with hunter trials in March. The Pinehurst Harness Track, on the National Register of Historic Places, has been the winter home for standardbreds for more than 50 years.

Beyond horses and golf, there are other places of interest in the Pinehurst area. The Malcolm Blue Farm in Aberdeen is an example of the small farms of Scottish immigrants who settled the area in the 19th century. Weymouth Center in Southern Pines is the site of the North Carolina Literary Hall of Fame. Weymouth Woods Sandhills Nature Pre-

---

the Raleigh-Durham airport for jet service. Interstate 95, the East Coast's major north-south interstate, is about 45 minutes east of Pinehurst near Fayetteville. Amtrak provides passenger rail service with a station in Southern Pines.

Health: Moore Regional Hospital is a 400-bed, acute-care, not-for-profit facility serving a 15-county region. With a medical staff of 190 physicians, a professional staff of more than 3,700 and more than 750 volunteers, the hospital has a reputation for excellence in cardiology, cancer care and other specialties.

Housing options: The Pinehurst area offers a wide range of housing choices, from large luxury homes in the "old town" area of the Village of Pinehurst for $1 million or more to small houses or mobile homes for less than $75,000. Among area developments: **National Golf Club** in Southern Pines, (800) 471-4339, offers single-family homes from $489,000 and golf-course lots from $125,000. **Pinehurst Resort** has golf-course lots for $100,000-$490,000. **Pinewild Country Club of Pinehurst**, (800) 826-7624, has golf-course lots from around $70,000, including a $20,000 golf club membership fee. At **Whispering Winds at Whispering Pines**, homesites with views of the golf course and pond start at $70,000. At **Whispering Sands at Whispering Pines**, homesites with views of the golf course and pond start at $70,000, townhomes start from the $120,000s, and duplexes start in the mid-$200,000s. **Beacon Ridge at Seven Lakes West**, (800) 200-4653, surrounds Lake Auman and features homes from the low $200,000s to over $2 million. Homesites start at $30,000, including country club membership. **Foxfire** offers homes from the high $100,000s, and **Talamore Villas**, (910) 692-7207, has two-bedroom furnished condos from around $185,000. **Longleaf of Southern Pines**, (800) 522-9426, has townhomes from the low $200,000s and single-family homes with golf-course views from the $300,000s. The Pinehurst area also has several assisted-living communities, including **Belle Meade Resort Retirement**, (910) 246-1000; **Quail Haven Village**, (910) 295-2294; and **Oakdale Heights**, (910) 695-0011.

Visitor lodging: Accommodations range from historic inns to modern motels. The rambling 222-room, wood-frame Pinehurst Resort retains the charm of its early days as the Carolina Hotel. Rates are $182-$436, depending on season, including breakfast and dinner. High season is April-May and September-November, (800) 487-4653. The Holly Inn, also in the Village of Pinehurst and affiliated with the Pinehurst Resort, is smaller, with 77 rooms and eight suites, but even more charming, with rates of $155-$480, including breakfast and dinner, (800) 487-4653. Another small hotel, with 11 rooms, is the Magnolia Inn, also in the Village of Pinehurst. Packages including breakfast and dinner and green fees at selected courses are $280-$530, double occupancy, for two nights, (800) 526-5562. Among chain motels in the area are Hampton Inn, $69-$89, (910) 692-9266, and Springhill Suites by Marriott, $89-$94, (910) 695-0234. Many golf developments offer packages that include greens fees and short-term condo rentals from about $140 per night, double occupancy. For information: Pinehurst Area Realty, (910) 295-5011; Tin Cup Golf and Travel, (888) 465-3857; or First Tee Golf Packages, (800) 781-1165.

Information: Mooree County Chamber of Commerce Pinehurst Area Convention and Visitors Bureau, P.O. Box 2270, Southern Pines, NC 28388, (800) 346-5362 or www.homeofgolf.com. It concentrates mostly on golf information for visitors but can provide limited retirement information. Sandhills Online (www.sandhills.org) has information about the area and links to local businesses.

serve is a 898-acre wildlife reserve with hiking trails and a pond in Southern Pines.

About 35 miles northwest of Pinehurst is Seagrove, renowned for its pottery. In Colonial times, potters from England were attracted to this area because of its deposits of fine potting clay. Now, nearly 100 pottery studios are scattered along U.S. Highway 220, and the North Carolina Pottery Center has exhibits of pottery from around the state.

Asheboro, 50 miles northwest of Pinehurst, is home to the North Carolina Zoo. This 1,500-acre zoological park has 1,600 animals and 60,000 exotic plants. Pine-hurst is about two hours from Myrtle Beach and the Wilmington area, the closest beaches. Real estate agents say they lose some prospects who want to live on the coast but gain others seeking to avoid the threat of hurricanes. The North Carolina coast has been hit hard by hurricanes in recent years, and residents have had to evacuate several times.

At an elevation of around 500 feet, Pinehurst has some low rolling hills, but the nearest mountains are three to four hours away in the western part of the state. Normally Pinehurst gets little snow, and it usually disappears by the next day, residents say.

But the Millers looked at a number of areas before selecting Pinehurst, including several places in Arizona, Southern California, Florida and coastal South Carolina. "They were all too crowded, too hot, too flat, too expensive or too something," says Jim, 63, who was an engineer with Boeing before he retired.

And that brings up one of the things that Jim says he especially likes about Pinehurst. He says residents are accepted for what they are now, rather than what they did before retirement. Jim, a 13-handicap golfer, and other retirees say it's rare for anyone even to ask what they did before they retired. ●

Portsmouth, New Hampshire

Residents enjoy a low-key lifestyle in this beautiful 17th-century town on New Hampshire's seacoast

By Mary Lu Abbott

Spring comes late in Portsmouth, but it's ever so sweet after the long winters in New Hampshire. Lilacs perfume the air, flowering Japanese crab apple trees are laden with white blossoms and tulip gardens come in more colors than a new box of crayons.

It's time to get outdoors and celebrate. Classrooms of children scatter across the green, exploring four centuries of buildings that trace the port's heritage at the outdoor living history museum, Strawbery Banke, site of the original settlement in 1623. Joggers skirt the adjacent Prescott Park gardens along the Piscataqua River, where cargo ships make their way to the docks. At Market Square, around the 1854 North Church with its landmark white spire, residents and students from the nearby University of New Hampshire take time to drink coffee and welcome the warm rays.

Less than 20 years shy of turning 400 years old, Portsmouth has a nice patina about it, which has contributed to its ranking as one of the country's best places to live in recent years. Literally, it's a small town — the population is about 21,000 and the newspaper runs the police log, listing all activity, from arrests down to reports of missing cats. Yet it evokes the feeling of a cosmopolitan city, vibrant but manageable. One visit here can hook you — or at least it did for some retirees seeking a new home.

Jeff and Margaret Caro had spent a year looking around New England for a retirement destination. Portsmouth hadn't crossed their minds. On the way back to their Long Island home after taking their son to college, Margaret noticed Portsmouth off Interstate 95 as they crossed the Piscataqua River from Maine into New Hampshire. On a whim she suggested they stop.

"We drove into downtown and when we got on Congress Street, which is in the heart of town, Margaret turned to me and said, 'This is where I want to live,'" recalls Jeff, 61. "It was so beautiful, all the old buildings," says Margaret, 49.

Some structures date to the early 1700s, though more are from the early 1800s, when after several disastrous fires, the city required brick construction. Many early mansions were lost, but a 1716 one survives. The commercial center of town for centuries, Market Square now has wide brick sidewalks that help make it a gathering place for friends to stop and chat.

On one side of the square facing the church is Bankers Row, and on another side, the Athenaeum, an elegant 1805 building that houses one of the country's oldest private libraries. Some side streets are as narrow as an alley, and within a few blocks is the port. There are no skyscrapers. "The ambiance struck her immediately," Jeff says.

In the early 1990s, Jeff and Margaret decided they had "had enough" of their high-pressure executive positions with major companies. Only the two of them, and a dog, were left at home. Though they had children in college, they felt they no longer needed as much income or as large a home. They wanted to downsize for retirement, buy a small business, run it together and have time to enjoy life. Jeff was born in Boston and Margaret likes history so they had focused on New England locations.

They returned to give Portsmouth in-depth consideration and found its attributes hard to beat. They moved here in 1992, purchasing a home and a small business that made all types of indoor and outdoor signs.

"Here you've got the ocean. You're 45 minutes from the White Mountains, 45 minutes or so from Boston and Portland (ME)," Margaret says. "You've got four seasons — and four seasons of outdoor events."

Besides liking the central location, Jeff says, "It had an ambiance we absolutely loved, a relatively small-town feeling. It's a very artistic community in the sense that it has a lot to offer in theater, the outdoors, parks, and it has the history. It had a working town feeling, which we loved," says Jeff, noting the port at the foot of downtown is active with cargo ships, tankers, tugboats and all types of vessels coming and going. "You say, 'Wow, this town is alive and it works, and there are people doing things. It's real.'"

"It's not an artificially constructed town," Margaret says. Though it does draw summer visitors who enjoy New Hampshire's 18 miles of coastline that run southward from the city, it's not really a tourist town.

"People actually work and live in the old buildings (downtown), and we loved that ambiance, and we liked the openness of the people. They're very friendly and outgoing, which sort of surprised me. We were expecting crusty New Englanders, and that was not the case at all," Jeff says. "It was welcoming, it was comfortable, it was open, it was beautiful."

Founded in 1623 as Strawbery Banke and renamed Portsmouth in the mid-1600s, it was settled mainly by commercial venturers who soon were building ships and setting up wharves and warehouses to handle goods going to and from the fledgling band of Colonies. A naval shipyard opened in 1800 and remains active today, repairing nuclear submarines. Portsmouth always has been a center of world trade and thereby a melting pot of cultures, leading to its motto, "City of the Open Door."

The town was a rather serendipitous find for John and Nancy Grossman. They lived in Redondo Beach in Southern California, where he was an executive with a publishing firm and she was an artist and writer. When John commented that it might be time to leave his company, Nancy pounced on the idea.

"I was ready," she says. "Then we faced the question, 'If you could move anywhere, where would you want to go?' First we started with a map and x-ed out whole sections of the country that we knew we didn't want to live in, and that left basically the Northeast coast." She was from Connecticut and New York City and he was from Cincinnati, so

moving back East was getting them closer to their roots.

They looked at where their children were living, and one was in Nashua, NH, southwest of Portsmouth on the Massachusetts border. About the same time, after a high school reunion, Nancy renewed a friendship with a classmate who was living in Portsmouth and raved

Portsmouth, NH

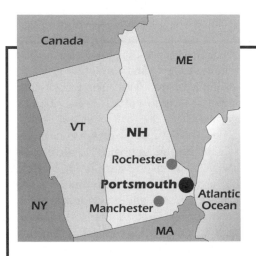

Population: About 21,000
Location: In New Hampshire's Seacoast Region at the mouth of the Piscataqua River, which flows into the Atlantic Ocean. Across the river is Maine, with Kittery facing Portsmouth. It's on I-95, about halfway between Boston, 55 miles south, and Portland, 50 miles north.

Climate High Low
January 34 15
July 83 59

Average relative humidity: 56%
Rain: 50 inches
Snow: 71 inches
Cost of living: Above average
Average housing cost: $376,798 for single-family homes, $304,949 for condos in Portsmouth. In the area, single-family homes average $425,000. Housing in the historic district or on the waterfront generally is higher.
Sales tax: None
State income tax: State taxes interest and dividends only, at a rate of 5%, with a number of investments excluded. Tax applies to those with more than $2,400 ($4,800 for couples) in taxable interest and dividends.
Income tax exemptions: Those age 65 and older get a $1,200 exemption from the interest-dividends tax.
Estate tax: None
Inheritance tax: None

Property tax: In Portsmouth, $15.72 per $1,000 in valuation, with homes assessed at about 85% to 90% of market value in a citywide revaluation in 2006. Property tax on a $376,798 home would be about $5,331.
Homestead exemption: There's a city exemption of $125,000 to $225,000 off assessed value, varied by age, for those 65 or older with incomes of $30,000 or less if single, $37,000 or less for couples, and assets of less than $100,000 (excluding home). The homeowner must be a New Hampshire resident for at least five years to receive the exemption. There are also city exemptions for veterans, the blind and disabled. Statewide, there's a low- and moderate-income homeowner's property tax relief for those with income of $20,000 or less ($40,000 for couples).
Religion: Within Portsmouth and the surrounding towns are places of worship for most religions and denominations.
Education: The city has Granite State College, with classes for students of all ages, plus six other colleges. The University of New Hampshire is located at Durham, only 12 miles inland, and many students come into Portsmouth.
Transportation: Trolleys and buses serve the city and surrounding towns. There's limited air service from Portsmouth International Airport. The nearest major airport is at Manchester, NH, 35 miles west, or Boston, about an hour's drive south, or Portland, ME, slightly less than an hour north.
Health: The Portsmouth Regional Hospital is a full-service 144-bed facility with more than 200 physicians and a Heart and Lung Center with the latest in cardiac care.
Housing options: There are few planned communities other than some

around golf courses. You will find subdivisions and neighborhoods, some with such amenities as a pool and tennis courts. New construction around Portsmouth starts in the high $300,000s, though you will find garden-style condos from the $160,000s, says Ann Cummings of RE/MAX Coast to Coast Properties in Portsmouth, (888) 349-5678. Houses on or near the water or with views will be quite expensive, and historic housing is limited. She says small homes built in the 1940s-1960s can be found from the high $200,000s, and the Elwyn Park area has ranch homes from the 1960s-1970s from the high $200,000s, though updating likely would be required on the low-priced ones. Going a few miles inland to Dover or Exeter will net a savings on price. **Sterling Hill at Exeter**, (603) 778-1800, an active-adult community southwest of Portsmouth, offers 128 maintenance-free, shingle-style condos. There's a clubhouse, picnic areas and walking trails; prices start at $300,900.

Visitor lodging: About 10 minutes from downtown, Wren's Nest Village Inn is a family-owned motel with rooms, cottages and Jacuzzi suites, $59-$179, (888) 755-9013 or www.wrensnestinn.com. In the historic downtown waterfront district, Sheraton Harborside Portsmouth has 200 rooms starting at $99 off-season, (603) 431-2300 or www.sheratonportsmouth. com. There are several B&Bs in historic homes. The chamber of commerce lists lodgings in its visitor's guide.

Information: Greater Portsmouth Chamber of Commerce, 500 Market St., P.O. Box 239, Portsmouth, NH 03802, (603) 436-3988 or www.portsmouthchamber.org. Also, City of Portsmouth, City Hall, 1 Junkins Ave., Portsmouth, NH 03801, (603) 431-2000 or www.cityofportsmouth.com.

about it. So they came to see Portsmouth.

"I woke up early Sunday morning and walked downtown, and I came back and said, 'Nancy, this is where I want to live,'" says John, 71. Nancy, 57, already was sold on the town.

"Portsmouth was beautiful, walkable and historic and had all the elements of a Northeast community, and we subsequently found out, without the major drawback that most Northeast communities have — that you have to live there three to four generations before they accept you. Portsmouth had had an Air Force base here so they were used to people coming and going, and they were very accepting of newcomers," John says. Nancy says she finds that inland towns aren't as open.

They wanted to be near the coast, so they looked at towns along the shore from Newburyport, MA, into Maine. They had seen Portsmouth in fall, when the entire region becomes a palette for artists, but Nancy returned in February, drove hundreds of miles "getting the lay of the land, and I became convinced this was where we wanted to be," she recalls.

In scanning the real estate situation, she saw a sign on a "gigantic place" for $99,900 and thought that if such large homes were that inexpensive, they would have to find an investment for the proceeds expected on their California home. So she suggested to John that they look for a home to start a bed-and-breakfast business, and he was game. It was only when they got a real estate agent and started looking that they learned the $99,900 price tag was for a condo inside the "gigantic place." By then, though, they were excited about owning a B&B. They bought Governor's House, which had been the home of a governor, and started an innkeeping business in 1992.

"It's not a pretentious kind of place. Nobody dresses (up). People accept you for who you are, not what you wear, what you drive," Nancy says of the 50-and-better segment of the population. "People are more practical. If it's a messy winter night, they're going to wear their galoshes and look ridiculous, and they don't care."

Unlike the Caros and Grossmans, Marsha and Gerry Sieve knew Portsmouth.

A son-in-law was from New Hampshire, and he and their daughter lived in Portsmouth. "Every time we visited, we'd say, 'Oh, we could live back here. This is wonderful.' We could hear the foghorns if it was bad weather," says Marsha, 61.

Sailing and boating enthusiasts, the Sieves love the coast and the ocean. In Gerry's career with Eli Lilly and Co. pharmaceuticals, they had lived numerous places in the United States and Europe. In Massachusetts they had gotten interested in sailing. When they began to think of where to retire in the early 1990s, they were living in Lake Forest in the Chicago area.

They considered retiring to a vacation home they had in northern Michigan but decided it was rather isolated. They loved the amenities in the Chicago area, but being near family was important. They rejected the idea of moving to Texas, where one daughter lived, and Vermont, where a son lived. "We always had thought we ought to move over here," says Gerry, 63. "You have the arts available here. You don't have to go to Boston. The first year we got season tickets to the repertory theater, and we still go," Marsha says.

They looked along the New Hampshire coast up to Kennebunkport, ME, about 20 miles north. They were seeking a water view and a newer home so there wouldn't be much maintenance. In 1994, they found what they wanted in New Castle, on an island in the mouth of the river, a community of about 1,000 residents. It's less than a square mile, encompassing a large island and a couple of smaller islands, connected to Portsmouth by bridges. All residential and recreational, New Castle has an oceanside park, marina, yacht clubs and beaches. It's also home to a grand historic hotel, the 1874 Wentworth by the Sea, which was shuttered for years and fell into ruin but was rebuilt by Marriott into a hotel-spa.

"It's a gorgeous spot," Marsha says of their setting. "We have so much beautiful wildlife. We see heron and egret. We can look across the water and see the tankers going in and out. It gives you the chills. You see so much happening — it's an exciting spot. We're three minutes from golf, and our boat is right across the street at the marina."

The little town dates to 1623 as a fishing village. "You can't buy a quart of milk anywhere but you can buy lobster from the lobsterman. That's kind of nice," Gerry says. Stores and other services are within a couple of miles, easily accessible across the bridges.

All three couples moved to Portsmouth at one of the best times for buying homes, the Caros and Grossmans in 1992 during an economic slump after the closing of Pease Air Force Base here and the Sieves in 1994 early in the recovery.

"Timing is everything. We were fortunate," says Jeff Caro, noting that they bought for less here because of the recession but quickly got full asking price for their Long Island home because of a high demand in their area. The Caros moved into a neighborhood called The Woodlands, developed in the early 1980s, with a pool and tennis courts. Their home was built in 1985 and was vacant for several years. "The house was a very good value. We bought at a price much lower than what it cost. It was a steal, frankly," Jeff says.

The Sieves moved into a neighborhood that started in the 1980s but didn't sell because of the recession, and houses sat empty for about seven years before a developer bought and redid them as the market was picking up.

The market is drastically different today, all three couples caution. Home prices have jumped — particularly for anything in the historic area or near the water — making availability of affordable housing limited.

"If we came in now, we'd have to pay almost twice for our house," Marsha Sieve says. Property in New Castle now starts in the $400,000s.

"For people with a limited income, it's going to be hard to come in and buy a home here now for a decent price. If you can buy the home, you're probably going to be fine (on costs of living), though property taxes are high," says Jeff Caro.

"The biggest barrier here is the cost of homes," says Margaret Caro. "I watch the papers. You can have a small ranch house at 1,200, 1,300 square feet and you're at $200,000 minimum, and then you have to fix it up. It's very hard to find a small home." She says many people moving into the area want homes of 3,000 square feet or larger.

The average housing price in Portsmouth is $376,798. When you take in outer areas, the prices rise to an average of $425,000. New construction starts in the high $200,000s.

The Grossmans sold their B&B in 1996 and truly retired (though Nancy still writes and paints some). They thought briefly of moving but decided they really enjoyed living in Portsmouth. They bought a small 1930s house a few blocks from the waterfront. It's close to the Strawbery Banke museum complex of historic buildings and overlooks a 1740 home of the man who served as secretary to George Washington, who frequently visited Portsmouth. "We love the fact that we can walk to almost every place we want to go. We got rid of one car," John says.

"We thought we were spending a lot then (on the B&B), but now it's worth more than twice what it was then. It's crazy," Nancy says.

With no state sales tax or state income tax — other than one on interest and dividends, with a number of investments excluded — property taxes are the major source of revenue. In the summer of 2002, Portsmouth hired a firm to do a citywide revaluation of property. Assessments had been based on 1994 valuations. In the revaluation, home values rose dramatically, sometimes more than doubling.

The Grossmans say their property was originally valued at about $200,000 and now is about $500,000, a 150 percent jump.

State law now requires property revaluations at least every five years — the last revaluation was completed in 2006.

It's easy to speak up and have your voice heard here, the residents say, in part because the state is small. But it plays a key role in national politics, the state with the first presidential primary each election.

"The (presidential) primary season here is fascinating," Nancy Grossman says. "You can see any of the candidates in rooms of 50 people or less. You can ask questions and you can listen to and see these people interacting with people in a way you just can't in any other highly populated state."

"You really get to know your legislators because there are so many of them," she says, noting the state House of Rep-

resentatives has 400 members, nearly as large as the U.S. House.

Marsha Sieve recalls the day George W. Bush came to New Castle to announce he was running for president. "We biked five minutes from our house to where he made his announcement, and all the media was there. We were in our biking gear, and we asked him questions," she says. "You don't get that close to candidates most other places," Gerry says.

The couples say you can be as involved as you want in community endeavors. Nancy Grossman is doing an artist-in-residency project with an elementary school, is involved with a historic home and is writing a book on the street names in Portsmouth. John is on a committee to plan a new library and is a member of the Portsmouth Advocates, who work to preserve the historic district. They volunteer as ushers at The Music Hall downtown, a restored 1870s theater saved from the wrecking ball. Among major events is the Telluride by the Sea film festival, which brings the best works from the acclaimed Telluride Film Festival in Colorado. Bill Pence, director of the local festival and co-director of the Colorado event, lives in Portsmouth.

Marsha Sieve helps her garden club do civic projects by tending community grounds and volunteers at Strawbery Banke. Gerry is a trustee of the New Castle Trust Fund, which handles donations and fund raising for the community, among other work.

The Caros sold their business in 2002, considering themselves officially retired, but both wanted to stay active and productive, contributing but not in high-pressure jobs. Jeff has become a counselor for SCORE, the Service Corps of Retired Executives, providing programs and individual assistance for small businesses. He also volunteers one day a week as a consumer specialist in the state attorney general's office. He and other volunteers help the legal staff investigate reports of consumer fraud. Margaret wanted to continue working some and has started a financial consulting business. They both do other volunteer work.

All of the couples say the cultural scene is a major attraction, with five performing arts theaters, a summer arts fes-

tival on the waterfront and art galleries. Some of them first thought they'd be going to Boston for cultural outings, but they've found the local scene so good that they don't need to seek entertainment elsewhere.

Gerry and Marsha Sieve say they've seen changes for the better in eight years. At first it was hard to find good Italian bread, proscuitto and other specialty items, which now are available. "This area has gotten significantly more cosmopolitan in the time we've been here," Marsha says. "When we first came here, if you didn't want fried clams, forget it. Now there are some really good restaurants," says Gerry, citing a French bistro they enjoy.

None of the couples minds the winters. The Sieves do escape for several months to their home in Florida. The Caros get outdoors in all seasons, enjoying snowshoeing in winter. The Grossmans are happy to have defined seasons after living in Southern California, where there's not much change in the weather. Nancy found the lack of seasons in California "disorienting," and John says it got boring.

"You had to figure out what month it was," Nancy says. "Here there's no question. But the reality is that here winter lasts six months. We've had winters that were nothing and winters that it never stops snowing, one storm after another." With short summers, there's an urgency to get out and make the most of pretty days.

The area isn't without problems. The Sieves say their electricity rates are high. "My electric bill when I'm not here is twice as much as my electric bill in Florida when I'm there and running my air conditioner, in the same size house," says Gerry, adding that their New Hampshire house is not all-electric and they have oil heat. He says they probably run the air conditioning less than two weeks in New Hampshire. He says his car registration fees run about $1,500.

"The thing that surprised me when we moved here was that everybody already knew what we were going to be doing," says Nancy Grossman. "I wasn't used to my next-door neighbor knowing what I was doing in California. People (here) read the newspaper and really keep up with what's going on. The anonymity in my life was gone. In small towns, you don't have that (anonymity)." But she says it's a very caring community and that neighbors look out for each other.

The Grossmans are concerned about the downtown, which now mainly has shops unique to Portsmouth, residents living above the stores and a mixture of people on the streets, from young professionals to college students, kids with spiked and colored hair, Harley and Honda bikers, families and retirees, everyone friendly. There's everything from high-end restaurants with nationally acclaimed chefs to pubs on the waterfront. But, the Grossmans say, major chains such as Starbucks and the Gap are coming in with the budget to pay higher rent and forcing up rates so that it's difficult for mom-and-pop stores and downtown residents to afford to stay there.

But most retirees give the area a thumbs-up, with a caveat — if you can afford it.

"We've really been happy. It's a beautiful piece of heaven. Of all the places we've lived, including three places in Europe, the seacoast of New Hampshire is right there at the top in beauty, and the quality of life is outstanding," says Marsha Sieve. Two more of the Sieves' children liked the area so well that they have moved here, so the Sieves now have three children and seven grandchildren within three miles of their house.

"Come and do a lot of footwork or rent and get to know the area before you decide where you want to live. We originally thought we'd want to be in the country right outside town somewhere," but after staying in town they realized they liked it better than the suburbs, says Nancy Grossman.

The Caros think that active people who enjoy the arts and outdoors, from boating to mountain biking and hiking to skiing, would be happy here. "If you have preconceived prejudices, throw them away. They don't belong here. This is an open community, and I'm better because of that," Jeff says.

"There's no place we'd prefer to be," Margaret says. ●

Port Townsend, Washington

A sense of history lingers in this 19th-century seaport
on Washington's Olympic Peninsula

By Stanton H. Patty

Port Townsend always has been a dreamscape. Back in the 1890s, the picturesque seaport in the northwestern corner of Washington state boasted that it was on the way to becoming the "New York of the West." That was when city fathers were certain that a railroad northward from the Columbia River would bypass Seattle and roll into Port Townsend. It never happened.

But later, as big-city residents began searching out quiet zones for their retirement years, dreams did come true in old Port Townsend. "We live in paradise," says Helen Cleveland, a Port Townsend resident since 1995. "But, shhh, we don't want everyone to know what a wonderful place this is."

Helen and her husband, Robert, moved to Port Townsend from Minneapolis by way of adventurous working years in Australia, Singapore and Manhattan. Robert, 64, retired from a career in merchant banking and sales. English-born Helen, 60, was a librarian and office manager. Now they have a 2,300-square-foot home near Port Townsend's airport, with a splendid garden of rhododendrons and azaleas — and what Helen describes as a "knock-dead" view of 10,778-foot-high Mount Baker across Puget Sound in Washington's Cascade Range.

Another happily retired couple in Port Townsend is Richard and Anne Schneider, who built a vacation home in Port Townsend in 1993. For the next three years Dick Schneider split his

Population: 8,430 in the city, 26,700 in Jefferson County.

Location: On Puget Sound in the northeastern corner of Washington state's Olympic Peninsula, about 52 miles by highway and ferry north and west of Seattle. There are views of the Cascade Range to the east and the Olympic Mountains to the west. Elevation in the Port Townsend area ranges from sea level to 350 feet.

Climate:

	High	Low
January	44	35
July	71	51

Weather is mild because the city is sheltered by the "rain shadow" of the Olympic Mountains.

Average relative humidity: 60%

Rain: 16 inches

Snow: Rare

Cost of living: Generally average, but food prices tend to be higher than in Seattle because of transportation costs.

Average housing cost: $277,000 in Port Townsend, $287,950 in Jefferson County.

Sales tax: 8.2%

Sales tax exemptions: Groceries and medical prescriptions.

State income tax: None

Intangibles tax: None

Estate tax: Applicable to taxable estates above $2 million.

Property tax: The city tax rate is $10.8137 per $1,000 of assessed valuation. The tax on a $277,000 home in the city is about $2,995.

Homestead exemption: Homeowners age 61 or older, with a gross household income of $35,000 or less, are eligible for certain property tax exemptions.

Religion: Several denominations are represented, with at least 30 places of worship in the Port Townsend/Olympic Peninsula region.

Education: Port Townsend has a branch of Peninsula College, which has its headquarters in nearby Port Angeles. Washington State University has a branch campus in Port Hadlock, about six miles southeast of Port Townsend. Both offer programs for older adults.

Transportation: Jefferson County International Airport is served by air-taxi operators with charter flights to Seattle, Washington's San Juan Islands, Vancouver and Victoria in neighboring British Columbia and other points. There is no scheduled air service to or from Port Townsend. Jefferson County Transit is an integrated system serving Jefferson, Clallam and Kitsap counties for transportation around the Olympic Peninsula. Within Port Townsend, there is free shuttle service between the port area and the city's historic districts. Washington State Ferries operates between Port Townsend and Keystone on Whidbey Island, with crossings taking about 35 minutes each way. The most direct way to reach Port Townsend from Seattle is to ride the Bainbridge Island ferry (Washington State Ferries) from downtown Seattle to Bainbridge Island, then take State Route 305 northwest about 13 miles, past Poulsbo, to State Route 3 and follow signs for seven miles to the Hood Canal Bridge. Cross the bridge and turn left. About one-half mile later, there is a sign pointing toward Port Townsend. About five miles after that, turn right on State Route 19. Continue about 22 miles to the town of Chimacum and to a four-way stop on State Route 19. Route 19 joins State

time between Port Townsend and his investment-business office in Southern California.

"Then one day I had a great revelation," Dick recalls. "I asked myself, 'Why am I leaving this great place?' Right then, I decided to retire, and here we are."

The Schneiders have a waterfront home on two acres of property — plus a 48-foot boat for cruising through British Columbia and other destinations. They didn't wait for their Social Security years to retire — Dick is 59, and Anne is 58 — and they thoroughly researched their options. "We spent 10 years looking for a retirement place," Dick says. "This is it."

Another couple who took special care in choosing a retirement community was Bobby and Rose Morrison, who both were working in the California prison system when they began methodical retirement planning. That was in 1987, and they already had set 1996 as their retirement date.

Bobby, 62, was based in Sacramento, in the central office of the California Department of Corrections, implementing wheelchair access and other such facilities for disabled inmates. Rose, 54, was a nurse consultant, helping to oversee medical care for a dozen prisons.

"We had a target," says Rose. "We're planners. First, we made individual lists of key things we wanted in a retirement place. Then we merged our lists and prioritized."

Among their prime factors: a close-to-nature saltwater setting, adequate medical facilities, a quality library system, strong cultural assets and proximity to a major city for shopping and the arts. Port Townsend, population 8,430, met all the requirements for the Morrisons and many of their retired neighbors.

The retirees also are aware that they reside in one of the Pacific Northwest's history-rich communities. Port Townsend was founded in 1851, six months before settlers reached nearby Seattle. Farming, logging and seafaring were the first industries.

Because of its commanding site at the entrance to Puget Sound, the U.S. government soon designated Port Townsend as headquarters of a busy customs district. The stampede to the Klondike gold fields was under way. A steady procession of vessels steaming to and from Alaska — through the waters of neighboring Canada — were required to check in with customs inspectors at Port Townsend. There also was a growing trade between Puget Sound and Asia.

Saloons, brothels and assorted other nefarious enterprises crowded Water Street, the main drag. Port Townsend was a brawling port with a reputation almost as wicked as that of San Francisco's Barbary Coast. Proper families built fine Victorian homes on a bluff above the harbor, and stairways linking the bluff with downtown were declared "off limits" to the soiled doves of Water Street.

Just as the 19th century was ebbing, Port Townsend had high hopes of con-

Port Townsend, WA

Route 20 about seven miles south of Port Townsend. Follow Route 20 into Port Townsend. The trip normally takes one and a half to two hours.

Health: Jefferson Healthcare, with 42 beds, is Port Townsend's only hospital. Air-ambulance service to medical centers in Seattle is available through Jefferson Healthcare. At last count, the Port Townsend area had 32 physicians and 15 dentists. Kah Tai Care Center in Port Townsend is a nursing home with 94 beds. Victoria House, (360) 379-8223, close to downtown Port Townsend, is an assisted-living facility with 39 apartments for residents needing various levels of care. Studio apartments at Victoria House rent for $2,580 to $5,460 a month; one-bedroom apartments range from $2,940 to $5,820. Other assisted-living facilities are situated in the town of Sequim ("skwim"), a major center for retirees, about 28 miles west of Port Townsend.

Housing options: Popular with Port Townsend retirees are the Kala Point and Cape George neighborhoods. **Kala Point**, about four miles south of the city center, near the airport, has a mix of single-family dwellings, townhouses and time-share and for-sale condominiums. Amenities include beach access, walking trails, tennis courts and boat launches. Prices range from $359,000 for a two-bedroom house to $1 million for a waterfront home with generous acreage. Three-bedroom condominiums are priced at in the $300,000s. **Cape George**, on Discovery Bay some eight miles west of Port Townsend, features beach access, a marina, swimming pool, community club, a workshop for hobbyists and views of the Olympic Mountains. Cape George is divided into three zones — first is The Colony, a residential area with single-family homes priced from about $300,000 to over $1 million. A second zone, The Village, has less expensive properties, ranging from the $200,000s to $375,000. Some modular and mobile homes are permitted in The Village. The third zone, The Highlands, is in forested property behind The Colony and The Village. Home prices in that zone range from about $195,000 to $380,000.

Visitor lodging: Accommodations include hotels, motels and bed-and-breakfast inns. Options include the 48-room Port Townsend Inn downtown, with rates from $54 to $128 a night, double occupancy, (800) 216-4985. Bishop Victorian Hotel has 16 suites downtown, with rates from $119 to $200, (800) 824-4738. Blue Gull Inn, a six-room B&B in Port Townsend's historic district, has rates from $95 to $140 year-round, (888) 700-0205.

Information: Port Townsend Chamber of Commerce and Visitor Information Center, 2437 E. Sims Way, Port Townsend, WA 98368, (360) 385-7869 or (360) 385-2722. On the Internet, visit www.ptguide.com.

necting to a major railroad out of Portland, OR. Speculators framed Water Street with showy buildings built of brick. Promoters laid 25 miles or so of railroad track toward Portland. Property values soared, and boosters dubbed Port Townsend "the inevitable New York."

But the dream crashed in 1904 when civic leaders were handed a telegram with the news that the Union Pacific Railroad had decided to go to Seattle instead. Downtown construction projects halted so suddenly that carpentry tools were found years later in the upper stories of unfinished business buildings. Perhaps half of the town's 7,000 or so citizens departed over the next year.

Port Townsend survived — frozen in time as a museum of a town — until a few years ago when it was rediscovered by city dwellers. Now most of this treasure of a town on Washington's Olympic Peninsula is preserved as a national historic district. The sturdy brick buildings along Water Street are restaurants, galleries and offices. Many of the elegant Victorians on the virtuous bluff are bed-and-breakfast inns.

And retirees such as Bob and Helen Cleveland are happy to be a part of this contented community. "The only way they will ever get me out of Port Townsend is feet first," vows Helen.

The Clevelands and many of their friends are active in Centrum, a thriving, nonprofit center for the arts at adjacent Fort Worden State Park. Retirees volunteer as ushers, for office work and other chores. Centrum features workshops and festivals that range from jazz to classics, from writers' conferences to teacher training.

Maybe you remember seeing Fort Worden in the movies. The former military post was the setting for "An Officer and a Gentleman." But Port Townsend's transplants didn't need directions from Hollywood to find Port Townsend. "I call it serendipity," says Anne Schneider.

The Schneiders had considered several areas for retirement, including Arizona, New Mexico, Colorado and California. Then one day in 1990, while on vacation, they happened to drive through Port Townsend on the way to catch a ferry to nearby Whidbey Island.

"Suddenly, we realized Port Townsend was what we had been looking for," Dick Schneider remembers. "We stopped at a real estate office and asked them to show us some properties. Right after we returned home (to Dana Point, CA), I went to my office and called the Realtor in Port Townsend and arranged to buy a waterfront lot."

Among Port Townsend's assets, the Schneiders say, are fascinating people. "It's an eclectic mix of successful, well-traveled people who have chosen to be here — just great people," Dick says. Anne Schneider puts it this way: "There's a heart and soul to this town."

Jefferson Healthcare, Port Townsend's only hospital, offers excellent care, Dick says, and the stylish community is attracting talented young physicians. Also available, for critical-care patients, are air-ambulance helicopter flights to medical centers in Seattle. "But our hospital can handle a lot of heavy-duty stuff," Dick says.

Dick Schneider stays busy with boating and gardening and as a board member of the Port Townsend Marine Science Center. Anne Schneider is president of the Centrum board and serves with Working Images, an organization that provides appropriate clothing for women leaving the welfare rolls for the work force. Somehow the Schneiders still find time to travel and have plans to participate in a study cruise to the Antarctic.

Bob and Helen Cleveland are among Port Townsend's more adventurous retirees. In 1969, they went to Australia as migrants, at a time when Australia was seeking newcomers with strong skills. They stayed six years.

"We went without a position, but the odds were good for Americans," Bob recalls. Soon Bob was named an assistant to the chairman of a merchant bank in Sydney.

It was on the way to Australia that the Clevelands met a couple from Vancouver, British Columbia, who suggested they visit Port Townsend. "We did, and we liked it instantly," says Helen Cleveland. "This definitely is God's country."

Both volunteer at Centrum events. They hike and camp through the Olympic Peninsula, including outings in nearby 897,000-acre Olympic National Park. Bob is a fly-fishing enthusiast who finds productive catch-and-release waters in the area's streams and lakes.

Their travel schedule also is full. "We're just back from Nepal, India and Japan," Helen says. "Next will be Ireland."

Bobby and Rose Morrison hope to visit Europe, but they might have a difficult time tearing themselves away from Port Townsend for a few weeks. "There are two deer walking around here as I am talking to you," Bobby says. "It's a great sight — as long as they don't eat my azaleas."

The Morrisons have a three-bedroom house with a 10- by 40-foot outdoor deck that overlooks a serene half-acre of trees and shrubs. "We hear birds and know that there are four-footed types out there," Bobby says. "This is special."

The Morrisons consider their neighbors special, too. "The people here are very nice, very honest, very open and intelligent," Bobby says. "They are willing to accept ideas and to express opinions. I guess we are 'closet hippies.'"

There isn't much time for loafing on the Morrisons' schedule. Rose Morrison volunteers at the Port Townsend Visitor Center and at Centrum. The couple also tries to walk at least two miles a day, often with a dachshund named Mischief. "Sometimes, on gray days, we miss the sunshine," admits Bobby Morrison. "Then we toss another log on the fire and cuddle up and everything's OK."

Capt. George Vancouver, the English navigator, put Port Townsend on the map when he sailed by in 1792 aboard the HMS Discovery. Vancouver sighted what he described as "a very safe and capacious harbor." He named it Port Townshend for his friend, the marquis of Townshend. American settlers dropped the "h," and that's the way it stayed.

George Townshend, the marquis, never saw his namesake town. But his younger brother, Charles, certainly left his mark on America. It was Charles Townshend who was responsible for imposing the detestable tax on tea and other goods that resulted in the Boston Tea Party.

"There's a real sense of history here," says Bobby Morrison. "And it's just a darned nice place." ●

Poulsbo, Washington

This charming town in Washington is dubbed "Little Norway on a Fiord"

By Stanton H. Patty

Poulsbo, in the Puget Sound region of Washington state, is a retiree-friendly community of saltwater marinas and verdant parks tucked into a fiord not far from Seattle and the snow-crested Olympic Mountains. "Velkommen" (welcome), Poulsbo says to newcomers, with echoes of its proud Scandinavian heritage.

Dolph and Frances Jaeger heard the call. They have lived many places, but now their roots are spread in this one-time Norwegian-style fishing village. "The more we travel, it's a delight to come back home," Dolph says. "I'd like to think this was our last move."

The Jaegers traveled the world when Dolph was serving 24 years as a Navy officer. They resided in London, Hawaii, California, Boston and other duty stations. Later, Dolph became a real estate broker. In 2001 they moved 10 miles from a roomy, split-level house with a smashing view on Puget Sound's Bainbridge Island, to a manufactured home in Poulsbo.

It was time to downsize, they decided, and to get involved in a community they find both exciting and caring. "And as friendly as can be. We love it here," Frances says.

The Jaegers met on a blind date 54 years ago in Astoria, OR, a historic port city at the mouth of the Columbia River. They were married three and a half weeks later. "I came to Astoria to get a (Navy) ship and won a bride," Dolph says.

Another relocated couple, Dr. Roger J. Meyer and his partner, Sydney Costigan-Cotton, are busy writing and compiling historical books to benefit worthy causes such as the Bremerton Symphony and the Olympic College Scholarship Fund in the neighboring Kitsap County city of Bremerton. Their most recent publication is "Poulsbo Past Times," a look back at the life and times of Poulsbo and other Kitsap County communities. The Poulsbo-North Kitsap Rotary Club, North Kitsap Herald newspaper and several businesses sponsored the book.

Roger, 76, a noted pediatrician, still is a part-time clinical professor at his alma mater, the University of Washington in Seattle. Sydney, a journalism graduate from the same university, finds time to teach piano and to volunteer as a teacher and librarian at a nearby elementary school.

Why did they choose to settle in Poulsbo (population 7,273)? "It's a jewel of a setting with the mountains and the water," says Seattle-born Sydney. "Safe, enjoyable and beautiful, a wonderful place for families."

Roger, who describes Poulsbo as a "lovely, terrific little community," moved here from Chicago about 10 years ago. He had been dean of the School of Public Health and a professor of pediatrics at the University of Illinois. For Sydney, 74, moving from Seattle to Poulsbo was a sort of homecoming. Her grandmother, Lillian Costigan, was a Poulsbo pioneer who settled here in 1916. Sydney's son, Peter Harris, now a coastal surveyor in Australia, was reared in Poulsbo and sharpened his interest in oceans as a youngster at Poulsbo's top-rated Marine Science Center.

Peter recently discovered a giant submerged coral reef — larger than the famed Great Barrier Reef — off Australia's shores. He returned to Poulsbo to lecture about the find at the Marine Science Center.

For Pearce and Alberta Dressel, it took "a lot of looking" before they decided on Poulsbo for their retirement place about eight years ago. Pearce, 77, a former nursing-home administrator, and Alberta, formerly in the jewelry business, say Poulsbo's civic spirit was among the qualities that attracted them.

"There is a real sense of community here," Alberta says. "People just close ranks and get things done. And there is a nice mix of people, young and old." The Dressels moved from the Olympia area (Olympia is the state's capital) and chose a manufactured home with a view of the lofty Olympic Mountains to the west. Their unit is in Viking Park near Poulsbo's North Kitsap High School. All Viking Park residents are homeowners; no rentals are allowed.

Living in Poulsbo offers a slower tempo and lower housing costs than in busy Seattle, about 22 miles southeast by highway and ferry. But, retirees say, it's good to have the cultural attractions of Seattle only an hour or so across the briny. The Dressels aren't traveling much beyond Seattle these days. "It's so lovely here that there's no need to go running around," Alberta says.

William A. (Bill) Moore, 80, and his late wife, Marjorie, moved to Poulsbo in 1980. Bill, who had built what he describes as a "great big place" upon moving here, decided to stay in Poulsbo after his wife's passing in 1999 — and to welcome his daughter and son-in-law into his 5,000-square-foot, two-level home.

When Bill's daughter, Karla Therriault, asked if he would like them to move in with him, Bill knew he would love it. So, Karla's husband, Ted, an attorney, left a Seattle law firm and, with Karla, opened a property-management company in Poulsbo. Their office is the lower floor of the Moore home. Bill also has a son, William H. Moore, a successful farm-implement dealer in nearby Hansville.

Hansville, Poulsbo, Port Gamble, Kingston, Indianola, Keyport, Suquamish, Bremerton, Silverdale: They are unfamiliar names to outsiders, but known around the Puget Sound area as good-neighbor communities, clustered mostly in the north end of Kitsap County. Into this charmed fiordland more than 100 years ago came Ivar B. Moe and other Norwegian pioneers. The majestic mountains and sheltered waterways reminded them of their scenic Scandinavian homeland.

For many years, Norwegian was the only language spoken by the early settlers along Dogfish Bay, later renamed Liberty Bay, Poulsbo's picture-postcard waterfront. In 1886, Ivar Moe filed an application for a post office and pro- posed naming the town Paulsbo (Paul's Place, in Norwegian). But postal offi- cials misread Moe's handwriting and listed the new post office as Poulsbo. And so Poulsbo it is.

Hardy commercial fishermen sailed three-masted schooners from Puget Sound into Alaska's stormy Bering Sea to

Poulsbo, WA

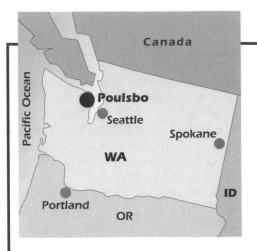

Population: 7,273 in the city; 260,500 in Kitsap County.

Location: Poulsbo is in the northern part of Washington state's Kitsap County. It is a popular destination for boaters and other travelers and is a gateway to the moun- tains and hiking trails of the Olympic Peninsula. Seattle is the largest neighbor city in the Puget Sound region. Getting to Seattle from Poulsbo requires a short drive and then a crossing aboard passenger- and-vehicle vessels of Washington State Ferries. Another important neighbor is Bremerton, a longtime Navy community about 20 miles south of Poulsbo.

Climate: High Low
January 45 34
July 75 53

Rain: Annual average is 30-35 inches.

Snow: Rare, occurring mostly in Decem- ber.

Average relative humidity: About 60%

Cost of living: Above average but about 20% lower than in Seattle for housing and utilities.

Average housing cost: $325,000, based on recent home sales.

Sales tax: 8.6%

Sales tax exemptions: Groceries and medical prescriptions.

State income tax: None

Estate tax: Applicable to taxable estates above $2 million. For more information, call the Washington State Department of Revenue, Estate Tax Section, (360) 570- 3265.

Property tax: Within the city of Poulsbo, the tax rate is about $13 per $1,000 of

assessed valuation. Taxes are assessed on 100% of valuation, although the assessed value typically runs a year or so behind the actual market value. With exemptions noted below, the tax on a $325,000 home would be about $1,690 on incomes up to $25,000; $3,315 on incomes up to $30,000. Without exemp- tion, the tax would be about $4,225.

Homestead exemption: Persons 61 or older or disabled receive an exemption on owner-occupied homes. Those with incomes up to $25,000 are exempt from voter-approved taxes and exempt from regular taxes on the first $60,000 or 60% of assessed value, whichever is greater. For incomes up to $30,000, exempt from voted levies and from regular taxes on the first $50,000 or 35% of assessed value, whichever is greater, up to a maximum of $70,000. For incomes up to $35,000, exempt from voted levies only. Assessed values are frozen for all the above classifi- cations beginning with the first year one qualifies.

Religion: More than a dozen churches serve several denominations.

Education: Olympic College, a two-year community college, with its main campus in Bremerton, opened a 20-acre branch campus in the Olhava section of Poulsbo in early 2004. Olympic also has a Puget Sound branch in Shelton, WA. Total enroll- ment for the three campuses is about 12,000. Additional information: (800) 259-6718 or (360) 394-2700 in Poulsbo.

Transportation: Getting to Poulsbo from Seattle begins with a ferry trip to Bain- bridge Island, then a short drive into Pouls- bo on State Highway 305. Ferry fare between Seattle and Bainbridge Island is $9.05 to $11.75 for a car with a senior driver, depending on season. Other senior passengers (age 65 or older) are charged $3.00. Regular adult fares: $10.60 to $13.30 for car and driver, depending on season, $6.10 for foot passengers. Addi- tional information: Washington State Fer- ries, (206) 464-6400 or www.wsdot.wa. gov/ferries. Public transportation in the

Poulsbo area is provided by Kitsap Transit, which covers Kitsap County. Basic fare is $1 for up to two hours of travel, 50 cents for those age 65 or older or disabled. Kit- sap Transit also offers door-to-door trans- portation for elderly and disabled persons in a program called ACCESS, which must be booked a day in advance. Additional information: Kitsap Transit, (800) 501-7433 or www.kitsaptransit.org.

Health care: The closest full-service hos- pital is Harrison Hospital in Bremerton, about 20 miles south of Poulsbo. Harri- son has an emergency room in a smaller facility in Silverdale, about 10 miles south of Poulsbo. There also are several clinics and assisted-living facilities in the area. The North Kitsap Senior Center, on Front Street in downtown Poulsbo, serves "chuckwagon" lunches Monday, Wednes- day and Friday for $2.50. The center also offers a schedule of games and craft ses- sions. The senior center is open to per- sons age 55 or older, (360) 779-5702. Kitsap County publishes a Senior Resources Directory that is available from the senior center or the Greater Poulsbo Chamber of Commerce. It covers topics ranging from home health care to legal assistance.

Housing options: Poulsbo offers a mix of housing that includes modest single- family homes, manufactured homes, con- dominiums and luxury homes with water- front property. Prices range from about $170,000 to more than $1 million.

Visitor lodging: Holiday Inn Express, $79 to $125 based on double-occupan- cy, depending on season, (800) 465- 4329 or (360) 697-4400. Poulsbo Inn and Suites, $99 double, (800) 597-5151 or (360) 779-3921. There also are several bed-and-breakfast establishments in the Poulsbo area.

Information: Greater Poulsbo Chamber of Commerce, P.O. Box 1063, Poulsbo, WA 98370, (360) 779-4999 or www poulsbochamber.com. City of Poulsbo, P.O. Box 98, Poulsbo, WA 98370, (360) 779-3901 or www.cityofpoulsbo.com.

harvest cod by hook and line, then delivered their catches to the Pacific Coast Codfish Co. here in Poulsbo for curing and drying. It was one of the largest seafood-processing plants in the Northwest.

Codfish translates into a dish called lutefisk on Poulsbo's festival days. Lutefisk — dried cod usually cured in, of all things, lye — is boiled and served piping hot with potatoes and other vegetables. Lutefisk lovers consider it a Norwegian delicacy; detractors call it a "national disgrace."

Willing locals and visitors enjoy lutefisk at Poulsbo's First Lutheran Church annual lutefisk dinner on the third Saturday of each October. The church, founded in 1888, crowns a bluff overlooking downtown Poulsbo and Liberty Bay. The Sons of Norway and their ladies also carry on a lutefisk dinner tradition each November in a lodge that dates to 1916.

No wonder Poulsbo still is known as Washington's "Little Norway." Dolph Jaeger describes lutefisk as "not all that bad, I kind of like it." He estimates that the First Lutheran Church must serve "more than a ton" of lutefisk at its annual get-together. "They have meatballs, too," Frances Jaeger notes. Pearce Dressel's take on lutefisk: "No, thank you."

Jim Lee Martin, former executive director of the Greater Poulsbo Chamber of Commerce since March of this year, is impressed by the spirit of volunteerism in Poulsbo. "It's really something — everyone works together," he says.

An example, Martin says, is Poulsbo's Raab Park, which includes an award-winning youth garden, a playground and an off-leash area for dogs. Retirees and children join in growing crops there, with generous donations of produce going to needy persons. The project also is designed to teach young persons gardening skills and the rewards of conservation efforts. Guest speakers for youngsters cover topics ranging from butterflies to bird feeders.

"Volunteers do many good things for the community," says Alberta Dressel. "All the service clubs — Rotary, Kiwanis, Lions, Soroptimists and others — are involved." Her husband, Pearce, is active in the 100-member Poulsbo North Kitsap Rotary Club and volunteers part time at the chamber of commerce office. "I've

never been so busy in my life, keeping up with all the things he's involved in," Alberta says.

Sydney Costigan-Cotton describes Poulsbo as a town where the residents "have a tremendous attitude about giving back to the community." It was in that spirit that Sydney and her partner, Dr. Roger Meyer, compiled a book last year to benefit the all-volunteer Bremerton Symphony. It was the 60th anniversary of the financially strapped orchestra. They titled the book, "Symphony Notes." It sold out, with all proceeds going to the symphony and a scholarship fund for musicians.

Sydney, a talented pianist, is the musician in the Meyer/Costigan-Cotton partnership. "I play the didjeridu (an ancient musical instrument of Australia's aboriginal people) and the harmonica — but not in public," Roger jokes. Their next book is a story about their two families, for their families.

Roger's single-level, three-bedroom home — with a view of the Olympic Mountains — is in Indianola, just northeast of Poulsbo. "This is a great place to live," Roger says. "But if you don't like the close-to-nature quiet life and deer eating your roses, well that could be a problem."

Bill Moore has no problem filling his time, either. Before retiring from a sales position in Seattle, he built his "great big place" here in Poulsbo, situating it on three acres of property. "The first three things you do when you get here is buy (1) a pickup truck, (2) a chain saw and (3) a tractor," he says. "You need all those with three acres."

Later, Bill added a riding mower to his list of essentials. "I'm busy all the time," he says. Bill commuted to Seattle by automobile and Washington state ferry for six years before retiring here at age 62. He positioned cars on both sides of the ferry route to smooth the commutes.

"Some of my friends thought I was foolish to retire so early," he recalls. "I fooled them. I'm still around." He still enjoys ferry travel on occasional trips to Seattle. "The ferry is great — it keeps you on schedule, and you get acquainted with a lot of nice people," he says. Many of those "nice people" are his neighbors and fellow Rotarians in Pouls-

bo. They include both civilian and military retirees (nearby Bremerton is a major Navy community), and Bill describes them as "interesting people who have had interesting lives."

Seattle beckons with an array of shops and visitor attractions. But, say Bill and his friends, there is little need to travel to Seattle just for shopping. There is a large shopping mall, the Kitsap Mall, in Silverdale, only about 10 highway miles from Poulsbo.

Seniors also find adequate health-care facilities on the Kitsap Peninsula. Harrison Hospital, a 300-bed, full-service hospital, is in Bremerton, about 20 miles south of Poulsbo. Harrison Hospital also has an emergency room at a smaller facility in nearby Silverdale. There also are several clinics in the area.

"We're in good health, fortunately, and we still like to travel," says Dolph Jaeger. One might think that Dolph and Frances have had enough of world travel after more than two decades of Navy service, but the couple recently completed a 1,000-mile trip along Europe's Danube River. They plan to spend Christmas on the Rhine River, and they are hoping to visit Ireland and South Africa. Their favorite places include the Norwegian coast and New Zealand.

Meanwhile, at home here in Poulsbo, both are busy with volunteer work. Dolph drives a bus for senior outings once a week. Along for the ride is Parade, Dolph's golden retriever. Parade was trained as a guide dog but changed careers, so to speak, when he was judged "too friendly" for guide service. Frances is active in the Sons of Norway Ladies Club and quilts at the Port Madison Lutheran Church, a small country church on neighboring Bainbridge Island.

Poulsbo, with its inviting marinas and Scandinavian character, has become a popular destination for boaters and other visitors. But its residents are determined to preserve the town's small-town charm. They take their cue from Norway's late King Olav V, who visited Poulsbo in 1975.

The king's parting remark, as quoted in "Poulsbo Past Times" by Dr. Roger Meyer and Sydney Costigan-Cotton: "I like your town. Keep it the way it is." ●

Prescott, Arizona

This cool retreat is set high in the pine-clad mountains of central Arizona

By Ron Butler

It doesn't take long to discover why people from back East and up North are settling in Prescott, and why well-heeled Silicon Valley residents are building second homes and retirement homes in the piney oasis of ponderosa that surrounds town like a shimmering green shawl.

You may have to give it a few days, but it soon will become obvious why this mile-high town of 38,930 people in central Arizona is growing so rapidly as a retirement destination, as is its next-door neighbor, Prescott Valley. At first glance, Prescott probably won't knock your socks off. There are too many boxy homes going up amid magnificent old Victorian houses, and too many weathered wooden structures that should be abandoned or torn down.

But list climate among the attractions. Midway between the state's lowest desert and its highest mountains, Prescott offers four distinct seasons. Many newcomers attracted to Arizona's laid-back lifestyle find the scorching desert summers too hot to handle, and Prescott is the perfect alternative.

That's what sold Bill and Lola Jolly, 75 and 70 respectively, who moved to Prescott in 1991 from Fullerton, CA, where Bill was a retail furniture executive and Lola worked as a real estate agent. They had been coming to Prescott for years to visit California friends who had settled there. "We were never here when the weather wasn't perfect," says Bill. "Even when it snows, the snow disappears in a couple of hours. We have snow chains for our car but have never had them out of the box."

The Jollys live in a three-bedroom home in a planned development in the Antelope Hills area on the Prescott-Chino Valley border, not far from the Prescott Airport (catering to small, private and light craft) and immediately adjacent to the Antelope Hills Golf Course, a 36-hole public course. Also in Prescott are two private golf courses, the Prescott Golf and Country Club and Quailwood Greens. An avid golfer, Bill's retirement present from his firm was a golf cart.

Thus, about eight miles from downtown Prescott, Bill and Lola can look through the large picture windows in their living room and see lush green fairways in one direction or track light aircraft gliding through dense blue sky in another. Scenes from "Planet of the Apes" were filmed in the rocky outcropping of nearby Granite Dells.

But they don't spend that much time at home. "The fine arts department at Yavapai Junior College offers marvelous entertainment," says Lola. "There are good museums, antique shops, a fine library and several good bookstores. I think we've eaten at every restaurant in town."

Lola and Bill both volunteer one or two days a week at the downtown visitors center. There also are special classes for adults at Yavapai College and an active community bridge club. Bill, a fighter pilot in Hawaii during World War II, adds the action at Bucky's Casino and seasonal horse racing to the entertainment mix. The casino, located on a hilltop in what formerly was a Sheraton Hotel, is operated by the Yavapai Prescott Indian tribe.

For many, Prescott's strong sense of history is a major selling point and the inspiration, perhaps, for its city slogan, "Everybody's hometown." The Palace Bar on historic Whiskey Row no longer has gambling tables and painted ladies, but it has lost little of its frontier flavor over the years, and the sound of spurs is as common as the jingle of pocket change.

Outside on its central pediment, the Palace Hotel wears the Great Seal of the Territory of Arizona. When President Lincoln named Arizona a territory in 1864, Prescott was declared its capital by order of the first territorial governor, former congressman John N. Goodwin. Arizona's seat of government moved to Tucson in 1867, back to Prescott 10 years later, and finally to Phoenix in 1889.

As frequently happened during the days of the early West, a time when towns were constructed almost entirely of wood, Prescott was devastated by fire. In its heyday, Whiskey Row had more than 20 saloons going full blast, 24 hours a day, filling the glasses of thirsty miners and cowboys. Three local breweries helped meet the demand. In 1900, a drunken miner knocked over a kerosene lamp in a boarding house and the resulting inferno destroyed five hotels, 25 saloons and more than 50 downtown businesses. When the flames came swooping in, undaunted patrons at the Palace lifted the massive bar, carried it out the door and across the street, and set it up on the courthouse lawn, where libations continued to flow.

Prescott also is where the rodeo was born. Cowboy competitions were common during the early days of the American West. By matching roping and riding skills, ranch against ranch, the hard-working cowboys let off steam and had themselves a ball doing what they did best. As part of its Independence Day celebration in 1888, Prescott sponsored a cowboy competition, the nation's first, making it a signature community event. The Prescott Frontier Days Rodeo has been a July Fourth weekend tradition ever since, now the oldest continuous celebration of leather and sweat in existence and one of the most popular.

Thousands of cowboys and cowboy types — tourists, vagrants, "buckle bunnies" (young women who follow the rodeo cowboys) and other assorted revelers — come pouring into town, filling the hotels and spilling over into the hills beyond. They sleep in pickup trucks, camp trailers and in bedrolls and sleeping bags just off the highway. The rules of the rodeo have been refined and standardized over the years, but little else has changed since the very first one was staged in Prescott. The dust and enthusiasm are still blinding.

More local history can be explored in 525 buildings that have been placed on the National Register of Historic Places. The town plaza, shaded by cottonwoods, is the star attraction. Its historic white granite Yavapai County Courthouse, built in 1916 in handsome Neoclassic Revival style, represents the justice and order that eventually came to the wild and bawdy West.

Among Prescott's legendary lawmen was George Ruffner, who was Arizona's oldest peacemaker when he died in 1933 at the age of 71. A local newspaper wrote of Ruffner, the first Arizonan elected to the Hall of Great Westerners at the Cowboy Hall of Fame: "He possesses nerves of steel, utmost calm in moments of danger, and his name has become a terror to the outlaws and toughs that infest the territory."

Prescott, AZ

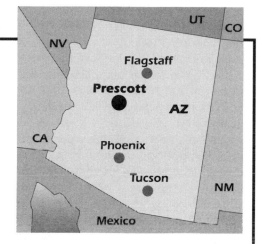

Population: 38,930 in Prescott, 190,628 in Yavapai County.

Location: Prescott is located in central Arizona amid the largest stand of ponderosa pine in the world. The community is 96 miles northwest of Phoenix and 90 miles southwest of Flagstaff.

Climate:

	High	Low
January	50	22
July	89	57

Rain: 19 inches

Snow: 21 inches

Cost of living: Above average

Average home price: $330,000 in Prescott.

Sales tax: 8.35%

Sales tax exemptions: Groceries and prescription drugs

State income tax: For married couples filing jointly, graduated from 2.87% of taxable income up to $20,000 to 5.04% minus $2,276 on amounts over $300,000. For single filers, graduated from 2.87% of taxable income up to $10,000 to 5.04% minus $1,138 on amounts over $150,000.

Income tax exemptions: Social Security benefits and up to $2,500 on federal, Arizona state and local government pensions are exempt.

Estate tax: None.

Inheritance tax: None

Property tax: Residential property is assessed at 10% of market value, with property taxes ranging from 7.76% to 10.32% of assessed value, depending on location. Taxes on a $330,000 home, without exemption, would range from about $2,560 to $3,406.

Homestead exemption: Those who are disabled or whose spouse died while residing in Arizona can receive an exemption of $3,000 off assessed value. To qualify, the full cash value of one's home must be less than $203,860.

Religion: Prescott has dozens of houses of worship, representing virtually every denomination.

Education: Yavapai Community College is a public two-year institution offering both university transfer credits and occupation education. Prescott College is a four-year liberal arts college. Embry-Riddle Aeronautical is a four-year university offering bachelor degrees in the fields of aviation and engineering.

Transportation: Interstate 17 is 36 miles east of Prescott via Highway 69 or 169. Prescott is 52 miles south of Interstate 40 via U.S. Highway 89. Local bus service, Greyhound connections and shuttle to Sky Harbor International Airport in Phoenix are available.

Health: Yavapai Regional Medical Center has 136 beds and is fully accredited. Northern Arizona Veterans Administration Health Care System offers 25 beds, plus 120 beds for domiciliary care and a 90-bed nursing home care unit and long-term care facilities. Other area facilities include Las Fuentes Care Center, Peppertree Square of Prescott, Prescott Samaritan Village, Meadowpark Care Center, Mountain View Manor, Center for Adult Day Care, Mi Casa Care Home Group and Margaret T. Morris Center (for Alzheimer's care).

Housing options: Medium-priced and luxury condominiums, townhouses, patio homes and ranch-style homes, plus other styles of one- and two-story single-family homes, are all available, as are mobile homes. Among new-home developments is **Pinon Oaks**, (877) 829-4150, a development planned for 640 homes. A new section of 59 lots opened in 2005, with floor plans ranging from 1,800 to 4,400 square feet in size with home-and-lot packages starting in the high $300,00s. At the **Viewpoint at Prescott Valley**, (928) 775-2000, homes by eight different builders range in size from 1,400 to 2,700 square feet and start in the low to mid-$200,000s.

Visitor lodging: SpringHill Suites by Marriott, within walking distance of the Prescott plaza, is conveniently located in a retail center near restaurants, stores and a supermarket, (888) 287-9400 or (928) 776-0998. Rates for double occupancy are $129 seven days a week, including buffet breakfast, free local calls, a pool and workout facilities. The renowned Hassayampa Inn, (800) 322-1927 or (928) 778-9434, opened its 200 guest rooms in 1927 right off the plaza. Meticulously maintained, it offers the romance and luxury of a bygone era, highlighted by its gourmet Peacock Room for elegant dining. Rates for standard double occupancy range from $99 to $159, depending on season, including a full breakfast in the Peacock Room. Other hotels include the Antelope Hills Inn, Hampton Inn, Prescott Resort and Conference Center and Super 8. In total, Prescott offers 1,300 rooms in 32 hotels and motels and 19 bed-and-breakfast inns.

Information: Prescott Chamber of Commerce, 101 S. Cortez, P.O. Box 1147, Prescott, AZ 86302-1147, (928) 778-2193 or www.prescott.org. Prescott Area Coalition for Tourism, (800) 266-7534 or www.visit-prescott.com.

Bucky O'Neill was another Prescott hero who wore a badge. Sheriff, mayor and one-time newspaperman, he helped organize the famous Rough Riders during the Spanish-American War, rode alongside Teddy Roosevelt and died in combat on a Cuban hillside. An equestrian statue, erected on the square by the State of Arizona in 1907, honors O'Neill. These days the statue overlooks square dances and band concerts held on warm summer evenings.

No one views Prescott with more of a sense of communal purpose and pride than Don and Annette Schiller, both 62, who moved from Irving, TX. Originally from California, Don, whose background includes cable television management and production as well as alarms and security systems, bought property in Prescott in 1989 and eventually built a two-story, three-bedroom home, all gables and picture windows — "I wanted to bring the outside inside" — in what's now known as the Timber Ridge development.

Since arriving in Prescott, Don has immersed himself in community activities — Rotary Club and the chamber of commerce as well as youth group activities such as the Youth Exchange, Chamber of Commerce Youth Division, Boy Scouts and Big Brothers/Big Sisters. For the past five years he has appeared as Santa Claus, raising money for the Prescott Big Brothers organization. During our interview, his cell phone rang incessantly.

Don's wife, Annette, is a retired schoolteacher who now enjoys teaching nature studies to young children at the Highlands Center for Natural History. She is a past president of the American Association of University Women. Don and Annette both like to travel in Scotland and the Philippines, and they frequently hike in the woods near their home. Their son, Brad, is a lighting designer and programmer in Texas. He and his wife, Margaret, have a 3-year-old son, Matthew.

The arrival of Ginny, 48, and John Van Vliet, 57, was more circuitous. They came by Winnebago after traveling around the country for two years, from Mississippi to Southern California, before deciding to settle in Prescott. "It met our budget, wants and needs," says Ginny, who previously worked as a sign language interpreter for General Motors. Husband John was human resources director for the Miller Brewing Co. and worked briefly as a Harley Davidson representative in Milwaukee. Both now own Harleys and frequently ride around the countryside or "90 miles down the hill to Phoenix." The growing number of Hell's Angels bikers in town gives more bark than bite, says Ginny.

The Van Vliets live in a single-family subdivision in the Yavapai Hills east of Prescott. Their three-bedroom home has huge picture windows and decks. The Flying U Court, where they live, is adjacent to the Bar Circle A ranch, which belonged to early cowboy film star Tom Mix before he was killed in a car accident in Florence, AZ.

John likes to golf, and Ginny belongs to a ladies luncheon group. Since settling in Prescott three and a half years ago, they've been to glitzy Las Vegas seven times. The casinos and restaurants in Las Vegas, 268 miles away, counter limited options in Prescott, says Ginny.

As for Lola Jolly, the former California real estate agent, she notes that the local junipers "are killers for anyone with allergies" when asked about drawbacks, but she says that buyers can get twice as much for their real estate dollar.

And Don Schiller, affiliated with the Prescott Chamber of Commerce on a volunteer basis, can find nothing at all on the downside. "Every time I drive back from town through that beautiful pine forest, I can't help but be thankful that I'm not on those choking freeways in Texas or Los Angeles," he says. ●

Punta Gorda, Florida

Florida city offers a sense of the past and an eye to the future

By Karen Feldman

When Spanish explorer Juan Ponce de Leon set sail in search of the fountain of youth, he made his way to Florida's shores, starting at the northeast in St. Augustine and wending his way down to Southwest Florida.

At Charlotte Harbor, he encountered the Calusa Indians and, judging from the fierce defense of their territory, became convinced that this was where the magical fountain must be. Why else would the Calusas fight so hard?

For Ponce de Leon, what is today Punta Gorda proved not to be the site of eternal youth, but of untimely death in 1521, when the Calusas killed him in battle.

Both the Calusas and the search for the fountain of youth are history. But many of the city's 14,344 residents find that simply living in this waterfront city, with its historic brick streets, miles of canals, manicured parks and golf courses, can be curative in itself. For those 50 and older, who comprise more than 65 percent of the city's population, it can come close to heaven.

Harriet Mielke, 62, moved to Punta Gorda from Detroit with her husband, Leonard, in 1992 and now volunteers at the chamber of commerce for Charlotte County, of which Punta Gorda is the county seat. "When I talk to prospects who visit the chamber, I tell them we have found Utopia," the former Detroit Public Schools employee says.

"It's a really diverse community," says Julie Mathis, executive director of the chamber. Recent publicity has focused attention on the area, drawing the curious who "come here and fall in love with it," she says.

It's a common occurrence. Bob and Jackie Meatty, both retired from the U.S. Department of State's Foreign Service, moved to Punta Gorda in 1995 from Alexandria, VA. They had seriously considered retiring in Charleston, SC, and checked out spots all along the Atlantic Coast from North Carolina on down.

After one visit to Punta Gorda, they decided it was where they wanted to be. They rented for five months, then purchased a single-family home with a large family room on a canal in Punta Gorda Isles, an upscale community where many homes are built on a multitude of canals that offer direct access to Charlotte Harbor and, beyond that, the Gulf of Mexico.

For Bob Meatty, 59, it was the "climate, lifestyle, ease of water access and a home on a canal" that convinced him. For 62-year-old Jackie, it was all those things as well as a lower cost of living. Jackie misses some of the cultural opportunities of the Washington, DC, area but happily lives without the metropolitan traffic.

As for Bob, "I don't miss anything." Low crime, moderately priced housing, lots of outdoor activities and a subtropical climate are the main attractions for them and for other Northerners looking for their place in the sun.

Although no one is sure of the exact spot at which Ponce de Leon landed, the city lays claim to the explorer and maintains Ponce de Leon Park on a choice piece of unspoiled land that looks out on Charlotte Harbor. His statue stands sentry over the park's entrance. Each March, the town celebrates his landing — with men dressing up as conquistadors and crossing Charlotte Harbor by boat to claim the city.

Other than the Calusas, most found the area inhospitable with its almost impassable crush of plants and ferocious mosquitoes. Eventually the English found their way to the region, settling a bit north of the harbor along the Peace River. In 1885, Col. Isaac Trabue from Kentucky bought the land from the British and named it Trabue. When the city incorporated in 1887, it returned to the more popular Spanish name, Punta Gorda. Trabue Cottage, the colonel's home, still stands.

Today, the city's downtown area has won recognition as a state historic district, and the city's Streetscape program is restoring its Old Florida look by adding to the historic red-brick streets, planting more trees and installing street lamps, benches and brick planters. Old wooden homes are being restored and have become highly sought real estate.

The city's residents are content to leave the busier pace and commercial development to Port Charlotte, its neighbor to the north across Charlotte Harbor. In Punta Gorda's downtown, cozy shops and restaurants share space with City Hall and the soon-to-be-replaced county courthouse.

In Punta Gorda Isles, just west of downtown, almost everyone has a car but also is likely to have one or more other forms of transportation: boats, bicycles and golf carts. It's not uncommon to see residents tooling along neighborhood streets in their golf carts, whether or not they are headed to the golf course.

For the Mielkes, it was their interest in boating through which they initially made friends. The Detroit couple didn't know a soul in Punta Gorda when they moved.

"The first year was very hard," Harriet Mielke says. "Once we joined the yacht club, though, we met a lot of people." After that, they made still more friends through tennis and golf. "This is a place where you can get up in the morning and find 10 people to play golf with," she says. "It's a great party town."

Ed and Barbara Ring found much the same thing 12 years ago when they moved to Tropical Gulf Acres, a rural subdivision about seven miles south of the city limits. Their early friendships came through church and the Tropical Gulf Acres Civic Association, recalls Ed, 65.

But, even before that, Barbara, 63, says, "While we were building our home, our neighbors came by to chat."

The Rings had spent the better part of their married life traveling as Ed rose through the ranks in the U.S. Marines. They moved first to Port Charlotte but, after a couple of years, decided they "wanted a slower, quieter lifestyle," Ed says.

They were drawn to Tropical Gulf Acres because it was still relatively unde-

Punta Gorda, FL

Population: 17,168 in Punta Gorda, 159,574 in Charlotte County.

Location: On the southwest Gulf Coast, 100 miles south of Tampa.

Climate: High Low
January   74   53
July   91   75

Average relative humidity: 56%

Rain: 52.55 inches

Cost of living: Below average

Median housing cost: $207,323 in the county. About $300,000 in the city.

Sales tax: 7%

Sales tax exemptions: Groceries, prescription drugs and most professional services.

State income tax: None

Intangibles tax: None. The tax was repealed as of Jan. 1, 2007.

Estate tax: None

Property tax: From $16.0141 to $16.7111 per $1,000 in Punta Gorda, with homes assessed at 100% of market value. Annual tax on a $300,000 home is about $4,404 to $4,596 with the homestead exemption noted below. The rate in unincorporated Charlotte County is $15.3893 to $17.2920 per $1,000, excluding special taxing districts in some areas.

Homestead exemption: $25,000 off assessed value of permanent, primary residence.

Religion: There are 20 churches and one synagogue in Punta Gorda and 40 churches and one synagogue in neighboring Port Charlotte.

Education: Edison Community College offers two-year associate degrees on the Punta Gorda campus. Florida Southern College Charlotte-DeSoto in Port Charlotte, a satellite of Florida Southern College in Lakeland, offers a bachelor of liberal arts degree, with some credit given for life experiences. The program is geared to students 40 and older. Florida Gulf Coast University is about 40 miles south in Fort Myers. It offers undergraduate and graduate degrees.

Transportation: Interstate 75 runs through the east side of the city, with access about a mile from downtown. Southwest Florida International Airport is about 35 miles south and easily reached via I-75. Charlotte County Airport, just east of the city, is a general aviation airport for smaller planes but no commercial lines.

Health: Charlotte Regional Medical Center is a 208-bed hospital offering 24-hour emergency care, a cardiac care unit, sports medicine and rehabilitation, two wellness centers, diabetes and sleep disorder centers, and treatment for psychiatric and chemical dependency disorders. In nearby Port Charlotte are Columbia Fawcett Memorial Hospital, a 254-bed full-service, acute-care hospital with 24-hour emergency treatment, and Bon Secours-St. Joseph Hospital, a 212-bed not-for-profit facility with 24-hour emergency services, a women's center and an affiliated nursing home, hospice care and assisted living.

Housing options: Single-family homes are the primary form of housing with prices ranging from $180,000 in modest neighborhoods to $2 million to $3 million for more lavish dwellings that sit along the edge of Charlotte Harbor. There also are manufactured-home communities with options under $100,000. **Punta Gorda Isles**, (800) 445-6560, just west of downtown, is a community that began in the early 1960s and continues to grow today. Most of the homes are on canals. Prices start from the high $400,000 for an older two-bedroom home. New waterfront homes start in the $500,000s and go up to about $2 million. Downtown Punta Gorda, a state historic district, features mainly wooden structures, many of which have been refurbished in recent years. Convenient to downtown shops, waterfront parks and I-75, these in-demand properties start at $250,000. **Burnt Store Marina**, south of the city, has a spectacular location on a wide stretch of Charlotte Harbor. This gated community offers waterfront condominiums from the $200,000s, courtyard homes from the $300,000s, and estate homes from the $400,000s to $2 million and up. There's a large marina, tennis courts and a restaurant on the property. **Burnt Store Meadows**, south of Burnt Store Marina, has more modest homes, with lots starting in the low $100,000s. Burnt Store Colony, a manufactured-home community, is geared to those 55 and older, with a clubhouse, pool, tennis courts and shuffleboard. Prices start in the $100,000s for a package of land shares and a double- wide mobile home. Call Burnt Store Properties, (888) 381-7779. **Blue Heron Pines**, a golf-course community for those age 55 and older, offers new manufactured homes starting in the low $100,000s and resales from $80,000 to $120,000. Amenities include a clubhouse, exercise room and heated pool, (800) 635-4834. On the east side of the city is Ventura Lakes, which offers manufactured homes starting in the $70,000s, a security gate, tennis courts, shuffleboard and clubhouse, (941) 575-6220 or (888) 575-6220.

Visitor lodging: Best Western in downtown Punta Gorda overlooks Charlotte Harbor, $119-$149 with discounts for AAA and AARP members, (800) 525-1022 or (941) 639-1165. Days Inn is just off I-75, $89-$125, (941) 637-7200. Other options include Punta Gorda RV Resort, $29 per day, $176 weekly, (941) 639-2010; Fisherman's Village Resort Club, $140-$190, (941) 639-8721; and Burnt Store Marina and Country Club Resort, $89-$99 summer, $150-$195 winter, (800) 859-7529.

Information: The Punta Gorda Chamber of Commerce, 1200 W. Retta Esplanade, Suite E 43, Punta Gorda, FL 33950, (941) 639-3720 or www.puntagorda-chamber.com.

veloped and, as a result, most of their neighbors were birds and other wildlife. Their two-acre parcel sits on the banks of a pond.

Barbara says, "To me it's home — what we have been looking for after a nomadic military life. We have a bass in our pond that grew from a few inches to a foot long since we moved here and now follows us as we walk the bank of the pond. We feed him Cheerios."

The subdivision's 39 lakes attract osprey, ring-necked ducks "and a hawk that takes baths in the pond" behind the house, she says.

Nature's not far off even for those who live in more populated portions of the city. It's not uncommon to see fish leaping gracefully out of the water in backyard canals, or to see large turtles plodding along the roadside or sunning on a sea wall. Tiny lizards, called anoles, scamper about on sidewalks and climb screens around most homes.

Manatees, lumbering but docile sea mammals, make their way into the harbor and canals during cold weather, seeking warmer waters and the tons of sea grasses they need to eat to survive. Dolphins leaping about in the harbor, or playing in the wake of powerboats, are familiar sights. So are osprey, eagles, pelicans and all sorts of other birds.

Even the less-welcome alligator makes an occasional appearance, posing log-like in a canal, sunbathing in grasses along the shore or, once in a while, getting disoriented and scurrying for cover under a car in the driveway. Feeding gators is illegal — the more accustomed they become to being fed by humans, the bolder they grow and the more likely they are to become aggressive. Those that venture too close to homes are picked up by wildlife officials.

Parks are numerous, too. Punta Gorda has six city parks, and there also are 34 county parks, four state facilities, and a federal wildlife refuge. There also are 15 public beach access sites, although none are in Punta Gorda itself. There's a small beach on Charlotte Harbor in Port Charlotte and, on the northwestern end of the county, access to the Gulf of Mexico in Englewood. South of Englewood is Boca Grande, an upscale island from which some of the world's best tarpon fishing takes place.

About 45 miles south, off the coast of Fort Myers, are the renowned beaches of Captiva and Sanibel islands. Sanibel is ranked one of the top three places in the world for shell collecting. There are several excellent public beaches and many places to dine and stay.

While residents describe Punta Gorda as on the sleepy side, there are quite a few things to see and do when not boating, fishing, playing golf or tennis.

There are lots of shops downtown and still more at the waterfront complex Fisherman's Village, which also has a marina and restaurants. For more extensive shopping, the Port Charlotte Town Center has department stores, more than 100 specialty shops and a food court.

The Florida Adventure Museum contains four exhibit galleries and offers traveling exhibits from around the country. The focus is on Florida-related themes. For artists and those who would like to be, the Visual Arts Center offers classes, programs, workshops and exhibits.

Babcock Wilderness Adventures consist of swamp buggy tours high above the waters of the 8,000-acre Telegraph Cypress Swamp and elsewhere on the 90,000-acre Crescent B Ranch, where visitors will see unspoiled Florida interpreted by well-trained guides.

The Charlotte Harbor Environmental Center offers environmental education and recreation, including guided tours of four miles of nature trails. And the Peace River Wildlife Center in Ponce de Leon Park protects and preserves native wildlife that has been orphaned, displaced or injured. Visitors are welcome.

Annual events include the aforementioned observance of Ponce de Leon's Landing in March. This also is the height of the tourist season and the month when the boys of summer head to the state for baseball spring training. The $6 million Charlotte County Stadium, a few miles northwest of Port Charlotte, is the former spring training home of the Texas Rangers. The Boston Red Sox train in Fort Myers, and the Minnesota Twins play just south of Fort Myers.

In April, the two-day Florida International Air Show swoops above and into Charlotte County Airport, featuring expert aerobatic and ground displays. The U.S. Navy Blue Angels and Army Golden Nights are frequent participants.

May brings warmer temperatures and fewer visitors, but the fun continues with the annual Charlotte Harbor Fishing Tournament and the annual Chili Challenge for Charity, which benefits the YMCA. At Christmas there's the Peace River Lighted Boat Parade and Holly Days, when Punta Gorda businesses hold open houses.

Volunteer opportunities abound at places such as the Charlotte County Chamber of Commerce, the Visual Arts Center, the Florida Adventure Museum, Port Charlotte Cultural Center and Charlotte Regional Medical Center. At the hospital, golf-cart driving volunteers give visitors lifts from their cars to the hospital entrance.

While Charlotte County was once the fastest-growing county in the nation, hurricane damage in 2005 contributed to a decline in population. However, long-term population growth will likely prevail, as has been the overall trend with the state of Florida and coastal development.

The Meattys, the Mielkes and the Rings have no plans to relocate. "We like living where we are," Ed Ring says. "There's no place nicer." ●

Rancho Mirage, California

The warmth of the desert, clear blue skies and a relaxed lifestyle
draw retirees to this Southern California town

By Mary Lu Abbott

From its beginning, Rancho Mirage has been a sybaritic place, an escape for enjoying the good life, more about fun than work. The rich and famous first frolicked in the oasis built in the scrubby desert of Southern California. Now celebrities are joined by thousands of retirees.

In the early 1900s, astute ranchers saw opportunity amid the cactus and sand beyond the fledgling community of Palm Springs in the Coachella Valley east of Los Angeles. They began developing guest ranches and hotels that attracted Hollywood stars of the 1930s.

After World War II, the valley boomed, and in what would later be incorporated as Rancho Mirage, country clubs with golf courses began to attract presidents and other prominent visitors as well as the movie crowd. For years, publisher-philanthropist-diplomat Walter Annenberg entertained world notables at his winter estate in Rancho Mirage, and after his death in the fall he was interred here.

Luxury hotels added to the greening of the desert, and the wealthy built winter vacation homes with views of the surrounding mountains. Former President Gerald Ford made news by whacking people with golf balls and eventually bought a home in one of the early Rancho Mirage developments, Thunderbird Country Club. Celebrities such as Dinah Shore, Frank Sinatra and Bob Hope have given generously of their time and money to benefit the community, the Hopes donating land and helping raise millions of dollars for the Eisenhower Medical Center in Rancho Mirage.

Like many retirees who settle here, Shelby and Paul Cheek had vacationed in the area many times. His position with an insurance company had taken them to San Francisco, Los Angeles, San Diego and then Great Falls, VA, just before retirement. They considered retiring to San Diego but decided it was too booming and congested with traffic.

"I've always loved the desert — the mountains, blue skies, calmness," says Shelby, 61. "You can be on the floor of the desert and drive 45 minutes up the mountain and be in snow." As they desired, though, they've left their snow shovels behind.

The beauty of the valley can mesmerize, particularly in the early morning and late evening when the surrounding mountains take on a velvety blue hue. A string of towns stretching from Palm Springs, the farthest west, through Cathedral City, Rancho Mirage, Palm Desert, Indian Wells, La Quinta and Indio nestles against the jagged San Jacinto Mountains, which top 10,000 feet, and the adjacent Santa Rosa Mountains, only slightly lower.

Coming over the mountain pass from Los Angeles on Interstate 10, one quickly senses a more relaxed resort feeling. Towering palm trees line broad boulevards, and flowers bloom in profusion, thanks to regular showers by sprinklers. At times it's hard to believe you're in the desert, with all the greenery, fountains, waterfalls and lakes accenting properties and golf courses. Even a $50 million shopping-entertainment complex called The River at Rancho Mirage boasts a man-made river running around it.

Beyond the beauty of the desert environment, the Cheeks were drawn by the people they met here. "There are very nice people from all walks of life," says Paul, 63, noting a diversity in backgrounds of residents.

"Most people we know are transplants from somewhere else," adds Shelby. "I can't think of a single person we know who has lived here all of their life. Most of us don't have families here. Your neighbors are like family. People come here to retire and enjoy life. They're very active."

The Cheeks moved to the Rancho Las Palmas country club community of condos in 1997, and among their new family of friends were Norman and Joan Waitt, who came from Sioux City, IA, where he was a cattle broker and she was in real estate. In the mid-1990s, they vacationed at the Marriott Rancho Las Palmas resort, rented a condo at Rancho Las Palmas for a couple of years and then bought in the community in 1996 after looking at other destinations and around the valley.

"We considered Sanibel and Captiva islands (in Florida) and Mesa, AZ, but when we discovered Rancho Mirage, this was it," says Joan, 71. "We liked the climate. Winter couldn't be better. It has wonderful theater. Everything is so handy — we're 10 minutes from top restaurants and El Paseo or the Palm Desert Mall shopping. We have a shopping center right next door for the necessities. Rancho Mirage has a wonderful library, which I use a lot."

"Other places just didn't have the options Rancho Mirage has," says Norman, 71, who adds great golfing to the amenities available.

In nearly 18 years here, retirees Dale and Marion Cowle have watched an explosion of growth throughout the valley, in population and development. Rancho Mirage itself now has about 15,518 residents, still small but about double what it was in the early 1980s.

"We liked the area because it was quiet, peaceful and not overpopulated," Dale says. "We're still happy here. We get a little selfish and spoiled. When the traffic gets heavy and we have to wait for (restaurant) reservations, it's a little inconvenient. But on balance, it's wonderful.

"Rancho Mirage has more a small city feel as opposed to Palm Desert, which is getting commercial and big, and La Quinta is going to be huge. This (Rancho Mirage) is a comfortable place to live," he says.

The Cowles, who are in their 70s, came from Ames, IA, where he owned a broadcast station. They had wintered in the desert but visited other sites before deciding to retire here. They considered

Longboat Key off Sarasota on the west coast of Florida.

"The traffic was horrible. That was one of the things that turned us against retirement in Longboat Key, and we thought it was too humid," Dale says. In the years they've been here, Dale says, "we have yet to have a boring day. We've never been at a loss to find

Rancho Mirage, CA

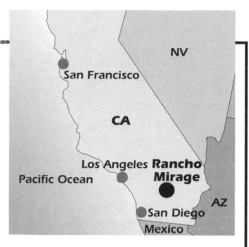

Population: About 15,518 permanent residents in Rancho Mirage, another 12,000 seasonally in winter. About 330,000 people live year-round in a string of towns in the valley, and that number increases to more than 500,000 in winter.

Location: In the Coachella Valley, about 110 miles east of Los Angeles (two to three hours by car) and 11 miles southeast of Palm Springs. Its northern edge abuts Interstate 10. The desert valley surrounded by mountains extends about 40 miles and includes the following communities, which run shoulder to shoulder, linked by Highway 111: from the west, Palm Springs, Cathedral City, Rancho Mirage, Palm Desert, Indian Wells, La Quinta and Indio. Desert Hot Springs and Thousand Palms are on the northern fringes, across I-10.

Climate: High Low
January 70 41
July 107 74
Sunny, dry climate with warm days, cold nights in winter and hot days, pleasant evenings in summer. Daytime temperatures often top 100 degrees from June into September and can exceed 110 degrees, but low humidity tempers the heat somewhat. Rainfall is minimal, usually coming between October and February. Valley elevation ranges from about 250 feet to 8,516 feet at the Mountain Station of the Palm Springs Aerial Tramway atop the San Jacinto Mountains, which borders the towns.

Average relative humidity: 26.5%

Rain: About 5 inches annually.

Snow: Rare in the valley but mountains are snowcapped in winter.

Cost of living: Above average

Average housing cost: $735,400. Besides multimillion-dollar estates, there are nice homes on golf courses starting slightly under $500,000 and condos starting around $225,000.

Sales tax: 7.75%

Sales tax exemptions: Groceries, prescription medicines and services.

State income tax: For married couples filing jointly, the rates range from 1% on the first $12,638 to 9.3% (plus $3,652) on amounts above $82,952. For single filers, rates run from 1% on the first $6,319 to 9.3% (plus $1,826) on amounts above $41,476.

Income tax exemptions: Social Security and railroad retirement benefits are exempt.

Estate tax: None. The state's "pick-up" portion of the federal tax was eliminated Jan.1, 2005.

Property tax: From 1% to 1.25% of the property value, which is the purchase value the first year and then escalates about 2% a year; exact rate will vary by area. Taxing jurisdictions can add special assessments. Basic tax on a $500,000 home, with the $7,000 exemption noted below, would run about $4,930 to $6,163 a year. Those 62 or older with income less than $39,699 may be eligible for a rebate of up to $473 on taxes.

Homestead exemption: $7,000 off the value of owner-occupied homes.

Religion: There are numerous places of worship for all faiths within a short drive from anywhere in the valley.

Education: Adult education classes are available at the two-year College of the Desert in adjoining Palm Desert. California State University at San Bernardino has a Palm Desert Campus, which is a separate branch of the CSU system.

Transportation: Palm Springs International Airport is less than 20 minutes away. Of the Los Angeles airports, Ontario and John Wayne are closest, at slightly under two hours by car, and Los Angeles International Airport is about two and a half hours away. The SunLine Transit Agency has a SunBus serving towns throughout the valley at low fares.

Health: The valley has outstanding medical facilities and physicians in all specialties. Rancho Mirage is home to the Eisenhower Medical Center, the major health facility in the valley, which includes the Betty Ford Center. Other communities in the valley also have medical facilities.

Housing options: A popular option is The Springs Country Club, with homes also starting in the $400,000s. The **Rancho Las Palmas Country Club**, an older development, has resale single-story condos, many on the golf course, also starting in the $400,000s. Among agents: **Windermere Real Estate**, (800) 869-1130 or (760) 200-1490, handles both real estate sales and vacation rentals.

Visitor lodging: The valley has more than 300 hotels in all price ranges. Summer rates usually are considerably lower than winter prices. Beware: Some resorts charge an extra resort fee of $14 a day. In Rancho Mirage, options include the Westin Mission Hills Resort, (800) 544-0287, from about $200 a night, and the Rancho Las Palmas Marriott Resort and Spa, (760) 568-2727, from about $150; special reduced rates often are available. Country Inn and Suites by Carlson, (760) 340-5516, has rooms from about $100 a night. Windermere, (800) 869-1130, has condo rentals in 10 country club communities in the area, including Rancho Las Palmas, starting from about $200 in low season.

Information: City of Rancho Mirage, 69-825 Highway 111, Rancho Mirage, CA 92270, (760) 324-4511 or www.ci.rancho-mirage.ca.us. Rancho Mirage Chamber of Commerce, 42-464 Rancho Mirage Lane, Rancho Mirage, CA 92270, (760) 568-9351 or www.ranchomirage.org. Palm Springs Desert Resorts Convention and Visitors Authority, 69-930 Highway 111, Suite 201, Rancho Mirage, CA 92270, (760) 770-9000 or www.palmspringsusa.com.

something to do here."

Among the most popular activities are golf and tennis. Few places can rival this resort valley, with its estimated 100 golf courses and a climate that allows play year-round. Rancho Mirage itself has about a dozen golf courses in its 24.7 square miles. Some estates have their own golf courses. The valley hosts major golf and tennis tournaments and is noted for its polo matches.

But there's more than the outdoor sports here, say the Cowles, who do not play tennis or golf. Dale does walk about four miles daily and they both work out with a personal trainer.

Like many other retirees, the Cowles do a lot of volunteer work. He serves on the board of a bank and has been a Rotary president, and they're both active at Temple Sinai and the Mission Hills Country Club, the setting for the popular Dinah Shore women's golf tournament. The Cheeks are active in their country club, and Paul volunteers for the annual Bob Hope Chrysler Classic golf tournament. The Waitts are active with their church and golf groups.

The communities of the valley have grown shoulder to shoulder. For visitors it's sometimes hard to know which town you're actually in, particularly Rancho Mirage and Palm Desert, where homes or shops on one side of an avenue may be in one community and those across the street are in the other town. Both Gerald Ford Drive and Frank Sinatra Drive go through Rancho Mirage and Palm Desert.

The River at Rancho Mirage is a 30-acre complex at Bob Hope Drive and Highway 111, the ribbon that laces all the communities. City officials say it has become the town center. Barry Foster, the economic development director for Rancho Mirage, says the city "worked for over 20 years on attracting the right commercial development for this key location. It has been immensely gratifying to see how The River has become a gathering spot."

While Rancho Mirage has a vibrant commercial sector, it also has restrictions about developments. Along Highway 111, it has sought upscale retailers to serve the community and said no to "big box" stores and fast-food chains with drive-through windows.

If not within a few blocks of their homes, certainly within 15 minutes or so, residents can find nearly everything they need or want in the way of dining, shopping or entertainment. Bordering Rancho Mirage, Palm Desert's posh El Paseo, with landscaped medians, alfresco cafes and upscale boutiques, rivals Rodeo Drive in Beverly Hills for see-and-be-seen strolling and shopping. Valley retailers range from Home Depot to high-end jewelers, a large outlet mall and big-name department stores. Restaurants run the gamut from bistros with rising chefs to chain restaurants.

About a dozen theaters in the valley stage all kinds of live productions and concerts. The noted McCallum Theatre for the Performing Arts in Palm Desert is literally across the street from Rancho Mirage, and in nearby Civic Center Park, free movies and concerts are presented throughout the summer in a setting that can rival the show. The Palm Springs Desert Museum is another major cultural arts venue for the valley.

Two American Indian museums record early history of the area, and in Rancho Mirage itself, a Children's Discovery Museum is a fun, hands-on learning center. There's hiking in the adjacent mountains, and Highway 74 is the popular Palms to Pines Highway, taking you from the desert floor to the cool mountain community of Idyllwild in less than an hour.

"Our kids love it here, too. They have a wonderful place to come visit," Dale Cowle says.

There are medical facilities throughout the valley, but the best known is Rancho Mirage's Eisenhower Medical Center, which has benefited greatly from donations by Walter Annenberg, Bob and Dolores Hope and other celebrities. The complex also includes the renowned Betty Ford Center for alcohol and drug dependency, the Annenberg Center for Health Sciences and the Barbara Sinatra Children's Center.

Rancho Mirage is mainly residential, except along Highway 111. The 2000 census indicates the average age of Rancho Mirage is 61. The community has about 50 planned residential developments, many of them gated neighborhoods, and much of the housing is second homes or retirement places. Single-story homes on large lots are common, as are price tags of $1 million and up.

However, there are homes on golf courses for under $500,000 and nice condos for $225,000 and up. Though overall it is an upscale community, it does have a range of housing, with some mobile home parks and affordable senior housing complexes, including a new gated community with a clubhouse, pool and spa.

"We found that to get the quality of life we wanted, on a golf course, the accommodations here were affordable. There is a variety of accommodations to choose from — high end and lower — depending on your lifestyle," Paul Cheek says.

The tremendous growth over the last two decades has raised questions about the impact on the water supply, an important issue throughout Southern California, where rain is minimal, usually less than 10 inches a year. "Fortunately the Coachella Valley sits on top of one of the largest aquifers in the country. There are no restrictions on development because of the water supply, but the city works diligently with the Coachella Valley Water District on promoting water conservation in new and existing development," says Foster, the economic development director.

The Waitts say they think the basic staples cost about the same in Rancho Mirage as they do in Sioux City, where they have kept a home and still spend half the year. "The only difference is the price of property, and they have a lot more high-dollar places here — shops and restaurants — than in Sioux City," Norman says.

"We have had people tell us that it's expensive to live here. We haven't found that to be the case," Dale says. "We don't think it's any more expensive than Minnesota (where he grew up and still visits) or Iowa. There are trade-offs. Taxes are more reasonable. Cooling here is expensive, but so was heating in Ames, IA."

Dale says his cooling bill was topping out at $1,000 a month in the hottest periods, but after putting in two new energy-efficient units, his bills dropped to about $600 for their 4,000-square-foot home. About four years ago, the Cowles moved from the neighborhood where they had bought in 1985 to a small gated community with only seven homes. "We have spectacular views of the mountains here," he says, noting they enjoy seeing the snow atop the peaks in winter but are happy not to have to deal with it close-up.

The couples find little fault with the area. "I miss the changing of the leaves in the fall — and that's all," Marion Cowle says. She thinks some of the drivers are "crazy," and Dale doesn't like the freeway congestion encountered toward Los Angeles.

Norman Waitt also thinks motorists here "all drive like race car drivers" compared to Sioux City. "There's nothing I dislike. I wouldn't like the summer temperatures, but we go back to Sioux City," Joan says.

Shelby Cheek does caution about the desert environment. "You either really love it or don't care for it at all," she says, noting she's of the former persuasion.

Paul says the desert does have seasons but they're "just a lot more subtle." Shelby notes that nights get "very cold" in winter, averaging in the low 40s. Spring and fall nights are cool, and even in summer the temperatures can drop 30 degrees or more once the sun goes down. Despite the low humidity, summers are very hot, Shelby warns, noting it had been 116 degrees this past season. She and her husband sometimes escape to San Diego, which is cooled by sea breezes. She suggests that people considering retirement here visit at different times of the year to experience the variations in weather.

While some people come to the desert to escape allergy problems, others may have trouble here, Shelby cautions. Both she and Paul have allergies. "In the desert, you have blowing sand and here you have something blooming year-round. A tree that loses leaves here is budding out again by the time all the leaves come off" because of the warm climate, she says.

Shelby says most people welcomed The River of Rancho Mirage complex with its restaurants, theaters and shops, but personally she wasn't too happy since it is close to where they live and it increased traffic and noise, at least after first opening.

All the couples highly recommend Rancho Mirage. "It's just a really nice place to live. Spend some time getting acquainted with the area. You can live at the high or low end, so the cost of living is not prohibitive," Paul says.

"We've done a lot of travel throughout the world, and we never found any place that was as comfortable as Rancho Mirage," says Dale Cowle after nearly 18 years here. "It's the best of all worlds." ●

Reno, Nevada

The "biggest little city" is a winner with retirees

By Adele R. Malott

Although loudly dressed in neon, Reno's casinos are no match for nature's compelling colors arrayed along the banks of the Truckee River as it travels from Lake Tahoe in the soaring Sierra Nevada through the heart of town and on to Pyramid Lake. The Truckee's route is one that was used by hundreds of thousands of emigrants on their way to the riches they hoped to find in California's gold fields. A few stayed on in the lush green valley now called the Truckee Meadows, which eventually became Reno and the neighboring city of Sparks.

Reno — known as the "biggest little city" — now often seems a secret closely held by its residents. Nearly everyone in the United States will recognize the city's name, but few could tell you much about it beyond historic references to easy divorce, prizefights, gaming or the beauty of nearby Lake Tahoe.

Today the Truckee's banks are marked by walking and biking paths and provide a venue for cultural events like big band dances, the symphony, opera and ballet. Artists' studios can be found in the restored Riverside Casino. Festival events are held nearly every month of the year, and a downtown skating rink adjoins the river in winter. Beyond downtown, theaters, community centers and parks decorate the river.

Reno's downtown has been freshened up with streetlights, banners and markers to help visitors find their way. The Nevada Museum of Art, the oldest cultural institution in the state, has undergone various name changes and opened in a spacious new facility in 2003, with a renewed focus on its collections, education and outreach. A new hotel-spa-casino with the look of Tuscany, the Siena, sits on the Truckee River adjacent to the National Automobile Museum.

And there is a buzz about what might be planned for the former river's-edge site of the historic Mapes Hotel, where the likes of Marilyn Monroe stayed while filming "The Misfits." While an outdoor ice-skating rink opened there in November 2005, future development plans may include a $4 billion public plaza.

Festivals give Reno the feeling that a party is always going on somewhere in town. Among the more popular are Hot August Nights, a tribute to 1950s music, cars and culture; Artown, 30 days of music, dance and art, mostly free each July; a hot-air balloon festival; food festivals like the Best of the West Rib Cook-off in Sparks; and ethnic festivals honoring the Greeks, Italians and Basques.

The Basques, who migrated to states like Nevada from the Pyrenees Mountains of Europe, have left a special legacy in the number of family-style restaurants in Reno and surrounding communities. Always popular, the meals are a bargain. Many a savvy newcomer will take the opportunity to find out more about Reno by visiting with tablemates during a Basque dinner.

Reno is populated by independent people who are careful and conscientious in reaching decisions about their city's future and not easily swayed by crowd preferences or what Las Vegas, nearly 500 miles south, is doing. Many neighborhoods have mature trees offering shade to popular walking areas like the milelong circle around Virginia Lake and the Crooked Mile along the Truckee. New areas are following suit by incorporating walking paths in their design.

New residents — many of whom arrive as a result of word-of-mouth recommendations from friends and family — quickly become Reno advocates. Wanda Dingwall, a widow who moved to Reno from Denver the day after she retired in 1999, says Reno simply is "more manageable" than most places. She points to attractions being within an easy distance of one another — most within 15 minutes — and with little traffic to interfere.

Reno is "just right" in many ways for Wanda, who cites its "perfect size, mild climate, wonderful people" and a "vast array of cultural activities." The bonus for Wanda is that Reno is a "fantastic place to grow roses." Indeed, Reno has a comprehensive municipal rose garden in Idlewild Park along the river. Aficionados share expertise on pruning and soil preparation at workshops held each spring.

Wanda chose Reno in part because her daughter lives here and "really likes it." Wanda selected a single-family home in a new golf course community on the east side of Sparks where a fitness center and social club are available to her.

Reno was just one possibility when Wanda began looking for a place to relocate. So was the Four Corners area where Colorado, New Mexico, Arizona and Utah meet. In evaluating the two, she felt Four Corners was too isolated for her needs and, she says, "I really needed some culture." Wanda is now urging her sister to make the move to Reno, too.

Judy and Ken Heitzenrader lived in San Marino, CA, and then bought a home in Palm Desert for retirement. When they found they didn't care for that area, they looked north to Reno, where their son lives, and chose a model home on the west side of Reno. Reno has "all kinds of recreational options, cultural activities, nature trails. It fills all our needs," Judy says. As president of the Reno-Sparks Newcomers Club, she sees up to 20 new members join the club every month.

"Reno reminds us of Fresno, where we lived when we were younger," Judy says. "It has the medical facilities that we'll need — and it has a Costco," she laughs. It also has the desert lights and shadows that her artist husband covets in his painting. And the city's central location provides rich opportunities for the couple to discover assets in nearby areas, such as Nevada's mining history in Virginia City, the Gold Country in Auburn, CA, and the snowy peaks of the

Sierra Nevada range that surround beautiful Lake Tahoe.

The area around Reno is a treasure trove of things to do and see. A drive north on Nevada Route 447 leads to Pyramid Lake with good fishing and views of a robin's-egg-blue lake surrounded by a landscape that changes with the passing clouds. It was Pyramid Lake that Charlton Heston parted as the Red Sea in the film, "The Ten Commandments."

It also is home to the Anaho Island National Wildlife Refuge, a white pelican rookery. Fascinating for city folk is the fish hatchery operated by members of the Paiute tribe, which is trying to save the prehistoric cui-ui (pronounced kwee-wee) from extinction. The tribe also has a new museum and visitors center that provides insights about the area's

Reno, NV

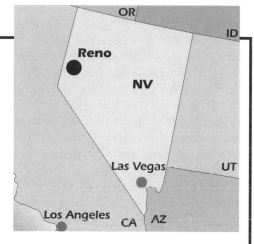

Population: 200,000 in Reno and 80,000 in neighboring Sparks, with an estimated population of 385,000 in the metropolitan area.

Location: Tucked into the rain shadow of the Sierra Nevada, Reno and Sparks are located in Washoe County. Often referred to as the Truckee Meadows, the area is a circular green valley at an elevation of 4,500 feet. Some 530 miles to the east is Salt Lake City, 120 miles west is Sacramento and 450 miles south is Las Vegas.

Climate: High Low
January 45 21
July 92 51
The moderate year-around climate offers four distinct seasons with golf possible most of the year and winter skiing within an hour at any of Lake Tahoe's many ski resorts. Temperatures may vary 30 to 40 degrees in a 24-hour period, virtually guaranteeing cool nights summer and winter.

Average relative humidity: 31%
Rain: 7.5 inches
Snow: 25.3 inches
Cost of living: Above average
Housing cost: Median home price is $353,000, while an average two-bedroom apartment rents for about $847 per month.
Sales tax: 7.375%
Sales tax exemptions: Prescriptions, groceries and utilities.
State income tax: None
Estate tax: None, except the state's "pick-up" portion of the federal tax, applicable to taxable estates of more than $2 million.
Property tax: Property is assessed at 35% of appraised or market value. The state limits the rate of property tax to $3.64 for each $100 of assessed value. The rate is $3.6477 per $100 in Reno, $3.6168 in Sparks, and $2.7002 in Washoe County. Tax on a $353,000

home in Reno would be about $4,508; in Sparks, about $4,471; in the county, about $3,336.

Homestead exemption: Nevada offers a property tax/rent rebate program for those 62 and older who meet specific income requirements as well as property tax exemptions for veterans and widows.

Religion: Choices range from nondenominational congregations to those representing faiths from around the world.

Education: The University of Nevada at Reno, a land-grant college established in 1862, is within 10 minutes of Reno's downtown. In addition to offering nearly 175 degree programs, UNR also has the nation's only judicial college for the training of trial court judges. It also offers a lifelong learning program called Elder College, with extensive lectures and enrichment programs for seniors and discounted tuition.

Transportation: Eleven airlines serve Reno, as do Amtrak and various bus lines. Citifare provides local service throughout the metropolitan area. Citilift serves the elderly and handicapped.

Health: Some 1,500 hospital beds in 12 medical and psychiatric facilities — including three major medical centers and a Veterans Administration hospital — are available in the Reno-Sparks area. There are a number of skilled-nursing facilities.

Housing options: Nearly 30 specialty retirement and life-care communities are available to seniors, including Promenade on the River, (775) 786-8853, an independent-living community for seniors on the riverfront with 84 villa apartments featuring 31 distinct floor plans. Rates, which cover all costs from three daily meals to a day spa, range from $1,695 to $4,425 a month. An additional occupant is $450 per month. Another community for independent seniors is Sky

Peaks, (775) 747-9555, in the northwest section of Reno, with monthly rents averaging $1,750 for a studio, $2,250 for one bedroom and $3,000 for two bedrooms, with all services included except telephone.

Visitor lodging: Hotel-casinos and motels are available throughout the metro area. For hotel facilities, availability and rates, call the area's reservations line at (800) 367-7366 or visit www.renolaketahoe.com. Reno's rates vary with the season and reflect heavy bookings during popular festivals and weekends. Among favorites of residents are the Atlantis, (800) 723-6500, near the new convention facility, where a tower room starts at $49 in winter and $299 in summer. John Ascuaga's Nugget in Sparks, (800) 648-1177, has a rate of $58-$124 in its tower, while the downtown Siena, (877) 743-6233, quotes $99-$299. The Marriott Residence Inn, (800) 228-9290, charges $144 and up for a one-bedroom with kitchen.

Information: Reno-Sparks Chamber of Commerce, 1 E. 1st St., No.1600, Reno, NV 89501, (775) 337-3030 or www.renosparkschamber.org. A relocation package is available for $18, including shipping. An extensive list of senior resources also is available. Reno-Sparks Convention and Visitors Authority, P.O. Box 837, Reno, NV 89504, (888) 448-7366 or www.rscva.com.

past. Beyond Pyramid Lake is the Black Rock Desert.

To the southeast, modern-day explorers can discover the adobe remnants of Fort Churchill State Park, built in 1860 as an outpost to protect settlers and Pony Express riders and to house the U.S. Army during the Civil War, making it a prime site for Civil War re-enactments today. To the south is Carson City, with its silver-domed state capitol building and a good museum in what was once the U.S. Mint building. History buffs will seek out the city's fine old homes and the State Railroad Museum for glimpses of the past and insights into the lives of such early residents as Mark Twain's brother, once secretary of the state of Nevada.

To the east is Lake Tahoe, a year-round playground for those who love the outdoors. A skier's paradise with 15 alpine and 13 cross-country ski areas in winter, Tahoe transforms itself into a summer beauty offering water sports, boating and fishing in the deep-blue alpine lake. The Great Tahoe Rim Trail, 150 miles around the lake, was started in 1984 and was recently completed by the determined volunteers who have cleared the path for hikers.

Four major casinos serve up gaming with special events like slot machine tournaments along with variety shows and name stars for entertainment. Scattered throughout the area are historic towns like Virginia City with surrounding mountains veined with silver and gold, and Genoa, Nevada's first settlement, as well as signature golf courses designed by the likes of Arnold Palmer and Jack Nicklaus.

Fred Sennewald, who retired 11 years ago, is a practical man who watches the numbers. He worked as a civil engineer with Redwood City, CA, for 15 years and decided "people didn't know how to enjoy life." As a result, he retired early and went to San Jose State University for a master's degree in leisure studies. Since then he has been teaching classes in retirement strategies and how to "live smarter, not harder."

Fred confesses he had marked off everything on his "to do" list except to start a workshop about enjoying life. So he began looking for a two-bedroom apartment that would accommodate an office. Rents quoted in the Silicon Valley were "not in the cards," so he visited Reno and found an apartment in a complex with an extensive fitness center, tennis and swimming facilities.

But he didn't really want to move away from his grandkids at the time, so he stayed put. He later renewed his interest in Reno when he discovered that the apartment complex he had originally chosen had increased its rents only $25 in five intervening years, making it a value. Now he travels to San Jose frequently to visit his grandkids.

"You have to want to get involved" in your community, Fred says. He didn't know anyone in Reno, but he joined the Reno Singles Club, worked on a Veterans Day Parade and signed up for the RSVP Clown Arounds, a group of volunteers who entertain at community events.

"Besides all the events and activities going on here all the time, you can get to them without being stressed out and park free, too," says Fred, who is content with his choice. One of the spots for these events and activities is the University of Nevada at Reno, where new buildings seem to pop up like mush-

rooms to house burgeoning programs, including a wide selection of lectures and programs available free or at a low fee to Reno's mature residents.

Crowded conditions and the hectic pace were what sent Judy and Howard Lenfestey looking for something different. While they moved to Reno from Los Altos, CA, in 1998, they had started to think they "wanted out" of the San Francisco Bay area a couple of years earlier. They had opportunities to visit Reno for many years and had seen the city in its different seasons and moods, watching it develop and add more amenities.

While a less-expensive housing market and tax conditions were appealing, the low-stress atmosphere and the leisure outdoor opportunities available were more important to the Lenfesteys. They admit they did not get involved in community activities right away. That was delayed as they cared for sick family members. But when they joined the Newcomers Club, they began to build a network of friends through several of the 50 different interest groups.

Judy Lenfestey is amused at the reactions of disbelief when she tells old friends that she and her husband retired to Reno. But it isn't long before she finds those friends impressed when they come to visit and see all the activities available, particularly those tied to the arts and outdoors.

The Reno-Sparks Chamber of Commerce says the information they mail goes to seniors at a three-to-one ratio. And many new residents, eager to keep Reno their very own secret, joke about building fences at the California border as one way to keep Reno a manageable, low-stress place to live. ●

Rio Grande Valley, Texas

Retirees find inexpensive living, friendly neighbors and a bicultural ambiance in sunny South Texas

By Mary Lu Abbott

If the words "Texas" and "tropics" seem at odds in your mind, then picture this: green parakeets screeching in palm trees, red-crowned parrots flocking in brush lands and butterflies painting gardens a myriad of bright colors. Add to that rosy and purple bougainvillea tumbling over adobe walls and the scent of oranges, grapefruit and lemons wafting through the air.

Welcome to the Rio Grande Valley, at the very southernmost tip of Texas. Draw a line across the Gulf of Mexico and you're on similar latitude as Miami and the Florida Keys. Sunny and warm — some might say hot — year-round.

At a junction of temperate and subtropical ecological systems and on two migratory flyways between North and South America, the Valley rewards its residents and thousands of bird-watching visitors with sightings for the record book. More than 500 species of birds and 300 species of butterflies have been seen in the Valley, the number and variety of spottings drawing birding enthusiasts from all over the world. Many of the birds, including some found nowhere else in North America, live here year-round while others are seasonal visitors.

Likewise, retirees have discovered that the Rio Grande Valley is a good place to call home. Many seniors first come here seasonally, enjoying winters when daytime temperatures normally in the 60s and 70s allow golfing, fishing, birding and other outdoor pursuits.

After experiencing its other attributes, retirees often resettle here year-round. Besides the weather, the Valley has a favorable economic climate with a cost of living that is considerably lower than average. It has colleges, cultural attractions and extensive health facilities. Its cities and small towns welcome retirees, catering to them with a variety of programs and services. And, Mexico is literally the next-door neighbor, creating a bilingual, bicultural environment throughout South Texas.

Encompassing four counties, the area known as the Valley stretches along the Rio Grande from the towns of Roma and Rio Grande City eastward to Brownsville and South Padre Island on the Gulf of Mexico. Numerous small towns dot the area, some melding into the larger cities of Brownsville, McAllen and Harlingen. Many who retire in the Valley are from the Midwest — the area was settled by Midwestern farmers in the late 1800s — and the warm climate often is the deciding factor for them.

Former residents of St. Louis, Jim and Hope Golliher considered the mountains of the Carolinas and places in Arkansas and Florida for retirement. They found property in the Carolinas too expensive and winters too disagreeable in Arkansas, and Hope didn't care for Florida. While in the Air Force, Jim had been stationed in Harlingen and remembered that he liked it, so they came to visit and found it suited them best.

Besides the weather, they liked the small-town atmosphere, the stable economy, economical cost of living and proximity of medical facilities. But there was something more: "I didn't want any place you couldn't grow palm trees," says Jim, 65, a former stockbroker. "We have 23 palm trees in our yard." The Gollihers moved in the fall of 2000 to a home in Harlingen Country Club, a golf-course community with a clubhouse.

Hal and Sandy Schultz settled in the Valley in 1988 when he took early retirement; both were with the U.S. Postal Service. At first they split their time between the Valley and their home in Eagan, a suburb of St. Paul, MN. By 1997 they grew tired of moving twice a year and moved permanently to their home in Mission, in the McAllen metropolitan area.

"We liked to travel and had been to every state. In Florida, Arizona and Texas, we looked for retirement locales," says Sandy, 60. "Florida was too humid. We wanted to be near a college town for theater, cultural and sporting events."

They came to check out Austin but encountered a cold winter and went to the Valley. "The weather was gorgeous. We decided then that this was the place for us," Sandy says.

Hal, 62, says they first rented a place in Weslaco, between Harlingen and McAllen, then explored the area and decided that the upper Valley — the McAllen area — had more amenities and activities they sought after being urbanites. The McAllen-Edinburg-Mission metropolitan area, one of the fastest-growing in the country, had a population of 569,463 in the 2000 census. McAllen, with about 120,000 residents, is the financial, retail and health center of the Valley. Mission has about 58,000 residents but is adjacent to McAllen and seven miles from Edinburg, site of the largest university in the area, the University of Texas-Pan American.

The Valley's weather, friendly people and abundant fresh produce brought Bill Miller, 76, a former salesman, and his wife, Jean, 72, to Edinburg in 1994. Formerly residents of Gurnee, IL, between Chicago and Milwaukee, WI, the Millers had considered retiring in Kentucky, Tennessee, Florida, New Mexico, Arizona and Austin, TX.

"We spent a month at a time in different places. We saw so many people leave the North and come south and then in a year be back home because they didn't like it," says Jean, a former teacher. "We read a lot and traveled."

They bought a mobile home and lived in the Valley a year before making a final decision to sell their home in Illinois. "This just fit our niche," Jean says. "We like a town with activities. Edinburg is the county seat and has a university, a wonderful campus. There's symphony and theater. McAllen has a civic center, too.

"Prices are at a level retirees can handle," says Jean, noting that eating out is quite inexpensive. For instance, a neighborhood restaurant offers a breakfast of two eggs with bacon, ham or sausage, hash-brown potatoes or refried beans and a biscuit for $1.69.

Jean notes that health factors also were a consideration in their move. "I'm an asthmatic, and I haven't been to an allergist since we moved here," Jean says.

One of her greatest joys is having citrus outside her door. "I can go out and pick oranges and grapefruit. I have six grapefruit trees, three oranges and one lime in my yard," she says. Jean and Bill have a manufactured home in Orange Grove RV Park, a master-planned community with about 500 units, a clubhouse and a pool.

Retirees note that farmers markets and roadside fruit stands sell fresh produce at low prices, and with several growing seasons, there nearly always are good selections. The Valley's renowned Rio Star red grapefruit is considered sweeter than Florida grapefruit by many people, and the farms produce a number of varieties of oranges, Hal says.

"After a harvest, a lot of produce is left in the fields. Many of us go out and glean the fields (pick up remaining produce). We take a percentage to the homeless shelters and keep some for ourselves and neighbors. Some neighbor is always coming by offering cabbage, carrots or something. Maybe hundreds go out to the fields," Hal says.

The Valley has been ranchland since Spanish colonial days. Reynosa, in Mexico across the river from McAllen, was settled in 1749; Laredo to the north in 1755; and Matamoros, across the river from Brownsville, in the late 1700s. After Texas won its independence from Mexico in 1836, a dispute arose over the new border, with Texas claiming the Rio Grande and Mexico declaring the boundary far-ther north at the Nueces River, which flows into Corpus Christi Bay.

After the Republic of Texas became a state in 1845, Fort Brown was built by the Rio Grande, setting off battles that led to the Mexican-American War. The American victory enlarged the United States by one-third, bringing in territory that today stretches from West Texas to California and north to Wyoming.

Around Fort Brown, Brownsville grew as a major port and industrial center along with its Mexican neighbor Matamoros, a heritage that remains true today with the increased commerce across the border fostered by the North American Free Trade Agreement. The remaining buildings of old Fort Brown today are part of the University of Texas at Brownsville and Texas Southmost College campuses.

With the realization that the area was

Rio Grande Valley, TX

Population: It's estimated that there are more than a million residents in the Valley's four counties. The largest metro area is McAllen-Edinburg-Mission with about 658,248 residents. The Brownsville-Harlingen-San Benito area has about 371,825 residents. McAllen has an estimated 120,000 residents, Brownsville about 160,000, Harlingen about 62,000, Edinburg about 58,000 and Mission about 58,000. With the populations of Matamoros and Reynosa across the Rio Grande in Mexico, the region has 2.2 million residents.

Location: The area known as the Rio Grande Valley is a delta along the river, extending about 100 miles from South Padre Island on the Gulf of Mexico inland to the town of Roma. From Brownsville, on the river border with Mexico, U.S. Highway 83 links the towns westward. At the southernmost tip of Texas, the Valley is 272 miles south of San Antonio.

Climate:

	High	Low
January	69	50
July	93	76

Average relative humidity: 63%
The subtropical climate fosters growth of palm trees, aloe vera, groves of citrus trees and fields of vegetables. Freezes are rare, though winter can bring some cool weather. Summers are hot and humid, and September is usually rainy.

Rain: 27 inches

Snow: Extremely rare

Cost of living: Below average. Food and housing costs are particularly low.

Average housing cost: About $98,644 in Harlingen, $110,000 in McAllen, $95,000 in Edinburg, $135,000 in Mission and $117,000 in Brownsville.

Sales tax: 8.25%

Sales tax exemptions: Groceries, prescriptions and over-the-counter medicines (including dietary supplements), certain agricultural products and equipment.

State income tax: None

Intangibles tax: None

Estate tax: None

Property tax: Taxes range from about $24 to $28 per $1,000 valuation with homes assessed at market value. Besides city, county and school taxes, levies may be assessed by road, fire and irrigation districts.

Homestead exemption: $15,000 exemption from school taxes for all homeowners. Those age 65 or older or disabled qualify for an additional $10,000 exemption and a school tax amount ceiling. Disabled veterans may receive an exemption of up to $12,000 off the home's value, depending on disability rating. City, county and school taxing entities give homeowners age 65 and older additional exemptions ranging from $3,000 to $15,000 off valuations.

Religion: There are numerous places of worship throughout the Valley, representing all faiths.

Education: The University of Texas-Pan American in Edinburg is the largest campus, with about 17,000 students and numerous cultural programs and events. The University of Texas at Brownsville and Texas Southmost College have over 10,000 students. South Texas Community College has several sites in the Valley, and Texas State Technical College is located in Harlingen. Continuing-education programs are available. Also, the Harlingen Chamber of Commerce sponsors a Center for Cre-

a fertile delta, the Valley became heavily agricultural around the turn of the 20th century as Midwest farmers were drawn by the long growing season. Today more than 40 crops are raised in the area. Though perhaps best known for its citrus, the Valley also has large acreage in cotton and grain sorghum and produces many vegetables, among them the noted sweet Texas 1015 onion.

The Valley stretches for about 100 miles, with U.S. Highway 83 threading the towns along the Rio Grande. Mexico is paces away, accessible via a number of international bridges. Increased trade across the border over the last few years has re-energized the Valley, contributing to a more urbanized environment. An expressway links the major towns, and large shopping centers with name retailers have located along the route.

Because of the heritage of exchange between the borders, the population of the Valley is about 90 percent Hispanic. None of the three couples interviewed speak Spanish, though some have taken Spanish lessons. But they all enjoy the bicultural lifestyle.

"The Valley people are very, very friendly. It's like when you were a child and knew all of your neighbors. You can go to the supermarket and come home with a new friend," says Jean Miller. "You would expect cultural differences, but we get along very well with everyone. The Hispanics are hard-working, family-oriented people."

Jim Golliher calls the Hispanics in the area "the most polite and generous people of any nationality I have ever known. Just the other day, for the second time in my life, I ran my car out of gas, loaded with groceries and a dog. Just as I pushed it off the road, a gentleman came along and gave us a ride home. He couldn't speak a word of English."

Jim and Hope often cross the border. "At the place I get my hair cut now (in Nuevo Progreso), they have asked us to come down along with all their customers and have dinner in their home," Jim says.

The area still attracts many Midwesterners. Hal Schultz says Mission has a small-town atmosphere. "Aladdin Villa, our development, is very tight-knit and friendly. Most of the residents are from the upper Midwest. If you don't go to church, they will call to find out if you're OK. Our roof needed work, and a neighbor insisted on going up on the roof and worked on it all day. That sort of thing is normal here," Hal says.

Hal and Sandy first bought a small home in Aladdin Villa, a 55-and-older retirement community, and recently built

---

ative Retirement with programs for those 55 and older.

Transportation: Airports at Brownsville, Harlingen and McAllen serve the Valley. Valley Transit Company buses serve towns in the area. Brownsville and McAllen have city bus services. The Harlingen Express is an urban demand response system providing transportation mainly for seniors and the disabled to medical facilities, shopping centers and other businesses on a reservation basis.

Health: State-of-the-art health-care facilities are available from Brownsville to McAllen, and the area is served by emergency helicopter. The Regional Academic Health Center has a medical school, research facility and public health institute at different sites in the Valley. McAllen and Harlingen have medical complexes with several hospitals, and Brownsville has a regional medical center and other hospitals. Several smaller towns also have hospitals. All fields of medicine are covered.

Housing options: A wide range of options is available, from manufactured housing communities to country club estates. Among the choices: **South Padre Island Golf Club**, which hosts the Texas Senior Open tournament, (956) 943-3622, is a gated residential community in Laguna Vista, between Brownsville and South Padre Island. Single-story townhomes start at $99,500 and two-story waterfront townhomes start at $250,000. Lots begin at $40,000, lot-and-home packages at $175,000.
Impact Properties, (956) 425-7098, handles homes in several country club and golf course communities in the Harlingen area. **Stuart Place Country Club** in Harlingen, (956) 428-1000, is an active-adult community built around 11 lakes, has a variety of home styles from patio homes to larger homes on two lots. The average home price is about $110,000, with patio homes starting at $85,000 and larger homes at $180,000. In Mission, **Bentsen Lakes**, (956) 994-8900 (NAI Rio Grande Valley) is a gated community with lots from $59,900 and home-and-lot packages starting at $219,000 and **Sharyland Plantation**, (956) 585-9595, has 14 communities. There are assisted-living and continuing-care communities.

Visitor lodging: Throughout the Valley are lodgings in all price ranges, including several hundred RV parks and many apartments for six-month rentals ($350-$600). South Padre Island has many condos. Among options: Renaissance Casa de Palmas, a historic hotel in McAllen, (956) 631-1101, from about $90-$110. The Inn at Chachalaca Bend in Los Fresnos, (888) 612-6800, from $100, including breakfast. Note: The Valley, particularly South Padre Island, is a favorite escape for high school and college students at spring break during March and into April.

Information: The Rio Grande Valley Partnership/Chamber of Commerce, P.O. Box 1499, Weslaco, TX 78599, (956) 968-3141 or www.valleychamber.com. Brownsville Chamber of Commerce, 1600 University, Brownsville, TX 78520, (956) 542-4341, and Brownsville Convention and Visitors Bureau, P.O. Box 4697, (800) 626-2639 or www.brownsville.org. Harlingen Area Chamber of Commerce, 311 E. Tyler, Harlingen, TX 78550, (800) 531-7346 or www.harlingen.com. McAllen Chamber of Commerce, 10 N. Broadway, McAllen, TX 78501, (956) 682-2871, (877) 622-5536 or www.mcallencvb.com. South Padre Island Chamber of Commerce, 600 Padre Blvd., South Padre Island, TX 78597, (956) 761-4412 or www.spichamber.com, and South Padre Island Convention and Visitors Bureau, 7355 Padre Blvd., South Padre Island, TX 78597, (800) 657-2373 or www.sopadre.com.

a slightly larger home on one of the last lots available there. The community of over 1,000 residents has a pool, woodworking shops, ballroom and outdoor games.

"We had no trouble selling our home. A San Diego couple who's retiring bought it. They're square dancers and had met someone who lived at Aladdin Villa," Hal says. The McAllen area is known as the square-dance capital of the world. Each February, the annual Texas Square Dance Jamboree draws more than 2,000 dancers, and on any given day enthusiasts will be able to swing their partner at some dance in the area. While none of the three couples interviewed are square dancers, some assist with the jamboree as one of their volunteering activities.

All are active in community work. "This is a volunteering community. Everything is done by volunteers. It's a primary hobby of many people," Hal says. He and his wife are McAllen Chamber of Commerce "Amigos," working at the chamber information desk. They also participate in HOSTS, Help One Student To Succeed, an elementary school program that pairs adults on a one-to-one basis with children with learning problems. They act "as a mentor, as a teacher, as a friend — it's been very successful," Sandy says.

Jim and Hope volunteer at the Creative Retirement Center, established by the Harlingen Chamber of Commerce to provide learning opportunities for those 55 and older. Jim serves as program director and Hope is the hospitality chairwoman. Monthly lectures and excursions include such offerings as "Report Card on NAFTA," a look at how the trade agreement functions today; "Water, Agriculture and Ranching in South Texas;" "History and Culture of a Shared Border;" and "Habitat and Birding in the Rio Grande Valley." The Gollihers also volunteer at the Loaves and Fishes food kitchen.

Bill and Jean give their time and talents at the McAllen Chamber of Commerce and help greet newcomers to their neighborhood.

There's no lack of things to do in the Valley, particularly nature-oriented outings. There are more than 30 birding areas, including about a half dozen wildlife refuges from dry brush country to wetlands. A new World Birding Center

is taking shape along a 120-mile stretch of the historic river road. Five of the nine network sites were open at press time.

Golfers have a choice of about 30 courses, and both freshwater and saltwater fishing are less than an hour's drive from most places. There's a professional baseball team with a new stadium at Edinburg. South Padre Island, a major resort with a long stretch of beautiful beach on the Gulf of Mexico, is within easy reach, about 25 miles east of Brownsville and about 70 miles from McAllen.

There are historical museums, two vintage airplane collections, the acclaimed Gladys Porter Zoo at Brownsville, a cultural arts center and several theaters and other entertainment venues for ballet, symphony and visiting performers.

Jean Miller says they miss some of the entertainment they had in Chicago and Milwaukee, "but we have community concerts here, a band and productions at Pan Am University."

Hope Golliher, 46, likes the variety of restaurants available. "It's like a mini-St. Louis in terms of ethnic restaurants. We didn't lose a lot when we moved here," says Hope, who previously worked with a brokerage firm.

All agree that health-care facilities are on par with the urban areas where they previously lived. There are extensive medical facilities throughout the Valley. The Regional Academic Health Center in Harlingen has an upper-level medical school and is part of a Valley-wide system that includes a public health institute and a medical research facility. McAllen has three major hospitals and a cancer center, and Harlingen has a medical complex with three hospitals and the Regional Academic Health Center. Brownsville has three hospitals, and Edinburg, Mission and a couple more towns have at least one hospital each.

For the Schultzes and the Gollihers, the lower cost of living was a factor in choosing the Valley, and while the Millers didn't think about it at the time they moved, they now appreciate that their money goes further here.

None of the couples finds much fault with the area, but it's not without some problems. In Mission, controversy centers on the presence of toxic chemicals found in some property near an abandoned chemical warehouse complex that was found to be polluted and

underwent cleanup by the Environmental Protection Agency. Residents are awaiting the results of more testing, but a lawsuit already has been filed.

The couples note that with the border so close, there is some drug trafficking and theft. FBI reports show that towns in the Valley do have higher-than-average crime rates, but none of the couples felt unsafe or considered the crime a serious problem. Many of the crimes are larceny-theft, such as shoplifting or taking bicycles or motor vehicle parts, without the threat of violence or use of force.

None of the couples seems to mind the warm weather. The hot, humid summers can seem stifling to some people unaccustomed to the weather here, but the Valley does have strong breezes. "The summer here is better than the winter there," Hal says of the Valley heat versus the Minnesota cold.

With its proximity to the Gulf, there is a threat of hurricanes. Hal says one reason he chose Mission is that the town is about 70 miles inland and would not bear the brunt of a hurricane.

The Valley gets two major influxes of tourists. Thousands of "Winter Texans," many of them retirees in RVs, come in late fall to escape the cold in the North. Spring brings large numbers of high school and college students on break, mainly heading to South Padre Island for sun and suds and across the border to Matamoros.

Hal says roads are busier in winter, although it still doesn't take him long to get anywhere, but Bill Miller says highway expansion sometimes can make getting around more difficult. Traffic can be heavy along the U.S. 83 expressway, which still is under construction in some areas.

Bill adds that there's considerable dust in the air when fields are being plowed and the wind blows, and Hope Golliher doesn't like it when the sugar cane fields are being burned.

The couples consider the Valley the paradise they wanted. "It's just about the perfect place. The quality of life is at a high level," Bill says.

"Small-town Northern residents feel very comfortable here — and those looking for year-round golfing," Hal says, also noting it's a good place for bird and butterfly enthusiasts and square dancers. His wife, Sandy, adds, "Movers and shakers, jet-setters would be bored here." ●

Rockport, Texas

Artists and anglers are drawn to the relaxing ambiance of this Texas Gulf Coast town

By Mary Lu Abbott

For more than 600 miles Texas fronts the Gulf of Mexico, with a strand of barrier islands and bays, long beaches, a bounty of wildlife and noted resorts from Victorian Galveston on the upper coast to Miami Beach-modern South Padre Island adjacent to Mexico. In the middle area known as the Coastal Bend is a quiet little town called Rockport, so small on some maps that you may have to pull out the magnifying glass to spot it.

Hummingbirds and butterflies by the thousands don't have trouble finding this place, though, and neither do the magnificent big whooping cranes, which make a 2,600-mile migration yearly from Canada to their winter refuge outside Rockport.

By the thousands, visitors of all kinds have homed into Rockport for years, drawn to fish, to bring families to a pretty beach on gentle bay waters, to enjoy the wildlife — and to retire. It's blessedly away from interstate freeways — but on major migratory flyways — and while certainly progressive and up-to-date, it retains a feeling of a kinder, gentler lifestyle.

In the still of the evening, a bright yellow kayak slips across the protected Little Bay near downtown, a fisherman casts a line from a pier and a great blue heron stands statue-still in the water, contemplating his own catch. The long-legged wading bird is easily 3 feet tall and looks somewhat scrawny — until its feathers fan out. With an awesome wingspan, the bird transforms into majesty in flight.

The town is situated on Aransas Bay, protected by a large barrier island. Fishing boats bob in the small harbor downtown, and sea gulls hang in the salt breeze, which over the years has sculpted many trees into graceful arcs inland. No wonder artists have come here by the scores, helping contribute to Rockport being featured among choices for "The 100 Best Art Towns in America."

Looking for a place to buy a second home that would become their retirement spot, Glenn and Valerie Guillory toured the entire Gulf Coast from Naples, FL, to South Padre Island, at the tip of Texas.

"We hadn't spent a lot of time on the coast, but we knew we were water people and that when we did retire we wanted to be on the coast," says Glenn, 62. They found an island retreat in Belize that they fancied for retirement until they decided it was "an idea more attractive in the abstract than when you actually pursue it in reality," he says.

They were considering the city of Corpus Christi, about 35 miles south, when they decided to stop in Rockport because they had heard so much about it. "It's a beautiful location, and it's small but has enough amenities that you don't feel you're in the outback. It's quaint, with the shrimping industry," Glenn says.

The Guillorys came here from Houston. Glenn and Valerie had gone to high school together in Lake Charles, LA, but their paths separated. After college, she went into education in Lake Charles, and he became a manager with an oil company based in Houston and traveled worldwide. Both were divorced when they met again at their 32nd class reunion, and they married in 1992.

In 1993, with Glenn working in Houston and Valerie a counselor in a suburban school system, they bought what they intended to be a vacation home in Rockport and came on weekends. Then Valerie interviewed for a counseling position in the Rockport schools.

"I asked her, if she got the job, what we were going to do, and she said, 'Well, you can retire or you can commute to Houston,'" says Glenn. He already had 30 years with his company so he took early retirement.

Similarly, Todd and Martha Pearson were looking for a vacation home. They had a financial planning business in Burleson, south of Fort Worth, and had mentally scoped out possibilities for

retirement as they visited places over the years. "We both have a history of liking the water. I grew up in Michigan near the lakes, and we seem to gravitate toward the water," says Martha, 58.

From Pecos in West Texas, Todd, 61, had grown up visiting family here in summers. "My grandfather had a little cottage in Rockport, so I spent a lot of time here fishing," Todd says, noting his other grandfather retired to the adjacent town of Fulton and an uncle also lived in the area. Over the years, Todd, Martha and their daughter had vacationed here.

In 1995, they bought a second home on Rockport's Key Allegro, an island on Aransas Bay with canals into Little Bay, in part to test the town for retirement. In their financial planning seminars, they counseled pre-retirees to visit potential retirement towns at varying seasons, not just the idyllic time. "We took our own advice," Martha says.

They found themselves lingering longer on their weekend visits and in 1998 decided Rockport was the place where they would retire. They bought another bayside home more suited for full-time living and worked with their son-in-law to gradually take over their business. They planned to cut back their work in Burleson one day a week each year and fully retire within four to five years, but they enjoyed the more relaxed lifestyle in Rockport so much that they retired in two years, moving there permanently in 2000.

A restful seaside setting, their home has a wall of windows overlooking an expanse of blue water, which laps gently at a protective bulkhead. "Our Aransas Bay is unmatched anywhere on the Texas coast. We're fortunate to have such nice water," Todd says. He notes that the city constantly monitors and tests the health of the bays to protect the environment, which not only is a major tourist draw but also a vital habitat for more than 400 species of birds and other wildlife.

Also coastal enthusiasts, Jim and Jackie Mays grew up in the Corpus Christi area and spent most of their working years in Houston, he in law practice and she in banking. They made a semiretirement move to Rockport in 1996 and have watched the town change.

"Rockport used to be a sleepy fishing village, but it's not sleepy anymore. It has attracted a lot more people and a lot more development," says Jim, 64. "Most of us are here because we like the water and water-related activities, especially fishing. We were very fond of the coast and coastal activities. Jackie likes birds, and I'm a fisherman."

The Mayses had a beach house in Port O'Connor, about 70 miles north, but decided Rockport offered more amenities for retirement. "We came to slow down and eventually retire," Jim says. They bought an 18-month-old home in the Rockport Country Club neighborhood, and he opened a law office. In the last couple of years, he has decreased his workload and now only occasionally goes into his office.

One reason Rockport has changed — awakened, perhaps — is because of the influx of retirees and their community involvement, the couples say.

"A lot of people come down here at a point in their lives when they still have a lot of energy. They come here with successful backgrounds, well-educated, and they want to make a contribution. They have the business and professional experience and the energy to share that in community activities," Jim says.

"A beauty of Rockport is that you can come here to retire from your profession but you can still be very active and make

Rockport, TX

Population: About 8,000 residents in Rockport, 1,500 in adjacent Fulton and 24,000 in Aransas County. Summer visitors and Winter Texans from the North swell population seasonally by 8,000 or so.

Location: Noted as a resort, art community and major bird-watching area, Rockport is on the central Gulf Coast of Texas, about 35 miles north of Corpus Christi, 170 miles southeast of San Antonio and 180 miles southwest of Houston. It's on Aransas Bay, protected from the open gulf by a barrier island.

Climate:

	High	Low
January	64	50
July	90	79

Average relative humidity: 66%

Rain: 37 inches

Snow: Rare

Cost of living: Below average

Average housing cost: $128,141 in Aransas County, including single-residence homes, condos, and mobile homes.

Sales tax: 8.25%

Sales tax exemptions: Groceries, prescription and over-the-counter medicines and dietary supplements, most professional services.

State income tax: None

Estate tax: The state eliminated its "pick-up" portion of the federal tax as of Jan. 1, 2005.

Property tax: The tax rate in Rockport is 2.1649 per $100 valuation, with homes assessed at 100 percent of market value. Tax rates in adjacent Fulton are slightly less; for homes in the county the rate is 1.9092 per $100. Taxes on a $137,295 home with no exemptions run about $3,041 a year. See below for available exemptions.

Homestead exemption: There are several taxing entities, and their exemptions vary. Regular exemptions range from 20% off the value to $15,000 off, and over-65 exemptions run from 20% plus $3,000 off to $25,000 off the value.

Religion: The area has about 30 places of worship, including several congregations that date to the 1860s-70s.

Education: There are four colleges in the area, the closest in Corpus Christi: Texas A&M University-Corpus Christi and Del Mar Community College. Del Mar offers leisure learning classes and senior programs in Corpus Christi and in Rockport.

Transportation: There is no in-town bus but there is service to other towns in the region. The nearest airport is in Corpus Christi, about 45 minutes away.

Health: Rockport has a couple of small medical clinics, including one associated with a major hospital system in nearby Corpus Christi. The regional medical center is 75-bed North Bay Hospital in Aransas Pass, about 10 miles south, which has acute care and most other services. More extensive medical care is available in Corpus Christi, which has several larger hospitals.

Housing options: Popular **Key Allegro,** an island on Aransas Bay with canals, has little remaining vacant land, but some people are replacing smaller, older homes with new ones. Resale homes are available, usually from the high $300,000s, though newer homes go from about $950,000 and up. Among options are two new developments built amid live oaks between Highway 35 and the Fulton Beach Road by the bay in neighboring Fulton. **Heron's Roost,** (361) 729-4214, has homesites from about $58,000. The **Rockport Country Club Estates,** with an 18-hole golf course, has homes from the low $200,000s and rising to over $2 million. Small condos on the water start at about $85,000s.

Visitor lodging: Hoopes' House Bed & Breakfast, (800) 924-1008, an 1890s Victorian home facing the harbor, has eight rooms, including four in a garden wing with private entrances adjacent to a pool; rates are $190 a night. The Lighthouse Inn at Aransas Bay, (866) 790-8439, is a new boutique resort hotel on the waterfront, with rooms from $89 to $169. The Inn at Fulton Harbor, (866) 301-5111, has rooms from $104 summer, $79 winter, with special weekly rates.

Information: Rockport-Fulton Area Chamber of Commerce (Where to Retire magazine), 404 Broadway, Rockport, TX 78382, (800) 242-0071 or www.rockport-fulton.org.

a contribution to the community in a lot of different ways," Jim says.

"It's a unique community in a lot of respects," Todd Pearson says. "A very large portion of the population are people who came here from somewhere else, and they came with a history of successes behind them. These are people who are involved in their community. They have an expectation of being able to affect the qualify of life in their community."

"It's a very diverse community," Glenn Guillory says. "We're a very volunteer-oriented community."

All three couples exemplify this action-oriented nature of retirees in Rockport, lending professional expertise on volunteer boards and projects. Todd and Glenn have gone a step further — getting into politics and now serving the community as elected leaders. Todd is mayor and Glenn is county judge, overseeing administrative matters.

When they moved here permanently, Todd and Martha wanted quiet time to themselves. "For nine months, we did not do much with other people. I think that was an important time. We consciously decided to be anonymous. It was a nice transition. We did a lot together, arranging the house, golfing, bike riding. We got caught up and then it was time to think about what we wanted to do here," Martha says.

"I played golf and fished for a year. I got caught up on that," Todd says.

There was a vacancy on the Rockport City Council, Todd notes, and little interest among residents to run. "It was something I knew I could do. I had served in Burleson so I understood city government," says Todd, who ran and won.

He took office as a councilman in 2001 and served one year. Because of term limits the mayor was not seeking re-election in 2002, so Todd ran and was elected to a two-year term. A city manager oversees the day-to-day operations, and as mayor Todd runs city council meetings and represents the city in most official functions. He is paid a small monthly fee.

"It's a great place to be mayor. There's such responsiveness out of everybody," Todd says.

Glenn enjoys telling people that "one of the few things I've failed in life is retirement." While his wife was busy starting a new counseling program in the Rockport schools, Glenn fished and did a number of things he'd never had time to do before, among them learning the art of glass-blowing. His colorful, creative work accents their home and has been in charity auctions.

He delved into volunteer work, becoming president of the Rockport Center for the Arts, which serves as a cultural and social hub, offering exhibits, classes and numerous events. He also lent his time and expertise in economic development work for the Rockport-Fulton Area Chamber of Commerce.

Glenn had given no thought to politics until a friend was leaving his position as an Aransas County commissioner and suggested that Glenn seek the office. Glenn ran against eight opponents, most of whom were longtime residents — and he won.

"I think people wanted a change," Glenn says. "Enough people had come into this community from outside that they recognized the community was growing and there was no way to stop it, but they wanted to channel that growth in progressive ways. I offered that to the community."

The next election he ran unopposed. When the county judgeship was split into two jobs — one law court judge doing the judicial work and a county judge handling the administrative end — Glenn was appointed the county judge, managing the money, contracts and employees. Last year he ran for the position and won a four-year term.

"My philosophy always has been that we're going to have growth, but we don't want uncontrollable growth. We want what I call sustainable growth. We need our children to have jobs, but we don't want to destroy the quality of life that we all came here for. We don't want high-rises on the beach. We try to manage the growth and channel it into what's good for the community," he says.

The town was founded in 1867 and became the county seat of Aransas County when it was formed in 1871. With large herds of cattle in the area, it became a meatpacking center. When trains arrived in the 1880s, tourism flourished and it remains a mainstay of the economy. During both world wars, ships were built here, and the shrimping industry thrives today, along with pleasure fishing in bay waters for flounder, redfish, trout and other species and offshore for large catches, including billfish.

The town has a number of historic homes, some dating to the 1860s, and the Rockport Center for the Arts adjacent to the harbor occupies an 1890s Victorian home. Several congregations of worship date to the 1860s and early 1870s. One of the state's noted architectural landmarks is the Fulton Mansion, an ornate 1870s French Second Empire house facing Aransas Bay in Rockport close to where it abuts the town of Fulton. Built by cattle baron George Fulton, the home was quite innovative at the time, with modern plumbing, heat and gaslights.

Over the years Rockport grew rather slowly, a fishing village popular with summer vacationers and in more recent years an artists' community, with a number of galleries and a major art festival. Since 1990, the town population has mushroomed from 4,753 to about 8,000 residents who have moved to the "charm of the Texas coast," as the chamber of commerce tags Rockport-Fulton. The chamber's visitor center even calls its volunteer greeters "charmers."

"We've got two interesting problems, nice problems to have," Glenn Guillory says. "One is the growth factor and the other is that the community expands greatly in summer and in the winter, and then we have festivals. We have to be prepared to serve a community quite a bit larger than those who live here, and that's always a challenge."

Todd Pearson adds that the police department has to be able to provide safety and security for the 30,000 or more people who may come for festivals, including the Fulton Oysterfest, the Rockport Art Festival, the Hummer/Bird Celebration and the Rockport Seafair. Todd says all police officers serve full time, and three positions are being added in the next budget year. There are police on boat patrol and on bikes, as well as in cars. He says there's little crime, petty property thefts being the most common.

An estimated 8,000 to 10,000 "Winter Texans," retirees mainly from the Midwest, arrive in the fall and stay into spring. The majority come in RVs. Besides being active with cookouts, fish frys, dances and themed events such as Michigan Day or Wisconsin Day, the winter visitors lend a helping hand throughout the community, the couples say.

"Every February we have the Winter Texans Trash-Off. We have a huge party and prizes for the teams that bring in the most trash. The Winter Texans love to do it," says Valerie Guillory, 62, who served as president of the Clean Team. She says some groups of Winter Texans call to volunteer for trash pickups as soon as they arrive.

Jim Mays says that while the increased growth has brought more car and boat traffic, it's not a serious problem. In fact, after living in a big city, one thing Jackie Mays, 61, likes about Rockport is the proximity of everything. "I like that everything is so close and easy to get to. Any place we want to go, we can get there quickly," Jackie says.

The couples have found it easy to make friends and get involved. Jim became president of the board of the Texas Maritime Museum adjacent to the Rockport Harbor. A small museum with a lighthouse, it has excellent exhibits on the maritime history of the state from the Spanish explorers to oil drilling. It's currently participating with other area museums to tell the story of a French ship lost in nearby waters in the 1600s.

Both Jim and Jackie are active with their church, one of the town's oldest congregations. Jackie has made friends while playing mahjong, an Oriental dominolike game that is very popular in the area, and Jim has taken up fly-fishing and has a boat.

Jackie walks each morning with a group of friends on trails at the Rockport Beach Park, adjacent to the harbor and on a peninsula between Aransas Bay and the interior Little Bay. The park also is the site of the Connie Hagar Wildlife Sanctuary, where herons, egrets, roseate spoonbills and many other birds live. The mile-long beach is the state's first to earn the Blue Wave environmental certification given by the Clean Beaches Council. A bandstand in the beach park is the site of free summer concerts.

Todd Pearson has served on the boards for the chamber of commerce, the United Way, the maritime museum and the North Bay Hospital, the regional medical center in nearby Aransas Pass. The Pearsons joined the Rockport Yacht Club, which Martha notes is a social gath-

ering spot even for those who don't own boats, and they golf at the country club. She tutors in the schools and trains volunteers. The Pearsons say there's a good camaraderie among those living in the 750 residences on Key Allegro, many of whom are retired.

Glenn Guillory says, "We thought our social life was going to slow down here, and it has increased exponentially. A weekend doesn't go by that there aren't several functions. We have groups who get together and have parties — like 20 couples will have a party, invite all their friends, get a band and there'll be 300 or 400 people."

The Guillorys have been active in the museum, the arts center, the historical society, the yacht club and the chamber. Glenn belongs to a men's club called the Coast Watchers, which meets weekly for lunch. "Our motto is, 'We do nothing, and we do it well,'" he says.

In 1998, Valerie Guillory was honored as the Texas counselor of the year for her work in creating a special middle-school program in Rockport. She retired in 1999 and was voted citizen of the year by the chamber of commerce to honor her civic work. As president of the Clean Team, she helped usher the town into the Keep America Beautiful program and beautify the downtown area. She was a founding member of the education foundation board, which helps raise funds for the schools, and chaired the first event to honor outstanding students in the schools. She helped the county set up a counseling agency for low-income people in need, serves on the Mental Health/Mental Retardation board and leads computer classes for the mentally retarded.

Diane Probst, executive director of the chamber of commerce and a longtime resident of the community, has welcomed the influx of retirees. "We glean so much from their expertise and knowledge. We're very lucky. They want the town to be pretty and want to get into leadership and help. It's a sophisticated small town," she says.

Jim Mays says, "You hear people talk about the old Rockport and the new Rockport. Old-timers sometimes aren't real pleased with the influx of others. Their voice and presence is felt and the attitude is different from the people who grew up here 45 or 50 years ago. But I

think we've integrated pretty well."

The downtown business area adjacent to the bay is small (newer chain stores are on the main highway a few blocks inland) but has interesting art galleries, shops and places to eat. A proposed harborfront boardwalk with Victorian-style hotel, shops, convention facility, residences and restaurants is in the talking stage. The town has several newer restaurants, with innovative menus, to complement tried-and-true seafood spots. While there are major grocery stores and some clothing shops here, people go to Corpus Christi for more extensive shopping.

Housing prices have risen, particularly for waterfront property, which is getting scarce, but still they're comparatively low for a coastline. The average housing price is running about $128,141, including houses, condos and mobile homes. Marilyn Simmons, an agent with Key Allegro Sales, (800) 385-1597, says, "There's a little bit of everything here." Small waterfront condos start at $73,000 and go up to $640,000. The average price for a waterfront home is $483,300, figured on homes ranging in price from $84,900 to $1.6 million.

Of course, any coastal town has a natural downside: It is subject to hurricanes and, indeed, a good portion of downtown Rockport was destroyed in 1919.

The Guillorys lived in two homes on the bay, but Valerie worried about the "water beating on the house." So they now have a home slightly off the bay.

It's hot here in the summer, the Pearsons caution. Winters are mild. "If you don't like heat and humidity and wind or the water, this is not for you. We all suffer bad-hair days here," says Martha Pearson. "If you like to dress up and wear hose, this isn't the place. We're normally very casual."

Jim Mays says Rockport is well-suited for "anyone who enjoys water activities and who is community-minded." Glenn Guillory adds that it's appealing for those who want to escape crowded cities but still have social and cultural amenities.

Martha Pearson treasures the quality of life here, a pace that allows time to develop and nurture friendships and to appreciate the beauty of the setting. "We're better grandparents, better parents, better friends," she says. ●

Ruidoso, New Mexico

Cowboys, creative souls and lovers of the outdoors find an easy fit in the high country of New Mexico

By Ellen Barone

With awe, retiree Frank Amigo, 69, glances out a wall of glass that graces his luxurious chalet-style cedar home situated near the ponderosa- and piñon-forested mountain community of Ruidoso. "What a life," he exclaims.

Frank ought to know. He's had four lives so far — a rowdy boyhood in rough, tough Harlem and a rebellious stint as a soldier before college, followed by a successful career with the U.S. Department of Defense. In 1989 he retired and transformed himself into the talented and respected wood-turner and silversmith he is today.

You might suppose that Frank's odyssey from Harlem gang member to New Mexico artist could have ended anywhere. But ask any of the fiercely partisan cadres of eccentric, risk-oriented citizenry of Ruidoso, and you'll see that his story is simply one of many proving the region's power to inspire new beginnings and journeys of the heart.

What's behind the magic? "Peace and quiet, land and light," suggests retiree Jacqueline Ste. James, who moved here 12 years ago from San Diego. "And, the absence of people." When you consider that New Mexico ranks as the fifth-largest state in the union, with 121,511 square miles, and has only one area code for a population of approximately 1.8 million, one-third of whom reside in Albuquerque, you'll understand what she means.

It was four years ago when Frank Amigo and his wife, Elizabeth, traded the congestion and high taxes of metropolitan Maryland for retired life in Ruidoso. Frank's sister followed a year later, relocating nearby from New Jersey. But these newcomers are certainly not the first, nor the last, to succumb to the allure of the area. Since the first stream of Anglo settlers arrived in Lincoln County in what was then a sleepy Old West outpost, it has had a magical effect on those who discover it.

Like many out-of-state retirees, the Amigos didn't just happen upon Ruidoso. They discovered it through word-of-mouth. "A guy in Frank's office always talked about Ruidoso even though he'd only visited it once years ago," recalls Elizabeth. "I grew up in Oklahoma, and my family spent summers in the mountains of northern New Mexico and southern Colorado. Frank and I continued the tradition, spending four weeks out West every summer, always with an eye for retirement possibilities," she says. "So naturally, when our house sold back East, we came west to look for land.""We liked Ruidoso immediately," Frank adds, "and unlike Santa Fe or Colorado, land and building prices are still reasonable." Eighteen months after purchasing an 11 acre homestead, the Amigos moved into their custom-built home in Alto, a scenic community on the outskirts of town.

The lure of inexpensive land was also what first attracted John Hershey and Susan Mentley to Ruidoso from Chicago. "Each winter I found myself more and more irritated. We wanted out of the traffic, congestion and harsh winters," John says. "Our attraction was the Southwest, but we didn't want another large city, Santa Fe included. So we made a list of towns that might fit the bill and contacted each chamber of commerce for more information. In Ruidoso's relocation kit, we spotted a full-page ad for five-acre plots at $19,900. Living in Chicago, that caught our attention."

Vic and Sherry Dunham first started coming to Ruidoso in 1980, and spent at least two weeks of every year in the area for the next 20 years before settling in permanently in 2000. "This was our 28th move in 40 years," Sherry says.

Vic adds that while it may be their 28th move, it also is their last one. Vic's military career took the Dunhams to cities and towns across the nation and abroad. But as soon as they could put down roots, they chose to make their home in Ruidoso.

Both are natives of Denver, and their Colorado friends questioned their decision to move to Ruidoso. "Sure, cost was a player. The weather is right, four seasons but milder winters. Property taxes are reasonable. Plus, two of our sons live in El Paso (2.5 hours south)," Vic says.

Some 180 miles southeast of Albuquerque, Ruidoso is a beautiful paradox. For its citizens who wish it to be sophisticated, the town succeeds. There's fine cuisine, the $22 million Spencer Theater for the Performing Arts, the Smithsonian-affiliated Hubbard Museum of the American West, and community choir and orchestra. And for its citizens who wish it to be a laid-back mountain paradise, where solitude, wilderness and simple comforts reign, the town succeeds at that, too.

"We wanted a place that our kids (and grandkids) would like, so that when they come there'd be plenty to do — horseback riding, golf, mountain biking, skiing," says Sherry Dunham. "Like the field of dreams, we built it and they come — by the droves."

To most Americans, New Mexico is picturesque, Old Spanish, American Indian, desert mesas, pueblos and cowboys, land and light. It's a tantalizing combination of fact and fantasy carefully crafted by Hollywood films, tourist board propaganda and the popularizing of "Santa Fe style" by fashion designers and interior decorators. But the essentials are genuine: a combination of cultures, history and landscape that exists nowhere else.

For years most retirees to New Mexico have pointed their compasses north, to Albuquerque or Santa Fe. But those hearts more suited to Wild West action and natural wonders can follow in the footsteps of Billy the Kid to Ruidoso and surrounding historic Lincoln County — Billy's stomping grounds and home of the infamous Lincoln County Wars.

In the days of Billy the Kid, Apache

raids were common and a frightening concern for 19th-century Hispanic and Anglo settlers. Today Ruidoso borders the Mescalero Apache Reservation, but settlers and natives live side-by-side in peace. Casino Apache is a welcome attraction, as are the tribal-owned Inn of the Mountain Gods (a four-star resort completed a multimillion-dollar reconstruction in May of 2005), the top-ranked Inn of the Mountain Gods Golf Course, and Ski Apache, the nation's southernmost ski area. Unlike the parched landscape of New Mexico's Navajo Reservation in the northwest corner of the state, the Mescalero Apache Reservation boasts an abundance of natural resources and lush, forested landscapes.

For horse lovers, neighboring Ruidoso Downs Race Track offers thoroughbred and quarter horse racing Memorial Day to Labor Day, concluding the season with the world's richest quarter horse race, the All American Futurity.

Beyond cowboys and Indians, for a compact town Ruidoso packs a lot into a little. "We wanted small-town without small-mindedness," says native Chicagoan Susan Mentley. On a Southwestern odyssey that took Susan and John to Prescott, AZ, St. George, UT, and Las Cruces and Silver City, NM, the twosome chose Ruidoso for their retirement. "Our first stop on that scouting trip was Ruidoso," says John Hershey. "We liked it immediately, even put a deposit down on this land after only a day. We left for the other towns with a 'let's see if we can top Ruidoso' attitude. Nothing could."

Arizona, rather than New Mexico, was where retirees Bob and Sandy Budnick thought they'd end up after first trying lakefront retirement in Wisconsin. Lifelong residents of Minnesota's Twin Cities, Minneapolis-St. Paul, the Budnicks' original plan was to spend winters in Arizona and summers in Wisconsin. After a few years, however, they decided that they'd be better suited to a year-round residence in a milder climate.

"We wanted a place where we could be outdoors year-round," Sandy says. Bob adds, "I wanted mild winters, but not if it meant blazing summers (like Phoenix or Tucson) that would keep me inside an air-conditioned house. At this altitude, even when it snows, the sun is warm. Our winter parkas haven't seen action since we left Wisconsin."

Like most homes in Ruidoso, the Budnicks' custom-built home doesn't include air-conditioning. With summertime averages in the low 80s, there's rarely any call for it. "Our friends up North think we live in a sweltering desert," Sandy says. "They don't have a clue."

While warmed by an annual average of 300 days of sunshine, Ruidoso has four distinct seasons. Situated at approximately 7,000 feet in the foothills of the Sacramento Mountains, it enjoys a high-altitude climate — warm, sunny days and crisp, clear nights.

Straddling the banks of the Ruidoso River (more like a stream), Ruidoso,

Ruidoso, NM

Population: The city of Ruidoso has a permanent population of about 9,000. The population in surrounding Lincoln County is 19,814.

Location: Nestled at 6,937 feet in the foothills of the Sacramento Mountains, Ruidoso is 180 miles south of Albuquerque (the state's most populous city) and 209 miles south of Santa Fe (the state capital). It's also 114 miles from Las Cruces, 75 miles from Roswell and 50 miles from Alamogordo.

Climate: High Low
January 45 19
July 82 47

Average relative humidity: 31%

Rain: 23 inches annually

Snow: 47 inches annually. (Average annual snowfall at Ski Apache is 180 inches.)

Cost of living: Below average

Average housing costs: $194,779 for a single-family residential home in Ruidoso.

Sales tax: The gross receipts tax is 7.6875% for the city of Ruidoso and 6.1875% in nearby Ruidoso Downs.

Sales tax exemptions: Prescription drugs, groceries and medical services.

State income tax: New Mexico uses a four-bracket, graduated-rate table. For single filers, ranges from 1.7% of taxable income of $5,500 or less to 6% of taxable income over $16,000. For married couples filing jointly, ranges from 1.7% of taxable income of $8,000 or less to 6% of taxable income over $24,000.

Income tax exemptions: Depending on income level, taxpayers who are 65 and older may be eligible for a deduction from taxable income of up to $8,000 each. Social Security benefits are not exempt. Unreimbursed and uncompensated medical expenses not already itemized on the federal 1040A schedule for the same year may be eligi-

ble for a tax deduction.

Estate tax: None

Property tax: $23.18 per $1,000 within the Ruidoso city limits, $18.479 per $1,000 outside the city limits. Homes are taxed at 33.3% of appraised value minus exemptions such as head-of-family ($2,000) or veterans ($3,500 in 2005; $4,000 in 2006) exemptions. Tax on a $194,779 home within city limits would be about $1,503 without exemptions.

Homestead exemptions: New Mexico residents who are 65 or older and who have a modified gross income of $16,000 or less for the tax year qualify to claim a property tax rebate. The rebate may not exceed $250 for married taxpayers filing jointly ($125 for married taxpayers filing separately, or single taxpayers). Also, those over 65 with an income of $19,700 or less qualify for valuation limitation, which freezes the assessed value of a home beginning with the first year one qualifies. Homeowners must reapply yearly. For more information, call the Lincoln County assessor, (505) 648-2306.

Religion: More than 39 churches repre-

which is Spanish for "noisy," got its start in the 1890s as a trading post. Twelve-thousand-foot Sierra Blanca, where mountain lions, black bears, deer and elk roam, towers majestically just outside of town. With high-country scenery and half-cowpoke, half-artsy charm, Ruidoso nurtures an affordable and creative atmosphere while providing a staging area for hikers, equestrians, hunters and skiers.

Bereft of Starbucks and a mall, Ruidoso has no high-rise buildings and no parking meters. Residents collect their mail at the post office, and the single movie house has three screens. For some, business hours are flexible with an "open when we're here, closed when we're not" mentality, also known as a "gone skiing" outlook on life. Gift shops cater to the pressed-jeans set. Thriving art galleries serve visitors hungry for Western lore and tradition. But when you see working cowboys on the street in Ruidoso, they may look like they belong on a movie set, but it's not a tourist act.

"Ruidoso's slow pace envelops you. There's something about this town that opens people up, and you find yourself talking with perfect strangers," local resident Leland DeFord, a Texas transplant, offers in explanation of why it's so easy to make friends here.

Locals and visitors alike meet over lattes at Sacred Grounds. Most mornings you'll find 62-year-old Mel Hayes, a retired Delta Airlines employee from Indiana, holding court at a sun-drenched cafe table. Three years ago Mel left Ruidoso but returned a year later. "We knew you'd be back," one of the coffeehouse regulars told him. "There's no place worth living that isn't here."

It's easy to be intoxicated by Ruidoso's charms — the scenery, Old West ways and even the skies. On summer afternoons when rainstorms are prevalent, double rainbows arch across the mesas. Flaming sunsets burnish the sky with lush hues of purple, pink and orange. And at night, electrical storms can turn clouds into glowing apparitions with lightning bolts streaking from one to another.

Drawbacks are few. There's concern over water shortages, management of growth and the threat of fire, and Ruidoso's high-altitude location can present problems for some. It's a three-hour drive to the nearest commercial airport, although there's an excellent regional airport just outside town for private pilots. For serious shopping at malls or large department stores, residents must drive 180 miles to Albuquerque or 133 miles to El Paso.

Frank Amigo thinks that's a small price to pay for paradise. "I'm still a young kid in a gang in Harlem, and I walk down the driveway to my workshop and I wonder how did I get this — how am I so lucky?" he says with a sweep of his hand that takes in an expansive view of grazing does and their spotted fawns. ●

---

senting 19 denominations hold worship services throughout the county.

Education: Continuing-education programs, in addition to undergraduate and graduate programs, are available at the Ruidoso branch of Eastern New Mexico University (ENMU-Ruidoso), (505) 257-2120. Continuing-education (noncredit) courses are available at half-price for students 62 and older, and ENMU offers degree courses at $5 per credit hour, a substantial savings from regular fees.

Transportation: There's no public transportation, but Shuttle Ruidoso offers daily airport shuttles to El Paso, and various group transports to the racetrack, casinos and Spencer Theater, among other venues. (877) 903-7483 or www.ruidoso. net/shuttle. Albuquerque International Airport, (505) 842-4366, is located approximately 175 miles north of Ruidoso via Interstate 25. The El Paso International Airport, (915) 780-4749, is 137 miles south via Highway 54. Locally the Sierra Blanca Regional Airport, (505) 336-8111, serves corporate jets and private planes.

Health: Lincoln County Medical Center (LCMC) is an affiliate of Presbyterian Healthcare Services. LCMC provides high-quality, low-cost, accessible health care, including 24-hour emergency services, labor and delivery facilities, an intensive care unit and numerous diagnostic services such as ultrasound imaging, mammography, CAT scanning and magnetic resonance imaging (MRI). Major regional health facilities are located nearby in Alamogordo and Roswell. Ruidoso also supports a talented roster of some two-dozen alternative and holistic health-service providers. The Ruidoso Care Center, (505) 257-9071, offers assisted living in addition to recovery and rehabilitation services.

Housing options: Ruidoso's housing options range from rustic cabins and vacation condominiums to luxurious homes. Throughout the city a good inventory of properties range from the low $100,000 to $400,000 and up. For high-end homes in master-planned residential and golf developments just outside of town, **Alto Lakes Country Club,** (505) 336-4231, or **Kokopelli,** (505) 336-1818, are options. The **Ranches of Sonterra,** www.sonterra.org, a premier acreage residential community situated several miles north of the village, offers upscale homes on large lots, priced from $43,000 to $125,000. For more information on real estate and housing, call the Ruidoso Valley Chamber of Commerce, (877) 784-3676 or www.ruidosonow.com.

Visitor lodging: Visitors to Ruidoso can choose from hotels, motels, bed-and-breakfast inns, cabins and lodges, condominiums, campgrounds and RV parks. Chain hotels include Hawthorn Suites, with rates from $119 to $199, (888) 323-5216 or www.ruidosohawthorn.com, and Comfort Inn, with rates of $59-$159 throughout the year, (866) 859-5146 or www.comfortinnruidoso.com. For complete lodging accommodations, including cabins, condos, hotels, motels, B&Bs, inns, lodges, vacation rentals and resorts, call Ruidoso Central Reservations, (888) 257-7577 or www.ruidoso.net/reservations.

Information: Ruidoso Valley Chamber of Commerce, 720 Sudderth Drive, Ruidoso, NM 88345, (877) 784-3676 or www.ruidosonow.com. Ruidoso Visitors Information, (888) 268-8811, www.ruidoso.net. Additional information: New Mexico Department of Tourism, (800) 545-2070 or www.newmexico.org.

St. George, Utah

"Utah's Dixie" blends history with a spectacular setting

By Jerry Camarillo Dunn Jr.

St. George exerts an attraction that's like love at first sight. Falling for St. George is as easy as one-two-three. First, the town has a gorgeous setting in southwestern Utah. Overhead, the sky is bonnet blue, with high clouds streaming like white ribbons. Behind town, the sandstone cliffs look like pleated skirts of red wool.

Second, there's the green patchwork created by the area's nine golf courses — a huge lure for retirees. Some people call St. George "the other Palm Springs."

Third, there's the climate of this high desert hot spot. Just ask John and Audrey Castle, both 76, who moved here in 1992 from Midland, MI. "We have sunshine at least 300 days a year," exults John, his native English accent coming as a surprise in the wild West. "We love the lack of rain and snow."

Well, yes, he admits, summer days do drive the thermometer well above 100 degrees. "But it's very dry heat, so it doesn't bother you. If you stood out in the middle of the street, of course, you'd get plenty hot — you'd probably get killed, too! But you have air-conditioning in your home and in your car."

As for winter, St. George is blessedly mild, with daytime temperatures of 55 to 65 degrees. "It's a long way from an English winter," says John. "Thank goodness!"

Before retiring, John was in the "education racket" as he jokingly calls it, teaching business administration at Michigan's Northwood University. Audrey worked at a daycare center. When they decided to retire, it didn't take the Castles long to decide on St. George, even after touring other appealing places in their search for the perfect retirement spot.

"We flew in on Friday and bought our house on Saturday," John recalls. "We just said, 'This is it.' " And they weren't alone: Between 1990 and 1995, St. George's population grew by two-thirds. Retirees make up 30 percent of the residents.

The Castles purchased a three-bedroom townhouse in a Southwestern-style condominium complex in the Green Valley district. On their patio they enjoy barbecuing and looking out at Pine Valley Mountain, whose peaks tower more than 10,000 feet high. The condo complex has a swimming pool where John and Audrey often spend an hour or so exercising under radiant blue skies.

Those skies also spread over some of southwestern Utah's most stunning canyonlands scenery — particularly Zion National Park, just 43 miles east of St. George. Zion is a place of big fundamentals — rock, water and sky — where everything seems exalted. Even the names on the map spell out glories: Angels Landing, East Temple, Great White Throne.

On a 6.5-mile scenic drive into the heart of the canyon, one stop is Weeping Rock, where a seep of water on a vertical cliff creates a hanging garden of scarlet monkey flowers and ferns.

Nearby, the easy Narrows Trail follows the Virgin River, the liquid force that carved the canon. Motorists also stop at the visitors center to hear informative talks about local geology and wildlife. ("If you could unhinge your jaws the way a rattlesnake does to swallow a mouse," a park ranger tells a mesmerized crowd, "you could gulp down a watermelon.")

Another popular drive from St. George is the two-hour trip on Interstate 15 to Las Vegas. "If we want to live it up, we just get in the car and go," John Castle says. "We make three or four trips a year."

Glittering Las Vegas offers a strong contrast with homespun St. George, which has about 60,000 residents. "St. George is reasonably small, with a slow pace of life and not much traffic, yet it still retains some of the advantages of a bigger city," John says. "The shopping, for instance, is pretty good here."

In fact, St. George is the regional shopping hub. The enclosed Red Cliffs Mall boasts more than 50 stores and shops, while Zion Factory Stores and The Promenade offer an equal number of stores selling everything from sporting goods and discounted name-brand clothes to books.

Speaking of books, says John Castle, "The public library is very good here. We can always get any book we want."

Another factor in the Castles' decision to move to St. George was the town's low crime rate. A possible explanation for the civic tranquility: "St. George is heavily influenced by the Mormons, who make up about 70 percent of the population," John says. "Their influence is very beneficial, especially their family values and good, clean living."

Not surprisingly, the history of St. George has a lot to do with Mormons. The town got its start in 1861 when Brigham Young, president of the Church of Jesus Christ of Latter-day Saints (Mormons), sent a group of 309 pioneer families to grow cotton and wine grapes in this unlikely terrain. Other products included silk, dried fruit, molasses and pecans. Because so many of the settlers hailed from the South, the region was nicknamed Dixie. The St. George area is still known as "Utah's Dixie."

Young also saw the health benefits of the warm climate — he suffered from rheumatism — so the Mormon leader became St. George's first snowbird, leaving Salt Lake City and building himself a tidy winter home with a white picket fence. Today new residents enjoy looking at the house's historic furnishings, including a piano hauled across the plains in a covered wagon, silverware forged from melted-down coins and a wooden rocking chair made by Brigham Young himself.

As you gaze across the townscape, it's hard to miss the gleaming white St. George Temple, which the Mormons completed in 1877 at a cost of $800,000. Unless you're a church member, you'll find it buttoned up tighter than a starched shirt. There is a visitors center, however, where earnest church members are on hand to discuss their faith and educate people about the temple, the first one west of the Mississippi River.

A few blocks away stands the St. George Tabernacle. To build the walls, huge slabs of limestone were brought from local quarries, while wooden trusses were made of logs hauled from the mountains 32 miles away.

St. George, UT

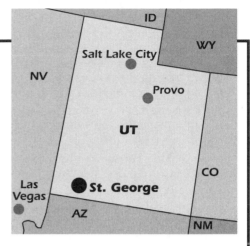

Population: About 60,000 in St. George, and 125,000 in Washington County.

Location: St. George lies at 2,880 feet above sea level in a valley in far southwestern Utah, six miles from the Arizona border. Red sandstone cliffs form a backdrop for the city. St. George is 120 miles from Las Vegas and 305 miles from Salt Lake City, Utah's capital. Zion National Park is 43 miles away.

Climate: High Low
January 54 27
July 102 69
St. George has approximately 300 days of sunshine each year.

Rain: 8 inches, primarily in April and May.

Snow: About one snowstorm per year, lasting only a few hours.

Cost of living: Slightly below average.

Average home price: A single-family home averages $270,078. A condominium sells for about $151,528.

Sales tax: 6.25%

Sales tax exemptions: 67 exemptions statewide, including prescription drugs, hearing aids and prosthetic devices.

State income tax: For married couples filing jointly, graduated from 2.3% of taxable income up to $1,726 to 7% on amounts over $8,626. For single filers, graduated from 2.3% of taxable income up to $863 to 7% on amounts over $4,313.

Income tax exemptions: There are exemptions in pensions and taxable Social Security benefits of up to $4,800 for each taxpayer under age 65 and up to $7,500 for those age 65 and older if they meet specified income limitations.

Inheritance tax: None

Estate tax: None

Property tax: $10.354 per $1,000 valuation, with primary residences assessed at 55% of market value. Annual tax on a $270,078 home would be $1,538.

Homestead exemption: None

Religion: While St. George's population is about 70 percent Mormon (Church of Jesus Christ of Latter-day Saints), two dozen other churches are active, including Assembly of God, Baptist, Catholic, Christian Science, Episcopal, Lutheran, Methodist and Presbyterian.

Education: Founded in 1911, Dixie State College, (435) 652-7500, is a comprehensive community college serving 5,500 students. The college's Institute for Continued Learning, (435) 652-7670, specifically for retirees and pre-retirees, offers classes ranging from archaeology and Spanish to bridge, along with field trips, discussion groups and special events. For a $45 fee, seniors can take classes all year.

Transportation: Interstate 15 links the city to Las Vegas (two hours south) and Salt Lake City (four hours north); there are three exits in St. George. Local bus and taxi services are available, as well as transportation services for those who need assistance with medical appointments. For air travel, SkyWest offers six departures daily to Salt Lake City, and the St. George Shuttle makes seven daily round trips to McCarran Airport in Las Vegas. A new regional is planned, slated for completion in 2010.

Health: Dixie Regional Medical Center, (435) 634-4000, is a comprehensive community hospital that opened a second campus in 2003 and totals 196 beds. Other health-care services include the Snow Canyon Clinic, Color Country Health Express, IHC Health Center and the St. George Medical Clinic. Services available include cardiology, behavioral medicine, cancer treatment, radiology, rehabilitation, intensive and critical care, pediatric care, obstetrics, chronic wound healing, home and hospice care, outpatient surgery and treatment and 24-hour emergency service.

Housing options: Housing comes in a variety of sizes and styles, with home prices in St. George and nearby communities ranging from $25,000 for manufactured homes to more than $3 million for estates. At **Entrada at Snow Canyon**, (435) 656-5600, a Southwestern-style development with a top-rated golf course, prices start at $549,000 for patio homes and rise to $1 million for villas; home lots range from $175,000 to $660,000. **SunRiver St. George**, (888) 688-6556 or (435) 688-1000, is an active-adult golf development where homes begin at $190,000; there is an indoor pool, fitness center, tennis courts and lawn bowling. **Coral Canyon**, (435) 688-1500, is a golf-oriented community on 2,700 acres, with homes starting at $184,000 to $593,000. There is a trail system for hiking and biking. St. George's assisted-living facilities include **Sterling Court**, (435) 628-1400; **Cliff View**, (435) 628-1117; and **The Meadows**, (435) 628-0090.

Visitor lodging: In the downtown historic district, Greene Gate Village Historic Bed and Breakfast Inn is a cluster of restored 1870s pioneer homes, $65-$165, (800) 350-6999 or (435) 628-6999. The Green Valley Spa offers one-bedroom condos by the night from $100-$200, and a spa stay (accommodations, full meals, fitness instruction, guided hikes) requires a three-night minimum and is priced for double occupancy from $1,100 per person (spa treatments are extra), (800) 237-1068 or (435) 628-8060. St. George's other accommodations include national chains (Holiday Inn, Quality Inn, Hampton Inn, Best Western, Motel 6) and several bed-and-breakfast inns.

Information: St. George Area Chamber of Commerce, 97 E. St. George Blvd., St. George, UT 84770, (435) 628-1658 or www.stgeorgechamber.com. Other helpful Web sites: www.sgcity.org, www.sou thernutah.com and www.utahsdixie.com.

Another hub of local history is the Jacob Hamblin Home in the adjacent community of Santa Clara. Built in 1862 by a Mormon missionary to the Paiute Indian tribe, this stone-and-timber homestead played host to Saturday night dances and Sunday school classes alike. Spread on the wooden floor are mountain lion and buffalo skins once used as blankets and rugs in pioneer days.

Local history is something you'll learn about if you drop by St. George's Chamber of Commerce Visitors Center, which is partly staffed by retiree volunteers like Curt and Ann Olson, both 64, who moved here from Decorah, IA. "There are lots of opportunities to volunteer in St. George," says Ann, a former junior high school library and computer lab supervisor. Retirees donate their time at the Dixie Regional Medical Center, usher for a concert series and volunteer to help out at the annual Huntsman World Senior Games.

"These games are attended by retired people from all over the world," explains Curt, who managed an insurance association before his retirement. "They compete at just about everything — basketball, tennis, golf, bowling, racquetball, swimming, and track and field. They play softball and even bridge."

The Olsons themselves play bridge at the Elks Club every Monday night. On Tuesdays they have a standing golf date with another couple. "Golf" is a magic word in St. George. Eight of its courses lie within 15 minutes of each other, and they include several of Utah's top-rated links, known for challenging designs, scenic features, careful maintenance and year-round play. During winter, balmy temperatures make it a breeze to play a full 18 holes.

"Golfing is also more affordable here than in Phoenix or Las Vegas," Ann points out. "And on city courses, local residents can buy a punch card that really reduces the fees. It gives you 20 rounds of nine holes for just $120 in summer and $160 in winter.

"There are courses for every kind of golfer," she says. "If you're learning and don't hit a very long ball, you'd feel quite comfortable playing a course like Dixie Red Hills. The St. George Golf Club is flat and easy. And the front nine at Southgate Golf Club is very easy for someone who's not very good yet."

Sunbrook is tougher. It was rated by a national golf magazine a few years back as Utah's top course. A challenger is the area's newest course, Entrada. Designed by Johnny Miller, it features rolling dunes, black lava beds and winding arroyos.

SunRiver St. George, a 50-plus community, is built around a golf course that has views of red rock cliffs and Pine Valley Mountain. At Coral Canyon, the challenges range from a labyrinth of dry washes to red rock outcroppings.

Besides golf, another popular outdoor activity takes place in October — the famous St. George Marathon. A qualifying race for the Boston Marathon, it winds through high desert terrain and attracts about 6,200 runners, including a number of retirees.

All year around, the St. George Recreation Center provides locals with a fitness room, racquetball courts and a new gym, while the Sand Hollow Aquatic Center has both competition and leisure pools.

All that exercise builds up an appetite, and St. George offers more than 50 restaurants. "If you come from San Francisco, you might not find St. George up to your dining standards," cautions Ann Olson. "We don't have gourmet restaurants with the wine and the atmosphere, although we do have several very nice restaurants."

Utah's strong Mormon influence has created liquor laws different from those in most places, she explains. Unless you eat something, you can't order a drink in a restaurant. And many restaurants don't have liquor licenses, period. "If you like to relax with a cocktail and then go in to dinner, you won't find that available," Ann says. "And if you like beer with your pizza, you're out of luck. There's no beer at any pizza place in St. George.

"One nice thing about all this is that we don't have bars," she says. "So St. George doesn't have the type of atmosphere where people go sit in a bar and stagger out at midnight."

Churchgoers find that all the major denominations are thriving in St. George. And Ann likes the fact that the town has plenty of things to keep residents busy night and day. The $25 million Tuacahn Center for the Arts in nearby Snow Canyon — named for a family called Snow, not for icy weather — presents Broadway plays. "You sit outdoors in a beautiful red rock amphitheater, and the performances are very good," she says.

During summer, "St. George Live" offers tours of historical sites led by local residents costumed as pioneers. Besides these offerings, there are nearby state parks, ghost towns and canyons. The Olsons like to hook up their fifth-wheel trailer and camp at Zion, Snow Canyon or Panguitch Lake. And Curt regularly goes fishing in local reservoirs stocked with trout. "I've been catching my limit," he says happily.

Like many retirees, the Olsons also enjoy touring throughout the West. "We've been roaming for the past eight years, from Reno to Phoenix," Curt says. "And you know what? In all that traveling, we haven't found anyplace we like better than St. George." ●

San Antonio, Texas

A colorful history and international flavor add spice to this Texas city

By Julie Cooper

It was March 6, 1836, when 189 valiant defenders of the Mission San Antonio de Valero fell at the hands of Mexican General Santa Anna and his troops, giving rise to the independence battle cry, "Remember the Alamo," as the fort is better known. More than 17 decades later, the Alamo and its poignant past are remembered fondly by thousands of visitors who annually pay homage to the most famous historical site in Texas.

For Ray and Barbara Clark, those fond feelings extended to the entire Alamo City, where they were stationed early in Ray's military career.

They couldn't forget the life they once had in San Antonio and finally fulfilled a dream to move back in retirement.

"We'd been trying to get back to San Antonio for 25 years," Barbara confesses. When Ray retired as an Air Force master sergeant in the mid-1970s, the couple was set to move to nearby Austin, where Ray had a job lined up with Texas Instruments. But family obligations took them back to Barbara's hometown of Evansville, IN.

The couple owned and operated a number of businesses in the Evansville area, including the 11th Frame Lounge and Cross-Eyed Cricket family restaurant. When retirement finally did dawn, the Clarks once again turned their eyes to the Lone Star State.

The eighth-largest city in the United States, San Antonio has one of the lowest costs of living among major cities. The seat of Bexar (pronounced Bear) County, San Antonio has a population of about 1.24 million. The population of the metropolitan statistical area, which includes Bexar, Comal, Guadalupe and Wilson counties, is 1.72 million.

Whether they live in outlying Converse, Universal City or Garden Ridge, communities popular among newcomer retirees, most residents say they're from San Antonio. The city is about a three-hour drive from the Texas Gulf Coast and about four hours to the Mexico border. San Antonio is in south-central Texas and enjoys an average temperature of 68.7 degrees. Its proximity to the Texas Hill Country, with its rich history of 19th-century German settlements and wildflower-dotted pastures and roadsides in spring, is a big draw for Texas residents.

San Antonio ranks No. 1 with Texans as a vacation destination. Four interstate highways, five U.S. highways and five state highways make getting there a snap. The San Antonio International Airport serves the city and surrounding area and is just 13 miles from the downtown River Walk, an area along the San Antonio River that is packed with restaurants, clubs and shops. City attractions also include historic Market Square, museums, theme parks and scores of savory Mexican restaurants.

Before settling near San Antonio, the Clarks spent two years crisscrossing America in a 34-foot recreational vehicle. They found their 1,800-square-foot dream house in Carolina Crossing, a new gated community in Schertz, a booming community of 25,000 just north of San Antonio in Guadalupe County. The Clarks thought about a condo or garden home but wanted a small yard for their schnauzer, Shotzie. They bought a model home the same day it went on the market in February 1996.

"We saved a good $1,200 to $1,300 a month by moving to San Antonio," says Barbara, 68. Ray, 67, estimates that the neighborhood includes about 30 percent active military and 30 percent retirees. Military retirees can use the exchange, commissary and pharmacy at Randolph Air Force Base in nearby Universal City.

The military presence in south-central Texas is a big plus with retirees. Lackland and Brooks Air Force bases lie on the south side of town, while Randolph Air Force Base sits on the northern edge. San Antonio's former Kelly Air Force Base was recently phased out, its runway now the Kelly Field Annex operated by Lackland. Fort Sam Houston, northeast of downtown, has been an Army base since 1845.

If they so choose, the Clarks could use the medical services at Brooke Army Medical Center, but they prefer to use an HMO to supplement Medicare. "The medical facilities are tremendous," Ray says. Major hospital systems include Baptist, Methodist, Christus Santa Rosa, Southwest General and Nix Medical Center, among the 36 hospitals serving the area.

The Air Force is part of the reason that Schertz has seen its population jump from 10,500 in 1990 to 25,000, according to city manager Kerry Sweat. "The large number of persons retired from the military is really how Schertz began," says Sweat of the town once called Cutoff. "We have a lot of the advantages of the big city. We're close enough to enjoy it and still be a small town," he says.

Part of what they enjoy about San Antonio is a history that is a colorful draw for vacationers and residents alike. In 1718, Father Antonio Olivares, a missionary in south Texas, helped establish Mission San Antonio de Valero (the Alamo) and Villa de Bexar, the military outpost. The missions continued to grow as the Franciscans moved to convert the local Native Americans to Christianity. These missions still stand today along the historic Mission Trail and are active Catholic parish churches.

The flavor of Mexico is very much in evidence in multicultural San Antonio. In April, San Antonio holds its biggest party of the year when it celebrates Fiesta, a 10-day festival commemorating the area's rich history and cultures. Parades, parties, special exhibits, concerts and coronations are just some of the activities.

Fans of Western movies — whether it is John Wayne's "The Alamo" or Errol Flynn's "San Antonio" — won't be disappointed in the cowboy history that the area retains. Each February the city immerses itself in all things Western with the San Antonio Rodeo and Stock Show.

Trail riders and chuck wagons make a journey from all parts of South and Central Texas to meet up for the start of the

16-day rodeo, fair and livestock show.

Lascelles Wisdom, 55, doesn't have to wait for February to enjoy saddles and

San Antonio, TX

Population: 1.24 million in San Antonio, 1.5 in Bexar County.

Location: In south-central Texas at the edge of the Gulf coastal plains, about 140 miles north of the Gulf of Mexico, 78 miles south of Austin, 270 miles south of Dallas and 197 miles west of Houston. Elevation is 701 feet.

Climate: High Low
January 63 39
July 94 69

Average relative humidity: 50%

Rain: 28 inches

Cost of living: Below average

Median housing cost: $134,000

Sales tax: 8.125%

Sales tax exemptions: Groceries, prescriptions and over-the-counter medicines (including dietary supplements), certain agricultural products and equipment.

State income tax: None

Intangibles tax: None

Estate tax: None

Property tax: Paid to the city, county, local school districts and a host of other special taxing districts. Taxes are assessed at 100% of the current market valuation. Rates are .698534 per $100 valuation in Bexar County, .578540 in San Antonio, .5975 in Converse and .7791 in Schertz (plus 1.74 for the school district). There are 12 school districts in Bexar County with tax rates from 1.63 to 1.79 per $100 valuation.

Homestead exemption: Each taxing entity caps exemptions for homeowners 65 and older at a different amount, the highest being the city of San Antonio at

$65,000. Bexar County exempts the first $50,000, and the Alamo Community College District exempts $30,000. Guadalupe County exempts 1% plus $10,000 of the appraised value of a residential homestead. For homeowners under age 65, there is a $3,000 flood exemption, a $5,000 river authority exemption and a $15,000 school district exemption in Bexar County. Other exemptions may be available, depending on the neighborhood in which you live.

Religion: More than 1,200 churches represent every denomination. There are nine synagogues.

Education: There are four campuses in the Alamo Community College District: Northwest Vista College, Palo Alto College, St. Phillip's College and San Antonio College. The University of Texas at San Antonio was established in 1973 as part of the UT system. Trinity University is a top-rated liberal arts school established in 1869. The University of the Incarnate Word is a Catholic university with an enrollment of about 5,000. St. Mary's University is the oldest Catholic University in Texas with three undergraduate schools, master's and doctoral programs and the only law school in San Antonio. The UT Health Science Center at San Antonio includes medicine, nursing, dental, allied health sciences and graduate-level biomedical science. Our Lady of the Lake University offers undergraduate degrees in more than 40 areas, master's degrees in nine programs and a doctorate in psychology and leadership studies. The National University of Mexico also has a downtown campus offering classes in Spanish, English as a second language, Mexican arts, history, literature and computers.

Transportation: Via Metropolitan Transit serves the metropolitan area. Funded through a .5 percent sales tax, VIA operates a fleet of 428 buses. Bus fare is 80 cents and there are discounts for senior citizens and people with disabilities. The Park & Ride system serves special events

such as Fiesta, Spurs games and events at the Alamodome.

Health: The San Antonio area has more than 35 hospitals, including three military hospitals, mental health centers and rehabilitation centers. The Cancer Therapy and Research Center, a joint venture with UT Health Science Center, is dedicated to the cure and prevention of cancer and offers outpatient treatment and clinical research. The 700-acre South Texas Medical Center is the largest in Texas and represents a combined annual budget of $2.5 billion. The Center has more than 26,000 employees.

Housing options: There are more than 145,000 rental housing units, including apartments, townhouses and duplexes in all sections of the metropolitan area. San Antonio's hottest area is in the northwest. Newer developments include **The Ridge at Carolina Crossing**, from $110,000; **The Springs at Stone Oak**, from $160,000; and **Mainland Square**, from the $90,000s. There also are build-to-suit sites of one-half to five acres starting in the mid-$40,000s. There are more than 47 retirement and life-care communities, which include assisted living, residential care and Alzheimer's care.

Visitor lodging: There are 25,000 rooms in hotels, motels, resorts and bed-and-breakfast lodgings. The Westin La Cantera offers room rates of $199-$269. A sister hotel, the 513-room Westin Riverwalk, opened in November 2000; rates start at $169, (800) 937-8461. Historic hotels on or near the San Antonio River Walk include the Menger Hotel, La Mansion del Rio, Fairmount and St. Anthony Wyndham Historic Hotel.

Information: San Antonio Convention and Visitors Bureau, 201 E. Market St., San Antonio, TX 78205, (800) 447-3372 or www.sanantoniocvb.com. The San Antonio Chamber of Commerce, P.O. Box 1628, San Antonio, TX 78296, (210) 229-2100 or www.sachamber.org. The chamber has a Guide to San Antonio relocation package for $15, plus $7 postage and handling, (888) 242-3068.

spurs. The recent retiree from Long Island, NY, has indulged his love of horses by purchasing eight thoroughbred racehorses. He stables them at Retama Park Racetrack, a facility 15 minutes northeast of downtown San Antonio that offers thoroughbred racing July through October.

Lascelles and his wife, Netilda, 64, moved to San Antonio just last October. The Wisdoms had checked out Florida and South Carolina, where many of their friends had moved, as likely retirement spots. They chose Texas in part to be close to their daughter, Lorraine Smith, and her family.

Retirement came early for Lascelles when he accepted a buyout from Long Island Lighting Co. after 26 years as a welding engineer. He says he and his wife never considered staying in New York. "It is very expensive to retire and live in New York," Lascelles says. "My house was paid for, but the taxes were $8,200 a year."

The Wisdoms traded a five-bedroom "high ranch" for a newly built four-bedroom home in Converse in the northeast part of Bexar County. Netilda, who retired as an assistant rehabilitation aide in a nursing home, has tentative plans to do volunteer work. Currently, though, she's busy furnishing her new home. The Wisdoms left much of their furniture in New York rather than move it.

The median selling price for a single-family home in San Antonio is $134,000. The average monthly rental rate on a two-bedroom, two-bath unit is $710.

"I used to visit Lorraine and fell in love with San Antonio," Netilda says. "The people here are, let me say, different. The people here are friendly," she says with added emphasis.

There is an international flavor that permeates San Antonio. According to 2000 census figures, 59 percent of the population is Hispanic, 32 percent is Anglo and 7 percent is African-American. The low number of African-Americans among the populace does not bother the Wisdoms, both natives of Port Antonio, Jamaica.

"Where I lived in Jamaica, we were one people," Netilda says. "When we moved to Long Island, about 2 percent of the population was black," Lascelles adds.

Other recent retirees also have found San Antonio to be a friendly place to live. "It's amazing how friendly the people are," says Nan Birmingham, 75. A former contributing editor for Town & Country magazine, Nan was ready to say goodbye to the New York winters and find a slower pace of life. She moved to San Antonio in 1998, partly to be closer to her only grandchild, Caitlin. Caitlin and her parents live 25 minutes away.

"I've finally stopped looking over my shoulder," Nan says, chuckling about the "innate suspicion" that many New Yorkers have for passers-by when it comes to crime. "I'm getting over it now," she says.

Nan sold her townhouse in the Bronx and opted to rent a spacious one-bedroom apartment in the Meridian, a gated complex near San Antonio's Quarry Market. Her ground-floor apartment borders the green space that backs into the complex. Nan estimates that a similar apartment in New York City would go for $3,500 a month — a far cry from the $1,270 a month she pays, and that includes use of a pool, health club, security and party room.

"I figure I've cut my overhead probably in half," says Nan, who likes to breakfast on her plant-filled terrace. She has turned half of her expansive kitchen into an office with computer and couch.

A native of California, Nan says she briefly considered San Francisco for retirement, and she watched a number of her friends retire to Florida and New Mexico. Besides traveling, which she does two to three months of the year, Nan enjoys the San Antonio Museum of Art, where she holds museum membership. One of the top art museums in Texas, SAMA is home to the Nelson A. Rockefeller Center for Latin American Art.

Other art draws include the McNay Art Museum, where admission is free but the art is priceless. The museum is housed in a Spanish Colonial Revival-style mansion built in 1927. It holds Cézanne, Picasso and bronzes by Rodin. And the Southwest School of Art & Craft is the place for learning the arts. Classes include photography, painting, ceramics, weaving and carving. The school is housed in the Old Ursuline Academy, begun in 1851.

Both Nan Birmingham and the Clarks pitch Central Market as a fun spot to go near downtown. "It's my favorite place," Nan says. "When everyone said, 'Oh, you have to try the Central Market,' I envisioned Texas pickup trucks and fresh vegetables in an outdoor setting." She was surprised to find valet parking at a store once dubbed "Gucci B" by San Antonians. Central Market is part of the HEB Grocery Co., which has its corporate headquarters in San Antonio. A cooking school that offers weekly classes is another reason that Nan, a former cooking instructor, likes Central Market. And, "the price is right," she says.

The Clarks, who have authored a cookbook, frequently make the 20-mile drive from their home to Alamo Heights for a special shopping foray at Central Market. The longer growing season and proximity to Mexico mean more fresh fruits and vegetables at good prices almost year-round in San Antonio stores.

But if eating out is on the menu, there is more to the city than tacos and tamales. Former restaurateurs, the Clarks admit to a love affair with Tex-Mex food and appreciate the spicy stuff. "We eat out about three times a week," says Barbara, noting that she and Ray usually stop for lunch when they are running errands. The early influences on the city's restaurants were Mexican and German, but the wide variety today boasts American, Continental, Chinese, Italian, Vietnamese, Indian and steakhouses too numerous to count.

On the negative side, what do retirees find to complain about? "The standing joke is we're running a B&B," Barbara says. The Clarks find their home popular among vacationing friends and relatives, but Barbara and Ray like to travel as well. They made five or six trips to Mexico in 1999 — "especially when friends come to visit," Barbara says.

Three months into their retirement, the Wisdoms were still adjusting to the way Texans drive. "I've got to get used to the driving in the center lane — those arrows are turning left and right and I don't know where to go," Lascelles says.

The Clarks are busy counting their blessings. "There's hardly a day that goes by that one of us doesn't say, 'I love Texas' or 'I love my house,' " Barbara says with a laugh. "I love Texas," Ray quips in agreement. "I love the attitude of the people here, and the patriotism," he adds. ●

Sanibel, Florida

Retirees enjoy unspoiled natural beauty and a casual lifestyle on this tranquil Florida island

By Karen Feldman

While many Florida beachfront communities have been all but overrun with high-rise condominiums and commercial development, Sanibel Island stands out for its steadfast refusal to go with the flow. This barrier island off the Southwest Florida coast has fewer than 6,200 permanent residents, miles of well-tended bike paths and thousands of acres of unspoiled nature sanctuaries teeming with wildlife. The residents are careful to cultivate culture as well as nature, supporting playhouses, art centers, galleries, boutiques, restaurants and hotels.

What's missing? Not much, other than traffic lights, beachfront high-rises and all except one of the usual fast-food franchises. So it's not surprising that a move to Sanibel is the retirement dream of — and logical step for — many people who vacation there year after year.

That was the case for full-time residents Bob Hanger and William (Bill) and Tina Hillebrandt. Bob's first trip to the island was by car ferry from the mainland in 1962, to visit his first wife's aunt. He fell in love with the island, and when he retired from his sales job with Merck & Co., the decision to move came easily.

"We knew we were going to come here. We had already bought a lot here," says Bob, 81. "We never considered retiring anywhere else."

He and his wife moved south in October 1981, driving over the causeway and settling into a three-bedroom home with swimming pool. When his wife died, Bob remained, eventually remarrying.

In 1986, the Hillebrandts were looking for a quiet getaway from their home in Omaha when a friend told them about Sanibel Island. "We'd never heard of it," says Tina, 43. "We had no idea what we were coming to. It was magical."

They arrived after dark. "When we walked out the door in the morning, it took our breath away," says Bill, 58, a retired freight transportation executive.

They rode bicycles around the island for a few days and bought a condo before they left. "We borrowed against my retirement plan," Bill says. "We really went out on a limb."

They visited a few weeks each year until they moved full time in 1992. As is the case for many who move to the island, cost wasn't their primary consideration. "We were paying the same amount of taxes on the house we owned in Omaha at the time," says Tina.

What really sold them, says Bill, was "the natural philosophy of the community, the preservation, the conservation." In the 1970s, the county commission approved a measure that would allow a total of 90,000 people to live on the island. Residents balked. They held a referendum, incorporated as a city and promptly reduced the maximum allowable population to 9,000.

That sort of active environmental concern draws a lot of residents, says Keith Trowbridge, executive director of the Sanibel-Captiva Chamber of Commerce. "Sixty-five percent of the island is sanctuary," he says. "It's tranquil and serene. There are a lot of community activities and three live theaters. People are retiring earlier today; they're healthy, 50 or 55, and have 30 years to look forward to. They'd better get busy doing something."

Finding ways to stay busy on Sanibel is not difficult. Activities, classes and cultural and volunteer opportunities abound. Because of its roomy beaches along the gentle gulf, Sanibel is a popular vacation destination for Americans and Europeans. That, in turn, has created a wealth of well-stocked boutiques and galleries as well as a sophisticated dining scene.

Despite the inevitable reduction in pace to island time that occurs when crossing the causeway, residents also like the fact that their peaceful getaway is close to the rest of the world. Southwest Florida International Airport is growing rapidly, with more flights going to more cities, many nonstop, including Frankfurt and London.

Add in low crime and that no-nonsense attitude toward growth control, and its appeal as a retirement haven looms large. And many people aren't putting off the dream of an island lifestyle until the traditional retirement years.

"We're seeing a lot of early retirees, people in their 40s and 50s, many of whom have made their money in the stock market," says Pam Pfahler, a real estate agent with John Naumann Associates on Sanibel. "We're also seeing some with younger families who are able to locate their homes anywhere and work from their home office." With real estate appreciating at a nice clip, it's an attractive market for those with money to invest.

Count Debbie and John Friedlund among that younger group who couldn't wait for retirement to relocate. They vacationed on Sanibel more than 20 years ago and found returning to the Chicago area very difficult. "We tried to like winter but we just didn't," Debbie Friedlund says. "On that vacation in 1979 we talked to Realtors and never looked back."

Although they would continue working, they knew they wanted to live out their retirement years on Sanibel. Today, at 49, the couple recently sold their island motel and Debbie has retired, although John still works. While she has no paying job, she keeps busy.

"There are lots of organizations here depending on volunteers, like the library, the chamber of commerce and CROW (Clinic for the Rehabilitation of Wildlife)," she says. "They all have training programs in place; you know what's expected of you. You feel like you're needed and really making a difference. I have to be careful not to overdo it."

She devotes time to CROW, a rehabilitation center for injured native animals, such as burrowing owls, hawks, snakes and turtles. She also helps the Sanibel-

Captiva Conservation Foundation with beach patrols, a summer ritual during which volunteers help protect nesting sea turtles and their eggs and help guide hatchlings to the sea.

The Hillebrandts do turtle patrols, too, and early one morning last summer happened on a huge endangered loggerhead turtle laying her eggs. "I was late for tennis, but I didn't care," Bill says.

With the advent of mosquito control and air conditioning, today's residents live a far more comfortable existence than their forebears did. Researchers believe people lived on Sanibel Island 2,500 years ago, not long after it became an island, rising from the sea as a persistent ridge of sand. Archaeologists have found evidence of the prehistoric Calusa Indians, who eventually died out. Later, Cuban and Indian mullet fishermen came next, living in thatched structures.

Eventually, settlers on the island and wealthy cattle farmers across the bay requisitioned a lighthouse, a 104-foot tower built in 1884 that still stands today. The beach around that structure is one of the island's most popular, with broad expanses of sand, lots of shells washing up with the tides, sprawling sea grape trees and gnarled driftwood facing an aquamarine gulf.

In the 1920s, the island began drawing famous visitors looking for a place to get away from it all. When his isolationist views earned Charles Lindbergh the public's scorn, he and his wife, Anne, became regular visitors. Thomas Edison sailed from his winter home in Fort Myers to study native plants and savor the beach. Poet Edna St. Vincent Millay vacationed there in the 1930s.

In 1935, Pulitzer Prize-winning political cartoonist Jay Norwood "Ding" Darling began the first of many winters on

Sanibel, FL

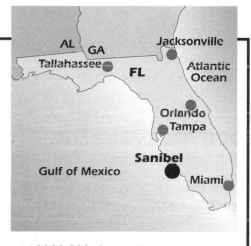

Population: 7,074 permanent residents with a seasonal peak population of 33,000.

Location: A barrier island off the coast of Fort Myers in southwest Florida, Sanibel Island is 145 miles south of Tampa and 158 miles west of Miami.

Climate:

	High	Low
January	72	52
July	91	73

Average relative humidity: 52 percent

Rainfall: 53 inches

Cost of living: Above average

Median housing cost: $700,000

Sales tax: 6%

Sales tax exemptions: Groceries, prescription drugs and some professional services.

State income tax: None

Intangibles tax: None. The tax was repealed as of Jan. 1, 2007.

Estate tax: None

Inheritance tax: None

Property tax: $18.1632 per $1,000 of assessed value, with homes assessed at 100% of market value. Yearly tax on a $700,000 home with homestead exemption below is about $12,260.

Homestead exemption: $25,000 off the assessed value of a permanent, primary residence.

Religion: There is one synagogue as well as several churches on the island, including multidenominational, United Church of Christ, Catholic, Episcopal, Unitarian-Universalist and Christian Scientist. Other religions meet on neighboring Captiva Island and on the mainland in Fort Myers.

Education: There's only an elementary school on the island, but the Sanibel Community Center and BIG Arts hold a variety of classes and seminars, including various types of art, music and current events. On the mainland, Edison Community College in Fort Myers offers a variety of two- and four-year degrees as well as adult education classes. Also in Fort Myers is Florida Gulf Coast University, the state's newest university. It offers distance learning, many degree programs and special events.

Transportation: There is no public transit system operating on Sanibel Island. A number of shuttle services transport passengers to and from Southwest Florida International Airport in Lee County. Taxi service also is available.

Health: There are no hospitals, but numerous physicians have offices on Sanibel, including dentists, internists, ophthalmologists and other specialists. HealthPark of the Islands services many of the medical needs of the community, from routine check-ups to emergencies and minor surgery. Lee Memorial Health System's HealthPark Medical Center on the mainland about five miles from the causeway offers a full range of services in a well-appointed structure as well as seminars, senior services and discounts.

Housing options: Housing along the beach is in demand and hard to come by. A four-bedroom, three-bath home on the beach starts at about $3 million, while beachfront condos start in the high $600,000s for one bedroom and the mid-$800,000s for two bedrooms. Inland homes are selling for upwards of $500,000, with most averaging in the $700,000s. Lots start in the $300,000s inland and run to about $3 million on the beach.

Visitor lodging: Because of the island's popularity as a vacation destination, there are dozens of choices. Rates are highest from Christmas to Easter. Among the options are: Best Western Sanibel Island Beach Resort, a beachfront motel, $149-$499, double occupancy, (800) 528-1234. Brennen's Tarpon Tale Inn offers cottages and motel rooms within walking distance of the beach, $79-$199, (239) 472-0939. Casa Ybel Resort is a beachfront all-suites resort, $275-$525, (800) 276-4753. Holiday Inn Beach Resort is a beachfront hotel, $177-$299, (800) 443-0909. Song of the Sea is a beachfront European-style inn, $179-$469, (800) 231-1045.

Information: Sanibel and Captiva Islands Chamber of Commerce, 1159 Causeway Road, Sanibel, FL 33957, (239) 472-1080 or www.sanibel-captiva.org.

the island and its neighbor, Captiva, which is still more sparsely developed and more expensive than Sanibel. A staunch conservationist, he campaigned for federal protection of the fragile and unique environment on Sanibel. The result is the 6,400-acre J.N. "Ding" Darling Wildlife Refuge, which occupies a third of Sanibel Island.

Take a walk, bike, car or tram ride along the five-mile Wildlife Drive in the refuge and come upon alligators sunning themselves, raccoons and possums foraging for a snack, and a host of birds, including roseate spoonbills, great white egrets, Florida scrub jays, white ibis, ospreys, red-shouldered hawks, bald eagles, cormorants and herons.

Long renowned as one of the top three areas in the world for shell collecting, Sanibel takes its reputation seriously. Every spring since 1937, the Sanibel Community Association has held the Sanibel Shell Fair and Show. It began as a small affair on someone's porch with a few islanders displaying their prized finds. Over the years it's outgrown the community center, spilling out onto the grounds as well.

The Bailey-Matthews Shell Museum bills itself as the only museum in the United States devoted entirely to the shells of the world, featuring exhibits of shells and shell-related subjects, shells in tribal art, and a collection of tree snails. There's even a name for that telltale posture struck when the urge to reach down and pick up a beautiful shell from the beach becomes irresistible. It's called the Sanibel Stoop, and it can be seen on every beach on the island at all times of the day.

The island is fast becoming as culturally well-endowed as it is environmentally appealing. BIG Arts (Barrier Island Group for the Arts) is in its third decade of promoting arts on the island, offering concerts, workshops, films, lectures, discussion groups and a Thanksgiving weekend arts and crafts fair.

The Schoolhouse Theater, Sanibel's only professional musical theater, is affectionately named after its orginal schoolhouse building. It now offers an intimate approach to live theater in newer facilities. The Pirate Playhouse at the J. Howard Wood Theatre houses a professional regional theater company, bringing actors, directors and designers from throughout the country for drama, classics and comedies.

Tina Hillebrandt has been a board member there, although she's had to cut back because of illness in the family this year. She remains active in the church. A certified massage therapist, she also donates massages to women who pay for them by doing something nice for someone else.

In November Bill will finish his term on the city council, and he is past president of the conservation foundation board and remains active in the organization. "There are so many wonderful, legitimate things to do around here — not busy work," Bill says. "We get a chance to give back because we've been given so much."

Tina says, "We've got life down to three questions: Can you live where you want to live, be with people you want to be with and do what you want to do? If you can get one out of three, you're living a good life. Bill and I are living a dream. We have all three."

Tina and Bill Hillebrandt started making friends on that very first visit in 1986 and still socialize with some of those people today. They both play tennis, bicycle and enjoy boating. One of their favorite activities is watching the sunset every night.

"There's something to be said for sitting, periodically taking that daily pause," Bill says. "There are lots of nice places just to pause — on the beach, on the bay, in the middle of "Ding" Darling (refuge), you can pause and look up anywhere and see beautiful things."

They've moved five times, first from condo to condo, then two houses on the beach and now to a three-bedroom home with a dock on the bay, which seems the best fit so far. "We didn't know it at the time, but when we bought our first condo we got into the Sanibel real estate market at a pretty good time," Bill says. "Our investment then made it possible for us to be here now."

As for their old life back in the Midwest, "that was then and this is now," he says, adding that they stay in touch with family and old friends. "It's amazing how many more people come to see us in Florida than in Omaha."

If there's anything about their current life that's bothersome, it might be the traffic during the busy winter months. "Like Tina says, traffic and no-see-ums (gnats) are God's reminders that we're not in paradise," Bill quips. But he adds, "It's a choice. The community wisely made the decision to keep the road two lanes, relatively rural. We've lived in small towns and big cities. Sanibel is another small town; it's just surrounded by water. But that's part of its charm."

To those considering a move there, Tina kids, "The bugs are big, there are live animals roaming the streets and you really should consider Montana." Her husband adds: "The traffic is terrible; the taxes are outrageous. But other than that, we'd love to see you."

Joking aside, they caution that the life they love on Sanibel isn't for everyone. "When the sun goes down, it really gets dark," says Bill. "There are no street lights, no traffic lights. People half-kiddingly say that 9 p.m. is Sanibel's midnight, but it's true that there's not much going on after that. For a lot of people, it's not their bag. But we found it appealing." ●

San Juan Islands, Washington

Low-key and secluded, these islands in northwest Washington boast charming villages and spectacular scenery

By Stanton H. Patty

In the San Juan Islands, the times seem perpetually kinder and gentler — sort of like the old "Happy Days" television show, say David and Sondra Bayley, who were vacationing from the Los Angeles area when they found the spot they thought was perfect for retirement.

Other retirees found equally compelling reasons to move here. Richard and Victoria Baker retired from high-voltage jobs in Southern California to become innkeepers. Jim and Carolee Maya took early retirement from California teaching careers — and then Jim became known as Captain Jim, skipper of a whale watching charter boat. Ron and Carol Duke retired, rented a truck and moved their belongings from the hectic Seattle area to a place where "people really care about people."

All of these retirees set a course for the San Juan Islands, a string of saltwater pearls in northwestern Washington state. Canada's British Columbia is a near neighbor across the water. "It's a great place to live," says Captain Jim. "I have this incredible feeling of safety and peacefulness."

At last count (depending on whether tallies were made at high or low tide) there were more than 700 islands and islets in the archipelago. Only 40 or so are inhabited, some by lone occupants. Most of the islands' 15,000 residents live on four islands: San Juan, Orcas, Lopez and Shaw. The principal islands are as different as chinook salmon and Dungeness crab, favorite bounties of the San Juans.

San Juan Island (population 6,500), home of the islands' largest community, Friday Harbor, is where most retirees have settled. And it's where most visitors go ashore from island-hopping ferries, floatplanes and fast catamaran shuttles from Seattle. There are no highway connections to the San Juans. The only way to reach the islands is by water or air. And that's just fine with most of the contented islanders.

"I like the ferry — I like the distance that it creates," says Sondra Bayley, 66, former owner of a court-reporting agency in the Los Angeles area. Sondra and her husband, David, 58, a retired community college instructor, built their retirement home 12 miles northwest of Friday Harbor.

Friday Harbor (population 2,098) is the seat of San Juan County, which covers all of the islands. It's a snug harbor where sailing yachts, powerboats and commercial fishing vessels are moored almost hull to hull in summer. There's a merry fugue of whistle toots as ferries arrive and mewing gulls wheel overhead. Cyclists pedal off the ferries and go exploring on country roads to catch views of killer whales (orcas) prowling the waterways.

Orcas Island (population 4,500) is the largest of the San Juans with almost 57 square miles of charming hamlets and dazzling scenery. The commercial center is Eastsound, which actually is on the north end of the island. (Yes, one needs a compass to navigate in the San Juans.) Hikers and cyclists on Orcas ascend 2,047-foot Mount Constitution, the highest point in the San Juans, for summit views that sweep from British Columbia to Washington's Cascade and Olympic mountain ranges.

Lopez Island (population 2,200) is another favored destination for cyclists because of its mostly flat terrain, uncrowded beaches and cozy bed-and-breakfast inns. Lopez residents still wave greetings at each passing car and bicycle.

Shaw Island (population about 150) has a small county park with limited camping and picnicking facilities. Most of the eight-square-mile island is private property. Members of a local order of Roman Catholic nuns have been operating the ferry landing there for more than 15 years.

The San Juans have been attracting visitors ever since Capt. George Vancouver, the English navigator, sailed by in 1792. Vancouver described the islands thusly in his log: "The serenity of the climate, the innumerable pleasing landscapes, the most lovely country that can be imagined . . ."

Sailors, pirates, smugglers, soldiers and a few pioneer settlers followed. Soon villages took root. Then boaters from Seattle and other Puget Sound cities made the San Juans a popular rendezvous. One visit to these getaway islands today and a traveler might be tempted to settle in the San Juans forever.

But island life may not be for everyone, retirees caution. "If you come here, you need to be comfortable with yourself, comfortable with your partner," David Bayley says.

Sondra Bayley suggests that newcomers rent awhile before building or buying an island home.

"Some people come with unrealistic expectations and are soon out," she says. The Bayleys visited Mexico "and all the pretty places people go in the West" before considering retirement in the San Juans. In 1988, well before they actually retired, they made a down payment on a lot. They returned the following two years and camped on their property, "experiencing it," David recalls. Then it was time to build.

The lifestyle also attracted Richard and Victoria Baker, the proprietors of Wildwood Manor, a three-story bed-and-breakfast inn that crowns a wooded knoll on the northeast side of San Juan Island. Opening the B&B was a dramatic lifestyle change for the former Californians. Richard, 65, is a retired Los Angeles fire chief. Victoria, 59, used to be a deputy sheriff in Los Angeles County.

They decided to "check out" the San Juans after friends, who had honeymooned in the area, brought home enthusiastic reports. "We came to visit, saw the property we wanted, and that was it," Richard says.

Victoria, who had studied architecture after retiring from police work, designed their 4,500-square-foot, Queen Anne-style Victorian. Now Wildwood Manor, looking like a small castle in the wilderness, offers three guest rooms and a smashing saltwater view across San Juan Channel to the Cascade Mountains. The top floor is reserved for the Bakers' children and grandchildren when they visit from California and Colorado.

Volunteerism is a major activity for Friday Harbor-area retirees. Victoria is a past president of the local Kiwanis service club. Richard served as president of the Lions Club. He also is a past commander of the Friday Harbor Power Squadron, an educational organization that promotes boating safety. "We've met a lot of wonderful people here," he says.

First-rate medical care is a priority for San Juans residents. Seniors make up 26 percent of the county's population, the highest percentage in Washington. There are no hospitals in the San Juans, but three islands — San Juan, Orcas and Lopez — have emergency clinics and

San Juan Islands, WA

Population: 15,190 total on all islands; 6,500 on San Juan Island, including 2,098 in Friday Harbor, 4,500 on Orcas Island and 2,200 on Lopez Island.

Location: In northwestern Washington state, about 80 air miles north of Seattle. Only four islands — San Juan, Orcas, Lopez and Shaw — are served by Washington state ferries.

Climate:

	High	Low
January	43	35
July	70	50

(The above figures are averages. Temperatures and rainfall vary from island to island.)

Average relative humidity: 40%

Rain: 20.98 inches

Snow: Up to 6 inches some years, depending on location.

Mild climate with warm, sometimes breezy, summers and cool, often damp, winters. The sun shines an average of 247 days a year. Severe windstorms are rare.

Cost of living: Slightly above average. Most goods are shipped to the islands by ferries or by air. Gasoline arrives by barges.

Median housing cost: $494,000 is the

median price for a single-family home in the county. Waterfront homes fetch considerably higher prices.

Sales tax: 7.7%

Sales tax exemptions: Groceries and medical prescriptions.

State income tax: None

Intangibles tax: None

Estate tax: Applicable to estates above $2 million.

Property taxes: They range from $5.6384 per $1,000 of assessed valuation to $7.82664, depending on levies approved by voters for schools and other programs. Property is assessed statewide at 100% of market value. The annual tax on a $494,000 home, without homestead exemption, would range from about $2,748 to $3,866.

Homestead exemption: None, except for those age 61 or older (or disabled) with household income less than $35,000.

Religion: Eight places of worship on the four main islands, representing Protestant and Roman Catholic denominations.

Education: Skagit Valley College, based in Mount Vernon, a mainland neighbor, operates the San Juan Center campus in Friday Harbor. The center offers a two-year liberal arts degree and has a variety of classes designed for seniors. Senior courses include genealogy, literature and history. In addition, seniors (age 60 or older) are able to audit regular classes; prices vary. Several classes are taught by retired academics. Additional information: San Juan Center, (360) 378-3220.

Transportation: Access from the mainland mostly is by state ferries and air taxis.

There is no public transit system in the islands. However, the San Juan County Health and Community Services Department has senior centers on San Juan, Orcas and Lopez islands, and these centers operate vans for both on-island and off-island trips. There also is van service for twice-weekly lunches at the senior centers, and lunches are delivered to shut-ins.

Health: There are emergency/primary care clinics on San Juan, Orcas and Lopez islands. The Friday Harbor clinic, the largest, has four physicians on staff. Top-rated paramedics are on duty aboard the three islands. Serious cases are transported by helicopter or ferry to hospitals in mainland cities.

Housing options: Most islanders buy or build single-family homes that usually include some acreage. A few condominiums are available in Friday Harbor and in Roche Harbor, both on San Juan Island. Prices range generally from $250,000 to about $450,000.

Visitor lodging: In Friday Harbor, Inns at Friday Harbor, $125-$235, (800) 752-5752. Hillside House Bed and Breakfast, $95-$275, (800) 232-4730. On Orcas Island, Orcas Hotel, $89-$208, (360) 376-4300. Rosario Resort, from $89, (800) 562-8820. On Lopez Island, Lopez Islander Resort, $80-$143, (360) 468-2233.

Information: San Juan Islands Visitor Information Service, P.O. Box 65, Lopez Island, WA 98261, (888) 468-3701or www.guidetosanjuans.com. Other sources: San Juan Island Chamber of Commerce, (360) 378-5240; Orcas Island Chamber of Commerce, (360) 376-2273; Lopez Island Chamber of Commerce, (360) 468-4664.

paramedic units.

Richard Baker, who had two open-heart surgeries before moving to San Juan Island and knows about skill levels from his years as a firefighter, gives the local paramedics and volunteer fire department "excellent" ratings. The InterIsland Medical Center on San Juan Island (Friday Harbor) is staffed by four physicians. There also is a family physician in private practice on the island. Patients requiring care beyond the island clinics' capabilities are transported to hospitals in nearby cities — Anacortes, Mount Vernon and Bellingham — or to more distant Seattle.

Anacortes (Anna-COURT-ess), about 80 highway miles north of Seattle, is where most San Juans-bound visitors board Washington state ferries. It, too, is on an island, Fidalgo, but it is connected by bridges to the Washington mainland. Mount Vernon is on Interstate 5, on the way to Anacortes. Bellingham, also on I-5, is some 90 miles north of Seattle.

All three are "off-island" shopping destinations for San Juans residents. Bellingham also is the southern terminus of the Alaska Marine Highway, the state of Alaska's seagoing ferry system.

"This is a fabulous place to retire," says Wendy Stephens, director of senior services for San Juan County's Department of Health and Community Services. "Our retirees are fabulous people. They are creative and resilient folks who have had rich experiences through the Great Depression and world wars. We love working with them." There are additional senior centers on Orcas and Lopez islands.

Transportation is another major concern for San Juans retirees. They depend mostly on the state ferries that cruise to and from the islands from the Anacortes gateway. The ferries that carry islanders and their vehicles also bring tourists, sometimes swarms of visitors that crowd the ferries. The result can be aggravating boarding delays, especially in Friday Harbor and over on Orcas Island.

Canny residents bound for "off-island" excursions have devised a way to beat the crowds. They park their cars in a waiting line along a pier as soon as a fully loaded ferry departs, then go home to have breakfast or lunch until shortly before the next scheduled ferry is due to arrive.

"It's difficult to be resentful of tourists," says Victoria Baker. "After all, most of us came here as tourists."

In fact, Jim Maya, 63, a retired high school theater teacher, has a new career that caters to tourists: whale watching. It is a business, but for Maya it's pure joy as he pilots his 22-foot charter boat, Annie Mae, on whale-watching trips from Friday Harbor in search of killer whales.

Pods of resident killer whales, known around the Northwest as orcas, voyage through the San Juans. At times the local orcas are joined by transient whales bound for distant waters. "It's a very exciting time out there," Captain Jim says. "Those whales are about the most magnificent creatures on earth — wild, intelligent and beautiful."

The Mayas retired early to move in 1990 from Gilroy, CA, to the San Juans. "We could have stayed in California and retired at 62 or 63 to get the max out of our retirement, but we just wanted to live here," Jim says. Jim also organizes San Juan Island's annual Santa Ship program. Santa, you see, reaches salty Friday Harbor by boat, not with reindeer.

It would be nice, the Mayas say, if San Juan Island had a shopping mall and department stores. But they don't miss smog, traffic congestion and what they remember as the "frantic" pace of California. "The tradeoffs have been incredible," Jim says. "I can be in my boat in 15 minutes, catching salmon. This is the dream spot of the United States for a boater."

Another couple who came first as tourists were Ron and Carol Duke, frequent visitors to the islands before moving from the Seattle area in 1998. Ron, 64, had been a mailer at a Seattle newspaper. Carol, 62, is a retired history teacher.

They were attracted to San Juan Island by what Carol describes as the "warm and welcoming people here." An added incentive was that their son, Andy, operates a sporting goods store in Friday Harbor.

"We had heard that it takes a long time for people to accept you in a small town, but we haven't found that to be true at all," Carol says. "We have a grandson, Henry (14 months old), and when I take him for walks everybody knows Henry and they say, 'Hello, Henry.' It's nice."

The Dukes built a modest 1,870-square-foot home on a hillside two miles north of Friday Harbor. It's not waterfront property, but does have a saltwater view. Their advice to couples who are thinking of retiring to the San Juans: "Come and rent for a year. See if this is the lifestyle you want."

But you may not want to wait too long to try the San Juans. Waterfront property at appealing prices is in short supply. "Mother Nature is not making new islands," warns Jim Knych, a Friday Harbor real estate agent. ●

Santa Fe, New Mexico

Spanish, Mexican and American Indian influences enrich this culture-loving city in northern New Mexico

By Ellen Barone

There's something special about Santa Fe, a place where movie stars blend into the high desert landscape as easily as its low-lying adobe buildings. Since the first stream of Anglo settlers arrived centuries ago to what was then a sleepy American Indian pueblo, Santa Fe has had a magical effect on those who discover it.

Perhaps it's the awe-inspiring natural setting — the bittersweet scent of piñon that drifts through the clear air, the dazzling blue sky, the casual way that locals roll into Spanish and back again to English, or the vibrant colors used to accent window frames and doors — that draws celebrities to Santa Fe. Whatever it is, it has attracted artists, musicians, writers and, now, an increasing number of retirees.

For Tony Bonanno, a retired regional chief ranger for the National Park Service, the city cast its spell a quarter of a century before he would eventually call it home. "I used to come to Santa Fe in the early '70s on business, but something about the place stayed with me," he says. "As a career ranger, I've lived in a lot of beautiful places — Zion, the Grand Canyon, Shenandoah, the Blue Ridge Mountains and, most recently, Cape Cod. In Cape Cod, visitors would admire my historic seafront home with its sweeping ocean views and ask where else I could live that could beat that. Surprisingly I found myself answering, Santa Fe."

It was in the early years of the 20th century that people began to take notice of Santa Fe's inspirational qualities. Its growing reputation as a wellspring for artists and dreamers attracted a steady trickle of intellectuals, writers and other creative types lured by the desert and the unaffected appeal of its American

Population: About 68,041 in Santa Fe, 138,705 in Santa Fe County.

Location: Nestled at 7,000 feet in the foothills of the Rocky Mountains, the capital city of Santa Fe is 54 miles northeast of larger Albuquerque and its international airport.

Climate:

	High	Low
January	40	16
July	85	53

Average relative humidity: 46%

Rain: 14 inches annually

Snow: 32 inches annually

Cost of living: Above average

Average housing cost: The median cost of a single-family detached home is $393,440 in the city and $380,000 in the county.

Sales tax: The gross receipts tax is 7.5625% in the city and 6.25% in most other parts of Santa Fe County.

Sales tax exemptions: Prescription drugs, groceries and some medical services.

State income tax: New Mexico uses a four-bracket, graduated-rate table. For single filers, ranges from 1.7% of taxable income of $5,500 or less to 6% of taxable income over $16,000. For married couples filing jointly, ranges from 1.7% of taxable income of $8,000 or less to 6% of taxable income over $24,000.

Income tax exemptions: Depending on income level, taxpayers who are 65 and older may be eligible for a deduction from taxable income of up to $8,000 each. Social Security benefits are not exempt. Unreimbursed and uncompensated medical expenses not already itemized on the federal 1040A schedule for the same year may be eligible for a tax deduction.

Estate tax: None

Property tax: In the city of Santa Fe, $17.494 per $1,000 in valuation; in the county, $17.035 per $1,000. Homes are taxed on 33.3% of their market value. There is a $2,000 head-of-family exemption, $4,000 veteran exemption and complete exemption from property taxes for disabled veterans. Tax on a $393,440 home in the city would be about $2,292, without exemptions.

Homestead exemption: New Mexico residents who are 65 or older who have a modified gross income of $16,000 or less for the tax year qualify to claim a property tax rebate. The rebate cannot exceed $250 for married taxpayers filing jointly ($125 for married taxpayers filing separately, or single taxpayers). Also, those over 65 with an income of $19,000 or less qualify for valuation limitation, which freezes the assessed value of a home beginning with the first year one qualifies. Homeowners must reapply yearly.

Religion: Santa Fe boasts 50 Christian churches, two synagogues, two Buddhist temples and dozens of other spiritual centers supporting many other beliefs.

Education: The city enjoys substantial higher educational opportunities with University of New Mexico Extended University-Santa Fe, Santa Fe Community College, Southwestern College, University of Phoenix-Santa Fe and St. John's College. Southwestern College is a graduate institution specializing in experimental education in the mental health fields. Both UNM-SF, (505) 428-1234, and Santa Fe Community College, (505) 428-1777, are known for their adult and continuing-education programs.

Transportation: The local bus line, Santa Fe Trails, (505) 955-2001, operates a citywide public bus system from 6 a.m. to 10:30 p.m. Adult fares are $1 one way or $2 for a day pass. A monthly pass costs $20 for adult riders and

Indian culture. Its primitive ruggedness inspired the writings of Willa Cather, D.H. Lawrence, Aldous Huxley and Robert Frost, the photography of Ansel Adams and the work of physicist J. Robert Oppenheimer, creator of the atomic bomb.

Today Santa Fe is no larger than Bloomington, IN, or Camden, NJ. Yet Santa Fe stands out among cities its size for its flair — for architecture, art, cuisine and dress — known from Bangkok to Madrid.

A cultural hybrid — equal parts Wild West and New Age, American Indian and Hispanic, old money and old hippie — Santa Fe is an odd mixture, but one that works. It's a place where massage therapists outnumber computer programmers, where bolero ties pass for formal wear, and where the sense of escape from the ordinary is immediately apparent. It's a place where you can spot the locals by their well-worn cowboy boots and lack of a wristwatch. It's a place where you can order a margarita with your breakfast burrito and no one will think anything of it, and where art openings and operas complement rodeos and wilderness adventure.

Santa Fe has been dubbed "the City Different," and the reputation is apt. "It's really a wonderful place, a beautiful place, a spiritual place," says Kim Perry, a 46-year-old marketing consultant who specializes in promoting environmentally responsible development — a controversial subject in the drought-prone state. "If you're not touched by Santa Fe's natural beauty, you're jaded. The landscape here is very primitive and a constant reminder of nature," she says.

Creativity and controversy, innovation and originality are characteristics that seem as much a part of Santa Fe as adobe walls and dramatic skies. And when a place spurs passion the way Santa Fe does, it's only natural that people come back for more.

Come back they do. "Ever since my first visit to Santa Fe in 1989, I sought out every excuse to return. I began to visit more and more often — twice, three times, then up to four times a year — before moving here," explains Peter Rachor. A 44-year-old baby boomer, he cashed out of the telecommunications rat race two years ago, relocating to Santa Fe from San Francisco and ending an exciting career that racked up 3.5 million frequent-flier miles.

"I lived all over the U.S. and abroad, from Hong Kong and London to San Diego and DC, relocating 11 times for work. The 12th — and last — move was for me. It's been better than I had hoped for," he says.

Like a growing number of boomers who mix retirement relocation with second or continuing careers, Peter is working again, this time for the Univer-

Santa Fe, NM

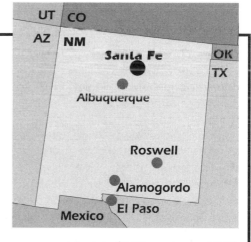

$10 for senior citizens, students and the disabled. Fares are inclusive of all one-way transfers. Door-to-door services are also available through private organizations such as Capital City Cab Co. and Roadrunner Shuttle Services. Albuquerque International Airport is located approximately 54 miles south of Santa Fe via Interstate 25. The Santa Fe Municipal Airport serves corporate jets, private planes and one commercial flight to Denver.

Health: Modern technologies, combined with many alternative therapies, contribute to Santa Fe's reputation as a center of healing for body, mind and spirit. St. Vincent Regional Medical Center, the largest medical center in northern New Mexico, is a full-service medical center providing a regional trauma center, FirstCARE urgent care clinic, rehabilitation therapy, behavioral health services, comprehensive cancer treatment, a pediatric intensive care unit, a women's services wing, general surgery, cardiac labs and a pain management clinic. Numerous other health-care organizations and HMOs are also available.

Housing options: Santa Fe's housing options range from modest to luxurious.

Homes start below $300,000 at developments such as **Rancho Viejo**, (888) 707-5454; and **Nava Adé**, (505) 982-8388. Throughout the city homes vary from the simplest of structures to the swankiest of estates ranging from $175,000 to $2 million and more. Offering housing alternatives uniquely suited to the needs of seniors are **Sierra Vista Retirement Community**, (505) 986-9696; **Ponce de Leon**, (505) 984-8422; **El Castillo Retirement Residences**, (505) 988-2877; **Kingston Residence**, (505) 471-2400; **Rosemont Assisted Living**, (505) 438-8464; and **La Vida Hermosa**, (505) 474-8031.

Visitor lodging: Visitors to Santa Fe can choose from hotels, motels, bed-and-breakfast inns, condominiums or RV parks. Options include the Fairfield Inn Santa Fe, $59-$109 including continental breakfast and free high-speed Internet connection in every room, (800) 758-1128. Hilton of Santa Fe is located within the centuries-old adobe walls of the original Ortiz Hacienda, just steps from the historic downtown Plaza, from $139, (800) 336-3676. Hotel Santa Fe is the city's only American Indi-

an-owned hotel, $129 and up, (800) 825-9876. In the heart of Santa Fe's downtown historic district is the Inn of the Governors, which has 100 rooms, 34 with kiva fireplaces, $154 and up, (800) 234-4534.

Information: The Santa Fe Chamber of Commerce, 8380 Cerrillos Road, Suite 302, Santa Fe, NM 87507, (505) 983-7317 or www.santafechamber.com. Santa Fe Convention and Visitors Bureau, 201 W. Marcy St., P.O. Box 909, Santa Fe, NM 87504-0909, (800) 777-2489 or www.santafe.org. For a detailed relocation package contact the chamber of commerce or order online at www.santafechamber.com/about_santafe/relocation.html.

sity of New Mexico with the title of "entrepreneur in residence" — a liaison between faculty and commercial corporations. "I wanted a change. In the past I traveled constantly. This time I was looking for something a bit like what I'd done, but not with the same intensity," he says.

Tony Bonanno wasn't quite ready to kick back completely either. He views his current situation not as retirement, but as "the next chapter." Ten years ago he moved to Santa Fe from Cape Cod as regional chief ranger for the Southwest with the National Park Service. Five years later, after more than 25 years with the service, he officially retired.

However, Tony shows no sign of slowing down. "There's no shortage of things to get involved in," he says, listing his numerous volunteer activities. As an amateur photographer turned professional, he donates his art and time as a board member of the Santa Fe Artists' Emergency Medical Fund, an organization created to help offset emergency health-care costs for struggling artists. He also serves on two state regulatory boards and has launched a successful photography business. "I don't know how I ever had time to work," he jokes, echoing a sentiment shared by many retirees.

Santa Fe, New Mexico's capital city of 68,000, offers something for just about anyone: artistic, athletic, spiritual, political, imaginative, outdoorsy or adventurous. Bob Seery, 63, relocated to Santa Fe two years ago from Cincinnati, OH. "Santa Fe has everything we wanted — an abundance of art, archaeological sites and Native American culture, world-class opera and cuisine. The city is culturally and aesthetically diverse with something going on all the time, yet it's relatively small compared to other places we've lived," he says.

For the past 15 years Bob and his wife, Mary Ellen, have been coming to Santa Fe. For six years before buying their current house, they owned a vacation condominium. For Bob, an established ceramics collector, Santa Fe — the third-largest art market in the United States, surpassed only by New York and Los Angeles — was an obvious choice when it came time to choose a retirement destination.

But it was Mary Ellen, a college pro-fessor at the University of Dayton, who was really the driving force behind the move, even though she continues to work in Ohio. Mary Ellen started her teaching career five years ago at the age of 56, after obtaining her doctorate. "I'm very fortunate. I love my job and am not yet ready to give it up. But I also love Santa Fe. So really I have the best of both worlds. As long as I have the energy to maintain two lives, I will," she says. "I come every chance I get." That usually means three months in the summer, a week in October, three weeks at Christmas and two weeks for spring break.

Murphy Scurry, a 69-year-old retired physician from Galveston, TX, and his wife, JoEllen, also had been frequent visitors to Santa Fe before retiring here permanently. Murphy started visiting New Mexico in the mid-1940s when his mother started a summer camp for boys near Cimarron, a mountain settlement two and half hours north of Santa Fe. "I spent nearly every summer of my childhood and adolescence at the camp," he says. "Later, after JoEllen and I got married, we bought three acres from the camp and built a cabin. When it started to get hot in Galveston, we'd head for the mountains."

Many Americans who have heard of, but never visited, Santa Fe share a common misconception about its weather — they think it's scorching hot. While warmed by an annual average of 300 days of sunshine, Santa Fe has four distinct seasons. Situated at 7,000 feet in the foothills of the Sangre de Cristo Mountains ("Blood of Christ," a reference to the red hue that colors the mountains at sunset), Santa Fe enjoys a high-altitude climate — sunny days and crisp, clear nights.

It snows in Santa Fe, beginning some years in mid-October. "I like the four seasons," says Peter Rachor, an avid skier and outdoorsman. "There's nothing wrong with snow when it comes with sunshine," he adds. But when Texans and Oklahomans are laid out flat with July and August heat, people in Santa Fe are enjoying balmy summer days in the 80s, with low humidity and cool evenings.

An agreeable climate and rugged mountain vistas were the deciding factors in choosing Santa Fe as a retirement destination for Peter's mother, Gail Rachor. "I woke up in Peter's guest room on Christmas morning with warm sunlight streaming through the window looking out onto snowcapped mountains and suddenly decided that this was where I want to die," says the 66-year-old Michigan native. "I started looking for houses immediately."

However, housing in Santa Fe can be an expensive proposition. The median home is nearly $400,000. But given the 32 percent increase in Santa Fe County's senior population between 1990 and 1998, many, like mother and son Rachor, feel it's worth the price.

For Murphy and JoEllen Scurry, buying a home within walking distance of Santa Fe's downtown plaza, the city's heart and soul for the past 400 years, was an important yet costly consideration. Less expensive housing options are available in new developments popping up all over the city's outskirts, but, "Santa Fe's weather allows you to be outside year-round, and we wanted to be able to walk to restaurants and activities," JoEllen says.

A community that feels metropolitan without the metropolis, Santa Fe is a town for strolling. Offering more than 200 restaurants, 250 art galleries, 13 museums and an abundance of antique shops and stylish boutiques, it's worth taking the time to walk. Thanks to city codes, there are no high-rises blocking the scenic mountain views.

For centuries the Pueblo tribes have lived alongside the area's Mexican and European settlers, and the blend of cultures spills onto the streets. American Indian vendors spread their turquoise and silver jewelry across a sea of hand-woven blankets under the portal of the sprawling Palace of the Governors, built in 1610 as the original capitol of the Spanish government.

The city's tricultural heritage is most evident in its cuisine. With recipes that show the influence of more than 2,000 years of American Indian culture (beans, corn and squash), some 400 years of Hispanic inclusion (chiles, cilantro, cumin, onions, garlic, wheat, rice and both beef and pork) and a liberal dash of American inventiveness, Santa Fe restaurants serve up a cornucopia of sensory feasts.

While most people savor Santa Fe's

cultural diversity, some deride it as a "faux adobe Disneyland." Many find deep spiritual resonance in its tolerance for alternative lifestyles; others are appalled by how wealthy "Santa Flakes" have embraced sacred American Indian rituals. "Santa Fe isn't for everyone," Peter Rachor admits.

The fact is that Santa Fe is popular because it's different from anywhere else in the country. But it's not Eden. Water issues, traffic messes and growth problems lurk beneath the city's enchanting atmosphere. In addition, its high-altitude location can present problems for some.

But talk to a few retirees here and you'll find that those who decide to stay are avid converts — enthusiastic, renewed and vocal on their newfound faith in their new hometown. ●

Sarasota, Florida

Culture and sunshine glow bright in this Gulf Coast town

By Karen Feldman

In some areas of the country, arts and cultural groups are struggling to make ends meet. Many cities have trouble funding opera and ballet companies, a symphony orchestra, theaters, film fests and museums. But Sarasota has all that — plus a front row seat for sunsets over the crystalline Gulf of Mexico.

Set midway between Tampa and Fort Myers along the Gulf of Mexico, Sarasota oozes natural appeal, offering the laid-back lifestyle one would expect of a beach community. But it also has style, with easy access to sophisticated shopping, cutting-edge restaurants, scores of golf courses and a citizenry that values culture and the arts as much as the area's abundant natural charms.

It's not surprising that the county has drop-dead gorgeous beaches — 35 miles of them, in fact. It's also got miles of waterfront property along Sarasota Bay. Lesser-known natural attractions include Myakka River State Park, where modern-day visitors can explore old Florida along 40 miles of trails, and Lemon Bay, a slender waterway that serves as a nursery area for 230 fish species.

The impetus for what has become a culturally rich subtropical community came from John Ringling. Best known for his circus, which he based in Sarasota in 1927, the entrepreneur had diverse interests, amassing a fortune through investments in real estate, railroads and oil. His business dealings brought many well-heeled colleagues and friends to the area, and some of them also decided to stay.

What began as a circus tycoon's winter retreat has evolved into a city of modest proportions that has amassed big-time attractions. Cultural draws include Asolo Theatre, Sarasota Opera, Florida West Coast Symphony, Sarasota Jazz Society, Sarasota Ballet of Florida, Van Wezel Performing Arts Hall, Golden Apple Dinner Theatre and numerous small play houses and art galleries.

Two of the city's crown jewels lie along the edge of Sarasota Bay near downtown. The John and Mable Ringling Museum of Art, the couple's winter residence and a circus museum are all open to the public. The Marie Selby Botanical Garden covers nine lush acres just a few minutes south of the Ringling estate. The gardens have world-class collections of air plants, orchids and Amazonian bromeliads, and Selby has been named one of the top 10 botanical gardens in the United States.

Downtown Sarasota is also home to a bustling arts and shopping district, with busy galleries, boutiques and restaurants. An enterprising company, Florida Ever-Glides, gives downtown tours on Segway transporters from an office across from Towles Court, a thriving art colony.

For sports fans, major league baseball's Grapefruit League hits Florida every February and March. The Cincinnati Reds hold their spring training in Sarasota. It's also where the Sarasota Red Sox, the Class A team of the Boston Red Sox, step up to the plate from April through September.

Sarasota claims to be the first place in the country in which golf was played. At last count, the county had some 85 courses with several more under development.

Added bonuses are the barrier island communities that flank the coast: tony Longboat Key, the more casual Siesta Key and, in between the two, St. Armands Circle, with its upscale boutiques, bistros and clubs set around a meticulously manicured circle. Nearby is Mote Marine Laboratory, which serves as a living classroom and the base of extensive marine research, especially on sharks and dolphins.

This treasure trove of activities provides entertainment and countless ways in which to get involved in the community.

"I don't know how we got everything done before," says retiree Karen Williard, who lives in Sarasota with her husband, Dick, part of the year and in Mooresville, NC, the rest of the time. Dick, 62, started visiting former in-laws in Sarasota during the mid-1960s, and later bought a winter home while still living mainly in North Carolina. After they married 12 years ago, Karen, 56, quickly fell under Sarasota's spell as well. The couple's frequent trips to Sarasota made retiring there a logical choice.

Both are avid golfers. Dick, a retired commercial pilot, works out at the YMCA five days a week. Karen plays tennis and takes aerobic dance classes. They also have season tickets to programs at the Asolo Theatre and attend other shows throughout the season.

Her passion is cooking, so they eat at home more often than not. Meanwhile, Dick keeps up with the stock market and business news and maintains the gardens.

"I love Sarasota because there's so much to do," Karen says. "Almost any shopping you'd want is here, and it's easy to get around. Everything is kind of on a grid, so it's easy to get from point A to point B, except for traffic sometimes. I like it even in winter when we have cold snaps. It's still pretty — still green, and there are still flowers. Even if it's cold, there's still a blue sky. When I go north in the wintertime, it's so gray and dreary."

For Sophia and Joe LaRusso, their move to Sarasota was sheer serendipity. The couple lived in Croton-on-Hudson in New York's Westchester County. Sophia, 63, worked as director of operations for an international family planning organization, setting up field offices all over the world. Joe, 71, was an administrator at several New York hospitals, including Bellevue, Montefiore and Rikers.

They were sophisticated New Yorkers who'd never heard of Sarasota. As they looked ahead to retirement, "we never considered Florida," Joe says. "Our view was that it was flat and there was nothing going on."

Then a couple of golf-loving, long-time friends discovered Sarasota. Sophia received the call at work. She says a friend told her, "I've found the perfect place for us all to retire." Sophia recalls expressing skepticism.

Nonetheless, the LaRussos headed south for a short visit to see for themselves. To their surprise, they fell for the combination of tropical idyll and cultural wonderland that is Sarasota.

"If it didn't have the arts, it would just be another place in Florida," Sophia says. "There are more things to do than you can think of. We call it Florida's cultural coast."

Perhaps because of their shared background in education, Sharon and Tom Giles researched their way to Sarasota, where they retired in 1994. The couple, who lived in a Chicago suburb, started their search for a place to retire five years before they planned to actually leave their jobs. They started with a big list that included Arizona, California, North Carolina, South Carolina, Georgia and Florida, Tom says.

Sarasota, FL

Population: There are 54,639 residents within the city limits, 358,307 in Sarasota County.

Location: About 55 miles south of Tampa on the Gulf of Mexico, the county measures 572 square miles, with 35 miles of beachfront.

Climate: High Low
January 71 49
July 91 72

Average relative humidity: Ranges from 58% to 83%

Annual rainfall: About 51 inches

Cost of living: Above average

Median housing cost: $326,300

Sales tax: 7%

Sales tax exemptions: Some food and medicines.

State income tax: None

Intangibles tax: None. The tax was repealed as of Jan. 1, 2007.

Estate tax: None

Inheritance tax: None

Property tax: $17.68 per $1,000 of assessed value. With a $25,000 homestead exemption, the annual tax on a $326,300 home would be $5,327.

Homestead exemption: $25,000 off assessed value of primary, permanent residence.

Religion: All major religions and many smaller ones are represented in the Sarasota area, which has more than 200 houses of worship.

Transportation: The Sarasota-Bradenton International Airport is served by a variety of major airlines that fly to points throughout the United States and Canada, with connections to foreign cities as well. Tampa International Airport (about an hour's drive) is served by all major airlines and offers flights throughout the world. U.S. Highway 41 is the main commercial thoroughfare that runs north and south through Sarasota, while Interstate 75, just east of the city, connects the area as far south as Miami and north into the Midwest. Sarasota County Area Transit, (941) 861-1234 or www.scgov.net, provides bus service throughout the county.

Health: Sarasota is served by Sarasota Memorial Health Care System, an 826-bed public regional medical center with a full range of services, including the third-largest cardiac program in the state. Doctors Hospital of Sarasota is a 168-bed acute and general care facility. Lakewood Ranch Medical Center is a new, 120-bed acute care hospital with a staff of over 300 physicians and health professionals.

Housing options: Condos, conventional single-family neighborhoods and deed-restricted communities are available in a wide range of prices. **Lakewood Ranch,** (800) 307-2624, (941) 907-6000 or www.lakewoodranch.com, is northeast of the city. It has a variety of neighborhoods offering condominiums, townhomes, garden homes, single-family homes and estate homes. Prices start in the mid-$200,000s and rise to about $4 million. Downtown is seeing a renaissance in housing, with many new condominium developments under way. Prices have jumped significantly since the Ritz-Carlton built a hotel and condominiums there in 2001. The area is flanked by the bay and surrounded by the arts, sidewalk cafes and a new retail center. Condos start in the mid-$300,000s for a modest two-bedroom unit upwards to about $6 million for waterfront penthouses with about 4,000 square feet of living space. Older homes south of downtown start at $400,000 and rise to the millions. Along the barrier islands, prices are higher. Longboat Key properties range from the mid-$500,000s up to about $16 million. On Siesta Key, expect to spend from about $600,000 on up to the millions for Gulf-front homes. **Cascades,** (941) 752-2095 or www.levittandsons.com, also in the northeast region of the county, is an active-adult community offering single-family homes from the $300,000s to $400,000s. Marcia McLaughlin is a retiree relocation specialist with **RE/MAX Properties** in Sarasota, (800) 708-6689 or www.homesinparadise.com.

Visitor lodging: The Cypress is a B&B next to a marina and park, with rooms done in various motifs, $150-$240, (941) 955-4683. Holiday Inn Lakewood Ranch costs $84-$152, (941) 782-4400. Hyatt Sarasota is a large-scale hotel near downtown with on-site parking, $164-$329, (941) 953-1234. The Ritz-Carlton, Sarasota, a luxury hotel with up-to-date amenities, is $199-$409, (941) 309-2000. Hotel prices throughout the area are lowest from mid-April to mid-December.

Information: Sarasota Convention and Visitors Bureau, 655 N. Tamiami Trail, Sarasota, FL 34236, (800) 522-9799, (941) 957-1877 or www.sarasotafl.org. The Sarasota Chamber of Commerce, 1945 Fruitville Road, Sarasota, FL 34236, (941) 955-8187 or www.sarasotachamber.org.

They spent a couple of weeks in each place, then narrowed the list to three: Palm Desert, CA; Asheville, NC; and Sarasota/Bradenton. They spent four to six weeks in each place before deciding on Sarasota.

"After looking at all of those, we really felt we were most compatible with the Sarasota/Bradenton area," says Tom, 68, a retired high school principal. "I wanted to be close enough to a large town to have access to major league (sports) and relatively good access to airport transportation. We both enjoy water, and my wife is a beach nut."

Even after deciding on Sarasota, they opted to rent for six months, which gave them time to thoroughly explore before investing in a home. "We'd heard too many stories about people who picked a location, then three or four months later decided it really wasn't what they wanted," says Sharon, 66, who taught elementary school.

They had plenty of options to explore. Sarasota's real estate scene is white-hot these days, with lots of new developments under construction and a large inventory of existing homes on the market, says Jim Soda, an agent with Prudential Palms Realty. There's a lot of property available in almost all price ranges.

Among the hottest spots is Lakewood Ranch, northeast of the city and east of Interstate 75. "It's a master-planned community that's so well planned," Soda says. It has its own hospital, Lakewood Ranch Medical Center, which opened in 2004, a new elementary school, lakes, golf, and a Main Street shopping district featuring high-end boutiques, restaurants and national stores.

The various neighborhoods within the development offer a range of housing plans, including condominiums, townhomes, garden homes, single-family homes and estate homes. Prices start in the mid-$200,000s and rise to about $4.7 million.

Downtown is seeing a renaissance in housing, too, with many new condominium developments under way. Flanked by the bay and surrounded by the arts, sidewalk cafes, and a new retail center that includes a Whole Foods store, a growing number of people want to live there. Condos start in the mid-

$300,000s for a modest two-bedroom unit and go upward to about $6 million for waterfront penthouses with about 4,000 square feet of living space.

Old homes that are south of downtown start at $400,000 and risr to the millions, in large part because of their choice location in the center of everything. Along the barrier islands, prices are higher. Longboat Key properties range from the mid-$500,000s up to about $16 million. On Siesta Key, expect to spend from about $600,000 to the millions for Gulf-front homes.

The Founders Club, a new development with 262 home sites and a Robert Trent Jones golf course, is also east of the city and I-75. Lots start in the high $400,000s, with homes priced at about $300 per square foot.

The Gileses bought an existing home that needed work in the northeastern part of the county. "Tom is a visionary," Sharon says. "He could see the possibilities. I walked in, turned around and walked out," she says of the first time they saw the house.

They ended up buying the 3,000-square-foot home with three bedrooms. They added a swimming pool and large screened-in porch around it, from which they have a prime view of the golf course.

The Williards decided on a two-bedroom condo villa in Sunrise Country Club. In April, they moved to a bigger condo unit at Bent Tree Country Club, in Sarasota's northeastern area. With about 1,925 square feet, it has two bedrooms and a den, two baths and a living room-dining room combo, an eat-in kitchen and a lanai (screened porch). To modernize the 10-year-old condo, they replaced the carpet with tile and installed new appliances, kitchen countertops and window treatments.

The LaRussos built a home in Longwood Run, a development in northern Sarasota. With about 2,800 square feet, the three-bedroom home has a Spanish villa design with a large outdoor area that's walled in to hold a pool and garden. The home sits on a natural lake that will not be developed, so they have a ringside seat on the natural habitat. The lushness was a big part of the appeal.

"We'd come from Westchester with its lush trees and didn't want to live in an area that was bald," Sophia says. They liked that the developer built the homes

between stands of trees, rather than leveling everything.

When they retired in 1994, the LaRussos made Sarasota their permanent home, and both have thrown themselves into making a difference. "I've gotten more involved than I ever was up north when I was working," Sophia says.

For five years, she co-hosted "Working Women Today," a biweekly cable TV show that featured interviews with local professionals. She serves on the board of the Community Foundation of Sarasota County, chairing the grant committee that awards $4 million to $6 million each year to worthy community projects; is on the board of the West Coast Black Theatre Troupe; works with the Junior League of Sarasota on endowments; volunteers on an advisory board for Cyesis, a public school for pregnant teens and their children; sits on the board of Take Stock in Children; belongs to the American Business Women's Association; and has her own business as a wellness consultant. She also manages to fit in some golf and tennis time. When she wants to unwind, she cooks.

While Sophia is busy with her pet projects, Joe has his own set. He's the past president of the Mental Health Community Centers; serves as president of Theatre Works; sits on the board of their homeowners association, where his committee oversees roofing issues; and plays tennis three times a week and golf twice a week. He recently enrolled in the Florida Studio Theatre's improvisation school, indulging a passion he's had since he was a child.

"It's very nice to be involved," Joe says. "It's nice to give something back to the community." His wife adds, "It's important not to just feel isolated and do nothing but things from which you benefit personally. When looking to relocate, you want to look at places that give social opportunities as well as a lot of volunteer opportunities. I find that when you are involved, your spirit, your life are so totally different. When you give, you get back more than you give out."

The Gileses share that philosophy. Shortly after moving in, Sharon was invited to join the housing development's women's club and the garden club. After visiting Selby Gardens just a few days after arriving, she decided to volunteer there. She served a two-year term as president of the Selby Garden Associates, whose 150 members volunteer at the gardens and serve as ambassadors in the community.

Tom, who'd been involved with the United Way in Illinois, contacted the Sarasota chapter, which directed him to a number of organizations in need of help. He's signed on with Volunteer Connections, which matches volunteers with nonprofit groups; Brush-Up Sarasota, which paints homes for people who can't do it themselves; and PALS (Partnerships and Alliances Linking Schools), which recruits and trains volunteers for the schools. Additionally he also conducts Selby Garden tours.

The Gileses also work part time, helping coordinate Elderhostel programs that take place in Sarasota. Tom, an avid baseball fan, even teaches during the spring training Elderhostel program. He lectures on subjects such as baseball history, the old Negro League and other related topics, and accompanies groups to four spring training games where they can meet some of the players.

They believe their careful planning paid off. "We miss our friends in Chicago, but they come down," Sharon says. "When we told our friends we were moving, they said, 'What are you thinking?' But we made the right choice — no regrets." ●

Saugatuck-Douglas, Michigan

Serenely quiet, yet bursting with energy, this resort draws retirees to the Lake Michigan shore

By Mary Lu Abbott

Barbara and Mac McDonald had lived in a suburb outside Detroit for years but never had explored the Lake Michigan shoreline 200 miles west until his relatives from England came for a visit. A friend had highly recommended Saugatuck, a small resort community in the lower part of West Michigan.

"It's very close to paradise," says Mac. "I come from England, and Saugatuck is the nearest thing to an English village I've come across. We both love the peace and quiet."

As they were making plans to build a home here, though, their daughter expressed concern because it was so quiet. "She came in the winter and said, 'Are you sure about this?' She came back in the summer and went into town with a couple of friends and then said, 'This is a really neat place you retired to.' Along with the peace and quiet, we have a town bursting with energy in the summer," Mac says.

Since the early 1900s, Saugatuck has been a popular resort, attracting people mainly from the Midwest to its beautiful lakeshore, the Kalamazoo River and forests. Lake steamers brought tourists from Chicago and other cities, and the wealthy built homes amid the trees along the bluffs, where they have sweeping views of the lake.

America's Great Lakes are a sight to behold, particularly the shore of Lake Michigan lapping the west coast of Michigan. The water is deep blue and stretches to the horizon like an ocean. Sandy beaches attract swimmers and sunbathers as if this were the Atlantic Seaboard, and everything from small fishing boats to big yachts slowly navigate the Kalamazoo River into the lake. The wind has sculpted sand dunes so tall they rightfully earn the term hills.

The main part of Saugatuck is set on the Kalamazoo River, which widens into a large lakelike harbor where about 900 yachts and sailboats are moored. A couple of parks and a boardwalk promenade with flowers front the river, which forms the border with the neighboring village of Douglas.

The setting seems made for artists, and, indeed, Saugatuck and Douglas has become a noted artists colony. Chicago artists came to Saugatuck in the early 1900s and started the Oxbow School of Art, which now is associated with the Art Institute of Chicago and has classes in all kinds of media during the summer. Saugatuck has more than 30 galleries and Douglas adds several more.

Before deciding to move to Saugatuck, the McDonalds looked along the West Michigan shoreline at other towns, but they liked the combination of serenity and activities at Saugatuck. Barbara, 60, retired from teaching in 1992, and a few years later they bought five acres of wooded land on Indian Point about four miles outside town on the Kalamazoo River. They built a home and moved here about seven years ago. Mac, who is from Yorkshire in England, is a writer and continued his work, commuting to Detroit as necessary for his clients. He sold his business and retired in 1998.

The McDonalds enjoy Saugatuck's seasonal rhythm of life. "I love the spring," says Barbara, an avid birder. "We have magnificent dogwoods and beautiful oak trees, and I look forward to the return of the birds — Baltimore orioles, hummingbirds. You know, the first ones you are going to see are redwing blackbirds, and once they start to come, you can sort of kiss the snow goodbye. Our springs are usually very nice and lingering because of the temperate climate of the lake. Then we move into the glorious summertime where you have bright sun and the water. Our favorite season is fall with the colors and return of the geese. We measure life in quarters."

"We overlook 800 acres of marshes on the other side of the river, the biggest wetlands between the Upper Peninsula (Michigan) and Kentucky," says Mac, 58. "We see bald eagles all the time, coyote, deer, sandhill cranes, blue heron, egrets. Around the river, there's lots of life. One of the amazing things we love is we're on the migratory path of the Canada geese. When they come in, the sky becomes black with them. They roost overnight and take off in the morning. The noise they make — that's quite an experience," Mac says.

"The geese come in honking," Barbara says. "In October they gather up and get ready to leave and they come back in the spring, around February. It's a very active bird area."

Mac says their view across the marshlands changes all the time. "Even in winter it's still beautiful. You can see rusts and yellows and mustard colors. In summer it's totally green," he says.

The seasons also were an important reason Bobbie and Bob Gaunt chose to retire to Saugatuck. An executive with Ford Motor Co., Bobbie relocated 11 times in 29 years. Her last assignment was as president and CEO for Ford Canada, which took her to the Toronto area. Bob was in marketing and communications in Detroit, which they considered their main home, and took early retirement in the late 1980s. Bobbie retired in 2000. During her career she was transferred to California and was excited about the sunny weather, but they both soon realized they missed the seasons.

"Winter is beautiful here but in a quieter way. The river is frozen with ice and snow across it, and the starkness is compelling. Lake Michigan freezes, and when you go to the beach, it's like waves are frozen in motion. It looks like a moonscape," says Bobbie, 56.

The Gaunts discovered Saugatuck in the early 1990s, bought a condo as a second home and within two years purchased a house with more room because so many of their family and friends loved to visit. When she retired, they decided to relocate here.

"We like the culture of the community — we both love the arts — and the diversity the community has to offer," says Bobbie, noting that besides the galleries, the Saugatuck area has performing arts, great restaurants and a mixture of people, with many from Chicago and cities in Indiana as well as from Michigan. Saugatuck is about 140 miles from Chicago, about 190 from Detroit.

"We like the small-town atmosphere,"

Bob says. "It's a composite of everything you find in a city you like except you don't have the distance to travel."

In 1999 they bought a home on the river about midway between Lake Michigan and downtown Saugatuck. It was a place they had admired for years. They enjoy being on the water. "We can see over a hundred boats coming and going on the river. It's a fun pastime on a Saturday night or a nice sunny day to sit out

Saugatuck-Douglas, MI

Population: About 3,000 in Saugatuck-Douglas area.

Location: On the eastern shore of Lake Michigan, in southwestern area of Michigan. It's about 140 miles from Chicago, 190 miles from Detroit, 40 miles southwest of Grand Rapids and only 10 miles south of Holland.

Climate:

	High	Low
January	31	18
July	83	60

Average relative humidity: 64%

Rain: 36 inches

Snow: About 100 inches

Cost of living: Average to slightly above average.

Average housing cost: About $329,000. Condos are available from the high $100,000s.

Sales tax: 6%

Sales tax exemptions: Most groceries, prescription drugs and vitamins.

State income tax: Residents pay a flat rate of 3.9%. Tax is based on adjusted gross income as reported on federal return.

Income tax exemptions: Michigan exempts federal, state and local pensions and Social Security benefits. It allows an exemption of private pensions up to $39,579 (adjusted annually) for each taxpayer; however, this amount is reduced by the amount of any public pension claimed. Those 65 and older can exempt up to $8,828 (adjusted annually) per taxpayer in dividends, interest and capital gains; however, this exemption is reduced by the amount of pension exemption claimed.

Estate tax: None

Property tax: In Saugatuck, the rate is $41.428 per $1,000 in value (on homesteads, higher if it's not your homestead),

with property assessed at 50% of taxable value. The approximate tax on a $329,000 home would be about $6,815. In Douglas, the rate is $36.651 per $1,000 (on homesteads), at same assessment rate. The approximate tax on a $329,000 home would be about $6,029.

Homestead exemption: If it is your homestead (your main residence, where you're registered to vote and where you file IRS returns), you pay a lower property tax rate than if it is a second residence. Those with incomes of less than $82,650 are eligible for a homestead property tax credit.

Religion: There are 10 churches in the Saugatuck-Douglas area and 170 representing 49 denominations in Holland, about 10-15 minutes away.

Education: Hope College in Holland has a Learning in Retirement program with classes, and the Grand Rapids Community College has classes on health, computers and on finding new community leadership roles in retirement.

Transportation: Interurban Transit Authority provides van service door-to-door in the area.

Health: Saugatuck-Douglas has a doctor and a lab associated with the Holland Community Hospital, a 213-bed facility. Holland has numerous physicians and a wide range of health care. More extensive health care is available in Grand Rapids, about 40 minutes away, which has about 10 medical complexes and a developing medical research institute.

Housing options: Range of options includes reasonably priced condos, new single-family houses, older homes in town and homes in a nearby golf-course community. In Douglas, **Summer Grove** is a small neighborhood of attractive cottages

with porches and picket fences, starting in the mid-$200,000s. Between Saugatuck and Holland, the **Ravines Golf Club**, with an Arnold Palmer course, has 90 homesites, with new homes from the high $300,000s. Laura Durham, broker-owner of Mill Pond Realty, (269) 857-1477, says many retirees prefer buying within walking distance of town, where they find older homes for remodeling.

Visitor lodging: The area is a popular summer getaway for residents in Illinois (particularly Chicago), Indiana and from inland Michigan towns. There are numerous B&Bs, inns, motels and cottages for rent. Among options: Lake Shore Resort is a congenial family-run motel on a bluff overlooking the lake, with a heated pool, spacious grounds, hiking trail and its own beach. It's open mid-May through mid-October; rates start at $75 off-season, $150 in summer, including continental breakfast, (269) 857-7121. The Saugatuck-Douglas Visitors Guide from the visitors bureau noted below lists area accommodations with pictures.

Information: Saugatuck/Douglas Convention and Visitors Bureau/Chamber of Commerce, P.O. Box 28, Saugatuck, MI 49453, (269) 857-1701 or www.saugatuck.com.

and have a cocktail and check them all out. It's a no-wake zone, so the boats have to go slow, and there's no noise," says Bob, 71.

Bobbie says it always has been important to them to have a relaxing, rejuvenating home environment, and this home and its setting were ideally suited to their needs. She says she feels fortunate every day to live here.

"We're surrounded by history. The tree outside our bedroom I've been told is the oldest white pine in the area. Another aspect I liked here is the community is environmentally sensitive…and protective of the sand dunes, the wildlife, the forests," Bobbie says.

Saugatuck dates to 1830, Douglas to 1870. In the early days, there was a community called Singapore near where the river flows into the lake. Lumber was the major business, and much of the lumber to rebuild Chicago after the Great Fire of 1871 came from this area.

By the late 1800s the lumber business gave way to fruit orchards and boat building, with more than 200 vessels built here around the turn of the century. With the demise of those two industries, tourism became the major force. There still are orchards and pick-your-own-fruit farms in the area, and a company builds custom yachts with price tags that can top $4 million.

Today the Saugatuck-Douglas area has about 3,000 residents. The number swells to 15,000 to 20,000 in summer, as many people vacation or spend the season here, either in housing or on their boats. Winter is quiet, but the town still has numerous events, including festive holiday celebrations. Tourists still come on weekends for snowmobiling, cross-country skiing or quiet getaways to one of the numerous area B&Bs. There are extensive ski trails at Saugatuck Dunes State Park by the lake.

The small-town village lifestyle was the compelling factor for Judy and David Mauger. Judy had lived in the Detroit area, in nearby Holland and in Wisconsin. When she became a single parent, she searched Michigan for the best place to raise children, decided a village would be better than the suburbs and settled in Saugatuck.

"I figured I'd have more help here," she says, noting that in a small town, residents are more likely to watch out for each other and keep tabs on children's activities away from home. She thought this also would be a good place to retire, figuring the children would come see her in a resort town.

She loved the village life, but in the early 1990s she met and married David and moved to nearby Holland. David, an engineer who had worked in Wisconsin, New York and Connecticut before coming to Holland, had a home on Lake Macatawa with a dock for his boat. It was a choice location that he loved, and they had planned to retire there.

"It's a lovely town and it was a lovely home and a beautiful place, but it wasn't village life," says Judy, 64. "It's just different living in a village rather than in a city. No matter how nice the town or city is, there's not the intimacy that a village has." A sales representative, she took early retirement in the mid-1990s, then found she was lonely at home because most people in the neighborhood were away at work.

So around 1997, when David retired, he "indulged" her, Judy says, and agreed to move. Being close to the water was important to him, so they found a marina community in Douglas, where they bought property, and David, 71, oversaw the building of their condo. They've been here more than four years now and he calls Saugatuck and Douglas "great."

"It is loaded with fascinating people," Judy says. "It's attracting people who are doers. People who come here don't expect to sit on the beach all day and do nothing. They come here because there's a very active life and they can participate and increase their skills or use the developed skills they have."

Judy says the leader of her aerobics class has been a co-producer and director of the Broadway show "Fosse" and now is starting a theater group in Saugatuck. The area also has attracted retirees who have worked on historic preservation projects and now devote energy to helping preserve the heritage of Saugatuck and Douglas.

The main part of Saugatuck — The Flats, The Hill and the waterfront area across the river — has about three dozen historic buildings that now house shops, galleries and restaurants, and some still are homes. A large number of buildings from the mid-1800s remain, including several from the 1850s along Butler, one of the main streets. Italianate, Gothic Revival and Craftsman styles are common.

The Wilkins Hardware Co. has been operating in its building since 1904, and a traditional drugstore in business 75 years still has an old-fashioned soda fountain. A small hand-cranked ferry still takes passengers back and forth across a narrow part of the river. Saugatuck has approximately 200 shops. Douglas is more residential but has a downtown with shops, galleries and restaurants in restored buildings.

The calendar of events is packed. Summer brings a chamber music festival, the Waterfront Film Festival, boating events and a major Fourth of July celebration. Art 'Round Town starts in summer and extends through spring, presenting outdoor sculptures specially chosen from among regional artists for display in Saugatuck and Douglas. Seasonally, a trolley provides tours to see all the sculptures.

The Red Barn Playhouse has summer theater, and the Lakeshore Community Arts Pavilion is the venue for ongoing live productions. The Woman's Club of Saugatuck has frequent events, including jazz concerts several times a year. The historical society has monthly programs, and there are frequent special film screenings. There are several golf courses in the area, including a noted one designed by Arnold Palmer.

Judy Mauger says it's very easy to get involved with civic activities. She and David volunteer with a program for one-to-one tutoring of first graders in reading. He serves on the Douglas village council and is working to put bicycle paths in the area. He's also a member of the Holland Rotary. She started a women's investment club and works with the historical society, recently coordinating a St. Patrick's Day party to help fund some of its projects.

Bobbie Gaunt is chairperson of the Lakeshore Community Arts Pavilion, and she and her husband both work with arts groups. She also still serves on two corporate boards and a university board and remains an active mentor. The McDonalds have been supporters of the Oxbow school and some other arts programs, and Mac works with the Kalamazoo River Association, a group of citizens who do bird counts and are environmental watchdogs, trying to assure that the river is not polluted.

Mac considers the friendliness of the people in western Michigan one of the major attractions. "It's quite amazing," says Mac, who believes that people are more open here than in eastern Michigan. He also says the pace of life is more relaxed and easygoing in western Michigan.

When the McDonalds made the decision to come here, Barbara says, "We knew absolutely no one. People said, 'How can you go someplace and not know anyone?' It wasn't a concern to us. We were in this house less than a week and we had neighbors coming around, inviting us to brunch, introducing themselves and welcoming us to the neighborhood. It became a very strong community we belong to now."

Bobbie Gaunt says, "We haven't lived anywhere where we've had the number of friends we have here. If they don't see you in a few days, they call or come over to make sure you're OK." When Bob had to have surgery unexpectedly in Detroit, friends in Saugatuck took care of their place, and when they arrived home they found groceries at the door, people came with food and someone plowed snow off their driveway, she says.

Because Bobbie returns frequently to Detroit for board meetings, they still see doctors there but will transfer to closer care. Health care in Saugatuck-Douglas is limited, though Judy Mauger says there's a "wonderful general practition-

er." The couples say Holland, 10 miles away, has good health care with a hospital and a variety of doctors, but for specialties and more serious medical issues, most residents go to major medical complexes in Grand Rapids, about 40 miles away.

The couples say their cost of living is comparable to where they've lived before. They all say the farmers market in Holland, which runs from late spring through Thanksgiving, has excellent produce, and Barbara McDonald thinks it saves them money on food. There's no specific cost-of-living index for Saugatuck, though for Holland it's slightly below average. But Saugatuck has limited lower-priced housing.

The couples don't find any faults with the area, but they offer some caveats. They all emphasize that Saugatuck and Douglas are small towns. "There's a big difference in living in large cities vs. in a small town — everything from the pace to the people that you know," says Bobbie Gaunt. "You're much more visible in a small town. Everybody knows everybody. In a big city there's a degree of anonymity. When you move to a place where the population is 1,000, you lose that anonymity and that's an adjustment."

Bob calls living here "terrific" but laughs that "news travels fast in a small town." Things residents say or do may quickly become known, unlike in a metropolitan area where residents may not see anyone they know when they go out. But there are benefits of the closeness among residents, Bobbie points

out, as the Gaunts discovered in the caring, responsive nature of everyone when Bob had surgery.

David Mauger says, "I never lived in a small town, but I really like it. I've gotten involved, and it's very nice because you know most of the people in town." His wife adds that there's always interaction as you see people in the post office or restaurants, and the casual encounters often lead to brainstorming ideas for projects. "You're always among friends," Judy says.

While Saugatuck and Douglas are small, they have big-city diversity, including a gay community, the couples say. The Gaunts and the McDonalds say they think the communities appeal most to people who are comfortable with all kinds of diversity. The McDonalds say the communities are a mixture of conservative and liberal — conservative thinking with small-town, old-fashioned values in that the historical society works to preserve and protect the historic districts, but relatively liberal in that people are open-minded and accepting of how people want to live their lives.

For city residents who want to escape the fast-paced, high-stress lifestyle, this is a good place to slow down, yet still be active and have many of the cultural advantages they've enjoyed.

"I love the sheer beauty of the place. I still find it breathtaking," says Barbara McDonald. "I love the charm of the town no matter what season. I love the beauty of all the woodlands around, all the water. Just being surrounded by the beauty, I just find it wonderful." ●

Scottsdale, Arizona

A Phoenix suburb blends Southwestern and Mediterranean architecture
with beautiful desert scenery

By Ron Butler

Forty years ago, Scottsdale was little more than a dirt road and a couple of saloons — Lulu Belle's and the Pink Pony. Then word got out and Scottsdale was swept up in the phenomenal Arizona population explosion that today makes the Phoenix-Scottsdale area one of the fast-growing urban centers in the country.

Just being in Scottsdale is an event — imagine living there. Situated seamlessly between Phoenix, Paradise Valley, Carefree and Tempe, Scottsdale's population is now over 225,000. Known for its outstanding architectural and landscape design, the impressive city also has impressive numbers — about 125 art galleries (the biggest art center this side of Santa Fe), four libraries, 32 indoor theaters, one outdoor theater, over 30 parks, four bowling alleys. There are three municipal swimming pools, 30 golf courses, over 200 tennis facilities, eight museums, a civic center, baseball stadium, a Center for the Arts and the Scottsdale Community College.

Its downtown Civic Center Senior Center is groundbreaking in concept. "As part of the city of Scottsdale, we give our community a place to have fun, a place to be safe, and help to enhance the quality of life, especially for our senior population," says Human Services spokeswoman Cathie McDaniel. The center looks like a bank or office building outside, but inside there's a wide variety of social and recreational programs, health screenings, special events, organized outings, discussion groups and classes in everything from computer techniques to Spanish language. Only the special classes and concert and theater outings require fees. Everything else is free.

Throw in gorgeous desert scenery with proud mountain landscapes and a near-perfect climate, and it makes you wonder why Nancy and Ned Benedict, 52 and 59 respectively, took so long to move there. They came from San Fran-

cisco three years ago. Ned spent 32 years as a career pilot for Federal Express. Nancy, his co-pilot if you will, is a homemaker.

The Benedicts live in a sprawling five-bedroom, three-and-a-half-bath ranch-style home in a gated, master-planned community north of town called Terravita, meaning harmony of life and land. Frequent visits to relatives in the area made them forsake San Francisco for the Arizona desert.

Golf is a big priority with the Benedicts. (Membership fee for the Terravita Club is $25,000. Greens fees for guests range from $30 to $125, depending on season.) The couple also enjoys excursions into the desert and trips to towns such as Tucson, Bisbee and Douglas in the southern part of the state to soak up all that Western ambiance. They enjoy eating out, with Roy's Pacific Rim Cuisine their current favorite, offering seared lemon grass-crusted salmon with watercress-ginger sauce, and grilled spiny lobster with bean thread noodles and macadamia nuts.

Eating out also is a favorite activity of Dr. Melvin Breeze, 85, and his wife Elizabeth, 84, who moved to Scottsdale from Portland, OR, five and a half years ago. They count 44 restaurants within walking distance of their Forum Pueblo Norte senior living community, and have tried them all.

Melvin is a retired pediatrician and gynecologist; Elizabeth was on the home economics staff at Oregon State University. Married in 1937, they have five children and five great-grandchildren.

It was a medical convention at the Wigwam resort in nearby Litchfield and subsequent conferences in the area that introduced Melvin to the glories of desert living. He liked the people and loved the climate. He and Elizabeth have taken two apartments in the Forum, a Sunrise Senior Living retirement property, and combined them to make one large apartment with four bedrooms, a

guest room and possibly the largest-screen TV set this side of the big sports bar on Scottsdale Road.

The Forum also has its own health-care center and an assisted-living community. Services include three meals a day, downtown shuttle service, weekly housekeeping, free local calls, utilities, maintenance, heated swimming pool, shuffleboard and a putting green along with a wide range of organized social and cultural activities. The Breezes are members of the Scottsdale Center for the Arts and enjoy a full active life outside the Forum as well.

Norman and Cathy Arthur, 63 and 52 respectively, gave up the good life in Hawaii for the good life in Scottsdale and now reside in a gated community in the mountain foothills in the north part of town. He's a retired civil engineer; she's a computer consultant who still takes part-time assignments. They enjoy the desert scenery and often are part of it, taking long hikes and jogging 10 miles a day. They're often thrilled to spot a coyote or a bobcat or a pair of javelinas (wild pigs) along the way. They enjoy several challenging trails among the sheer red cliffs of Camelback Mountain, the area's best-known landmark, and they also play tennis but have an aversion to golf.

Their tastefully decorated home, with four bedrooms and three baths, is filled with Western artifacts and art — Hopi Kachina dolls, desert paintings, Indian blankets. The Arthurs also have a cabin in the summer recreation area of Pinetop, but it was primarily economic considerations that made Scottsdale a retirement choice. The cost of living in Scottsdale is about half of what it was in Hawaii, and there are all those pesky volcanoes.

They have a 17-year-old son living at home and another at school. The community has no age restrictions, so the Arthurs enjoy an eclectic group of neighbors, ranging from empty-nesters to retirees and even a couple of newlyweds on their second and third marriages. They like to read so it's not unusual to find them browsing the shelves at the fine downtown bookstores such as the Antiquarian Shop. Here serious collectors can pick up a signed, first edition of John Steinbeck's "In Dubious Battle" for $8,000, a first edition of Ernest Hemingway's "Death in the Afternoon" for $4,000 or Arthur Conan Doyle's "Hound of the Baskervilles" for $4,000.

Victor and Ann Phillips, 72 and 70 respectively, gave up Ohio's frigid winters to worship "el sol" in Scottsdale 12 years ago. They lived in Oxford, a charming little town of cobbled streets and unique shops where both were affiliated with Miami University, he (following a 24-year military career) in business and she in library arts. They

Scottsdale, AZ

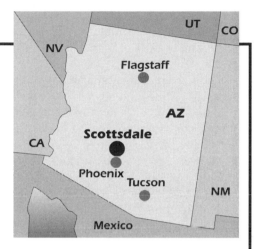

Population: 225,680

Location: In south-central Arizona, bordered by Phoenix, Paradise Valley, Carefree and Tempe in the Valley of the Sun.

Climate:

	High	Low
January	65	39
July	105	80

Humidity: 23%

Rain: 7.05 inches of rain per year.

Cost of living: Above average

Median housing costs: Home prices range from $120,000 to $6 million, averaging $282,000 for a three-bedroom home. Condos average about $226,500.

Sales tax: 7.95%

Sales tax exemptions: Groceries and prescription drugs.

State income tax: For married couples filing jointly, graduated from 2.87% of taxable income up to $20,000 to 5.04% minus $2,276 on amounts over $300,000. For single filers, graduated from 2.87% of taxable income up to $10,000 to 5.04% minus $1,138 on amounts over $150,000.

Income tax exemptions: Social Security benefits and up to $2,500 on federal, Arizona state and local government pensions are exempt.

Estate tax: None

Inheritance tax: None

Property tax: Tax rates vary depending on location and school district. For a resident living in the Scottsdale Unified School District, the rate is $9.2992 per $100 of assessed value. Homes are assessed at 10% of market value. The annual tax due on a $282,000 home would be about $2,622.

Homestead exemptions: None. In Maricopa County, seniors age 65 and over with incomes under $27,792 ($34,740 for couples) can qualify for valuation protection, which freezes the full cash value of the homeowner's primary residence.

Religion: Scottsdale has hundreds of churches and synagogues representing virtually every denomination.

Education: Scottsdale Community College offers an associate degree with credits transferable to university levels and technical degrees. A wide range of continuing-education classes and community service programs also are available. Arizona State University, the state's largest university with an enrollment of nearly 50,000, is located in the neighboring community of Tempe.

Transportation: Nearly everyone in Arizona drives, but those who don't will find Scottsdale taxis among the most expensive anywhere. Figure about $1.50 a mile in this sprawling area. Valley Metro provides wheelchair-accessible bus service throughout Scottsdale with connecting service to major Phoenix and other regional transportation routes. The Scottsdale Trolley offers free transportation throughout downtown Scottsdale year-round. Dial-a-Ride is a low-cost transportation program operating in Scottsdale and Tempe for disabled persons and those 65 and older. Proof of age (Medicare card or photo identification) is required. The Scottsdale Airport, one of the busiest single-runway facilities in the country, accommodates business and recreational flyers.

Health: Scottsdale is home to one of the three branches of the Mayo Clinic, a multispecialty outpatient clinic with more than 300 physicians and a medical support staff of more than 3,500. Scottsdale Healthcare is the largest single employer in Scottsdale with more than 4,000 staff members and 1,350 active physicians.

Housing options: Medium-priced and luxury condominiums, townhouses, patio homes, ranch-style homes and two-story homes are all available in Scottsdale, making housing options one of its most attractive features. Of the more than 100,000 dwelling units currently occupied in Scottsdale, approximatly 70 percent are owned and 30 percent are rent-

ed. Scottsdale has several nationally recognized planned communities, such as **McCormick Ranch, Gainy Ranch, Scottsdale Ranch, Desert Highlands, Grayhawk, Desert Mountain, Troon, Terravita, McDowell Mountain Ranch** and **Scottsdale Mountain**. For information, call Neighborhood Resource Guide, (480) 312-7251.

Visitor lodging: Options range from glittering five-star resorts like the world-famous Phoenician, $295-$635, (480) 941-8200, and the Fairmont Scottsdale Princess, $159-$509, (480) 585-4848, to short-term rentals like the Abode Apartment Hotel, (480) 945-3544. Days Inn Fashion Square, (480) 947-5411, is immediately adjacent to Scottsdale's most prestigious shopping mall and offers rates ranging from $54 for a standard room in low season to $110 during the high season. For visitor information online, see the Scottsdale Convention and Visitors Bureau site at www.scottsdalecvb.com.

Information: Scottsdale Chamber of Commerce and Convention and Visitors Bureau, 7343 Scottsdale Mall, Scottsdale, AZ 85251, (866) 475-0535 or (480) 421-1004. Arizona Office of Senior Living, 3800 N. Central Ave., Suite 1500, Phoenix, AZ 85012, (602) 280-1300, provides out-of-state retiree prospects with free relocation information. Web sites to check out include www.scottsdalecham ber.com.

raised four children.

Today, home is a comfortable, art-filled, two-bedroom casita in the Classic Residence of Scottsdale, a senior living community by Hyatt and the Plaza companies that offers virtually all the amenities of a luxury resort. These include 24-hour concierge service, one meal a day (lunch or dinner), weekly housecleaning and linen service, shuttle service and a wide variety of health and fitness programs.

The scenery is all mountains and lofty saguaros. Ann, who keeps busy with volunteer church, library and bilingual school classes, complains that a persistent family of javelinas has been eating her flower garden, roots and all.

With their obvious love for art (their home is filled with Western oils, bronzes and tie-dye prints), the Phillipses couldn't have settled in a more compatible community. Scottsdale's art scene is world famous. Sculptor Bob Parks' magnificent downtown fountain with four life-sized Arabian stallions frolicking about — the most photographed landmark in Scottsdale — sets the tone.

For the past 20 years, Scottsdale galleries have treated visitors and locals to Thursday night Art Walks, the oldest such art event in the United States. Many of the best-known galleries are concentrated along Marshall Way and Main Street (the arts and antique district), with others clustered in the Fifth Avenue shopping area and Old Town. Buck Saunders Gallery on East Camelback Road, now closed, was the first major gallery to feature the work of the late Ted DeGrazia, Arizona's best-known, most-loved artist, and was long his exclusive representative.

For the downside of living in Scottsdale — ah, and you thought there wasn't any — progress seems to be the main culprit. Nearly everyone echoes the same complaint — too many people, too much traffic, limited bus service, too much building and banging. "There's so much work," says Ned Benedict, the former Federal Express pilot, "that many unqualified workers are filling the work force, taking forever to show up for a job when you call them, and then doing shoddy work."

Yet for all of its glitz and development, there's something about Scottsdale that calls to mind the small towns in Italy or Spain where old men spend their time sitting around the town square, sipping coffee or wine and discussing the cares of the day. You see the same men in downtown Scottsdale — but they're at trendy outdoor cappuccino bars, and they dress better. ●

Seaside, Florida

An upscale new town sports an old-fashioned look in the Florida Panhandle

By Karen Feldman

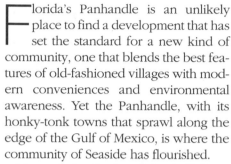

Florida's Panhandle is an unlikely place to find a development that has set the standard for a new kind of community, one that blends the best features of old-fashioned villages with modern conveniences and environmental awareness. Yet the Panhandle, with its honky-tonk towns that sprawl along the edge of the Gulf of Mexico, is where the community of Seaside has flourished.

Most of the Panhandle's Gulf Coast developed helter-skelter as entrepreneurs crammed in as many motels, surf shops, eateries, and tattoo and piercing parlors as the market would bear. Apparently it will bear a lot, as the solid mass of commercial development along U.S. Highway 98, the main route along the Gulf, reveals.

But turn onto County Road 30A, and the development becomes less dense, the beach widens and palms line the roads of upscale condo communities. The scene sets the stage for Seaside, a testament to what can happen when one man with conviction turns his vision into reality.

That's what developer Robert Davis has proved with his creation of Seaside. While Seaside may not be a household name, anyone who has watched "The Truman Show," a movie starring Jim Carrey, has seen the idyllic 80-acre town with its pastel-hued cottages and white picket fences lining red-brick streets.

What Davis had in mind was a new type of community created by culling the best aspects of towns of the past. To find out what those were, Davis and his wife spent two years driving around Florida studying towns, their architecture and the qualities that gave them character. He and his team of architects then compiled the features that were to become the basis for this model town. Among these were white picket fences of varying designs around each home, screened porches with large overhangs, galvanized metal roofs, dirt footpaths and native landscaping.

What started as a couple of cottages built for about $65,000 each now encompasses 480 homes with prices that start at $825,000 and go upwards of $5 million. There are a dozen restaurants, an amphitheater for community events and a town center to which people walk for shopping and socializing. Across the highway is a large expanse of sugar-sand beach upon which the Gulf of Mexico laps gently.

Begun in 1982, Seaside is still relatively young. Virtually all the empty lots have been sold and most have been built upon. Besides restaurants, there are shops, a gourmet supermarket, a bank, post office, chapel, clinic, fitness club and a small charter school. Yet to come are and a significant number of full-time residents. Currently, about 10 percent of the homeowners occupy their cottages year-round, and another handful is in residence about half the year. Most homeowners spend a few weeks there annually and rent their homes to beach-loving vacationers the rest of the time.

Carroll and Felton Temple consider Seaside their primary residence, although they spend half the year in Charlotte, NC. Carroll, 67, is a retired medicinal chemist who worked for the Southern Research Institute in Birmingham, AL. Felton, 66, is a medical transcriptionist who still works when she chooses.

During the 43 years in which they lived in Birmingham and raised a family, the Temples took many trips to Florida's Panhandle. It was during one of those trips in 1983 that they happened upon Seaside. Even then the fledgling community caught their eye. "There were three or four cottages here," Felton recalls. "I screamed for my husband to stop. I tried to get my husband interested in building a house, but he wouldn't do it."

Instead, they spent at least one vacation a year at Seaside, renting cottages owned by others. After eight years, Carroll came around. When they couldn't

find an existing house to suit them, they built the four-bedroom cottage they dubbed Blue Heaven. The name comes from the University of North Carolina at Chapel Hill, where Carroll did his graduate work. The school's colors are blue and white and are referred to as Blue Heaven.

Blue also happens to be Felton's favorite color. Not surprisingly, the cottage is painted blue outside and "has a blue theme running more or less inside," Felton says. "One bedroom is blue with peach, another is blue with yellow, and so on."

While the couple's home is larger than many of the so-called cottages at Seaside, its whimsical name and decor are typical of the community's ambiance. Each cottage has a name neatly posted on the white picket fence or near the door, along with the homeowners' names, including those of their children and sometimes pets as well. The cottages have names such as Salad Days, Dreamweaver, Hakuna Matata, Freckles, Plum Lazy, Sun-kissed and Ooh-La-La.

Felton says the couple didn't look anywhere else when they decided to build a second home. "We never considered any other place but Seaside. The Gulf is so beautiful. I liked the concept of little Victorian houses and cobblestone streets. You can't describe how pretty it is to anybody. They have to see it for themselves," says Felton, who notes that they put their cottage into the Seaside rental program during the summer, when it's too hot there for their tastes, and head north to Charlotte.

Charles and Sarah Modica discovered Seaside in much the same way as the Temples. In 1983, when they were vacationing at Panama City Beach, they drove out to see Seagrove Beach, just down the road from Seaside. From the road, they "saw a man sitting on the porch of a red house with his two dogs on his lap," Charles recalls. "That was Robert Davis and he was talking about what the city would look like."

At the time, Seaside consisted of two cottages on an unpaved street. "I said, 'Sarah, this man is crazy. Let's go,'" says Charles, who also thought the asking price of $65,000 for a house was on the high side back then. But his wife had other ideas, and the Modicas bought a lot and built the home they still occupy on Tupelo Street. Although it was to be a summer home, a respite from their grocery business in Alabama, Davis encouraged them to start an ice cream and sandwich shop on the beach. Sarah stayed and ran it while Charles continued to operate their grocery store in Alabama.

Seaside continued to grow and 10 years ago, Davis persuaded the Modicas to open a gourmet grocery store there. Charles, who was 61 at the time, object-ed that he was too old to start a new business, but Davis persisted. So the Modicas traveled around to see gourmet establishments in New Orleans and else-where, then opened their store, Modica Market, which is stocked floor-to-ceiling with everything from basics like toilet paper and onions to high-end wines, gourmet breads, cheeses and fresh seafood. Their son, Charles Jr., is now part of the business as well.

Although Charles Sr., now 71, and his 67-year-old wife had visions of retiring at Seaside, he can't foresee that day com-ing. The business, open seven days a week, is booming. He walks to work and enjoys his customers, including the children whose parents set up accounts at the store so the kids can go in and buy what they want on their own. "It's a close community," Charles says. "They take care of one another. It's like living in paradise."

While Seaside can't yet be considered a retirement town, it has the potential to become one. Most Seaside homebuyers now are well-heeled baby boomers with families who are looking for an invest-ment or ensuring themselves a retire-ment place in the sun in a few years.

"If you look at fairly recent research on what people want out of a retirement community, what the plurality want is a small town with urban amenities," says developer Robert Davis. "College towns fit that bill rather well, and so does Sea-side, with the added benefit of having a beach and warm weather, unlike Hanover (NH) and Amherst (MA)."

Davis, whose iconoclastic approach to development initially was ridiculed, only to later win high praise and many

Seaside, FL

Population: During summer, about 2,500 when rental homes are at maxi-mum capacity. During winter, about 200.

Climate:

	High	Low
January	61	42
July	89	74

Average relative humidity: 49%
Rainfall: 60 inches
Cost of living: Well above average
Median housing cost: $1.85 million
Sales tax: 7%
Sales tax exemptions: Groceries, medi-cine and most professional services.
State income tax: None
Intangibles tax: None. The tax was repealed as of Jan. 1, 2007.
Estate tax: None
Property tax: $9.4344 per $1,000 in Seaside, with homes assessed at 85% of market value. The annual tax on a $1.85 million home, with exemption noted

below, is about $14,600.
Homestead exemption: $25,000 off the assessed value of a permanent, pri-mary residence.
Religion: There is a small nondenomina-tional chapel in Seaside. In neighboring cities, houses of worship include Episco-pal, Lutheran, Presbyterian, Roman Catholic, United Methodist, Unity, Jewish and interdenominational.
Education: The Seaside Institute is a nonprofit organization devoted to expanding the concept of town planning and living. It sponsors intellectual and cul-tural events throughout the year. The Seaside Neighborhood School is a char-ter school offering classes for about 90 students in grades 6 through 8.
Transportation: The self-contained com-munity encourages foot and bicycle traf-fic. The airport shuttle provides service to the Bay County Airport/Fanin Field in Panama City, 35 miles east of Seaside; Okaloosa County Airport in Fort Walton Beach, 45 miles west of Seaside; Pensaco-la Airport, 80 miles west of Seaside; and Tallahassee Airport, 140 miles east of Sea-side. US Airways and Atlantic Southwest Airlines/Delta serve all four airports; Northwest Airlink serves Bay County, while Northwest flies into Okaloosa and Pensacola. American and Continental also serve Pensacola.

Health: Seaside's comprehensive health-care facility has a resident physician and visiting specialists. Nearby are the Bay Medical Center and Sacred Heart Hospital on the Emerald Coast.
Housing options: Options range from one-bedroom condos, which start at $825,000, to furnished beachfront cot-tages that cost upwards of $5 million.
Visitor lodging: The Cottage Rental Agency, (800) 277-8696 or www.cottage rentalagency.com, serves as the agent for about 280 privately owned rental cot-tages in the area. Rentals are least expen-sive in winter, rising in spring and fall and highest in summer. Reservations should be made well in advance, as Seaside has a high percentage of returning visitors and many arrange accommodations while in town for the following year. Rental cottages range from one to six bed-rooms and are classified as Grand, Premier or Classic, depending on location, size, interiors, and appliances. Grand rates start at $589 per night, Premier rates start at $385 per night, and Classic rates start at $205 per night. Josephine's French Coun-try Inn, (800) 848-1840 or (850) 231-1939, offers bed-and-breakfast accommo-dations for $175-$295.
Information: Seaside Community Realty Inc., P.O. Box 4730, Seaside, FL 32459, (888) 732-7433 or www.seasidefl.com.

awards, is blunt about his dislike for the growing trend of adult-only housing developments spreading across Florida and other retirement states. "What people are looking for, I think, at least in this generation of preretirees, is a place very unlike the summer camps for the elderly," he says. "These concentrations of one age group, I think it's unhealthy for us as a culture and unhealthy for people who are so concentrated."

Davis, who is 55 and owns a home in Seaside, says, "I don't know many of my friends who picture themselves going off to live with our own age group. I would find it completely deadly. Yet I know a lot of people go to these places even if they don't want to segregate by age because the suburban environment where we have spent most of our lives is so completely unsupportive of people without driver's licenses.

"Seaside represents a place where people without driver's licenses can do just fine," he says. "They can walk to most of the things they need on a daily basis, and there's a van that will run errands for them, take them to the airport — basically, there's no reason that they need a driver's license to live comfortably."

Comfortable living without a car is what Seaside is all about. Even those who can drive are encouraged to park their cars at their cottages and leave them there for the duration of their stay. As a result, pedestrians, bicyclists and skaters have the streets to themselves.

The heart of the community is Central Square, where much of the commercial element is clustered. There's the MM Fitness Studio, an attorney's office, clothing stores, art galleries, a real estate broker, a wine bar and the Seaside Institute, a nonprofit organization that offers educational and cultural programs. Modica Market is nearby.

An outdoor amphitheater provides a communal gathering spot for a variety of activities, such as concerts, a summer film series and storytelling. There are wine festivals twice a year, architectural tours, a conference for writers and other cultural events.

Across the highway are more shops and eateries. PER-SPI-CAS-ITY, an open-air market like those found in Italy, features stalls with all sorts of clothing and accessories. There's also Piazza Nancy Drew, an open area with shops on which the fanciful paintings of well-known designer Nancy Drew create festive fronts. Bud & Alley's bistro and rooftop bar overlook the Gulf and feature rustic coastal cuisine such as crab cakes and seafood stew.

Among Seaside's most distinctive features are the nine beach pavilions that frame the entrances to the beach, providing access over the high dunes as well as bathroom facilities and yet another opportunity for architecture to shine. The pavilions, each designed by a different architect, also are popular gathering spots for watching the sun set. All lead to a smooth beach virtually devoid of shells. Big blue beach umbrellas shading lounge chairs line up like so many sandpipers facing the water. Besides the beach, amenities include three swimming pools, six tennis courts and a croquet lawn.

The town is divvied up into various smaller neighborhoods, such as Ruskin Place Artist Colony, where artists can create and sell their works on the ground floor, while townhomes with a New Orleans flavor occupy the upper floors. And although it was the town's beauty and location that prompted the Temples to build there, there's no disputing that it was a good investment. "Our house has more than doubled in value since we built it — almost tripled," Felton says.

Despite the storms that wreaked havoc along the Florida coast in 2004 and 2005, overall property values have appreciated significantly in recent years, and will likely continue to do so. Due to the town's stringent building methods, homes are situated at a safe distance from storm surges. Stacey Brady, Seaside's public relations director, says that a beach restoration project, completed in 2006, revitalized area beaches.

When Robert Davis' grandfather, Birmingham department store owner J.S. Smolian, bought the remote 80-acre property in 1946, his family considered his $100-an-acre investment foolish. Davis inherited the land in 1978, and in the early 1980s, the most expensive lots ran about $20,000. "Those lots today would probably sell for $1 to $2 million," says Jacky Barker, real estate broker for Seaside.

One-bedroom penthouses start at $825,000. These properties are frequently situated in a mixed-use zone on top of a downtown building, with water views. Cottages start at about $1.4 million and rise to about $5.8 million. A typical cottage for sale costs $1.58 million, a price that includes the land on which to build a main house, as the guest cottage was built first.

"People buy here because there is a sense of community," Barker says. "A lot of the folks have been renting here and their families just love it. They get to know other families. The children can roam the streets here without the parents having to worry about it."

When they do put their properties up for sale, there's very little flexibility in the price. "Some have more than one property," Barker says. "Their attitude is, 'If I'm going to sell it, this is what the price is going to be.'"

While they may be trailblazers, the Temples find Seaside almost ideal for retirement living. The only drawbacks, Felton says, are that "it's a little hot in the summer and they don't have very extensive medical facilities yet."

The Temples find plenty to keep themselves occupied, even in the winter when there are less than 200 people in residence. Felton likes to read and do needlepoint. Carroll likes to paint. They both like to take long walks around the town and along the beach.

"We also like to try out the different restaurants," Felton says. "The facilities for eating seafood around here are wonderful." To others considering retiring in Seaside, she only has one piece of advice: "Just do it." ●

Sedona, Arizona

Fall under the spell of the red rocks of central Arizona

By Ron Butler

It's the classic picture-postcard town: a main street lined with attractive low-rise wood and stucco buildings that hint of the West of long ago. It's set in the heart of Arizona's fabled Red Rock Country where canyon walls stand frozen in time like the upswept wings of giant birds, and monoliths of flaming red rock reach majestically toward the sky.

It's a place where ancient mystics once stood tall to peer into the heavens. Heaven seemed that close.

Two hours north of Phoenix, at an altitude of 4,300 feet, Sedona is located well above the desert heat and below the mountain snow. Spring-fed Oak Creek Canyon glistens through thickets of cottonwood trees just off the main highway. The massive buttes and giant mesas of red sandstone are everywhere like lush color photos brought instantly to life.

Sedona's staggeringly beautiful setting is what stops artists, writers, photographers and casual holiday travelers dead in their tracks and keeps them coming back. It's as though Revlon, Gauguin and Technicolor all came together to gift-wrap the town in the cinnamon colors of fall every day of the year.

The red comes from a high concentration of oxidized iron — hematite. The 280-million-year-old landscape, once a prehistoric sea, is the result of eons of erosion — cloudburst, wind, running water, broiling temperatures, cold, melting snows, gravity — giving the land its ancient dignity. According to an American Indian legend, the red landscape came about when First Woman had twin grandsons, Monster Slayer and Born for Water. As the "People" began to emerge from the Third World into the higher realm of the Fourth, the women began to bear deformed children. Monster Slayer thought they were beasts and killed them, turning the landscape red with their blood.

"It's called red rock fever," says Sedona councilwoman Susan Solomon, "the thing that sweeps over visitors and makes them act so impulsively, as though any delay might make it all vanish and go away." Susan and her husband, Paul, both 54, came to Sedona on a week's timeshare vacation from their Cupertino home in California's Silicon Valley, and by the second day they were

---

Population: About 10,700. However, the town seems larger because of its healthy tourism industry.

Location: Sedona spreads across the boundaries of two north-central Arizona counties, Coconino and Yavapai. It's a two-hour drive north of Phoenix, two and a half hours from the Grand Canyon and 30 miles (40 minutes) south of Flagstaff.

Climate:

	High	Low
January	55	30
July	96	65

Located in the high Southwestern desert under a rim of the Colorado Plateau, Sedona enjoys mild weather throughout the year. Sunshine and clean air abound at Sedona's elevation of 4,500 feet.

Average relative humidity: 38% (69% mornings)

Rain: 17.15 inches annually

Cost of living: Above average

Average housing cost: About $550,000. Prices generally range from $250,000 for small residences to the millions for more exclusive, hideaway properties.

Sales tax: 9.525% in Coconino County, 9.35% in Yavapai County.

Sales tax exemptions: Groceries and prescription drugs

State income tax: For married couples filing jointly, graduated from 2.87% of taxable income up to $20,000, to 5.04% minus $2,276 on amounts over $300,000. For single filers, graduated from 2.87% of taxable income up to $10,000, to 5.04% minus $1,138 on amounts over $150,000.

Income tax exemptions: Social Security benefits and up to $2,500 of federal, Arizona state and local government pensions are exempt.

Estate tax: None

Inheritance tax: None

Property tax: The city of Sedona has no set property tax, but residents are taxed for special districts based upon property values, and both Coconino and Yavapai counties impose property tax in Sedona. Homes are assessed at 10% of market value. Rates range from 6.85% to 9.05% of assessed value, depending on location. When compared to other areas, many people find Sedona property taxes to be reasonable. Taxes on a $550,000 home would range from about $3,769 to $4,977. In addition to title and registration fees, Arizona assesses a vehicle license tax in lieu of a personal property tax on all vehicles registered in Arizona. This is based on the manufacturer's base retail price for the vehicle when new, less depreciation. Vehicle value is decreased 60% the first year and 16.25% for each subsequent year. The tax rate is $2.80 ($2.89 for used vehicles) per $100 of the vehicle's taxable value.

Homestead exemption: None

Religion: More than 20 churches, representing most faiths, serve the area. Many churches characterize themselves as non-denominational, such as the Chapel of the Holy Cross, which presents an imposing sight atop a sandstone ridge south of town.

Education: Coconino Community College offers continuing-education courses in nearby Flagstaff, (800) 350-7122. Yava-

out looking for land.

"We made studies, talked to people, and in June '95 bought what we thought would be a second home here," Susan says. "Ah, but red rock fever still had held. Instead, Paul, a professor at San José State, took an early retirement at age 50, we pulled up stakes and here we are."

The Solomons have one of the town's older homes, built in the '60s. They like their privacy but embrace Sedona's almost fierce sense of community. "People come here from all over the world, and from all areas of life," Susan says. "Retired people. Yuppies, tied to their computers. Artists, writers — you name it."

Susan has a doctorate in English and a background in publishing. She's a movie buff — "They don't get much better than 'American Beauty' or 'The Hours,'" she says — and she currently has 25 hours of film for a planned documentary she refuses to discuss for fear the project will be jinxed. Husband Paul has just published an economics textbook with McGraw-Hill. Their 24-year-

old son is in a writing program with the Actors Studio in New York. They have four dogs. Dinner with the Solomons — Susan loves to cook — is never dull.

Red rock fever is also what captivated frequent Arizona visitors Carl and Sylvia Saban, 68 and 69 respectfully, and brought them from LaGrange, IL, to retirement in a contemporary Southwest home at the mouth of Red Rock State Park in the Village of Oak Creek. Parents of three grown sons, including twins, and a daughter, they live in a home built on the site of what was the corral and bunkhouse in the 1965 movie, "The Rounders," starring Glenn Ford and Henry Fonda.

The street they live on, Broken Arrow, is named after the movie of the same name about the friendship between Cochise and American scout Tom Jeffords, starring Jeff Chandler as the Apache chief and Jimmy Stewart as the scout. Much of the movie was filmed right there.

Hollywood discovered color during the heyday of Western films, and one after another of the great directors —

John Ford, Delmar Daves and others — brought their larger-than-life stars to film against the magnificent scenery. In fact, so many Westerns were filmed in Sedona that, until recently, a Western film festival was held every year at a theater called The Flicker Shack. However, box-office interest in old Westerns disappeared in a cloud of dust, and the theater was replaced by a glitzy six-screen movie house that shows far more contemporary fare.

Carl Saban, who was a quality control manager with Reynolds Aluminum, and Sylvia, who was in budget management and sang professionally, are actively involved in everything Sedona has to offer. She immerses herself in its staggering array of cultural activities, including theater, dance, art and music, and he embraces the outdoors with a vengeance, hiking, mountain climbing and attending regular yoga classes at the Hilton Spa that he says helps make climbing 1,200 foot Humphrey's Peak a piece of cake.

They entertain visitors frequently. "Of course, everyone who comes here from

Sedona, AZ

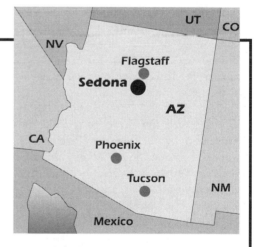

pai College in Prescott, which awards associate degrees, conducts courses in Sedona Center, (888) 204-4406. The Adult Community Center of Sedona also offers programs of interest, (928) 282-2834.

Transportation: If you don't have a car in Sedona, you walk. Scheduled van and charter ground transportation is available, focusing mainly on service between Sedona and Phoenix Sky Harbor International Airport.

Health: Sedona boasts a wide range of physicians, surgeons and dentists, with many specialties represented. Sedona's outpatient facility contains both emergency and cancer centers, lab, X-ray and a mammography unit. There's a 99-bed hospital in Cottonwood (20 miles west), a 238-bed hospital in Flagstaff (30 miles north) and a walk-in "urgent care" clinic. Six ambulances, an emergency search and rescue team, technical rescue team and a medical evacuation helicopter serve the area.

Housing options: Home design and

characteristics in Sedona are probably some of the most varied in the country. Housing is predominantly single-family residences, with some condominium developments. There are also several mobile home parks and subdivisions. Recent real estate listings ranged from $186,000 for a one-bedroom condo to $6.5 million for a 20-acre ranch. **Sedona Winds Independent Living** has restaurant-style dining, housekeeping, transportation and Alzheimer's care, (888) 522-4446.

Visitor lodging: Names like Hilton, Radisson, Quality Inn, Comfort Inn, Best Western and Super Eight are represented along with numerous unique, family-run, independently owned motels, lodges and bed-and-breakfast inns. After several owners and a few shaky starts, Enchantment Resort now hits its stride as Sedona's leading full-service luxury hotel resort. With Boynton Canyon as its stunning backdrop, Enchantment offers 220 guest rooms, studios and suites, and a spectacular new spa. Rates, single or double,

begin at $195, (800) 826-4180. Los Abrigados Resort & Spa is a 40-suite resort adjacent to the popular Tlaquepaque shopping complex. It boasts three restaurants, and rates begin at $225. At the more affordable Los Abrigados Lodge, rates begin at $139. For reservations at either, call (800) 258-2899.

Information: Sedona-Oak Creek Canyon Chamber of Commerce, P.O. Box 478, Sedona, AZ 86336, (928) 282-7722 or (800) 288-7336. Web sites: www.visitsedona.com, www.sedonachamber.com or www.experiencesedona.com.

out of town wants to see the Grand Canyon. It's two and a half hours north. We were there three times in one week recently," Sylvia says.

Also popular for outdoor buffs are the Pink Jeep Tours that course the desert and explore the ancient cliff dwellings around Sedona. The area feels sacred. Early American Indians believed that the towering spires of rock were pillars that held up the sky. Your guide, who likely looks like an American Indian with long hair tied into a braids, lots of polished silver and faded denim, but who may well be from someplace like Detroit, will tell you to be quiet and listen to the music of silence. Indeed, this is a strange and spiritual place.

It attracted Joel and Robin Staadeker, 56 and 54 respectively. They are movers and shakers in every sense of the word. They moved to Sedona from San Diego, where Joel was the president and chief executive officer of Allegiant Technologies. Robin is a lawyer with a doctorate in philosophy. They moved to Sedona four years ago with the idea of finding a more livable hometown for their then pre-teen daughter, Erin.

As Robin puts it, "We wanted to trade manscape for landscape, and we found it in Sedona." It wasn't an easy choice. The Staadekers drove 10,000 miles throughout the Southwest, looking, studying and evaluating their options. Santa Fe got high marks, but they found life there too intense. After three days in Sedona, they were convinced. They now live in a 50-year-old one-story home in a riparian area of cottonwoods and mesquite trees along the banks of Oak Creek, about as far from the boardrooms and chaos of big business as anyone can get.

As with most of Sedona's 10,000-plus residents, the Staadekers are strongly protective of the town they now call home. Joel is a member of the board of Keep Sedona Beautiful, Robin heads Sedona Recycles, a not-for-profit recycling center, and co-chairs the Task Force on Aging. She also is vice president of a grassroots citizens group committed to preserving the beauty of State Route 179.

"Sedona will reach its 'build-out' capacity by 2015," Robin says. "We've got to control all the building and banging." In other words, she and others don't want to tamper with perfection.

The town's showiest face is Tlaquepaque, a gracefully walled shopping complex styled after the market square of a small village outside of Guadalajara, Mexico. Its Spanish colonial bell tower, taller than the highest trees in Sedona, is a local landmark, attracting visitors from near and far to its many shops and restaurants.

Just beyond the complex is the block-long, red-stone Garland Building, where a concentration of shops deal in American Indian crafts, paintings and jewelry. Garland's, a Sedona institution, claims to feature "the world's largest selection of Navajo rugs." Tarry long enough and you'll no doubt see a family of Navajo weavers arrive with their latest works for sale. The women will be dressed in traditional full-length skirts, bright velveteen blouses and silver and turquoise beads.

Initial negotiations will be in English, slow and polite, the Indians looking down at the chocolate tile floor or up at the beamed ceilings as though to find the prices there. Bargaining is in the Navajo tongue, which the store buyers speak fluently. The Navajo reservation, the largest American Indian reservation in North America, is about a four-hour drive from Sedona. The weavers will want to get home before dark.

It's not surprising that a town as pretty as Sedona would attract more than its share of major artists. Surrealist Max Ernst was the first to take up residence. Zoe Mozert, famous in the 1930s and '40s for the Esquire magazine calendar girls, was another. The famed Cowboy Artists of America was founded in 1965 in Sedona's Oak Creek Tavern, as a brass marker outside attests. Work by artist Ted DeGrazia, who painted Southwest Indians with stylish brilliance in a palette of dazzling colors, can be found almost everywhere in Arizona. Paintings purchased for a song in the early days have put many a student through college today.

Of late, dozens of psychics, astrologers, tarot card readers, healers, spiritual advisers, channelers and palm readers have set up shop in Sedona to enhance their powers through the natural energy centers known as "vortexes." If you go into a restaurant and order soup, the pretty waitress who stares at you isn't necessarily coming on. She's probably reading your aura.

The downside of living in Sedona? Disadvantages are painless. Sylvia Saban misses the ethnic diversity of food when shopping — all the exotic things she could find back in Chicago. Can't anyone out here make a loaf of rye bread with a hard crust? And because the population is so small, she spends far too much time when she goes to the supermarket because she has to stop and talk with everyone.

Robin Staadeker doesn't like the growing profusion of timeshares. Film buff Susan Solomon is unhappy because she hasn't as yet run into Al Pacino or Nicholas Cage, both of whom recently bought homes in Sedona. But not to worry. With a population of less than 11,000, it shouldn't take long. ●

Shepherdstown, West Virginia

Youthful energy, community spirit and Colonial history make
a winning combination in this West Virginia college town

By Jim Kerr

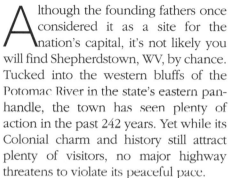

Although the founding fathers once considered it as a site for the nation's capital, it's not likely you will find Shepherdstown, WV, by chance. Tucked into the western bluffs of the Potomac River in the state's eastern panhandle, the town has seen plenty of action in the past 242 years. Yet while its Colonial charm and history still attract plenty of visitors, no major highway threatens to violate its peaceful pace.

Had the Potomac been deep enough to navigate this far, things might have been different. Instead, Washington, DC, about an hour and a half to the southeast, got the capital role. And while a bridge along Route 34 across the river and into Maryland is well traveled, outsiders generally find themselves here because of forethought rather than pure serendipity.

"We really didn't know anything about Shepherdstown until we came here for our anniversary vacation in 1993," says Marty Broadhurst, now retired here with his wife, Nan. "We stayed at the Bavarian Inn, a well-known resort along the river. But instead of turning left and heading back across the bridge on our way home, we decided to turn right and come into town for lunch. There was an art fair going on. We were smitten. We became friends with the owner of a house for sale, and we've lived here for the past eight years."

Marty, a government physicist for 30 years, and Nan, a systems engineer with the World Bank, originally thought they wanted to retire to a small town in New England. Not only was Shepherdstown closer to where they lived near Gaithersburg, MD, it also had the right proportions and mix of attractions for them.

The town is barely eight by seven blocks. The main thoroughfare, German Street, runs downhill toward the river, where neatly packed two- and three-story brick buildings contain shops, restaurants, bookstores and other businesses, including the Opera House, one of the nation's oldest movie theaters. Other historic buildings have been converted to civic uses such as a library, hotel-museum and the War Memorial Building, which now headquarters the town's very active Men's Club.

There is no stoplight in Shepherdstown, although the four-way stop sign at the corner of German and Duke streets is said to be the busiest intersection in Jefferson County. The traffic, which moves steadily, consists mainly of commuters headed either northeast into Maryland, south toward the county seat at Charles Town, or west to Martinsburg, WV. Few cars head east toward the river and the town center.

Despite the town's compact and small-town nature, there is a distinct energy here. Much of it is generated by the nearly 4,000 students at Shepherd University, founded in 1872, where myriad events related to the liberal arts school include concerts, art shows, lectures and an annual four-week series of plays in July called the Contemporary American Theater Festival.

"We go to so much more here in terms of plays and concerts than we ever did in DC," says Nan Broadhurst. "First of all, we can walk to them. And they're very diverse and interesting, from live theater to Saturday night River House concerts with all types of music, from cello to guitar. And it costs $10."

Marty, 71, and Nan, 60, are among a growing segment of retirees here in Shepherdstown. They spent eight months fixing up their old-fashioned bungalow-style home built in 1923. It was the large front porch that captured Nan's fancy, and the huge garden space out back allowed Marty to replant more than half the 200 azalea bushes that he moved in several trips from Gaithersburg.

A cozy living room with a wood-burning stove hosts daily guests, and newspapers that line the ceiling of Marty's basement workshop date to 1935. Now well-established in the community, the Broadhursts have found a seemingly endless assortment of civic and social activities that have left them wondering how they ever found time to work at regular jobs. Yet, even with Marty's involvement in the Men's Club and Nan's interest in the Arts and Humanities Alliance of Jefferson County, both have found time to volunteer as Care Givers, helping the elderly and disabled, while taking up painting as a hobby.

Being at the heart of the action seems to be a Shepherdstown tradition. Established originally as Mecklenburg in the 1730s, the town's many cottage industries included a gunsmith who made long rifles. When the American Revolution broke out, a company of men organized in Shepherdstown marched the 600 miles to Boston in 24 days to reinforce George Washington's beleaguered troops.

Later, from 1850 to 1924, mules pulled shallow-draft barges up the Chesapeake & Ohio Canal along the north bank of the Potomac, giving local farmers access to outside markets. The railroad eventually made the canal obsolete, but it is preserved today as a national historic park, with hiking and biking for 184 miles from Georgetown to Cumberland.

At a bend just south of town, the same shallowness of the river that had eliminated Shepherdstown from competition for the nation's capital also led to its greatest crisis. Early in the Civil War, on Sept. 17, 1862, the Battle of Antietam was fought at nearby Sharpsburg, MD, and when Confederate forces retreated across the river at the shallow bend known as Pack Horse Ford, cannonballs and Union forces followed.

Between 5,000 and 8,000 Confederate casualties from the single bloodiest battle in American history filled every house, church, alley and street in Shepherdstown, and many who died from their wounds are buried in Shepherdstown's cemetery. Antietam National Battlefield, which is only a few miles from Shepherdstown, gets 250,000 annual visitors, yet curiosity seems to attract only a fraction of them across the Potomac to take a look at the town.

Shepherdstown was renamed in 1798 for Thomas Shepherd, an early settler and benefactor who recognized a swift-moving stream here as a good source of power for a grain mill. Now known as the Town Run, the stream still travels unabated under the visitor center, the main street and the Blue Moon Cafe before plunging into the Potomac.

Besides its namesake, the town has a long history of other pioneer innovators, including James Rumsey, who first successfully tested the steamboat here in 1787. But in the past decade, it has been largely the task of inventive and resourceful newcomers to preserve and shape the town for the future.

Pam and Rusty Berry arrived a decade ago to escape more frenetic lives working with computers and communications in Arlington, VA. "There were empty storefronts, a lot of inexpensive student housing and little to do in the evening," remembers Pam, 57. "But it was quaint, and the people were extraordinarily friendly. They invited us to potluck dinners. It was like they had known us forever."

With some trepidation, Rusty, 50, acquired and reopened the Opera House movie theater, built in 1909 but shut down since the 1950s. He reduced the number of seats to 130 in the 20-foot-wide and 190-foot-deep building, brought in the best projection equipment that the space allowed, and completely renovated the theater.

"Rusty worked full time on renovations while I commuted to Washington by train for a year," Pam says. "We were still unpacking the popcorn machine, putting seats in and selling tickets for the 8 p.m. show when the theater opened on Feb. 19, 1992. People were lined up around the block. It's frequently full, depending on the movie, and we have a clientele that extends as far as Cumberland, MD."

Across the street from the Opera House, Pam opened and expanded what had been a food market into the Sweet Shop, a bakery and cafe, in 1993. The couple now lives in an apartment above the theater, renting out the third floor to college students.

About half the student population, roughly three times the size of the town's permanent population, commutes from

---

Population: Shepherdstown has a year-round resident population of 1,500, plus 3,700 students attending Shepherd University. The nearest city with a population of 50,000 or more is Frederick, MD, 27 miles away. Martinsburg, WV, with 16,000 inhabitants, and Charles Town, the Jefferson County seat with about 4,000 residents, are both located about 11 miles from Shepherdstown.

Location: On a bluff above the Potomac River on the border with Maryland in West Virginia's Eastern Panhandle. The town is 65 miles west of Washington, DC.

Climate: High Low
January   41   22
July   87   65

Average relative humidity: 68%

Rain: 40.5 inches annually

Cost of living: Above the state average, but well below large urban areas nearby, such as Baltimore and Washington.

Average housing cost: While there are increasing housing options in the surrounding area for under $300,000, including condos and townhouses, homes within the historic town limits are rarely available for under $500,000.

Sales tax: 6%

Sales tax exemptions: There are no taxes on prescriptions.

State income tax: There is a graduated income tax rate ranging from 3% on taxable income up to $10,000 to 6.5% of income over $60,000.

Income tax exemptions: Under age 65, there is an exemption for federal and some state pensions of up to $2,000 per taxpayer and a full exemption for those in the state and local police, sheriffs and firefighter's pension system. For those age 65 and better, there is an exemption of up to $8,000 in all income. Social Security benefits subject to federal tax are taxable.

Estate tax: None, except the state's "pick-up" portion of the federal tax, applicable to estates of more than $2 million.

Property tax: In incorporated Shepherdstown, the rate is $1.4062 per $100 of assessed value, which is 60% of market value. A house that sold for $400,000 would be assessed at $240,000 and the annual tax would be $3,375. In the county, a house costing $400,000 would be assessed at 60% and taxed at 1.2534% annually or $3,008. Residents pay either town or county property taxes, but not both. There is a personal property tax of $2.5068 in the county and $2.8124 in the town on each $100 of value on items such as automobiles and recreational vehicles.

Homestead exemptions: The first $20,000 of the assessed value of a home is exempt from property taxes for citizens over 65.

Religion: There are 11 churches of various denominations.

Education: Shepherd University, with 3,700 full-time students, two-thirds of them commuting from surrounding areas, is a public school affiliated with the state university system. Tuition is low with four-year degree programs in business and liberal arts studies and some emphasis on music and the performing arts. Seven other colleges with enrollments of more than 2,000 are within 50 miles of Shepherdstown. More than 50 percent of the resident population has a bachelor's degree or higher.

Transportation: Route 45 connects Shepherdstown with Interstate 81 about 12 miles west at Martinsburg, WV. Inter-

surrounding communities, while the rest live in college dorms, apartments and boarding houses. The campus, which consists of 28 buildings adjacent to the business district, is anchored by McMurran Hall, a building of beautiful hand-cut stone originally built as a town hall in the 1860s. Its hand-wound clock tower still strikes the hour.

This combination of Old World ambiance with youthful energy, community spirit and entrepreneurship has encouraged a small wave of new residents and retirees escaping urban enclaves in the east. "People here are not only nice, they're interesting," says Lillian Kinser, who has lived here with husband Glen since 1993. "A lot of them are well-educated and have backgrounds in government."

Glen, 63, had lived in a dozen locations as an ecology instructor and training officer for the U.S. Fish and Wildlife Service before he and Lillian, also with the service, moved here from Annapolis.

The agency maintains a large training facility near Shepherds- town, and when the couple retired a few years ago, they decided this was the place to stay. "We talked a lot about moving to the Outer Banks of North Carolina, which we've visited 14 times," Glen says. "But we liked our house and we liked the town. While it has changed in the past 10 years, it really hasn't changed much."

Their 3,000-square-foot bungalow-style house, built in 1928, is a solid work of craftsmanship. It has six bedrooms, including two on the ground floor, and plenty of room for a recent family reunion of 19 relatives. The couple has filled the house with antiques and odds and ends bought at auctions around the area. Glen, whose "serious hobby" is woodcarving, has a shop and studio in the house, and he travels around the county to various craft shows.

When they feel a need for city amenities and entertainment, the couple makes the two-hour drive into Washing-

ton, Baltimore or Annapolis to visit museums and art exhibits. Many residents also commute to DC by train; a rural station in Duffield is only a few miles out of town. Another is in Martinsburg, 10 miles away, and still another is 11 miles down the Potomac at Harpers Ferry, a town whose own Civil War past has largely eclipsed Shepherdstown's role with Antietam.

Wings were added to McMurran Hall in 1866, when Shepherdstown briefly became the county seat. In 1871, the county seat was moved to Charles Town, where it remains today. Charles Town's race track and 2,000 slot machines, along with nearby Harpers Ferry National Historical Park, draw the vast majority of tourists to this corner of the state.

It was Shepherdstown's more subtle appeal as a quaint and historic retreat that prompted Jim Ford and Jeanne Muir to leave good-paying jobs in Boston and invest in a bed-and-breakfast inn here. In September 2002, they sold their 1,500-

Shepherdstown, WV

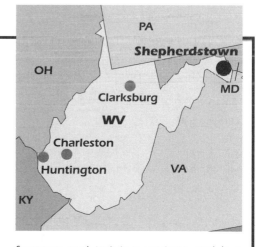

state 70 at Frederick, MD, 26 miles away, connects with U.S. highways 340 and 34, which run west to Shepherdstown. The closest regional airport is Hagerstown Regional 20 miles away, and the closest international airport is Washington Dulles about 43 miles away. There is daily commuter train service to Washington's Union Station from three stations within 10 miles of Shepherdstown.

Health: Jefferson Memorial Hospital is 10 miles away in Ranson, WV, and City Hospital is 11 miles away in Martinsburg. Other community hospitals are in Hagerstown, MD, and Winchester, VA. Washington DC's Johns Hopkins is about 70 miles away, an hour-and-a-half drive.

Housing options: Few houses are for sale at any given time within the historic town's corporate boundaries, and anything priced between $350,000 and $500,000 is generally under contract quickly. A three-bedroom, 2,000-square-foot home was recently for sale at $240,000. Numerous options are offered immediately outside the town limits in a number of developments. Construction is under way on a new

and as yet unnamed townhome development east of downtown near the river. Lots are available at **Colonial Hills**, a subdivision near the Clarion Hotel property on the edge of town, with units priced from $385,000. **Deerfield Village**, a new subdivision with quarter-acre lots beyond the Clarion Hotel property on Route 480 west of Shepherdstown, has begun construction of 48 homes on 64 acres, with prices from $425,000. For information on all three subdivisions, call (304) 876-3737. Rental apartments are available in Shepherdstown. About 5,000 new housing units have been approved for construction in the county around Shepherdstown over the next five years.

Visitor lodging: The 73-room Bavarian Inn is Shepherdstown's premier resort. The European-style inn and restaurant was converted from the historic Greystone Inn by Carol and Erwin Asam 25 years ago and offers riverfront chalets from $95 and garden-view rooms from $85, (304) 876-2551. The 168-room Clarion Hotel and Conference Center is located on Route 480 just outside town. It's widely used for government-related con-

ferences and training sessions and is a full-service facility with rates that typically run $106-$125, (800) 252-7466. The Days Inn, located one-half mile from the historic district off Route 45, has 51 rooms starting at $78 with AAA or AARP discount, (304) 876-3160. The Thomas Shepherd Inn, located a block from downtown, has six elegantly furnished rooms with private baths and complete gourmet breakfast for two starting at $89, (304) 876-3715.

Information: Shepherdstown Visitors Center, P.O. Box 329, 102 E. German St., Shepherds- town, WV 25443, (304) 876-2786, or www.shepherdstownvisitorscenter.com.

square-foot home in Boston for $600,000 and bought the Thomas Shepherd Inn, built in 1868 as the parsonage for a Lutheran Church, for $710,000.

The price included not only the beautifully renovated 4,500-square-foot building and its six guest rooms, but also ample living quarters for Jim and Jeanne, as well as the B&B business, which had been successfully operated since 1983. The transition from city routine and corporate jobs to a more personal involvement in small-town life, while requiring some adjustments, has been a positive experience.

"We haven't known our neighbors in many places we've lived," says Jeanne, 43. "But here we're a part of so much going on, from helping to organize garden tours to working with a new economic council, which is setting up forums to attract new business and high-tech companies to the county."

Their elegantly furnished living room at the inn is often the venue for meetings, just as the Broadhursts often host friends for discussion groups and meditation. It seems that folks are getting together everywhere in Shepherdstown, whether it's a student study group down at Betty's Restaurant, a chess game at the local coffeehouse, or a meeting of the Men's Club.

Like the Town Run, a community spirit runs through here, alive and perpetually on the move. ●

Sierra Vista, Arizona

A frontier history, mountain views and cool nights in southern Arizona

By Ron Butler

Sierra Vista means "mountain view" in Spanish, and therein is the secret of its fabulous success. Along with providing knockout, often snowcapped scenery, the mountains form a protective barrier around a city that was originally founded to house military personnel and their families.

Fort Huachuca, one of the oldest active military installations in the nation, is situated within Sierra Vista, which is located 70 miles southeast of Tucson and 20 miles north of the Mexican border. It was the home of the famous 10th Cavalry Buffalo Soldiers who helped quell the warring Apaches.

Buffalo Soldiers, troopers of the all-black 9th and 10th U.S. Cavalry Regiments, played a decisive role in the settlement of the Old West. They guarded the mail, built roads and telegraph lines, mapped and explored, escorted stage-coaches and cattle drives, and for more than two decades, fought an elusive enemy who struck from ambush when least expected and disappeared like whispering ghosts.

These were the days that tried men's souls, wrote Capt. John G. Burke at the time. "To march into battle with banners flying, drums beating and pulse throbbing in unison with the roar of the artillery does not call for half the nerve and determination that must be daily exercised to pursue, mile after mile, over rugged mountains and through unknown canyons, a foe whose habits of warfare are repugnant to every principle of humanity."

Buffalo Soldiers were so named by the Indians partly because their skin color and hair reminded the Indians of the buffalo. It was also a designation of respect. Indian warriors learned quickly that the black men in blue uniforms would fight ferociously to the end when under attack.

Today, Fort Huachuca is a national historic landmark and a major military communications center or, more official-

ly, Command Headquarters of the U.S. Army Intelligence Center and School, Army Communications-Electronics Command and Electronic Proving Ground. As a tribute to their role in settling the West, Fort Huachuca maintains the Buffalo Soldier Museum where saddles, rifles, uniforms, amulets and horseshoe nails crudely bent into rings to be worn during fistfights can be seen. Admission is free with a pass obtained at the visitors gate.

Rather than overwhelm the town of 43,000, the large military presence adds a sense of security. Fort Huachuca has more than 12,000 military and civilian employees. The woman in the mall parking lot with her bundles and packages and the senior citizen tinkering out back on his antique Woodie always feel safe.

Delightful climate, clear air (at an elevation of 4,623 feet) and a relatively low cost of living all help explain why so many of the soldiers who serve at Fort Huachuca stay on after their discharge and why other visitors also see it as an ideal place to retire.

Sierra Vista is located in Arizona's high desert, an area of sand and rocks and occasional spurts of green, weather and season permitting. Fry Boulevard begins at Fort Huachuca's main gate and continues east, forming Sierra Vista's main drag, with motels, restaurants, bars, offices — the usual chain of life for any small Western town. The architecture is a mishmash of wooden frontier buildings next to stucco and modern structures, all put together during the ebb and flow of progress and periods of Fort Huachuca's military prominence. At the moment it couldn't be hotter.

You don't have to ask Jim and Jo Smith, 67 and 59 respectively, why they left Colorado Springs, CO, three years ago and selected Sierra Vista as the place they wanted to settle down and stay. He was a retired Navy radar engineer who spent six years in Alaska, and she was a

Delta Airlines ticket agent.

Both avid skiers, they became tired of the cold. They checked out Florida and found it too hot. They had visited Arizona often (thanks to a Delta Airlines pass) and finally decided on the gated, active-adult community of Winterhaven, little more than a putting green away from the Pueblo del Sol Country Club. (Family golf fees are $208 a month, and guest greens fees are $38.)

Although less active since developing heart problems in 1991 which forced his retirement, Jim enjoys biking and hiking wilderness trails in and around Sierra Vista, as does his wife. "The town has everything, and yet it has a laid-back, less-developed feel about it," Jim says.

"Well, maybe not everything," Jo adds. "We could always use more upscale shops and restaurants. I'd kill for a Trader Joe's. But then, Tucson is not that far away."

Indeed, facilities in Sierra Vista include nine parks, a community center, two riding clubs (the trails are spectacular), four libraries, a tennis club, 13 public ball fields, four public swimming pools, a community college and an extension branch of the University of Arizona. The San Pedro Riparian National Conservation Area, east of town, is world-famous for bird watching. Sites rich with Western history set among Dragoon, Mule and Whetstone mountains all shape the city's character.

"And we're only six or seven hours from Puerto Penasco for great fish and great fishing," says Jim, referring to the rapidly developing northernmost Mexican west coast resort, also known as Rocky Point. "We have an Outback Steakhouse here in Sierra Vista," says Jo, "and the fish is excellent. We also eat at the country club Grille a lot."

Sierra Vista is located in Cochise County, named for the famous Apache chief. Before there was Geronimo, there was Cochise. After the 1850 U.S. takeover of what is now Arizona and New Mexico,

Cochise and his band of Chiricahua Apaches operated from a rugged natural stronghold of heavily wooded domes, spires, cliffs and granite rock pinnacles in southeast Arizona, about 45 miles northeast of today's Wild West town of Tombstone. Not far from Sierra Vista, the area is called Cochise Stronghold.

Known as a master strategist and leader, Cochise was an imposing 6-foot-tall figure who was never conquered in battle. He also was never photographed. He died on June 7, 1874, and was buried in a grave in Cochise Stronghold where, as he wished, "only the rays of the morning sun would know its location." His grave has never been found.

Today, Cochise Stronghold is a popular recreation area with a small creek, a variety of campsites with grills and picnic tables, and hiking and wilderness trails. Manzanita, oak and juniper-covered hillsides are home to deer and javelina.

Sierra Vista, AZ

Population: 43,000

Location: Seventy miles southeast of Tucson, 20 miles northwest of the Mexican border town of Naco. Elevation is 4,623 feet.

Climate:

	High	Low
January	61	33
July	92	66

Average relative humidity: Almost none

Average rainfall: 14.71 inches

Cost of living: Lower than average. (One night's lodging in a first-class hotel costs $69-$79, dinner for two runs $35, and a night at the movies costs $4-$7.50.)

Median housing cost: $185,875

Sales tax: The city collects 1.60%, county charges 0.50%, and the state levies 5.60%.

Sales tax exemptions: Prescription drugs

State income tax: For married couples filing jointly, graduated from 2.87% of taxable income up to $20,000 to 5.04% minus $2,276 on amounts over $300,000. For single filers, graduated from 2.87% of taxable income up to $10,000 to 5.04% minus $1,138 on amounts over $150,000.

Income tax exemptions: Social Security benefits and up to $2,500 of federal and Arizona state and local government pensions are exempt.

Estate tax: None

Inheritance tax: None

Property tax: The tax rate is $11.34 per $100 in assessed valuation, with homes assessed at 10% of market value. Property tax on a $185,875 home would be about $2,108.

Homestead exemptions: None

Religion: With its strong Spanish Catholic base and an infusion of military personnel from all parts of the world, Sierra Vista offers dozens of places of worship.

Education: With six elementary schools, two middle schools, a new state-of-the-art Buena High School, the University of Arizona Sierra Vista campus and an extension of Cochise College, education is a high priority in the community.

Transportation: Located on State Highway 90 at State Highway 92, 30 miles south of Interstate 10. Sierra Vista has seven cab and shuttle services, and three car rental firms. The newly expanded Sierra Vista Municipal Airport offers links to commercial airline service in Phoenix via Great Lakes Airlines.

Health: The area has an 83-bed hospital, two nursing homes, 50 physicians, 22 dentists and eight chiropractors. The Sierra Vista Regional Health Center, with a full-service pharmacy, laboratory and medical records department, and the Veterans Administration Clinic at Fort Huachuca are prepared to cover virtually all medical needs and emergencies. The community also has several private resident-care homes and home health care agencies.

Housing options: The average rental rate for two-bedroom, two-bath apartments is about $600, depending on location. For much of the past decade, Sierra Vista has seen home sales volume totaling more than 900 units per year, beginning in the mid-$60,000s to $200,000 or more. Its mild year-round weather has fostered at least a dozen RV parks. Sierra Vista has two gated active-adult communities of new homes — **Winterhaven** and **Vista View Resort**. Winterhaven, a Castle & Cooke community, (800) 837-6841 or www.cc-winterhaven.com, has three distinct series of homes, some on or near the fairways of Pueblo del Sol Country Club. Prices start in the $200,000s. Residents enjoy such activities as social gatherings, exercise classes, swimming, a book club and arts and crafts. Vista View Resort, (866) 459-0775 or www.vistaviewresort.com, offers freestanding condos on a 99-year lease, so land and property taxes are included in the lease arrangement. Buyers can choose from liberal customizing options; prices start at about $97,000. Vista View amenities include a fully equipped gym, miniature golf course, walking trails, bocce ball and RV parking.

Visitor lodging: As a military and retirement town and a vacation destination, Sierra Vista has hotels, motels and bed-and-breakfast inns in all price ranges as well as RV camps and guest ranches. Among options: Gateway Studio Suites, $80, (877) 443-6200; Quality Inn and Conference Center, $79, (800) 458-0982; Sierra Suites, $69-$99, (520) 459-4221; Windemere Hotel and Conference Center, $85, (800) 825-4656; Comfort Inn and Suites, $78-$136, (520) 459-0515; Fairfield Inn Suites, Marriott, $89, (520) 439-5900. The city boasts about 1,200 rooms.

Information: Sierra Vista Chamber of Commerce, 21 E. Wilcox Drive, Sierra Vista, AZ 85635, (520) 458-6940 or www.sierravistachamber.org. Sierra Vista Convention and Visitors Bureau, 1011 N. Coronado Drive, Sierra Vista, AZ 85635, (800) 288-3861 or www.visitsierravista.com. City of Sierra Vista, www.ci.sierra-vista.az.us or (520) 458-3315.

Just west are the Chiricahua Mountains, the setting for Elliott Arnold's classic novel "Blood Brother" about the friendship between Cochise and American scout Tom Jeffords. It was made into the film "Broken Arrow," with Jeff Chandler playing Cochise and Jimmy Stewart as the scout. A prolific writer, Arnold wrote numerous books but none caught the public's imagination more than this one. Just about every home in Cochise County has a copy of "Blood Brother" on the bookshelves.

Arnold was a soft-spoken, sensitive man with deep blue eyes who liked Alexander Calder paintings and was as comfortable in Arizona Indian country as he was in New York City, where he died after a brief illness on May 13, 1980. Arnold's scrupulously researched book became a massive best seller (it was reprinted in 20 hardcover editions in 13 years, not to mention countless paperback editions) and was one of the first popular novels to depict the Native Americans sympathetically.

Another Fort Huachuca retiree who decided to stay in Sierra Vista is Wesley Hewitt, 41, who recently completed his 20-year military career as an instructor in unmanned remote-controlled spy plane operations, serving the past 10 years at Fort Huachuca. He and his wife, Donna, also 41, both originally from Long Island, New York, live in a ranch-style home in the east-side foothills. They have a son and daughter, 21 and 23, who have left the nest.

Donna, who worked at the customer service desk at the Sierra Vista Parks and Leisure Department, remains astonished at the town's growth in the past 10 years. "It's literally doubled in size," she says. "A badly needed mall opened in 1999."

Husband Wesley remains a strong supporter of Fort Huachuca, pointing out that it's easily the most tourist-friendly military installation in the United States. "It may be a fully active, mission-focused Army post, but it offers horseback riding stables, a golf course, a U.S. Army Military Intelligence Museum, the Buffalo Soldier Museum, sport shooting range, archaeological sites and nature preserves, all open to the public. There are nominal charges for golf, sport shooting and horse rentals," he says.

Drew Whiteside, 63, and his life part-ner of 20 years, Ruth Nolte, 58, made the move to Sierra Vista just more than a year ago from their home in northern Minnesota. Originally from Duluth, Drew is a dentist and Ruth is a nurse. They chose Sierra Vista as their retirement home because of the weather, the Old West flavor, the hiking trails and, says Drew, "because there are too many bugs in Minnesota."

Drew's brother also lives in Arizona, and the couple visited often before making their own move. They have a home in Vista View Resort, two miles from downtown, a gated and age-restricted community with a clubhouse and fitness center where homes begin at about $97,000s. They enjoy the proximity to such legendary Western towns as Tombstone (17 miles), Bisbee (20 miles) and Fort Bowie. "Ruth volunteers for everything," says Drew, including Meals on Wheels. "And she's studying Spanish."

And where does this dentist go to get his teeth fixed? "I go across the border to Mexico. Naco is only 20 miles away. I checked it out: modern equipment, clean and sanitary, about half the price," he says with a big smile. ●

Siesta Key, Florida

Get to this Florida isle fast, and then take it slow

By Karen Feldman

It would be impossible to pick a better name for Siesta Key, the eight-mile-long barrier island just offshore of Sarasota on Florida's Gulf coast.

Mature trees, lush foliage and winding streets abloom with hibiscus and bougainvillea soothe even the most stressed-out soul. The white-sand beaches — often voted the world's best — beckon visitors to sit down and enjoy. The gently lapping surf of the Gulf of Mexico provides the fluid show and soundtrack.

While it may seem worlds away from civilization, Siesta Key is just minutes from Sarasota, quite possibly Florida's most culturally blessed city. That "get away from it all without giving up anything" quality has ensnared even those convinced they couldn't move to Florida.

Take Jon and Paula Stein, for example. They were living in Canton, OH, in 1995 when Jon retired from the family scrap recycling and brokerage business. Paula, who was a family counselor and real estate saleswoman, among other things, eventually stopped working, too.

Both in their early 50s at the time, they set out to pick a place where they would be assured of an active retirement. They eliminated Breckenridge, CO, where they already owned a home.

"When we thought about where we wanted to go, we thought warm," Jon says. But Paula had ruled out the Sunshine State, too. "You'd have to shoot me before I'll move to Florida," she recalls thinking at the time.

Yet they found they liked Key West enough to buy a home. The ink on the contract was barely dry when a family emergency called them back to Ohio. The effort and time it took to get there from the remote island made them realize they needed to be closer to a big city and a major airport.

Jon's parents had owned a home on Longboat Key, a barrier island just north of Siesta, since 1972. Jon and Paula had visited often but couldn't see themselves living there. Despite their many trips to the region, they'd never been to Siesta Key, separated from Longboat only by one small island.

During one visit, they took a drive and headed south. "It was like entering a different world," Paula recalls of her first glimpse of Siesta Key. "We realized people lived here, raised families here, went to school here. I think that's what did it." They moved in 1998.

Jane Phelan and her husband, Bob, chose Siesta Key for the same reason in 1996. He's a retired airline pilot in his 70s who's seen most of the world. Jane, 58, is a former journalist who now has her own marketing company and works with the Siesta Key Chamber of Commerce.

Besides the mix of ages, Jane likes that there's a diversity in incomes, too. "There are very wealthy people who live on Siesta Key, but you also have upper-middle-class and regular working people," she says. "Not every single person is retired or plays golf or tennis. I think that makes for an interesting community."

The couple decided on Siesta Key for the usual reasons: It was warm and close to the action. "Here I am living at the beach and I decide I want to see a Broadway show at Van Wezel (Performing Arts Hall)," Jane says. "Fifteen minutes later, I'm pulling up and going in. That's when I pinch myself. We used to live on the eastern shore of Maryland. To go to the theater or opera, it was a two-hour drive to Washington."

On the island, residents can walk or ride their bicycles to a gourmet restaurant, a funky beach bar, the hardware store or the pharmacy. There are great places to run and kayak and there's a prime view of the sunset every night. The main draw is, of course, the beach.

"Siesta Key's public beach is probably the finest beach in the world," says Marcia McLaughlin, a real estate agent with RE/MAX Properties in Sarasota. It's something she says with conviction, not as sales rhetoric.

In the Great International White Sand Beach Challenge, held in 1987, sand from Siesta Key's Crescent Beach topped 30 other varieties, including some from the Bahamas and Caymans, to be named the world's finest, whitest sand. Powdery and dazzlingly white, Siesta Key's beaches are made of finely ground quartz crystals devoid of shell and coral, giving it a soft feel and keeping it relatively cool when other varieties would sear the soles.

The beach also won top honors for cleanliness, water quality and safety from noted coastal geologist Dr. Stephen Leatherman, also known as "Dr. Beach" because of his highly touted annual beach rankings. As if that weren't enough, the public beach also has free parking (a rarity in Florida these days), a place to change clothes and areas for volleyball, barbecue grills and playgrounds.

The island attracted residents long before there was a bridge connecting it to the mainland. Timucua and Caloosa Indians gathered shellfish and hunted game there centuries ago. By the late 1800s, the island had a small population of mostly fishermen. It was dubbed Siesta Key in 1907 when the Siesta Land Co. became the first developer to plat a subdivision there. The Roberts Hotel later welcomed luminaries such as Cecil B. DeMille, Bette Davis and Charlton Heston. In 1917, the first drawbridge connected the island to Sarasota. Two bridges now connect the island to the mainland.

In Sarasota, what began as a winter retreat for circus tycoon John Ringling has evolved into a small city with big-city culture. There's the Asolo Theatre, the Sarasota Opera, the Florida West Coast Symphony, the Sarasota Jazz Society, the Sarasota Ballet of Florida, Van Wezel Performing Arts Hall, the Golden Apple Dinner Theater and numerous small playhouses and art galleries.

During February and March, the Cincinnati Reds are in town for spring training, with the Sarasota Red Sox, the Class A team of the Boston Red Sox, stepping up to the plate from April through September.

Sarasota, said to be where golf first came to the United States from Scotland, today has some 85 courses with more on the way. Along the edge of Sarasota Bay near downtown Sarasota are the John and Mable Ringling Museum of Art, the couple's winter residence and a circus museum, all open to the public. The

Marie Selby Botanical Garden covers nine lush acres just a few minutes south of the Ringling estate. The gardens have world-class collections of air plants, orchids and Amazonian bromeliads.

The easily accessible downtown has a thriving arts and shopping district, with busy galleries, boutiques and restaurants. And an enterprising company, Florida Ever-Glides, gives tours by Segway transporters from an office across from Towles Court, a thriving art colony.

For a stylish turn, St. Armands Circle (on the little island between Siesta and Longboat) offers upscale boutiques,

bistros and clubs around a well-landscaped circle. Nearby is Mote Marine Laboratory, which serves as a living classroom and the base of extensive marine research.

Not only do all of these attractions provide entertainment, they offer countless opportunities to get involved. Retired doctors Patty and Frank Sturtevant, both 77, have to use calendars to track all of their volunteer activities.

In 1989, Patty Sturtevant retired from Loyola University Medical School, where she taught anatomy. The following year, Frank left GD Searle and Co., a pharma-

Siesta Key, FL

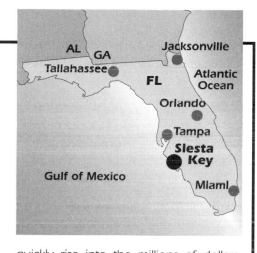

Population: About 24,000, half of which are seasonal residents.

Location: About 55 miles south of Tampa on Florida's Gulf coast, Siesta Key is an eight-mile-long barrier island connected to Sarasota by two bridges.

Climate:

	High	Low
January	72	51
July	92	75

Average relative humidity: Ranges from 58% to 83%.

Rainfall: 51 inches annually

Cost of living: Higher than average

Average housing cost: Median price is $350,000 in Sarasota County. Current figures for Siesta Key were unavailable but would be about $500,000.

Sales tax: 7%

Sales tax exemptions: Food, medicine and services.

State income tax: None

Intangibles tax: None. The tax was repealed as of Jan. 1, 2007.

Estate tax: None

Inheritance tax: None

Property tax: $14.7179 per $1,000 of assessed value. With a $25,000 homestead exemption, the annual tax on a $500,000 home would be $6,991.

Homestead exemption: $25,000 off assessed value of primary, permanent residence.

Religion: All major religions and many smaller ones are represented in the Sarasota area, which has more than 200 houses of worship.

Transportation: Siesta Key is connected to the mainland by Siesta Drive Bridge to the north and the Stickney Point Bridge

to the south. The Sarasota Bradenton International Airport is served by a variety of major airlines that fly to points throughout the United States and Canada, with connections to foreign cities as well. Tampa International Airport (about an hour's drive from Siesta Key) is served by all major airlines and offers flights throughout the world. U.S. Highway 41 is the main commercial thoroughfare that runs north and south through Sarasota, while Interstate 75, just east of the city, connects the area as far south as Miami and north into the Midwest.

Health: Sarasota is served by Sarasota Memorial Health Care System, an 828-bed public regional medical center with a full range of services, including the third-largest cardiac program in the state. Doctors Hospital of Sarasota is a 168-bed acute and general care facility. Lakewood Ranch Medical Center in Sarasota is a new, 120-bed acute care hospital with a staff of over 300 physicians and health professionals.

Housing options: Condos, conventional single-family neighborhoods and deed-restricted communities are available on Siesta Key. A standard two-bedroom, two-bath condo unit with about 1,000 square feet starts in the $500,000s, according to Marcia McLaughlin, a real estate agent with **RE/MAX Properties** in Sarasota, (941) 349-8899 or (800) 708-6689. That rises to $700,000 and higher on the bay and from $900,000 into the millions of dollars for footage on the Gulf. In the single-family market, homes start at about $375,000. For housing on the water — canal, bay or Gulf — prices

quickly rise into the millions of dollars.

Siesta Isles, a deed-restricted community, offers single-family homes that start at about $600,000 and rise to $1.5 million; it's on a canal and within a mile of the beach. Real estate agents and companies are listed on the Siesta Key Chamber of Commerce Web site at www.siestakeychamber.com. If you identify an area that you would like to try out, you may be able to secure a rental through local management companies.

Visitor lodging: The Beach Place, tropical garden cottages at Siesta Key Beach, pets welcome, starting at $130 nightly, $400-$1,400 weekly, depending on season. (800) 615-1745. Best Western Siesta Beach Resort, a renovated two-story hotel in Siesta Village near the beach, $94-$244, (800) 223-5786. The Capri, studio apartments facing a tropical garden and private beachfront, $80-$130 nightly, $435-$725 weekly. (941) 349-2626.

Information: Siesta Key Chamber of Commerce, 5118 Ocean Blvd., Siesta Key, FL 34242, (941) 349-3800 or www.siestakeychamber.com.

ceutical firm, where he'd worked as a research pharmacologist and expert witness. They moved from the Chicago area to Siesta Key shortly thereafter.

Their lives are as busy now as when they worked and raised their three daughters. Frank serves as a floor guide at Mote Marine and a tour guide at Selby Gardens. He's a member of SEEK (Scientists and Engineers Exploring Knowledge, a club that meets for educational lectures on all manner of subjects) and a local computer group. He also gives nature tours along the beach near their condo.

Both donate time to the symphony, for which they recently co-chaired a concert. And when there are afternoon and evening performances by the ballet, they take a turn bringing in a hearty dinner for as many as 30 dancers between shows.

Patty combines her scientific training with her passion of underwater photography to conduct research around the world. She's currently involved in a project with scientist and Mote founder Eugenie Clark and the University of Maryland. She also fits in a daily swim at the condo pool, takes regular aerobics classes and attends meetings of the local camera club, which attracts a lot of big-time photographers now retired and willing to share their knowledge.

The Steins devote considerable time and talent to the community, too. Both are trained mediators for the court system. Jon, who plays jazz clarinet and sax, often performs free for good causes and also has regular gigs at restaurants on the island and in downtown Sarasota. Paula has volunteered at the Humane Society and the Siesta Key Chamber of Commerce.

This is retirement? "We have jobs all the time, we just don't get paid," says Patty Sturtevant.

Vern Johnson, 72, likes to balance work and play. He's out on the tennis courts by 8:30 a.m. six days a week. On Tuesdays, he and as many as 31 like-minded neighbors from his condo development head to the mainland for a round of golf. "You have to have a reason to get up every morning," he tells the newly retired.

Since moving there full time in 1992, Vern has volunteered with a number of groups, including the Small Business Administration and Florida House, an eco-friendly demonstration home. Now he focuses on the Siesta Key Chamber of Commerce. There he works with the island's accommodation database, which helps match visitors with local lodging, and he represents the chamber regularly at events such as ribbon cuttings.

Vern, retired vice president of sales and marketing for NCR, and his wife bought a condo at the Gulf and Bay Club 16 years ago and moved in full time four years later. They moved from the Los Angeles area, but always maintained a house in Madison, WI, their home base.

His wife died six years ago, but he continues to live in the two-bedroom, two-bath condo they bought together. With about 1,450 square feet on the ground floor just footsteps from the beach, along with a full complement of recreational amenities at the development, he plans to stay where he is except for trips to see his four daughters and their families.

"I've got the weather, the activities," he says. "I can get to the Midwest in two hours and to Colorado in four. I'm not going anywhere. They'll have to carry me out of here."

The Sturtevants, who live in a sixth-floor condo in the Gulf and Bay Club, are similarly rooted. From windows on three sides of their 2,200-square-foot unit, they look out on the beach and Gulf. They found it was easy to make friends, particularly at their very social condominium complex, and there is always plenty to do indoors and out. "We made the right decision when we chose to live here," Patty says.

Housing on Siesta Key runs from modest cottages to multimillion-dollar estates with lots of condos and single-family homes in between. There are condo developments and conventional neighborhoods with single-family homes as well as deed-restricted communities. But real-estate prices are rising rapidly.

Condominium prices jumped about 25 percent three years ago and have been climbing 20 to 30 percent a year ever since, says Marcia McLaughlin, a real estate agent. A standard two-bedroom, two-bath condo unit with about 1,000 square feet starts in the $500,000s, she says. That rises to $700,000 and higher on the bayfront and from $900,000 into the millions of dollars for Gulf property.

In the single-family market, homes start at about $375,000. For something on the water — canal, bay or Gulf — prices quickly climb into the millions of dollars. Siesta Isles, a deed-restricted community, offers single-family homes that start at about $600,000 and rise to $1.5 million, with access via canal and within a mile of the beach.

It took the Steins two years to find just the right property on the island. Paula wanted to be on the water with a boat. Jon wanted a property where he wouldn't see other homes. The house they found is on a main canal that attracts all manner of birds, tortoises, lizards and the occasional snake. It's also on a street with an oak canopy, which forms a perfect curtain of privacy for the house.

Initially they fixed up the downtrodden two-bedroom, two-bath home that was there. But after living in it for five years, they decided to tear it down and start over. They built a 3,500-square-foot house with four bedrooms, three and a half baths and some extra rooms for good measure. They even took into account their future needs — or those of potential buyers — when they designed the new house.

There are only a few steps from the ground to the front door, rather than the original 17. The master suite, den, great room and kitchen are on the ground floor "so that when we get old and gray we don't have to go up and down stairs," Jon says. There's also a place for an elevator, which now serves as closet space.

With a big new house that has plenty of space for their two dogs and visiting family and friends, they find they aren't so eager to make annual trips to Europe or New York the way they did when they lived in Ohio.

"Every time somebody says, 'Let's go,' we think, 'Where could we go that's better than where we are?'" Paula says. "We're on permanent vacation." ●

Southern Delaware

Beyond beaches and boardwalks, parks and preserves
put emphasis on nature in rural Sussex County

Candyce H. Stapen

There's something about a beach. Whether strolling deserted sands on a mild winter day when the sun catches in the curl of a wave, or sitting on a blanket-laden shore in August watching kids toss a Frisbee as the surf splashes their ankles, beaches bring a special kind of joy.

Southern Delaware's 25 miles of ocean and bay shoreline stretch from Lewes (pronounced "Lewis"), a historic town on the Delaware Bay; south to Rehoboth, a bustling summer boardwalk resort; then to Bethany, a small oceanside town, and to Fenwick Island near the Maryland line.

Although differing in ambiance, the proximity of the towns to each other means it's just a short drive to any of the region's state parks, wildlife refuges and beaches. Residence comes with two other pluses: no sales tax (a statewide fiat) and easy access to big-city amenities in Wilmington (a drive of one and a half hours) and Philadelphia, Washington, DC, and Baltimore (each about a two-hour drive).

"Our dream retirement location had to have a beach," says Patricia Klosek, 53, a former facilities manager for a Baltimore insurance company who relocated to Bethany from Harford County, MD, outside Baltimore, in May 1999 with her husband, Alexander, 54, a former Baltimore police officer.

"We had been vacationing in Ocean City, MD, since we were teenagers, so we were familiar with the area," says Patricia, who resides in Ocean View, a little more than a mile from Bethany Beach. "We didn't want to be by the outlets in Rehoboth because it's too busy. We wanted to be within walking and biking distance from the beach. We wanted a family-oriented place."

Dubbed the "quiet resorts," Bethany Beach, about 20 miles south of Rehoboth, and Fenwick Island, offer a laid-back élan with access to the bay and the ocean. Unlike Rehoboth's bustling

boardwalk lined with stores and cafes, Bethany's mile-long promenade is more a relaxing place to stroll than a see-and-be-seen hangout.

What do the Kloseks do in Bethany? "Year-round, weather permitting, we go biking and take long walks on the beach. In summer we attend concerts in Bethany on Friday and Saturday evenings, and in November we take advantage of Rehoboth's film festival," Patricia says.

"People come to this area for the nature-based tourism," says Karen McGrath, executive director of Bethany-Fenwick Area Chamber of Commerce, "for activities such as bicycling, bird-watching and kayaking that don't require a great deal of athletic ability or skill."

Fenwick Island State Park lies between the towns of Bethany Beach and Fenwick Island, a long, thin finger of land with three miles of relatively uncrowded beaches. Visitors come early to watch the sun rise over the Atlantic, kayak and sail, picnic and swim, then watch the sun set over Little Assawoman Bay.

"For a lot of people, retiring to this area is a lifestyle change," says Betsy Reamer, executive director of the Lewes Visitor Center. "The big attractions are the beach and the bay. We're not urban, we're not crowded."

One of the Delaware Shore's charms is that along with developed beaches, state parks preserve acres of natural scenery. Prime Hook National Wildlife Refuge, 10 miles north of Lewes, features 10,000 acres of managed land. You can walk nature paths, paddle along a seven-mile canoe trail, and in spring and fall, watch the skies fill with thousands of migrating ducks, geese and songbirds. The Delaware Seashore State Park, south of Rehoboth, offers six miles of sands as well as bay and beach swimming.

Bordering Lewes, Cape Henlopen State Park is a prime spot for pier fishing

and crabbing, a time-honored Delmarva tradition. Delaware's largest beachfront park with 3,143 acres, Cape Henlopen attracts swimmers as well as hikers in search of gentle nature trails that wind past dunes or lead inland through pinewoods and cranberry bogs. Those who prefer to pedal can pick up a free bicycle, available on a first-come, first-served basis from the park's Seaside Nature Center.

Don Ridzon's favorite Lewes activity is surf fishing for bluefish or striped bass at Cape Henlopen State Park. Don, 59, is a former workforce analyst for the U.S. Department of Labor's Bureau of International Labor Affairs in Washington, DC, and his wife Marilyn, 58, is a retired professional organizer. Like many area retirees, they had been summering at the Delaware Shore for years and knew the area's beach allure. They moved to Lewes in September 2001 from Silver Spring, MD.

The Ridzons wanted more than just sand, sea and surf. "In thinking about retirement," notes Marilyn, "I wasn't crazy about living in the suburbs and I didn't want a golf community. I didn't want a town that disappears in winter. Both Bethany and Rehoboth lose about 70 percent of their population in winter, but Lewes loses only about 20 percent. I wanted a small town. And I wanted a community I could be active in."

The Ridzons found it easy to contribute to Lewes, which has a year-round population of about 3,000. "There's tremendous community involvement — all kinds of volunteer opportunities," says Don, a board member of the Friends of Cape Henlopen State Park. Marilyn volunteers with the Lewes Historical Society, helping to raise funds to restore the town's historic schoolhouse and other buildings.

Lewes, dubbed "the first town in the first state," celebrates its 375th anniversary this year. At the Zwaanendael Museum, visitors find out about the 32

Dutch settlers who came ashore in 1631, naming the area Swanendael, which means "Valley of the Swans."

The graceful birds may be scarce now, but flowers are plentiful. In spring and summer, planters filled with petunias,

Southern Delaware

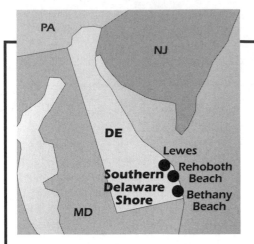

Population: 172,216 in the area. Year-round: 3,092 in Lewes, 15,267 in the Bethany-Fenwick area and about 1,600 in Rehoboth.

Location: Sussex County encompasses the lower third of Delaware, which is mainly small towns and beach communities extending to the Maryland state line. Lewes, located where the Atlantic Ocean meets the Delaware Bay, is 10 miles north of Rehoboth Beach and 85 miles from Wilmington, the state's largest city. Rehoboth is 116 miles from Philadelphia and about 120 miles from Washington, DC. Cape May, NJ, is a 90-minute ferry ride from Lewes.

Climate:

	High	Low
January	45	28
July	86	68

Average relative humidity: 60-70%
Rain: 41 inches annually
Snow: 12 inches annually
Cost of living: Lower than average
Average housing cost: There is a wide variety of property and housing available for rental and sale. Median home prices in Sussex County are $415,000 in the eastern part of the county, $210,000 central and $165,000 western. Home prices in the Bethany-Fenwick area range from $175,000 to $4 million.
Sales tax: None
State income tax: Delaware has a graduated tax rate ranging from 2.2% to 5.55% for income under $60,000 and 5.95% (plus $2,943.50) for the amount above $60,000.
Income tax exemption: Persons 60 years and older can exclude up to $12,500 in pension and other eligible retirement income. Eligible retirement income includes dividends, interest, capital gains, net rental income from real property and qualified retirement plans and government-deferred compensation plans. Those under age 60 receiving a pension can exclude up to $2,000. Social Security and railroad retirement benefits are not taxable in Delaware.
Estate tax: Through 2010, there are no estate taxes imposed by the state.
Property tax: In Lewes, the tax rate is $2.9103 per $100 of assessed value; in the Bethany-Fenwick area, Indian River School District, it's $2.9143 per $100 of assessed value; and in Sussex County the average is $3.38 per $100 of assessed value. Property is assessed at 50% of the 1974 market value. A Lewes home built in 2004 with a selling price of $410,000 has a yearly tax bill of about $1,200. Homeowners 65 and older can get a credit equal to half of the school property taxes, up to $500.
Homestead exemption: There is an exemption related to age and disability with income and residency restrictions.
Religion: There are 619 churches in Sussex County, including 17 in Lewes.
Education: Lewes has an Academy of Lifelong Learning program of classes. The Delaware Technical and Community College in Georgetown offers an extensive program of enrichment classes and activities for age 50 and beyond. Georgetown is 15 miles from Lewes and about 20 miles from Bethany Beach.
Transportation: Route 1 is the main highway in the eastern part of the county. Baltimore-Washington (BWI) and Philadelphia International airports each are about 115 miles from Lewes. Private limousine services are available, and a regional airport in nearby Salisbury, MD, has connector service. DART First State bus service is available year-round with stops in Lewes. Cape May-Lewes Ferry connects the Lewes terminal to the Cape May, NJ, terminal with year-round service.
Health care: Beebe Medical Center in Lewes has 158 beds and a 24-hour emergency room, www.beebemed.org.
Housing: A full range of housing options is available in the area. Currently under construction, **Bay Crossing,** (888) 222-4805, four miles from the ocean in Lewes, is a 55-plus retirement community by Pulte Homes, with attached villas and detached homes from the $360,000s. Near Millsboro, about eight miles from Rehoboth Beach and 11 miles from Lewes, **The Peninsula,** (866) 736-3352, is a new golf resort community with a variety of home options from the $360,000s. Between Rehoboth and Lewes, the **Coastal Club by Del Webb,** (888) 755-7559, a community for all ages, is expected to open in 2007. For those who want to live farther inland, in the western part of the county at Bridgeville, **Heritage Shores** is a new active-adult community with 2,000 homes planned by Lennar, (888) 337-0202, and Providence of Brookfield Homes, (866) 684-3348; there are homes of varying styles from the mid-$200,000s. Realty agents are listed on the Lewes Chamber of Commerce Web site, www.leweschamber.com.
Visitor lodging: Lewes offers nearly 400 rooms in hotels, motels, inns, B&Bs and guesthouses, and there are more than 4,000 rooms available in Sussex County. Inn by the Bay, from $100 off-season and from $150 in season, (866) 833-2565. The Holiday Inn Express, Bethany Beach, from $69 off-season and from $200 in season, (888) 465-4329. Lewes Chamber of Commerce has a listing of lodgings at www.leweschamber.com.
Information: Lewes Chamber of Commerce, P.O. Box 1, Lewes, DE 19958, (302) 645-8073 or www.leweschamber.com. Bethany-Fenwick Chamber of Commerce, P.O. Box 1450, Bethany Beach, DE 19930, (302) 539-2100 or www.thequietresorts.com. Rehoboth Beach-Dewey Beach Chamber of Commerce, P.O. Box 216, Rehoboth Beach, DE 19971, (800) 441-1329, (302) 227-2233 or www.beach-fun.com. Southern Delaware Tourism, P.O. Box 240, Georgetown, DE 19947, (800) 357-1818, (302) 856-1818 or www.visitsoutherndelaware.com.

geraniums and other blossoms line the main streets, adding to Lewes' seaside charm. The town is so decked out that it won first place in the America in Bloom contest in the category for towns under 5,000 in population.

In fact, it was the gardens that Marilyn visited on a tour before she moved here that clinched her choice of Lewes for retirement. "I'd only seen the front of the houses, but when I went in the back, everyone had a secret garden — small, charming and private. I liked that," Marilyn says.

The Ridzons purchased a home in the Village of Drake Knolls, a little more than a mile from the beach. "We're on a little bigger lot than most — three-quarters of an acre," Marilyn says. "I wanted to have one of those small, secret gardens."

The Ridzons enjoy bicycling the mile and a quarter from their house to the beach for breakfast at the Blue Moon or the Buttery. Another favorite outing is to take a 90-minute boat ride on the Cape May-Lewes Ferry to Cape May, NJ, a restored Victorian-era beach town known for its restaurants.

Along with the beach, Southern Delaware's easy proximity to East Coast cities for football games lured Carolyn Marshall, 62, and her husband Tom, 70, to Lewes in 1998 from Merrick on Long Island, NY.

"I always liked the area and being near the ocean and the bay, and I grew up in Lewes," says Tom, a retired physical education teacher and former college football coach. He and Carolyn, a former elementary school teacher, drive to football games at the U.S. Naval Academy in Annapolis, the University of Maryland in College Park and the University of Virginia at Charlottesville. "We still have grandchildren in the New York area and that's not too far away," Tom says.

Carolyn Marshall enjoys the Southern Delaware Academy of Lifelong Learning, classes for ages 50-plus taught by volunteers. She has signed on for courses in human origins, opera, Shakespeare, Arthur Miller, jazz, advanced gardening and other subjects. "I think when you go to school you're worried about taking tests. These classes are fun and great for socializing," she says.

Vera Altevogt, 77, took early retire-ment from her job as a clerk for Sea-grams in Baltimore and moved to Lewes in 1991 after her spouse died. "My husband and I used to come to Lewes to fish, and we brought the kids for vacations to Ocean City, MD, for two weeks every year," Vera says.

"My family thought I was crazy moving here by myself. I live in a mobile home development in Lewes. I have never regretted it. I like Lewes. It's a little town. It's easy to meet people. I learned pinochle and we have a group of seven women. We play cards in each other's homes every week and have dessert and coffee," Vera says.

Lewes' year-round community is also important to Don Ridzon. "What's also appealing to me as a retiree is that there is a quality medical center right in town, the Beebe Medical Center. That's one of the benefits of living in a year-round community rather than a more seasonal one," he says.

For those who like a lively, full-fledged beach town, there's bustling Rehoboth. Although Rehoboth proper is just one square mile, it buzzes in season with 100 eateries, specialty stores and a wide boardwalk, chock-ablock with visitors enjoying the sun, food and fun. Just outside the beach area on Route 1, shoppers head to Rehoboth's outlets, whose 130-plus low-price brand name shops include L.L. Bean, Brooks Brothers and Ralph Lauren.

"Rehoboth has a true old-fashioned boardwalk," says Helen Morgan, 65, a registered nurse. "There's a Funland with a Ferris wheel and kiddy rides, and a merry-go-round. Everybody takes their kids here, generation after generation. I took my kids here when they were little, and we had a beach house in the area. And now my kids are 32, 35 and 41."

Helen met Ralph Morgan, 68, in 1991 when he worked for the U.S. Postal Service in Georgetown, DE, about 12 miles from Rehoboth. Ralph retired in January 2000. When the Morgans married in 2003, Helen moved to Rehoboth from Wilmington, DE. Semi-retired, she works as an emergency room nurse in Wilmington one weekend a month. Although the Morgans have a Lewes mailing address, they live in Chapel Green, a development of 120 homes about eight miles from Lewes and eight miles from Rehoboth.

One advantage of being close to Rehoboth for the Morgans is the proximity to the town's Cape Henlopen Senior Center. "I go down to the senior center to do line dancing five days a week," Ralph says. "We also do rumbas, cha-chas, waltzes, polkas. It's fun. It's good exercise. It keeps your heart rate up and your blood pressure down."

Helen, besides keeping up with Ralph in dance class, volunteers. "I'm the president of the senior center. I participate in the shows to raise funds and I bring in people to discuss health issues like stroke prevention and disaster preparedness," she says.

"I also indulge in fishing," Ralph says. "You can always find something to do here — kayaking, sailing and a lot of golf courses."

The Bayside Course, a Jack Nicklaus design near Fenwick Island, features tree-lined fairways and marshland. Three miles from Bethany, Bear Trap Dunes' 27 holes have been rated among America's 100 Best Golf Courses by Golf Week, and The Rookery, an 18-hole golf course in Milton, borders wetlands that boast a breeding ground for herons.

How do the Morgans cope with Rehoboth's summer crowds? "We buy our groceries before Thursday and we do our home chores — cutting the grass — and those tasks on weekends. Line dancing is in the morning Monday to Friday. We're coming out of town when the beach people are coming in," Ralph says.

Southern Delaware's popularity has created a development boom, especially in the communities a few miles inland from the shore.

"When I moved to the Rehoboth area in 1987," Ralph says, "we didn't have Wal-Mart, K-Mart or chain restaurants like Ruby Tuesdays. There were fields across from where I lived. Development, I guess, is inevitable. But it's a nice place to be. You can always find something to do. When I take a walk on the beach, I always see a few porpoises in the water."

Carolyn Marshall notes, "More and more people are discovering the area because it's a gem." ●

Stuart, Florida

Residents enjoy the low-key, uncrowded feeling and serene beauty
around this Florida east coast town

By Karen Feldman

A river runs through the heart of Martin County, caressing the town of Stuart on three sides and capturing the fancy of growing numbers of youthful retirees looking for a piece of paradise.

The tranquil St. Lucie River affords plenty of water for recreation and serves as a scenic Florida backdrop for countless homeowners. It also provides convenient access to the Intracoastal Waterway and, beyond that, the Atlantic Ocean.

That bounty of comely waterways proves a powerful enticement for retirees like Leanna and Lewis Everett. The Richmond, VA, couple knew they wanted to live in a temperate Southern locale but weren't sure which one. They considered and ruled out the Bahamas, Naples and Miami. Because they love to fish and make frequent trips to the Bahamas aboard their 45-foot boat, ocean access was a primary consideration, Lewis says.

They found what they wanted at Sailfish Point, an upscale development on Hutchinson Island, the barrier island east of Stuart. The ocean was nearly at their doorstep and the area fit the bill on another front, says Leanna, 43. "We can be in Palm Beach or other places quickly if we need to, but we're not in the thick of it," she says. "There's plenty to do, but you're not in the traffic and hubbub all the time."

Stuart, the Martin County seat, "is a very quaint community," says Joe Catrambone, president and chief executive officer of the Stuart-Martin County Chamber of Commerce. With a resurging downtown, easy access to beaches, lots of riverfront, a multitude of golf courses, gated communities and very low density, it's a natural fit for active retirees.

"There is a huge number of boomers retiring in the next three to five years and we're going to get our share," he predicts. The county's strict regulation of growth and resulting low density set it apart from many Florida communities that have grappled with rampant development in recent years.

In some parts of Martin County, only one home is permitted for every five acres. In other spots, it's one unit per 20 acres. No buildings can be more than four stories high, and pristine wetlands are zealously preserved.

Not all developers may welcome such strict growth control, but it provides residents with lots of space and privacy, commodities that are getting scarce around the Sunshine State. That's not to say, however, that the region hasn't experienced growth. Between 1980 and 1990, Catrambone says, the county's population jumped from about 50,000 to 100,000.

To slow growth back then, he says, "The powers that be said, 'Let's not build roads and bridges and people won't come.' They were wrong." The result is that now, with a year-round population of 140,800 — rising to 163,000 in the winter — the 550-square-mile county continues to play catch-up to provide enough roads and bridges.

Nonetheless, the quality of life the area affords more than outweighs the fact that traffic moves slowly on occasion. And, with the recent slowdown in the real estate market, property prices are dropping somewhat, making a move to the region more affordable.

Georgia Gordon, a real estate agent with All Florida Realty Services in Stuart, says prices jumped about 27 percent between early 2005 and early 2006 but have begun to level off, following the national trend.

"Even with the decline (in sales prices), people are still making money," she says. "There's very good inventory. It's a buyer's market."

Condos built before 1990 are selling for $135,000 to $190,000 for a two-bedroom, two-bath unit with about 1,000 square feet of living space. Newer units of comparable size start in the low $200,000s and climb to about $475,000, depending on the community's amenities, she says.

Single-family homes with three bedrooms and two baths range from about $375,000 to $500,000 in a standard subdivision, rising to $650,000 or more in gated communities with amenities and lots that range from three-quarters of an acre to a full acre each.

Homes on the water can run from $850,000 to upwards of $1 million, and new condos under construction in the downtown area are in the same price range.

The county has a larger-than-average share of waterfront homes, as well as many properties big enough for horse enthusiasts to keep their animals at home. Even people who don't have horses like the concept of not being so close to their neighbors.

"People come here for the serenity of Martin County. If you like nightlife, you're only 30 minutes away from Palm Beach," says Catrambone of the chamber of commerce. Don't expect a lively night scene around Stuart "because we don't have it," he says.

That's all right with people who relocate here — even those who come from metropolitan areas. For Bill and Julie Paterson, water and warm weather were more important than a scintillating nightlife. The couple moved from Westchester County, NY, where Bill, 56, was a supervisor with the police department and Julie, 53, worked as a hair stylist.

When they retired in 1993, two of their four children still lived at home, so schools were important, too. They started out in a development in Palm City, just west of Stuart. Bill got involved in the homeowners association and served as president for eight years. At the same time, "my wife got tired of hearing me sing in the shower so she sent me for auditions at the theater," he says.

That's the Barn Theatre, a converted barn that houses the county's oldest community theater. Bill appeared in a couple of productions but found his niche on the board of directors, where he served as vice president, then president. Julie volunteers with Dogs and Cats Forever Inc., a private, no-kill animal rescue organization. Their volunteer work helped them meet a large circle of new friends.

They decided they wanted a home on the water and a place where their 6-year-old rottweiler, Tavan, could romp. They found a large home on the north fork of the St. Lucie River in neighboring Port St. Lucie. It has a lift where they can keep their 27-foot Sea Ray, but they

Stuart, FL

Population: About 17,000 year-round residents in Stuart and 140,800 in Martin County.

Location: Stuart is on Florida's east coast about 100 miles north of Miami and 250 miles south of Jacksonville.

Climate:

	High	Low
January	74	53
July	91	74

Average relative humidity: 70%

Rain: 49 inches annually

Cost of living: Slightly above average

Average housing cost: $261,200

Sales tax: 6%

Sales tax exemptions: Groceries and prescription drugs

State income tax: None

Intangibles tax: None. The tax was repealed as of Jan. 1, 2007.

Estate tax: None

Property tax: $19.05 per $1,000 of assessed value, with homes assessed at 90 percent of market value. On a $261,200 home with a $25,000 homestead exemption, annual taxes would be $4,002.

Homestead exemption: $25,000 off assessed value of primary, permanent residence.

Religion: There are some 40 houses of worship in Stuart with more in surrounding communities, representing all the major religions and several smaller denominations.

Education: Several educational venues are located in the area. The Treasure Coast Square mall is home to the county's adult education center. Miami-based Barry University offers degree programs at its Port St. Lucie campus. Florida Atlantic University operates campuses in Port St. Lucie and Jupiter to the south; at the Jupiter site, the Lifelong Learning Society provides non-credit liberal arts courses for mature learners. Indian River Community College runs a campus in Stuart, offering a range of courses and programs.

Transportation: Palm Beach International Airport, served by 17 airlines, is about 40 miles south of Stuart. Martin County Airport accommodates private planes. Amtrak (800) 872-7245, makes stops in West Palm Beach. The Tri-Rail commuter railway, (800) 874-7245, connects West Palm Beach to Miami. Some cruise ships depart from the Port of Palm Beach, (561) 842-4201.

Health care: Martin Memorial Health Systems is a not-for-profit network that includes two hospitals, the 236-bed Martin Memorial Medical Center and the 100-bed Martin Memorial Hospital South. Its services include emergency care, a surgical center, cancer care, rehabilitation, wellness and diagnostic imaging. The Frances Langford Heart Center is scheduled to open in August, where open-heart surgery and other cardiac services will be available. St. Lucie Medical Center in Port St. Lucie is a 194-bed, full-service hospital offering an outpatient surgical and diagnostic center, women's services, cancer care, orthopedics, MRI, laser surgery, emergency care, cardiac and trauma treatment and community outreach.

Housing: Condos built before 1990 sell for $135,000 to $190,000 for a two-bedroom, two-bath unit with about 1,000 square feet of living space, while newer ones of comparable size start in the low $200,000s and go to about $475,000. Single-family homes with three bedrooms and two baths range from about $375,000 to $500,000 in a standard subdivision. In gated communities with amenities and large lots, prices can run $650,000 or more. Waterfront houses cost $850,000 to upwards of $1 million, as do new luxury condos under construction downtown. **Mariner Sands**, (800) 437-2127, is a 728-acre master-planned golf community with 771 residences including condos, villas, townhomes, cottages and single-family homes priced from $225,000 to $1.3 million. **Willoughby Golf Club**, (772) 220-7877, is a 403-acre gated community with golf homes priced from the $400,000s to the $700,000s and estate homes from the $800,000s to $1.5 million. **Sailfish Point**, (772) 225-6200, is a 532-acre island community with a 77-slip, full-service marina, Jack Nicklaus golf course and condominiums, villas, patio homes, townhomes and single-family homes, with prices starting in the $800,000s. **Harbour Ridge Yacht and Country Club**, (877) 336-1801, in Palm City, is a gated golf community on the St. Lucie River featuring condos, patio, golf and custom homes from $200,000 to upwards of $2 million. **Pinelake Gardens and Estates**, (772) 287-1115, offers manufactured homes for $47,000 to $190,000. In neighboring Hobe Sound, **Portofino Villas**, (305) 692-2232, plans a clubhouse and 50 townhomes in island style; construction is scheduled to start this summer, with prices from the high $300,000s.

Visitor lodging: Best Western Downtown Stuart has 119 units, $89-$169, (772) 287-6200. Plantation Beach Club at Indian River Plantation offers 30 large, fully equipped condominiums with screened porches and water views, minimum two-night stay, $185-$320, (772) 225-0074. Ramada Inn has 118 rooms, $104-$189, (772) 287-6900.

Information: Stuart-Martin County Chamber of Commerce, 1650 S. Kanner Highway, Stuart, FL 34994, (772) 287-1088 or www.goodnature.org.

don't use the boat as much as they'd like because they stay so busy with other activities.

They are avid New York Mets fans and have been season ticket holders for the team's spring training games in Port St. Lucie for more than a decade. For them, March means baseball and lots of it.

Come April, "we kind of go through a little withdrawal," Julie says. "We're members of the booster club. We don't go anywhere without running into somebody we know."

Bill belongs to the Port St. Lucie Power Squadron of boating enthusiasts and the couple is active in the local Westchester Club, composed of former residents of Westchester County, NY. They also enjoy strolling in downtown Stuart's historic district, with its quaint shops and restaurants. The city offers pamphlets for a self-guided walking tour.

For those who aren't baseball fans or beach devotees, Stuart and its environs still boast plenty to do. In addition to the Barn Theatre, the Lyric Theatre, an art deco structure dating to 1925, presents professional shows and concerts. The Court House Cultural Center occupies the county's 1930s-era former courthouse, with two galleries that feature rotating art exhibitions. The Maritime and Yachting Museum maintains a collection of historically important artifacts and vessels, offering educational programs and vessel restoration.

Nature lovers can wander through the Hobe Sound National Wildlife Refuge, which sprawls over 1,100 acres and includes a 3-mile-long beach that's a popular nesting site for sea turtles. Also in Hobe Sound, just south of Stuart, is the 11,600-acre Jonathan Dickinson State Park where visitors can hike, bike, camp overnight, paddle a canoe and take guided tours. The county also has numerous tennis courts, community parks and public beaches.

The Patersons frequently travel, enjoying the convenience of cruising because the Port of Miami is so easy to reach. But travel provides a temporary diversion from the pleasure they get daily from their adoptive community. "We feel like we're on vacation all the time," Julie says. "We thank God all the time."

"We have a little slice of heaven right here," Bill adds.

That's a familiar sentiment among area retirees. Betty and Bill Saunders weren't planning to retire, but when a relative found them a great deal on a condominium in a development called Vista Pines, the Rochester, NY, couple jumped at it.

"We'd been down here visiting relatives off and on for years and really liked the area," says Betty, 65, who ran her own music school and taught in a community college for many years.

When they bought their 1,100-square-foot condo, "we were thinking we'd use it for vacations and possibly rent it out," Betty says. Then they spent a couple of weeks in their new home. "That second week we looked at each other and said, 'What are we doing? Let's just pack it up.' We never, ever second-guessed ourselves," she says.

They sold their 4,000-square-foot home in Rochester and became full-time Floridians. Because they got such a good deal on the condo, which is in an older development, they were able to afford to upgrade the two-bedroom, two-bath unit.

"We gutted the kitchen and redid everything, including the bathrooms," Betty says. "It's like a brand new place and it's so easy to take care of."

Although Betty retired, Bill, 67, has not. He runs his industrial supply business by phone and computer. Betty keeps busy with volunteer work. Within a month of moving, they joined a church and Betty signed on with the Treasure Coast Toastmasters Club, the same type of club she'd belonged to in New York. She has become the assistant choir director at the church, plays the piano for special events and works with the children who attend there.

She also directs the Vista Pines chorus and belongs to the Jensen Beach Chamber of Commerce. Through the chamber she wound up playing piano for a fund-raising gala that raises money for women with breast cancer. That led her to a piano engagement at the Barn Theatre, and she's now considering doing some acting.

"It's really neat how one thing leads to another," she says. "I'm doing things now I normally wouldn't have time to do. There are so many things

happening. It's just a wonderful community culture."

Bill Saunders makes jewelry in his spare time and volunteers at a gallery in Jensen Beach. He also works in about four rounds of golf a week at the Martin County Golf Club near their home.

Lewis Everett is a devoted golfer, too. He plays regularly at the Jack Nicklaus-designed private course at Sailfish Point, where members can golf without tee times. "We never wait more than 20 minutes to start," says Lewis, 65, noting that he enjoys the course being so close to their home.

When the Everetts bought property in Sailfish Point, Leanna was 35, so buying where there were other young, active people was a priority. Lewis, a retired vice chairman of a stock brokerage in Richmond, had a boss who lived in the area. After spending about five days visiting him, they decided to buy a home in the area, too, and settled on Sailfish Point.

"We knew when we pulled in the gates that this was it," Leanna says. "It's just the way the grounds were kept. It was where it was situated on the water, the golf course. It was out of the way, not in the middle of the city, but we could get into Stuart easily."

It had security, water on three sides, tennis, a spa — in short, virtually everything they were seeking. They bought the property in 1998, hired Miami architect Manuel Angles to design a Mediterranean-style home and moved in April 2000. The home has a water view from every room. The interior features a neutral color palette and a look that's formal yet welcoming, an important feature for the couple because they enjoy entertaining.

"It's a great house," Leanna says, and one that gets a lot of use. Their friends from Richmond, her family from Columbus, OH, and her father, who lives in Naples, visit regularly.

They've made new friends within the Sailfish Point community. "It's almost like a little city," Leanna says. "We met at yacht club events, golfing, dinner dances, things at the club."

The community provides for their varied interests, too. Lewis plays a lot of tennis and both of them work out regularly at the fitness center. Leanna takes kickboxing classes and serves on the development's real estate board and the architectural review committee.

The Everetts are full-time Florida residents but usually escape during the hotter months to their Virginia townhouse on Chesapeake Bay.

They have no plans to move. "We get to do every day what most people get to do two weeks a year," Leanna says.

The Patersons feel much the same way. "They'll probably throw my ashes in the river in the back yard," Bill Paterson jokes. He fishes in that river regularly, gets together with friends to play cards and keeps a close eye on the news now that one son, a first lieutenant in the Army, is stationed in Iraq.

"We're really enjoying our retirement," Bill says.

"And spending our kids' inheritance," says Julie. ●

Tallahassee, Florida

Oak-canopied lanes lend Southern ambiance to this Florida
capital city and university town

By William Schemmel

Bordering southwestern Georgia, the Tallahassee area has a Southern accent with piney woods, azaleas and dogwoods instead of the palmettos, palms and bougainvillea that visitors expect to see elsewhere in Florida. Canopy roads are Tallahassee's "beauty mark." Originally created as dirt and sand trails linking the county's cotton plantations, the paved, two-lane roads pass through leafy tunnels of live oak and laurel oak that are draped in Spanish moss. To preserve 65 miles of these roads from the pressures of development and transportation, a city ordinance officially designated five Canopy Roads and established a city-county agreement to maintain and preserve them.

It is this beauty, plus opportunities to stay active in a youthful population, that attracts retirees. "Tallahassee is a great place to retire if you like to keep busy," Edward Northcutt says cheerfully. More than 15 years after retiring as a marketing director of Eastern Airlines, Edward, 76, maintains a work ethic that keeps him in vigorous mental and physical health. The important difference in his working career and retirement life is that now it's all volunteer.

"On Mondays and Thursdays, my wife (Martha, 75, a retired real estate agent) and I deliver meals-on-wheels and do other work at Elder Care Services, a wonderful organization that does so much for people in this area who are too old or too disabled to do things for themselves," says Edward. "On Tuesdays I go to Kiwanis, on Wednesdays I'm a tour guide at the Florida State Capitol, and on Fridays I'm a docent at Pebble Hill, a historic hunting plantation at Thomasville, GA, 30 miles from Tallahassee," he says.

"If you want to sit around a golf course all day, then Tallahassee probably isn't the place for you," he adds, "but if you want to keep busy volunteering, there's plenty for you to do."

When they're not volunteering, the Northcutts keep fit by power walking in their northeast Tallahassee neighborhood and taking day trips to Florida Gulf Coast beaches and nature preserves an hour or two away.

The Northcutts lived in Florida's capital city in the late 1940s, then moved to Miami and on to Orlando, where Edward worked for 15 years as Eastern Airline's marketing manager at Walt Disney World. Eastern was then Disney World's "official airline."

"When I retired in 1985, my wife and I wanted to get out of the tourist market," he says. "We'd lived in Tallahassee before, and it felt like home, so we decided to move back. We haven't regretted it. It's a beautiful area, more like south Georgia than many other places in Florida," says Edward.

"It's the state capital, so government is really the main industry. Then we've got two major universities, Florida State University (about 40,000 students) and Florida A&M University (about 13,000 students), and Tallahassee Community College (about 14,500 students) and several smaller colleges, that offer opportunities for continuing education, as well as sports and other activities in which the community can participate," he says.

With a population of 171,600 — 263,400 in Leon County — Tallahassee has almost a small-town feeling compared with Miami (475 miles), Tampa-St. Petersburg (275 miles), Orlando (257 miles), Jacksonville (165 miles) and other Florida metropolitan areas. The city defies many Sunshine State stereotypes. For example, with nearly 70,000 college students, thousands of state government workers and young professionals, Tallahassee has a higher proportion of younger residents than most Florida cities. It's the perfect Florida destination for retirees who want to live in a community of all ages.

A temperate four-season climate is another big contrast with the rest of the

state. "We're not stuck with hot weather all the time," Edward Northcutt says. "We have definite spring, summer, fall and winter."

Hot and humid in midsummer, with frequent afternoon thunderstorms, Tallahassee and the rest of Florida's northwestern Panhandle get a brisk taste of fall. In January and February, occasional frosts and rare snow flurries wrap residents in sweaters and topcoats. Spring is glorious, with tens of thousands of azaleas, dogwoods, forsythia and other colorful plants brightening parks, gardens and roadways.

Like many other newcomers, the Northcutts relocated to northeast Tallahassee, the city's most popular residential area. "We bought (the late sportscaster) Red Barber's four-bedroom, three-bath house. It's a solid brick house in pretty much the same area where we lived before. This is one of the most desirable areas in Tallahassee. The annual property taxes on our house run about $2,000, which is about what we paid in Orlando," Edward says.

You can probably beat Tallahassee's real estate prices, admits Edward, but "you can't beat the lifestyle."

Large homes in Betton Hills, Bobbin Brook, Golden Eagle Plantation, Killearn Estates, Waverly Hills, Woodgate and other northeast quadrant communities range in price from the $300,000s to $800,000 and up, with some selling for $1 million or more. Area residents have easy access to upscale shopping, dining and recreation areas. Alfred B. Maclay State Gardens showcases 150 varieties of camellias and 50 types of azaleas. Maclay's Lake Hall recreation area has a boat ramp, swimming, fishing and picnic grounds.

Tallahassee's public park system includes several golf courses, tennis, basketball, racquetball and volleyball courts, swimming pools and softball and baseball fields. The cultural calendar is enlivened by local theater, dance and musical companies, touring performers and Broadway musicals. Art galleries are plentiful, and a number of city, state and privately operated museums are devoted to fine arts, science, history and natural history.

Tallahassee lists 122 sites on the National Register of Historic Places. Now a historical museum, the domed Old State Capitol has been restored to its 1902 appearance. In the 1970s the seat of government moved to the adjacent, 22-story "new" capitol building. Hernando DeSoto State Historic Site, less than a mile from the capitol, is the only place in North America confirmed as a site connected with the Spanish explorer's 1539-1540 trek through the Southeast.

Only a few years ago, housing prices in Florida's capital city were considerably below the state average, but home prices have been rising and now are considered above average. The average price of a 2,000-square-foot home in Tallahassee is $250,000.

"You can find affordable homes," says Michael Parker, Tallahassee's economic development director, "but you have to look for them." He defines affordable homes as equal in price to 80 percent or less of the city's median family income, times two, about $100,000.

Detached single-family homes are the most popular type of housing, making up 47 percent of all units that have

received construction permits since 1990, and 59 percent of all constructed housing units overall in Tallahassee (not counting mobile homes). Single-family homes are especially prevalent in the northern and eastern areas of the city. Mobile homes, which make up about 20 percent of the housing market, are most popular in the southern and western areas of the city.

College students looking for off-campus housing have created a strong demand for all types of housing. That also has helped increase rents and purchase prices.

Another retired couple, Bill and Della Kell, moved from Atlanta to the Bear

Tallahassee, FL

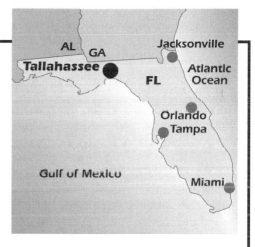

Population: 171,600 in Tallahassee, 263,400 in Leon County.
Location: Northwest Florida Panhandle, 475 miles northwest of Miami, 165 miles west of Jacksonville and 257 miles northwest of Orlando. Florida's Gulf of Mexico coast is an hour south of the city.
Climate: High Low
January 62 38
July 91 71
Tallahassee has hot, humid summers with frequent thunderstorms, and mild winters with occasional frost. Spring and fall are delightful.
Average relative humidity: 68%
Rain: 55 inches
Cost of living: Above average
Median housing cost: $163,700
Sales tax: 7.5%
Sales tax exemptions: Groceries, medicine and most professional services.
State income tax: None
Intangibles tax: None. The tax was repealed as of Jan. 1, 2007.
Estate tax: None
Inheritance tax: None
Property tax: $21.5760 per $1,000 valuation, with property assessed at 85% of market value. Annual tax on a $163,700 home, with homestead exemption listed below, is $2,463.
Homestead exemption: $25,000 off assessed value of primary, permanent residence.
Religion: More than 300 churches represent all major faiths.
Education: Florida State University

(about 40,000 students) and Florida A&M University (about 13,000 students) offer a comprehensive choice of day and evening credit and noncredit courses, as well as cultural, entertainment and athletic opportunities. Tallahassee Community College (about 14,500 students) has two-year programs in the arts and sciences.
Transportation: StarMetro, Tallahassee's public bus service, has more than 50 routes in the city.
Health: Tallahassee Memorial Health Care and Capital Regional Medical Center have complete acute-care services with a full range of surgical specialties, including 24-hour emergency care and outpatient services. Leon County has 536 licensed physicians.
Housing options: The city's northeast quadrant is the most popular residential area. Resale townhomes and estate homes in Killearn Estates, a golf-course community, range from $150,000 to $1 million. Killearn Lakes has a few remaining lots starting around $100,000 and homes ranging from $200,000 to $1 million and up. Other prestige subdivisions are Betton Hills, Bobbin Brook, Woodgate and Eastgate, with homes from the $300,000s to the $800,000s. With its large student population, the city has hundreds of apartment and condominium complexes and mobile home parks. In northwest Tallahassee, homes in Huntington Woods, Hartsfield Woods, Settlers Creek, Lakeview and other neighborhoods average about $175,000. **West-**

minster Oaks, (850) 878-1136, Tallahassee's only continuing-care retirement community, has homes and assisted- and independent-living apartments.
Visitor lodging: Holiday Inn Capital, near the state capitol and universities, has double-occupancy rates from $59 in January to $119 in summer and fall, (850) 877-3171 or (800) 465-4329. Amenities include a fitness center, pool, voice mail and data ports. Other major chain hotels are Best Western Pride Inn, (850) 656-6312; Courtyard by Marriott, (850) 222-8822; and Days Inn University Center, (850) 222-3219. Double-occupancy rates at the Wakulla Springs Lodge, (850) 224-5950, are $85-$105. Amenities include cable TV, phone and private bath.
Information: Tallahassee Area Chamber of Commerce, 100 N. Duval St., P.O. Box 1639, Tallahassee, FL 32302, (850) 224-8116 or www.talchamber.com. A relocation package for new residents is about $20.

Creek subdivision in northeast Tallahassee two years ago. They've also lived in St. Petersburg and spent 10 months in Iran when Bill, 79, was a telephone company executive. Homes in their neighborhood sell for $175,000 to $250,000 and up, Della says. The Kells pay about $2,000 in property taxes on their custom-designed, 1,700-square-foot home.

Like the Northcutts, the Kells keep active by volunteering with Elder Care Services. Bill also has volunteered with Habitat for Humanity. Other organizations that welcome retiree volunteers include Volunteer LEON, Retired Seniors Volunteer Program and Tallahassee-Leon County Shelter. Retirees are invited to join clubs that include the Florida Daffodil Society, the Rose Society, Amateur Radio Society and others that foster bridge, stamp collecting, model railroads, computers, investing, birding and preservation of vintage vehicles.

"We looked at some other areas for our retirement," says Della, 72, "but we chose Tallahassee for several reasons. We're within a day's drive from our daughter, who lives in Huntsville, AL, which is very important to us. And Tallahassee has a much more relaxed pace than other places we've lived. It has everything that big cities have, but it's just so much more convenient. We fell in love with it — it's a beautiful place, and we have wonderful neighbors. Many of the streets in Tallahassee have canopies of trees where you feel like you're in a forest and not a city."

Tallahassee's scenic beauty also attracted Charles and Mary Lou Watford back to Tallahassee in the mid-1980s after 13 years in Miami. "We're both from this area, and we both graduated from FSU, but we moved all around when Charles was with the telephone company," says Mary Lou, 63, a former school-teacher. "When we decided to take early retirement, we came back here by choice. After living in Miami, I've really enjoyed not being in a big city," she says.

"Tallahassee is a beautiful place," says Mary Lou. "When my sister and her husband were visiting us from Mississippi, they marveled at all our wonderful trees."

The Watfords designed their 2,800-square-foot home in northeast Tallahassee, with ample room for Charles to enjoy his hobby, growing camellias. There's also ample room for their children, who return frequently for football games and other activities at FSU.

"In the fall, our population increases by about 62,000 students, says Mary Lou, "but they're over on the west side, away from us. FSU and Florida A&M have all kinds of programs of which people who live in the area can take advantage. We can attend football and basketball games, and go to concerts, film and lectures, and they have courses in everything imaginable." The problem with all those students, Mary Lou laughs, "is they love this area so much, when they graduate, they don't want to go home."

The Watfords also participate in programs at the Tallahassee Senior Center. "We played a lot of bridge when we were younger, and recently took a refresher course at the senior center to get back into it. It's great mental exercise, especially for Charles, who's recovering from a stroke," says Mary Lou. She also suggests churches as an excellent way for local retirees to meet other people and to keep busy. "Our Baptist church has a very active senior choir and other programs for older adults," she says.

Many retirees, including the Watfords, spend free time exploring nearby state parks, wildlife refuges and Gulf of Mexico beaches. Tallahassee isn't a beach community, but the Gulf Coast's blinding white sands and turquoise waters are only about 90 minutes by car from the city. St. George Island State Park, consistently top-ranked nationally, is a big favorite of Tallahasseans. Recreational amenities on the island's nine miles of sandy shores include swimming, sun-bathing, camping, fishing, hiking and nature study. It's also happy hunting grounds for shell collectors.

St. Joseph Peninsula State Park, also ranked highly among beaches, is a 2,516-acre park surrounded by the Gulf of Mexico and St. Joseph Bay. Bird-watchers come to the park to observe some 209 species. While they're here, they enjoy the park's miles of sandy beaches, camping, fishing, hiking and boating.

Last fall, Mary Lou and Charles Watford and their visiting relatives drove down to the St. Marks National Wildlife Refuge, south of Tallahassee, to observe the annual migration of monarch butterflies heading south to Mexico for the winter. When the monarchs aren't the main attraction, the 67,000-acre sanctuary attracts flocks of birders. Seventy-five miles of marked trails are ideal for spotting more than 270 species of waterfowl, shore birds and long-legged waders.

The 16-mile Tallahassee-St. Marks Historic Railroad State Trail is another popular day outing. Once Florida's oldest operating railroad line, the abandoned roadbed has been transformed into an outdoor mecca for bicyclists, hikers, joggers, in-line skaters and horseback riders.

And at Edward Ball Wakulla Springs State Park and Lodge, between Tallahassee and the Gulf, retirees enjoy nature trails and brisk dips in 70-degree spring water. Glass-bottom boats provide views deep into the crystal-clear spring. Wildlife observation boats cruise into wilderness sections of the Wakulla River. Tallahassee residents can make an overnight or weekend trip of it at the historic Wakulla Lodge, which has a full-service restaurant.

It's among many attractions that are drawing more and more retirees to Tallahassee. "I've felt all along that retirement is going to be one of the biggest factors in this area's growth — but I don't want too many people to discover this place," laughs Mary Lou Watford. ●

Temecula, California

Retirees enjoy a small-town ambiance amid vineyards and rolling hills
in Southern California

Carole Jacobs

Sue and Jerry Turek still can't believe their luck. This time last year they were shoveling snow in suburban Chicago. Today the 60-year-old active retirees are living the good life in Rancho Vista, an upscale community in Temecula, where they both work part time as freelance consultants.

"We live so much nicer here than we ever lived there," says Sue, whose mission is to get all her friends to move to this sage-scrubbed Shangri-La located 60 miles north of San Diego. "I send them brochures of our historic downtown and beautiful wine country and they can't believe their eyes. I see flowered hillsides in February and I can hardly believe it myself," she says.

"We could never have afforded a house like this in Los Angeles," says Linda Cole, who with husband Bill, formerly with AT&T Corp., moved to Temecula from Redondo Beach, a seaside community outside Los Angeles. "We went from a dinky 900-square-foot house to a 2,400-square-foot single-family home in Rancho Highlands," an upscale development with a pool and tennis courts, she says. "From the size of our house to the quality of our life, everything went up except the cost."

A Midwest native, Linda says Temecula's small-town friendliness and four-season climate feels more like home than Redondo Beach ever did. "We lived there for more than 20 years and didn't know people who lived a few doors down. We've only been in Temecula a year and already it feels like we know everybody," says Linda, who didn't waste any time getting involved in community life. She currently chairs the Senior Golden Years Club — a sort of brat pack for seniors with more than 200 members.

Crystal-clear air, picture-perfect weather sans bugs, a low crime rate, quality medical care, a small-town atmosphere with big-city amenities, a wide variety of affordable housing, a state-of-the-art senior center with a politically active membership, plus a wine country that's giving Napa a run for its Riesling — it's easy to see why Temecula is the 10th-fastest growing city in California. The population increased by 7 percent to nearly 58,000 residents in 2000, and in 2006 the population was estimated at 90,000. Retirees account for about 9 percent of Temecula's overall population.

"We're really not what you'd consider a retirement mecca," stresses City Manager Shawn Nelson. Most of the growth is the result of young and middle-aged families moving in from San Diego and Los Angeles counties — a fact that makes what former Mayor Jeff Stone calls the town's "enormous investment in our seniors" even more remarkable.

Ringed by rolling hills that are Bonanza-brown in summer and Brigadoon-green in winter, Temecula inhabits a unique microclimate not unlike Tuscany — a mild, dry climate that is as ideal for wineries as for retirees. Pacific breezes whip up through the canyons and Temecula's aptly named Rainbow Gap and collide with drier desert air that results in thunderstorms. The clouds scoot off to reveal an Oz-land where double rainbows ring emerald hilltops and arch gracefully across the valleys to snowcapped peaks. It was this breathtaking natural phenomenon that inspired Temecula's first inhabitants, the Luiseno Indians, to name it Temecula, which means "where the sun breaks through the mist."

Call it love at first sight (they do), but it was largely the pleasant climate and bucolic scenery that inspired Dick and Fran Handley to abandon the Detroit heat, cold and gridlock 20 years ago and retire to Temecula. "We moved into a mobile home community and have been living in the land of wine and roses ever since," says Dick, formerly with the Detroit Department of Transportation.

Just one look was also all it took to encourage Rosemary and Richard Parsons to pull up roots in suburban Chicago and settle into an affordable senior housing community in Temecula. "We flew out one weekend, picked out a house, packed up and moved," says Richard, a retired paratrooper with the U.S. Army who has lived all over the world. "When it's 85 in Chicago, you're ready to fight," quips Richard. "In Temecula, it can be 100 degrees out, but you're never uncomfortable, and the nights are always cool." Adds Rosemary, "All my life I wanted to live in California near the ocean. Now we're only an hour away."

Norma Matkovich, 75, moved to Temecula in 1984 after having lived all over the world with her ex-husband, a military man. After her divorce, she wanted to live in a small town where she could make friends and feel like a part of the community. She chose Temecula for its natural beauty and small-town charm and has never looked back. "In Long Beach (her last stop before moving to Temecula) the only people you met were at work — you never ran into anyone you knew when you went shopping at malls," she says. "In Temecula, you have to get dressed in the morning because you never know who you're going to run into."

Ask retirees what they do for fun and a sense of community and it's not long before the Mary Phillips Senior Center comes up. "I've been all over the world and I've never seen anything like what our senior center offers," says Richard Parsons. "We have friends in Chicago who can't wait to retire and move here," he says, "and our son and two daughters already have. Not only is Temecula wonderful for retirees, but it's also a great place to raise grandkids."

Adds Dick Handley, "We were a little worried about not knowing anyone when we first moved here, but it was never a problem. With the senior center, it wasn't long before we made our own nuclear family." With a free daily lunch program plus Meals on Wheels, potlucks, dinner dances, far-flung field trips and a daily exercise schedule that could make Jane Fonda wilt, there's rarely a dull moment at the center. "Aerobics, weightlifting, swing dance, line dance, hip-hop, field trips to Las Vegas, classes in everything from Spanish and nutrition to driving and health insurance — they wear me out," says recreation director Candice Flohr of the seniors who frequent the center.

The center includes a 3,000-square-foot expansion housing a full kitchen, a billiards room, a library and three additional classrooms. It was named after the late Mary Phillips, "a feisty lady who pestered city council until they agreed to gut the old bus depot and turn it into a senior center," recalls Norma Matkovich, who lent her energies and "loud mouth" to the cause. Since then, Norma has served in a variety of capacities at the senior center and is currently treasurer of its Senior Golden Years Club. When the Golden Yearers, as they call themselves,

aren't raising funds for the less fortunate or donating holiday fruit baskets, they're likely to be gallivanting around Old Town terrorizing small restaurants, chuckles Dick Handley. "They see 27 of us coming at once and they just about tear their hair out," he grins.

Temecula also is an ideal place for single seniors to start anew, says Norma Matkovich. "One couple met here, married and took 55 of us with them on their honeymoon to Las Vegas," she says.

Still single herself, Norma says "there are enough men here to keep me busy. But I haven't met anyone yet I want to take home." She adds, "My married friends put up with me, and there's so much to do. And even with all the growth, Temecula still feels like the country."

In fact, Temecula appears to be expanding on all fronts. Beyond the beehive of the senior center lies Historic Old Town, Temecula's redeveloped nine-block historic district. Front Street, with boardwalks and lantern-style streetlights,

is lined with shops, antiques dealers, art galleries, Western-style restaurants and saloons (one still has a hitching post). A year-round farmers market is open on Saturdays. Festivals celebrate the town's colorful past as a stop on the Butterfield Stage route and location for Hollywood westerns as well as its more recent claim to fame as California's "other" wine country. Festivals include Old Town Western Days, a wine tasting and arts festival in May, an old-fashioned Fourth of July celebration, a film festival in September, the Temecula Tractor Race in October and a Christmas festival and parade.

Outside the time warp of Old Town lies modern-day Temecula, a sprawl of green where the sparkling Promenade Mall offers 110 specialty shops, major department stores, cinemas and a cluster of restaurants. Trendy baby boomers weren't far behind the retirees in moving to Temecula.

Other attractions include the five-acre Temecula Duck Pond, nine champi-

---

Population: About 90,000

Location: The Temecula Valley is located in Southern California, 85 miles south of Los Angeles and 60 miles north of San Diego. Elevations range from 1,980 feet in the east to 2,600 feet on the west.

Climate:

	High	Low
January	69	46
July	92	61

The weather is comparable to the Napa Valley, with warm, dry days and cool evenings. Although separated from the Pacific Ocean by the Santa Rosa range, the Rainbow Gap funnels a mild beach climate into the valley.

Average relative humidity: 25%

Rain: 24 inches

Cost of living: Above average

Average housing cost: $525,000

Sales tax: 7.75%

State income tax: For married couples filing jointly, the rates range from 1% on the first $12,638 to 9.3% (plus $3,652) on amounts above $82,952. For single filers, rates run from 1% on the first $6,319 to 9.3% (plus $1,826) on amounts above $41,476.

Income tax exemptions: Social Security

benefits and railroad pensions are exempt.

Estate tax: None

Inheritance tax: None

Property tax: 1.3%-1.4%, does not include special assessments in some parts of the city. The state reimburses up to $472 in property taxes for those 62 years or older, blind or disabled with federal adjusted gross incomes of $40,811 or less. The tax on a $525,000 home, with homestead exemption noted below, would range from about $6,734 to $7,252.

Homestead exemption: $7,000 off assessed value.

Religion: Most denominations are represented locally or in nearby communities.

Education: Temecula is within commuting distance of 22 private and public colleges and universities with a combined enrollment of more than 139,000 students. This includes nationally known private liberal arts schools like the Claremont Colleges and the University of Redlands. Impressive scientific work is being conducted at Harvey Mudd College, California State Polytechnic University at

Pomona and the University of California at Riverside. Loma Linda University boasts a renowned medical school. The University of La Verne College of Law is located in Ontario. Cal State San Marcos in nearby San Diego County offers classes in Temecula as does UCR Extension and the University of Redlands. There are five community colleges in the region, including Mount San Jacinto Community College, which also offers classes in Temecula.

Transportation: Riverside Transit Agency operates Dial-A-Ride, which provides curb-to-curb transportation for the elderly and disabled. Fixed-route bus service operates along major streets. Senior Van offers local transportation to and from the Mary Phillips Senior Center. Temecula is 55 minutes from San Diego International Airport, 45 minutes from Ontario International Airport, and 90 minutes from Los Angeles International Airport. Van and limo service to the three airports is $100-$250, $105-$144 and $138-$250, respectively.

Health: The 80-bed Inland Valley Medical Center in Wildomar and the Rancho

onship golf courses, the 6,000-acre Lake Skinner Recreation Area (for camping, fishing, boating, picnicking, horseback riding, hiking trails and outdoor swimming in a half-acre swimming lagoon), the 8,300-acre Santa Rosa Plateau Ecological Reserve and the century-old Glen Ivy Hot Springs Spa, where you can slather yourself with local mud or ease into a bubbly pool fed by natural hot springs.

Then there's Temecula's burgeoning wine country. Scattered in the rolling hillsides, it is home to more than 15 wineries ranging from small ma-and-pa establishments to grandiose estates featuring wine-tasting rooms, patio fountain cafes, gourmet restaurants and herb gardens. Almost a city unto itself, the wine district in toto and individual wineries host fetes galore, from barbecue suppers with hayrides to candlelight gourmet dinners, jazz concerts under the stars and even wine-stomping events where you can help press the grapes.

Housing options for seniors currently range from quality apartment units and luxury condominiums to single-family homes, says Gloria Wolnick, marketing coordinator for the city of Temecula. Vicki MacHale, activities director for the Vintage Hills Planned Community Association, says nearby Sun City and Banning also offer a wide variety of senior housing for all income levels.

Temecula real estate agent Gene Wunderlich, director of the Southwest Riverside County Association of Realtors, predicts that a wider range of housing options for retirees, from inexpensive mobile home parks and senior housing facilities to upscale golf communities and acres for custom estates, will encourage even more people to consider Temecula as their retirement home.

"With one of the best affordability indexes in a state notorious for high-priced real estate, 50 percent of Temecula's residents can afford a medium-priced home," says Wunderlich, adding that Temecula is especially a bargain for retirees who move from more upscale areas of neighboring Orange and San Diego counties. "They can sell their homes there and buy a palace out here," he says.

Sue and Jerry Turek agree. Their new four-bedroom home with a backyard pool cost $298,000 — and that's $50,000 less than what they got for their smaller 70-year-old home in Chicago.

All Temecula residents are benefiting from a recent tax cut, while a recreational tax approved by residents is paving the city with lush greenbelts and regional parks stocked with tennis, basketball and squash courts, baseball fields and swimming pools.

"It's a win-win situation," says Wunderlich. "From volunteering to drive unarmed patrol cars to raising money for charities, our seniors are a highly visible and vibrant part of the community. I've had people in their 70s and 80s tell me they don't want to live with a bunch of old people. They want to contribute to the community and be appreciated, and in Temecula, they really are." ●

Temecula, CA

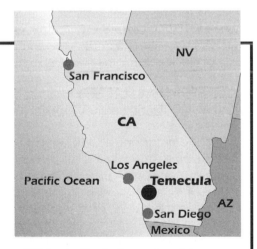

Springs Medical Center in Murrieta, a 96-bed facility, both have radiology and oncology departments. Inland Valley also is the regional trauma center, with 13 beds devoted to emergency care and two for trauma.

Housing options: The Fountains at Temecula, (951) 506-1579. This gated community has 346 apartment homes plus a fully appointed clubhouse with planned activities, a pool and therapeutic spa, library, computer learning center, putting greens and covered parking. Other properties for seniors include **The Colony** in neighboring Murrieta. Built in the mid-1980s, the golf community includes nearly 300 single-story houses in Spanish or Southwestern architecture priced from the $300,000s. Another option is **Murrieta Hot Springs**, a 30-year-old golf and retirement community for residents age 55 and over, just outside Temecula on the grounds of the former Murrieta Hot Springs Resort. Housing ranges from condos and manufactured homes to vacant lots where you can move your own mobile or manufactured home. A clubhouse with swimming pool serves as the community's social hub. Prices for mobile homes average $192,000, and condo prices average $230,000. **Temeku Hills Golf Community**, (951) 774-1300, is a California mission-style community of single-family homes set in rolling hills at the 72-acre Temeku Hills Country Club. The community is popular with active retirees and features special senior recreational and service programs at its clubhouse. Prices for four-bedroom homes start at $420,000. Assisted-living communities include **Chancellor Place of Murrieta**, (951) 696-5753, which offers independent living in large studio and one-bedroom suites with full baths and kitchenettes for older seniors who require assistance. The property overlooks a golf course and is within walking distance of a shopping center. Call for pricing and available specials. **Sterling Senior Communities**, (951) 506-5555, is a new 179-unit senior apartment complex on 21 acres. The community has an independent-living complex of 52 apartments, an assisted-living complex of 74 apartments and an Alzheimer's complex of 53 beds. The independent-living quarters range from studios at $1,945 to two-bedroom apartments starting at $3,415.

Visitor lodging: Options include Best Western Country Inn, $89-$139, (800) 528-1234; Comfort Inn, $77-$150, (951) 296-3788; Embassy Suites, $99-$189, (951) 676-5656; Loma Vista B&B, $89-$195, (951) 676-7047; Temecula Creek Inn, $189-$299, (951) 694-1000; and Holiday Inn Express, $110-$140, (951) 699-2444.

Information: Temecula Valley Chamber of Commerce, 27450 Ynez Road, Suite 124, Temecula, CA 92591, (951) 676-5090 or www.temecula.org.

Tucson, Arizona

Bunk down in an artsy Arizona city with cowboy spirit

By Ron Butler

Call it an intriguing mix of modern sophistication and Old West imagination. Tucson long has been known as a ranching center but largely has shed its swaggering cowboy image, emerging instead as an alternative for refugees in search of a sunny escape. The city's skyline is impressively modern, with its dramatic glass towers worthy of any major urban center.

But Tucson likes to play up its Old West roots. A bean burrito and a cold beer is still a breakfast standard. The city's Sun Tran bus drivers all wear cowboy hats. Travel posters proclaim that "Geronimo Slept Here."

Amid the culture and the boom times, a genuine feel of the Old West, with its galloping, wide-open spaces and dusty bravado, still exists. You'll find it in honky-tonk bars like the Maverick, where the two-step is the popular dance of choice. Cowboys and cowgirls, often wearing matching shirts and jeans, glide around the dance floor as though on roller skates.

You'll find it in steakhouses that serve entrees too big for Easterners, and in art museums that celebrate the works of Remington, Russell, Maynard Dixon and local son Ted DeGrazia, who died 20 years ago, leaving an artistic legacy known around the world. You'll find it in places like Bisbee, Benson, Tombstone and Yuma, all within an easy drive.

But most of today's cowboys wear gold neck chains and boots that have never stepped in mud. And with its 530,000-plus population (center of a sprawling 890,000 overall base), Tucson is one of the fastest-growing cities in the United States. It supports its own professional theater company, dance company, opera and symphony.

And above it all are Tucson's marvelous mountains — the Santa Ritas, Santa Catalinas and Rincons — serving as subliminal road signs for motorists. On rare rainy days when clouds hang low in the sky and obscure the mountain details, drivers lose all sense of direction. They head up the wrong streets, south instead of north, east instead of west. Such days, however, are not common. In fact, sunglasses are sold by corner street vendors the way umbrellas are peddled in Seattle or New York.

It's no wonder that newcomers like Bob and Liz Davies, 66 and 65 respectively, picked Tucson as the place to retire after 15 whirlwind years back East. Bob, a nuclear physicist who has a suitcase full of degrees, worked for power companies in Washington, DC.

"In many ways it's a small-scale version of Washington," says Bob. "There's an impressive number of really good restaurants, and the range and level of hotels is incredible."

Both like to eat out, with a growing fondness for Mexican restaurants, such as La Fuente. A strong Spanish flavor makes Tucson unique in its own right. Some of the best Mexican food in the country is offered in the family-owned restaurants of south Tucson, among them El Minuto, Mi Nidito, El Dorado and Xochmilco. (As a general rule, Mexican food gets blander — and more expensive — the farther north one goes in the area.)

Bob and Liz live in the Tucson foothills in a home designed by a follower of Frank Lloyd Wright. At night the city provides an unfailingly spectacular light show. But like the finest of jewels, its luster is kept at a relatively dim twinkle. This is done not to conserve energy but out of consideration for the scientists and astronomers at famous Kitt Peak and other key observatories where the world's most powerful solar telescopes peer into the galaxies. Ironically, in the telescope's shadow, Yaqui, Pima and Tohono O'odham Indians still consult tribal medicine men for their aches and pains, and still harvest the desert for cactus fruit and building materials.

The couple also owns a mountain "escape home" in Pinetop near Show Low. The Apache-owned land is a cool summer retreat for many Tucson and Phoenix desert-dwellers, but Bob and Liz prefer it in the spring, fall and winter, a place for true family bonding when one or more of their three adult children — two sons and a daughter — come to visit.

"We feel safe here," says Liz Davies. "And it feels right. It seems we had to drive at least 75 miles to get anywhere in Washington. Here, we're where we want to be."

These are the words echoed almost exactly by Chuck and Connie (Charles and Carolyn) Osborn, 74 and 73 respectively, who migrated from Texas six years ago, following trial stop-offs everywhere from central Massachusetts to the Oregon coast. They live in a ranch-style home in the gated retirement community of Copper Crest just west of Tucson. "There's plenty to do here," Connie says. "We go to the symphonies, bike in the Tucson mountains, collect ancient Indian pottery."

Trekkers and bikers are in for a treat. Within its dry sierras, canyons and mesas, Tucson and its southern Arizona boundaries contain 27 varieties of cactus and a wide assortment of flora, wildlife and bird life. Desert walks are popular, especially at sunrise. You may have to dance a little jig to stay warm at first, but the sun quickly warms the desert and brings it to life.

Also celebrating the desert is the Arizona-Sonora Desert Museum, an internationally known zoo founded nearly 40 years ago, part of the 16,000-acre Tucson Mountain Park 12 miles west of town. Its "cages" are sand dunes, water holes, dry washes, rock caves, shrubs and trees. Glass-panel viewing allows visitors to watch otters and beavers cavort underwater. The museum maintains the precise natural habitat of the animals, fish, birds and insects it houses and protects — everything from mountain lions to tarantulas and javelinas to rattlesnakes. The result is a zoo that's not a zoo at all — always the best kind.

Along with the wildlife exhibits, underground limestone caves can be explored. They're part of the Earth Sciences Center, which includes meteor and mineral displays. Visitors are encouraged to examine the stones and even study them under magnifying glasses. The Arizona-Sonora Desert Museum is the state's second most popular tourist attraction after the Grand Canyon.

Tucson's Saguaro National Park, elevated six years ago from national monument status to the nation's 52nd national park, consists of thousands of acres of candelabrum-shaped cactuses that annually attract more than 700,000 visitors. Many of the towering plants, some more

Tucson, AZ

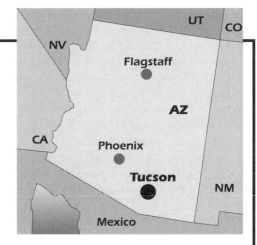

Population: 532,000

Location: In Southern Arizona, 60 miles north of the Mexican border.

Climate: High Low
January 64 38
July 99 74

Average relative humidity: 26%

Average rainfall: 11 inches

Cost of living: Average

Average housing cost: The median sales price for a new home is $199,000.

Sales tax: The state imposes a 5.6% retail sales tax, and Tucson imposes 2%.

Sales tax exemptions: Groceries and prescription drugs.

State income tax: For married couples filing jointly, graduated from 2.87% of taxable income up to $20,000 to 5.04% minus $2,276 on amounts over $300,000. For single filers, graduated from 2.87% of taxable income up to $10,000 to 5.04% minus $1,138 on amounts over $150,000.

Income tax exemptions: Social Security benefits and up to $2,500 in federal and Arizona state and local government pensions are exempt.

Estate tax: None

Inheritance tax: None

Property tax: The tax ratio is figured on 10% of the "full cash value," which is typically 80% to 85% of the market value. For every $100,000 in property value, owners can expect to pay $1,400-$1,600 in property taxes, depending on location.

Homestead exemption: None

Religion: Tucson, predominately Catholic, boasts literally hundreds of places of worship. One of Arizona's most striking landmarks, the Mission San Xavier del Bac, was established in 1700 and has been in continual use ever since.

Education: Education is one of Tucson's highest priorities, with its public school system providing general and college-preparatory courses. The University of Ari-

zona offers bachelor's, master's and doctorate degrees in a wide field of study. Pima Community College, with five local campuses, is a two-year college serving all county residents.

Transportation: Tucson International Airport is 10 miles south of downtown. Sun Tran Transit provides bus service throughout Tucson. General fare is $1; seniors 65 and over ride for 40 cents. A pocket guide is available containing detailed schedules, (520) 792-9222. Long-distance bus service is provided by Greyhound, (800) 231-2222.

Health: Tucson boasts some of the most sophisticated health care available, including University Medical Center, Kino Community Hospital, Northwest Medical Center, Tucson Medical Center, El Dorado Hospital, St. Mary's Hospital and St. Joseph's Hospital. Even before such state-of-the-art medical facilities became available, doctors across the country recommended Tucson's dry desert air for patients with respiratory problems.

Housing options: The metro area is home to 37 builders offering homes in 152 subdivisions. Homes are available in every style and price range, from affordable to very expensive. Newer homes offer a wide variety of single-story and multistory designs and include gas and electric utilities, garages for up to four cars, rounded interior corners and lots with horse privileges. Styles are overwhelmingly Spanish with earth tones, stucco finishes and tile roofs. The region includes 20 master-planned communities, several of which include golf courses. Nine are age restricted. Among options: **SaddleBrooke** by Robson Communities is an active-adult community set in the foothills of the Santa Catalina Mountains. Residents enjoy 36 holes of championship golf, lighted tennis courts and scores of additional amenities at its MountainView Country Club, (800) 733-

4050 or www.robson.com. **The Academy Village** is a unique active-adult community in the Rincon Valley east of Tucson. Founded by Dr. Henry Koffler, president emeritus of the University of Arizona, its heart is the Arizona Senior Academy, a nonprofit lifelong-learning organization that offers cultural and educational programs. All residents are members of the academy. Townhomes and single-family homes are available, (877) 647-0171 or www.theacademyvillage.com.

Visitor lodging: Tucson has shed its bunkhouse image. Resort hotels such as Westin's La Paloma, Loews Ventana Canyon, the posh Canyon Ranch Spa and Hilton's El Conquistador give new focus to Tucson as a principal resort center in the American Southwest, although Tanque Verde and a number of excellent dude ranches still thrive. Relatively new are bed-and-breakfast inns, but they've proliferated so quickly that the phone book lists about 70. The grand dame of Tucson hotels is the Arizona Inn, from $149. Three-night tennis, golf and spa packages are available, (800) 933-1093.

Information: Metropolitan Tucson Convention and Visitors Bureau, 100 S. Church Ave., Tucson, AZ 85701, (520) 624-1817, (800) 638-8350 or www.visit tucson.org. Tucson Metropolitan Chamber of Commerce, P.O. Box 991, 465 W. St. Mary's Road, Tucson, AZ 85701, (520) 792-1212 or www.tucsonchamber.org.

than 60 feet high, have stood tall since before the time of Coronado. Columnar, lofty, and majestic, their limbs raised to the heavens as though in prayer, the saguaro is the symbol of the Arizona desert. No Tucson travel ad is complete without one, nor is any Hollywood Western. They've even been transported to Spain and Italy to authenticate the scenery for "spaghetti Westerns."

Saguaro National Park actually consists of two sprawling sections of the Sonoran Desert, east and west of town about 30 miles apart. Designated driving loops offer a close-up look at the towering plants that grow in such profusion nowhere else in the world.

Survival is the first commandment of all living things, and plants — even blades of grass — stand far apart on the desert so that their roots will not compete for water. Study the saguaro up close and you'll find that it is home to many small desert animals and birds. The red-capped, zebra-backed Gila woodpecker can make a nesting hole in the self-healing saguaro's pulpy interior in a matter of days. Many raise two or three broods a year and often make a new hole for each brood. The woodpecker's abandoned homes frequently house other birds that are unable to peck holes of their own.

The Southwest desert was long considered a scourge of man, arid and untamable, but now more and more people see in its raw, awesome beauty the last vestige of America's wilderness.

For Chuck Osborn, a retired Delta pilot and a military pilot before that, Tucson's appeal as a major center of aviation and aerospace activities couldn't be more obvious. "It's an aviation buff's dream come true," says Chuck, who works as a docent at the Pima Air and Space Museum. It sprawls over 65 acres of desert landscape 12 miles southeast of downtown and contains more than 200 historic aircraft, both military and civilian.

Nearly a quarter of a million visitors annually tour the indoor/outdoor museum where such stars as the Boeing B-29 Superfortress, the type of plane that dropped the first atomic bomb on Japan, and the SR-71, also known as the Blackbird, the world's fastest aircraft, are on view.

"By far the most popular exhibit is Air Force One, the DC-6 that was the last piston-driven aircraft used by Presidents Kennedy and Johnson and the only plane on display that the public may enter," says Chuck, as though addressing a new group of visitors to the museum.

"The same dry climate and constant sun that makes Tucson such an ideal location for military air base operations, such as Davis-Monthan Air Force Base, also make it a prize setting for a museum of this type," he says.

Between the museum and Davis-Monthan is the "bone yard" where literally thousands of planes, victims of peacetime and military attrition, are stored. Beyond that are several square miles filled with abandoned airplane parts stashed about in ghostly disarray — wings and engines, fuselages, frames and tail sections.

This is, indeed, aviation country. In 1911, only eight years after the Wright Brothers' first flight at Kitty Hawk, history's first recorded aerial "dogfight" took place just over the Mexican border in Sonora. Dean Ivan Lamb, a young Arizona pilot and soldier of fortune flying for the guerrilla general Pancho Villa, exchanged pistol fire with a Mexican federal army plane similar to his own — a Curtis "pusher-type" plane, literally a box kite pushed through the air by a giant propeller. Neither pilot was hit and the battle ended in a draw.

Guides, or docents, at the museum are all volunteers, mostly retired Air Force and commercial pilots. War stories abound, especially around the outdoor tables at the museum's snack bar — tales of the Flying Tigers and hits over the English Channel. The docents eat free of charge at the snack bar. "It's small compensation," says Connie Osborn with a smile, "for all the time they put in."

Jerry and Maria DiPietro, 61 and 54, picked Tucson because they're both in the wholesale travel business. They've seen everything and been everywhere. And they've done everything, including buying a home recently in Saddle-Brooke, one of 38 master-planned communities in the Tucson area. That means a 36-hole golf course, gyms, recreational facilities galore and a mountain view that will literally knock your white tennis socks right off.

"We haven't actually moved yet, but we're on our way," says Jerry from his office in Maine, where he primarily handles European-bound travel groups. "We had pretty much decided on Arizona, where we visited often. But where? We went through the usual process of elimination. Phoenix and Scottsdale were too crowded — too much traffic. Green Valley was too out of it."

Both Jerry and Maria follow a "stay active, stay healthy" routine with a concentration on tennis. "OK, there's no ocean in Arizona. But we're from Maine. We've had the ocean," Maria says. "And there's the city itself, with all its laid-back appeal."

The DiPietros like to read. Tucson probably has more successful writers per capita than any place else in the country, the desert and its survival their common ground. Authors such as Charles Bowden ("Blue Desert," "Desierto," "The Secret Forest") and Richard Shelton ("Going Back to Bisbee") follow a course set by the late naturalists Joseph Wood Krutch and Edward Abbey in defining, preserving and protecting the stark, awesome landscape. Tom Miller ("Jack Ruby's Kitchen Sink," "Trading With the Enemy") and Byrd Baylor ("Desert Voices") also call Tucson home. Larry McMurtry ("Lonesome Dove") spends enough time here to be a local, as does Jim Harrison ("Legends of the Fall"), who has a small ranch in Patagonia near the Mexico border. N. Scott Momaday, Leslie Marmon Silko, Simon Ortiz and other Native American authors add to the city's literary luster.

The city of Tucson was established more than 200 years ago as a presidio, or walled city, to protect citizens from warring Indians. Part of the presidio's wall was uncovered when excavation began 50 years ago for the Pima County Courthouse downtown. A section of the wall was preserved and is now on display in the courthouse vestibule. The courthouse itself was designated a national historic landmark in 1957.

Downtown Tucson and its impressive glass and steel skyscrapers reflecting images of the past — including a statue of Pancho Villa on horseback — has been reclaimed in recent years, following a period in which the closure of several department stores made the city somewhat of a ghost town after dark. But largely led by tourist demand, galleries, high-end shopping, boutiques and cafes have given the city new life.

Visitors only have to stroll the downtown El Presidio area north of City Hall to see a well-preserved portion of the city's past. The Old Town artisan area, where the popular La Cocina restaurant is located, includes a sprawl of old adobe buildings where the work of more than 150 artists is offered for sale. Some of the buildings go back to 1862. Stretching back even further are buildings in the Mexican-flavored El Barrio section of south Tucson. Only recently have Tucson city fathers begun to mine — and preserve — the treasures of the Old Pueblo's historic past.

That history is just another aspect of Tucson that draws relocating retirees. "Everything you want is here," says Bob Davies. ●

Venice, Florida

Residents praise the civic spirit and cultural riches of this Florida Gulf Coast town

By Jay Clarke

From its beginnings in 1925, Venice was destined to be different from other Florida cities. Unlike most communities that arose haphazardly in Florida during the 1920s land boom, Venice was planned down to the last byway before the first spade of sand was turned. It even incorporated the then-little-employed concept of zoning to separate business property from residences.

That heritage makes today's Venice one of the most livable cities in Florida. Graceful palms outline Venice Avenue, many blocks of which are still lined with stately Mediterranean-style mansions of yesteryear.

Downtown has grown and become modern, but archways and red-tile roofs still mark many 1920s-era buildings — and even some new structures have reverted to that earlier, elegant Northern Italian style of architecture.

Civic pride is strong. The Venice Foundation, dedicated to improving life in Venice, is the largest of its kind in Florida. And though its population is 20,000, the city has its own symphony, theater, art center and opera guild.

So when a go-getter like Terry Redman retired to Venice from Niles, MI, seven years ago, it's hardly surprising that he plunged right into efforts to make his new hometown even better. Now 59, Terry is a busy volunteer, chairing the county's parks board and working hard to create and improve parklands.

"It's a passion about something you enjoy doing," Terry says of his volunteer work. Currently he is putting his energy into improving a strip park on each side of the Intracoastal Waterway, which runs through the city. Already, Venetian Waterway Park has a paved walk- way, shelters, picnic sites and playgrounds. His wife, Sandy, 52, also keeps busy singing with the Sweet Adelines, a women's barbershop organization, and raising money for scholarships.

One reason Terry chose to retire to Venice is because it reminded him in some ways of Niles, the pleasant town where he was born, raised and worked. But Venice also had the attributes that he sought in retirement.

"I liked this community, I liked this lifestyle," he says. Venice's warm climate clinched the move. Neither he nor Sandy is fond of snow.

A school administrator, Terry moved here in 1996 upon his retirement. Sandy, also a school administrator in Niles, took a position in the Charlotte County school system here before retiring. "We had looked at Fort Lauderdale and West Palm Beach, but we liked small towns, and we had friends living in Venice," Terry says. "I found a property I liked — three acres on the water — and we built our home there."

Terry is a master gardener, and with three acres of land around his home, he has plenty of space to work with — and in this climate he can do it the year around. Since his home fronts the water, he and Sandy find it easy to go boating, which they both enjoy. Another plus: Friendly neighbors. "They're great. We have potluck dinners," Terry says, noting that they watch each other's homes and pick up newspapers when neighbors are away. "We take care of each other," he says.

Other retirees who were happy to say goodbye to snow are Mike and Linda Moultrie, who lived and worked in Arlington County, VA, a suburb of Washington, DC, before they moved to Venice. "It's not what brought us here as what drove us here," says Mike, 54. "I don't like the cold up North, the amount of leaves to rake, the unbearable traffic."

The couple had been visiting Venice every August for 10 years, he says, so they were familiar with the community. "More and more it kind of grew on us," says Mike, who retired from the Arlington Fire Department in June 2000 after more than 27 years of service. His wife, Linda, 55, was with the Arlington Police Department for more than 28 years and retired the same day.

Mike and Linda had purchased a home here before they retired but decided it wasn't what they really wanted. They sold it and bought a lot on the water to build a home. They moved to Venice in January 2001 and moved into their new house a year later.

"We like the area, the environment, the winter. We have a beautiful home, all the amenities, a large house, large pool, a boat on the water," Mike says. Boating, in fact, has become a favorite pastime for the couple. "We do as much boating as we can. It's just 19 minutes to the Gulf," Mike says. He and Linda also patronize restaurants on the water.

But while he likes his new home and lifestyle, Mike found the move to Florida traumatic in other ways. "I wasn't prepared for going from a 56-hour week to doing nothing," says Mike, who now does some consulting work. "Linda adjusted better. She volunteers three days a week at a thrift store and works for a lady who baby-sits pets." Mike says it also took time to make new friends. "We have made friends, but it's taken nearly 19 months," he says.

Monty Andrews, 64, was another retiree who was looking for ways to keep busy. Monty and his wife, Jan, 63, discovered the rewards of volunteering after they moved to Venice from Omaha, NE, where he had worked as an industrial engineer.

"At first, I didn't do anything, but I tired of playing golf," Monty says. Now he's active in several volunteer positions, and he has turned from golf to senior softball. "It's tremendously popular," he says. "Four to five hundred play here in the winter, and the Legends, the national champions, come from here." Monty says he made many friends through the softball connection.

Like Monty, Jan finds great rewards in volunteering. "If it's nothing more than visiting a nursing home, it's a joy, such a joy," says Jan, who had worked as an administrative assistant for a health company before they moved to Venice. Monty remembers the satisfaction they both felt when they taught an 88-year-old woman to use a computer.

Bolstering the volunteer movement in Venice, Monty says, is the "phenomenal" cooperation between the city government and the public. "When the city didn't have enough money for July 4 fireworks a couple of years ago, volunteers raised $10,000 just by standing around with a cup," Monty says. "Our reward was a most fantastic display."

Jan says she and Monty also looked at Naples and Fort Myers but thought Venice was better located. Contributing to that decision was the fact that Monty had lived in nearby Sarasota 35 years before, and "I always said I would come back."

Their move to Florida drew some resistance from family members, but Jan and Monty have few regrets. They have two sons, one living in Nebraska and the other in Chicago. "They didn't want us to move from Omaha, but it's our life. We miss our friends," Monty says, but he and his wife have gotten involved locally and are excited about Venice. Jan puts it succinctly: "I don't miss Omaha," she says.

Many retirees find that Venice's attributes far outweigh any regrets. Ronnie Bell, 70, who moved here from Philadelphia in 1981, says her husband, Bill, 71, a former police officer, was determined to relocate. "'We're not staying in Philadelphia. There's got to be someplace better,' he kept telling me," says Ronnie. "He left after midnight on the day he retired. I was here waiting. We've never regretted moving."

Ronnie says they also looked at several other Florida towns — among them Lehigh Acres, Port Charlotte and Naples — before settling here. "We liked the sleepy little town of Venice," she says.

Bunny Theobald, 80, is another retiree who never looked back after moving to Florida. "My husband morphed into a butterfly when we moved here," says Bunny, who moved to Venice from Memphis, TN, in 1985. His wardrobe

Venice, FL

Population: 20,818. Population doubles in winter.

Location: Venice is on Florida's Gulf coast between Sarasota and Fort Myers.

Climate:

	High	Low
January	72	53
July	89	71

Average relative humidity: 62%

Annual rainfall: 47 inches

Cost of living: Slightly above average

Average housing costs: $244,734 for a two-bedroom home, $264,000 for a condominium.

Sales tax: 7%

Sales tax exemptions: Food, medicine

State income tax: None

Intangibles tax: None. The tax was repealed as of Jan. 1, 2007.

Estate tax: None

Inheritance tax: None

Property tax: The Sarasota County rate is $14.6599 per $1,000. In Venice, the total rate, including city taxes, is $18.1719. The tax on a $244,734 home in Venice, with homestead exemption noted below, would be $3,993.

Homestead exemption: $25,000 off assessed value of primary, permanent residence.

Religion: There are seven places of worship in Venice and many more in neighboring Sarasota.

Education: Manatee Community College, a two-year state facility in Venice, offers courses in more than 90 fields of study, (941) 408-1300. In nearby Sarasota are the Sarasota-Manatee branch of the state's University of South Florida, (941) 359-4296, which has numerous degree programs; Eckerd College, (941) 957-3397, which has a Program for Experienced Learners; and Webster University, (941) 358-3840, a leader in practical graduate school education.

Transportation: Sarasota-Bradenton Airport, serving 1.5 million passengers a year, is 29 miles northwest. Tampa International Airport is 77 miles north, and Southwest Florida International Airport at Fort Myers is 56 miles south. Sarasota County Area Transit (SCAT) provides bus service throughout the county, (941) 861-1234. Take Care Transport provides nonemergency transportation, (941) 923-3434.

Health: Bon Secours Venice Hospital in downtown Venice has 342 beds and 24-hour emergency care. Twenty miles north of Venice in Sarasota is 826-bed Sarasota Memorial Hospital, and 20 miles south is 100-bed Englewood Community Hospital. Both have 24-hour emergency care.

Housing options: In addition to private homes, Venice has five retirement residences, six assisted-care facilities and six skilled-nursing homes. Additional ones are located in nearby Sarasota. The new **Venetian Golf & River Club** is being developed on the Myakka River by WCI Communities. It features a golf course, lakes, wetlands, a nature park, and river and golf clubs for socializing. Twenty home designs are offered, with prices ranging from the $300,000s to the millions. All homes will be constructed using green building principles devised by the Florida Green Building Coalition. For information, call (800) 924-4486.

Visitor lodging: Venice has almost three-dozen hotels and motels whose rates vary according to season (summer is low, winter is high). Best Western Ambassador Suites, (800) 685-7353 or (941) 480-9898, has an outdoor heated pool, continental breakfast and rates of $90-$180. Other options: Hampton Inn, (800) 426-7866 or (941) 488-5900, $79-$189; Veranda Inn, (941) 484-9559, $65-$95; and Holiday Inn, (800) 237-3712 or (941) 485-5411, $89-$130.

Information: Venice Area Chamber of Commerce, 597 Tamiami Trail South, Venice, FL 34285, (941) 488-2236 or www.venicechamber.com.

changed from suits and ties to "bright clothes" when they moved to Venice, she says.

Her husband died a year later, but Bunny hasn't let that tragedy hold her back. "I love being busy," says Bunny, an energetic octogenarian who lives in a condo. "I go to the yacht club, play bingo, go bowling, go to the theater, go to parties." She has no problem making friends and says she doesn't miss Memphis because there are "too many fun things to do here."

Another benefit is that most retirees find living in Venice less expensive than in their former home cities. "The cost of living is lower here, and there's no heavy insurance burden," says Jan Andrews. Terry Redman says property taxes also are lower.

Mike Moultrie puts the cost of living here on par with Washington. "But you can build a very nice home for almost nothing relative to up North," he admits. He says he recently had his home reappraised and was pleased to find it was worth much more than when he built it.

Being located close to Sarasota (about 20 miles), the cultural capital of Florida's Gulf Coast, Venice is blessed with cultural opportunities worthy of much larger cities. Only three other counties in the United States enjoy a higher per-capita attendance at cultural events.

Sarasota has its own symphony, ballet and opera as well as 10 theaters and 30 art galleries, including the world-famous Ringling Museum of Art. Its Van Wezel Performing Arts Hall, known locally as the "Purple Cow" because of its color, is busy almost every evening during the winter season.

In Venice itself, the Little Theatre gives performances on three stages. Plays on the main stage have included "Grease" and "Guys and Dolls." The 75-member Venice Symphony puts on six sets of classical and pops concerts in the winter. The Venice Art Center displays art in seven venues and also conducts classes and workshops the year around.

Of special interest to prospective retirees is the proximity and quality of medical facilities. Downtown Venice has a 342-bed hospital, Bon Secours, and two other hospitals are less than 40 minutes away. In nearby Sarasota is the large and nationally recognized 826-bed Sarasota Memorial Hospital. The other is the 100-bed Englewood Community Hospital. All three have 24-hour emergency care.

With a population that is heavily senior, Venice offers a wide variety of services for the 55-plus population, among them two large centers whose activities are directed mostly to older adults. The Senior Friendship Center offers programs such as caregiver support, volunteer work, meals programs, day centers and other services keyed to older adults. The Venice Community Center in downtown Venice is not specifically aligned to seniors, but 90 percent of its clientele are over 55, according to program coordinator Annette O'Kon. Activities include antique shows, art classes, dancing and concerts.

While Venice is named after the famous Italian city, it never had canals. It began life in 1925 when the Brotherhood of Locomotive Engineers bought 50,000 acres from Dr. Fred Albee and set out to build a farming and railroad retirement town. Boston architect John Nolen earlier had created an innovative but never-implemented design for the city for Albee, and the Brotherhood stuck to that plan.

When the Florida land boom fizzled in the late 1920s, the Brotherhood lost millions and Venice almost became a ghost town. It recovered somewhat in 1932, though, when the Kentucky Military Institute established a winter school here. But more lasting fame came in 1960 when the Ringling Bros. and Barnum & Bailey Circus made Venice its winter headquarters. For 31 years, until 1991, the annual trek of circus wagons, elephants and clowns from a train to their quarters was a highlight for the city's winter residents.

Today, Venice is a thriving city building on its rich heritage. That suits Jan Andrews fine, except for one thing: Too many other people have discovered the life she has learned to love here and are moving in, she laments. ●

Vero Beach, Florida

This town on Florida's Atlantic coast wins praise for its cultural scene and well-kept appearance

By Karen Feldman

Few people conduct as exhaustive a search as Dennis and Doris Murphy did when they set out to find the ideal place to retire. The Murphys spent three years exploring the East Coast before buying an oceanfront lot in Vero Beach.

"We have literally — with our own eyes — seen every piece of coastal land from Charleston, SC, to Florida," says Dennis Murphy, 61.

Lifelong residents of the Washington, DC, area, the couple retired 12 years ago after selling the computer company Dennis founded. They lived on a sailboat for eight years, visiting 88 countries and traveling 44,000 miles, keeping an apartment in Boca Raton for occasional respites.

When they decided to go ashore and build a home, they knew exactly what they wanted. "After living near the tropical zone for seven or eight years, we decided warm is better than cold," Dennis says. "We wanted to be on the East Coast where the prevailing winds come from the east and we could get to the Bahamas easily."

It had to be on the water, but not in an isolated area or one teeming with T-shirt shops and tattoo parlors. They drew up a list of candidates, crossing them off as they visited each one. They liked Charleston, SC, but it was too cold in winter. They considered Naples on Florida's west coast, but Vero Beach won out because of its small-town coziness combined with a wealth of culture.

"We wanted a neighborhood, a community," says Doris Murphy, 62. "Vero just kind of had it all for us." The Murphys find Vero Beach a perfect fit. "This town is remarkably open and friendly," Dennis says. "Even when we were the new people on the block we were warmly received."

It's a recurring theme among those who relocate to Vero. "It's the laid-back, very friendly attitude we have that makes visitors think, 'Maybe I'd like to live here the rest of my life,'" says Lori Burns, director of tourism and marketing for the Indian River County Chamber of Commerce.

Mike Joyce, 63, fell in love with the area the first time he visited from his home in Dayton, OH, where he was the director of distribution for a marketing company. He continued making visits until 1999, when he moved to Vero Beach full time.

In June 2001, he was volunteering at the McKee Botanical Garden when he met Mary Ann Collins, a widow who also volunteered at the subtropical garden that is listed on the National Register of Historic Places. They still volunteer there as well as at their church. They take long rides along the bicycle path that parallels Highway A1A, sharing a picnic lunch or dinner on the beach. They also travel a lot, visiting friends in Canada and hiking out West.

The town's location makes it an easy two-hour drive to Disney World, and it's little more than an hour to West Palm Beach. But it's the quality of life in their own town that they like best. "It's small so we don't have the traffic problems that other communities have," says Mary Ann, 59. "It's very pretty, too. All the developments have all this gorgeous landscaping."

There are no high-rises or neon signs. Instead, there are plenty of trees, well-kept waterfront parks with lots of beach access and developmental safeguards put in place by forward-thinking city fathers to ward off the over-development and commercialization that have befallen other retirement areas. As a result, Lori Burns says, Vero attracts "a marvelously affluent, culturally and environmentally savvy group of people."

That would aptly describe Evelyn Wilde Mayerson and her husband, Don. The 60-something Mayersons have been married more than 40 years. He is an attorney, and she is an author and professor emeritus of the University of Miami English department. They bought their Vero Beach home in 2001 and moved in full time in May 2002.

"When we left Miami we didn't know one person in Vero Beach," Evelyn says. That changed quickly. "I find the community very receptive to new people who are enthusiastic and feel good about themselves," she says.

The Mayersons are native Miamians who spent 10 years in Philadelphia, then returned to Florida, settling into South Beach, the upscale heart of Miami Beach. But "traffic was getting difficult," Don says. "Someone offered us a lot of money for the place we had, and we thought it was a good time to sell. We were ready for a new adventure."

They bought a home in Windsor, a 350-unit development by renowned urban planners Andres Duany and Elizabeth Plater-Zyberk, who designed Seaside in northern Florida. "Before we bought the house, I fell in love with Windsor," Evelyn says. "It's designed like a village so you can walk to anything."

Their 3,300-square-foot home is smallish by Windsor standards. The property has two houses — a large one and a smaller guest house that Don uses for an office. The four-bedroom, three-and-a-half-bath complex has a Charleston-style exterior that blends with its neighbors, complete with a tin roof, wooden plantation shutters and an overhanging porch. Fifteen-foot walls frame the perimeter of the property for added privacy.

The home's interior Evelyn describes as "a very lean and mean spare minimalist style" with a large living room and dining room space adjoining an L-shaped kitchen, all of which is built around the swimming pool.

The development has a well-equipped gym where the Mayersons work out and an 18-hole golf course designed by Robert Trent Jones Jr. Both have taken up golf since retiring. Don plays tennis and Evelyn is taking tennis and bridge lessons. She also serves on the board of the community theater, volunteers at the museum of art and is active in the Indian River Literary Society.

Like the Murphys, the Mayersons treasure the town's many cultural opportunities. The Riverside Theatre presents plays, celebrity shows and travel and lecture series. The Vero Beach Theatre Guild is a community theater that offers several plays a year. The Indian River County Historical Society depicts the region's history, while the McClarty Treasure Museum tells of Spanish shipwrecks in area waters and the treasures they held.

Other attractions include baseball at Holman Stadium, where the Los Angeles Dodgers hold spring training and their minor league team, the Vero Beach Dodgers, plays through the spring and summer. The Vero Beach Polo and Saddle Club holds weekly matches January through April.

The Mayersons have orchestrated an ideal existence, spending summers at their home in Vermont and the rest of

Vero Beach, FL

Population: About 18,058 residents live within the 12-square-mile city of Vero Beach, the county seat of Indian River County.

Location: About midway down Florida's east coast, about 100 miles southeast of Orlando and 135 miles north of Miami. Interstate 95, U.S. Highway 1 and State Road A1A run north and south. State Road 512 and State Road 60 run east and west, with access to I-95. Florida's Turnpike runs south to Miami and northwest to Orlando and beyond.

Climate: High Low

January 72 50
July 88 73

Average relative humidity: 58%

Rain: 53 inches

Cost of living: Slightly below average

Average housing cost: $250,000 for a single-family home in Vero Beach.

Sales tax: 7% (6% assessed by the state, 1% assessed by the county)

Sales tax exemption: Food and medicine

State income tax: None

Intangibles tax: None. The tax was repealed as of Jan. 1, 2007.

Estate tax: None

Inheritance tax: None

Property tax: There are several different taxing entities in Vero Beach. According to the assessor's office, property taxes will be about 2% or $20 per $1,000 of a home's full market value. With the $25,000 homestead exemption, the annual tax on a $250,000 home would be about $4,500.

Homestead exemption: $25,000 off assessed value of primary, permanent residence.

Religion: There are more than 100 places of worship in Vero Beach and surrounding Indian River County. They include all of the major Christian denominations as well as Greek Orthodox, Roman Catholic, Unitarian and nondenominational.

Education: A branch campus of Indian River Community College offers a range of two-year programs as well as personal and professional development courses. Webster University, Florida Atlantic University, Florida Institute of Technology and Barry University are within driving range.

Transportation: Melbourne International Airport is about 35 miles north. Airport limousine service and auto rentals are available at Melbourne and Vero Beach airports. Vero Beach Municipal Airport is a general aviation facility for private and corporate aircraft. The Council on Aging operates fixed-route bus service Monday through Saturday throughout the county. It's free to people of all ages but passengers must be able to board, get off the bus and carry packages themselves. The agency also runs a door-to-door service called Community Coach for seniors who are medically or nutritionally disadvantaged. There's a $1 charge each way, (772) 569-0903. Greyhound service, (800) 231-2222, is available with a depot at the Melbourne International Airport.

Health: Indian River Memorial Hospital in Vero Beach is a 335-bed, not-for-profit community hospital, offering medical, surgical, maternity, pediatric, rehabilitation, cancer center and emergency services. All rooms are private. Holmes Regional Trauma Center in Melbourne, affiliated with the University of Florida Health Science Center-Jacksonville, has a trauma team on duty around-the-clock, including the First Flight air ambulance. Sebastian River Medical Center in Sebastian is a 129-bed, for-profit acute-care hospital with services that include emergency, intensive care, cardiac and diagnostic.

Housing options: The island portion of Vero Beach is virtually built out. Condominium resales on the island start around $300,000 and single-family homes start at $500,000. On the mainland, two-bedroom, two-bath condos start at about $200,000 and three-bedroom, two-bath homes start at about $300,000. The popular Vero Beach Country Club area has single-family homes in the $300,000-range. **River Village at Grand Harbor**, (800) 826-8293, has single-family homes and condominiums starting in the $900,000. Construction has begun on a new section of golf villas, starting in the low $500,000s to the mid $600,000s. **Windsor**, (800) 233-7656, is designed as an urban village, with 350 homes starting at $2.2 million on up to about $17 million.

Visitor lodging: Disney's Vero Beach Resort is a large oceanfront property, $165-$1,105, (407) 934-7639 or www.dvcresorts.com. Howard Johnson's Express Inn is on the mainland, $65-$89, (772) 567-5171. Best Western Vero Beach is a two-story motor inn, $91-$150, (772) 567-8321.

Information: Indian River County Chamber of Commerce, 1216 21st St., Vero Beach, FL 32960, (772) 567-3491 or www.indianriverchamber.com.

the year in Vero Beach. "We live in two resorts," Don says. "Where do you go from there? We can't find places that are much nicer than where we live."

A booming housing market is proof that a lot of people feel that way about Vero Beach, a city that straddles the Intracoastal Waterway, with a portion on the mainland and another portion on a slender barrier island.

Although Indian River County's population has soared — rising from about 60,000 in 1980 to 125,000 in 2005 — Vero Beach has grown more slowly. It had 17,350 residents in 1980 and only 708 more than that in 2005. While the county is expected to grow to 154,000 people by 2020, projections put Vero Beach's population then at 18,245.

Real estate in this 12-square-mile city is a lot harder to come by than it was in the 1880s, when early settlers were lured to the region by the government's offer of 160 acres of high land for $50. It became a largely agricultural region, with citrus the predominant crop. The city was incorporated in 1910 and, like much of the state, experienced a real-estate boom in the mid-1920s.

In the past couple of years, yet another boom has occurred. While real estate usually rises in value gradually, Vero Beach real estate has taken a decided leap of late. The island portion, which is virtually built out, has appreciated the most, according to Linda Schlitt Gonzalez, broker for Coldwell Banker Ed Schlitt in Vero.

"Some places have risen 100 percent in 18 months," she says. "Areas where homes were $250,000 are now $500,000. Lots that were $250,000 are now $395,000. In central Vero Beach, for example, homes are now $550,000 and up. In Indian River County alone, there are nearly 200 homes and condominiums currently listed for over $1 million."

The trend on the island is to either tear down the existing home and rebuild or do major renovations. Single-family homes start at $500,000, while on the mainland they start at half that. Two-bedroom, two-bath condos start at about $200,000 on the mainland while a comparable island condo would start at $300,000 and climb to as much as $2 million.

The island is home to The Village of Sea Oaks, a 125-acre master-planned community of condominiums and maintenance-free villas. Its recreational focal points are the large tennis center and the Georgian-style oceanfront clubhouse, which has a fitness center, dining venues and pro shop. There also is a 48-slip marina.

The Murphys opted for a beachfront location, purchasing a lot in a 20-home development, also buying a home on the mainland, where they lived for two years while their 4,500-square-foot oceanfront home was under construction.

They put as much energy into the creation of their new home as they did in choosing its location. They designed the Mediterranean revival home themselves, including an elaborate computer system that gives them fingertip control of the whole property. Window shades automatically adjust to follow the sun, and the push of a button near their bed turns off all 121 lights and the music while arming the security alarm. They can check and set the temperature in any room and get early notice if someone is approaching the house.

"Dennis loves these electronic things," Doris says. "He calls the computer on his telephone from the airport and tells it to start heating the Jacuzzi."

Owing to the home's waterfront location, the Murphys chose to put their primary living area — living room, dining room, office and master bedroom — on the second floor for optimal views of the water, with a media room, bath and bar downstairs.

Despite such luxurious appointments, they don't spend much time lolling about. Doris, who both danced professionally and taught ballet, works out with a personal trainer. Dennis walks the beach for exercise. They both volunteer at the Episcopal church and are active with the Vero Beach Museum of Art, for which they've chaired two major events. Doris studies painting there as well. Dennis helps out at the Salvation Army, both on an advisory board and as one of many Christmas bell ringers.

They travel frequently, visiting their daughter and her family in Colorado, sometimes making the journey on their Honda Goldwing motorcycle. Other 2002 trips included a sailing trip on the Long Island Sound, two months in Ireland, trekking and sailing in Vietnam and Hong Kong and a cruise on the World ResidenSea along the West Coast. In between Dennis sailed with friends in a Caribbean race from Norfolk, VA, to Tortola, British Virgin Islands.

They don't foresee leaving anytime soon, although they never say never. "We always said in our golden years we're going to live on an island somewhere," Dennis says. "We have a couple on our list to think about later."

To those contemplating a move to Vero Beach, retirees who already have say it's a good choice for people who are active and plan to stay that way. "A lot of people are from someplace else, so I think they're kind of looking for people to socialize with," says Mary Ann Collins. She says that makes it easy to find new friends.

Evelyn Mayerson recommends getting involved in church and a club or organization, such as the local theater, art museum or botanical garden. "All you need is a smile on your face and a willingness to participate," she says. ●

Waynesville, North Carolina

Retreat to this North Carolina town tucked between the Great Smoky Mountains and a national forest

By Jim Kerr

From an overlook on the Blue Ridge Parkway in western North Carolina, the town of Waynesville peeps through the summer greenery a few miles north and more than 2,000 feet below. In fall, church spires protrude through maples and oaks dressed up in riotous color, and in winter, white, powdery snow dusts the tops of barns and the rolling hillsides, sparkling under sunny skies.

The dramatic changes make Waynesville a town for all seasons. Spring brings wildflowers and dogwood blossoms as nearby ski slopes close for the year, and warm weather ushers in a trickle of tourists that will become a river of lowlanders beating the heat in the months of July and August.

Nestled into a high valley at 2,713 feet, Waynesville shops, galleries, restaurants and other businesses open with the mountain laurel and rhododendron. Tourists and other patrons, including a sizable retiree community, stroll Main Street and take up positions on numerous benches to read, chat and watch the world go by on the town's brick sidewalks.

What with a 1932-era neoclassical courthouse, brick storefronts and streets, it could be Main Street USA half a century ago, except for today's headlines blaring from the news racks in front of the town's open-air news and magazine store, and the stoplight backup of shiny new SUVs and pickups with oversized wheels. Waynesville is today a rural enclave whose established popularity as a tourist retreat and retiree haven seems more like a good fit than an incongruity, even though the area is still relatively unknown compared with other mountain destinations.

"We never saw Waynesville or knew it existed until the last night of our weeklong search of the area," says Jack Surfus, who, with his wife, Judy, moved here from Fort Wayne, IN, five years ago. "It fit what we wanted, which was to be in the mountains in a climate without severe changes."

It doesn't normally get above the low 80s in the summer, nor colder than 20

Population: About 10,000 in town, 57,000 in Haywood County.

Location: At an elevation of 2,658 feet in western North Carolina, bordered on the northwest by Smoky Mountains National Park, to the south and east by the Nantahala and Pisgah national forests, and Balsam Mountains on the west.

Climate:

	High	Low
January	47	23
July	82	58

Average relative humidity: About 60%

Rain: 46 inches

Snow: 12 inches

Cost of living: Below the national average

Average housing cost: Average sale price of a home in August 2005 was $205,135, up from $184,318 during the same period in 2004, with sales covering a wide variety of homes in Haywood County.

Sales tax: 7%

Sales tax exemptions: Prescription drugs, eyeglasses, some medical supplies and most services.

State income tax: For married couples filing jointly, graduated from 6% of taxable income up to $21,250, to $14,537.50 plus 8.25% of amounts over $200,000. For single filers, graduated from 6% of income up to $12,750, to $8,722.50 plus 8.25% of amounts over $120,000.

Income tax exemptions: Social Security and Railroad Retirement Act benefits are exempt. Up to $2,000 of private retirement benefits, distributions from IRAs (up to the amount reported in federal income taxes) or up to $4,000 of government pensions may be exempt. Total deductions may not exceed $4,000 per person.

Estate tax: Applicable to taxable estates above $2 million.

Property tax: $0.42 per $100 of assessed value in the city of Waynesville and $0.61 per $100 of assessed value in the county. Tax on a $205,000 home would be about $2,112 in the city (city plus county taxes) and $1,251 in the county.

Homestead exemptions: North Carolina residents 65 and older, with combined incomes of $19,200 or less, are exempt from the first $20,000, or 50% of assessed value, whichever is greater. Home must be permanent place of residence.

Religion: There are 170 churches in the county covering a wide variety of denominations, although most are Protestant. There are two Roman Catholic churches. Lake Junaluska Assembly, a Methodist conference center, attracts thousands of people annually to meetings, retreats and other activities.

Education: Haywood Community College has 2,039 students involved in over 50 curriculum programs offering associate degrees, and 6,270 enrolled in continuing-education courses. The University of North Carolina at Asheville is 35 miles east and offers a diverse curriculum, including its Center for Creative Retirement. An Elderhostel program offers weeklong seminars for seniors. Western Carolina University is 40 miles southwest in Cullowhee.

Transportation: Interstate 40 runs through the middle of Haywood County. It connects to I-26 from the South Carolina coast, I-75 from the Midwest and U.S. Highway 441 from Atlanta and Florida. The Asheville airport is 40 minutes away with regional service and connections,

degrees in winter, where Jack and Judy live in a three-bedroom, mountainside home at 2,800 feet. But climate was only one requisite. Five years ago they made the western North Carolina circuit looking for retirement locales, spending nights in two different bed-and-breakfast inns.

"We met with realtors in Asheville (too big), Hendersonville (not enough mountains), Highlands and Cashiers (too expensive) and Dillsboro (too touristy)," Jack says. "The last night of our trip, the real estate agent brought us to this house." It's a rustic, three-bedroom cedar home with an overhanging deck, steep woodsy back yard and mountain view. Three weeks later Jack came back, looked around a bit more and made the owners an offer somewhat lower than their asking price, but good enough to cement a lasting friendship between the two couples.

The purchase also sparked a whirlwind time for Jack and Judy, who were both divorced when they met in 1997 through personal ads in the Fort Wayne

newspaper. In less than a month, they got married, retired from their jobs and moved. When they closed on the house in July 1998, they saw downtown Waynesville for the first time.

Shopping and churches turned out to be minutes away from their new house, as were good restaurants and even job opportunities. Jack, 70, a former general manager of a cheese company who hates to be idle, took a job delivering bread for a bakery two days a week and another part-time position as a clerk in a health food store. Judy, 65, a former medical secretary, does volunteer work for her church's Open Door soup kitchen and in the Haywood Regional Medical Center's surgery ward. They have two rambunctious golden retrievers and have formed a pet-sitting company called Critter Care, minding pets for others.

"The beauty of retirement," says Jack, "is not doing anything you don't want to do or being tied down to a schedule. Even with jobs, I work on other things, like my landscaping, when and where I want to do it."

Finding Waynesville in a roundabout or serendipitous way is not unusual. It may be the largest town in the county, with 10,000 inhabitants, and the Haywood County seat, but the area has always been somewhat off the beaten track. Forty-six miles of the Blue Ridge Parkway loop around the valley to the south, and mountain ranges border Haywood County's 546 square miles on all sides. Nineteen peaks within the county tower more than 6,000 feet, and Great Smoky Mountains National Park, the most-visited park in the United States, lies just north. They are all part of the Appalachian mountain chain, the oldest on Earth, dating back 500 million years.

Cherokee Indians, who broke away from the Iroquois of the Great Lakes, migrated to the Smokies around 1,000 A.D., and several centuries later, in 1809, Waynesville, named after Revolutionary Gen. "Mad Anthony" Wayne, was founded. It was a rough and rural area so isolated that the Civil War did not end here until a month after Robert E. Lee surrendered at Appomattox because

Waynesville, NC

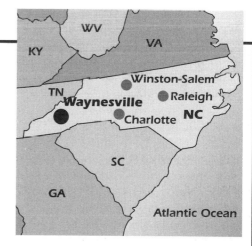

and Atlanta's Hartsfield International Airport is a two-and-a-half hour drive.

Health: Haywood Regional Medical Center has more than 100 doctors on staff practicing in more than 50 specialties. The center has 194 beds, employs 885 people and offers specialized programs in cardiology, spine surgery, sports medicine and vascular surgery. HRMC also has an urgent care center, a home care program and a 54,000-square-foot heath and fitness center.

Housing options: A wide variety of housing is available, from mobile homes to mansions in the mountains, hillside cedar and log homes to country club townhouses and single-family homes. While the sale price of a home has averaged between $184,000 and $205,000 over the past year, a three-bedroom, two-bath house in a good location starts at about $215,000. One-acre lots are available at an average price of $30,000, and construction starts at about $120 per square foot. Country club environments include **Waynesville Country Club**, (828) 456-3551, and **Laurel Ridge**, (800) 433-7274, where resales

start at $500,000. Two new townhouse and single-family home developments are currently under way: **Rolling Hills Estates** and **Glen Meadows of Waynesville**, (800) 419-0378, with townhouse prices starting around $200,000. Two assisted-living facilities are available, **Arrowhead Cove at Silver Bluff Village**, (828) 648-2044, and **Haywood Lodge and Retirement Center**, (828) 456-8365. Less-expensive housing is also available in three other Haywood County towns: Maggie Valley, Canton and Clyde.

Lodging: Waynesville is a popular tourist destination with more than 3,000 rooms in hotels and motels. In the center of town on Main Street, the Oak Park Inn, (828) 456-5328, has rooms for $50 to $79. Best Western-Smoky Mountain Inn, (800) 218-2121, has a scenic out-of-town location with rooms ranging from $49 to $109, including continental breakfast. There are many independent homeowners and agents renting homes, which average about $800 a week. Some in Waynesville include Carolina Mornings, (800) 770-9055; David's NC Mountain

Rentals, (877) 523-0890; and Mainstreet Realty, (800) 467-7144. B&Bs include Andon House, (800) 293-6190, from $100 a night, and Herren House, (800) 284-1932, from $110 a night, and The Swag Country Inn, (800) 789-7672, at the high end of the scale at $330 a night and up.

Information: Haywood County Chamber of Commerce, P.O. Drawer 600, Waynesville, NC 28786, (877) 456-3073, (828) 456-3021 or www.haywood-nc.com. Ask for a relocation package. Also, the Haywood County Tourist Development Authority, (800) 334-9036.

word had not filtered through the rugged mountains.

A railroad ushered in a logging and lumber industry in the 1800s, and tourism soon followed, as summer heat and humidity drove visitors to higher elevations, a practice very much in vogue today. Even though it's still less well known than other areas, the population is increasing steadily and real estate prices are rising as new residents find their way here.

In 1992, Janeen and Gene Barrett were returning to their home in suburban Toledo, OH, from a golfing trip to Myrtle Beach, SC. "We decided to take Interstate 40 through Asheville," Gene says. "We got lost looking for a subdivision and wound up in Waynesville. After that, we came back during different seasons over the next four years to see what all four were like."

"We spent a lot of time here staying at the Econo Lodge, and we already knew a lot of people before we ever moved here," he says. "We bought our lot on a cold, rainy day in January, and we knew if we liked it then, we would like it better every other time of the year."

They drew up plans for a local builder, with all living space on one floor, plus room for a basement. The three-bedroom, 1,700-foot home, located on a mountainside a few miles outside of town, is somewhat smaller than their previous 2,400-foot home, but it still has plenty of room for their combined children from previous marriages and Janeen's three grandchildren, who live in Ohio.

"My deal is, I want to see my grandchildren every three to four weeks," Janeen says. "I can get up to Ohio easily, and they love to come here to ski."

Waynesville offers something for everyone throughout the year. Winter and spring skiing at nearby Cataloochee Resort is followed by summer folk festivals, band concerts, square dances on the courthouse square, street dances, and numerous arts and crafts fairs. An enthusiastic performing arts community produces and performs plays at the 250-seat HART (Haywood Arts Repertory Theatre), and throughout the year residents enjoy a variety of good restaurants, most of which have sprung up because of the year-round tourists and new residents.

Gene, 64, a former teacher and school principal, does some substitute teaching in Waynesville and helps support his golf habit by working part time at nearby Lake Junaluska golf course, one of half a dozen public or semiprivate courses in the area. Janeen, 60, who worked for 34 years for the board of education in Rossford, OH, works with the Elderhostel program, a nonprofit organization that offers low-cost courses and seminars for seniors, and with the same church-sponsored soup kitchen where Judy Surfus volunteers.

"If you get out there," she says, "there are plenty of things to do. It's a two-way street, and you get back what you put in."

Jim and Ruth Hoyt would agree. Originally from Ohio, they moved here after living 19 years in Santa Monica, CA. Jim, who worked for a computer company, and Ruth, an elementary school teacher, both retired at age 55 in 1987, bringing along Ruth's father, who had grown up here. "My great-great-great-grandfather had settled here in 1800," Ruth says, "and I had visited many times as a child. We wanted to come back East to a four-season climate." Her 95-year-old aunt also lives here in a nursing home.

For less than a third of what they were paid for their Santa Monica home, they bought a large, sturdy house made from eight-inch-thick logs, located outside town at 3,400 feet in a development that backs up to Smoky Mountains National Park, a portion of which lies in Haywood County. Jim joined the Kiwanis Club and Ruth works with Friends of the Library, but their passion has been involvement with HART, where the couple works a weekly shift in the ticket box office during the March-to-November season. "There are no professional or paid staff except the executive director," Jim says. "It's all volunteers, and there's an amazing amount of local talent here."

A recent production of "The King and I" in the $850,000 HART theater drew rave reviews from locals, even though the actors can be found working regular jobs around the county. The economy is still largely agricultural, with about 27 percent of the work force, although the newly expanded Haywood County Regional Medical Center, with 870 staffers, is the third-largest employer.

Tourist accommodations, which include 3,000 rooms and hundreds of rental cottages, cabins and houses, attract ever-increasing numbers, and real estate prices have climbed more than 25 percent in the past decade. Prices tend to be somewhat lower in three other Haywood County towns — Maggie Valley, Clyde and Canton, all considerably smaller than Waynesville.

"A possible downside to living here," says Gene Barrett, "is the fact that this was a vacation spot for us for so many years. Now we have a house and a yard, and the whole perspective has changed. Maybe that's why we painted our front door the same color as the one in the Econo Lodge."

Other newcomers have simply jumped into the tourism industry themselves, taking on far more responsibility than the average retiree homeowner. On July 4, 1995, Don and Ann Rothermel found themselves in downtown Waynesville staring at a flyer in a real estate office window that said: "Needs some work." The two-story house depicted, a 1902 post-Victorian built by a lumber mill owner, "was a total disaster," Ann says. When Don insisted they see it, she refused to get out of the car. Then they bought it. Don, 65, an industrial model maker and contractor, and Ann, 63, an interior decorator and designer, quit their jobs in Orlando, FL, and moved up.

"The house had been vacant for eight years," Don remembers. "It took two years for it to warm up, and it had every varmint the country had to offer living in it."

In March 1996, they moved in with a space heater, slept in sleeping bags in the former "library," and proceeded to strip the dilapidated house to the bare bones. After months of relentless work and a remarkable transformation, the old house opened as the Andon House Bed & Breakfast. While the couple continues to pour their efforts into running and maintaining the business, they also get involved in the community art culture, sing in the church choir and entertain family and friends in the restored house minutes from downtown.

Like any neighborhood in or around Waynesville, vacant lots are filling here with new houses, and even though white lights in the night sky appear to be low-hanging stars, they are really houses along the mountainsides. And every year the dots of light increase. ●

Whidbey Island, Washington

Retirees find a place to pursue their dreams on this pretty Pacific Northwest island

By Stanton H. Patty

Up a country road on Washington state's Whidbey Island, there are clusters of purple heather, a ramshackle barn that may not last another winter, and the studio of one of the Pacific Northwest's celebrated artists. There you might find Georgia Gerber shaping a life-size sculpture of a little girl dancing with a playful bear and other critters.

"What's the story?" asks a visitor. "Whatever you want it to be," Georgia replies. "Let your imagination go."

Dr. Herb McDonald understands that invitation. The retired cardiologist, felled by heart disease a few years ago, has found a new life on this quiet island, only an hour or so from Seattle's smothering traffic. Now he is writing short stories about what he calls "slices of life" on Whidbey Island. Many of the stories involve the four dogs that share a saltwater-view home with Herb and his wife, Susan, a retired nurse. "I've always enjoyed creative writing," says the 65-year-old physician. "Now I have time to do it."

Another couple, Dick Curdy and Lynn Geri, also followed a dream to Whidbey Island. They moved to the island to open a bed-and-breakfast inn. Dick, 65, had been a high school English teacher for 24 years in Bellevue, a Seattle suburb. Lynn, 61, worked in counseling with several corporations. "We're having a great time, meeting wonderful people who come to stay with us," Lynn says.

Also having a wonderful time are Ed and Marie Parr, who conducted a methodical search of Northwest communities before deciding to settle on Whidbey Island. "We looked at many places with a critical eye," Marie recalls. The Parrs had decided in advance that their retirement spot should be near a major airport (Seattle-Tacoma International, in this case), have adequate medical facilities (Whidbey General Hospital), offer a first-rate golf course (Useless Bay Golf and Country Club) — and be more or less snow-free.

"I shoveled snow when we lived in Colorado. Now I don't have to do that anymore," says Ed, 74, a real estate consultant and developer in Berthoud, CO, north of Boulder, before he retired. Marie, 74, was a full-time mother of five and also held a real estate license.

Whidbey Island, anchored in Puget Sound just north of Seattle, is a favorite weekend retreat for the high-voltage Microsoft crowd. They come to browse the island's country towns and gardens, to go sea kayaking and beachcombing, to find blissful serenity. And some return to stay for good.

Whidbey's dazzling scenery, its mild climate and the appeal of slow-tempo living have peopled the 45-mile-long island with painters, potters, sculptors, writers — and now dozens of contented retired couples. "This is a place where people care about each other," says Georgia Gerber.

Georgia gave the island one of its top attractions, a beloved sculpture in the seaside village of Langley. "Boy and Dog" is the title. In the scene, a lifelike youth, in bronze, leans on a railing, daydreaming and looking toward distant, snow-streaked mountains. There is a bronze dog at his feet. Once someone left a leather leash beside the bronze dog, and there was speculation that it might have belonged to a visitor's pet that had died.

Georgia's eyes mist when told about the leash. The dog portrayed in the sculpture was her longtime companion. "I still miss him," says Georgia, who moved from Seattle in 1982 to build her studio on the island.

Langley, near the southern tip of Whidbey, is the magnet for most visitors aboard this seahorse-shaped island. The town of only about 1,000 residents offers stylish inns, art galleries and award-winning restaurants — all within one cozy square mile. "It's all about tranquility here," says Karen Davis, assistant manager at Langley's Saratoga Inn. "We don't hear traffic. We hear birds and squirrels and chipmunks. We're on 'island time.' Things move a little slower here, and we like it that way."

So do Whidbey Island's retirees. Marie Parr tells of daily breakfast gatherings at Sapori, a Langley cafe and bakery. "We laugh a lot," she says. "We're all retired authors, artists, musicians, business executives, lawyers, engineers and airline pilots. It's a wonderful mix. We share experiences, and then we go our own ways."

The Parrs discovered Whidbey during their first visit to the Northwest. They rented a car in Seattle and went exploring for a possible retirement site. While Ed Parr searched for his golf course, Marie was on the lookout for an easy-maintenance home. Marie had been injured seriously in an automobile accident before moving to Whidbey Island, and the crash caused her to give up golf — and their 40-acre ranch in Colorado. "The ranch was too much to handle," she says. "It was time for a change of lifestyle."

Once the decision was made to move to the Langley area, they bought and remodeled a two-bedroom home with a smashing view of Saratoga Passage, the scenic waterway between Whidbey and neighboring Camano Island. Do they feel isolated on an island where residents depend mostly on ferries to reach the mainland? "Not really," Ed says. "We have a good hospital and clinics here. If it were an extreme emergency, we could be airlifted to hospitals in Seattle."

The Parrs have traveled extensively in Europe and are planning a trip to Scotland and Italy. Ed has his heart set on playing Scotland's historic St. Andrews golf course. But they always are eager to return home to Whidbey Island. "This is just a very nice place," says Ed.

Dr. Herb McDonald, the cardiologist, was advised to retire about four years ago after undergoing coronary artery bypass surgery in El Paso, TX. His wife, Susan, then was working as a nurse in El Paso. "It was time, what with the stress and long hours," Herb says.

Herb knew Seattle from his days as a medical student at the University of Washington, and he also had attended school in Spokane in eastern Washington, so they decided to settle in the Northwest. They focused first on Washington's Olympic Peninsula communities, including Port Townsend and Sequim, before choosing Whidbey Island.

"One thing we knew for sure is that we didn't want to be in a big city," says Susan. "And we didn't want to live in a retirement community. We wanted to be in a place that had kids and adults, people younger and older than we."

The McDonalds reside in Coupeville, a picturesque Victorian town in the central section of Whidbey Island. Coupeville was founded in 1852 by a sea captain

Whidbey Island, WA

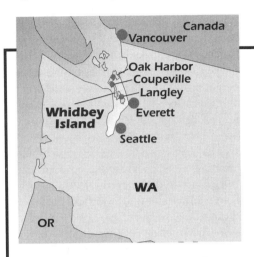

Population: 79,252 in Island County, which includes both Whidbey Island and neighboring Camano Island.

Location: In Puget Sound, about 35 miles north of Seattle by highway and ferry. There are three incorporated cities on Whidbey Island — Langley in the South Whidbey area, Coupeville in Central Whidbey, and Oak Harbor in North Whidbey.

Climate: High Low
January 46 36
July 73 51

Average relative humidity: 40%-90%, depending on location.

Rain: 18-35 inches, depending on location. Whidbey benefits from being sheltered in the "rain shadow" of the Olympic Mountains.

Snow: Rare

Cost of living: Slightly higher than average due to transportation costs.

Average housing cost: $277,950 in Island County.

Sales tax: 8.3%

Sales tax exemptions: Groceries and prescription drugs.

State income tax: None

Intangibles tax: None

Estate tax: Applicable to taxable estates over $2 million.

Property tax: Averages about 1% of assessed value. Tax on a home valued at $277,950 would be about $2,780.

Homestead exemption: Available to low-income senior citizens and disabled persons.

Religion: Whidbey Island has 64 churches representing many denominations.

Education: There are no four-year colleges or universities on Whidbey Island. Skagit Valley College, a community college, has campuses in Clinton (South Whidbey). Four-year degrees are offered through Chapman University's Academic Center at Whidbey Naval Air Station.

Transportation: Whidbey Island is served by Washington State Ferries from the mainland port of Mukilteo north of Seattle, and from Port Townsend on Washington's Olympic Peninsula. Ferries from Mukilteo call at Clinton in South Whidbey. Crossing time is about 30 minutes. Ferries operating from Port Townsend call at Keystone in Central Whidbey. Crossing time is about 45 minutes. The Deception Pass Bridge at the north end of the island, near Oak Harbor, connects Whidbey Island to Washington's highway system. Harbor Air offers scheduled commuter service between Oak Harbor and Seattle-Tacoma International Airport. Flight time is about 25 minutes. Island Transit, a free public bus system, operates on all of Whidbey's main roads.

Health: The 51-bed Whidbey General Hospital in Coupeville (Central Whidbey) has a 24-hour emergency room. Specialties include surgery, critical care, home health care, childbirth, physical and sports therapy, cancer care and diagnostic imaging services. There also are community clinics in Oak Harbor (North Whidbey) and Langley (South Whidbey). In addition, Naval Hospital Oak Harbor offers inpatient and outpatient services for active-duty military personnel and their families and for eligible retired military personnel and their eligible family members. Paramedic-staffed ambulances serve all points on Whidbey Island.

Housing options: Most island retirees live in single-family homes. There are few apartments for low- to moderate-income residents. A popular upscale development is Useless Bay Colony near Langley on the west side of the island. The colony has a limited number of condominiums, with prices beginning in the $200,000s. Single-family homes are priced from $319,000 to over $1 million. Features include a golf course and tennis courts.

Visitor lodging: Langley area: Harbour Inn, $79-102, (360) 331-6900, and Saratoga Inn, $115-$275, (360) 221-5801. Coupeville area: Coupeville Inn, $77-$135, (360) 678-6668 or (800) 247-6162, and Anchorage Inn, $85-$140, (877) 230-1313. Oak Harbor area: Acorn Motor Inn, $44-$89, (800) 280-6646.

Information: Langley Chamber of Commerce, 208 Anthes Ave., P.O. Box 403, Langley, WA 98260, (888) 232-2080, (360) 221-6765 or www.southwhidbey chamber.com. Central Whidbey Chamber of Commerce, P.O. Box 152, Coupeville, WA 98239, (360) 678-5434 or www.centralwhidbeychamber.com. Oak Harbor Chamber of Commerce, 32630 Highway 20, Oak Harbor, WA 98277, (360) 675-3755 or www.oakharborchamber.org.

who made his fortune by shipping the Northwest's tall timber to booming California. Coupeville's old-fashioned main drag, Front Street, is a favorite setting with Hollywood moviemakers. Celebrities and other travelers gather there to dine on just-harvested mussels at Toby's Tavern.

The McDonalds built a 2,300-square-foot house on 10 acres that overlook Penn Cove, where the tasty mussels are grown. The property is decked with madrona trees and Douglas firs and stretches down to the shore of the salt-water cove. "We have six children, so we also built a guest house," Susan says.

The McDonalds describe Coupeville as a vibrant community with a rich cultural menu and volunteer organizations that welcome newcomers. Susan is a board member of Concerts on the Cove, a group that sponsors a summer series of musical events running the scale from symphony to bluegrass. Always open to ideas, Concerts on the Cove even staged a rock concert for students at Coupeville High School's Performing Arts Center.

Meanwhile, when he isn't writing short stories or meeting with fellow members of a local group of writers, Herb serves on Whidbey Island's Community Health Advisory Board. The board's aim, he says, is to "stay ahead" of problems. Current projects include support for positive programs involving young persons and seniors.

Whidbey Island's only public hospital is the 51-bed Whidbey General Hospital in Coupeville. There also is a military hospital at Naval Air Station Whidbey Island, adjacent to the city of Oak Harbor near the northern end of the island. Herb McDonald rates Whidbey General as "good and getting better." He is especially pleased with the hospital's Patient First program that gives patients more involvement in treatment decisions.

Susan McDonald was a nursing supervisor at Whidbey General for a while after moving from El Paso, then retired to begin a new career in real estate. Much of the McDonalds' travel schedule involves trips to visit their children. They also go "off island" to Seattle about once a month to attend theater performances and to shop at Seattle's famed Pike Place Market with its array of fresh produce and seafood.

Last fall Susan traveled to Cuba with the Seattle Peace Chorus. "It was a fabulous trip, a real awakening," she says. The McDonalds say they have no regrets regarding their decision to snuggle into Whidbey Island. "Every time we come home, we know in our hearts that we made an excellent choice," says Susan.

Lynn Geri and Dick Curdy are the proud proprietors of the Brierly Inn, a bed-and-breakfast inn near the South Whidbey town of Clinton. Vehicle and passenger ferries commute between Clinton and the mainland city of Mukilteo north of Seattle. "It was nothing but a brier patch when we first looked at the property in 1998," says Dick in explaining how the inn got its name.

Lynn and Dick, partners for 14 years, bought that brier patch along with a 16-year-old Tudor-style manor house on five acres and opened their B&B. It's a peaceful place, they say, with towering cedars, meadows and a garden bright with rhododendrons, roses and other blossoms.

It's quite a change for Dick, the former schoolteacher, and Lynn, the former corporate counselor. "We were looking around for a business to buy," Lynn recalls. "There was a deli for sale on the island, but that didn't interest us. Then we found this beautiful house in a real-estate flier. Sometimes now we soak in the guest hot tub and ask ourselves: 'Do you know how lucky we are?' We just love it here."

The couple also considered Washington's sunny San Juan Islands before deciding on Whidbey. But, says Lynn, they wanted to be closer to their Seattle-area children — and they were concerned about being wholly dependent on ferries that serve the San Juans. That holiday archipelago has no highway connection to the Washington mainland. Whidbey Island has ferry service between Clinton and nearby Mukilteo, and a ferry that operates between Keystone on Whidbey Island and Port Townsend on the Olympic Peninsula. But there also is a highway connection to the mainland by way of the Deception Pass Bridge on the north end of Whidbey.

Now Dick spends quite a bit of time in the Brierly Inn's garden. He became a master gardener after moving to Whidbey Island, taking 65 hours of classes offered by Washington State University and the Island County Extension Service. Now, between chores at the inn, he volunteers at the acclaimed Meerkerk Rhododendron Gardens near the Whidbey community of Freeland and helps neighbors solve their gardening problems during clinics at weekend farm markets.

"It's a different tempo for us now," says Lynn Geri. "And we are counting our blessings every day." ●

Williamsburg, Virginia

Colonial heritage and college-town appeal draw retirees to the Virginia Peninsula

By Mary Ann Hemphill

It's not all fife and drums and horse-drawn carriages in Williamsburg. Although the heart of the city is Colonial Williamsburg, a major tourist attraction, the community also is a vibrant, rapidly growing town, home of the College of William and Mary and an area increasingly attractive to retirees.

The heritage of a Colonial past, the energy of a college and the warmth of a small town make an ideal blend. For Sandie and Tom House, it was love at first sight. Longtime residents of the Washington, DC, area, the Houses had thought of retiring to the West Coast. But before making the move, they wanted to see more of the sights on the East Coast.

In September 1987, they went to Williamsburg, spent the weekend in Ford's Colony, a planned community that offered hotel accommodations — and bought a house. They moved to Williamsburg on a part-time basis later that year, then full time in 1989 after Tom's retirement. Tom, 76, had been the president of the Frozen Food Institute, and Sandie, 58, was a dietician in the Navy Reserve when they moved to Williamsburg.

Mac and Marty MacDonald's decision was more deliberate. Mac, 75, was head of government sales activities for General Motors. Marty, 73, had worked part time in a nursery. They'd lived in Potomac, MD, for 14 years and had considered Maryland's Eastern Shore for retirement. They also had looked all along Route 17 north of Hilton Head, always mindful of their desire to live in a small college town.

Passing through Williamsburg in January 1987, Mac picked up the local newspaper while Marty browsed the shops. "I saw an ad for the Kingsmill area and called the real estate office there. Once we received the material, I told Marty, 'We've got to check this out. It looks terrific.'"

They visited Kingsmill and Mac was instantly convinced that it was where they should retire. "It was an affair of the

Population: 12,922 in Williamsburg (8% of the residents are ages 50-64, while approximately 12% are age 65 or better). Population in James City County is 41,370 (15% are ages 50-64 while approximately 11% are age 65 or better).

Location: On gently rolling hills of the Virginia Peninsula, midway between Norfolk (45 miles away) and Richmond (50 miles). It's 150 miles from Williamsburg to Washington, DC.

Climate:

	High	Low
January	48	31
July	83	65

Average relative humidity: 70%

Rain: 45.22 inches

Snow: 7.6 inches

Cost of living: About average.

Average housing cost: $350,080

Sales tax: 5% (4% state and 1% local). Groceries are taxed at a reduced rate of 2.5%.

Sales tax exemptions: Medicine, some medical equipment, home heating fuels, utility services and most other services. Reduced sales tax rate on groceries.

State income tax: For married couples filing jointly and single filers, the rate is graduated from 2% of taxable income up to $3,000 to 5.75% on amounts over $17,000.

Income tax exemptions: Social Security benefits are exempt. There is an $800 personal exemption for residents age 65 or older. There is a $12,000 deduction per person for residents 65 and older. (May not claim age deduction exemption if also claiming subtraction for disability income.)

Estate tax: On estates over $2 million, Virginia imposes a "pick-up tax" portion of the federal tax. The Virginia estate tax has been repealed for deaths after July 1, 2007.

Property tax: In the city of Williamsburg, $5.40 per $1,000 of assessed value. James City County, $7.85 per $1,000 of assessed value. Homes are assessed at 100 percent of market value. Tax on a $50,080 home would be $1,890 in the city and $2,748 in the county. Personal property tax for cars: In the city of Williamsburg, $35 per $1,000 of assessed valuation. James City County, $40 per $1,000 of assessed valuation.

Homestead exemption: Low-income persons 65 and older may qualify for exemptions in property tax rates.

Religion: There are more than 40 churches of varying denominations, as well as one synagogue.

Education: Founded by Royal Charter in 1693, the College of William and Mary is the second-oldest continuous institution of higher education in the country after Harvard.

Transportation: Williamsburg is just off Interstate 64. Amtrak serves Williamsburg with a train from Washington, DC, and the nearest airports are in Richmond and Norfolk as well as a small but fast-growing airport in newport News. James City County Transit provides local bus service for $1.25 per ride (transfer fee is 25 cents), and passengers over 60 can ride for half-price. Door-to-door Paratransit service, $2 one way or $4 round-trip, is available to anyone who can't ride a regular bus because of disability.

Health: The nearest hospital is the 139-bed Williamsburg Community Hospital. A new hospital, Sentara Williamsburg Regional Medical Center, opened in 2006. Specialized care is available at the

heart, not of the head," Mac says. Marty took a little longer to decide it was the right choice. "I had not considered a gated community or a golf area. I had played golf maybe once in my life," says Marty, who now plays twice a week.

Golf is a major attraction in Williamsburg. Golf Digest ranked Williamsburg 24th among the 50 greatest golf destinations in the world in 2000. There are almost 20 public and private courses, several of them in three planned communities.

Tom House hadn't played golf in 25 years, and Sandie never had played. Yet, "we said that golf would be the deciding factor," Sandie says. "If we liked it, we would stay. Otherwise, we would sell the Williamsburg house and move elsewhere." Obviously, golf clicked.

"Once we were here, we happily discovered the other benefits of the area," Tom says. "We liked the atmosphere of a college town, the ease of attending a football game, and the historical aspects of Colonial Williamsburg, Jamestown and Yorktown."

The many facets of Williamsburg's personality come together in Merchants Square, a two-block area (one block closed to cars) of shops, restaurants and outdoor dining patios. Here you'll find tourists resting on benches and students jogging, grabbing a sandwich or stocking up at the college bookstore. Adding to the mix are local residents shopping, dining or enjoying a summer evening concert.

In one direction from Market Square is Colonial Williamsburg, and in the other is the College of William and Mary, one of the top-ranked small public universities in the country. The college educated U.S. presidents Thomas Jefferson, James Monroe and John Tyler.

Colonial Williamsburg Historic Area ("CW" in local jargon) is 301 acres with 88 restored and scores of reconstructed buildings where character actors and talented craftspeople bring 18th-century Virginia to life. It is one point of the Historic Triangle, which also includes Jamestown, site of North America's first permanent settlement in 1607, and Yorktown, where the final major battle of the American Revolution was fought in 1781. Williamsburg also is well-located for access to other attractions.

Dudley Hughes, who relocated to Williamsburg in 1985, notes that the town has "access to the beach and to the mountains." Her husband, Tommy, adds, "It's three hours to Wintergreen for skiing, an hour to Virginia Beach for swimming, and two hours to Washington, DC." Norfolk and Richmond each are an hour away.

Making new friends was not a problem for Tommy and Dudley. They were part of a group of 12 couples who eventually relocated to Williamsburg from Chappaqua, NY, where Tommy had been vice president of sales for General Foods. Tommy, 83, and Dudley, 80, visited friends who had moved to Kingsmill. They liked the area and the people they met, so they bought a lot in 1983 and started building their home in 1985.

Williamsburg, VA

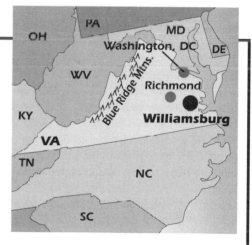

570-bed Riverside Regional Medical Center in Newport News, which is affiliated with the Medical College of Virginia in Richmond.

Housing options: At **Kingsmill**, (800) 392-0026, prices for single-family homes start in the $300,000s and go up to about $2 million. Condos and townhomes start in the mid $200,000s and go up to $1,395,000. In **Ford's Colony**, townhomes begin at $300,000 and single-family courtyard homes start at $429,000. Home sites, depending upon their size and location, range from $175,000 to $1,500,000, (800) 334-6033. (Check out the cost-of-living calculator at www.fordscolony.com.) **Governor's Land** has no condos or townhouses. Homes range from $557,000 to more than $1 million and lots begin at $155,000, (800) 633-5965. **Brickshire**, (888) 655-5263, has homesites with views of the golf course, lake or wooded scenery from the $110,000s and custom homes starting in the $300,000s. Contact real estate agents regarding resales at **Counselors Close** or **Port Anne**, neighborhoods located near **Colonial Williamsburg**. Several communities offer a mix of independent and assisted-living facilities. The newest is **WindsorMeade**, (877) 582-6385. Built on 106 acres, it will have 96 independent living villas and 85 apartments, as well as private licensed nursing beds and a memory support section. Its community center has bed-and-breakfast accommodations for visiting guests. **Williamsburg Landing**, (800) 554-5517, has cottage neighborhoods for independent living, assisted living and memory-impaired illnesses facilities and a 58-bed nursing center. A fitness and wellness center will open there in fall of 2006. **Chambrel at Williamsburg**, (800) 868-4654, also offers independent and assisted living. **Patriot's Colony**, (800) 716-9000, is an active retirement and assisted-living facility for retired military officers and senior government officials.

Visitor lodging: More than 10,000 rooms are available in local resorts, hotels, motels and bed-and-breakfast inns. For reservations, call the Williamsburg Hotel and Motel Association at (800) 899-9462. Colonial Williamsburg's Colonial Homes, which are former taverns, kitchens, offices and shops in the historic area, feature antique and reproduction furnishings and 21st-century amenities such as air conditioning and cable TV, $145-$450. The Woodlands Hotel and Suites is a new 300-room, contemporary hotel near the Colonial Williamsburg Visitors Center, $78-$195. All accommodations in Colonial Williamsburg can be booked at (800) 447-8679.

Information: Williamsburg Area Convention and Visitors Bureau, P.O. Box 3585, Williamsburg, VA 23187-3585, (800) 368-6511 or www.visitwilliamsburg.com.

Marty MacDonald knew "not a soul" when she moved to Williamsburg. Mac's interest in golf resulted in their first friends locally, and Marty joined the Kingsmill Women's Club, as most newcomers do. Marty calls their wide range of friends "just a great bunch of people." Sandie House says, "Ford Colony's Newcomers Club immediately plunges you into the social scene. Add an activity or two, and suddenly your dance card is full. If you're bored, it's your choice."

Kingsmill-on-the-James, Ford's Colony and Governor's Land at Two Rivers are planned golf course communities with households of families and retirees. Kingsmill is 2,900 acres of gently rolling hills, woods and ponds along the James River. Five minutes from Colonial Williamsburg, Kingsmill is both a prime residential area and a world-class resort. It has three golf courses, including the River Course, which hosts the October Michelob Championship at Kingsmill on the PGA Tour.

After several trips to look at the options in Kingsmill, the MacDonalds bought a single-family home in 1987. Eleven years later it was, in Mac's words, "time to get rid of the lawnmower," so they moved to a townhouse in the Wareham's Point neighborhood in Kingsmill.

Both the Hugheses and the MacDonalds extol Kingsmill. "We're just spoiled rotten here. We live in a beautiful setting with the bonuses of three golf courses, tennis, marina, restaurants and sports club with its fitness and spa facilities," Marty says. As for Tommy and Dudley Hughes, they moved 20 times in their first 21 years of marriage. "Of all the places we have lived," Tommy says, "Kingsmill people are the best. They go out of their way to be nice."

The Houses are equally ecstatic about Ford's Colony. Sandie is convinced that "there is no place we would rather live than Ford's Colony, and all of our friends here agree." Their house has a breathtaking panoramic view over a lake to the golf course.

But Sandie notes that you don't have to be a golfer to enjoy life at Ford's Colony. A multitude of special-interest groups includes calligraphy, tennis, computers, biking, travel and gardening. "If your particular interest is not among these, then let it be known and we'll probably start offering it," Sandie says.

Many cite the impressive Caring Neighbors program. Volunteers register to provide various services, including transportation for medical services, loan of cribs or rollaway beds for visiting grandchildren or guests, an information network on medical conditions and meal preparation for those needing help because of a family illness or death.

Ford's Colony has three golf courses, jogging trails, a 200-acre wildlife preserve and a AAA five-star restaurant on its 2,800 acres. There are courtyard homes, townhomes, and custom homes in Georgian, Colonial, Federal and Greek Revival styles.

With just 734 home sites on 71,482 acres, Governor's Land is less densely developed than the other two planned communities. About 60 percent of this land will remain open, and there are four miles of riverfront on the James and Chicahominy rivers. In addition to the private country club with its golf privileges on the Tom Fazio-designed course, plus tennis courts, swimming pools and dining facilities, there is the Two Rivers Harbor and Yacht Club with private boat slips.

Homes close to Colonial Williamsburg's historical area are generally very desirable. According to the Virginia Association of Realtors, the average sales price in the Williamsburg area was $350,080 in 2005.

Set in the Virginia countryside near Williamsburg is Brickshire, a golf community tucked amid gently rolling, wooded hills. It features an 18-hole Curtis Strange course, swimming and tennis, walking paths and equestrian facilities. Situated just off Interstate 64 midway between Williamsburg and Richmond, the community has homesites starting around $110,000 and custom homes from the mid $300,000s.

Colonial Williamsburg's Good Neighbor program gives local residents free admission to all sites and discounts admission tickets for friends visiting residents. Like most newcomers, the Hugheses "did all there is to do at first," but they still like to return with their guests. Marty MacDonald can't get enough of CW's gardens and Abby Aldrich Rockefeller Folk Art Museum.

Under the auspices of the College of William and Mary, the Christopher Wren Association offers a wide range of classes to those over 55 years of age. Sandie says she is "always taking something here," most recently classes on Theodore Roosevelt and on the 2002 Congressional elections. The $75-per-semester fee covers attendance in two courses. Marty has signed up for classes in art history and literature and takes advantage of William and Mary's program of letting those who are over 60 and who have lived in Virginia for a year audit classes at no charge.

Williamsburg's cultural scene is rapidly expanding. In addition to the folk art museum, Colonial Williamsburg has the DeWitt Wallace Decorative Arts Museum. The Muscarelle Museum of Art at William and Mary has permanent and changing exhibits of fine paintings and sculpture. The music scene is especially rich, including the 80-voice Choral Guild and the Williamsburg Symphonia. Each presents three major concerts during the year.

Tommy and Dudley Hughes have season tickets to the Williamsburg Players. "They are all local talent, and they are outstanding," Tommy says. Marty MacDonald volunteers at This Century Gallery, which sells works in all media by local artists as well as those from outside Virginia. Classes at this gallery inspired her husband, Mac, to resume acrylic painting.

These retirees also work seriously at keeping fit. All except Dudley are golfers. The Hugheses and Marty MacDonald regularly work out at Kingsmill's sports club. Physical fitness is always on the Houses' agenda, with daily walks and extensive work in their yard.

Despite the regular fitness routines, there's sometimes a need for medical care. Dudley recently had a knee replacement. Unlike husband Tommy, who had to go to Richmond when he needed both knees replaced several years ago, Dudley was able to have this done locally, thanks to the presence of a new orthopedic surgeon in Williamsburg. Those needing major cardio procedures, such as a bypass will have brand new facilities with the 2006 opening of the Sentara Heart Hospital in Norfolk, about an hour away.

Tom House, who was hospitalized in late 2001, praises the Williamsburg Community Hospital. "All was expertly done, with up-to-date care and excellent professionalism," he says.

Shopping opportunities, however, are limited despite an abundance of outlet malls. "Coming from DC, where we had everything, shopping in Williamsburg was a shock," Sandie says. Marty echoes Sandie's opinion. "There's no department store. We have to go to Richmond or Norfolk for the better stores," she says. Dudley handles the problem by doing a lot of catalog shopping. "There is no place around Merchants Square to get ordinary things, such as a pair of pajamas," she says.

Dining is a mixed scene with, as Marty MacDonald says, "lots of tourist places and just a few good restaurants." But in his years here, Tom House has noticed a big improvement, with more upscale restaurants opening.

Of Williamsburg's four seasons, summer, with its heat and high humidity, is the toughest — especially for the Hugheses. But Sandie House loves the heat and humidity. "It beats running around DC in a coat and tie in the summer," agrees her husband, Tom. "I can just put on shorts and a golf shirt." The MacDonalds escape into air-conditioning.

All agree with Mac MacDonald that growing pains are the area's biggest negative. "The traffic is getting worse, and highway construction is not keeping up with the growth because the state government is suffering a budget crunch. We worry where the water is coming from," Mac says.

But there are more than enough attractions to offset any drawbacks, local retirees say. Sandie House loves the area's beauty — "the water, the trees, the architecture."

"The cost of living is less than many other places, certainly less than New York," says Tommy Hughes. "It's a wonderful place to retire," says Tommy, who remembers when Williamsburg was "a sleepy little Southern town."

"Despite the growth, this is still a beautiful town," says Dudley Hughes. "Come on down — you'll love it." ●

Wimberley, Texas

Enjoy small-town flavor amid the hills of central Texas

By Nina Stewart

Outside of Austin, nestled at the edge of the beautiful Texas Hill Country where the Cypress Creek and Blanco River converge, is the Village of Wimberley. Residents and visitors have used many names to describe this picturesque community, but "heaven" is usually somewhere in the sentence.

In the 1850s the town was settled around a mill that did business with the extensive local ranching community. It was named after the mill's third owner, Pleasant Wimberley. In the 1900s, Wimberley's beauty was a haven known mostly to artists, locals and a few Houston and Dallas urbanites seeking respite from the big cities. Now it is home to a growing population of retirees and young families seeking excellent schools for their children.

"It combines the best of both worlds," says Dave Estey, 67. "We are close to Austin, San Marcos and San Antonio, and yet here in the hills, you can own property and not see signs of civilization." Congestion is what fueled the decision by Dave and his wife, Vicki, 61, to move to Wimberley from San Diego, CA, 18 months ago.

"I retired from the City of San Diego where I handled asset management," says Dave, "and Vicki was a health care administrator. We made a list of what we needed in a community and made some trips to such states as Colorado and Idaho. We were very deliberate about our search."

"We compared our list of priorities with a number of different communities," Vicki says. "We wanted good medical facilities and a nearby military base, since Dave is a retired Navy commander. We also wanted a community of highly educated people, and yet we wanted to have some land where we could feel as if we were at a retreat. We had a good feeling about Wimberley. The people are so genuine and friendly," she says. "We knew right away this was home."

The Esteys first learned of Wimberley from a friend who was working as a builder in the area. Their friend also was looking for the perfect retirement place and had accompanied the Esteys on other trips. The Esteys spent three weeks in Wimberley checking out the community. During that time they bought six acres known as Hilltop Place. Then they built a home for their elderly parents, a garage apartment for a sister and a house for themselves.

"Coming from California, land was inexpensive here," Dave says. "And also, because of the strict California regulations, we couldn't build what we have here," confirms Vicki. "We would have never gotten all of the permits in our lifetimes."

While land was inexpensive compared to California, the Esteys found the property taxes are a little higher than expected in Wimberley. Like many Californians, the Esteys had become accustomed to Proposition 13, which keeps the property taxes down in that state. "But, since there is no state income tax in Texas and other costs here are low, the increased property taxes are offset in other ways," Dave says.

"Wimberley is a community for active retirees," Vicki says. "Mostly the population is highly educated and progressive, with many having moved here to get out of the rat race. With the hills and canyons and creeks, there is so much to do outdoors. Hiking, fishing, swimming, hunting, bird-watching — it's a place for people who love the outdoors."

"Our son is a serious biker," Dave says, "and when he comes to visit, he finds it thrilling to bike here in the home area of Lance Armstrong. He will ride 30 miles along the roads before breakfast. And our three grandchildren love it here, too."

Vicki admits the humidity took some getting used to after years of California living. "The weather can sometimes be a challenge," she says. "I wasn't used to thunderstorms. However, I've never seen so many stars, and the peace and quiet is intoxicating."

"It's also a great place to volunteer and feel like you make a difference," Dave says. Both he and Vicki volunteer on advisory boards for the city council and participate in other community activities such as a New Neighbors program.

Glen and Bobbie Fryer, 74 and 71 respectively, also left a vacation destination to move to Wimberley. "We lived in Breckenridge, CO, for 10 years before coming here in 1995," Glen says. "Before that we lived in Houston for 23 years, where I worked for Rice University and Bobbie managed a credit union.

"Breckenridge started out as quaint, but it didn't do such a great job of controlling growth. If we can manage our town's growth properly, we should be able to keep Wimberley special for generations to come," says the former chairman of Wimberley's planning commission.

Wimberley was unincorporated until the year 2000. Since the vote to incorporate, village officials have worked to pass a number of planning and zoning ordinances designed to keep the community healthy and beautiful. "Not everyone likes the new rules," Glen says. "There are a number of people who have lived here all their lives, and they don't like regulation of any kind, even if it is best for the entire community. Change is difficult. We have some lively discussions," he laughs.

The acquisition city officials are most proud of is the historic Blue Hole, one of the top 10 swimming holes in the state and considered a treasure since the days of pioneers and Native Americans who lived along the shaded, clear stream of Cypress Creek. Dreams of developing a 129-acre tract with Blue Hole into a public park, complete with a one-mile nature walk into Wimberley's shopping square, became a reality when a local landowner purchased the property on behalf of the town. A combination of fund raising, grants and donations will finance the development, and it is on track.

"Blue Hole has been a favorite camping, fishing and swimming site for generations, even though it was privately owned. It's an important recreational spot that, as a public park, will add so much to Wimberley," Glen says. "In fact, Wimberley will have more public parkland than Austin," the state's nearby capital.

Gracious river living was the main feature that Glen and Bobbie found so attractive about Wimberley. "My sister lived here before we did," says Bobbie,

"and she has a lovely river home." The Fryers bought 5.5 acres with river frontage and built a guest home first. Then they added a stunning 3,500-square-foot stone home with 1,400 square feet of wraparound porches to complete the view. Collectors of fine Southwest and Native American art, they designed their home to showcase their treasures. Their penchant for gardening is indulged by the ample landscaping and flower beds they put in.

Building and real estate costs have gone up considerably in the eight years since they finished their home. "We paid about $100 per square foot to build, and

I think it's up to about $125 per square foot to build a quality home now," says Glen. "The property taxes here are also not cheap. We pay over $10,000 a year in taxes for this property." Plus, homeowner's insurance is pricey due to litigation over mold issues several years ago.

With Wimberley's beautiful shops, Olde Town Plaza and reputation as a haven for artists and musicians, one might assume the main economic engine is tourism. But, according to Glen, business and tourism account for only about 25 percent of the town's income. "I believe construction and the furnishing of homes is the real econom-

Wimberley, TX

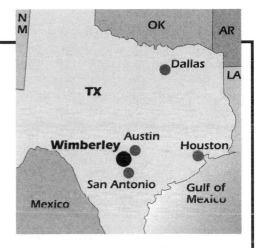

Population: 7,000 within city limits, 10,000 in the surrounding Wimberley area.

Location: Wimberley is located on Ranch Road 12, 12 miles west of Interstate 35 in south-central Hays County. It is 45 miles southwest of Austin, 60 miles northeast of San Antonio and 15 miles northwest of San Marcos.

Climate: High Low
January 60 38
July 95 71
At 1,012 feet on the edge of Edwards Plateau, Wimberley has mild winters and hot summers.

Average relative humidity: 60% in the afternoons

Rain: 37 inches per year

Snow: Trace amounts

Cost of living: Slightly above average

Average housing costs: The median housing price is $190,000, but older homes in town can be purchased for around $102,000, while large, new homes with river views can soar above $500,000.

Sales tax: 8.25%

Sales tax exemptions: Food, pharmaceuticals, certain agricultural products and equipment.

State income tax: None

Estate tax: The state eliminated its "pick-up" portion of the federal tax as of Jan. 1, 2005.

Inheritance tax: None

Property tax: $2.183 per $100 of assessed value, including school, county, road and fire district taxes. Depending

upon location, other taxing districts may apply. Taxes on a $181,000 home in Wimberley would be about $4,148, without exemptions noted below.

Homestead exemption: $15,000 for the Wimberley Independent School District, $10,000 for seniors age 65 and older, $10,000 for persons with disabilities.

Religion: There are 12 churches listed in the Village of Wimberley, but most denominations are well-represented in the Austin area.

Education: Advanced education opportunities abound in the area. Texas State University, with a 20,000-student enrollment in San Marcos, waives tuition for seniors age 65 and older. The largest public institution in the state with 50,000 students, the University of Texas at Austin is a 30-minute drive away.

Transportation: Austin-Bergstrom International Airport is 33 miles from Wimberley. San Antonio International Airport is 41 miles, and train and bus service is available from Austin and San Antonio.

Health: Central Texas Medical Center in San Marcos is eight miles from Wimberley, and a full range of health care is available in Austin. Local doctors in Wimberley include dentists, family practitioners, rehabilitation therapists, psychologists and chiropractors.

Housing options: A recent sample of the real estate market revealed a three-bedroom, 2,000-square-foot home on the Woodcreek Golf Course for $187,500; a three-bedroom, 2,100-

square-foot home on five acres at $269,000; and a three-bedroom, 2,600-square-foot home on Smith Creek for $350,000. Few rentals are found, and no apartments are available.

Visitor lodging: More than 50 bed-and-breakfast inns do a booming business in the Wimberley area, ranging from accommodations on the shopping square to creek-side living to ranch visits. At the renowned Blair House, rates of $135-$275 include breakfast and evening dessert, (877) 549-5450. Other options: Mountain View Lodge is located atop a ridge and offers hiking, swimming and continental breakfast, starting at $85, (512) 847-2992; Wimberley Inn, a quarter-mile from the Olde Towne Square, $89-$155, (512) 847-3750; Wimberley Log Motel, with cabins downtown or next to the Market Day area, $75 for up to four persons, (800) 660-0946.

Information: Wimberley Chamber of Commerce, P.O. Box 12, Wimberley, TX 78676, (512) 847-2201, www.wimberley.org or www.wimberleyonline.com.

ic engine here," Glen says. More than 50 percent of Wimberley's population is 45 or older.

Another economic boon to the community is the renowned Market Day, held on the first Saturday of every month from April to December and managed since the 1960s by the town's Lion's Club. Patterned after the market days of Europe, these special Saturdays are very popular. Thousands flock to Wimberley on Market Day to browse through more than 400 booths of unique art, crafts, clothing, produce, equipment, housewares and food. Come early, though, because parking fills up fast. It's the second-largest Market Day in the state.

Glen and Bobbie recommend visitors stay in one of the many charming bed-and-breakfast inns in the area to see how Wimberley suits them. Check out the local shops for antiques and artwork, take in the vistas atop Mount Baldy or embark on scenic drives along the Devil's Backbone, a highway atop hilltop ridges that is breathtaking during the spring wildflower season. Besides Wimberley's proximity to Austin and San Marcos, Canyon Lake is only a half-hour away. Historic Blanco and Johnson City are also within short drives.

Birding is an especially popular activity here, with several endangered species making Wimberley Valley their home. In October, the area is also host to migrating monarch butterflies, which blanket the hills and valley with rich color. The area enjoys 300 days of sunshine a year and 37 inches of rainfall on average. With the wildlife, landscape and wildflowers, artists have plenty to work with.

According to Bobbie, it is impossible not to get involved in the community. She enjoys the Institute of Cultures, which celebrates Wimberley's history, and the garden and civic clubs. The Wimberley Players is a theater group that regularly provides good entertainment at Greenhouse Theatre. The Corral, an outdoor theater, plays first-run movies on Friday, Saturday and Sunday nights. Seniors own the senior center and help

with the thrift shop, the visitor's center and the Crisis Breadbasket for those in need. The senior center moved to the new, $1.5 million Wimberley Community Center located in the heart of the village in 2006.

Retirees seeking to further their education can attend classes at Texas State University in San Marcos or the many colleges in Austin, such as the University of Texas. A good guide to living in Wimberley can be found in a book titled, "Welcome to Wimberley: Now What Do I Do?"

Cindy and Richie Colvert, both 55, found Wimberley to be the perfect place for them. "We lived in Austin in the 1980s and loved it, but Richie's job as vice president of a food company forced a move to Oklahoma," Cindy says.

When their two girls grew up and moved away, Cindy and Richie revisited Austin in 2001 but found the huge growth the city had undergone in the 1990s caused too much traffic congestion for their liking. "We drew a circle around Austin," Cindy says, "and took some drives to visit the smaller towns in the outlying areas. We remembered how wonderful Wimberley was, and when we visited, it looked very much the same as how we remembered it. It had everything we wanted: good health care in Austin, a good airport (Austin-Bergstrom International Airport), and yet it still had that small-town feel and friendliness where people care about one another."

When it came time to choose a house, Richie says, "I wanted to be near a golf course, and Cindy wanted a good back yard next to a nature area or park. We got both here at Woodcreek." Their large house in Oklahoma sold in three weeks, according to Richie, and the couple was determined to downsize and slow down their lives. They found the perfect home on a cul-de-sac in the incorporated community of Woodcreek, which has a golf course. The community is composed of a mix of retirees and young families.

"I haven't regretted a moment of it," says Cindy, a former schoolteacher.

She enjoys the back yard with the family dog, Jackie, and watches the squirrels, deer and hummingbirds feed on the greenway behind her yard. "I never tire of it. I also like that this community is environmentally conscious," she says, "and filled with so many talented people."

Her and Richie's favorite place to go on Friday nights is the bluegrass jam at Charlie's on FM 2325. "You've never heard so much great music in your life," Cindy says. Musicians come from miles around to jam from about 9 p.m. until the wee hours of the morning, and patrons get an opportunity to have dinner while listening to sweet, spontaneous strains from nearly every type of instrument imaginable.

While they didn't need to do so, both Richie and Cindy decided to work in order to stay active and meet new friends. Cindy is employed as the assistant to the town's city secretary, where her outgoing personality is a definite attribute, and Richie works in a local bank. "It's a welcome change to the type of work pace I maintained for so many years," Richie says. "And, it allowed us the time to go to our daughter Griffin's college basketball games."

According to City Administrator Steve Harrison, the Colverts' experience is not unusual. "Many retirees come to Wimberley and decide to work or volunteer in the community," he says. "We have 12 very active citizen groups who work to ensure the city's future, and most of them have retired from something else. We are very lucky to have a community of involved citizens from all walks of life."

Steve should know. He retired from the U.S. Secret Service and moved his family from California to Texas, where he is heavily involved in his second career in city management. The Harrisons live on a 66-acre ranch in a neighboring community where they, too, can enjoy the delights of the Texas Hill Country with good schools, majestic vistas and a lower-than-average crime rate. ●

Winter Garden, Florida

This central Florida town boasts a charming downtown, plenty of volunteer opportunities and proximity to theme parks

By Jay Clarke

When it came to winters in the North, Joe Hembrooke wanted out. "I was tired of shoveling snow — of cars rusting out," says the former school superintendent in the Delaware Valley. In 1995, he was ready to leave the Catskills area of New York and retire to a warmer climate.

His wife, Chesta, 55, wanted to move to Philadelphia, where her mother lived, but was willing to go to Florida under two conditions. She wanted to live within easy reach of a major airport and Disney attractions. "So we put a circle around Orlando and started looking," says Joe, now 69.

That led the Hembrookes to the Winter Garden area. "Disney World is 25 minutes away," Joe says. "The airport, 30 minutes."

Winter Garden itself was pretty well built out, and like other newcomers looking to build or buy new, Joe and Chesta scouted the outlying area and eventually constructed a house in the adjacent town of Ocoee. "It's bigger in square footage than (our former) house, but smaller in property," Joe says. More importantly, he says, "We're happy as can be."

A different incentive brought Colin and Donna Kelly to Winter Garden in 2000. "We had been coming down here from Springfield, IL, for some years to visit our daughter and grandchildren," says Colin, 61. When retirement became a possibility, they bought in Hyde Park, a manufactured home development in Winter Garden. "We intended to stay here in winter and go back to Illinois in the summer," Colin says. But the Kellys liked Winter Garden so much that they decided to sell the house in Illinois and live here year-round.

Winter Garden is listed on the National Register of Historic Places and possesses a charming downtown signaled by a distinctive clock tower. Quaint stores line each side of brick-paved Plant Street, including the venerable Edgewa-ter Hotel, built in 1927 and restored in the mid-1990s after being closed for 32 years. In its heyday, the 22-room hotel hosted the Washington Senators baseball team every year during spring training and was the lodging of choice for the affluent anglers who came to fish in nearby Lake Apopka.

Close to Plant Street is the city's old fire station, where the Winter Garden Recreation Department conducts a variety of programs for seniors, including monthly trips to theme parks, festivals and performances as well as weekly walks. Nearby are two museums, the Heritage Museum and the Railroad Museum. And living near Orlando is a huge perquisite that always is cited by relocating retirees.

It goes without saying that Orlando is one of the world's hubs of recreation. Three large theme parks — Walt Disney World, Universal Orlando and SeaWorld Orlando — tempt visitors of all ages, particularly the children and grandchildren of area retirees. The fact that relatives are eager to visit is an important bonus to retirees moving away from their families.

The Kellys are well ensconced in Winter Garden now, but it wasn't an easy adjustment at first, admits Donna, 63. "I miss the routine of the North and was lost until it was re-established. It's hard for a lady to go to a smaller home. Women get attached to knickknacks; it's hard to let them go. Also, it took two years to get to know people," she says.

Making friends was easier for Ray and Joline Krolicki, who moved here from Kent Island, MD, in 1996. One of their daughters, working for Disney, already lived in the Orlando area, and Joline's parents had moved here in 1982. So there was no doubt where the Krolickis would go when they retired. "We had visited many times before we moved here," says Joline, 62.

While there are a couple of things she and Ray, 65, miss from their previous home, they have no regrets about leaving Maryland. "Every winter, when I go outside to get the newspaper, I say, 'Thank God I live here,'" Joline says. And even though both had tickets to University of Maryland football games when they lived in Kent Island, they don't miss attending those either.

"I'll tell you a story," says Joline, who lives in a single-family home they built here in 1996. "I was watching a (University of Maryland) game on television here and saw everyone wearing heavy coats. Then it began to snow. And I was in shorts. No, I don't miss that at all."

Both she and Ray were high school department heads in Maryland, he in accounting, she in English. About a year and a half after their move, Joline says she got bored and went back to work, though not as a teacher. She runs the volunteer program at the hospital nursing home in Winter Garden.

Ray hasn't gone back to work, but he volunteers a great deal. "He put in 107 hours last month at the nursing home," Joline says. Colin and Donna Kelly also volunteer there, as does Gene Bosquet, 75.

Gene is another retiree who has kept quite busy since he and his wife, Dorothy, moved here from Attleboro, MA, in 1988. In addition to volunteering at the nursing home, he writes a 20-page newsletter for a mall every month, publishes the Hyde Park newsletter and teaches digital photography to seniors. That's not all. "I walk four miles a day, and I've just finished 5,000 miles," he says.

Gene also had a sister who lived in the area, but that wasn't the only reason he and his wife moved to Winter Garden. "We liked the climate," says Gene, who was in sales before he retired. "The living is good here."

While Gene is still more active than much younger men, Dorothy had to curtail most of her activities when she lost her eyesight. However, she still teaches line dancing and manages to travel independently by public transportation.

Colin and Donna Kelly also keep busy. Both volunteer at the nursing home, and Colin, who is named after but not related to a World War II hero of the same name, drives a shuttle. They also save time for some fun. Says Colin, "I swim, shoot pool and travel. We have year-around passes to Disney World. I see the money (that they spend at the theme park) as money for physical fitness because I walk a lot there." As for Donna, she enjoys crafts shows and says she and Colin take a lot of trips.

Keeping occupied is important for retirees, Joe Hembrooke agrees. "People who retire had better have something to do with their time," he says. "At first I wondered why I had retired, so I found a part-time job. I went to work for Disney just to do something. I also worked part time as a movie theater cashier." Now Joe and his wife volunteer for two organizations that help the needy, Bread of Life and Stars of west Orange County. "I personally founded Stars," he says. "My wife and I developed the program, and the chamber (of commerce) endorsed it."

Stars helps needy students. "We get supplies for kids — backpacks, school supplies," he says. In 2004 the program helped 4,200 children in 13 elementary schools in west Orange County. Joe also is a full-time volunteer at his church and umpires Little League games. Both he and his wife were previously married, and they have 10 grandchildren between them — seven in Florida, three in New York. "We see them once a year, either here or there," Joe says.

Winter Garden, FL

Population: Over 23,000

Location: Winter Garden is located in central Florida about 12 miles west of Orlando in west Orange County.

Climate: High Low
January 70 49
July 90 73

Average relative humidity: 62%

Rain: 50 inches annually

Cost of living: Slightly below average

Average housing cost: About $250,000 for an existing single-family home.

Sales tax: 6.5%

Sales tax exemptions: Food and medicine

State income tax: None

Estate tax: None

Inheritance tax: None

Property tax: $17.9051 per $1,000. Tax on a home valued at $250,000 would be about $4,029 (with $25,000 homestead exemption noted below). For information, call the Orange County Property Appraiser's Office at (407) 836-5044.

Homestead exemption: $25,000 of assessed value of primary, permanent residence.

Intangibles tax: None, the tax was repealed as of Jan. 1, 2007.

Religion: There are 24 churches in Winter Garden and 18 in Ocoee representing a variety of denominations.

Education: Options include the University of Central Florida, (407) 823-2000 or www.ucf.edu; Valencia Community College, (407) 299-5000 or www.valenciacc.edu; and Lake-Sumter Community College, (352) 243-5722 or www.lscc.edu.

Transportation: Orlando International Airport is 20 miles from Winter Garden. It's an easy drive to Interstate 75 to the Upper Midwest, Interstate 95 to the Northeast and Interstate 4 across Florida.

Health: Winter Garden is in the West Orange Healthcare District. Health Central has 171 beds and a 24-hour emergency room. Orlando Regional Medical Center has 517 beds and a 24-hour emergency room. Walk-in clinics include Florida Hospital's Centra Care, Health Alliance Family Care Center and ExpressCare.

Housing options: Literally thousands of housing opportunities are available in the booming Orlando area. Much of Winter Garden has been built out, but in the neighboring city of Ocoee and other parts of west Orange County, many projects offer a variety of housing styles. In Winter Garden there is a large manufactured home community, **Hyde Park**, (888) 388-3883. Other homebuilders with developments in the area include **KB Home**, (321) 354-2500 or www.kbhome.com; **Park Square Homes**, (407) 529-3000 or www.parksquarehomes.com; and **Ryland Homes**, (407) 872-1203 or www.ryland.com. **Keene's**

Pointe is a Castle & Cooke development of 14 neighborhoods in west Orange County. It boasts golf cottages, custom homes and estates with attended and gated entries and a Jack Nicklaus Signature golf course. A new phase of 70 premium lakefront and golf-course lots opened in 2006. Located in Windermere on former orange groves, the lakeside development is not age restricted, (407) 876-8879 or www.cc-keenespointe.com. A variety of rental apartments are offered in the Winter Garden/Ocoee area, starting at around $560 a month for a one-bedroom unit. Rental companies include: Country Gardens, (866) 358-1205 or www.forrent.com/countrygardens; Wilson Co., (813) 281-8888 or www.wilsoncompany.com; Villa Tuscany, (888) 747-2425 or www.forrent.com/villatuscany; and Westpointe Villas, (866) 255-7525 or www.cameoprofessionals.com. Assisted-living communities in the area include Golden Pond Communities, (407) 654-7217; Health Central Park, (407) 656-2151; Quality Health Care, (407) 877-6636; and Summerville Assisted Living, (407) 299-2710.

Visitor lodging: Best Western, $74-$89, (407) 656-5050. Edgewater Hotel, $75-$120, (407) 905-0114. Courtyard by Marriott, $99-$109, (407) 573-1010. Red Roof Inn, $66-$74, (407) 347-0140.

Information: West Orange Chamber of Commerce, 12184 W. Colonial Drive, Winter Garden, FL 34787, (407) 656-1304 or www.wochamber.com. City of Winter Garden, (407) 656-4111 or www.cwgdn.com. City of Ocoee, (407) 905-3100 or www.ci.ocoee.fl.us.

While Joline Krolicki was able to land a job here, Donna Kelly found the going more difficult. "I do tatting and smocking, but that's not a go for a business here," says Donna, who also plays the keyboard. She found work playing at local functions, but she says the job market is not adequate to support all the retirees who expect to supplement their retirement incomes by working either full or part time. She suggests that retirees who want to continue working in some capacity should check out job availability in their areas of interest before they make the decision to move.

But not everyone is a new retiree to Florida. Elaine Ausmus moved to Winter Garden before there was a Disney World, before Orlando became a name known worldwide, before the mass influx of retirees to Florida. "We lived in Chicago Heights. My husband, George, was a general contractor, but he had emphysema and his doctor advised him to get out of Chicago," says Elaine, now 79.

"He liked Mexico, but I said no way. We also thought of moving to Arkansas," Elaine says. They made their move to this area in 1967. What finally convinced them, Elaine says, was a storm that dumped snow on Chicago at a rate of an inch per hour.

Elaine lost her husband some years back and now spends a lot of hours volunteering. She plans trips for her church

and works in ambulatory surgery at a hospital. And like just about everyone else in central Florida, she doesn't like the traffic. "It's gotten worse in the past two years," she says in resignation.

Driving on main thoroughfares like Interstate 4 at rush hour can be pure stop-and-go frustration. "There are too many people," Gene Bosquet complains. Joe Hembrooke agrees, and thinks the area is growing much too fast. "Houses are going up all over the place. The traffic is just awful," he says.

On the other hand, there are good reasons why retirees are moving to Winter Garden — and incentives are not limited to the fine weather. Most retirees agree that a lower tax burden makes it less costly to live here than in their home states. Colin figures costs of living are about the same here as back home, "though taxes are less here." Joe also pegs the cost of living about the same. "I thought it would be a lot cheaper here, but food and housing are about the same," he says. He concedes, though, that taxes "are much lower here, probably by half." Joline finds living here much less expensive than in Maryland. "There's no income tax, and real estate taxes are less," she says.

Taxes are creeping up, though. Real estate is increasing in value and decreasing in availability in Winter Garden, which celebrated its 100th anniversary in 2003. As a result, many newcomers are

buying or building homes in the adjacent city of Ocoee. Residents can drive to nearby Orlando for anything they can't find in Ocoee or Winter Garden.

"We're fortunate to live near a large city," Joe says of Orlando. "We have the greatest doctors, the best of restaurants and we're just a half-mile from the West Oaks Mall." Joline also praises the ready access to facilities here. "We had to drive 20 miles to get to a grocery store in Maryland," she recalls.

Those who want to further their education can take courses at the University of Central Florida, which has become one of the state's largest schools with over 40,000 students. Top-quality medical services are within easy reach, as are malls that range from upscale stores like Neiman Marcus to budget outlet shops.

Joe Hembrooke says there isn't much he misses about his former home. His wife misses the change of seasons, "but she goes back to Pennsylvania to see the trees." As for Joline Krolicki, she says she's happy here but misses the seafood that is such a major part of the diet in Maryland. "They just don't know how to prepare crabs here," she says. And Donna Kelly had never heard of fire ants until she moved here. "Now I can't walk outside on my bare feet," she says.

But that's the trade-off, retirees note. Back in Illinois, folks don't walk in snow on their bare feet, either. ●

Winter Park, Florida

Once sampled, this Florida town is hard to forget

By Jay Clarke

As a career diplomat, Tom Donnelly lived and worked in many parts of the world and saw its wonders, but he settled in Winter Park when it came time to retire. "Winter Park is like a disease," he says. "Once you're infected, you never get it out of your system."

But it's a good sort of infection — the best, in fact — and Tom, 61, succumbed to the Winter Park bug early in life.

When Tom was growing up, "my aunt and uncle lived here, so I often visited," he says. "Then my parents moved here when I was in my senior year of high school, and I went on to Rollins," a private liberal arts college in Winter Park.

But he didn't see much of Winter Park in the years that followed, as his career took him from country to country around the world. He spent time in many attractive destinations, but it's not hard to understand what brought him back to Winter Park.

"First, it's pretty," he says. "Second, it has a sense of itself, a community spirit, and it's real friendly."

Tom retired from the U.S. State Department in 1994, and today he leads an active life in his second-time-around hometown. He serves in several volunteer positions in the community, works with computers and is interested in genealogy. He has served on the Rollins College alumni board, as well as the boards of the Albin Polasek Museum and the Florida Hospital Foundation's SHARES Program, and in Rotary at both the local and regional levels.

"I'm active in Rotary because it has more international activity than other clubs," he says. He especially likes the SHARES program because it sends surgeons and doctors overseas to treat needy residents in Third World countries like Mexico and Peru, where he served as a diplomat.

And he still travels widely, visiting friends he made abroad. "I go to Mexico six or seven times a year and also to Europe. I just spent five weeks in Germany." He also hosts many visitors. "I'm single and live alone," he says, "but I've got a million house guests."

Winter Park's close proximity to Orlando, five miles south, guarantees him a steady stream of visitors. Upscale Winter Park is within striking range of, and also offers respite from, the area's busy theme parks. But even before the famous theme parks were built, Winter Park was a magnet for tourists. Founded in the 1880s as a resort for wealthy Northerners escaping harsh winters, the town was known for area lakes and citrus groves. Today visitors can shop at upscale boutiques or go boating on lovely Lake Osceola. The town's sidewalks and canals are lined with feathery date palms, colorful azaleas and posh homes.

Another retiree who never forgot a brief stint in Winter Park is John Corbett, 63, who moved back with his wife, Sharon, in the mid-1990s. "I had lived here in 1968-1970," the former petroleum executive says, "and I had always planned to come back." He bought a home in Winter Park in 1993 before he retired, but he spent only a brief time in it.

"My wife and I decided to keep the home and rent it out because we both wanted to come back. We moved back in 1996," he says.

John was raised in Tallahassee and went to college there at Florida State University, but his career took him to a number of cities. "I worked in Atlanta four different times and in Houston four different times," he says. He also worked in Fort Wayne, IN, for a spell.

For the Corbetts, settling into Winter Park life was easy. "When I left Winter Park in 1970, I had a lot of friends. When I came back, they were still here and I picked up where I left off," he says.

This is the second marriage for both John and Sharon, and they have seven children between them — six boys and one girl — but only one lives in Winter Park. "Several times I thought of settling in Atlanta, where we have many kids, but it has too much sprawl," he says. Instead, their children, who range in age from 25 to 38, visit them in Winter Park. Trips to their parents' home allow them to enjoy area attractions as well as the Corbetts' company.

Like Tom Donnelly, the Corbetts keep busy. "I volunteer at church and at the YMCA. Membership there is very reasonable. I exercise there, run with a group twice a week and work out two or three times a week," John says. His wife, Sharon, 51, still works, so her days are filled.

Inevitably there are things one misses from previous homes. "I do like pro sports, and they don't have that here," with the exception of basketball, John says. "But you learn to do things on your own — you run, go biking, go boating."

And just as inevitably, there are compromises one makes wherever one lives. There's not much John doesn't like here. "It's a little cooler than I'd like," says John, who likes things hot. But even Central Florida's burgeoning population and crowded roads don't faze him. "After living in Atlanta and Houston, I see no traffic problem here," he says.

Still another world traveler who made it back to Winter Park is Gene Sullivan, former executive director of the Hong Kong Tourist Association. Gene spent the last eight years before his retirement in Hong Kong, but he also had early ties to Winter Park. Like Tom Donnelly, Rollins College was his alma mater.

That was a factor that brought him back to Winter Park in 1998, but it wasn't the only one. "I wanted a warm climate — and it's nice to live in a college town with a theater, classes and an intellectual community," he says. "There are good restaurants and shops here, and Winter Park is adjacent to Orlando, which has a good international airport."

Actually, Gene and his wife, Barbara, had become Florida residents of sorts some years back when they bought a condo in New Smyrna Beach, to which they vacationed every now and then. When they retired, though, they moved first to Longwood, another Orlando suburb, before settling in Winter Park. "Originally, we were looking for a gated community," Gene says, "but we found Winter Park very safe. We can leave for weeks and not worry about being burglarized."

But unlike the Corbetts, Gene and Barbara found it less easy to meld into the community as newcomers. "Moving into an established community, meeting people, was difficult. It wasn't easy to make friends. It would have been easier to retire into a retirement community, where everyone is your peer," he says.

They now have a good circle of friends and undoubtedly will develop more. Time is on their side. Gene is 61, his wife 62, and both have many active years ahead of them. Both their children are grown, single and living elsewhere — one in Washington, DC, the other in Connecticut.

So the Sullivans travel frequently and keep busy with volunteer work. "I work with what we call the Paunch Corps (as opposed to Peace Corps). These are retired people who go to developing countries to help. Their expenses are paid, but they get no salary," he says. The two organizations Gene is involved with are the International Executive Service Corps and the Citizens Democracy Corps, both funded by the Agency for International Development in Washington. He also serves on the Rollins College alumni board, volunteers at his church and has led escorted tours.

Gene admits that at first he missed Hong Kong and his glamorous lifestyle there. "We had a driver and a maid," he says. But he doesn't miss those conveniences now. "I have a lot of independence," he says.

Independence is a good thing to have in Winter Park, an affluent suburb of Orlando that has no neon signs, no parking meters, no large adult retirement complexes, gated communities or mobile homes. Single-family homes here are on the expensive side, but the rewards of living in an upscale community are substantial.

Brick-paved Park Avenue, lined with oaks and dotted with old-time streetlights, is one of Florida's premier shop-

Winter Park, FL

Population: 28,512 (18.6% are 65 or older)

Location: Winter Park is a suburb of Orlando, about five miles north of downtown Orlando.

Climate:

	High	Low
January	72	50
July	92	73

Average relative humidity: 60%

Annual rainfall: 50.26 inches

Cost of living: The overall cost of living in the Orlando area is just below the national average, but housing prices in Winter Park are higher than average.

Housing costs: Home prices in Winter Park vary drastically, depending on the proximity to downtown. The average home price is about $500,000, ranging from older homes starting at $200,000 to new construction downtown in the millions. Median price of homes in the overall Orlando region is $221,000.

Sales tax: 6.5%

Sales tax exemptions: Groceries, medicine, professional services.

State income tax: None

Intangibles tax: None. The tax was repealed as of Jan. 1, 2007.

Estate tax: None

Inheritance tax: None

Property tax: $18.6369 per $1,000 of the value. Tax on a $200,000 home would be approximately $3,087, with homestead exemption noted below.

Homestead exemption: $25,000 off assessed value of primary, permanent residence.

Religion: Winter Park has 39 churches.

Education: Rollins College, a private residential institution, has about 3,800 students and a student faculty ratio of 11 to 1. It is the only comprehensive liberal arts college in Florida. Valencia Community College, offering two-year associate degrees in the Orlando area, has a Winter Park campus with 2,400 students. The University of Central Florida, a state school with more than 42,000 students in eight colleges, is the major institution of higher learning in the Orlando area; its main campus is 13 miles east of downtown Orlando.

Transportation: Excellent domestic and international air service is available from Orlando International Airport, 30-40 minutes away. Amtrak has service to New York, Los Angeles and Miami from the Winter Park train station. A tri-county bus service called LYNX provides local public transit.

Health: Winter Park Memorial Hospital, a general acute-care facility, has a 24-hour emergency room, cancer center and walk-in medical center. Several other options are available in nearby Orlando. Three nursing homes are in Winter Park; a number of others are elsewhere in the Orlando area.

Housing options: Winter Park has single-family homes and apartments but no gated communities. There are nine retirement residences in the city or close by. Some provide assisted living or Alzheimer's care. No short-term or monthly condo rentals or mobile homes are allowed in Orange County.

Visitor lodging: Rates are seasonal, higher in winter and lower in summer. Rates at Park Plaza Hotel are $110 and up, (407) 647-1072. Rates at Best Western Mount Vernon Inn are $104 and up, (407) 647-1166. Rates at Park Inn, (407) 539-1955, are $59 and up and Ramada Inn, (407) 644-8000, is $69 and up. Many other motels cluster around highways close to the city.

Information: Winter Park Chamber of Commerce, P.O. Box 280, Winter Park, FL 32790, (407) 644-8281 or www.winterpark.org. Ask for a free relocation guide.

ping streets. One large store is dedicated exclusively to products for dogs. A former movie theater, the art deco Colony, has become a Pottery Barn. Other chic shops on the street include Banana Republic, Ann Taylor, Williams-Sonoma, The Gap and Peterbrooke Chocolates.

Living up to its name, Winter Park has more parks and recreation facilities per capita than any other city in Florida. Best known is Central Park, a comfortable six-acre spread shaded by large oaks directly across the street from the fancy shops of Park Avenue. "Popcorn Flicks," featuring free movies and popcorn, are held in the park on the third Thursday of every month. Cross-park traffic halts every now and again to let sleek passenger trains ease into the Amtrak station there.

Gracing the city as well are eight properties on the National Register of Historic Places — the three-acre Albin Polasek Museum and Sculpture Gardens, the 1883 All Saints Episcopal Church, the 1871 Comstock-Harris House, the 1899 Edward Hill Brewer House, the Winter Park Country Club, the Woman's Club of Winter Park, and the Annie Russell Theatre and Knowles Memorial Chapel, both on the grounds of Rollins College.

And culturally, Winter Park has much to offer. The block-long Morse Museum of American Art holds the world's most comprehensive collection of the works of Louis Comfort Tiffany, including the restored chapel he created for Chicago's 1893 Columbia Exposition.

On the Rollins College campus, the Cornell Fine Arts Museum, the oldest collection in Florida, houses more than 5,000 works of European and American paintings, sculpture and decorative arts. It is regarded as one of the nation's top college art museums. Another prestigious institution is the Albin Polasek Museum and Sculpture Gardens, which encompasses the estate and gardens of the renowned Czech-American sculptor.

Art also comes to Winter Park several times yearly in the form of festivals. Biggest is the Winter Park Sidewalk Art Festival, which draws more than 350,000 during its three-day run in Central Park every March. It features artists from all over the country. The Winter Park Autumn Art Festival, held in October, showcases works by Florida artists.

Music, too, draws many visitors to the city, particularly during the annual Winter Park Bach Festival, which was founded in the 1930s. Winter Park's respected Annie Russell Theatre stages productions during much of the year, and a new professional company, the Winter Park Playhouse, specializes in musical theater and comedies from New York.

Having a college in town is a major asset. Rollins, founded in 1885, has been ranked by U.S. News & World Report as one of "America's Best Colleges." Its 70-acre campus, dotted with Spanish Mediterranean buildings, is the locale for The Bach Festival concert series, lectures, seminars and other cultural activities.

Such cultural opportunities are powerful lures for retirees. So are the salubrious climate and Winter Park's ready access to shopping, restaurants and recreation.

"There's plenty of entertainment in Orlando, and for shopping we have a mall nearby," says Carol Dean, 75, who with her Air Force pilot husband Bob, now 80, retired from the military to Winter Park in 1970.

Another appeal is that Winter Park is affordable. "I find the cost of living no different than in other places," says John Corbett. "Property taxes are higher than in Orlando, but Winter Park's quiet is worth the tax money."

"The cost of living is a lot less than in Hong Kong, less than in Miami, less than in Washington," says Gene Sullivan. "But the value of living is as good as anywhere in the United States."

Tom Donnelly agrees. "It's affluent but not stuck up," he says.

Housing, on the other hand, is not inexpensive. Almost every lot in Winter Park's eight square miles is already built upon, and home prices keep spiraling upward. "We bought our house for about $35,000 and now it's worth over $200,000," says Carol Dean. Of course, that increase has come over 32 years, but prices have risen most sharply in the past few years.

Another factor in housing prices is that Winter Park is pretty much built out. "Smaller houses are being torn down to build big ones," notes Tom Donnelly. But that's fine with John Corbett. "One thing I like here is that it's protected. There's nowhere to build," he says.

Perhaps that's what keeps Winter Park so desirable. There's a continuity to the city and its people that often is missing in developing cities. "There's something about this community that I have not felt in other places," says Tom Donnelly. ●

Woodstock, Vermont

In the Vermont foothills, a rural setting satisfies cosmopolitan cravings

By Mary Lu Abbott

From inside their hilltop home, Joe and Cindy Carroll gaze over a 180-degree, ever-changing view of the meadows, woods and hills of rural Vermont. "It's like living on a painter's canvas," Joe says. On this day, rain has put a sheen on the blanket of white and the sun has burst forth. "It looks like diamonds in the snow," says Joe, adding that they find every day brings changes in the natural beauty in the foothills of the Green Mountains outside Woodstock.

"We're in love with it," Cindy says. "Each day I say I'm glad I moved here."

For the Carrolls, both 62, living in a house at the end of a country road outside a town of only 3,250 people is about as far removed from their previous life as possible. Since the 1960s, home for the Carrolls had been the populous San Francisco Bay Area and high-tech, fast-lane Silicon Valley. He was with Lockheed Martin and she with IBM.

Joe laughs that he was thinking about retirement from the day he started work, but actually they hadn't made any serious plans until 1997. After his treatment for cancer, they took an extended vacation, and when they returned they realized how stressful their work was, Cindy says. Joe made plans to retire in early 1999 and she retired early in 2000, but they didn't anticipate moving from the Bay Area anytime soon.

Over the years they had visited Woodstock several times on side trips when coming to see friends in Massachusetts. They liked Woodstock's beauty, small-town charm and good restaurants, so on a trip after they retired, they decided to rent a home in the area and stay a month in the summer of 2001.

"We figured if we ever moved from the Bay Area, it would be a place that had a college, good medical support, cultural events, good places to eat and multiple ages," says Joe, noting they didn't want an age-restricted retirement community.

They discovered that the Woodstock area met their criteria. They began looking at property, fell in love with a contemporary home on 24 acres about four and one-half miles from the center of Woodstock, bought it and relocated in the summer of 2002.

The month they spent "testing" life here, Joe says, "We kept saying, 'It just feels right.'"

Woodstock strikes most visitors that way — it looks and feels like the quintessential, perfect little town. There are no fast-food outlets, neon signs or "big-box" stores. People come to the post office to pick up their mail and greet each other on the street.

F.H. Gillingham & Sons General Store, the state's oldest such store, has served the community since 1886. A wonderland with every widget you could need, it has wooden floors and shelves filled with the widest imaginable range of products large and small, from wine to body shampoo, kids toys, lawn furniture, candy, nails and more.

Woodstock miraculously pulls off a blend of life at two different turns of centuries, partly small country town, partly cosmopolitan center. A covered bridge still channels traffic across the winding Ottauquechee River to The Green, the town's center. Cows graze the outlying hillsides, and farmers produce their own special cheeses and tap the maple trees in spring to make syrup.

Residents gather at the Town Hall to discuss city plans, see movies and enjoy regular music, theater and dance programs brought by the Pentangle Council on the Arts. In the surrounding hills and valleys, chefs have opened their "dream" restaurants, indulging customers with their individualized takes on gourmet cuisine.

Facing The Green are beautiful 1800s homes and the elegant Woodstock Inn & Resort, considered among the top hostelries in the world and an integral part of the town's history. Though built

in the 1960s by Laurance S. Rockefeller, the classic inn traces its heritage to a town-meeting tavern on this site in 1792, which then became a hotel for stagecoach passengers.

Settled in the mid-1700s, Woodstock was an agricultural and industrial community with a variety of businesses and tradesmen, augmented by numerous sawmills, gristmills and woolen mills around the outlying hills and streams. By the late 1800s, industry subsided and Woodstock became a summer retreat for the wealthy who wanted to escape the polluted cities for the clean mountain air. In 1892, the old hotel was replaced with the first Woodstock Inn, which became a year-round retreat, with everything from a golf course to a ski hill. The town proudly claims in the early 1930s that it built the country's first rope tow, helping launch skiing as a major industry.

To this day, Woodstock remains small and bucolic, but within 15 miles, at White River Junction, two major interstate highways intersect, providing fast routes to Boston, New York and Canada. Across the Connecticut River from White River Junction is New Hampshire and a few miles up the highway, about 20 miles from Woodstock, is Hanover, home to renowned Dartmouth College. Its medical school is associated with the Dartmouth-Hitchcock Medical Center a few miles south in adjacent Lebanon, which has branches throughout the region, including Woodstock.

Like the Carrolls, Jann and Bruce Macdonald hadn't thought that much about where they would retire but unexpectedly found the best of both worlds here — a scenic, quiet and rural setting that also satisfies their cravings on a cultural and intellectual level. Bruce, who retired in 2000 after a career with the BBDO Worldwide advertising and marketing agency, and Jann spent 28 years overseas in London and Moscow. They had owned vacation homes in Spain and Florida but sold them and were also selling their New York City apartment in the late 1990s when they began to ponder where they would live when they returned to the States.

"Florida was not for us. In fact, year-round sunny places were not for us," Bruce says they discovered over the years, noting they had particularly liked Seattle and Vancouver. "To us, a change of season was important. The idea of living in Arizona or Florida or Greece or Spain didn't have the appeal of living someplace that had a real sense of seasons and ideally, four seasons that stood up on their own and had their individual draws."

"We loved New England. It's where we had spent most of our time. New England is so beautiful that we wanted to come back, but we didn't know Vermont that well," Jann says. Also, having children with families in England and Italy oriented them to the East Coast for convenient travel to Europe.

A couple of years before retirement, they came to Vermont to vacation in the winter and friends suggested they look at Quechee, a neighboring village east of Woodstock. It dates to the 1760s and was the site of a number of mills. When industry died out in the 1900s, Quechee (pronounced kwee-chee) nearly became a ghost town, but it was revitalized starting in the 1970s when developers began a 5,200-acre planned country club resort community called Quechee Lakes in the surrounding hills.

A potter named Simon Pearce bought and restored the old village mill in 1981 to start his glassblowing business. His work has become well-known, and other craftsmen have been drawn to the area. Only about 900 people live in the village, and the Quechee Lakes community has about 1,300 residences, though many are second homes and occupied mainly in the summer.

The Macdonalds fell in love with Quechee and within three days had bought a home at Quechee Lakes. "We looked in Norwich, Woodstock, Lebanon, Hanover and around, but we saw this one in Quechee and when we walked in, we said, 'This is it, this is what we want,'" Jann says. Their home, built in the mid-1980s, has cathedral ceilings, open spaces and views of the valley and mountains.

"It's such a lovely little community, very well-managed," Jann says of Quechee Lakes. It has two golf courses, tennis, swimming pool, polo field and a clubhouse, to which all residents automatically belong (no initiation fees, but there are yearly fees). It even has its own small ski hill.

Their friends wondered how and why the Macdonalds, who were so urban-oriented, would be happy in a rural setting, but the Macdonalds quickly found a real camaraderie of interests.

"We have an amazing amount of cultural advantages you wouldn't expect to find in a community this size," says Bruce, 68. "We have the sort of things you'd expect to find in San Francisco or Boston but not in a rural area." In particular, he notes Northern Stage, which offers musicals and other live productions, including some New England premieres, at the 1890s Briggs Opera House

Population: About 3,250 in Woodstock, about 900 in neighboring Quechee year-round. The population swells in summer, and on weekends during the peak fall foliage season, 10,000 or more visitors come through the area.
Location: In what's known as central Vermont, Woodstock is in a rural valley in the foothills of the Green Mountains, about 15 miles west of the New Hampshire border. It's about 20 miles from Hanover, NH, home of Dartmouth College, and is convenient to Interstate 91, the major connection from Canada into New York City, and Interstate 89, which connects Vermont and New Hampshire to Boston. Quechee and the planned community Quechee Lakes are about halfway between Woodstock and the New Hampshire border.
Climate:

	High	Low
January	27	1
July	71	54

Average relative humidity: About 60%
Rain: 42 inches annually
Snow: About 100 inches annually
Cost of living: Above average

Average housing cost: The median sale price is $359,000.
Sales tax: 6% (9% on restaurant meals and lodging)
Sales tax exemptions: There are 46 exemptions from sales tax, including medical items, food, residential fuel and electricity and clothing and shoes under $110.
State income tax: For married couples filing jointly, ranges from 3.6% on taxable income up to $49,650 to $25,120 plus 9.5% on amounts over $326,450. For single filers, from 3.6% on taxable income up to $29,700 to $26,625 plus 9.5% on amounts over $326,450.
State income tax exemptions: Social Security benefits and all pensions are taxable. Railroad retirement benefits are taxable at the federal level, but exempt from Vermont income tax. There are also some income-based rebates on the state level. There is no tax on interest income from Vermont or U.S. government obligations.
Estate tax: None, except the state's "pick-up" portion of the federal tax, applicable to taxable estates above $2 million.
Property tax: $2.32 per $100 of assessed value in the village of Woodstock (one-square-mile area at center of town), $2.08 in the Woodstock town (outside the village), with homes assessed at 100% of market value. Yearly tax on a $359,000 home, without any rebates, would be about $8,329 in the village, about $7,467 outside. Property was reappraised in 2002, the first time in 10 years.
Homestead exemption: Vermont residents with incomes of less than $47,000 may be eligible to receive a property tax rebate and those with incomes of less than $110,000 may be eligible for a school property tax "prebate." There is also an exemption of at least $10,000 off a home's appraisal value for veterans.
Religion: There are six places of worship in Woodstock and more in neighboring towns within a drive of 15 minutes or so.
Education: Dartmouth College in Hanover, NH, about 20 miles from Woodstock, has an Institute for Lifelong Education with ongoing classes on a variety of subjects for adults, and Lebanon College at Lebanon, NH, about 15 miles from Woodstock, has lifelong learning

in White River Junction. Opera North has summer opera and other programs at a restored opera house in Lebanon, NH, across from White River Junction, and at Dartmouth in Hanover, both the Hood Museum of Art and the Hopkins Center for the Arts have frequent events and live productions. In addition, there's community theater throughout the area.

The Macdonalds discovered the Institute for Lifelong Education at Dartmouth, known as ILEAD, which has three semesters a year of adult classes on a wide variety of subjects. "ILEAD is so popular that people are demanding a summer session," says Bruce, noting he and Jann have enjoyed taking three "heavy" courses a year.

Two other couples, David and Joan Blackwell and Donald and Norma Griffith, are among the many who bought second homes here and then retired to them because they loved the area. The Blackwells lived in suburban Springfield, MA, in the western part of the state, south of Woodstock on Interstate 91. An insurance executive, David had attended

company meetings at the Woodstock Inn. Seeking a place for a second home, the Blackwells took a map and drew a circle around the area within a drive of 2.5 hours from Springfield. "We thought we might someday retire wherever we picked," David says.

"We ski and it had golf," Joan says about Woodstock. David adds, "We liked the small-town country living and we were near Dartmouth at Hanover. It's a cultural center and has a great hospital."

"Massachusetts is known as 'Tax-achusetts' — it's a high-tax state. We were determined to go to New Hampshire because it has no income tax. We stayed in Woodstock and went over to look in New Hampshire. Vermont is prettier," David says. They bought a home in Woodstock in 1980.

At retirement, they decided they liked Woodstock but also wanted another place to spend some of the year, seriously considering Carmel, CA, and Sedona, AZ, and finally buying a home in Sedona. After five years of splitting time between the two homes, they sold

the one in Sedona.

"We didn't spend enough time there to make it work. We were coming back and forth for holidays," Joan says. "We still go but we rent."

They've lived in Woodstock since 1987, and about eight years ago they built a new, contemporary house on 2.5 acres of land about a mile from the center of town. "We're hidden in the woods," says David, adding that wildlife is nearly too plentiful. "The deer eat everything. We've seen fox, mink, fisher cats (a large member of the weasel family). There are turkey and moose."

Like so many residents, the Blackwells enjoy the outdoors in all seasons. Both in their 70s, they're still avid downhill skiers and go every morning when the snow is good. Woodstock has its own ski area, Suicide Six, which is more family-oriented. Killington, one of Vermont's big resorts, is only about 20 miles away.

From Connecticut, Donald and Norma Griffith bought a second home here in the late 1970s, mainly for skiing, but as it was in the country, they also enjoyed

Woodstock, VT

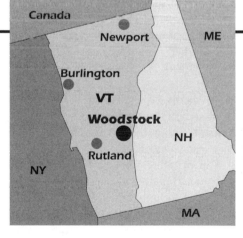

classes. The Woodstock Senior Center also has classes.

Transportation: Woodstock is a walkable town, though many retirees live in the outlying countryside. From the area there are buses and trains into Boston and New York and a bus to Boston Logan Airport, about 2.5 hours away. There's a small airport at Lebanon, NH, about 15 miles away, but most residents fly from Manchester, NH, slightly more than an hour away, or Boston.

Health: Locally the Dartmouth-Hitchcock Ottauquechee Health Center provides a range of general care and is linked with the Dartmouth-Hitchcock Medical Center in Lebanon, NH (about 15 miles), a regional complex covering all health fields. Most residents go to the main Dartmouth medical center. There's also a veterans hospital in nearby White River Junction, linked with the Dartmouth center, and another hospital in nearby Windsor.

Housing options: Homes and land are available in Woodstock, in the surrounding countryside and neighboring villages and towns. There's limited availability of

housing under $300,000. Nearby **Quechee Lakes**, a 5,200-acre development in rolling hills, has lots, single-family homes and townhomes, augmented with a country club, golf course and other amenities. For new property, call (888) 592-2224, and for resales, call (888) 654-9560, or visit www.quecheelakes.com. Prices for new, three- and four-bedroom townhomes start in the high $400,000s, new homes start at $425,000; resales may be available under $400,000.

Visitor lodging: The Shire Motel, a charming family-operated lodging with upscale furnishings, overlooks the Ottauquechee River and is within walking distance of the shops, galleries and restaurants in Woodstock. Rooms start at around $80 off-season, $128 in summer, (802) 457-2211 or www.shiremotel.com. The renowned Woodstock Inn & Resort has skiing, golf, tennis, spa services, outstanding dining and rooms from $149; inquire about value season dates when prices are lower, (800) 448-7900 or www.woodstockinn.com. There are numerous B&Bs and inns in the area,

including the new Victorian Maple Leaf Inn in the woods outside the nearby village of Barnard. Rooms start at $160, with gourmet breakfast, (800) 516-2753 or www.mapleleafinn.com. Note: Rates go up in fall during peak foliage weeks and early reservations are a must.

Information: Woodstock Area Chamber of Commerce, P.O. Box 486, VT 05091, (888) 496-6378 or www.woodstockvt.com. For Quechee and Quechee Lakes: Hartford Area Chamber of Commerce, 1856 Main St. (P.O. Box 106), Quechee, VT 05059, (800) 295-5451 or www.quechee.com.

growing vegetables. "We had looked in New Hampshire and Maine. We weren't interested in the Cape (Cod) — too much hassle with traffic. This was a simple shot up the interstate for us every weekend. There's not much traffic except in the fall," says Donald, who was a sales executive with a security systems firm.

"We had two favorite places — here and on the Maine coast. What we saw over there (in Maine) that we liked, we felt we couldn't afford, and what we could afford we didn't like. We kinda had our hearts set on this place," Donald says.

They bought an 1813 home on six acres of land overlooking the Ottauquechee River about 3.5 miles from town. They both love their home and the location. "We can't see any houses from our home. It's quiet. We have a bear, a moose, fox, deer, turkey, ducks," Norma says. She spends a lot of time gardening, tending to flowers and vegetables, including squash, corn, carrots, spinach, onions and tomatoes.

"You can't start planting until about Memorial Day and then you hope and pray the first frost doesn't come until the end of September," Donald says.

They live on a dirt road — "about 70 percent of the roads in Vermont are dirt, and people aren't in a hurry to get them paved either. The only drawback is April, when the roads turn into mud ruts. If you're smart, that's a good time to take vacation," Donald says.

The Griffiths, who are in their 70s, still use an old-fashioned wood stove in the kitchen, though it's not the primary source of heat or cooking. "We fire up the wood stove in winter nearly every day. We cook certain things on it — stews, soups. We used to chop wood. Now we usually buy it and store it," Donald says.

By the time they retired in the 1980s, they had become involved in the community and knew Woodstock was the place for them. They liked the local ownership of businesses, the golf course and the cultural attractions, including local theater and programs at Dartmouth.

"It's a wonderfully welcoming community," Donald says. "There are all different types of people, those who are extremely wealthy and those who work

hard for a living. I like to blend in with both. The people are the main attraction — I enjoy all the people and the organizations."

"I think we have a well-managed town. We have a town manager who has been here since the mid-1980s, and I think he does a superb job. We have the good old annual town meeting where you vote on the budget. It's the most interesting day to sit there and see the little conflicts between the farmers and out-of-staters who own property and the people in the village. I hope it never ends — it's a great institution," Donald says.

"Another reason the town is so wonderful is because of so much effort and money that Laurance Rockefeller put into here. He did a lot of things. A little illustration: They were putting in new sidewalks back in the 1980s and when they were digging up the old sidewalks, he said go ahead and bury all the wires and take down the telephone poles, and he picked up the tab. Any land he has given to the town that causes any loss of tax revenue he found a way to supplement the money so the town doesn't suffer. He did things without a lot of fanfare," Donald says.

Rockefeller formerly owned the Woodstock Inn & Resort and its amenities, including the golf course and indoor sports center, which local residents use. Rockefeller and his wife, Mary French Rockefeller, also donated her family mansion and forest lands to become the state's first national park, the Marsh-Billings-Rockefeller National Historical Park. On the outskirts of town, the park is the only site focused on the history and evolution of land conservation in America. It includes a 20-mile network of footpaths and carriage roads. Across from it, the Rockefellers established the Billings Farm & Museum to continue the farm's working dairy and make it a living history museum to illustrate rural Vermont life.

Another working farm in the area, Sugarbush, is family-operated and welcomes visitors to see its production of cheeses and maple syrup. It also has a nature trail through its maple groves. To access it, you cross the red Taftsville Covered Bridge, built in 1836, one of the longest and oldest such bridges in the state. Across from the bridge on the

highway between Woodstock and Quechee is the tiny Taftsville Historic District, with its country store that dates to 1840. Step inside and you'll find more than 40 Vermont cheeses, local maple syrup, wines (there's a winery in the valley) and the village post office.

Despite New Englanders having a reputation of being reserved and perhaps not as open to outsiders, all the couples interviewed commented on the warm welcome they received and the friendliness of people in the area.

"It's a very friendly small town. People stop at the post office and talk to each other. We have a large retired population here, but we also have a young population, too. It's a normal mixture," says David Blackwell. "Woodstock is made up of people from elsewhere. There are few natives here."

After living in Moscow and other cities with such large populations that people tend to be brusque, Bruce Macdonald recalls how surprised he was in Woodstock. "Cars actually stop when you cross the street and wait for you to pass. I remember being so overwhelmed by the courtesy here. Most of us were brought up with some small-town values, and you come back and find they still exist in a place like this. Maybe the best part of being rural is being in a gentle way the sort of community you remember as a kid."

"People are so outgoing and so warm," says Jann Macdonald. "I broke my leg on Halloween and the assistance has just been staggering. Food came through the door in droves. They're so helpful and attentive. They take over if there's an accident."

The Carrolls, who've been there less than a year, had a similar experience when Joe had to have surgery. "People were concerned about me. I didn't realize how many people knew about the situation," Joe says. Cindy adds, "You know your neighbors here. When he got out of the hospital, people brought food. It's like when I grew up as a kid, the way people take time for people up here." And, she says, "the care and concern of the facility at Dartmouth-Hitchcock was above and beyond anything we experienced in the Bay Area."

"Woodstock has such a sense of community. It's hard to describe how welcoming, gracious and friendly the people are. You just get meshed into the community immediately," Cindy says. She's already involved with the Rotary. She also volunteers at the Vermont Institute of Natural Science, which has a raptor refuge and nature preserve in the area, and the Pentangle Council on the Arts.

There's no shortage of volunteer opportunities, and the couples say their help is always welcome. Donald Griffith oversees the Rotary's food shelf project, supplying groceries to a local church that gives it to needy families, and he organizes the Christmas tree sale in December. He and Norma volunteer at the Senior Center, which has classes and trips and serves lunch daily. He serves on the boards of the Senior Center and a residential home for seniors and is active with the American Legion.

The Blackwells also volunteer at the Senior Center. David has been an officer for a charitable group raising funds to assist people with health care needs. He has also been chairman of a campaign to raise money for the local school district to offset the unreimbursed amount Woodstock sends to the state to share with other districts. He serves as a docent at the Billings Farm & Museum, among other volunteer work.

Bruce Macdonald is on the boards for the Quechee Club, the Friends of Hopkins Center & Hood Museum of Art, the Children's Hospital of Art and Opera North. Jann is active with the ladies golf association at Quechee and is president of the Quechee Garden Club, which takes on beautification projects for the village, sponsors two students in college and works with garden clubs in Woodstock, Hanover and other communities.

The availability of outdoor activities in all seasons is a major attraction, the couples say. "We can walk out our door and go on an incredible hike," says Cindy Carroll. She and Joe also bike, and he's an avid photographer. The Appalachian Trail winds through the area, as do other trails for hiking, biking, horseback riding and cross-country skiing. The Quechee Gorge has trails and a campground. Fly-fishing, kayaking and canoeing, as well as tennis and golf, are popular in summer.

The entire state is environmentally oriented. Residents take pride in and work to preserve the natural beauty of the area. There are no billboard signs on highways, and there are rigid controls on businesses to curb pollution.

In fall, Vermont becomes an artist's palette of reds, oranges, golds, browns and purples. It's the prime tourist season. Donald Griffith says from late September to late October the population can swell to 10,000 to 15,000 at times because of "leaf-peepers." Traffic on the two-lane highway through Woodstock, the main east-west route across this part of Vermont, can get bumper to bumper, but residents say it clears out in the evenings.

Winters can be severe, usually with snow on the ground from early December to April, but residents who've been here a long time say the roads are quickly cleared. "We have a wonderful road department," says Donald Griffith. "We can get a 12-inch to 18-inch snowstorm and within a matter of two to two and a half hours, our road is cleared." The winter of 2002-2003 brought major snowstorms. It was the first winter season for the Carrolls, and it was a big change

from California. But they said despite the heavy snowfall, they never were housebound.

No one finds much fault with the area, but they do note that housing costs and taxes are relatively high, though that depends on where you've lived previously. Home prices average about $359,000. There are a number of million-dollar homes, but housing under $300,000 is limited.

The couples say Woodstock is a good match for retirees who are active, enjoy outdoor activities in the summer and winter, like to get involved with community projects, like cultural programs and, perhaps most importantly, want a quieter, small-town lifestyle. Joan Blackwell cautions that Woodstock doesn't have a lot of nightlife. While there are cultural events and good dining, the town is rather quiet at night. Jann Macdonald says there's always something to do or see for those who want to be active, but if you seek quiet solitude in the mountains, you also can find that.

"It's a rural environment, but in education, culture and things to do, it's a robust community," says Donald Griffith. "The only thing I'd caution about, when you're coming for the first time, beware of the speed limit — it's 25 mph and they adhere to it."

"People who are real sun bunnies and really need to be in sun all the time shouldn't come here," says Bruce Macdonald. This area is for those "for whom a sense of season is important, for whom the visual is important," he says.

"It's not just a matter of having four seasons, it's four spectacular seasons. This place has the best of all four seasons," Bruce says. ●

Also Available
From Vacation Publications

Retirement Relocation Magazine

Print Cost Here

☐ Where to Retire, one-year subscription (six issues), $18

_____

Retirement Relocation Books

☐ America's Best Low-Tax Retirement Towns, Eve Evans and Richard Fox, $16.95 _____

☐ Choose the Southwest (Retirement Discoveries for Every Budget), John Howells, $14.95 _____

☐ Choose Mexico (Live Well on $600 a Month), John Howells and Don Merwin, $14.95 _____

☐ Choose Costa Rica (A Guide to Retirement and Investment), John Howells, $14.95 _____

☐ Choose the Northwest (Includes Washington, Oregon and British Columbia), John Howells, $14.95 _____

Retirement Relocation Special Reports

☐ SR1 How to Plan and Execute a Successful Retirement Relocation, 48 pages, $4.95 _____

☐ SR4 Should You Retire to a Manufactured Home? 32 pages, $4.95 _____

☐ SR5 Retiring Outside the United States, 48 pages, $4.95 _____

☐ SR7 America's 100 Best Master-Planned Communities,
Where to Retire Special Issue (coming July 2007), $4.95 _____

☐ SR8 America's Most Affordable Retirement Towns, 48 pages, $4.95 _____

☐ SR19 How to Get the Most Out of Your Social Security, 32 pages, $4.95 _____

Subtotal _____

Texas residents only add 8.25% sales tax
Add $2.50 postage and handling per book. Add $2.25 total postage and handling
for any number of Special Reports. Postage included in magazine subscription price.

Tax _____

Postage _____

Total Due _____

_____
NAME

_____
ADDRESS

_____
CITY, STATE, ZIP

Check the appropriate boxes and fill in the price for each title ordered. Total at the bottom.
Include your payment and return this order form or a copy to: Vacation Publications, 5851
San Felipe Street, Suite 500, Houston, TX 77057. For faster service call (800) 338-4962 or
order online with a credit card at www.wheretoretire.com.

Notes